Intermediate Mathematics

A REFERENCE GUIDE AND PROBLEM SETS

Book Staff and Contributors
Paul Thomas *Director, Mathematics*
Harold Lawrance Jr. *Content Specialist*
Jill Tunick *Senior Text Editor*
Karen Ingebretsen, Ellen Loeb, Anja Maguire *Text Editors*
Suzanne Montazer *Creative Director, Print and ePublishing*
Carol Leigh, Stephanie Shaw Williams *Print Visual Designers*
Jayoung Cho *Cover Designer*
Lee Horton *Senior Picture Editor*
Laura Creach, Megan Simmons, Peter Whittekiend *Mathematical Accuracy Editors*
Martin Donnelly, Michael Melnyk, Megan Simmons *Writers*
Amy Eward *Senior Manager, Writers*
Susan Raley *Senior Manager, Editors*
Elizabeth Lerner *Senior Project Manager*
Nols Myers *Director K–8, Program Management*

Lynda Cloud *Executive Vice President, Product Development*
David Pelizzari *Vice President, K¹² Content*
Kim Barcas *Vice President, Creative*
Christopher Frescholtz *Senior Director, Program Management*

Lisa Dimaio Iekel *Director, Print Production and Manufacturing*

About K12 Inc.
K12 Inc., a technology-based education company, is the nation's leading provider of proprietary curriculum and online education programs to students in grades K–12. K¹² provides its curriculum and academic services to online schools, traditional classrooms, blended school programs, and directly to families. K12 Inc. also operates the K¹² International Academy, an accredited, diploma-granting online private school serving students worldwide. K¹²'s mission is to provide any child the curriculum and tools to maximize success in life, regardless of geographic, financial, or demographic circumstances. K12 Inc. is accredited by CITA. More information can be found at www.K12.com.

ISBN: 978-1-60153-442-2 (online book)
ISBN: 978-1-60153-454-5 (printed book)

Printed by Quad/Graphics, Versailles, KY, USA, April, 2015

B
Intermediate Mathematics
A REFERENCE GUIDE AND PROBLEM SETS
K12

Contents

CHAPTER 4 Multiplication and Division

CHAPTER 5 Fractions

CHAPTER 6 Combined Operations

CHAPTER 7 Ratio, Proportion, and Percent

CHAPTER 8 Proportion Applications

CHAPTER 9 Plane Figures

CHAPTER 10 Circles and Measurement

CHAPTER 11 Solid Figures

CHAPTER 12 Probability and Statistics

Appendices

How to Use This Book

This book contains 12 chapters. Each chapter begins with an opener and a Foundations topic that provides a review of prerequisite math skills. The chapter then presents a series of explanatory topics and problem sets. Finally a Chapter Review problem set concludes the chapter.

The **Chapter Opener** introduces the subject that will be covered.

In This Chapter describes the concepts and skills covered in the chapter and gives a real-world example of what you will learn.

Topic List is a list of specific topic titles.

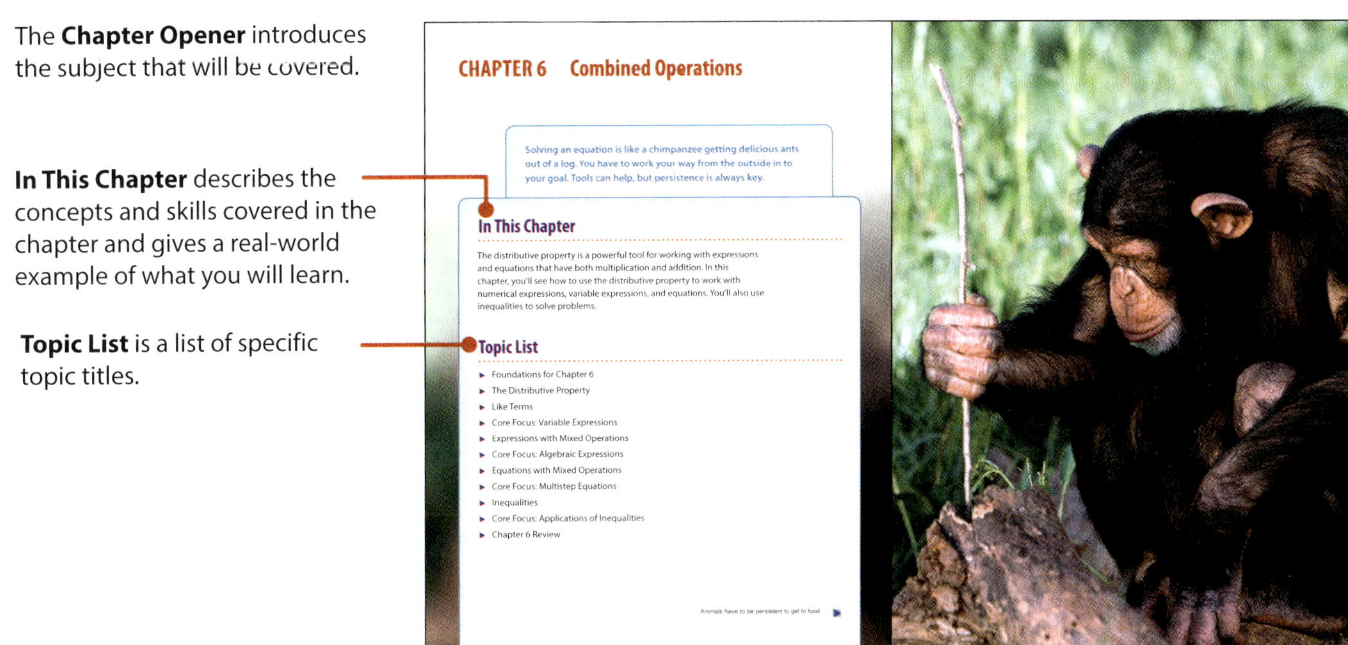

CHAPTER 6 Combined Operations

Solving an equation is like a chimpanzee getting delicious ants out of a log. You have to work your way from the outside in to your goal. Tools can help, but persistence is always key.

In This Chapter

The distributive property is a powerful tool for working with expressions and equations that have both multiplication and addition. In this chapter, you'll see how to use the distributive property to work with numerical expressions, variable expressions, and equations. You'll also use inequalities to solve problems.

Topic List

- Foundations for Chapter 6
- The Distributive Property
- Like Terms
- Core Focus: Variable Expressions
- Expressions with Mixed Operations
- Core Focus: Algebraic Expressions
- Equations with Mixed Operations
- Core Focus: Multistep Equations
- Inequalities
- Core Focus: Applications of Inequalities
- Chapter 6 Review

Animals have to be persistent to get to food

The **Foundations** topic provides a chance to identify and review your skills as you get ready for the math in the chapter.

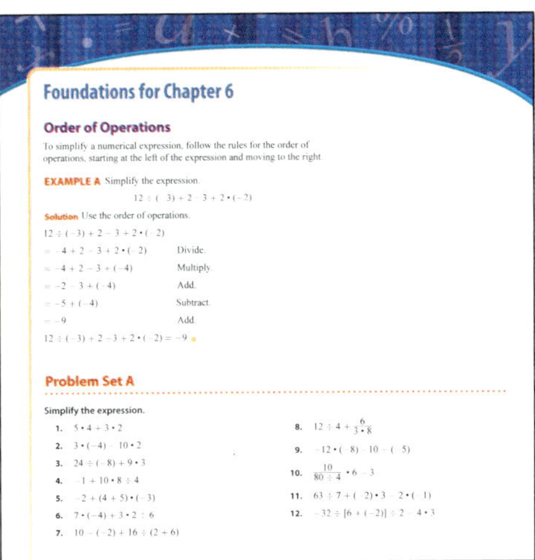

Foundations for Chapter 6

Order of Operations

To simplify a numerical expression, follow the rules for the order of operations, starting at the left of the expression and moving to the right.

EXAMPLE A Simplify the expression.

$$12 \div (-3) + 2 - 3 + 2 \cdot (-2)$$

Solution Use the order of operations.

$12 \div (-3) + 2 - 3 + 2 \cdot (-2)$
$= -4 + 2 - 3 + 2 \cdot (-2)$ Divide.
$= -4 + 2 - 3 + (-4)$ Multiply.
$= -2 - 3 + (-4)$ Add.
$= -5 + (-4)$ Subtract.
$= -9$ Add.
$12 \div (-3) + 2 - 3 + 2 \cdot (-2) = -9$

Problem Set A

Simplify the expression.

1. $5 \cdot 4 + 3 \cdot 2$
2. $3 \cdot (-4) - 10 \cdot 2$
3. $24 \div (-8) + 9 \cdot 3$
4. $-1 + 10 \cdot 8 \div 4$
5. $-2 + (4 + 5) \cdot (-3)$
6. $7 \cdot (-4) + 3 \cdot 2 \div 6$
7. $10 - (-2) + 16 \div (2 + 6)$
8. $12 \div 4 + \frac{6}{3 \cdot 8}$
9. $-12 \cdot (-8) - 10 - (-5)$
10. $\frac{10}{80 \div 4} \cdot 6 - 3$
11. $63 \div 7 + (-2) \cdot 3 - 2 \cdot (-1)$
12. $-32 \div [6 + (-2)] \div 2 - 4 \cdot 3$

Each Foundations topic has three sections, one for each skill you should review. Each section concludes with a problem set for you to do to make sure you are ready for the chapter.

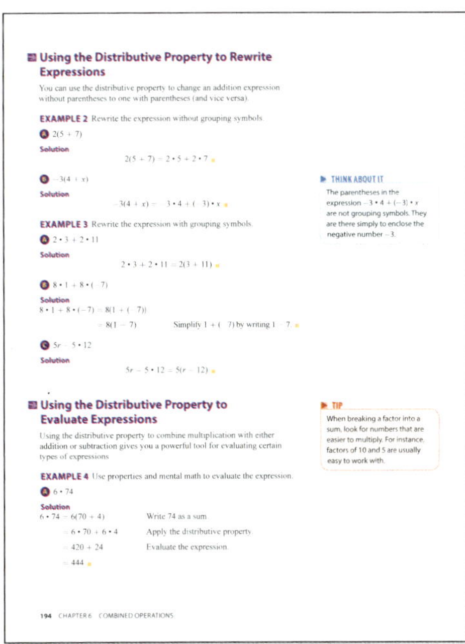

Using the Distributive Property to Rewrite Expressions

You can use the distributive property to change an addition expression without parentheses to one with parentheses (and vice versa).

EXAMPLE 2 Rewrite the expression without grouping symbols.

A $2(5 + 7)$

Solution

$$2(5 + 7) = 2 \cdot 5 + 2 \cdot 7$$

B $-3(4 + x)$

Solution

$$-3(4 + x) = -3 \cdot 4 + (-3) \cdot x$$

THINK ABOUT IT

The parentheses in the expression $-3 \cdot 4 + (-3) \cdot x$ are not grouping symbols. They are there simply to enclose the negative number -3.

EXAMPLE 3 Rewrite the expression with grouping symbols.

A $2 \cdot 3 + 2 \cdot 11$

Solution

$$2 \cdot 3 + 2 \cdot 11 = 2(3 + 11)$$

B $8 \cdot 1 + 8 \cdot (-7)$

Solution

$8 \cdot 1 + 8 \cdot (-7) = 8(1 + (-7))$
$= 8(1 - 7)$ Simplify $1 + (-7)$ by writing $1 - 7$.

C $5r - 5 \cdot 12$

Solution

$$5r - 5 \cdot 12 = 5(r - 12)$$

Using the Distributive Property to Evaluate Expressions

Using the distributive property to combine multiplication with either addition or subtraction gives you a powerful tool for evaluating certain types of expressions.

TIP

When breaking a factor into a sum, look for numbers that are easier to multiply. For instance, factors of 10 and 5 are usually easy to work with.

EXAMPLE 4 Use properties and mental math to evaluate the expression.

A $6 \cdot 74$

Solution

$6 \cdot 74 = 6(70 + 4)$ Write 74 as a sum.
$= 6 \cdot 70 + 6 \cdot 4$ Apply the distributive property.
$= 420 + 24$ Evaluate the expression.
$= 444$

194 CHAPTER 6 COMBINED OPERATIONS

Each topic has explanations and examples.

Definitions, formulas, and other information in boxes in the text provide valuable reference information.

Problem Set pages follow each set of reference pages.

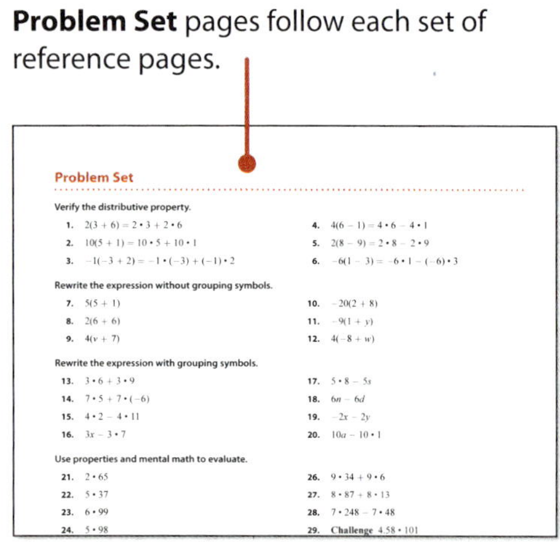

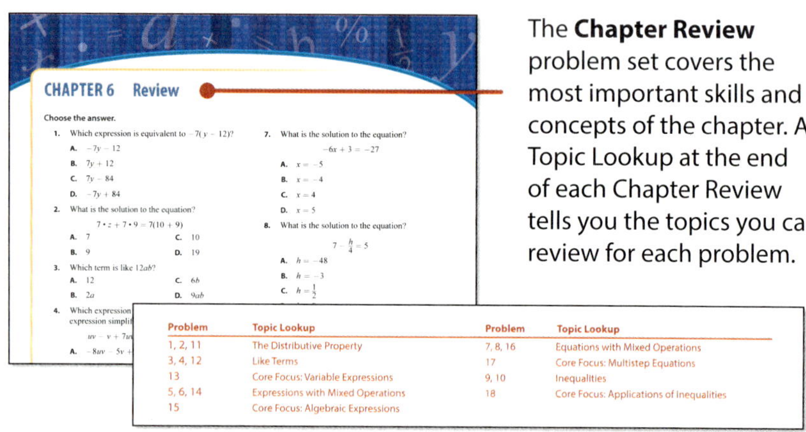

The **Chapter Review** problem set covers the most important skills and concepts of the chapter. A Topic Lookup at the end of each Chapter Review tells you the topics you can review for each problem.

The end of each topic is where you will do the math so you can learn the math.

Appendices

The appendices include quantitative and general reference information.

Quantitative Reference Information

- Nutritional Data
- Mobile Phone Data
- Sugar Consumption Data

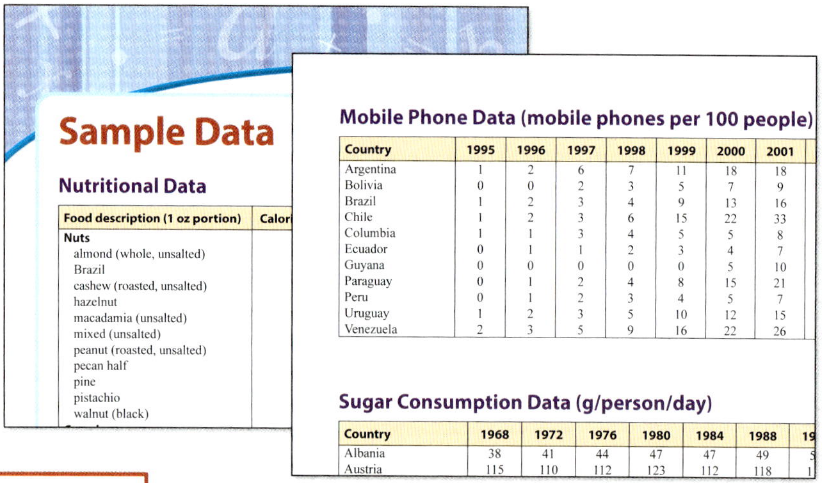

General Reference Information

- Pronunciation Guide
- Glossary
- Symbols
- Properties
- Formulary
- Selected Answers
- Illustrations Credits
- Data Sources
- Index

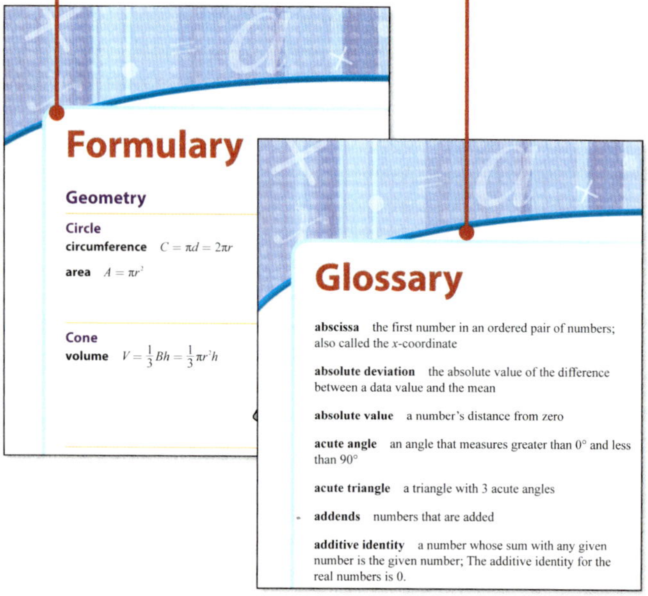

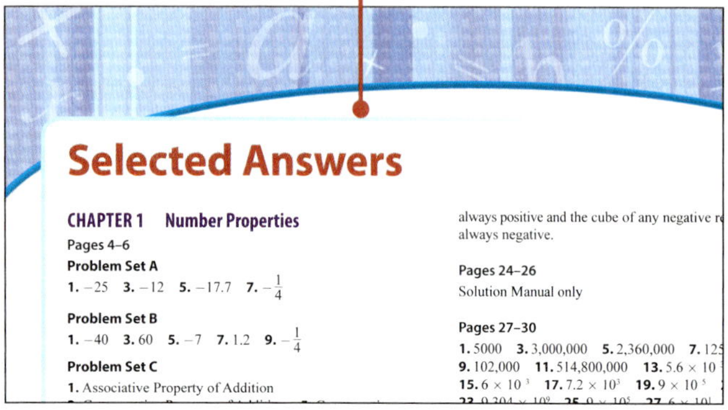

Introduction

Welcome to *Intermediate Mathematics*

This reference guide accompanies the online portion of K12 Inc.'s Intermediate Mathematics program. The topics and problem sets in this reference guide explain and illustrate how to solve problems. They make sense on their own, but they are not the entire story. The online component of the course is critical. Online you will see text, interactive pieces, and multimedia tools that provide the rest of the story.

Intermediate Mathematics A The first step in the middle school sequence covers fractions, ratios, and rates, as well as negative numbers. Geometry topics include finding areas of triangles and quadrilaterals, as well as finding volumes of prisms. Statistical graphs and measures of center and variability are also introduced.

Intermediate Mathematics B The second step in the middle school sequence covers proportional relationships, operations with rational numbers, and linear equations. Geometry topics include working with two-scale drawings, simple geometric constructions, and other two-dimensional shapes. Statistical topics include understanding how to use samples.

Intermediate Mathematics C The third step in the middle school sequence covers topics such as carrying out algebraic reasoning, using linear equations as models, and solving linear equations and systems of linear equations. Functions are introduced, as are the geometric concepts of angles, distance, similarity, congruence, and the Pythagorean theorem.

Get to Work

Math is learned at the tip of a pencil. As you work through the topics in this book, you will see worked examples that show you how to solve some problems. The most important part of each topic, however, is the problem set at the end. Reading problem solutions can help you find good strategies and best practices for solving problems, but only when you solve problems yourself will you really learn math.

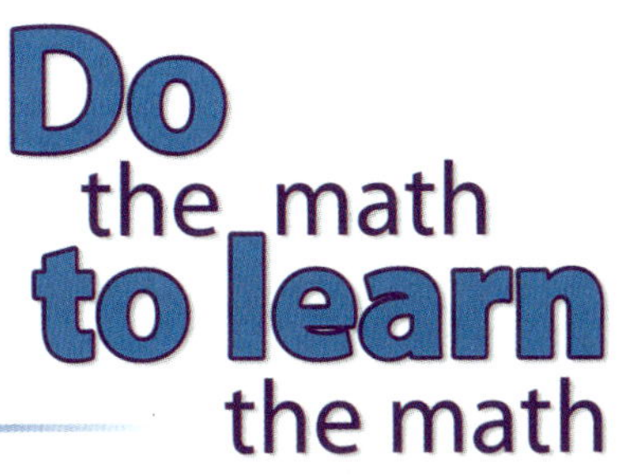

CHAPTER 1 The Basics

Let's start at the very beginning; it's a very good place to start. Just as you need to know basic grammar and vocabulary as you begin to learn any language, you need to know some basic building blocks as you begin to learn algebra.

In This Chapter

In this chapter, you'll focus on the building blocks of basic algebra. Building on your understanding of numbers and operations, you'll use the order of operations to evaluate numerical expressions and interpret, write, and evaluate expressions to solve real-world problems.

Topic List

- Foundations for Chapter 1
- Order of Operations
- Variable Expressions
- Writing Expressions for Word Phrases
- Related Equations
- Solving Problems
- Core Focus: Word Problems
- Core Focus: Interpreting Expressions
- Chapter 1 Review

You won't get far if you don't know basic grammar and vocabulary.

出発ロビー
Departure Lobby
起飞大厅　출발로비

搭乗口
Gates
登机口　탑승구
3
4·

出口
Exit
Baggage Claim
出口 行李提取处
출구

到着ロビー
Arrival Lobby
到达大厅　도착로비

観光・総合案内所
Information
询问处　안내
レンタカー
Rent a Car　租赁汽车
ホテル予約
Hotel Reservation
ご搭乗手続
Check-in
登机手续

Foundations for Chapter 1

Simplifying Expressions

To simplify a numerical expression involving just addition and subtraction, perform all the operations in the expression from left to right. Do the same for expressions with just multiplication and division: Work from left to right.

EXAMPLE A Simplify.

A-1 $3 + 8 - 6$

Solution Add or subtract from left to right.

$$\begin{aligned} 3 + 8 - 6 &= 11 - 6 \\ &= 5 \end{aligned}$$

A-2 $24 \div 8 \cdot 2$

Solution Multiply or divide from left to right.

$$\begin{aligned} 24 \div 8 \cdot 2 &= 3 \cdot 2 \\ &= 6 \end{aligned}$$

Problem Set A

Simplify.

1. $20 - 8 + 10$
2. $5 \cdot 4 \div 2$
3. $81 \div 9 \cdot 5$
4. $15 + 5 - 10$
5. $100 \div 5 \cdot 3$
6. $6 - 5 + 19$
7. $14 \cdot 3 \div 7$
8. $12 + 8 - 15 - 5$
9. $8 \cdot 2 \cdot 2 \div 16$
10. $90 \div 9 \cdot 3 \div 10$

Translating Expressions

To translate an expression into a word phrase, use words to describe the operation performed in the expression. Combine these words with the numbers in the expression.

EXAMPLE B Translate the variable expression into a word phrase.

B-1 $x - 10$

Solution Think about the word that means "the answer to a subtraction problem." Treat variables just like numbers.

the difference of x and 10 ■

B-2 $9 \cdot t$

Solution Think about the word that means "the answer to a multiplication problem." Treat variables just like numbers.

the product of 9 and t ■

Problem Set B

Translate the variable expression into a word phrase.

1. $12 + v$
2. $5 \cdot q$
3. $9 \div p$
4. $t \cdot 11$
5. $3 - a$
6. $16 \div c$
7. $7 \cdot r$
8. $x + 20$
9. $k \div 5$
10. $10 + f$
11. $m + 0$
12. $23 - g$
13. $n \div 0.8$
14. $b - \frac{1}{2}$

Information Needed to Solve Word Problems

Sometimes a problem contains information that is not needed to solve the problem. Determine what the problem is asking. Identify any information needed to answer that question, and ignore all other information.

EXAMPLE C Alden bought 3 lb of peaches and 6 lb of plums. The peaches cost $1.99/lb, and the plums cost $2.49/lb. How much money did Alden spend on plums?

C-1 Identify the information that is needed to solve the problem.

Solution The problem asks for the amount of money Alden spent on plums. To solve this problem, you would multiply the number of pounds of plums Alden bought by the cost per pound of plums. You do not need to find the cost of the peaches.

Needed information Alden bought 6 lb of plums. The plums cost $2.49/lb. ■

C-2 Identify the information that is not needed to solve the problem.

Solution **Not-needed information** Alden bought 3 lb of peaches. The peaches cost $1.99/lb. ■

Problem Set C

For each problem:
(a) Identify the information that is needed to solve the problem.
(b) Identify the information that is not needed to solve the problem.

1. Jack is 4 years older than Ryan. Ryan is 6 years older than Pete. If Pete is 3 years old, how old is Ryan?
2. Alicia walks at a speed of 8 kmph and jogs at a speed of 10 kmph. How long would it take for Alicia to walk 12 km?
3. A rectangle has a length of 4 cm, a width of 3 cm, and an area of 12 cm^2. What is the perimeter of the rectangle?
4. One vial of solution contains 20 mL distilled water and 1 mL of the active ingredient. How many milliliters of distilled water are in 3 vials of the solution?
5. A shape has 8 sides that each measure 2 mm and 8 angles, some obtuse and some acute. What is the perimeter of the shape?
6. Mai's science quiz scores are 95, 82, 90, and 88. She wants to earn a score of at least 90 on her next quiz. What is Mai's highest quiz score?

Order of Operations

Addition, subtraction, multiplication, and division are operations.

When an expression has more than one operation, you must use the **order of operations** to simplify it. To **simplify a numerical expression** means to find its value.

ORDER OF OPERATIONS

Step 1 Multiply and divide from left to right.

Step 2 Add and subtract from left to right.

TIP

Simplifying a numerical expression means the same as evaluating a numerical expression.

Simplifying Expressions Without Grouping Symbols

EXAMPLE 1 Simplify.

A $1 + 2 \cdot 5$

Solution

$1 + 2 \cdot 5 = 1 + 10$ Multiply.

$= 11$ Add. ■

B $6 \div 2 \cdot 3$

Solution

$6 \div 2 \cdot 3 = 3 \cdot 3$ Divide.

$= 9$ Multiply. ■

C $5 \cdot 2 - 6 \div 2$

Solution

$5 \cdot 2 - 6 \div 2 = 10 - 6 \div 2$ Multiply.

$= 10 - 3$ Divide.

$= 7$ Subtract. ■

NOTATION

$\cdot$ and $\times$ A raised dot and an $\times$ both mean multiplication.

D $12 + 55 \div 5 - 2 \cdot 10 + 9$

Solution

$$\begin{aligned} 12 + 55 \div 5 - 2 \cdot 10 + 9 &= 12 + 11 - 2 \cdot 10 + 9 && \text{Divide.} \\ &= 12 + 11 - 20 + 9 && \text{Multiply.} \\ &= 23 - 20 + 9 && \text{Add.} \\ &= 3 + 9 && \text{Subtract.} \\ &= 12 && \text{Add.} \end{aligned}$$

Simplifying Expressions with Grouping Symbols

Grouping symbols are symbols such as parentheses ( ), brackets [ ], and braces { }. Perform all operations inside grouping symbols first. If there is more than one set of grouping symbols in an expression, perform the operations in the innermost set of grouping symbols first.

ORDER OF OPERATIONS WITH GROUPING

Step 1 Perform operations within grouping symbols.

Step 2 Multiply and divide from left to right.

Step 3 Add and subtract from left to right.

EXAMPLE 2 Simplify.

A $5 \cdot (2 + 7)$

Solution

$$\begin{aligned} 5 \cdot (2 + 7) &= 5 \cdot 9 && \text{Add inside the grouping symbols.} \\ &= 45 && \text{Multiply.} \end{aligned}$$

B $20 \div (10 \times 2)$

Solution

$$\begin{aligned} 20 \div (10 \times 2) &= 20 \div 20 && \text{Multiply inside the grouping symbols.} \\ &= 1 && \text{Divide.} \end{aligned}$$

C $24 - [4 \cdot (6 - 5) + 5]$

Solution The parentheses are inside the brackets. Use the order of operations to simplify $6 - 5$ first.

$$\begin{aligned} 24 - [4 \cdot (6 - 5) + 5] &= 24 - [4 \cdot 1 + 5] && \text{Subtract inside the parentheses.} \\ &= 24 - [4 + 5] && \text{Multiply inside the brackets.} \\ &= 24 - 9 && \text{Add inside the brackets.} \\ &= 15 && \text{Subtract.} \end{aligned}$$

THINK ABOUT IT

If we remove one set of grouping symbols from each expression in Example 2,

2A

$$\begin{aligned} 5 \cdot 2 + 7 &= 10 + 7 \\ &= 17 \end{aligned}$$

2B

$$\begin{aligned} 20 \div 10 \times 2 &= 2 \times 2 \\ &= 4 \end{aligned}$$

2C

$$\begin{aligned} 24 - 4 \cdot (6 - 5) + 5 &= 20 + 5 \\ &= 25 \end{aligned}$$

Placing Grouping Symbols to Get a Specified Value

You can get different values for an expression by changing the placement of grouping symbols.

EXAMPLE 3 Place grouping symbols in the expression $90 - 10 \div 2 + 3$ to get expressions that have the values 16 and 82.

Solution

Get the value 16:

$$\begin{aligned}(90 - 10) \div (2 + 3) &= 80 \div 5 \\ &= 16\end{aligned}$$

Get the value 82:

$$\begin{aligned}90 - (10 \div 2 + 3) &= 90 - (5 + 3) \\ &= 90 - 8 \\ &= 82\end{aligned}$$

TIP

Solve Example 3 by trial and error. Experiment by including different parts of the expression in parentheses.

Simplifying Expressions with a Fraction Bar

The fraction bar represents division. It can be used as a grouping symbol.

EXAMPLE 4 Simplify.

A $\dfrac{60 \div 3}{2 + 2}$

Solution

$\dfrac{60 \div 3}{2 + 2} = \dfrac{20}{4}$ Simplify the numerator and denominator separately.

$= 5$ Divide the numerator by the denominator.

B $\dfrac{3 \cdot (17 - 5)}{4 + 9 - 1}$

Solution Use the order of operations to simplify the numerator and denominator.

$\dfrac{3 \cdot (17 - 5)}{4 + 9 - 1} = \dfrac{3 \cdot 12}{4 + 9 - 1}$ In the numerator, subtract inside the parentheses.

$= \dfrac{36}{12}$ In the numerator, multiply. In the denominator, add and subtract from left to right.

$= 3$ Divide.

THINK ABOUT IT

You can write the expression $\dfrac{60 \div 3}{2 + 2}$ as $(60 \div 3) \div (2 + 2)$.

Application: Business

EXAMPLE 5 A plumber charges \$25 to make a visit plus \$65/h. Suppose the plumber works on a project for a total of 3 h. Write and simplify an expression to find how much the plumber will charge for the project.

Solution

total charge	=	\$25 for the visit	+	3 h at \$65/h	
	=	25	+	$3 \cdot 65$	Write an expression.
		$= 25 + 195$			Multiply.
		$= 220$			Add.

The plumber will charge \$220 for the project.

Problem Set

Simplify.

1. **(a)** $8 \div 4 + 4$
   (b) $8 \div (4 + 4)$
2. **(a)** $3 + 10 \div 10 + 3$
   (b) $(3 + 10) \div (10 + 3)$
3. **(a)** $(15 - 2) \cdot 3 \cdot 2$
   (b) $15 - 2 \cdot 3 \cdot 2$
4. $21 + 17 \cdot 2 - 15 + 1$
5. $5 + 18 \div 3$
6. $24 \div 4 \div 3 + 1$
7. $25 \cdot 5 \div 5 - 20$
8. $35 - 5 \cdot 2 + 16 \div 4$
9. $21 \div 7 \cdot 3 - 4 \cdot 2$
10. $24 \div (3 + 5)$
11. $(4 + 16) \cdot 8 - 2$
12. $47 + [3 \cdot 8 \div (3 + 1)]$
13. $36 \div (3 \cdot 2) - 1$
14. $9 \cdot [2 + (35 - 5 \cdot 3)] + 7$
15. $29 + (5 \cdot 2) \div (10 - 8)$
16. $[16 \cdot (4 + 1)] \div 10$
17. $\dfrac{28}{4 + 3}$
18. $\dfrac{10 \cdot (2 + 4)}{14 + (7 - 1)}$
19. $\dfrac{(8 + 4 \div 2) \cdot 2}{10 \div (1 + 1)}$
20. $21 + \dfrac{15 \cdot 2}{9 \div 3}$

Place grouping symbols in the expression to get an expression that has the given value.

21. Get the value 35: $23 + 3 \cdot 5 - 1$
22. Get the value 67: $5 \div 5 + 6 \cdot 2 + 9$
23. Get the value 10: $9 + 3 \cdot 5 \div 2 + 4$
24. Get the value 14: $3 \cdot 5 + 9 \div 3$
25. Get the value 3: $17 - 5 \div 1 + 3$

Solve.

26. Apples cost \$2/lb and grapes cost \$3/lb. Brad bought 6 lb of apples and 5 lb of grapes. Write and simplify an expression to find how much money Brad spent.

27. Li planted a flower that was 6 in. tall. It then grew 2 in./wk for 4 wk. Write and simplify an expression to find the new height of the flower.

28. At the swim meet, a swim team had 2 swimmers finish their race in first place, 3 swimmers finish in third place, and 2 swimmers finish in fourth place. The chart shows the points earned for each place finished. Write and simplify an expression for the total number of points the swim team received.

Place finished	Points earned
fifth	1
fourth	3
third	5
second	8
first	10

29. The temperature of a liquid starts out at 65°C. The liquid is cooled and its temperature falls 6°/h for 4 h. The temperature of the liquid is then increased by 10°. Write and simplify an expression to find the final temperature of the liquid.

30. A tank holds 400 gal of water. A crack forms and 20 gal of water leak out every hour. Write and simplify an expression to find how much water is in the tank after 12 h.

31. Ann read 3 pages per day every day for 9 days. Jamal read 2 pages per day every day for 14 days. Write and simplify an expression to find how many more pages Jamal read than Ann.

32. **Challenge** Part of the floor shown is covered by tiles. Each tile is 1 ft wide and 2 ft long. There are 265 tiles. Write and simplify an expression to find how much of the floor, in square feet, is not tiled.

Variable Expressions

An **expression** is a group of mathematical symbols.

Expressions can contain numbers, variables, and operation symbols. A **numerical expression** consists of numbers and one or more operations.

A **variable** is a symbol that represents a value. In most cases, variables are letters, such as x, y, a, and n. Most variables in this book will be lowercase and italicized.

A **variable expression** consists of one or more variables and one or more operations; it may also contain numbers.

Numerical expressions do not contain variables. Variable expressions do.

Numerical expression	Variable expression
$8 - 6 \cdot (3 + 1)$	$8 - 6 \cdot (a + b)$
$\frac{25}{8 - 3}$	$\frac{x}{y - z}$

A numerical expression has only one value. But a variable expression can have different values, depending on the values that are substituted for its variables.

Evaluating Expressions

To **evaluate a variable expression**, replace all the variables in the expression with numbers and simplify. Remember to use the order of operations when simplifying.

When working with variable expressions, there are a few ways to show multiplication. You may be used to using the multiplication $\times$, but in algebra, you will most often see a raised dot. Also, you can show multiplication by putting a number right next to a variable. For instance, $6a$ is the same as $6 \cdot a$ and $6 \times a$.

REMEMBER

Multiplication can be shown in different ways. All of the following mean "six times the quantity three plus one":

$6(3 + 1)$
$6 \cdot (3 + 1)$
$6 \times (3 + 1)$

EXAMPLE 1

A Evaluate $7n + 5$ when $n = 8$.

Solution

$7n + 5 = 7 \cdot 8 + 5$ Substitute 8 for n.

$= 56 + 5$ Multiply.

$= 61$ Add. ■

THINK ABOUT IT

Vary means "change." Thus, when a variable changes its value, the value of the expression changes, too.

B Evaluate $x - y + 2$ when $x = 11$ and $y = 3$.

Solution

$x - y + 2 = 11 - 3 + 2$ Substitute 11 for x and 3 for y.

$= 8 + 2$ Subtract.

$= 10$ Add. ■

C Evaluate $\frac{c - 5d}{10 \cdot (2d + 1)}$ when $c = 200$ and $d = 4$.

Solution

$\frac{c - 5d}{10 \cdot (2d + 1)} = \frac{200 - 5 \cdot 4}{10 \cdot (2 \cdot 4 + 1)}$ Substitute 200 for c and 4 for d.

$= \frac{200 - 20}{10 \cdot 9}$ Simplify the numerator and denominator separately.

$= \frac{180}{90}$

$= 2$ Divide. ■

Application: Temperature

EXAMPLE 2 To approximate the temperature in degrees Celsius after an increase in altitude of f feet, you can use the expression $b - 2 \cdot \frac{f}{1000}$, where b is the beginning temperature. A hiker climbs 4000 ft to a summit from a parking lot, where it is 35°C. Approximate the temperature at the summit.

Solution

$b - 2 \cdot \frac{f}{1000} = 35 - 2 \cdot \frac{4000}{1000}$ Substitute 35 for b and 4000 for f.

$= 35 - 2 \cdot 4$ Divide.

$= 35 - 8$ Multiply.

$= 27$ Subtract.

The temperature at the summit is about 27°C. ■

Application: Sports

EXAMPLE 3 The distance around a rectangle is its perimeter and is given by the expression $2l + 2w$, where l represents length and w represents width. Find the perimeter of a soccer field that is 100 yd long and 60 yd wide.

Solution

$2l + 2w = 2 \cdot 100 + 2 \cdot 60$ Substitute 100 for l and 60 for w.

$= 200 + 120$ Multiply.

$= 320$ Add.

The perimeter of the soccer field is 320 yd. ■

TIP

Variables are often the first letters in the words they represent, such as l for length and w for width.

Problem Set

Evaluate the expression for the given value(s).

1. $7 + 10y$ when $y = 6$
2. $30b$ when $b = 0$
3. $\frac{35}{n-1}$ when $n = 6$
4. $x + 2x$ when $x = 4$
5. $\frac{4 \cdot (8 - b)}{b}$ when $b = 2$
6. $12 + g \cdot (9 \div g)$ when $g = 3$
7. $16 + a \cdot a$ when $a = 3$
8. $5x + 18x$ when $x = 6$
9. $3z + 4 + z$ when $z = 5$
10. $(8 + 3a) \cdot a$ when $a = 2$
11. $k + k \div 2$ when $k = 20$
12. $\frac{25 - n}{n}$ when $n = 5$
13. $\frac{df}{e}$ when $d = 2, f = 9$, and $e = 3$
14. $m + \frac{n}{m} \cdot 9$ when $m = 4$ and $n = 36$
15. $k + m \div 2$ when $k = 40$ and $m = 10$
16. $\frac{a}{c} + \frac{b}{c}$ when $a = 24$, $b = 12$, and $c = 4$
17. $\frac{a}{b - 2c}$ when $a = 27$, $b = 15$, and $c = 3$
18. $(2 \cdot 3q + 1) \div p$ when $q = 4$ and $p = 25$
19. $9 \cdot (x - 7) - y$ when $x = 11$ and $y = 19$
20. $7c - 4 + d \div 3$ when $c = 10$ and $d = 33$
21. $\frac{v - 2w + 12}{w + 5}$ when $v = 68$ and $w = 4$
22. **Challenge** $\frac{r - \frac{15}{s}}{12 - 2s} \cdot \frac{3 \cdot \left(\frac{r+s}{2}\right)}{\frac{r-3}{2} + s}$ when $r = 23$ and $s = 3$

Solve.

23. Doctors use the expression $\frac{c}{h}$, where c represents total cholesterol and h represents HDL (good) cholesterol, to find a patient's cholesterol risk ratio. Doctors are concerned when the ratio is greater than 4.
    - **(a)** Find the risk ratio for a patient whose total cholesterol value is 141 and good cholesterol is 47.
    - **(b)** Find the risk ratio for a patient whose total cholesterol value is 108 and good cholesterol is 36.
    - **(c)** Should the risk ratio for either patient give the doctor reason for concern?
24. The area of a parallelogram is given by the expression bh, where b represents the length of the base and h represents the height. Find the area of a parallelogram whose base is 16 in. and whose height is 9 in.
25. To find the length of an object in inches when you know its length in feet f, you can use the expression $12f$. How many inches long is an 8 ft long sofa?

26. The expression $\frac{c}{4} + 37$ can be used to approximate the current temperature in degrees Fahrenheit, where c is the number of times a cricket chirps in 1 min. What is the approximate temperature if a cricket chirps 60 times in 1 min?

27. The volume of a cone is given by $\frac{Bh}{3}$, where B is the area of the base of the cone and h is the height of the cone. Find the volume of a cone whose base is 153 in^2 and whose height is 11 in. (Hint: Your answer should be in cubic inches.)

28. To find the average of three bowling scores, a bowler uses the expression $\frac{g_1 + g_2 + g_3}{3}$, where g_1, g_2, and g_3 are the scores for each game.

    (a) Find the bowler's average when his scores are 147, 165, and 150.

    (b) Find the bowler's average when his scores are 210, 265, and 191.

    (c) A bowler's average for three games is 150. Two of his scores were 150 and 155. What was his other score?

29. **Challenge** The volume of a sphere is given by $\frac{4\pi r^3}{3}$, where r is the radius of the sphere. Estimate the volume of a sphere whose radius is 8 cm by using 3 for π. (Hint: $r^3 = r \cdot r \cdot r$.)

Writing Expressions for Word Phrases

To solve problems, you sometimes need to translate word phrases into variable expressions.

You can use the table to help determine what operation is indicated by a particular word phrase.

MATCHING WORDS AND PHRASES TO OPERATIONS

Addition	Subtraction	Multiplication	Division
plus	minus	times	quotient
more than	less than	product	separate into equal groups
increased by	decreased by	of	
sum	difference	combine equal groups	
total	shorter		
longer	younger		
older			

Think carefully when you translate. The phrases in the table do not automatically indicate particular operations. For example, "two is less than six" is written $2 < 6$; there is no subtraction involved.

Translating Word Phrases into Variable Expressions

EXAMPLE 1 Translate the word phrase into a variable expression.

A the sum of 16 and a number

Solution Possible variable expression:

$16 + n$ — The word *sum* indicates addition. Use any letter for the variable. ■

B 6 less than twice a number

Solution Possible variable expression:

$2x - 6$ — To represent 6 *less than* a quantity, you need to subtract 6 from that quantity. In this case, the quantity is twice a number, or 2 times a number. ■

C 20 students separated into equal groups

Solution Possible variable expression:

$\frac{20}{n}$ or $20 \div n$ You do not know how many equal groups, so use a variable for the number of equal groups. Use division to separate into equal groups. ■

D the number of seconds in m minutes

Solution Variable expression:

$60m$ You need to combine m "groups" with 60 s in each group. Use multiplication to combine equal groups. ■

> **TIP**
>
> Order matters in subtraction and division. In Example 1B, $6 - 2x$ is incorrect. In Example 1C, $\frac{n}{20}$ and $n \div 20$ are incorrect.

> **THINK ABOUT IT**
>
> In Parts A, B, and C, the answers are given as possible expressions because they could contain different variables.

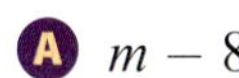

Translating Variable Expressions into Word Phrases

You can write a word phrase for a variable expression in more than one way.

EXAMPLE 2 Translate the variable expression into a word phrase.

A $m - 8$

Solution Possible answers include:

the difference of m and 8

8 less than m

m minus 8 ■

B $bc + 2$

Solution Possible answers include:

the product of b and c, increased by 2

2 more than the product of b and c ■

C $b \cdot (c + 2)$

Solution Possible answers include:

the product of b and the sum of c and 2

b times the quantity c plus 2 ■

> **THINK ABOUT IT**
>
> Notice that the parentheses in Example 2C form an expression whose meaning is different from the expression in Example 2B.

Application: Age

EXAMPLE 3

A Sam's mom is 2 years older than 5 times Sam's age. Write a variable expression to represent the age of Sam's mom.

Solution Variable expression:

$5s + 2$ Let s represent Sam's age. To represent 2 years older, add 2. The word *times* indicates multiplication. ■

B The ages of three sisters are consecutive odd whole numbers. Write a variable expression to represent the age of the oldest sister if the age of the youngest sister is y.

Solution Consecutive whole numbers, such as 5 and 6, have no whole numbers between them. Consecutive odd whole numbers, such as 5 and 7, have no odd whole numbers between them.

Notice that to get from an odd whole number to the next consecutive odd whole number, you add 2. Therefore, the ages of the sisters are y, $y + 2$, and $y + 4$.

The variable expression for the age of the oldest sister is $y + 4$. ■

REMEMBER

Expressions show relationships between different entities.

REMEMBER

Whole numbers are the numbers 0, 1, 2, 3, ...

Problem Sets

Translate the word phrase into a variable expression.

1. 15 less than a number
2. the product of 18 and a number
3. the quotient of a number and 7
4. a number increased by 1
5. 25 decreased by the sum of 6 and a number
6. 10 more than 3 times a number
7. combine 6 groups of n items
8. the difference of twice a number and 3
9. the difference of 3 and twice a number
10. the sum of 16 and 4 times a number
11. the quotient of the sum of 3 and a number and the number
12. n items separated into m equal groups
13. x inches shorter than 22 in.
14. the total of 14 and the difference of a number and 2
15. **Challenge** 5 times the product of 2 and 1 less than a number

Translate the variable expression into a word phrase.

16. $g + 24$
17. $2 \cdot (3 - x)$
18. $k \div 2j$
19. $3mn$
20. $3 + m + n$
21. $\frac{2}{n + 3}$
22. $\frac{500}{n} + 1$
23. $(a + b) - (2c + d)$

Solve.

24. Cassie is 4 cm shorter than Maria. Write a variable expression to represent Cassie's height.

25. Write a variable expression to represent the sum of four consecutive numbers if the least number is p.

26. There are 100 flowers on a truck bed. A florist removes f flowers from the truck bed and divides the remaining flowers into 3 equal groups. Write a variable expression to represent the number of flowers in each group.

27. Isaiah is 3 years younger than twice Jack's age. Kaleb is 4 times Isaiah's age. Write a variable expression to represent Isaiah's age and then another to represent Kaleb's age.

28. The heights of 3 boys, in inches, are consecutive even whole numbers. Write a variable expression to represent the height of the shortest boy if the height of the tallest boy is n inches.

29. Dario recycled b bottles and c cans and received 5¢ for each. Write a variable expression for the amount of money Dario earned by recycling the bottles and cans.

30. Mahal bought p pounds of grapes at \$2.99/lb. She paid for the grapes with a \$20 bill. Write a variable expression for the amount of change Mahal received.

31. **Challenge** The sales tax on an item is 5% of the item's value. Write a variable expression for the sales tax of the item. Then write a variable expression for the total cost of the item.

32. **Challenge** The width of a rectangle is 2 cm more than half its length. Write a variable expression to represent the width of the rectangle. Then write a variable expression to represent the perimeter of the rectangle.

Related Equations

You can use related equations to solve equations.

If you start with 5 and add 2, the result is 7. If you subtract 2 from 7, the result is the number you started with: 5. A set of related equations all communicate the same relationship between three values, but in different ways. Any time you have an addition equation, you could write two subtraction equations that describe the same relationship between the values.

RELATED EQUATIONS FOR ADDITION AND SUBTRACTION

For any *a*, *b*, and *c*:

$$\left.\begin{aligned} a + b &= c \\ a &= c - b \\ b &= c - a \end{aligned}\right\}$$ All three are related equations.

Example

$$\left.\begin{aligned} 5 + 2 &= 7 \\ 5 &= 7 - 2 \\ 2 &= 7 - 5 \end{aligned}\right\}$$ All three are related equations.

Writing Related Equations for Addition and Subtraction

A good strategy for writing a set of related equations for addition and subtraction is to identify the sum and write the addition equation first. Then, to write the subtraction equations, subtract each different addend from the sum.

EXAMPLE 1 Write a complete set of related equations for the given equation.

A $8 + x = 14$

Solution The sum is 14. Subtract 8 from 14 in one subtraction equation, and subtract x from 14 in the other subtraction equation.

$$\begin{aligned} 8 + x &= 14 \\ x &= 14 - 8 \\ 8 &= 14 - x \end{aligned}$$

TIP

The equation $14 - 8 = x$ is equivalent to $x = 14 - 8$. The equation $14 - x = 8$ is equivalent to $8 = 14 - x$.

B $21 = 35 - p$

Solution Because p is subtracted from 35, the sum in the addition equation is 35. Subtract 21 from 35 in the other subtraction equation.

$$\begin{aligned} p + 21 &= 35 \\ 21 &= 35 - p \\ p &= 35 - 21 \end{aligned}$$

Writing Related Equations for Multiplication and Division

Just like addition and subtraction, multiplication and division are also inverse operations, so you can write related equations using those operations.

RELATED EQUATIONS FOR MULTIPLICATION AND DIVISION

For any nonzero a, b, and c:		Example	
$ab = c$ $a = \frac{c}{b}$ $b = \frac{c}{a}$	All three are related equations.	$5 \cdot 2 = 10$ $5 = \frac{10}{2}$ $2 = \frac{10}{5}$	All three are related equations.

A good strategy for writing a set of related equations for multiplication and division is to identify the product and write the multiplication equation first. Then, to write the division equations, divide the product by each different factor.

EXAMPLE 2 Write a complete set of related equations for the given equation.

A $4y = 24$

Solution The product is 24. Divide 24 by 4 in one division equation, and divide 24 by y in the other division equation.

$$4y = 24$$
$$y = 24 \div 4$$
$$4 = 24 \div y$$

B $\frac{63}{a} = 9$

Solution Because 63 is divided by a, the product is 63 in the multiplication equation. Divide 63 by 9 in the other division equation.

$$9a = 63$$
$$\frac{63}{a} = 9$$
$$\frac{63}{9} = a$$

TIP

You can show division with either a division symbol or a fraction. $24 \div 4$ is equivalent to $\frac{24}{4}$.

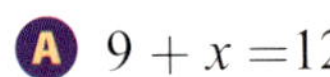 Using Related Equations to Solve an Equation

When you find a related equation that has the variable alone on one side of the equation, you can simplify to find the solution.

EXAMPLE 3 Solve using a related equation.

A $9 + x = 12$

Solution

$9 + x = 12$	Use a related equation that has the variable alone on one side of the equation.
$x = 12 - 9$	
$x = 3$	Subtract. ■

B $7y = 28$

Solution

$7y = 28$	Use a related equation that has the variable alone on one side of the equation.
$y = \frac{28}{7}$	
$y = 4$	Divide. ■

Problem Set

Write a complete set of related equations that contain the given equation.

1. $11 + 7 = 18$
2. $20 - 16 = 4$
3. $3 \cdot 4 = 12$
4. $\frac{44}{11} = 4$
5. $35 = 7k$
6. $3 = \frac{18}{e}$
7. $r \div 5 = 4$
8. $3t = 60$
9. $6 + h = 13$
10. $4.5c = 9$
11. $n + 16 = 28$
12. $120 = 2 \cdot d$
13. $m = 1.8 + 0.2$
14. $p = 24 \div 8$
15. $g + \frac{1}{2} = 5\frac{1}{2}$
16. $42 - 12 = w$
17. $\frac{75}{w} = 15$
18. $5 + x = 11.2$
19. $b \cdot 10 = 35$
20. $\frac{90}{j} = 45$

Translate the sentence into an equation. Then write the two related equations.

21. The sum of a number and 19 is 25.

22. The product of 7 and a number is 84.

Write the related equation that has the variable by itself on one side of the equals sign. Then simplify the other side.

23. $14 + b = 27$

24. $\frac{32}{s} = 4$

25. $4n = 84$

26. $40 - f = 27$

27. $r + 21 = 81$

28. $\frac{a}{11} = 11$

29. $3n = 39$

30. $x - 50 = 15$

Solve.

31. After selling x cans of soup from a 192-can shipment, a store had 51 cans left. Write and solve an equation to find how many cans, x, were sold.

32. A dozen eggs costs $2.52. Write and solve an equation to find the cost of 1 egg.

33. **Challenge** A child separated c crayons into 3 equal groups. There were 16 crayons in each group. Show how you could use related equations to find the value of c.

34. **Challenge** When the Mason family began their trip, the odometer on their car read 46,792 mi. After driving x miles, the odometer read 47,912 mi.

(a) Write an equation that represents the situation.

(b) Identify the solution by writing the related equation that has the variable by itself on one side and then simplifying the other side.

(c) Check your solution by substituting it back into the equation you wrote for Part (a).

Solving Problems

Problems are easier to solve when you have a plan.

PROBLEM-SOLVING PLAN

Step 1 ***Identify*** Read the problem and identify the unknowns. What is given? What are you being asked to find? Write it down in words. If you can, estimate the answer.

Step 2 ***Strategize*** Select and define variables and variable expressions for all the unknowns.

Step 3 ***Set Up*** Write an equation, inequality, system of equations, or whatever other tools you need that model the problem that is being solved.

Step 4 ***Solve*** Solve the model (equation, inequality, system, and so on). Answer the question.

Step 5 ***Check*** Check your answer for reasonableness and accuracy with the original problem statement.

Application: Transportation

EXAMPLE 1 Three times as many cars as trucks went over a bridge. Nineteen trucks went over the bridge. How many vehicles in all went over the bridge?

Solution Use the problem-solving plan.

Step 1 ***Identify***

Given The number of cars is 3 times the number of trucks. There were 19 trucks.

Need to find total number of vehicles

Step 2 ***Strategize*** Let t = number of trucks. Then the number of cars = $3t$.

Step 3 ***Set Up***

$\text{cars} + \text{trucks} = 3t + t$ Write an expression for the sum of the numbers of cars and trucks.

Step 4 ***Solve***

$3t + t = 3 \cdot 19 + 19$ Substitute 19 for t.

$= 57 + 19$ Simplify.

$= 76$

Seventy-six vehicles went over the bridge.

Step 5 ***Check*** Estimate to check for reasonableness. There were about 20 trucks. There were about $3 \cdot 20$, or 60 cars: $20 + 60 = 80$, which is close to 76. The answer is reasonable.

TIP

You can solve the problem without using a variable, because the number of trucks is known. But writing variables and variable expressions is a useful skill; you will need it in later topics.

Application: Geometry

EXAMPLE 2

A A playground is shaped like a square. Each side is 78 ft long. How many times did Maria run around the entire border of the playground if she ran 4992 ft?

Solution Use the problem-solving plan.
Step 1 ***Identify***

Given The playground is square, and each side is 78 ft long. Maria ran 4992 ft.

Need to find how many times Maria ran around the border

Step 2 ***Strategize*** Let n = the number of times Maria ran around the border.

Step 3 ***Set Up***
$4 \cdot 78 = 312$ All 4 sides of a square have equal length.

$312n = 4992$ Write an equation.

Step 4 ***Solve***

$$n = \frac{4992}{312} = 16$$ Use a related equation to solve for n.

Maria ran around the entire border 16 times.

Step 5 ***Check*** The distance around the playground is about 300 ft. Since $300 \cdot 16 = 4800$, the answer is reasonable. ■

B What are the possible lengths of a rectangle if the length must be 10 in. longer than the width and the area must be less than 35 in^2? Use only whole numbers for the dimensions.

Solution Use the problem-solving plan.
Step 1 ***Identify***

Given length = width + 10; area < 35

Need to find possible lengths for the longer side of the rectangle

Step 2 ***Strategize*** Let w = width. Then length = $w + 10$.

Step 3 ***Set Up*** Area < 35, so length • width < 35.

$$(w + 10) \cdot w < 35$$

Step 4 ***Solve*** Substitute whole numbers for w, starting with 1.

$(w + 10) \cdot w < 35$	$(w + 10) \cdot w < 35$	$(w + 10) \cdot w < 35$
$(1 + 10) \cdot 1 \stackrel{?}{<} 35$	$(2 + 10) \cdot 2 \stackrel{?}{<} 35$	$(3 + 10) \cdot 3 \stackrel{?}{<} 35$
$11 < 35$ ✓	$24 < 35$ ✓	$39 \not< 35$

The possible lengths are 1 + 10 and 2 + 10, or 11 in. and 12 in.

Step 5 ***Check*** Using a length of 11 in., the dimensions are 1 in. by 11 in. Using a length of 12 in., the dimensions are 2 in. by 12 in. In each case, the length is 10 in. greater than the width and the area is less than 35 in^2. The answers are reasonable. ■

REMEMBER

The area of a rectangle is the product of its length and width.

Problem Set

Use problem-solving plan to solve.

1. In a zoo, there are 5 times as many monkeys as there are bears, and the number of bears is 2 fewer than the number of elephants. The zoo has 6 elephants. How many monkeys does the zoo have?

2. Joey has nickels and dimes in his pocket. The number of dimes is 3 times the number of nickels. If Joey has 8 nickels, what is the total value of the money he has in his pocket?

3. Shawna's book report must have a minimum number of words. She counted the number of words she already wrote and realized she still has to write at least 4 times as much as she already wrote. What is the minimum number of words the book report must have if Shawna already wrote 125 words?

4. The number of cars in a store's parking lot during a Special Saturday Sale is about 250 greater than the number in the lot on a regular day. If there are about 700 cars in the lot during the Special Saturday Sale, about how many cars are in the lot on a regular day?

5. What are the possible lengths of a rectangle if the width must be 8 in. less than the length and the area must be between 100 and 200 in^2? Use only whole numbers for the dimensions.

6. What are the possible lengths for the side of a square if the distance around the square must be less than 25 m? Use only whole numbers for dimensions.

7. Mei drove a total of 504 mi in 9 h. Find her average rate of speed given that distance is the product of rate and time.

8. It takes Francis about 25 min to walk to his best friend's house. He figured that he spent a total of 7 h and 30 min walking back and forth to his friend's house last month. How many times did he walk to his friend's house last month?

9. A walking loop is made up of five connecting trails. Three of the trails are 1820 ft long and the other two are 965 ft long. How far does Mrs. Johansson walk if she walks the loop 2 times? 6 times?

10. The elevation at the start of a trail is 3780 ft and the elevation at the end of the trail is 5865 ft. Assuming the gain in elevation is fairly constant throughout the trail, about how many feet are gained every hour if it takes a hiker 3 h to hike the trail? 5 h?

11. The ages of three cousins are consecutive even whole numbers. The sum of the youngest and oldest ages is 16. How old is the oldest cousin?

12. The sum of the measures of the three angles in any triangle is 180°. If one of the angles is a 90° angle, what are the measures of the other two angles if the measure of the larger angle is 10° more than the measure of the smaller angle?

13. At a museum, adult tickets to a special exhibit cost $5 and children's tickets cost $2.50. A group of children and adults has budgeted $50 for the exhibit. Two adults must enter the exhibit. How many children could they take with them? How many fewer children could they take if the price of the children's ticket is raised by 50¢?

14. Donald drove a total of 279 mi at an average rate of 62 mph. How long did the trip take?

15. Doug is 1 year older than twice Cheryl's age. Ed is 3 times as old as Doug, and he is between 70 and 90 years old. Find the possible whole number ages that Cheryl could be.

16. A bird feeder is shaped like a rectangular prism. Its base measures 6.3 cm by 3.8 cm and its height is 16.6 cm. Alonzo bought a box of bird seed measuring 40 cm by 18 cm by 9 cm. About how many times can Alonzo fill the bird feeder completely?

Core Focus: Word Problems

THE CORE CONCEPT

Many real-world problems involve arithmetic using rational numbers that are not whole numbers.

Calculations with Rational Numbers

When a problem involves fractions or decimals, start by translating the problem statement into an expression as you would for problems involving only integers. Then follow the rules for the order of operations to simplify the expression.

EXAMPLE 1 The tank in Sabina's car holds 12.7 gal of gasoline. Currently, the tank is $\frac{3}{4}$ full.

A How much gasoline is in Sabina's tank currently? Round to the nearest tenth of a gallon.

Solution Multiply the capacity of the tank by the fraction representing how full the tank is:

$$12.7 \cdot \frac{3}{4} = \frac{38.1}{4} \approx 9.5$$

There are currently about 9.5 gal of gasoline in Sabrina's tank. ■

B Sabina's car can travel an average of 28.3 miles per gallon of gasoline. Explain how Sabina would estimate the number of miles traveled since she last filled the tank. Round to the nearest mile.

Solution Find the number of gallons of gasoline used:

$$12.7 - 9.5 = 3.2$$

Multiply this amount by the average miles per gallon:

$$3.2 \cdot 28.3 = 90.56 \approx 91$$

Sabina traveled about 91 mi. ■

REMEMBER

A **rational number** is a number that can be expressed as a ratio $\frac{a}{b}$, where a and b are integers and $b \neq 0$. A rational number can be written as a fraction, a decimal, or a percent.

REMEMBER

To multiply a decimal by a fraction,

Step 1 Multiply the decimal by the numerator of the fraction.

Step 2 Divide the result by the denominator of the fraction.

Q & A

Q How far would Sabina travel on 2 tanks of gas?

A about 696 mi

EXAMPLE 2 Dean had \$45.92 in his bank account.

A He withdrew $\frac{1}{3}$ of the amount in his account to buy a book.

How much did Dean withdraw?

Solution

$$\frac{1}{3} \cdot \$45.92 = \frac{\$45.92}{3} \approx \$15.31$$

Dean withdrew \$15.31. ■

> **REMEMBER**
> Unless told otherwise, round amounts of money to the nearest cent.

B How much does Dean have left in his bank account after the withdrawal?

Solution

$$\$45.92 - \$15.31 = \$30.61$$

Dean has \$30.61 left in his account after the withdrawal. ■

C Dean withdraws another \$5.50 from his bank account. How much is left in his bank account now, and what fraction is this amount of the original \$45.92 in his account? Write the fraction as a percent rounded to the nearest hundredth, and then convert to a percent.

Solution

$$\$30.61 - \$5.50 = \$25.11$$

Dean has \$25.11 in his account after this second withdrawal.

Divide this amount by \$45.92 to find the fraction of the original amount in the bank account that remains:

$$\frac{\$25.11}{\$45.92} = \frac{\$2511}{\$4592} \approx 0.55$$

About 55% of the original amount in Dean's bank account remains after the two withdrawals. ■

Problem Set

Solve.

1. Neyra earned \$140.43, \$163.78, and \$139.62 from three paychecks. Neyra deposits $\frac{1}{4}$ of each paycheck into a college savings account.
   - **(a)** Find each amount that Neyra deposited into her college savings account from her paychecks.
   - **(b)** What is the total amount that Neyra deposits into her college savings account from these paychecks?
   - **(c)** Use the distributive property to show that Neyra could have found the total amount deposited into her college savings account by summing the amount of all three paychecks and then multiplying this sum by $\frac{1}{4}$.

2. David makes pancakes according to the recipe on the box of pancake mix. The recipe calls for $2\frac{1}{2}$ cups of pancake mix, 1 cup of milk, and 2 eggs. The recipe makes enough pancakes for 6 people.
   - **(a)** David wishes to make enough pancakes for 9 people. How much of each ingredient does he need?
   - **(b)** Suppose David wishes to make enough for 10 people. Explain why he could have trouble following the recipe exactly in this case.

3. A recreation center sponsors three sports teams. The table shows the number of players on the three sports teams. The total budget for all three sports is \$25,000.

Team	Number of players
tennis	16
soccer	23
volleyball	14

   - **(a)** The coaches of all three teams decided to split the \$25,000 based on the fraction of the number of players on each team. Write the fraction of the number of all players on each team. Explain how you could use this fraction for each team to calculate its budget. Find the amount each team would receive.
   - **(b)** The recreation center decides to split the budget another way. Each team gets \$5500. What remains after each team gets \$5500 is split according to the fraction of the number of all players on each team. Find the amount each team would receive when the recreation center uses this method to divide the \$25,000 budget.

Core Focus: Interpreting Expressions

THE CORE CONCEPT

To solve many problems, you must translate word phrases into variable expressions, equations, or inequalities. There are usually many ways to model any problem.

Working with Multiple Representations

EXAMPLE 1 Ilya sold 10 veggie burgers on Tuesday. On Wednesday, she sold w veggie burgers. On Thursday, Ilya sold t veggie burgers. Each veggie burger sold for \$5.

Both the expressions $5(10 + w + t)$ and $50 + 5t + 5w$ represent combined sales, in dollars, of veggie burgers for all three days. Explain how each expression represents the combined sales.

REMEMBER

You can use the distributive property in some situations to rewrite an expression. Look for a factor common to all terms in the expression.

Solution Add the number of veggie burgers sold on the 3 days to get the total number of veggie burgers sold:

$$10 + w + t$$

Multiply the total number sold by the price per veggie burger to get the combined sales:

$$5(10 + w + t)$$

Each veggie burger sells for \$5 so total sales on Tuesday, Wednesday, and Thursday were 50, $5w$, and $5t$ dollars. Add these amounts to get the combined sales for all three days:

$$50 + 5w + 5t$$ ■

Modeling Word Problems

EXAMPLE 2 A water tank has 25 gal of water. Water begins to flow from a pipe into the tank at a rate of 6 gal/min. At the same time, water begins to drain from the bottom of the tank at a rate of 2 gal/min. The expression $25 + 4m$ represents the amount of water in the tank, in gallons, after m minutes. Explain how the expression represents this amount.

Solution Find the amount of water that enters the tank from the pipe: $6m$. Find the amount of water that drains from the tank: $2m$.

Subtract the amount that drains from the amount of water that enters:

$$6m - 2m$$

Add this amount to the initial amount of water in the tank:

$$25 + 6m - 2m$$

Simplify:

$$25 + 6m - 2m = 25 + 4m$$ ■

▶ **THINK ABOUT IT**

What flow rate into the tank would cause the amount of water in the tank to be constant?

Problem Set

Solve.

1. Kellie and Hoda share a savings account. This month Kellie was able to place k dollars in the account 5 times during the month. Every time Kellie made a deposit, Hoda took h dollars from the account. On the last day of the month, Hoda deposited a check for $250 in the account. Each expression represents the change in the amount of money in Kellie and Hoda's bank account by the end of the month. Explain how each expression represents this change.

Expression X: $5k - 5h + 250$

Expression Y: $5(k - h) + 250$

2. Casey bought 4 shirts on Monday. The price of a shirt was d dollars. On Friday, the price of a shirt was reduced by $3. Casey bought 2 shirts at this reduced price.

(a) Each expression represents the total amount Casey spent on shirts. Explain how each expression represents this total amount.

Expression W: $4d + 2(d - 3)$

Expression Z: $6d - 6$

(b) Suppose that the price of a shirt on Friday was reduced by $5 instead of $3. How would Expressions W and Z change? Show your work.

3. On Saturday, Tom biked for h hours at an average speed of 14 kmph. On Sunday, Tom biked for 2 more hours than he did on Saturday, riding at the same speed.

(a) Write a variable expression for the number of kilometers Tom biked on Saturday.

(b) Write a variable expression for the number of kilometers Tom biked on Sunday.

(c) Tom biked a total of 70 km on Saturday and Sunday. How many kilometers did Tom bike on Saturday? Explain your reasoning.

4. At the beginning of the year, Jubail had 11 video games, and he bought 1 more video game each month. At the beginning of the same year, Tyler had 3 video games, and he bought 2 more video games each month.

(a) Write a variable expression for the number of video games that Jubail had after m months.

(b) Write a variable expression for the number of video games that Tyler had after m months.

(c) After how many months did they both have the same number of video games? Explain your reasoning.

CHAPTER 1 Review

Choose the answer.

1. What is the value of the expression?

$$8 + 12 \div 4 - 3$$

A. 2
B. 8
C. 11
D. 20

2. What is the value of the expression?

$$8 \cdot (1 + 4) \div 2$$

A. 6
B. 10
C. 20
D. 24

3. What is the value of the expression $x - 2y + 4$ when $x = 7$ and $y = 3$?

A. 5
B. 8
C. 12
D. 19

4. What is the value of the expression $\frac{3u}{9 - v}$ when $u = -6$ and $v = 7$?

A. −9
B. −2
C. $-\frac{3}{2}$
D. $\frac{2}{7}$

5. Which variable expression represents the word phrase?

3 less the product of a number and 4

A. $3n - 4$
B. $3 - 4n$
C. $4 - 3n$
D. $4n - 3$

6. Which word phrase represents the expression?

$$\frac{n}{5} + 8$$

A. the quotient of a number and 5 decreased by 8
B. the quotient of a number and 5 increased by 8
C. the product of a number and 5 increased by 8
D. the sum of a number and 8 divided by 5

7. Which equation is related to the equation?

$$6 \cdot d = 42$$

A. $d = 6 \div 42$
B. $d = 6 \cdot 42$
C. $d = 42 - 6$
D. $d = 42 \div 6$

8. Which equation is related to the sentence?

The sum of a number and 4 is 13.

A. $n = 4 - 13$
B. $n = 4 + 13$
C. $n = 13 - 4$
D. $n = 13 + 4$

9. Shanie is 7 years younger than Emily, and Emily is twice John's age. John is 8 years old. What is Shanie's age?

A. 3 years old
B. 9 years old
C. 11 years old
D. 16 years old

10. The perimeter of a rectangle is 30. The length of the rectangle is 3 more than its width. What is the width of the rectangle?

A. 6
B. 9
C. 12
D. 18

11. Two rings are made from a metal alloy that is 90% pure gold. The 2 rings weigh 6 g and 8 g. How much more pure gold is there in the 8 g ring than in the 6 g ring?

A. 0.1 g
B. 0.2 g
C. 0.9 g
D. 1.8 g

Solve.

12. Davila had \$26 in her savings account. She deposited \$3 in her account every week for 4 wk. Then she withdrew \$10 from her account. Write and simplify an expression to find the amount of money Davila has in her savings account.

13. The formula for the volume of a rectangular pyramid is $V = \frac{1}{3}lwh$, where l is the length of the base, w is the width of the base, and h is the height of the pyramid. Find the volume, V, of a pyramid with a base length of 6 cm, a base width of 4 cm, and a height of 9 cm.

14. Finny is 5 more than twice Ana's age. Write a variable expression to represent Finny's age.

15. Write a related equation that has r isolated on one side of the equation. Then simplify the equation to find the value of r.

$$\frac{54}{r} = 9$$

16. Carlo worked 7 h less this week than Chris did. Chris worked half as many hours this week as Liana did. If Liana worked 36 h this week, how many hours did Carlo work this week?

17. A sandwich shop sells 23 bottles of apple juice on Monday, 19 bottles of apple juice on Tuesday, and 31 bottles of apple juice on Wednesday. Total sales of apple juice for the three days are \$120.45. For each day, write an expression for the apple-juice sales for that day. Simplify each expression.

18. Jenny earns \$50 each week walking dogs. She deposits \$5 of her earnings into a savings account for college, and she deposits the remaining amount into a checking account. Explain how each expression represents the total amount of money Jenny earns after w weeks.

Expression A: $w(5 + 45)$

Expression B: $5w + 45w$

Problem	Topic Lookup	Problem	Topic Lookup
1, 2, 12	Order of Operations	9, 10, 16	Solving Problems
3, 4, 13	Variable Expressions	11, 17	Core Focus: Word Problems
5, 6, 14	Writing Expressions for Word Phrases	18	Core Focus: Interpreting Expressions
7, 8, 15	Related Equations		

CHAPTER 2 Addition and Subtraction on a Number Line

You can find number lines on many things, such as thermometers, water-depth markers, or tape measures. You can use distances along these number lines to add and subtract numbers.

In This Chapter

Number lines are a great way to show how to add and subtract numbers. In this chapter, you'll look at how you can use a number line to add and subtract positive and negative decimals. You will also use integers to solve problems.

Topic List

- Foundations for Chapter 2
- Integers on a Number Line
- Adding Integers
- Subtracting Integers
- Core Focus: Distance
- Decimals on a Number Line
- Adding Decimals
- Core Focus: Additive Inverses
- Chapter 2 Review

Depth markers indicate how much of a boat is under water.

68
66
64
62
60
58
56
54
52
50
48

Foundations for Chapter 2

Identifying Points on a Number Line

DEFINITION

A **coordinate** is a number that locates a point on a number line.

A number line goes in two directions. Find the coordinate of a point by starting at zero and counting the number of units to the right or left. Positive numbers are to the right of zero and negative numbers are to the left of zero.

EXAMPLE A State the coordinate of each labeled point.

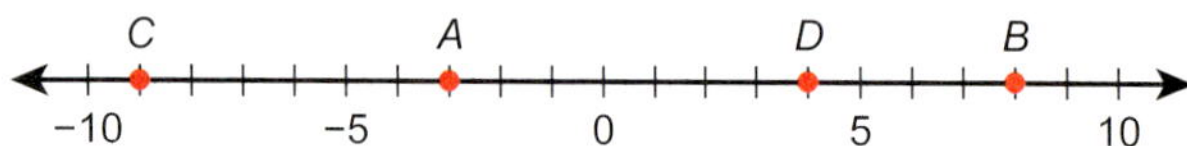

Solution

Point A is 3 units to the left of the origin. Its coordinate is -3.

Point B is 8 units to the right of the origin. Its coordinate is 8.

Point C is 9 units to the left of the origin. Its coordinate is -9.

Point D is 4 units to the right of the origin. Its coordinate is 4. ■

Problem Set A

State the coordinate of the labeled point.

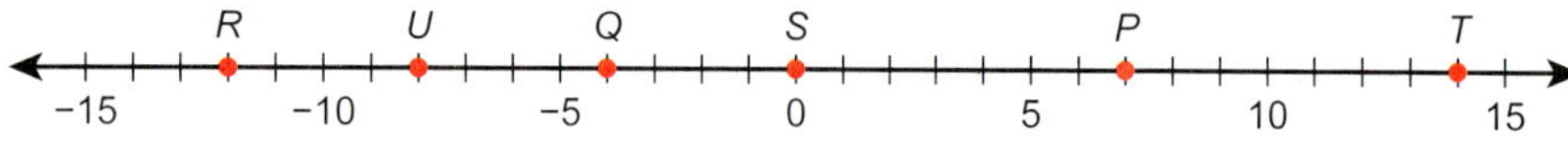

1. point P
2. point Q
3. point R
4. point S
5. point T
6. point U

Adding and Subtracting Whole Numbers

When adding or subtracting multidigit numbers, first line up the numbers by place value. Then add or subtract digits with the same place value, moving from right to left. Remember that you may need to regroup.

EXAMPLE B Add or subtract.

B-1 $256 + 179$

Solution Align numbers vertically by their place values.

$$\begin{array}{r} {\scriptstyle 1\,1} \\ 256 \\ +\,179 \\ \hline 435 \end{array}$$

$256 + 179 = 435$ ■

B-2 $627 - 249$

Solution Write the regrouped numbers directly above the digits they represent.

$$\begin{array}{r} {\scriptstyle \not{5}\;11\;17} \\ \not{6}\,\not{2}\,\not{7} \\ -\,2\;4\;9 \\ \hline 3\;7\;8 \end{array}$$

$627 - 249 = 378$ ■

Problem Set B

Add or subtract.

1. $95 + 63$
2. $82 - 47$
3. $126 + 315$
4. $261 - 83$
5. $553 + 364$
6. $104 + 973$
7. $956 - 481$
8. $201 - 108$
9. $497 + 203$
10. $721 - 654$
11. $604 - 581$
12. $179 + 823$
13. $810 - 657$
14. $671 + 809$

Adding Decimals

First align the decimal points of the two numbers. Add zeros, when necessary, so that the two numbers end with the same place value. Then add, and regroup any sums if necessary.

EXAMPLE C Add.

C-1 $3.58 + 4.7$

Solution Add zeros so that both numbers have the same number of place values after the decimal.

$$\begin{array}{r} {}^{1} \\ 3.58 \\ +\,4.70 \\ \hline 8.28 \end{array}$$

$3.58 + 4.7 = 8.28$ ■

C-2 $9.8 + 0.329$

Solution Align vertically so the decimal points in the numbers are aligned.

$$\begin{array}{r} {}^{1} \\ 9.800 \\ +\,0.329 \\ \hline 10.129 \end{array}$$

$9.8 + 0.329 = 10.129$ ■

Problem Set C

Add.

1. $1.23 + 5.6$
2. $0.35 + 3.01$
3. $0.82 + 31.16$
4. $1.362 + 4.5$
5. $0.709 + 0.88$
6. $61.98 + 539$
7. $134.5 + 6.589$
8. $10.86 + 0.097$
9. $4.07 + 391.08$
10. $89.04 + 1.67$
11. $0.095 + 8.25$
12. $7.628 + 0.407$

Integers on a Number Line

A number line goes in two directions. To the right of zero are positive numbers. To the left of zero are negative numbers.

Nonzero opposites are two numbers that are the same distance from zero on a number line. A **number line** can be used to compare and order numbers. Every number has its own corresponding point on a number line.

The set of **integers** is {. . ., −3, −2, −1, 0, 1, 2, 3, . . .}. It is the set of whole numbers and their opposites.

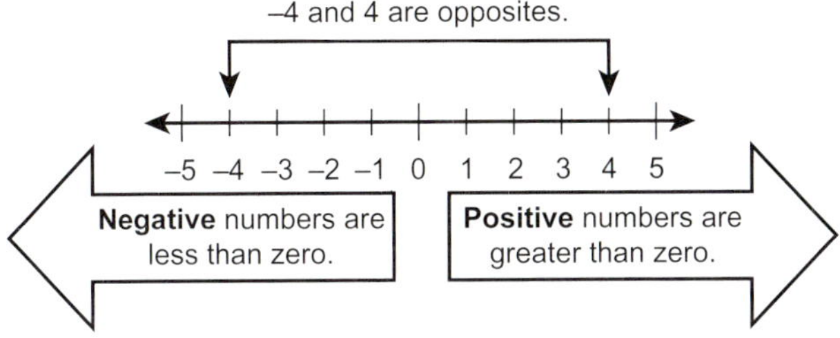

The opposite of zero is zero. Zero is neither positive nor negative.

THINK ABOUT IT

Zero is a whole number and an integer.

Identifying Coordinates of Points on a Number Line

A **coordinate** is a number that indicates the location of a point on a number line. The **origin** is the point on a number line with coordinate 0.

EXAMPLE 1 State the coordinate of each indicated point on the number line.

A point A

Solution Point A is the origin. The coordinate of point A is 0. ■

B point B

Solution Point B is 3 units to the right of the origin. The coordinate of point B is 3. ■

C point C

Solution Point C is 4 units to the left of the origin. The coordinate of point C is −4. ■

TIP

A number with no symbol in front is positive, so 3 represents positive 3. Some books use +3 to represent positive 3.

D point D

Solution Point D is 7 units to the left of the origin. The coordinate of point D is -7. ■

Graphing Integers on a Number Line

To graph an integer on a number line, begin at the origin, and then count the correct number of units right or left. Draw a dot to represent the point and label the point with its coordinate.

> **TIP**
> A point is the graph, or plot, of a number. A number is the coordinate of a point.

EXAMPLE 2 Graph the number on a number line.

A 6

Solution Since 6 is positive, it is to the right of the origin. Start at zero and count 6 units to the right.

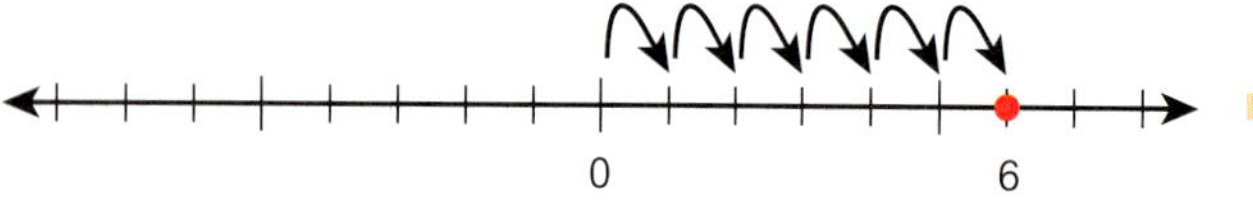

■

B -3

Solution Since -3 is negative, it is to the left of the origin. Start at zero and count 3 units to the left.

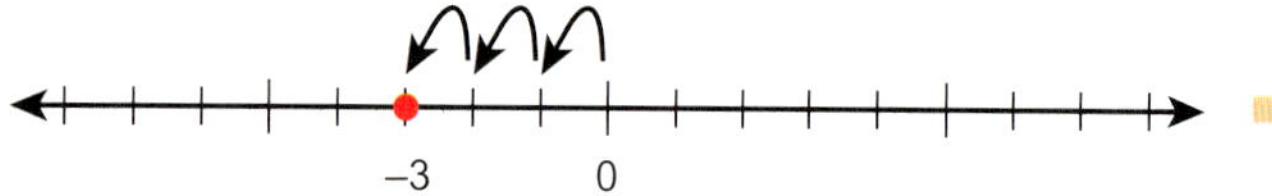

■

Comparing Numbers

Graphing numbers on a number line can help you compare them. Numbers increase in value as you move to the right. Numbers decrease in value as you move to the left. So, when comparing two numbers, the number to the left is less and the number to the right is greater.

EXAMPLE 3 Use a number line to compare the integers. Use $<$, $>$, or $=$.

A 2 and -4

Solution

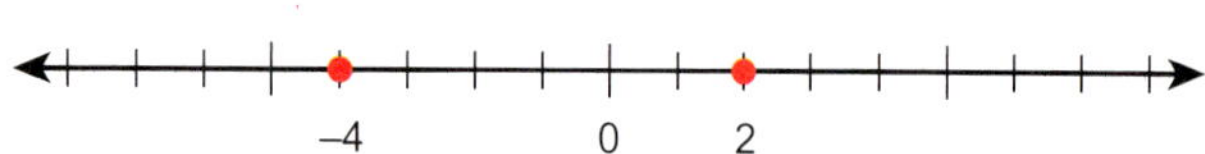

Because -4 is to the left of 2, you know that -4 is less than 2. So you can write either $-4 < 2$ or $2 > -4$. ■

> **REMEMBER**
> The inequalities $-4 < 2$ and $2 > -4$ are equivalent. You can say negative four is less than two or two is greater than negative four.

B -6 and -2

Solution

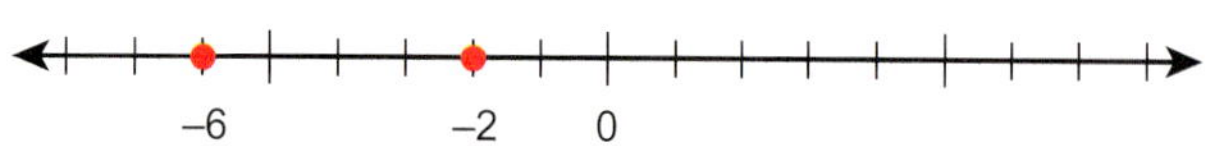

Because -6 is to the left of -2, you know that -6 is less than -2. So you can write either $-6 < -2$ or $-2 > -6$. ■

Absolute Value

The **absolute value** of a number is its distance from zero. Absolute value is indicated by the | | symbol. For example, read $|-4|$ as the absolute value of negative four.

EXAMPLE 4

A Find $|-4|$.

Solution

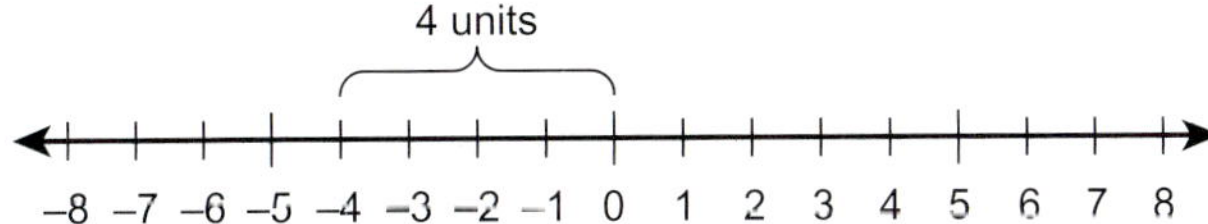

Since -4 is 4 units from zero, $|-4| = 4$. ■

B Find $|6|$.

Solution

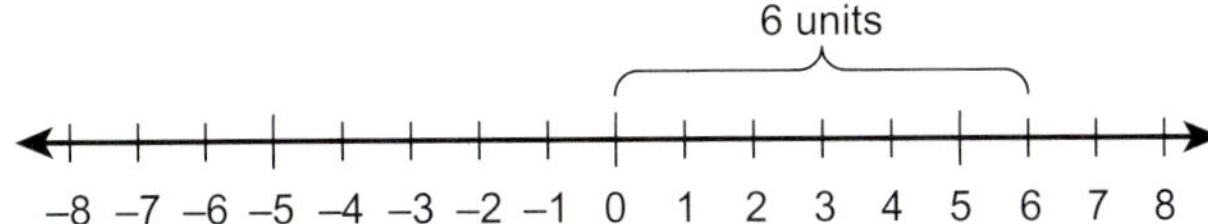

Since 6 is 6 units from zero, $|6| = 6$. ■

Opposite Numbers

Numbers are opposites if they are the same distance from zero but in different directions on a number line. Another property of opposites is that they have different signs (except for zero) but the same absolute value. For example, 12 and -12 are opposites because they have different signs, but $|12| = 12$ and $|-12| = 12$.

The $-$ sign is used to indicate opposite. You can read -2 as either negative two or the opposite of two. Read $-(-2)$ as the opposite of negative two. The opposite of -2 is 2, so write $-(-2) = 2$ and read it as the opposite of negative two equals two.

TIP

The same sign is used for opposite, negative, and subtraction.

EXAMPLE 5 Write the opposite of the integer.

A 3

Solution The opposite of 3 is -3. ■

B -10

Solution The opposite of -10 is 10, or $-(-10) = 10$. ■

C 0

Solution The opposite of 0 is 0. ■

THINK ABOUT IT

All numbers have opposites, not just integers. For example, the opposite of 3.4 is -3.4.

Identifying Integer Solutions of Absolute Value Open Sentences

You can use a number line to help identify integer solutions of simple equations and inequalities involving absolute value.

EXAMPLE 6 Identify all integer solutions of the equation or inequality.

A $|x| = 7$

Solution The absolute value of x is 7, so all values of x are 7 units from zero on a number line.

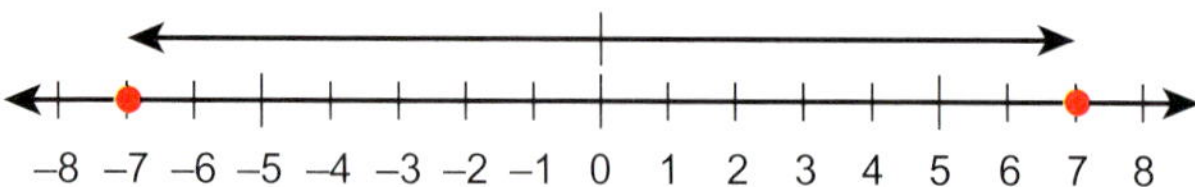

The integer solutions of $|x| = 7$ are -7 and 7. ■

B $|x| < 3$

Solution The absolute value of x is less than 3, so all values of x are less than 3 units from zero on a number line.

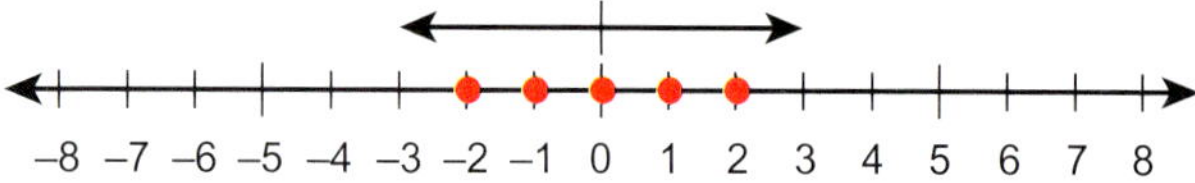

The integer solutions of $|x| < 3$ are -2, -1, 0, 1, and 2. ■

> **REMEMBER**
>
> An open sentence is an equation or inequality that contains one or more variables. A solution of an open sentence is a number that makes it true.

> **THINK ABOUT IT**
>
> There are many solutions of $|x| < 3$ that are not integers. Two solutions are -1.55 and $2\frac{3}{4}$.

Application: Weather

EXAMPLE 7 The table shows the temperatures for five cities on a particular day. Plot the temperatures on a number line. Then list the cities in order from coldest to warmest.

City	Temperature (°C)
Ottawa, Canada	-6
Los Angeles, CA	11
Seward, AK	-7
Houston, TX	6
Washington, DC	-1

Solution

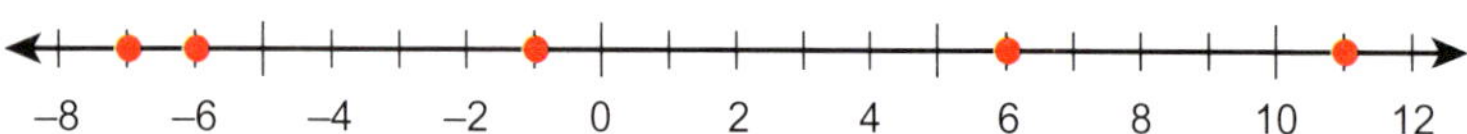

The cities from coldest to warmest are Seward, Ottawa, Washington, Houston, and Los Angeles. ■

Problem Set

State the coordinate of each indicated point on the number line.

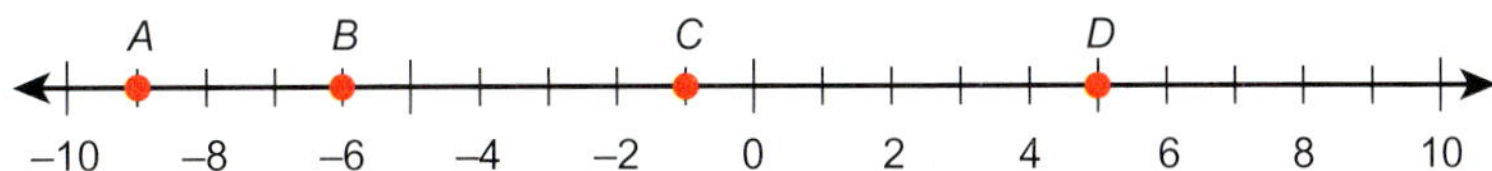

1. point A

2. point B

3. point C

4. point D

Graph the number on a number line.

5. -7

6. 0

7. 3

8. -6

Use a number line to compare the integers. Use $<$, $>$, or $=$.

9. 3 and -1

10. -8 and 4

11. -5 and 0

12. -2 and -6

For each value of *n*:

(a) Find the absolute value of n: $|n|$.

(b) Find the opposite of n: $-n$.

13. $n = 10$

14. $n = -15$

15. $n = -4$

16. $n = 8$

Complete the statement with $<$, $>$, or $=$.

17. $|-4| \; \square \; 4$

18. $|-3| \; \square \; |-8|$

19. $-6 \; \square \; |-10|$

20. $-|-5| \; \square \; 1$

Identify all integer solutions of the equation or inequality.

21. $|x| = 5$

22. $|x| = -3$

23. $|r| < 6$

24. $|x| < 1$

25. $|a| < -2$

26. $|n| > -1$

27. $|x| \leq 2$

28. $|s| \leq 1$

Solve.

29. Students are playing a game in which they draw cards and then add or subtract the integer shown on the card. The chart shows the students' scores at the end of the game. List the students in order from the lowest scoring student to the highest scoring student.

Name	Score
Alana	4
Haley	−7
Trent	0
Buan	−2
Jared	2

30. The chart shows the lowest recorded temperature in Boise, Idaho, by month, for 47 years. Name the months that had temperatures lower than the low temperature in April but higher than the low temperature in February.

Month	Temperature (°C)
Jan.	−27
Feb.	−26
Mar.	−14
Apr.	−7
May	−5
June	0
July	1
Aug.	1
Sept.	−5
Oct.	−11
Nov.	−19
Dec.	−31

31. A group of friends were playing miniature golf. The chart shows what their scores were at the end of the game. The player with the lowest score won the game. List the players in order of finish, starting with the winning player.

Name	Score
Olivia	−2
Emilio	3
Ramon	0
Leticia	−1
Max	−4

32. Order the numbers from least to greatest.

$$-7, |-4|, 3, -|6|, 0, -|-5|$$

Adding Integers

You can use a number line to add integers.

USING A NUMBER LINE TO ADD INTEGERS

Start at 0.

For positive integers, move right; for negative integers, move left.

The ending point of each move is the starting point for the next move. The ending point of the last move is the answer.

TIP

In any addition expression, the numbers being added are called addends.

Using a Number Line to Add Integers

EXAMPLE 1 Use a number line to find the sum.

A $3 + (-7)$

Solution Start at 0. Move 3 units right. From 3, move 7 units left.

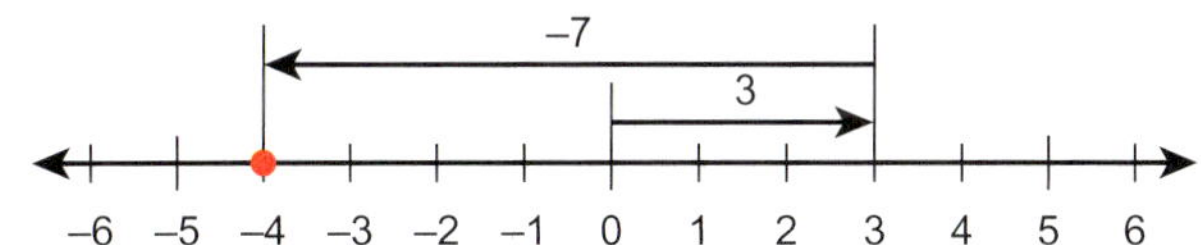

$3 + (-7) = -4$ ■

TIP

You can start with either integer.

$3 + (-7) = -7 + 3$

B $-4 + (-2)$

Solution Start at 0. Move 4 units left. From −4, move 2 units left.

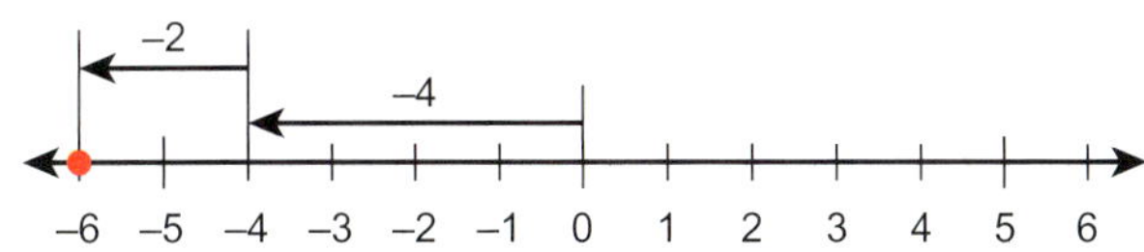

$-4 + (-2) = -6$ ■

Using Rules to Add Integers

In addition to a number line, you can also use rules to add integers.

RULES FOR ADDING TWO INTEGERS

If the signs are the same, add the absolute values of the integers. The sum has the same sign as the addends.

If the signs are different, find the difference of the absolute values. The sum has the same sign as the addend with the greater absolute value.

EXAMPLE 2 Find the sum.

A $-20 + (-13)$

Solution Both addends are negative. The sum will be negative.

$-20 + (-13) = -(|-20| + |-13|)$ The sum is negative.

$= -(20 + 13)$ Evaluate the absolute values.

$= -33$ Add. ■

B $-25 + 35$

Solution The addends have different signs. Because $|35|$ is greater than $|-25|$, the sum will be positive.

$-25 + 35 = +(|35| - |-25|)$ The sum is positive.

$= 35 - 25$ Evaluate the absolute values.

$= 10$ Subtract.

Check Use a number line.

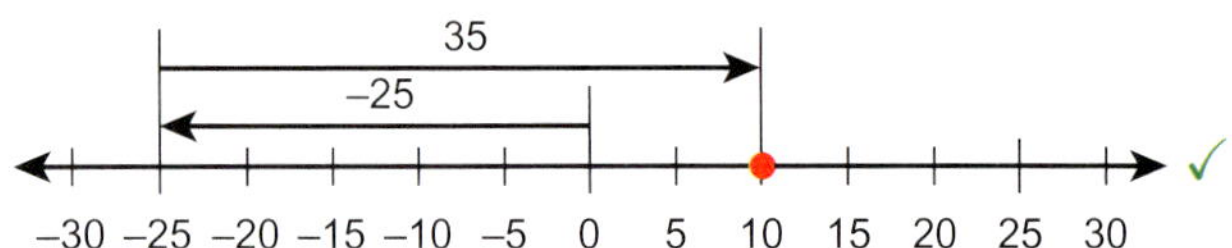

The sum is 10. ■

> **REMEMBER**
> Absolute value is always nonnegative.
> $|-25| = 25$
> $|35| = 35$

Evaluating Expressions

Evaluate variable expressions by substituting values for the variables and then simplifying.

EXAMPLE 3

A Evaluate $a + b$ when $a = 5$ and $b = -1$.

Solution

$a + b = 5 + (-1)$ Substitute 5 for a and -1 for b.

$= 4$ Add. ■

B Evaluate $x + y + z$ when $x = -43$, $y = -17$, and $z = -10$.

Solution

$x + y + z = -43 + (-17) + (-10)$ Substitute -43 for x, -17 for y, and -10 for z.

$= -60 + (-10)$ Add from left to right.

$= -70$ ■

Comparing Expressions

EXAMPLE 4 Select the symbol ($<$, $>$, or $=$) that makes a true statement.

A $3 + (-4) \;\square\; 5 + (-2)$

Solution

$3 + (-4) \;\square\; 5 + (-2)$	Evaluate the expression on each side.
$-1 \quad < \quad 3$	Since -1 is less than 3, use the $<$ symbol.

$3 + (-4) < 5 + (-2)$ ■

B $8 + (-20) \;\square\; -7 + (-10)$

Solution

$8 + (-20) \;\square\; -7 + (-10)$	Evaluate the expression on each side.
$-12 \quad > \quad -17$	Since -12 is greater than -17, use the $>$ symbol.

$8 + (-20) > -7 + (-10)$ ■

C $-3 + 8 + (-11) \;\square\; 10 + (-16)$

Solution

$-3 + 8 + (-11) \;\square\; 10 + (-16)$	Evaluate the expression on each side.
$-6 \quad = \quad -6$	Since -6 is equal to -6, use the $=$ symbol.

$-3 + 8 + (-11) = 10 + (-16)$ ■

TIP

To compare -12 and -17, plot them on a number line. The lesser number is on the left and the greater number is on the right.

Addition Properties

Here are two useful properties for addition.

ADDITION PROPERTIES

Property	Symbols	Examples
Identity Property for Addition The sum of any number and zero is equal to the number. Zero is called the **additive identity.**	$a + 0 = a$ $0 + a = a$	$-5 + 0 = -5$ $0 + 8 = 8$
Property of Inverses for Addition The sum of any number and its opposite is equal to zero. Opposites are also called additive inverses.	$a + (-a) = 0$ $-a + a = 0$	$3 + (-3) = 0$ $-10 + 10 = 0$ $-7 + (-(-7)) = 0$

EXAMPLE 5 Find the value of the variable that makes the statement true.

A $x + 5 = 0$

Solution The property of inverses for addition states that the sum of any number and its opposite is 0. Because the sum is 0, you know that x is the opposite of 5. So $x = -5$. ■

B $-4 + x = -4$

Solution The identity property for addition states that the sum of any number and 0 is equal to the same number. Because -4 plus x is equal to -4, you know that x is 0. So $x = 0$. ■

Application: Banking

EXAMPLE 6 The table shows deposits and withdrawals in a new bank account that is opened with the deposit on Monday. How much is in the account at the end of the week?

Day	Deposit or withdrawal ($)
Mon.	+50
Wed.	−27
Thurs.	+30
Fri.	−13

Solution

$$\begin{aligned} 50 + (-27) + 30 + (-13) &= 23 + 30 + (-13) \\ &= 53 + (-13) \\ &= 40 \end{aligned}$$

At the end of the week, the account contains $40. ■

Problem Set

Use a number line to find the sum.

1. $-7 + (-2)$

2. $4 + (-5)$

3. $-6 + 2$

4. $8 + (-3)$

Find the sum.

5. $17 + (-12)$

6. $-27 + 28$

7. $-22 + (-74)$

8. $45 + (-58)$

9. $-15 + (-25)$

10. $-100 + 42$

Evaluate when $a = -6$, $b = 2$, and $c = -7$.

11. $a + b$
12. $c + b$
13. $a + c$
14. $a + b + c$

Select the symbol ($<$, $>$, or $=$) that makes a true statement.

15. $8 + (-7)$ ☐ $7 + (-8)$
16. $-12 + (-4)$ ☐ $-20 + (-6)$
17. $9 + (-15)$ ☐ $-2 + (-4)$
18. $9 + (-20)$ ☐ $15 + (-3)$

Find the value of the variable that makes the statement true.

19. $x + (-7) = 0$
20. $-3 = -3 + x$
21. $x + (-15) = -13 + (-2)$
22. $4 + (-1) + x = 0$

Evaluate when $x = -12$, $y = 27$, and $z = -32$.

23. $|x| + y$
24. $|x + y|$
25. $|y + z|$
26. $y + |z|$
27. $x + |z|$
28. $|x + y + z|$

Solve.

29. The drama club is planning an after-play celebration. The chart shows the amount of money the club expects to gain (positive number) and the costs of each item for the party (negative numbers).

    (a) Will the drama club have enough money to pay for the party costs?

    (b) If it will, how much money will the club have left over? If it won't, how much more money will it need?

    (c) Explain your answer.

Party item	Amount ($)
income from tickets	800
cost of food	−523
cost of decorations	−125
cost of plates and cups	−80

30. This month, Nahla deposited $425 in her bank account. She withdrew $320 and then deposited $210. How much money is in her account after those transactions?

Subtracting Integers

In simple arithmetic, subtraction is the same as taking away. In algebra, subtraction is the same as adding the opposite.

To subtract an integer, you add its opposite.

SUBTRACTING INTEGERS

Properties	Symbols	Examples
To subtract an integer, add its opposite.	$a - b = a + (-b)$ $a - (-b) = a + b$	$1 - 5 = 1 + (-5)$ $10 - (-4) = 10 + 4$

Subtracting Integers

EXAMPLE 1 Find the difference.

A $2 - 7$

Solution

$2 - 7 = 2 + (-7)$ Rewrite as adding the opposite of 7.

$= -5$ ■

B $3 - (-5)$

Solution

$3 - (-5) = 3 + 5$ Add the opposite of -5.

$= 8$ ■

C $-4 - 11$

Solution

$-4 - 11 = -4 + (-11)$ Add the opposite of 11.

$= -15$ ■

D $-47 - (-7)$

Solution

$-47 - (-7) = -47 + 7$ Add the opposite of -7.

$= -40$ ■

THINK ABOUT IT

The rules for adding and subtracting integers apply to adding and subtracting all real numbers.

$-3.2 - 4.5 = -3.2 + (-4.5)$

$= -7.7$

Evaluating Expressions

Evaluate variable expressions by substituting values for the variables.

EXAMPLE 2

A Evaluate $a - b$ when $a = -1$ and $b = -6$.

Solution

$a - b = -1 - (-6)$	Substitute -1 for a and -6 for b.
$= -1 + 6$	Add the opposite of -6.
$= 5$ ■	

B Evaluate $20 - x - y$ when $x = 14$ and $y = -6$.

Solution

$20 - x - y = 20 - 14 - (-6)$	Substitute 14 for x and -6 for y.
$= 20 + (-14) + 6$	Rewrite using addition.
$= 6 + 6$	Add from left to right.
$= 12$ ■	

C Evaluate $c - d + f$ when $c = -2$, $d = 18$, and $f = -11$.

Solution

$c - d + f = -2 - 18 + (-11)$	Substitute -2 for c, 18 for d, and -11 for f.
$= -2 + (-18) + (-11)$	Rewrite using addition.
$= -20 + (-11)$	Add from left to right.
$= -31$ ■	

TIP

When substituting a negative value for a variable, use parentheses. Doing so helps prevent confusion between subtraction signs and negative signs.

Application: Geography

EXAMPLE 3 Driskill Mountain, Louisiana, has an elevation of 535 ft. In large portions of the city of New Orleans, the average elevation is -9 ft. What is the difference between those two elevations?

Solution Subtract the lower elevation from the higher elevation.

$$\begin{aligned} 535 - (-9) &= 535 + 9 \\ &= 544 \end{aligned}$$

The difference between the elevations is 544 ft. ■

Problem Set

Find the difference.

1. $-9 - (-10)$
2. $4 - (-9)$
3. $10 - (-10)$
4. $-6 - 8$
5. $5 - (-8)$
6. $0 - (-2)$
7. $-25 - (-31)$
8. $-46 - 37$
9. $13 - 23$
10. $50 - (-37)$
11. $-44 - (-34)$
12. $-20 - 30$
13. $51 - 59$
14. $18 - (-33)$
15. $-46 - (-77)$
16. $19 - 34$

Evaluate the expression for the given values of the variables.

17. $3 - y$ when $y = -4$
18. $b - (-8)$ when $b = -3$
19. $u - (-15)$ when $u = 10$
20. $27 - k$ when $k = -14$
21. $10 - w - 4$ when $w = -2$
22. $-8 - p - 5$ when $p = -5$
23. $1 - 9 - x$ when $x = -4$
24. $6 - q - (-7)$ when $q = 10$
25. $a - b + 7$ when $a = -4$ and $b = 6$
26. $8 - s + t$ when $s = -5$ and $t = -1$

Find the value of *x* that makes the equation true.

27. $7 - x = 24$
28. $30 - x = -15$

Solve.

29. The highest recorded temperature in South Dakota is 120°F. The lowest recorded temperature is −58°F. What is the difference between these temperatures?
30. The highest elevation in Africa is Kilimanjaro, Tanzania, at 5895 m. The lowest elevation in Africa is Lake Assal, Djibouti, at −156 m. What is the difference between these 2 elevations?

Core Focus: Distance

THE CORE CONCEPT

You can use a number line to calculate the distance between two points.

Calculating Distance on a Number Line

You can calculate the distance between two points on a number line using either of the following methods:

Step 1 Subtract the lesser coordinate from the greater coordinate.

Step 2 Take the absolute value of the difference of the coordinates.

EXAMPLE 1 Use both methods to calculate the distance between the points.

A Subtract the lesser coordinate from the greater coordinate.

Solution $2.4 - (-0.8) = 2.4 + 0.8 = 3.2$

The distance between the points is 3.2 units.

B Take the absolute value of the difference of the numbers (you can subtract in any order when using this method).

Solution

Greater number is subtrahend:

$$|-0.8 - 2.4| = |-3.2| = 3.2$$

or

Lesser number is subtrahend:

$$|2.4 - (-0.8)| = |2.4 + 0.8| = |3.2| = 3.2$$

Either way, the distance between the points is 3.2 units.

Q & A

Q When is the distance between two points not a positive number?

A If the two points have the same coordinate, the distance between them is zero.

EXAMPLE 2 The table shows the boiling points of 3 substances, rounded to the nearest integer.

Substance	Boiling point (°C)
carbon dioxide	−57
ether	35
Freon R-22	−41

A Plot and label the boiling points on a number line.

Solution

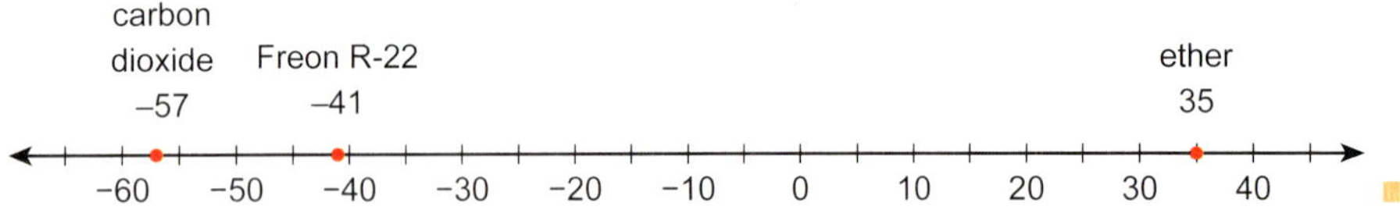

B Is the boiling point of ether greater than or less than the boiling point of Freon R-22? Explain.

Solution The boiling point of ether is greater than the boiling point of Freon R-22 because 35 is farther to the right than −41 is.

C Is the boiling point of carbon dioxide greater than or less than the boiling point of Freon R-22? Explain.

Solution The boiling point of carbon dioxide is farther to the left than the boiling point of Freon R-22 is, so the boiling point of carbon dioxide is less than the boiling point of Freon R-22.

D Calculate the differences between the boiling points of each substance.

Solution

Difference	Calculation of difference in boiling points	Difference in boiling points (°C)
carbon dioxide – ether	$\lvert -57 - 35 \rvert = \lvert -92 \rvert = 92$	92
carbon dioxide – Freon R-22	$\lvert -57 - (-41) \rvert = \lvert -57 + 41 \rvert = \lvert -16 \rvert = 16$	16
ether – Freon R-22	$\lvert 35 - (-41) \rvert = \lvert 35 + 41 \rvert = \lvert 76 \rvert = 76$	76

THINK ABOUT IT

Many real-world quantities can be either positive or negative.

List three besides temperature.

Problem Set

Solve.

1. Use both methods to calculate the distance between the points.

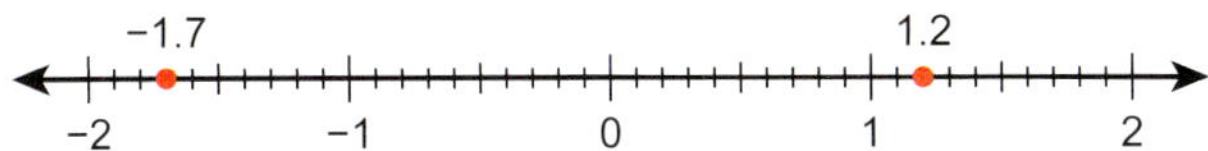

(a) Subtract the lesser coordinate from the greater coordinate.

(b) Find the absolute value of the difference between the two numbers. Show that the order of the numbers does not change the resulting value.

2. The table shows the freezing points of 3 substances rounded to the nearest integer.

Substance	Freezing point (°C)
sulfuric acid	11
radon	−71
nitric acid	−42

(a) Plot and label the values on a number line.

(b) Is the freezing point of sulfuric acid greater than or less than the freezing point of radon? Explain.

(c) Is the freezing point of radon greater than or less than the freezing point of nitric acid? Explain.

(d) Calculate the differences between the freezing points of each of these substances. Organize your work in a table.

Decimals on a Number Line

Integers are not the only numbers on a number line. Between any two integers, you can find countless other numbers.

You have seen that the set of whole numbers and their opposites is called the integers. Integers graphed on a number line look like this:

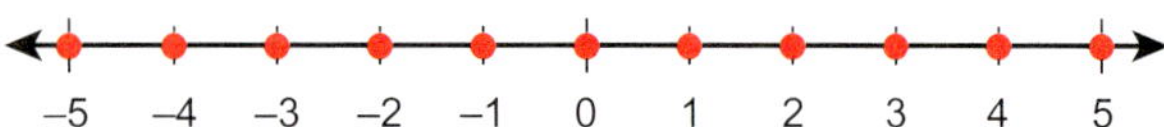

There are also numbers between integers that can be written in decimal form. The diagram shows some of the decimals between -1 and 1.

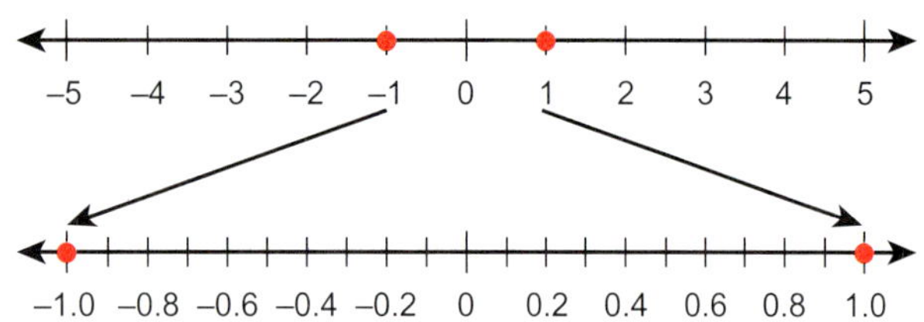

> ▶ **THINK ABOUT IT**
>
> Any integer can be written as a decimal by writing a 0 to the right of the decimal point. For example, $3 = 3.0$ and $-5 = -5.0$.

In fact, there are decimals between any two decimals you choose, no matter how close they are. For example, one decimal between 0.01 and 0.02 is 0.013. This property is described as density on a number line.

> ▶ **THINK ABOUT IT**
>
> A decimal between 0.00001 and 0.00002 is 0.000019.

DENSITY ON A NUMBER LINE

Between any two numbers on a number line, there are infinitely many other numbers.

Identifying Decimal Coordinates of Points on a Number Line

EXAMPLE 1 State the coordinate of each indicated point on the number line.

A 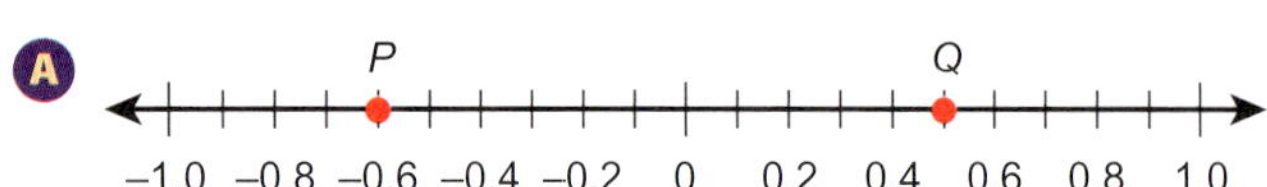

Solution Point P is 0.6 to the left of 0, so its coordinate is -0.6. Point Q is to the right of 0 and halfway between 0.4 and 0.6, so its coordinate is 0.5. ■

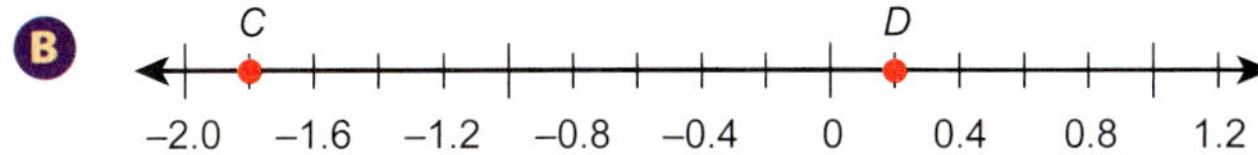

Solution The tick marks on this number line are 0.2 apart. Reading to the left from 0, the tick marks represent -0.2, -0.4, -0.6, -0.8, and so on. Point C is halfway between -1.6 and -2.0, so its coordinate is -1.8. Point D is halfway between 0 and 0.4, so its coordinate is 0.2. ■

Graphing Decimals on a Number Line

To set up a number line, decide what numbers to represent with equally spaced tick marks, which is called choosing a scale. Given a particular number to graph, you can choose different scales, but some scales are more appropriate than others. It is a good idea to include one or more integers in your scale because they are good reference points. It is often a good idea to include 0 because it separates negative numbers and positive numbers.

EXAMPLE 2

A Graph 1.4 on a number line.

Solution You can choose a scale in which tick marks are spaced 0.2 apart. Include several tick marks to the left of 0 and several tick marks to the right of 1.4. From 0, count by 0.2 until you get to 1.4. Draw a dot to represent the point for 1.4. Label 0, 1.0, and 1.4.

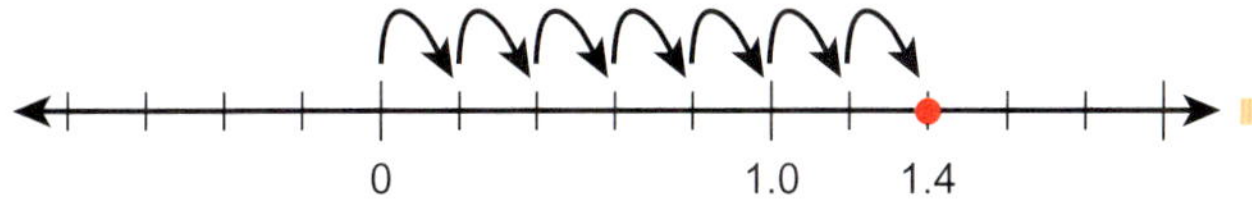

■

REMEMBER

People often read the decimal 1.4 as one point four, but more formally it can be read as one and four-tenths.

B Graph -0.7 on a number line.

Solution Because -0.7 is negative, it is to the left of the origin. Start at 0 and count 0.7 to the left. If your tick marks are spaced 0.2 apart, count three full spaces and another half space. Plot -0.7 halfway between -0.6 and -0.8.

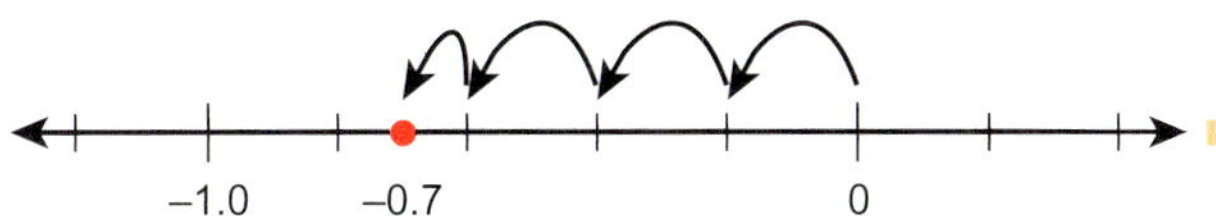

■

THINK ABOUT IT

For Example 2B, an alternate choice for a scale could have tick marks spaced 0.1 apart. Using that scale, -0.7 would be graphed directly on a tick mark.

C Graph -12.68 on a number line.

Solution The given number is in hundredths, but it would not be practical to use a scale in hundredths, containing 0. Such a scale would contain too many tick marks. It makes sense to use a scale that shows the integers -12 and -13 because -12.68 is between those two integers. You can draw the tick marks spaced 0.25 apart. Plot -12.68 between -12.50 and -12.75, closer to -12.75.

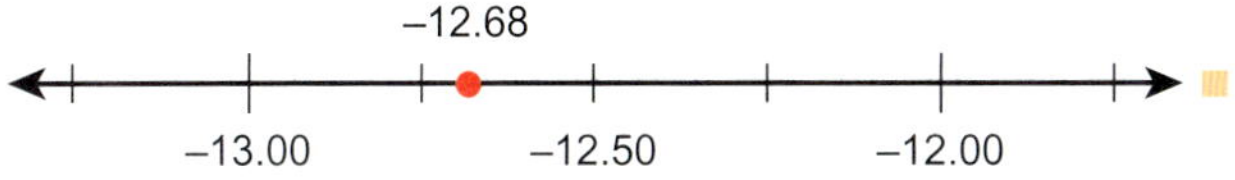

■

Comparing Decimals

Graphing decimals on a number line can help you compare them. Remember, when comparing two numbers, the number to the left is less than the number to the right.

EXAMPLE 3 Compare the decimals. Use $<$, $>$, or $=$.

A Compare -1.2 and 0.1.

Solution

Every negative number is less than every positive number, so you know that -1.2 is less than 0.1. You can write either $-1.2 < 0.1$ or $0.1 > -1.2$. ■

B Compare -0.4 and -2.4.

Solution

Because -2.4 is to the left of -0.4, you know that -2.4 is less than -0.4. You can write either $-2.4 < -0.4$ or $-0.4 > -2.4$. ■

C Compare -5.2 and -4.8.

Solution

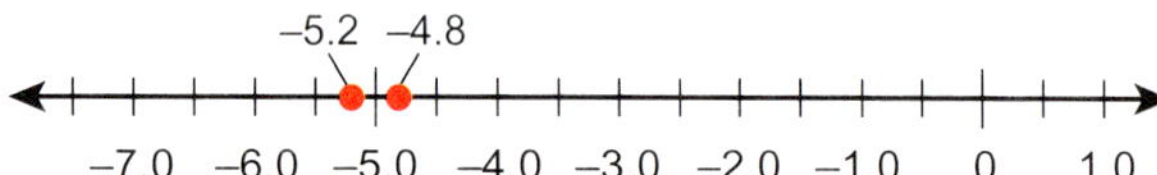

Because -5.2 is to the left of -4.8, you know that -5.2 is less than -4.8. You can write either $-5.2 < -4.8$ or $-4.8 > -5.2$. ■

> **TIP**
> To graph -5.2 and -4.8 on a number line, use -5.0 as a reference point.

Ordering Decimals

You can also use a number line to help you order decimals from least to greatest. First plot the decimals. Then list them in order from left to right.

EXAMPLE 4

A Write 0.8, -0.6, 0.4, and -1.0 in order from least to greatest.

Solution

From least to greatest, the decimals are -1.0, -0.6, 0.4, and 0.8. ■

B Write 0.3, −8.6, −6.2, and 2.8 in order from least to greatest.

Solution

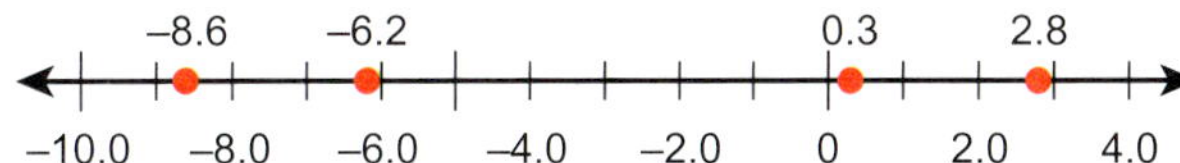

From least to greatest, the decimals are −8.6, −6.2, 0.3, and 2.8. ■

Application: Science

EXAMPLE 5 Students conducting an experiment measured the temperature of some different liquids. The table shows the data. List the liquids in order from coldest to warmest.

Liquid	Temperature (°C)
A	−7.2
B	5.0
C	−0.4
D	2.4
E	−5.5

Solution

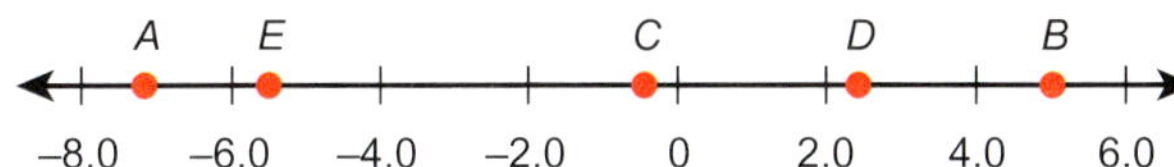

The liquids in order from coldest to warmest are A, E, C, D, B. ■

Problem Set

State the coordinate of the indicated point on the number line.

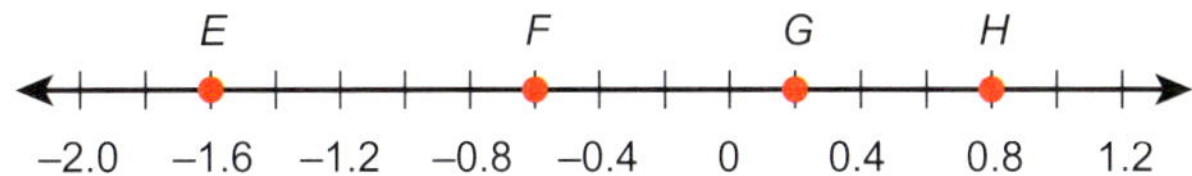

1. point E

2. point F

3. point G

4. point H

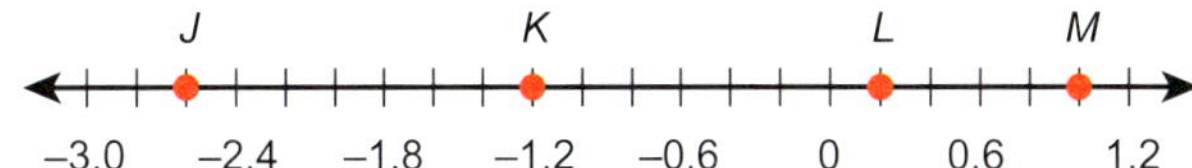

5. point J

6. point K

7. point L

8. point M

State the coordinate of the indicated point on the number line.

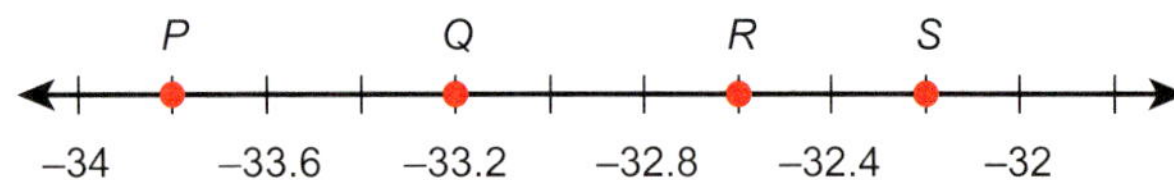

9. point P
10. point Q
11. point R
12. point S

Graph the decimal on a number line.

13. -2.4
14. 0.9
15. -8.65
16. 1.3
17. 0.1
18. -0.2

Compare the decimals. Use $<$, $>$, or $=$.

19. -2.4 ☐ 1.2
20. -0.6 ☐ -0.8
21. -1.24 ☐ -1.35
22. -8.75 ☐ -8.25
23. 4.95 ☐ 4.9
24. -7.342 ☐ -7.348

Write the decimals in order from least to greatest.

25. $1.3, -1.4, 0.9, -0.3$
26. $-1, 2.2, 0.2, -0.4$
27. $-0.5, 0.03, -1.9, 1.7$
28. $0.04, -0.5, -0.58, 0.002$

Solve.

29. The chart shows the temperatures of several cities. Put the cities in order of temperature from the coldest to the warmest.

City	Temperature (°C)
Oak Park	0.2
College City	−1.6
Snow Town	−1.4
Green Valley	−1.45

30. **Challenge** Write the decimals in order from least to greatest.

$|-4.3|, -3.2, -|4.1|, 0.6, -|-0.5|$

Adding Decimals

Adding decimals on a number line is similar to adding integers.

Using a Number Line to Add Decimals

As with integers, a negative decimal can be shown with a line segment pointing to the left, while a positive decimal can be shown with a segment pointing to the right.

> **REMEMBER**
>
> Check the scale of the number line you are using. The distance between tick marks in Example 1A is 0.2. The distance between tick marks in Example 1B is 0.1.

EXAMPLE 1 Find the sum.

A $-1.6 + (-0.8)$

Solution Start at 0. Move 1.6 units left. From -1.6, move 0.8 unit left.

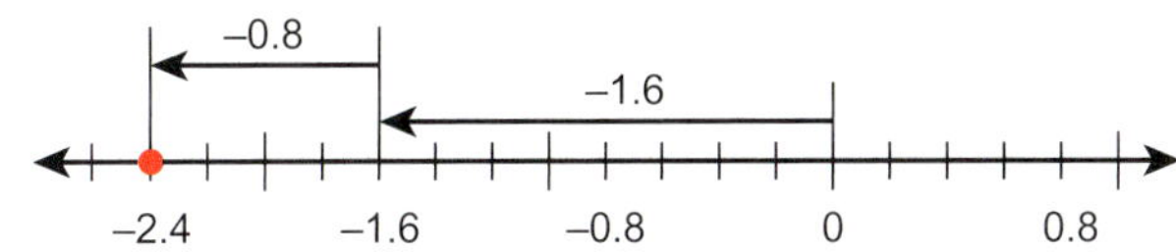

$-1.6 + (-0.8) = -2.4$ ■

B $0.5 + (-1.8)$

Solution Start at 0. Move 0.5 unit right. From 0.5, move 1.8 units left.

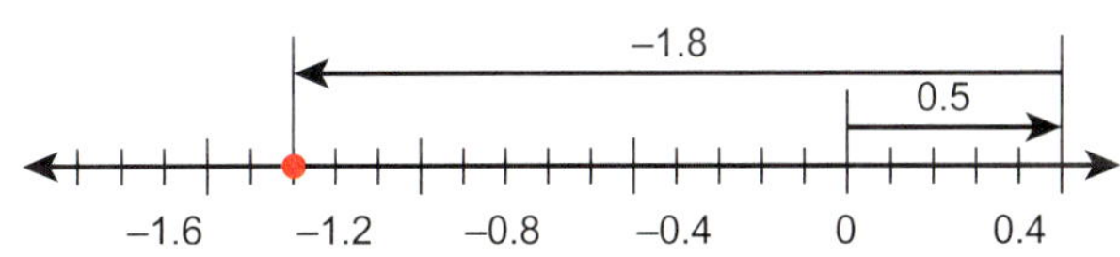

$0.5 + (-1.8) = -1.3$ ■

Adding Decimals Vertically

When you add decimals vertically, remember to align the decimal points. Use zeros as placeholders when necessary.

EXAMPLE 2 Find the sum.

A $34.14 + 12.6$

Solution

34.14	Align the decimal points.
+12.60	Write a zero as a placeholder.
46.74	Add. ■

B $0.85 + 11.678$

Solution

$$\begin{array}{r} \overset{1\,1}{0.850} \\ +11.678 \\ \hline 12.528 \end{array}$$

Align the decimal points. Write a zero as a placeholder.

Regroup as needed. Add.

Using Rules to Add Decimals

The rules for adding positive and negative decimals are the same as the rules for adding positive and negative integers.

RULES FOR ADDING TWO DECIMALS

If the signs are the same, add the absolute values of the decimals. Use the same sign as the decimals.

If the signs are different, find the difference of the absolute values. Use the sign of the decimal with the greater absolute value.

EXAMPLE 3 Find the sum.

A $-6.7 + (-1.3)$

Solution Both signs are negative. The answer will be negative.

$-6.7 + (-1.3) = -(|-6.7| + |-1.3|)$ Add the absolute values.

$= -(6.7 + 1.3)$

$= -8.0$ The sum has the same sign as the addends.

B $-27.8 + 14.3$

Solution The signs are different. Because $|-27.8|$ is greater than $|-4.3|$, the answer will be negative.

$-27.8 + 14.3 = -(|-27.8| - |-14.3|)$ Subtract the smaller absolute value from the greater absolute value. The sum has the sign of the decimal with the greater absolute value.

$= -(27.8 - 14.3)$

$= -13.5$

Evaluating Expressions with Decimals

Evaluate variable expressions by substituting values for the variables.

EXAMPLE 4

A Evaluate $a + b$ when $a = 1.5$ and $b = -2.8$.

Solution

$a + b = 1.5 + (-2.8)$ Substitute 1.5 for a and -2.8 for b. Subtract absolute values. Use the sign of the greater absolute value.

$= -1.3$

B Evaluate $-0.6 + r + z$ when $r = -5.09$ and $z = -1.2$.

Solution

$-0.6 + r + z = -0.6 + (-5.09) + (-1.2)$	Substitute -5.09 for r and -1.2 for z.
$= -6.89$	Add absolute values.

The sum is -6.89. ■

C Evaluate $c + d + f$ when $c = -2.2$, $d = -5.1$, and $f = 10.5$.

Solution

$c + d + f = -2.2 + (-5.1) + 10.5$	Substitute -2.2 for c, -5.1 for d, and 10.5 for f.
$= -7.3 + 10.5$	Add from left to right.
$= 3.2$ ■	

Using Related Equations to Solve Subtraction Equations

You can use related equations to solve subtraction equations. Just find a related equation with the variable alone on one side of the equation.

EXAMPLE 5 Solve the equation.

A $x - 3.2 = 6.04$

Solution

$x - 3.2 = 6.04$	Write the given subtraction equation.
$x = 3.2 + 6.04$	Write the related addition equation.
$x = 9.24$	Add. ■

B $n - (-0.9) = 1.25$

Solution

$n - (-0.9) = 1.25$	Write the given subtraction equation.
$n = -0.9 + 1.25$	Write the related addition equation.
$n = 0.35$	Add. ■

▶ **REMEMBER**

To add decimals, align the decimal points. Write zeros as placeholders if needed. Use the correct rule regarding positive and negative signs.

Application: Animals

EXAMPLE 6 Jess is tracking the movement of a garden snail toward a plant. The table shows the snail's progress each minute. A positive number indicates movement forward. A negative number indicates movement backward. What is the net forward progress of the snail toward the plant?

Minute	Distance traveled (ft)
1	+1.9
2	−0.5
3	+2.3
4	+1.1

Solution The net forward progress is the sum of the positive and negative numbers.

$1.9 + (-0.5) + 2.3 + 1.1 = 1.4 + 2.3 + 1.1$	Add from left to right.
$= 3.7 + 1.1$	
$= 4.8$	

The net forward progress of the snail toward the plant is 4.8 ft. ■

Problem Set

Find the sum.

1. $-1.4 + (-0.2)$
2. $-0.5 + 1.7$
3. $1.3 + (-2.4)$
4. $-1.8 + (-1.2)$
5. $-3.4 + 1.5$
6. $25.34 + 16.17$
7. $-10.25 + (-11.98)$
8. $-23.512 + 14.001$
9. $-0.66 + 0.14$
10. $6.13 + (-5.64)$
11. $15 + (-5.2) + (-1.4)$
12. $8.3 + (-0.044)$
13. $8.623 + 4.5$
14. $0.55 + (-6.8) + 2.05$
15. $0.02 + (-0.9)$
16. $-0.98 + (-0.06)$
17. $35 + (-0.023)$
18. $-0.985 + 0.87$
19. $-14.75 + (-2.25) + (-10.5)$
20. $0.011 + (-0.6) + 0.11 + (-2.03)$

Evaluate the expression for the given values of the variables.

21. $x + y$ when $x = -1.7$ and $y = -5.4$
22. $p + q$ when $p = -5.7$ and $q = 3.4$
23. $d + e$ when $d = 1.78$ and $e = -3.24$
24. $t + (-1.5) + s$ when $t = 1.23$ and $s = -4.01$
25. $-7.2 + m + n$ when $m = 14.78$ and $n = 0.875$
26. $u + v + (-2.15)$ when $u = -0.003$ and $v = -5.64$

Find the value of the variable that makes the equation true.

27. $-3.6 - a = -8.4$
28. $x - (-5.25) = 7.25$
29. $z - 2.4 = 4.2$
30. $2x - 3.5 = x - 3.5$
31. $4a - 2.5 = a - 10$

Solve.

32. A garden in the shape of a triangle is shown. What is the distance around the garden?

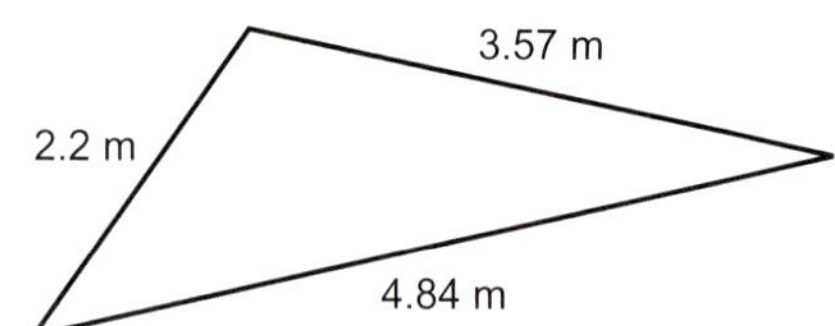

33. The table shows withdrawals in a bank account, which had a beginning balance of \$350. How much is in the account at the end of March?

Month	Bank account transactions (\$)
Jan.	−125.67
Feb.	−45.85
Mar.	−102.00

Core Focus: Additive Inverses

THE CORE CONCEPT

If the sum of two quantities is zero, the quantities are additive inverses.

Finding an Additive Inverse on a Number Line

ADDITIVE INVERSE PROPERTY

The sum of a number a and its additive inverse $-a$ is 0.

You can use a number line to represent additive inverses.

EXAMPLE 1 Yuna started a hike at sea level. She climbed to the top of a hill, at an altitude of 281 m. She descended the same route and finished her hike at sea level. How many meters in altitude did Yuna descend? Draw a number line to represent the situation. Explain your reasoning.

Solution Yuna ascended from sea level, which is 0 m, to 281 m above sea level. To represent her climb, start at 0 and move 281 units to the right on the number line. Since the sum of her gain in altitude and loss in altitude equals 0, the number that represents Yuna's descent must be the additive inverse of the number for her climb. To represent her descent on the number line, begin at 281 and move 281 units to the left, or -281 units.

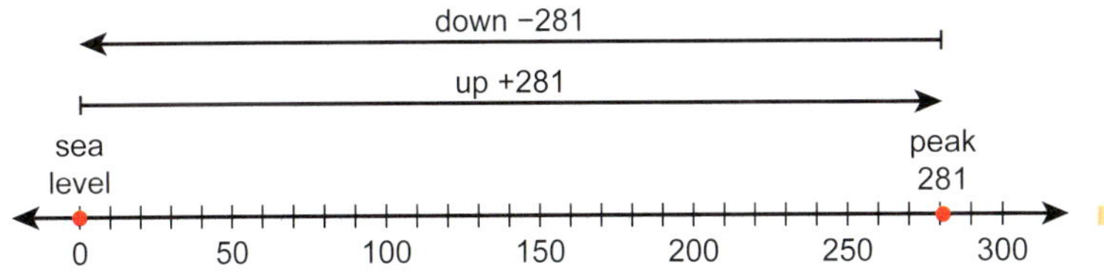

Check $281 + (-281) = 0$ ✓

EXAMPLE 2 In an American football game, a team loses 3 yd on first down. The team loses another 7 yd on second down.

A How many yards must the team gain on third down so that the overall change in yardage is 0? Show your reasoning using a number line.

REMEMBER

The additive inverse of a number is its opposite. For example, the additive inverse of -4 is $-(-4) = 4$.

REMEMBER

A number and its additive inverse have the same absolute value.

BY THE WAY

In American football, a down is an attempt to move the ball forward. A team has 4 downs to move the ball forward a total of 10 yd.

Solution A loss of 3 yd on first down is represented by moving 3 units to the left from 0. A loss of 7 yd on second down is represented by moving 7 units to the left from -3, leading to a total loss of 10 yd. This change is represented by the point -10 on the number line.

To end third down with no net change in yardage, the team must gain yardage to end up at zero. This change is represented by moving 10 units to the right from -10, ending up on 0.

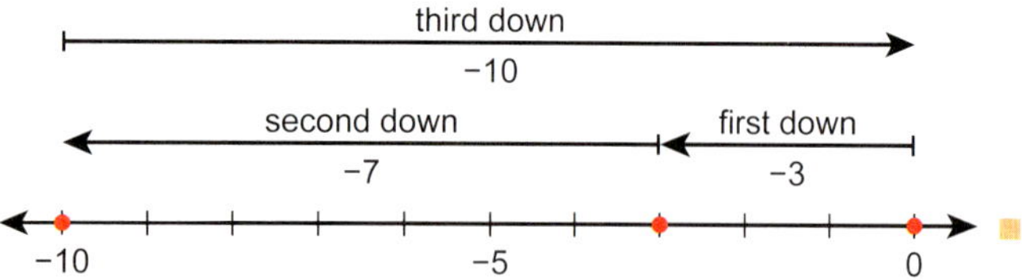

B Suppose that the overall change in yardage after 4 downs is 0 and that the team gained the same number of yards on both third and fourth downs. How many yards did the team gain on each of third and fourth downs? Show your reasoning using a number line.

Solution The team lost a total of 10 yd after first and second downs. To finish with 0 overall change in yardage, the team must have gained a total of 10 yd on third and fourth downs.

The 10 yd is divided evenly between third and fourth downs, so the team gained 5 yd on each down. This calculation is represented by moving 5 units to the right twice on the number line, ending up on 0.

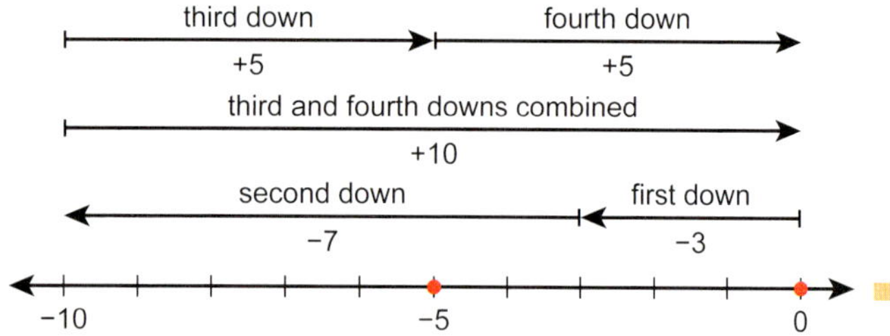

Check $-10 + 5 + 5 = 0$ ✓

▶ **THINK ABOUT IT**

Can you think of other real-world situations in which the end result is an overall, or net, change of 0?

Problem Set

Solve.

1. A scuba diver is 35 ft below the sea surface. How many feet must the scuba diver ascend to return to sea level? Explain your reasoning using a number line.

2. Charlie earned \$45 at his job. With the money he earned, he bought as many baseballs as he could and had no money left over. Each baseball cost \$9. How many baseballs did Charlie buy? Use a number line to represent the situation.

3. The table shows Asher's scores for the first three days of a golf tournament.

Day	Score above (+) or below (−) par
Thurs.	+2
Fri.	−3
Sat.	+5

What must Asher score on Sunday, the last day of the tournament, to have an overall score of even par (0 overall)? Use a number line to explain your reasoning.

4. A sodium ion combines with a chlorine ion to form a molecule of sodium chloride, which is common table salt. A sodium ion has a net charge of +1, and a chlorine ion has a net charge of −1.

   (a) What is the overall charge of 6 sodium chloride molecules? Explain your reasoning.

   (b) How many sodium ions must be combined with *n* chlorine ions to form *n* sodium chloride molecules? Use a number line to explain your reasoning.

CHAPTER 2 Review

Choose the answer.

1. What is the opposite of the coordinate of point A?

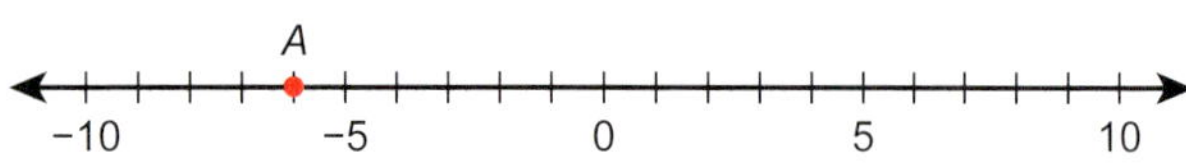

A. -6 **C.** 4

B. -4 **D.** 6

2. Which statement is true?

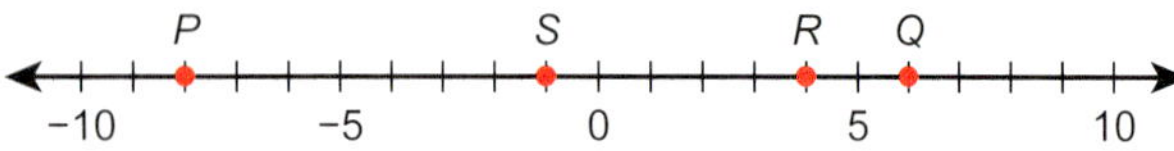

A. $P > S$

B. $R > Q$

C. $S < R$

D. $Q < S$

3. What are all the solutions to the equation?

$$|x| = -4$$

A. $x = -4$

B. $x = 4$

C. $x = -4, 4$

D. There is no solution.

4. What is the value of $b + c + d$ when $b = -8$, $c = 5$, and $d = -3$?

A. -16 **C.** 0

B. -6 **D.** 10

5. Which value of z makes the equation true?

$$-4 + z + 2 = -5$$

A. $z = -7$

B. $z = -3$

C. $z = 1$

D. $z = 7$

6. What is the value of $25 - (-61)$?

A. -86 **C.** 36

B. -36 **D.** 86

7. What is the distance between points U and V?

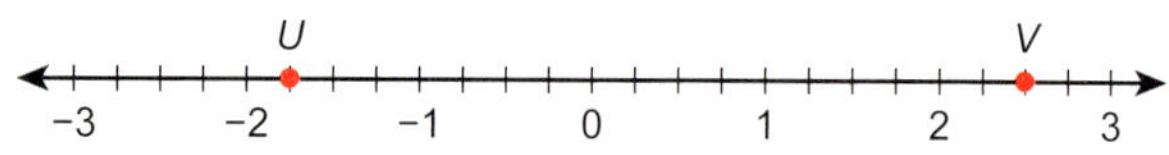

A. $\frac{3}{4}$

B. $1\frac{3}{4}$

C. $4\frac{1}{4}$

D. $5\frac{1}{4}$

8. Which statement is true?

A. $5.6 < -7.2$

B. $-2.5 > 1.3$

C. $-4.8 < -2.9$

D. $-0.5 < -6.1$

9. Which list of numbers is ordered from least to greatest?

A. 1.7, −1.3, 4.6, −5

B. −2.3, −4, 1.7, 5.2

C. 0.4, 2.2, −3.7, −6

D. −7, −2.5, 0.8, 3.9

10. Which value of z makes the equation true?

$$r - 6.34 = -2.5$$

A. $r = -8.64$

B. $r = -4.09$

C. $r = 3.84$

D. $r = 8.59$

11. Which is the additive inverse of -4?

A. -4 **C.** $\frac{1}{4}$

B. 0 **D.** 4

Solve.

12. Draw and label a number line containing the following points:

    (a) $A = -6$

    (b) $B = -2$

    (c) $C = 0$

    (d) $D = 7$

13. The table shows how many points Kamala received for the first three rounds of a card game.

Round	Points scored
1	5
2	2
3	−26

What is Kamala's total score after the three rounds?

14. The temperature in Novosibirsk, Siberia, at noon was 11°F. At 6 p.m., the temperature decreased by 5°. By midnight, the temperature decreased by another 18°. What was the temperature in Novosibirsk at midnight?

15. Plot the following points on a number line:

    (a) $J = -0.7$

    (b) $K = 2.5$

    (c) $L = 1.2$

    (d) $M = -3.9$

16. A rectangle has a length of 8.7 cm and a width of 3.2 cm. Find the perimeter of the rectangle.

17. A submarine is 145 m below sea level. The submarine descends another 93 m. How far must the submarine ascend to reach sea level? Explain your reasoning using a number line.

18. The table shows the elevation of four locations around the world.

Location	Elevation (m)
Niland, CA, USA	−43
Hiiumaa, Estonia	68
Caspian Sea, Russia	−28
Robles Point, Belize	4

(a) Graph and label the four elevations on a number line.

(b) Which elevation is closest to sea level? Explain your reasoning.

(c) What is the difference in elevation between Niland and the Caspian Sea? Explain.

(d) Find the difference in elevation between Hiiumaa and each of the other three locations.

Problem	Topic Lookup
1–3, 12	Integers on a Number Line
4, 5, 13	Adding Integers
6, 14	Subtracting Integers
7, 18	Core Focus: Distance

Problem	Topic Lookup
8, 9, 15	Decimals on a Number Line
10, 16	Adding Decimals
11, 17	Core Focus: Additive Inverses

CHAPTER 3 Addition and Subtraction Properties

Stock prices rise and fall all day long. These changes are important to investors and to investment firms. Each rise or fall can be understood in terms of subtraction, with the hope that the end result adds to the investors' or the companies' bottom line.

In This Chapter

This chapter focuses on properties for adding and subtracting numbers. In this chapter, you'll explore properties that will help you simplify expressions and solve equations.

Topic List

- Foundations for Chapter 3
- Subtracting Decimals
- Addition and Subtraction Properties
- Core Focus: Absolute Value and Distance
- Equations Involving Addition and Subtraction
- Addition and Subtraction Applications
- Core Focus: Distances Between Rationals
- Chapter 3 Review

As values go up and down, addition and subtraction can help you make sense of the changes.

-0.360
-2.362%
1.53B
09:30
13:00
533.01K
+0.600
+0.285%
112.38M
09:30
13:00
16.40M
-0.450
-1.911%
380.86M
09:30
18.14M
-0.400
-1.361%
528.80M
09:30
20.46M
-0.480
-3.625%
263.54M
09:30
420.00K
-0.250
9.63M

Foundations for Chapter 3

Subtracting Positive Decimals

Align the decimal points of the two numbers. If the numbers do not end with the same place value, write zeros as placeholders. Then subtract the digits in each place, moving from right to left. Regroup as necessary.

EXAMPLE A Subtract.

 7.28 – 1.96

Solution

$$\begin{array}{r} \scriptstyle 6\ 12 \\ \not{7}.\not{2}8 \\ -\ 1.94 \\ \hline 5.32 \end{array}$$

Check

$$\begin{array}{r} \scriptstyle 1 \\ 5.32 \\ +\ 1.96 \\ \hline 7.28 \ \checkmark \end{array}$$

The difference is 5.32. ■

A-2 13.8 – 3.17

Solution

$$\begin{array}{r} \scriptstyle 7\,10 \\ 13.\not{8}\not{0} \\ -\ \ 3.17 \\ \hline 10.63 \end{array}$$

Check

$$\begin{array}{r} \scriptstyle 1 \\ 10.63 \\ +\ \ 3.17 \\ \hline 13.80 \ \checkmark \end{array}$$

The difference is 10.63. ■

Problem Set A

Subtract.

1. 9.78 – 3.6
2. 14.67 – 0.15
3. 23.97 – 2.7
4. 86 – 0.5
5. 0.3071 – 0.007
6. 3.9 – 0.67
7. 2.4 – 1.33
8. 4.35 – 4.252
9. 10.03 – 1.7
10. 81.2 – 6.075

Adding or Subtracting Numbers on a Number Line

Start at 0 on the number line. For positive numbers, move to the right. For negative numbers, move to the left.

EXAMPLE B Use a number line to add or subtract.

B-1 $-2 + 7$

Solution Start at 0 on the number line. Move 2 units to the left. From -2, move 7 units to the right.

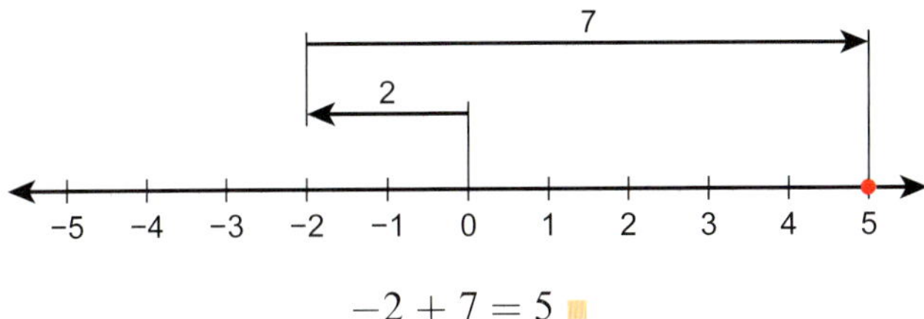

$$-2 + 7 = 5$$

B-2 $5 - 9$

Solution Rewrite subtraction as adding the opposite of 9.

$$5 - 9 = 5 + (-9)$$

Start at 0 on the number line. Move 5 units to the right. From 5, move 9 units to the left.

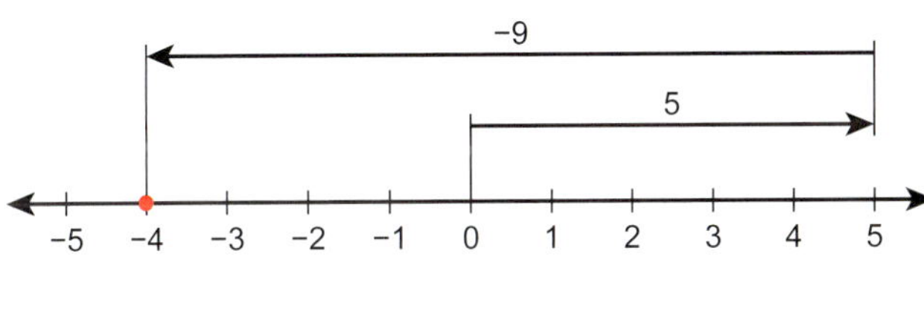

$$5 + (-9) = -4$$

Problem Set B

Use a number line to add or subtract.

1. $8 - 3$
2. $2 + 12$
3. $-4 + 7$
4. $10 - 5$
5. $-9 + 8$
6. $13 + 6$
7. $-7 - 5$
8. $12 + 6$
9. $8 + 9$
10. $7 - (-4)$

Solving Addition and Subtraction Equations

Solve an equation by finding its two related equations. Choose the equation with the variable by itself on one side of the equation. Simplify this equation.

EXAMPLE C Solve the equation by finding a related equation and simplifying it.

C-1 $x + 4 = 9$

Solution There are two related equations:

$$4 = 9 - x$$
$$x = 9 - 4$$

Only $x = 9 - 4$ has x alone on one side of the equation, so simplify it to find x.

$$x = 9 - 4 = 5$$

Check $5 + 4 = 9$ ✓

The solution is $x = 5$. ■

C-2 $-2 = m - 8$

Solution There are two related equations:

$$-2 + 8 = m$$
$$-2 - m = -8$$

Only $-2 + 8 = m$ has m alone on one side of the equation, so simplify it to find m.

$$m = -2 + 8 = 6$$

Check $-2 = 6 - 8$ ✓

The solution is $m = 6$. ■

Problem Set C

Solve.

1. $z + 2 = 8$
2. $j - 9 = 1$
3. $10 = 3 + y$
4. $q + 11 = 4$
5. $n - 5 = -7$
6. $12 = d - 9$
7. $-7 = -1 + x$
8. $k - 10 = -9$
9. $-3 = t + 12$
10. $-17 + a = -5$
11. $-9 - p = 1$
12. $14 = b - (-6)$

Subtracting Decimals

Before subtracting decimals that involve negative numbers, review the procedures for subtracting decimals vertically.

Subtracting Decimals Vertically

Remember to align the decimal points when you subtract, just as you do when you add. Use zeros as placeholders when necessary.

EXAMPLE 1 Find the difference.

A 129.52 − 14.2

Solution

129.52	Align the decimal points.
− 14.20	Write a zero as a placeholder.
115.32	Subtract. ■

B 20.56 − 8.473

Solution

20.560	Align the decimal points. Write a zero as a placeholder.
− 8.473	
12.087	Regroup as needed. Subtract. ■

TIP

You can check your subtraction by adding.

$$\begin{array}{r} 115.32 \\ +\ 14.20 \\ \hline 129.52 \end{array}$$

Using a Rule to Subtract Decimals

The rule for subtracting any number, including a decimal, is the same as the rule for subtracting an integer.

SUBTRACTING A NUMBER

To subtract a number, add its opposite.

$$a - b = a + (-b)$$

EXAMPLE 2 Subtract.

A $2.3 - 4.5$

Solution

$2.3 - 4.5 = 2.3 + (-4.5)$	Write subtraction as adding the opposite.
$= -(\lvert -4.5 \rvert - \lvert 2.3 \rvert)$	The signs of 2.3 and −4.5 are different, so subtract the absolute values. The difference has the sign of the number with the greater absolute value.
$= -(4.5 - 2.3)$	
$= -2.2$ ■	

B $24.3 - (-11.5)$

Solution

$24.3 - (-11.5) = 24.3 + 11.5$	Write subtraction as adding the opposite of −11.5.
$= 35.8$ ■	

C $-0.04 - (-10.1)$

Solution

$-0.04 - (-10.1) = -0.04 + 10.1$	Write subtraction as adding the opposite.
$= \lvert 10.1 \rvert - \lvert -0.04 \rvert$	The signs of −0.04 and 10.1 are different, so subtract the absolute values.
$= 10.1 - 0.04$	
$= 10.06$	The difference has the sign of the number with the greater absolute value. ■

Using Related Equations to Solve Addition Equations

Because addition and subtraction are inverse operations, you can solve an addition equation by subtracting. To solve a simple addition equation, write the related subtraction equation that has the variable alone on one side of the equation.

EXAMPLE 3 Solve the equation.

A $r + 7.5 = -3$

Solution

$r + 7.5 = -3$	Write the given addition equation.
$r = -3 - (7.5)$	Write the related subtraction equation that has the variable alone on one side of the equation. Then subtract.
$r = -10.5$ ■	

B $-2.4 + t = 1.05$

Solution

$-2.4 + t = 1.05$	Write the given addition equation.
$t = 1.05 - (-2.4)$	Write the related subtraction equation that has the variable alone on one side of the equation. Then simplify.
$t = 1.05 + 2.4$	
$t = 3.45$ ■	

C $x + (-0.85) = -1$

Solution

$x + (-0.85) = -1$	Write the given addition equation.
$x = -1 - (-0.85)$	Write the related subtraction equation that has the variable alone on one side of the equation. Then simplify.
$x = -1 + 0.85$	
$x = -0.15$ ■	

▶ TIP

For the addition equation $-2.4 + t = 1.05$, the two related subtraction equations are $t = 1.05 - (-2.4)$ and $-2.4 = 1.05 - t$.

Evaluating Expressions with Decimals

EXAMPLE 4

A Evaluate $a - b$ when $a = 3.1$ and $b = -4.6$.

Solution

$a - b = 3.1 - (-4.6)$	Substitute 3.1 for a and -4.6 for b.
$= 3.1 + 4.6$	Add the opposite of -4.6.
$= 7.7$ ■	

B Evaluate $b - a$ when $a = 3.1$ and $b = -4.6$.

Solution

$b - a = -4.6 - 3.1$	Substitute -4.6 for b and 3.1 for a.
$= -4.6 + (-3.1)$	Add the opposite of 3.1.
$= -7.7$ ■	

C Evaluate $u - 3.5 - s$ when $u = -4$ and $s = -0.1$.

Solution

$u - 3.5 - s = -4 - 3.5 - (-0.1)$	Substitute -4 for u and -0.1 for s.
$= -4.0 + (-3.5) + 0.1$	Write -4 as -4.0. Add the opposite of 3.5 and the opposite of -0.1. Add from left to right.
$= -7.5 + 0.1$	
$= -7.4$ ■	

▶ THINK ABOUT IT

For any numbers a and b, $a - b$ and $b - a$ are opposites. Examples 4A and 4B illustrate this property.

Problem Set

Find the difference.

1. $6.7 - 4.1$
2. $4.3 - 0.7$
3. $7.5 - (-6.9)$
4. $87.5 - 42.1$
5. $15.7 - (-2.6)$
6. $-7.45 - 2.17$
7. $-2.33 - (-1.05)$
8. $-4.037 - 1.057$
9. $-14.76 - 12.28$
10. $1.5 - 0.08$
11. $0.48 - 4.9$
12. $3.055 - (-0.26)$
13. $-0.1 - (-0.08)$
14. $658.23 - (-414.5)$
15. $-180 - 14.27$
16. $-56.87 - 23.25$
17. $62.1 - (-76)$
18. $-1.357 - (-2)$
19. $341.27 - (-78.5)$
20. $-79.432 - 54.6$

Evaluate the expression by substituting values for the variables.

21. $m - n$ when $m = -6.2$ and $n = 3.6$
22. $u - v$ when $u = 14.25$ and $v = -5.8$
23. $x - y$ when $x = 1.3$ and $y = 7.4$
24. $-7.1 - s - t$ when $s = 9.8$ and $t = -10.3$
25. $p - 14.832 - q$ when $p = 12.035$ and $q = -8.75$
26. $w - x - (-17.2)$ when $w = 134.7$ and $x = -4.003$

Find the value of the variable that makes the equation true.

27. $m + (-16.2) = 8.7$
28. $8.4 + b = -22.9$
29. $c + 3.4 = 4.3$
30. $1.5 = r + 4.5$
31. $8.7 = d + 8.7$

Solve.

32. Gwen is sketching the layout of a flower garden. The perimeter of her flower garden is 18.39 m. Gwen is going to fence in only the solid sides of the figure. She will not fence in the side indicated by the dashed line measuring 4.04 m. What is the total length of the sides that Gwen will fence in?

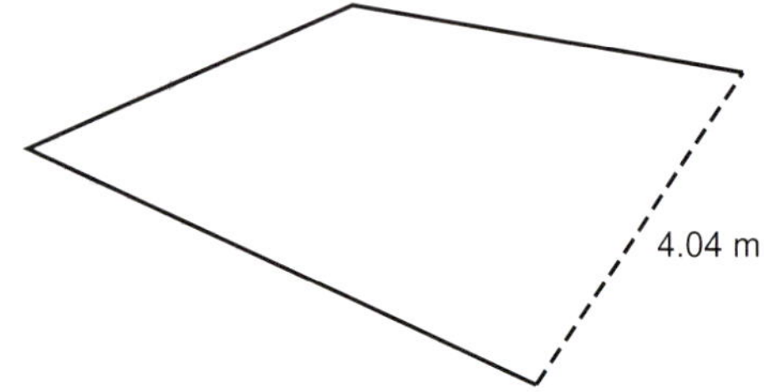

33. The temperature of a liquid was taken at different intervals. The temperature at one point was 1.35°C. When taken next, the temperature was −2.4°C. What is the change in the temperature of the liquid?

Addition and Subtraction Properties

You have already learned some properties of addition. Here are three more useful properties of addition.

ADDITION PROPERTIES

Property	Symbols	Example
Commutative Property Numbers can be added in any order.	$a + b = b + a$	$2 + (-5) = -5 + 2$ $-3 = -3$ ✓
Associative Property For three or more numbers, their sum is always the same, no matter how the numbers are grouped.	$(a + b) + c = a + (b + c)$	$(-1 + 7) + 4 = -1 + (7 + 4)$ $6 + 4 = -1 + 11$ $10 = 10$ ✓
Opposite of a Sum The opposite of the sum of two numbers is equal to the sum of the opposites.	$-(a + b) = -a + (-b)$	$-(5 + 3) = -5 + (-3)$ $-8 = -8$ ✓

Identifying Addition Properties

EXAMPLE 1 Identify the property shown.

A $-3 + 4 = 4 + (-3)$

Solution The order of the numbers being added is changed. The property shown is the commutative property of addition. ■

B $5 + (-8 + 10) = (5 + (-8)) + 10$

Solution The numbers being added are grouped differently. The property shown is the associative property of addition. ■

C $15 + (-7) + 5 = 15 + 5 + (-7)$

Solution The order of -7 and 5 is changed. The property shown is the commutative property of addition. ■

D $-(-1 + 7) = 1 + (-7)$

Solution The equation states that the opposite of the sum of -1 and 7 is equal to the sum of 1 and -7. The property shown is the property of the opposite of a sum. ■

TIP

Parentheses do not always indicate the associative property. In Example 1C, parentheses are used to separate negative signs from addition signs.

Using Addition Properties

Using the associative and commutative properties of addition can make some expressions easier to evaluate with mental math.

EXAMPLE 2 Use properties to rewrite the expression, and then evaluate it.

A $-87 + (-68) + (-13)$

Solution Use the commutative property to change the order of -87 and -68. Then use the associative property to group -87 and -13.

$$\begin{aligned} -87 + (-68) + (-13) &= -68 + (-87) + (-13) \\ &= -68 + (-87 + (-13)) \\ &= -68 + (-100) \\ &= -168 \end{aligned}$$

B $-36 + 419 + 136$

Solution Use the commutative property to change the order of 419 and 136. Then add from left to right.

$$\begin{aligned} -36 + 419 + 136 &= -36 + 136 + 419 \\ &= 100 + 419 \\ &= 519 \end{aligned}$$

Rewriting Subtraction as Addition to Use Addition Properties

The commutative and associative properties do not apply to subtraction. These examples illustrate this rule.

$$\begin{aligned} 3 - 1 &\neq 1 - 3 \\ 2 &\neq -2 \end{aligned} \qquad \begin{aligned} (8 - 2) - 5 &\neq 8 - (2 - 5) \\ 6 - 5 &\neq 8 - (-3) \\ 1 &\neq 11 \end{aligned}$$

However, by rewriting a subtraction expression as addition of the opposite, you can use the commutative and associative properties of addition.

EXAMPLE 3 Rewrite the expression using addition only. Then use addition properties so that you can evaluate the expression with mental math.

A $-18 + 34 - 12$

Solution

$-18 + 34 - 12 = -18 + 34 + (-12)$	To subtract 12, add -12.
$= -18 + (-12) + 34$	Use the commutative property.
$= -30 + 34$	Then add from left to right.
$= 4$	

B $42 - 27 + 8 - 3$

Solution

$42 - 27 + 8 - 3 = 42 + (-27) + 8 + (-3)$	Rewrite subtractions as additions.
$= 42 + 8 + (-27) + (-3)$	Use the commutative property.
$= (42 + 8) + (-27 + (-3))$	Then use the associative property to group numbers that are easier numbers to add.
$= 50 + (-30)$	
$= 20$ ■	

Solving Equations by Recognizing Properties of Addition

EXAMPLE 4 Solve the equation.

A $(7 + 4.14) + 8.2 = 7 + (y + 8.2)$

Solution By the associative property, $(7 + 4.14) + 8.2 = 7 + (4.14 + 8.2)$, so $y = 4.14$. ■

B $2 + (-0.4) + 5.06 = 2 + c + (-0.4)$

Solution By the commutative property, $2 + (-0.4) + 5.06 = 2 + 5.06 + (-0.4)$, so $c = 5.06$. ■

C $-(-5 + 4) = 5 + x$

Solution By the property of the opposite of a sum, you know that $-(-5 + 4) = 5 + (-4)$, so $x = -4$. ■

REMEMBER

The opposite of a negative number is positive. In Example 4C, the opposite of -5 is 5.

Application: Inventory

EXAMPLE 5 An inventory is a record of the number or amount of something. A librarian keeps track of the change in her inventory of books, as shown in the table. What is the net change in inventory for the week? Explain your steps.

Day of the week	Change in inventory
Mon.	+30
Tues.	−27
Wed.	+14
Thurs.	+26
Fri.	−3

Solution

$$\begin{aligned} 30 + (-27) + 14 + 26 + (-3) &= 30 + (-27) + (-3) + 14 + 26 \\ &= 30 + (-27 + (-3)) + (14 + 26) \\ &= 30 + (-30) + 40 \\ &= 0 + 40 \\ &= 40 \end{aligned}$$

The commutative property is used to change the order of the addends so that -27 and -3 are together from left to right. Then the associative property is used to group -27 and -3 as well as 14 and 26. Then the additions inside grouping symbols are performed. Finally, the numbers are added from left to right. The net change in inventory is $+40$. ■

Problem Set

Identify the property shown.

1. $-(6 + 2) = -6 + (-2)$
2. $14 + (-7) = -7 + 14$
3. $-4 + (-3 + (-10)) = (-4 + (-3)) + (-10)$
4. $12 + (-7) + (-8) = 12 + (-8) + (-7)$
5. $-(-7 + 3) = 7 + (-3)$
6. $(3.6 + 5.2) + 1.8 = 3.6 + (5.2 + 1.8)$

Use properties and mental math to evaluate the expression.

7. $42 + (-16) + 28$
8. $(63 + (-45)) + 5$
9. $-24 + 33 + (-6)$
10. $-45 + (17 + (-55))$
11. $(1 + (-15)) + (-35)$
12. $-94 - 51 + (-6)$
13. $-46 + 87 + 46$
14. $-62 + ((-18) - (-2))$
15. $6.2 + (-4 + 0.8)$
16. $1.3 + (-2.5) + 0.7$
17. $8.34 - (-6.32) - 0.34$
18. $-55.2 + (-6.8 - 15.1)$
19. $(9.8 - 0.3) + 12.3$
20. $2.25 + (-0.75 + (-0.37))$

Use the properties of addition to solve the equation.

21. $-(8 + 5) = -8 + m$
22. $(5 + 8) + 12 = 5 + (8 + a)$
23. $25 + (-6) + (-5) = 25 + (-5) + c$
24. $(4.2 + (-3.8)) + 2 = q + ((-3.8) + 2)$
25. $-(7 + y) = -7 + (-3)$
26. $-7 + 0.1 + (-3) = 0.1 + b + (-3)$

Find the value of the variable that makes the equation true.

27. $7 + x + (-17) = 2$
28. $-(5 + y) = 6$

Solve.

29. Spiro made the following deposits and withdrawals in his bank account:

    −\$25.00, +\$13.10, +\$50.00, −\$5.10

    What is the net amount of these transactions?
30. Hana's score in a game is determined by the sum of the numbers she selects. If Hana's numbers are −7, 14, 7, −3, and 6, what is her score?
31. A stock price starts at \$24, falls \$2, rises \$3, falls \$2, and rises \$3. What is the current stock price?
32. A football team gained 6 yd, lost 3 yd, gained 15 yd, lost 2 yd, lost 2 yd, and gained 7 yd. What is the net gain or loss?

Core Focus: Absolute Value and Distance

THE CORE CONCEPT

The distance between two different points is always a positive number. It doesn't matter whether you measure from point *A* to point *B* or from point *B* to point *A*; the distance is always positive.

Equidistant Points Occur in Pairs

For any two points with coordinates p and $p + q$, the distance between the two points is $|q|$. When you plot point p and try to plot a point that is q units away from p, there are two possibilities. Either q is negative (so the second point is to the left of p) or q is positive (the second point is to the right of p).

EXAMPLE 1 Frank climbed up a ladder to wash a window. At first, he climbed 7 rungs up the ladder. Then he changed his position on the ladder. His new position is 2 rungs away from his previous position.

A The two expressions represent Frank's possible positions on the ladder now. Represent each on a number line.

$$7 + 2$$
$$7 - 2$$

Solution A vertical number line usually has positive numbers increasing upward just as a horizontal number line increases to the right.

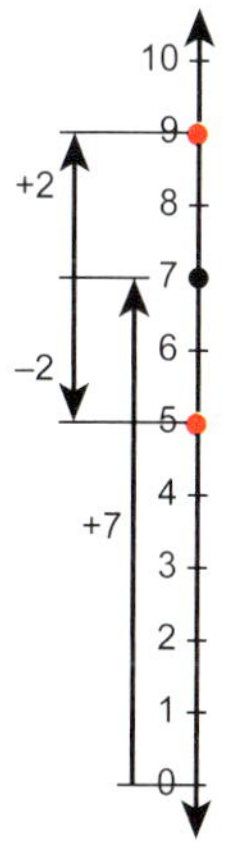

For these expressions, start at 0 and go up to 7 for the first addend. Then go up for the addend +2 and down for −2.

10
9
+2
8
7
6
−2
5
4
+7
3
2
1
0

B Explain how each expression in Example 1A represents traveling a distance of 2 rungs from Frank's previous position.

Solution The expression 7 + 2 represents going up 7 rungs and then going up 2 more rungs. Frank travels in the same direction (up) both times.

The expression 7 − 2 represents Frank going up 7 rungs and then going in the opposite direction (down) 2 rungs.

Since $|2| = 2$ and $|-2| = 2$, both cases represent traveling a distance of 2 rungs from the previous position.

REMEMBER

The absolute value of a number can never be negative.

Q & A

Q Suppose Frank's third position is 4 rungs away from his second position. How many rungs up the ladder could Frank be?

A Four possibilities exist.

$$7 + 2 + 4 = 13$$
$$7 + 2 - 4 = 5$$
$$7 - 2 + 4 = 9$$
$$7 - 2 - 4 = 1$$

EXAMPLE 2 Sadie drove 35 mi due west from her home along an east-west highway to visit her grandmother. After the visit, Sadie wanted to eat lunch. Sadie's GPS showed that a restaurant was 8 mi away along the same highway.

A Write two expressions that represent the possible positions of the restaurant from Sadie's home along the highway. Represent the two expressions on a number line.

Solution Two expressions to represent the situation are $-35 + 8$ and $-35 - 8$.

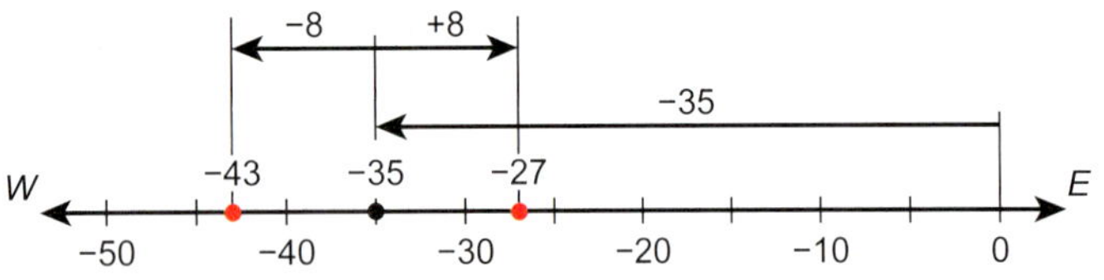

BY THE WAY

A global positioning system (GPS) is an electronic device that tells you your location on the earth by determining your distance from three or more satellites (and by using some fancy math).

B Explain how each expression in Example 2A represents the same distance from Sadie's grandmother's house.

Solution The expression $-35 + 8$ represents going 35 mi west and then going in the opposite direction, 8 mi east, to reach the restaurant.

The expression $-35 - 8$ represents going 35 mi west and then going another 8 mi west to reach the restaurant.

Since $|8| = 8$ and $|-8| = 8$, both cases represent Sadie traveling a distance of 8 mi from her grandmother's house, though the two trips are in opposite directions.

Problem Set

Solve.

1. Represent the expressions $2 - 6$ and $2 + 6$ on a number line. Explain how each expression represents a point a distance of 6 units away from a point with a coordinate of 2.

2. Soren is playing a board game with some friends. In the game, pieces can move forward and backward. On his first turn, Soren moves his piece 5 spaces forward from the start position. On his second turn, he moves his piece 3 spaces from its previous position.

   (a) The two expressions represent the two possibilities for the location of Soren's piece from the start position. Explain the situation each expression represents.

   Expression P: $5 - 3$
   Expression Q: $5 + 3$

   (b) Represent the expressions P and Q from Part (a) on a number line. Explain how each expression represents a change of 3 spaces from the previous position.

3. A shark is at a depth of 16 m below the ocean's surface. The shark's depth changed by 7 m.

   (a) Write an expression that represents the shark's depth if it descended 7 m.

   (b) Write an expression that represents the shark's depth if it ascended 7 m.

   (c) Represent the expressions from Parts (a) and (b) on a vertical number line. Explain how each expression represents the same change in depth.

Equations Involving Addition and Subtraction

To solve equations, you need to understand equivalent equations.

Equivalent equations are equations with the same solution or solutions. Related equations are equivalent, but you can also use properties of equality to create equivalent equations.

PROPERTIES OF EQUALITY

Property	Symbols	Example
Addition Property of Equality If you add the same number to both sides of an equation, you obtain an equivalent equation.	If $a = b$, then $a + c = b + c$ and $c + a = c + b$.	If $n = 3$, then $n + 2 = 3 + 2$. If $x - 4 = 9$, then $x - 4 + 4 = 9 + 4$.
Subtraction Property of Equality If you subtract the same number from both sides of an equation, you obtain an equivalent equation.	If $a = b$, then $a - c = b - c$.	If $r = 7$, then $r - 5 = 7 - 5$. If $x + 3 = 12$, then $x + 3 - 3 = 12 - 3$.
Substitution Property of Equality A value or expression may replace an equal value or expression.	If $a = b$, then either may replace the other in any expression.	If $x = 6$, then you can rewrite the expression $x - 10$ as $6 - 10$.

Solving Addition and Subtraction Equations

Addition and subtraction are inverse operations. To solve an equation, use inverse operations to obtain one or more simpler equations that are equivalent. When you obtain the simplest equivalent equation, you have the solution.

SOLVING ADDITION AND SUBTRACTION EQUATIONS

If a number is subtracted from a variable in an equation, you can add that same number to both sides of the equation to undo the subtraction.
If a number is added to a variable in an equation, you can subtract that same number from both sides of the equation to undo the addition.

EXAMPLE 1 Solve the equation. Check your answer.

A $x - 10 = -4$

Solution

$x - 10 = -4$

$x - 10 + 10 = -4 + 10$ To undo the subtraction, add 10 to both sides.

$x + 0 = 6$ Opposites sum to zero.

$x = 6$

Check

$x - 10 = -4$

$6 - 10 \stackrel{?}{=} -4$ Substitute 6 for x.

$-4 = -4$ ✓

The answer is correct. ■

> **TIP**
>
> We often don't show the step $x + 0 = 6$, but it's always implied.

> **THINK ABOUT IT**
>
> The equations
>
> $x - 10 = -4,$
>
> $x - 10 + 10 = -4 + 10,$
>
> and
>
> $x = 6$
>
> are all equivalent equations. The solution is given by the simplest equation, $x = 6$.

B $x + 15 = -10$

Solution

$x + 15 = -10$

$x + 15 - 15 = -10 - 15$ To undo the addition, subtract 15 from both sides.

$x = -25$

Check

$x + 15 = -10$

$-25 + 15 \stackrel{?}{=} -10$ Substitute -25 for x.

$-10 = -10$ ✓

The answer is correct. ■

Solving Equations Involving Decimals

Use the same strategies to solve equations with decimals that you use with integers.

EXAMPLE 2 Solve.

A $x + 5.3 = 15$

Solution

$x + 5.3 = 15$

$x + 5.3 - 5.3 = 15 - 5.3$ Subtract 5.3 from both sides.

$x = 9.7$ ■

> **REMEMBER**
>
> Check your solution by substituting it for the variable. A number is a solution if it makes the equation true.

B $23 = d - 9.5$

Solution

$23 = d - 9.5$

$23 + 9.5 = d - 9.5 + 9.5$ Add 9.5 to both sides.

$32.5 = d$ ■

Simplifying Before Solving

With some equations, it is easier to simplify one side of the equation before you perform an inverse operation.

EXAMPLE 3 Solve the equation.

A $-5.2 + x + 3.8 = 13$

Solution

$-5.2 + x + 3.8 = 13$	
$x + (-5.2) + 3.8 = 13$	Use the associative property to rearrange the addends.
$x + (-1.4) = 13$	Add -5.2 and 3.8 to simplify the left side.
$x - 1.4 = 13$	
$x - 1.4 + 1.4 = 13 + 1.4$	Add 1.4 to both sides.
$x = 14.4$ ■	

B $0 = -9.1 - (d + 3)$

Solution

$0 = -9.1 - (d + 3)$	
$0 = -9.1 + [-(d + 3)]$	To subtract $(d + 3)$, add its opposite, $-(d + 3)$.
$0 = -9.1 + (-d) + (-3)$	Apply the property of the opposite of a sum.
$0 = -12.1 + (-d)$	Add -9.1 and -3 to simplify the right side.
$0 + 12.1 = -12.1 + (-d) + 12.1$	Add 12.1 to both sides.
$12.1 = -d$	
$-12.1 = d$	If the opposite of d equals 12.1, then d equals -12.1. ■

Application: Landscape Design

EXAMPLE 4 A landscaper has 20 m of border for a garden. She has planned the lengths of three sides. What length is needed for the fourth side so that she can use the entire border?

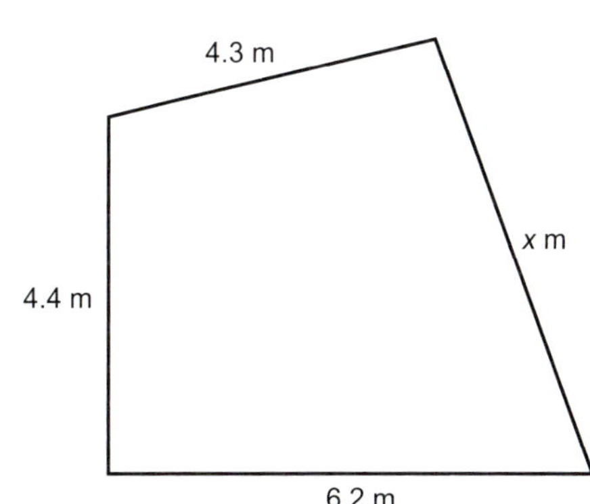

Solution

$$6.2 + 4.4 + 4.3 + x = 20.0$$
$$14.9 + x = 20.0$$
$$14.9 + x - 14.9 = 20.0 - 14.9$$
$$x - 14.9 + 14.9 = 20.0 - 14.9$$
$$x = 5.1$$

The length of the fourth side should be 5.1 m. ■

Problem Set

Solve.

1. $x - 16 = -36$
2. $m + (-12) = -8$
3. $23 = y + 6$
4. $-1 = b + (-3)$
5. $k - 7 = -24$
6. $m + (-13) = -19$
7. $-1 = a + 15$
8. $z + 11 = 21$
9. $x + 7 = 0$
10. $g + 11 = 9$
11. $x + (-14) = 5$
12. $k - 16 = -27$
13. $-31 = z + (-17)$
14. $-13 + s = -18$
15. $a - 5.1 = 1.7$
16. $y + 6.2 = -2.4$
17. $-8.4 = k + 0.6$
18. $a + 0.4 = -6.4$
19. $z + (-0.1) = 7.9$
20. $4.5 = g - 0.5$
21. $-2.2 = m + 0.8$
22. $-5 + y + (-6) = 5$
23. $7 + a + (-2) = 14$
24. $2 = y + (-4) + 11$
25. $-17 = -11 + z + (-8)$
26. $b + (-6) + 13 = 25$
27. $17 = -18 + 17 + b$
28. $14 + g + 3 = -36$

For each problem:
(a) Write an equation that models the problem.
(b) Solve the equation.
(c) Answer the question.

29. The sum of a number and 14 is −26. What is the number?
30. Sam purchased a calculator and a backpack. The total for the two items (without tax) is $151.48. The price of the backpack is $65.49. What is the price of the calculator?
31. Maggie wants to increase the number of cards in her collection to 325 cards. She now has 275 cards. How many cards does she need to buy?
32. The temperature is now −5°F. The temperature has dropped 12°F since midnight. What was the temperature at midnight?
33. The price of an item is $8.39. If the item is bought with a coupon, the price is $7.14. How much is the coupon worth?
34. **Challenge** If the mass of a rock were 4 kg heavier, its mass would be 3 kg more that twice what it is. What is the mass of the rock?

Addition and Subtraction Applications

Positive and negative numbers are used in many real-world applications.

Application: Nutrition

EXAMPLE 1 The table shows the amount of fiber in several types of fruit.

Fruit (100 g)	Grams of fiber
apple	2.3
apricot	2.1
banana	2.7
cherry	1.2
grapes	2.2
lemon	1.8
orange	1.8
peach	1.4
pear	2.1

A How much fiber is in a serving that contains 100 g of apple, 100 g of banana, and 100 g of orange?

Solution The apple has 2.3 g, the banana has 2.7 g, and the orange has 1.8 g. Add: $2.3 + 2.7 + 1.8 = 6.8$. The serving has a total of 6.8 g of fiber. ■

B How much more fiber is in 100 g of grapes than in 100 g of pear?

Solution Subtract: $2.2 - 2.1 = 0.1$.

The grapes have 0.1 g more fiber than the pear. ■

Application: Elevation

EXAMPLE 2 Mount Whitney, California, has an approximate elevation of 4418 m. The lowest point in Death Valley, California, has an elevation of −86 m. The shoreline of the Dead Sea, which is located on the border of Israel and Jordan, has an elevation of −413 m.

A What is the difference in elevation between Mount Whitney and the lowest point in Death Valley?

Solution Subtract the lower elevation from the higher elevation.

$$\begin{aligned} 4418 - (-86) &= 4418 + 86 \\ &= 4504 \end{aligned}$$

The difference in elevation between Mount Whitney and the lowest point in Death Valley is 4504 m. ■

B What is the difference in elevation between the lowest point in Death Valley and the shoreline of the Dead Sea?

Solution Subtract the lower elevation from the higher elevation.

$$\begin{aligned} -86 - (-413) &= -86 + 413 \\ &= 327 \end{aligned}$$

The difference in elevation between the lowest point in Death Valley and the shoreline of the Dead Sea is 327 m. ■

THINK ABOUT IT

In Example 2, subtracting elevations in the opposite order would have resulted in negative values, which is fine. When you get your solution, be sure to interpret any positive or negative signs.

Application: Temperature

EXAMPLE 3 The U.S. record for the greatest temperature change in 24 h occurred on January 23, 1916, in Browning, Montana. The temperature dropped from 44°F to −56°F. What was the change in temperature?

Solution Subtract the initial temperature from the final temperature.

$$\begin{aligned} -56 - 44 &= -56 + (-44) \\ &= -100 \end{aligned}$$

The change in temperature was −100°F, which was a decrease of 100°F. ■

Application: Sports

EXAMPLE 4 As of September 6, 2006, the indoor world record of 6.15 m for the pole vault was held by Sergei Bubka of Ukraine. The indoor world record of 2.43 m for the high jump was held by Javier Sotomayor of Cuba. What is the difference in these heights?

Solution Subtract 2.43 from 6.15.

$$\begin{array}{r} \overset{5}{\cancel{6}}.\overset{11}{\cancel{1}}5 \\ -\ 2.43 \\ \hline 3.72 \end{array}$$

Align decimal points. Regroup 1 whole as 10 tenths, and add 10 tenths to 1 tenth to make 11 tenths. Subtract.

The difference in the heights is 3.72 m. ■

Application: Ballooning

EXAMPLE 5 The changes in the height of a hot-air balloon were recorded at different times during a flight. Given that the balloon started and ended at the same height, what is the missing change in height, x?

Change in height (ft)	+1200	+775	−845	x	−475	+320	−620

Solution Because the balloon started and ended at the same height, the sum of all the decreases and increases is zero.

$$\begin{aligned} 1200 + 775 + (-845) + x + (-475) + 320 + (-620) &= 0 \\ 2295 + (-1940) + x &= 0 \\ 355 + x &= 0 \\ 355 + x - 355 &= 0 - 355 \\ x &= -355 \end{aligned}$$

The missing change in height is a decrease of 355 ft. ■

Application: Biology

EXAMPLE 6 The table shows the masses of four different monarch butterflies. Order the butterflies from least to greatest mass. Then find the difference in mass between the heaviest and the lightest.

Butterfly	Mass (g)
A	0.313
B	0.504
C	0.6
D	0.53

Solution To compare the masses, write them all with the same number of decimal places.

A 0.313
B 0.504
C 0.600
D 0.530

In order from least to greatest mass, the butterflies are A, B, D, C.

To find the difference in mass, subtract.

$$\begin{array}{r} \scriptstyle 5\,9\,10 \\ 0.\not{6}\not{0}\not{0} \\ -\ 0.313 \\ \hline 0.287 \end{array}$$

The difference in mass between the heaviest and lightest butterfly is 0.287 g. ■

Application: Personal Banking

EXAMPLE 7 The table shows Priti's bank account information. What is the missing amount? Is it a deposit or withdrawal? Explain how you know.

Beginning balance = \$268.42	
Deposit amount	Withdrawal amount
\$145.30	\$275.00
\$75.82	\$155.10
Missing amount = x	
Ending balance = \$53.82	

Solution

$268.42 + 145.30 + 75.82 - 275.00 - 155.10 + x = 53.82$

$59.44 + x = 53.82$ Simplify the left side.

$59.44 + x - 59.44 = 53.82 - 59.44$ Then subtract 59.44 from both sides.

$x = -5.62$

The missing amount is −5.62. It is a withdrawal of \$5.62 because it is a negative number. ■

Application: Amusement Park

EXAMPLE 8 A roller-coaster car starts at ground level, then rises 50 ft, drops 35 ft, rises x ft, and drops 12 ft. After the 12 ft drop, the car is 13 ft above the ground. What is the missing rise, x?

Solution

$$\begin{aligned} 50 - 35 + x - 12 &= 13 \\ x + 3 &= 13 \\ x + 3 - 3 &= 13 - 3 \\ x &= 10 \end{aligned}$$

The missing rise is 10 ft. ■

Problem Set

Solve. Assume all differences requested are positive differences.

The table shows the lowest elevation for each continent.

Continent	Lowest elevation (m)
Africa	−156
North America	−86
South America	−40
Antarctica	−2538
Asia	−411
Australia	−12
Europe	−28

1. List the elevations in order from lowest to highest.
2. What is the difference between the highest and the lowest elevations?
3. What is the difference between the lowest elevations for Africa and Europe?
4. Which two continents have the smallest difference between their lowest elevations?
5. The highest elevation in Asia is 8850 m. What is the difference between the highest and lowest elevations in Asia?
6. The highest elevation in South America is 6960 m. What is the difference between the highest and lowest elevations in South America?

The table shows the coldest recorded temperature for several cities.

City, State	Coldest temperature (°F)
Juneau, AK	−22
Los Angeles, CA	23
Denver, CO	−30
Bismarck, ND	−44
Philadelphia, PA	−7

7. List the temperatures in order from coldest to warmest.
8. What is the difference between the warmest and coldest temperature shown?
9. What is the difference between the Juneau temperature and the Los Angeles temperature?
10. Which two cities have the smallest difference in coldest temperature?
11. The difference between the Denver temperature and another temperature in the table is 23°F. Write an equation to represent this situation. Solve the equation. What city has the other temperature?
12. Which two cities have a coldest temperature difference of 37°F?

13. The table shows Amal's bank account information. What is the missing amount? Is it a deposit or a withdrawal? Explain how you know.

Beginning balance = \$426.30	
Deposit amount	Withdrawal amount
\$251.25	\$177.00
\$68.24	\$27.30
Missing amount = x	
Ending balance = \$135.50	

14. On July 21, 2007, Alan Webb set a U.S. record for the mile run at 3 min, 46.91 s. He broke the previous record of 3 min, 47.69 s, which Steve Scott set in 1982. What is the difference in these records?

15. A traffic helicopter hovered over an interstate to report on traffic. The table shows the changes in the height of the helicopter. Given that the helicopter started and ended at the same height, what is the missing change in height, x?

Increase or decrease in height (ft)				
+108	−375	+182	x	−134

16. The highest recorded temperature in the United States is 134°F, recorded in California. The lowest recorded temperature in the United States is −80°F, recorded in Alaska. What is the difference between these temperatures?

17. The difference between the elevations in a particular area is 46 ft. If the higher elevation is 32 ft, what is the lower elevation?

18. As of September 6, 2006, the world indoor shot put record for men was 22.66 m, held by Randy Barnes of the United States. The record for women was 22.5 m, held by Helena Fibingerová of Czechoslovakia. How much longer was Barnes's throw than Fibingerová's?

Sam, Ella, Anju, and Ben play a game by drawing cards. A black card represents a positive number. A red card represents a negative number. Each player selects 5 cards. The table shows the results.

19. What is the total score for each player?

20. List the players in order from the lowest score to the highest score.

21. What is the difference between the highest and the lowest scores?

Sam	**Ella**	**Anju**	**Ben**
+7	−8	+4	−10
−5	+2	−3	−2
−3	−1	−9	+8
+10	+6	+5	−7

Core Focus: Distances Between Rationals

THE CORE CONCEPT

The distance between two points on a number line is equal to the absolute value of the difference of their coordinates.

Distance Between Points on a Number Line

DISTANCE BETWEEN TWO POINTS

The distance between two distinct points is a positive number. The formula for finding the distance between two points with coordinates p and q is $|p - q|$.

You can use a number line to show that the distance between two different points is the same no matter which direction you travel.

Modeling a Real-World Distance Problem

You can use a number line to model the distance between two numbers. Plot the points on a number line, and then compute their difference.

EXAMPLE Brandon's dog is $10\frac{1}{2}$ in. tall. His parakeet is $6\frac{3}{4}$ in. tall.

A Represent the equations on a number line. Show how each equation relates to the pets' heights.

$$10\frac{1}{2} - 6\frac{3}{4} = 3\frac{3}{4}$$

$$6\frac{3}{4} - 10\frac{1}{2} = -3\frac{3}{4}$$

Solution

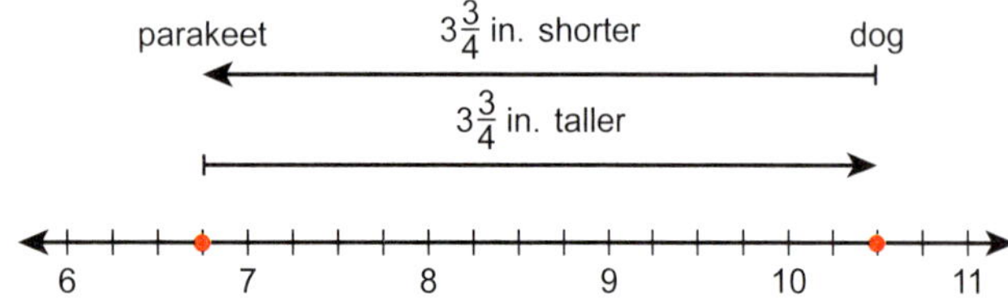

The difference $10\frac{1}{2} - 6\frac{3}{4} = 3\frac{3}{4}$ is positive, so it represents how much taller the dog is than the parakeet. The difference $6\frac{3}{4} - 10\frac{1}{2} = -3\frac{3}{4}$ is negative, so it represents how much shorter the parakeet is than the dog. ■

B Difference in height is commonly expressed as a number greater than or equal to 0, not as a negative number. How would you write an equation to ensure the pets' difference in height is a positive number, no matter what order the numbers are subtracted in? Explain your reasoning.

Solution Begin with the equations in Example A. Take the absolute value of each difference to ensure that the expressions each simplify to a positive number.

$$\left|10\frac{1}{2} - 6\frac{3}{4}\right| = 3\frac{3}{4}$$

$$\left|6\frac{3}{4} - 10\frac{1}{2}\right| = \left|-3\frac{3}{4}\right| = 3\frac{3}{4}$$ ■

Problem Set

Solve.

1. Point A has coordinate $-4\frac{1}{2}$ and point B has coordinate $2\frac{1}{4}$. Compute the two quantities $A - B$ and $B - A$. Explain how both quantities relate to the distance between the two points even though their signs differ.

2. Neyra has \$17.80 in her bank account. She wants to buy a lamp that costs \$24.
   - **(a)** Show on a number line how the equation $24 - 17.80 = 6.20$ represents the amount of money Neyra needs to buy the lamp.
   - **(b)** Show on a different number line how the equation $17.80 - 24 = -6.20$ represents how much the lamp's price would have to change for Neyra to buy it now.
   - **(c)** Describe how both equations represent this situation.

3. Yehuda and Joshua set sail from the same harbor. They sailed in opposite directions. At the end of the day, Yehuda had sailed 13.3 mi due north while Joshua had sailed 7.9 mi due south.
   - **(a)** On a number line, represent the distance Yehuda traveled that day. On the same number line, represent the distance Joshua traveled that day. Assume that north is in the positive direction.
   - **(b)** Write two different expressions to compute the distance between Yehuda and Joshua at the end of the day. Explain why both are valid expressions for computing the distance.
   - **(c)** Yehuda says that the distance between Joshua and him would be the same if instead Joshua had sailed 13.3 mi due south and Yehuda had sailed 7.9 mi due north. Is Yehuda correct? Explain your reasoning.

CHAPTER 3 Review

Choose the answer.

1. What is $-1.63 - (-28.1)$?

   A. -29.73 **C.** 26.38

   B. -26.74 **D.** 26.47

2. What is the value of the expression $x - y$ when $x = 4.51$ and $y = -2.97$?

   A. -2.54 **C.** 6.48

   B. -1.54 **D.** 7.48

3. What value of a makes the equation true?

   $$a + 10.8 = -7.5$$

   A. -18.3 **C.** 3.3

   B. -3.3 **D.** 17.3

4. What property is shown?

   $$-(38 + 17) = -(17 + 38)$$

   A. Associative Property

   B. Opposite of a Sum Property

   C. Distributive Property

   D. Commutative Property

5. What value of d makes the statement true?

   $$-7 + (-4.2) + 3 = d - 7 + 3$$

   A. -11.2 **C.** 4.2

   B. -4.2 **D.** 11.2

6. Which numbers are 6 units away from -2 on the number line?

   A. -8 and 4 **C.** -4 and 4

   B. -8 and 8 **D.** -4 and 8

7. What value of k makes the equation true?

   $$-48 + k = -17$$

   A. -65 **C.** 31

   B. -31 **D.** 65

8. What operation should be performed on both sides of the equation to isolate q?

   $$-5 = -34 + q$$

   A. Add 5.

   B. Subtract 5.

   C. Add 34.

   D. Subtract 34.

9. Mingyu went to a movie theater. Her movie ticket cost t dollars. She paid with a \$20 bill and received \$11.75 in change. Which equation represents this situation?

   A. $20 - t = 11.75$

   B. $11.75 - t = 20$

   C. $t - 20 = 11.75$

   D. $t + 20 = 11.75$

10. Ilya drove 34.7 km today. Yesterday she drove 70.9 km. How much more did Ilya drive yesterday than today?

    A. 36.2 km **C.** 114.5 km

    B. 45.2 km **D.** 115.6 km

Solve.

11. Point P has a coordinate of -4.6, and point Q has a coordinate of 1.5. Use absolute value to write an equation that shows the distance between point P and point Q.

12. At the beginning of the day, a stock's price was \$18.22 per share. At the end of the day, the stock's price was \$17.45. How much did the stock's price change that day?

13. Find the value of t that makes the equation true.

$$-(t + 2) = 6$$

14. The difference between a number and 27 is -15. Find the number.

15. The table shows the freezing points of several substances.

Substance	Freezing point (°C)
linseed oil	−20
turpentine	−59
propyl alcohol	−127
formic acid	8

(a) List the freezing points from lowest to highest.

(b) What is the difference between the warmest freezing point and the coldest freezing point?

(c) Which two substances have the least difference in freezing point?

(d) Hexane has a freezing point of $-95°$ C. Which substance's freezing point is closest to that of hexane?

16. On August 1, Helen's bank account contained \$46. On September 1, the balance changed by \$18 from the balance on August 1.

(a) Write two expressions that represent the possible amount in Helen's bank account on September 1. Represent the two expressions on a number line.

(b) Explain how each expression represents the same change in Helen's bank account.

17. A salad dressing recipe calls for $\frac{3}{4}$ oz of lime juice and $\frac{1}{8}$ oz of hot sauce. Draw a number line and label the points $\frac{1}{8}$ and $\frac{3}{4}$. Show on the number line how both of the following equations represent the difference in the amounts of lime juice and hot sauce needed.

$$\left|\frac{3}{4} - \frac{1}{8}\right| = \frac{5}{8}$$

$$\left|\frac{1}{8} - \frac{3}{4}\right| = \frac{5}{8}$$

Problem	Topic Lookup
1–3, 12	Subtracting Decimals
4, 5, 13	Addition and Subtraction Properties
6, 16	Core Focus: Absolute Value and Distance
7, 8, 14	Equations Involving Addition and Subtraction
9, 10, 15	Addition and Subtraction Applications
11, 17	Core Focus: Distances Between Rationals

CHAPTER 4 Multiplication and Division

Over a million wildebeest migrate between the Serengeti in Tanzania and the Maasai Mara in Kenya every year. How many will make it across the Mara River? How long will it take them to make the trip? Scientists use operations with rational numbers to understand wildebeest behavior and health.

In This Chapter

In this chapter, you'll extend your previous understanding of multiplication and division to signed (positive and negative) numbers as well as other rational numbers. This chapter also covers rounding and estimation as well as using equations to solve problems.

Topic List

- Foundations for Chapter 4
- Multiplying Integers and Decimals
- Dividing Integers and Decimals
- Multiplication and Division Properties
- Core Focus: Closure
- Rounding and Estimation
- Equations Involving Multiplication and Division
- Multiplication and Division Applications
- Core Focus: Modeling with Multiplication and Division
- Core Focus: Decimal Forms of Rational Numbers
- Chapter 4 Review

Wildebeest cross the Mara River as they migrate to find food and water.

Foundations for Chapter 4

Multiplying Decimals

To multiply two decimals, rewrite the problem vertically and multiply the digits in the upper factor by each digit in the lower factor. Add the partial products. To place the decimal point, count the number of digits after the decimal point in each factor and then add these two numbers. Count that many places (the sum of the number of digits after the decimal point in each factor) to the left in the product and place the decimal point there.

EXAMPLE A Find the product.

A-1 0.19 • 0.8

Solution Multiply each of the digits in the upper factor by the single digit in the lower factor.

$$\begin{array}{r} {\scriptstyle 1\ 7} \\ 0.19 \\ \times\ \ 0.8 \\ \hline 0.152 \end{array}$$

There are two digits after the decimal in 0.19 and one digit after the decimal in 0.8, so the decimal point in the product is three places to the left.

$$0.19 \cdot 0.8 = 0.152$$

A-2 3.6 • 0.74

Solution Multiply each of the digits in the upper factor by each digit in the lower factor. Add the partial products.

$$\begin{array}{r} 3.6 \\ \times\ 0.74 \\ \hline 144 \\ 2\ 520 \\ \hline 2.664 \end{array}$$

There is one digit after the decimal in 3.6 and two digits after the decimal in 0.74, so the decimal point in the product is three places to the left.

$$3.6 \cdot 0.74 = 2.664$$

Problem Set A

Find the product.

1. 3 • 1.5

2. 2 • 0.09

3. 1.2 • 43

4. 0.3 • 0.7

5. 2.09 • 20

6. 90.3 • 2.07

7. 0.11 • 84.4

8. 14 • 0.089

9. 5.8 • 0.37

10. 20.3 • 6.5

Dividing Decimals

To divide two decimals, rewrite the problem as long division. Convert the divisor to a whole number by moving the decimal point to the right. Place the decimal point in the dividend the number of places you moved it in the divisor. Perform the long division to find the quotient.

EXAMPLE B Find the quotient.

B-1 $0.96 \div 1.2$

Solution Rewrite the expression as long division.

$1.2\overline{)0.96}$

$12\overline{)9.6}$ Move the decimal point in both the divisor and dividend one place to the right.

$\begin{array}{r} 0.8 \\ 12\overline{)9.6} \end{array}$ Divide.

$0.96 \div 1.2 = 0.8$ ■

B-2 $0.42 \div 0.06$

Solution Rewrite the expression as long division.

$0.06\overline{)0.42}$

$6\overline{)42}$ Move the decimal point in both the divisor and dividend two places to the right.

$\begin{array}{r} 7 \\ 6\overline{)42} \end{array}$ Divide.

$0.42 \div 0.06 = 7$ ■

Problem Set B

Find the quotient.

1. $81 \div 9$
2. $8\overline{)0.24}$
3. $\frac{1.08}{12}$
4. $3.5 \div 0.5$
5. $\frac{0.44}{0.4}$
6. $1.5\overline{)0.06}$
7. $10 \div 0.25$
8. $\frac{0.091}{7}$
9. $65 \div 0.13$
10. $0.08\overline{)0.048}$

Solving Multiplication and Division Equations

MULTIPLICATION PROPERTY OF EQUALITY

If you multiply both sides of an equation by the same nonzero number, the equation is still true.

Solve the equation by isolating the variable on one side of an equation. For the product of a number and a variable, divide both sides of the equation by the number. For the quotient of a variable and a number, multiply both sides of the equation by the number.

EXAMPLE C Solve.

C-1 $-4d = 32$

Solution Undo the product on the left side of the equation by dividing both sides by −4.

$$-4d = 32$$
$$\frac{-4d}{-4} = \frac{32}{-4}$$
$$1 \cdot d = -8$$
$$d = -8$$

Check $-4(-8) = 32$ ✓

The solution $d = -8$ is correct. ■

C-2 $-13 = \frac{m}{6}$

Solution Undo the quotient on the right side of the equation by multiplying both sides by 6.

$$-13 = \frac{m}{6}$$
$$6 \cdot (-13) = 6 \cdot \frac{m}{6}$$
$$-78 = 1 \cdot m$$
$$-78 = m$$

Check $-13 = \frac{-78}{6}$ ✓

The solution $m = -78$ is correct. ■

Problem Set C

Solve.

1. $6d = 54$
2. $-8a = 32$
3. $-15 = 3x$
4. $\frac{y}{9} = 5$
5. $\frac{b}{-2} = 8$
6. $-42 = -7t$
7. $3z = -36$
8. $12 = \frac{q}{4}$
9. $\frac{w}{9} = -7$
10. $-\frac{1}{8}k = -2$
11. $0.4n = 20$
12. $-\frac{1}{3}v = 9$

Multiplying Integers and Decimals

The result of multiplying two or more factors together is the **product**.

Multiplying Integers

To find the product of two or more nonzero numbers, use these steps.

MULTIPLYING NONZERO NUMBERS

Step 1 Ignore the signs of the numbers. Multiply as usual.

Step 2 Give the product a sign.

- The product of two positive factors is positive.
- The product of two negative factors is positive.
- The product of a negative factor and a positive factor is negative.

TIP

The rules can also be stated this way:

If the signs are the same, the product is positive.

If the signs are different, the product is negative.

SIGN OF THE PRODUCT $a \cdot b$

		a	
		positive	**negative**
b	**positive**	+	−
	negative	−	+

EXAMPLE 1 Multiply.

A $3 \cdot 8$

Solution

$3 \cdot 8 = 24$ Multiply. Both factors are positive. The product is positive. ■

B $-4 \cdot (-7)$

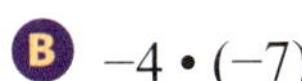

Solution

$-4 \cdot (-7) = +28$ Multiply. Both factors are negative. The product is positive. ■

C $-9 \cdot 5$

Solution

$-9 \cdot 5 = -45$ Multiply. One factor is negative. The other is positive. The product is negative. ■

Multiplying Decimals

Use the same rules to multiply decimals.

EXAMPLE 2 Multiply.

A $-0.2 \cdot (-6.5)$

Solution

$$\begin{array}{r} \overset{1}{6}.5 \\ \times\ 0.2 \\ \hline 1.30 \end{array}$$

Multiply 0.2×6.5.

$-0.2 \cdot (-6.5) = 1.30$ Both factors are negative. The product is positive. ■

B $4.2 \cdot (-1.3)$

Solution

$$\begin{array}{r} 4.2 \\ \times\ 1.3 \\ \hline 1\,2\,6 \\ 4\,2\,0 \\ \hline 5.4\,6 \end{array}$$

Multiply $4.2 \cdot 1.3$.

$4.2 \cdot (-1.3) = -5.46$ One factor is positive. The other factor is negative. The product is negative. ■

Multiplying Three or More Factors

To find the product of three or more factors, multiply one pair of factors. Then multiply their product by the next factor. Keep going until you have used every factor.

EXAMPLE 3 Multiply.

$$-8 \cdot 2 \cdot (-3)$$

Solution

$-8 \cdot 2 \cdot (-3) = -16 \cdot (-3)$ Multiply the first two factors.

$= 48$ Multiply the product by the third factor. ■

THINK ABOUT IT

You can choose any pair of factors to multiply first. The final answer will be the same. For example,

$$\begin{aligned} -8 \cdot 2 \cdot (-3) &= -8 \cdot (-6) \\ &= 48 \end{aligned}$$

Simplifying and Evaluating Expressions

EXAMPLE 4 Simplify.

$$3 + (-2) \cdot 6$$

Solution

$3 + (-2) \cdot 6 = 3 + (-12)$ Multiply. The product is negative.

$= -9$ Add. ■

> **TIP**
> When simplifying an expression, only do one step at a time.

EXAMPLE 5 Evaluate $3x - 4$ when $x = -7$.

Solution

$3x - 4 = 3 \cdot (-7) - 4$ Substitute -7 for x.

$= -21 - 4$ Multiply.

$= -25$ Subtract. ■

Determining the Sign of the Product of Several Factors

When you multiply three or more nonzero factors, you can determine the sign of the product by counting the number of negative factors. Every pair of negative factors makes a positive, which means that

- If the number of negative factors is even, the product is positive.
- If the number of negative factors is odd, the product is negative.

EXAMPLE 6 Give the sign of the product. Write *positive* or *negative*.

A $-6 \cdot 0.5 \cdot (-2) \cdot (-4) \cdot (-1)$

Solution

$-6 \cdot 0.5 \cdot (-2) \cdot (-4) \cdot (-1)$ There are four negative factors. The product is positive. ■

B $(-3)^5$

Solution

$(-3)^5 = (-3) \cdot (-3) \cdot (-3) \cdot (-3) \cdot (-3)$ There are five negative factors. The product is negative. ■

> **REMEMBER**
> An exponent tells how many times the base is used as a factor.

Problem Set

Multiply.

1. $12 \cdot 3$
2. $-4 \cdot (-2)$
3. $6 \cdot (-5)$
4. $7 \cdot (-2)$
5. $-8 \cdot (-15)$
6. $+5 \cdot (-13)$
7. $-9 \cdot (-8)$
8. $19 \cdot (-27)$
9. $+73 \cdot (+3)$
10. $-20 \cdot 6$

Multiply.

11. $-0.6 \cdot (-7)$
12. $3.4 \cdot (-1.5)$
13. $-2.4 \cdot (-3.2)$
14. $-5.6 \cdot 1.3$
15. $3.5 \cdot (-2.6)$
16. $15{,}000 \cdot (-2.5)$
17. $-2 \cdot 8 \cdot (-3)$
18. $-6 \cdot (-3) \cdot (-5)$
19. $2.5 \cdot (-2) \cdot 3$
20. $-8 \cdot (-4) \cdot (-5)$
21. $3.5 \cdot 4 \cdot (-5)$

Give the sign of the product. Write *positive* or *negative*.

22. $-5 \cdot (-3) \cdot (-2)$
23. $4 \cdot (-9) \cdot 7 \cdot (-4) \cdot (-7) \cdot 9$
24. $-1 \cdot (-1) \cdot (-1) \cdot (-1) \cdot (-1) \cdot (-1) \cdot (-1)$
25. -2^4

Simplify.

26. $20 - (-3) \cdot (-2)$
27. $-3 \cdot (-6) + (-5) \cdot 2$
28. $[4 - (-2) \cdot 3] \div 2$
29. $-4 \cdot (-1 + 6)$
30. $-3 \cdot 2 + (-2) \cdot 4$
31. $[(-6) \cdot (-8)] \div [(-3) \cdot (-2)]$

Evaluate.

32. $4t$ when $t = -16$
33. $-2a$ when $a = -4.1$
34. mn when $m = -3$ and $n = 8$
35. $4n + 9$ when $n = -3$
36. $st - 4$ when $s = 6$ and $t = -2$
37. $abc + 4$ when $a = -6$, $b = 2$, and $c = -3$

Dividing Integers and Decimals

The result of division is the **quotient**.

Dividing Integers and Decimals

If you can divide positive numbers, you can divide positive and negative numbers. The steps for the sign of a quotient are the same as the steps for the sign of a product.

DIVIDING NONZERO NUMBERS

Step 1 Ignore the signs of the numbers. Divide as usual.

Step 2 Give the quotient a sign.

- The quotient of two positive numbers is positive.
- The quotient of two negative numbers is positive.
- The quotient of a negative number and a positive number is negative.

TIP

The rules for signs when multiplying and dividing nonzero numbers are the same.

SIGN OF THE QUOTIENT $a \div b$

		a	
		positive	**negative**
b	**positive**	$+$	$-$
	negative	$-$	$+$

EXAMPLE 1 Divide.

A $-12 \div 3$

Solution

$-12 \div 3 = -4$ Divide. One number is negative. The other number is positive. The quotient is negative. ■

B $-5.5 \div (-1.1)$

Solution

$-5.5 \div (-1.1) = 5$ Divide. Both numbers are negative. The quotient is positive. ■

C $6 \div 1.5$

Solution

$6 \div 1.5 = 4$	Divide. Both numbers are positive. The quotient is positive. ■

Simplifying and Evaluating Expressions

EXAMPLE 2 Simplify.

$$\frac{12}{-4+2}$$

Solution

$\frac{12}{-4+2} = \frac{12}{-2}$	Simplify the denominator.
$= -6$	Divide. ■

> **NOTATION**
> A fraction is a way to show division. The expressions $a \div b$ and $\frac{a}{b}$ mean the same thing.

EXAMPLE 3 Evaluate $0.6b \div (0.2 - 0.5)$ when $b = 4$.

Solution

$0.6b \div (0.2 - 0.5) = (0.6 \cdot 4) \div (0.2 - 0.5)$	Substitute 4 for b.
$= (0.6 \cdot 4) \div (-0.3)$	Subtract inside parentheses.
$= 2.4 \div (-0.3)$	Multiply.
$= -8$	Divide. ■

Finding the Mean of Signed Numbers

The mean or average of a set of values is found by adding the numbers, then dividing by the number of values.

EXAMPLE 4 Find the mean of the set of numbers.

$$-3, 5, 0, 2, -1.5, -4$$

Solution There are six values, so to find the mean, divide the sum of the values by 6.

$\frac{-3+5+0+2+(-1.5)+(-4)}{6} = \frac{-1.5}{6}$	Simplify the numerator.
$= -\frac{1}{4}$	Divide. ■

Problem Set

Divide.

1. $21 \div (-3)$
2. $-45 \div 9$
3. $30 \div (-6)$
4. $-121 \div 11$
5. $-81 \div (-9)$
6. $-100 \div 10$
7. $-32 \div 8$
8. $63 \div (-7)$
9. $-4.5 \div (-5)$
10. $4.5 \div 9$
11. $-7.2 \div (-0.9)$
12. $3.6 \div 6$
13. $-3.2 \div 3.2$
14. $10{,}000 \div (-0.1)$
15. $-0.560 \div (-0.8)$
16. $-6.5 \div (\ \ 0.25)$
17. $3.75 \div (-0.125)$
18. $-8.14 \div 0.2$

Simplify.

19. $\dfrac{3-9}{-2}$
20. $\dfrac{6+(-4)}{-9+7}$
21. $[-5 \cdot (-5)] \div (1-6)$
22. **Challenge** $[(3-5) \div 0.2] \div 5$

Evaluate.

23. $\dfrac{t+5}{-6}$ when $t = 25$
24. $\dfrac{-1.2r}{6}$ when $r = -3$
25. $b \div 5c$ when $b = -60$ and $c = -1$
26. $\dfrac{m-1.1}{n+1.1}$ when $m = 5.6$ and $n = -0.6$

Find the mean of the set of numbers.

27. $-5, -6, -2, 0, 3$
28. $10, -12, -4, -6, 8, -10$
29. $-3, -6, 5, 12, 8, -7, -2, 3$
30. $-1.7, 2.5, -3.5, -1.1$

Multiplication and Division Properties

When you multiply or divide with 0, 1, or −1, you can use properties of multiplication and division to simplify.

THINK ABOUT IT

The number 0 does not have a sign. It is not positive or negative. The expression −0 is equivalent to 0.

MULTIPLICATION AND DIVISION PROPERTIES INVOLVING 0, 1, AND −1

Property	Symbols	Examples
Identity Property of Multiplication The product of any number and 1 is equal to the number. The number 1 is called the **multiplicative identity**.	$a \cdot 1 = a$ $1 \cdot a = a$	$5 \cdot 1 = 5$ $1 \cdot (-3) = -3$
Zero Property of Multiplication The product of any number and zero is equal to zero.	$a \cdot 0 = 0$ $0 \cdot a = 0$	$(-2) \cdot 0 = 0$ $0 \cdot 6 = 0$
Negative One Property of Multiplication The product of any number and −1 is equal to the opposite of the number.	$a \cdot (-1) = -a$ $(-1) \cdot a = -a$	$(-5) \cdot (-1) = 5$ $(-1) \cdot 4 = -4$
Identity Property of Division The quotient of any number and 1 is equal to the number.	$\frac{a}{1} = a$	$\frac{6}{1} = 6$ $\frac{(-2)}{1} = -2$
Division into Zero Property Zero divided by any nonzero number is equal to zero.	$\frac{0}{a} = 0$ (when $a \neq 0$)	$\frac{0}{(-3)} = 0$ $\frac{0}{4} = 0$
Negative One Property of Division The quotient of any number and −1 is equal to the opposite of the number.	$a \div (-1) = -a$ $\frac{a}{(-1)} = -a$	$4 \div (-1) = -4$ $\frac{(-2)}{(-1)} = 2$

Using Multiplication and Division Properties of 0, 1, and −1 to Simplify Expressions

EXAMPLE 1 Simplify.

A $-5 \cdot 0$

Solution

$$-5 \cdot 0 = 0$$

Use the zero property of multiplication. ■

B $\frac{-3}{-1}$

Solution

$$\frac{-3}{-1} = -(-3) = 3$$

The quotient of a number and −1 is the opposite of the number. ■

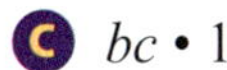

C $bc \cdot 1$

Solution

$$bc \cdot 1 = bc$$

Use the identity property of multiplication. ■

REMEMBER

The opposite of 3 is −3 because 3 lies 3 units to the right of zero and −3 lies 3 units to the left of zero.

Using the Commutative and Associative Properties of Multiplication to Simplify Expressions

Like addition, multiplication is commutative and associative for all real numbers.

MULTIPLICATION PROPERTIES

Property	Symbols	Example
Commutative Property of Multiplication In a product, you can multiply the numbers in any order.	$a \cdot b = b \cdot a$	$4 \cdot 6 = 6 \cdot 4$
Associative Property of Multiplication Changing the grouping of the numbers in a product does not change the product.	$(a \cdot b) \cdot c = a \cdot (b \cdot c)$	$(2 \cdot 3) \cdot 5 = 2 \cdot (3 \cdot 5)$

You can use properties to rearrange and group numbers so you can use mental math to simplify expressions.

EXAMPLE 2 Use properties and mental math to simplify.

A $5 \cdot 3 \cdot (-6)$

Solution

$5 \cdot 3 \cdot (-6) = 5 \cdot (-6) \cdot 3$	Commutative Property of Multiplication
$= -30 \cdot 3$	Multiply.
$= -90$	Multiply. ■

B $(4.65 \cdot 2) \cdot 5$

Solution

$(4.65 \cdot 2) \cdot 5 = 4.65 \cdot (2 \cdot 5)$	Associative Property of Multiplication
$= 4.65 \cdot 10$	Multiply inside parentheses.
$= 46.5$	Multiply. ■

C $2x \cdot 6y^2$

Solution

$2x \cdot 6y^2 = 2 \cdot x \cdot 6 \cdot y^2$	Use multiplication symbols.
$= 2 \cdot 6 \cdot x \cdot y^2$	Commutative Property of Multiplication
$= (2 \cdot 6) \cdot (x \cdot y^2)$	Associative Property of Multiplication
$= 12 \cdot xy^2$	Multiply.
$= 12xy^2$	Write without multiplication symbols. ■

REMEMBER

When you multiply a constant by a variable, you do not have to show the multiplication symbol.

$2x = 2 \cdot x$

$6y^2 = 6 \cdot y^2$

Using the Multiplicative Inverse

A **reciprocal** or **multiplicative inverse** is a number by which a given number must be multiplied to get a result of 1. The reciprocal of a nonzero number a is $\frac{1}{a}$. The reciprocal of a nonzero number $\frac{a}{b}$ is $\frac{b}{a}$.

RECIPROCAL PROPERTY OF MULTIPLICATION

For $a, b \neq 0$:	Example
$a \cdot \frac{1}{a} = 1$	$3 \cdot \frac{1}{3} = 1$
$\frac{a}{b} \cdot \frac{b}{a} = 1$	$-\frac{4}{3} \cdot \left(-\frac{3}{4}\right) = 1$

THINK ABOUT IT

The number 0 does not have a reciprocal. There is no number you can multiply by 0 to get a product of 1.

You can use this property to simplify expressions.

EXAMPLE 3 Simplify.

A $6 \cdot \frac{1}{6}$

Solution

$6 \cdot \frac{1}{6} = 1$ The numbers 6 and $\frac{1}{6}$ are reciprocals. Their product is 1. ■

B $b \cdot c \cdot \frac{1}{b}$

Solution

$b \cdot c \cdot \frac{1}{b} = b \cdot \frac{1}{b} \cdot c$ Commutative Property of Multiplication

$= 1 \cdot c$ Reciprocal Property of Multiplication

$= c$ Identity Property of Multiplication ■

C $\frac{2}{5} \cdot \frac{5}{2} \cdot (-4)$

Solution

$\frac{2}{5} \cdot \frac{5}{2} \cdot (-4) = 1 \cdot (-4)$ Reciprocal Property of Multiplication

$= -4$ Identity Property of Multiplication ■

Using Multiplication and Division Properties to Solve Equations

To **solve** an equation is to find the values of the variables that make the equation true. These values are called **solutions** to the equation. You can use properties to figure out the solution to an equation.

EXAMPLE 4 Solve the equation.

A $8 \cdot \frac{1}{n} = 1$

Solution

$8 \cdot \frac{1}{n} = 1$

$8 \cdot \frac{1}{8} = 1$ The product of 8 and $\frac{1}{8}$ is 1.

The solution is $n = 8$. ■

B $4 \cdot 3 \cdot t = 7 \cdot 3 \cdot 4$

Solution

$4 \cdot 3 \cdot t = 7 \cdot 3 \cdot 4$

$4 \cdot 3 \cdot t = 4 \cdot 3 \cdot 7$ Commutative Property of Multiplication

$4 \cdot 3 \cdot 7 = 4 \cdot 3 \cdot 7$

The solution is $t = 7$. ■

C $\frac{b}{7} = 0$

Solution

$\frac{b}{7} = 0$

$\frac{0}{7} = 0$ The quotient of 0 and 7 is 0.

The solution is $b = 0$. ■

TIP

For Example 4A, ask yourself, "What number must I multiply by 8 to get 1?"

THINK ABOUT IT

You could solve Example 4C using a related equation.

$\frac{b}{7} = 0$

$b = 0 \cdot 7 = 0$

D $(-4 \cdot b) \cdot 6 = -4 \cdot (6 \cdot 3)$

Solution

$(-4 \cdot b) \cdot 6 = -4 \cdot (6 \cdot 3)$

$(-4 \cdot b) \cdot 6 = -4 \cdot (3 \cdot 6)$ Commutative Property of Multiplication

$(-4 \cdot b) \cdot 6 = (-4 \cdot 3) \cdot 6$ Associative Property of Multiplication

$(-4 \cdot 3) \cdot 6 = (-4 \cdot 3) \cdot 6$

The solution is $b = 3$. ■

Problem Set

Name the property that shows the equation is true. Assume that no variable equals zero.

1. $7 \cdot 1 = 7$

2. $3 \cdot (4 \cdot 6) = (3 \cdot 4) \cdot 6$

3. $\frac{4}{5} \cdot \frac{5}{4} = 1$

4. $[5 \cdot (-6)] \cdot 1 = 5 \cdot (-6)$

5. $1 = 5 \cdot \frac{1}{5}$

6. $3bc = 3cb$

7. $(7 - 4b) \cdot 0 = 0$

8. $-2 \cdot h = h \cdot (-2)$

9. $9 \cdot 0 = 0$

10. $-2m(n - 7) = -2(n - 7)m$

Simplify. Identify the property or properties you use.

11. $3.5 \cdot 0$

12. $(6 - 9) \cdot 1$

13. $(7 \cdot 2) \cdot 5$

14. $\frac{2}{3} \cdot \frac{3}{2}$

15. $\frac{5 \cdot 0}{3 - 6}$

16. $5 \cdot 19 \cdot 2$

17. $3b \cdot 4c$

18. $\frac{5 \cdot (-6)}{5 - 6}$

19. $\frac{7}{8} \cdot \frac{r}{5} \cdot \frac{8}{7}$

20. **Challenge** $\left[\frac{3}{n} \cdot 5rs\right]\left[(-1) \cdot \frac{n}{3}\right]$

Use multiplication and division properties to solve.

21. $\frac{k}{-3} = 0$

22. $\frac{5}{8}b = 0$

23. $\frac{2}{3} \cdot \frac{m}{2} = 1$

24. $(5 \cdot 3) \cdot 6 = 6 \cdot (3 \cdot r)$

25. $3 \cdot (9 \cdot 8) = (3 \cdot b) \cdot 8$

26. $6 \cdot \frac{f}{6} = 1$

27. $-5.2 \cdot 3.6 \cdot z = -5.2 \cdot 2.1 \cdot 3.6$

28. $\frac{0}{b} = 0$

29. **Challenge** $\left(\frac{10 - r}{6}\right) \cdot \frac{6}{8} = 1$

30. **Challenge** $\frac{3x}{-1} = 12$

Core Focus: Closure

THE CORE CONCEPT

A set is **closed** under an operation if the operation performed on any two numbers in the set produces another number in the set.

Closure of Sets

Determine whether a set with a small number of elements is closed under an operation by testing combinations of numbers.

EXAMPLE 1 Determine whether the set $\{-1, 0, 1\}$ is closed under multiplication.

Solution Test each of the six possible combinations of elements in the set to determine if the product is a number in the set.

$-1 \cdot (-1) = 1$	$0 \cdot 0 = 0$
$-1 \cdot 0 = 0$	$0 \cdot 1 = 0$
$-1 \cdot 1 = -1$	$1 \cdot 1 = 1$

The set $\{-1, 0, 1\}$ is closed under multiplication since the product of any two elements in the set produces another element in the set. ■

Closure of Infinite Sets

EXAMPLE 2 Determine whether the set of whole numbers is closed under the given operation.

A addition

Solution Checking each pair of numbers is impossible. Test at least three pairs of numbers. Two whole numbers you should always test are 0 and 1 since they have special properties.

$0 + 5 = 5$	$10 + 6 = 16$
$1 + 7 = 8$	$8 + 0 = 8$
$2 + 11 = 13$	$125 + 312 = 437$

Each sum is a whole number. This solution is far from a proof, but these examples would support the conclusion that the set of whole numbers is closed under the operation of addition. ■

REMEMBER

An infinite set has a limitless number of elements.

REMEMBER

One counterexample is enough to show that a set is not closed.

B subtraction

Solution Checking each pair of numbers is impossible. Test at least three pairs of numbers. Include 0 and 1.

$10 - 0 = 10$ $\quad$ $18 - 18 = 0$
$6 - 1 = 5$ $\quad$ $9 - 11 = -2$
$2 - 7 = -5$ $\quad$ $125 - 129 = -4$

Although some differences are whole numbers, some differences are negative integers (-5, -2, and -4). Therefore, the set of whole numbers is not closed under subtraction. ■

EXAMPLE 3 Seth believes the set of integers is closed under division and provides the following examples to justify his claim. Is Seth correct? Explain.

$6 \div 1 = 6$ $\quad$ $24 \div (-6) = -4$
$20 \div 5 = 4$ $\quad$ $0 \div 3 = 0$
$-18 \div (-2) = 9$ $\quad$ $-320 \div 2 = -160$

Solution Seth is not correct. Each of his examples does result in an integer, but Seth did not consider an example such as $-8 \div 3$, which results in the fraction
$-\frac{8}{3}$ or $-2\frac{2}{3}$ (not an integer). You must try to think of every possible type of combination to determine whether a counterexample exists. ■

THINK ABOUT IT

Division by zero is undefined, so you can't use division by zero as an example.

Problem Set

Solve. Show all work.

1. Determine whether the set of integers is closed under subtraction. Show your reasoning.
2. Tina believes the set of natural numbers is closed under division and provided the following examples to justify her claim. Is Tina correct? Explain.

$8 \div 4 = 2$	$14 \div 7 = 2$
$16 \div 16 = 1$	$10 \div 2 = 5$
$12 \div 2 = 6$	$4444 \div 4 = 1111$

3. Give an example of a set that is not closed under multiplication. Provide a counterexample proving that the set is not closed.
4. Is the set of rational numbers closed under addition? Show your reasoning.

Rounding and Estimation

To estimate, you usually need to round numbers.

To round a number to a specified place value, use the steps for rounding.

ROUNDING A NUMBER TO A SPECIFIED PLACE

Step 1 Identify the digit in the specified place.

Step 2 Look at the digit in the next place to the right.

Step 3 If the digit to the right is greater than or equal to 5, increase the digit in the specified place by 1. If the digit to the right is less than 5, do not change the digit in the specified place.

Step 4 Drop all digits to the right of the specified place.

Rounding Numbers

EXAMPLE 1 Round the value to the nearest hundredth, tenth, unit, and ten.

A 42.738

Solution

nearest hundredth	42.738	$8 \geq 5$, so round to 42.74.
nearest tenth	42.738	$3 < 5$, so round to 42.7.
nearest unit	42.738	$7 \geq 5$, so round to 43.
nearest ten	42.738	$2 < 5$, so round to 40. ■

B 3.551

Solution

nearest hundredth	3.551	$1 < 5$, so round to 3.55.
nearest tenth	3.551	$5 \geq 5$, so round to 3.6.
nearest unit	3.551	$5 \geq 5$, so round to 4.
nearest ten	03.551	$3 < 5$, so round to 0. ■

REMEMBER

The symbol $\geq$ means greater than or equal to.

One way to estimate the value of an expression is to round every number in the expression and then perform the indicated operations. Even when you use a calculator, it is still a good idea to estimate to see if your answer is reasonable. If your answer is not reasonable, you may have pressed an incorrect calculator key.

Estimating the Value of an Expression

EXAMPLE 2

A Estimate 163.74 + 78.3 − 19.095 by rounding to the nearest ten.

Solution Round each number to the nearest ten. Then perform the indicated operations.

$$163.74 + 78.3 - 19.095 \rightarrow 160 + 80 - 20 = 220$$

The estimate for 163.74 + 78.3 − 19.095 is 220. ■

B Estimate \$3.84 + \$16.26 + \$5.14 by rounding to the nearest dollar.

Solution Round each amount to the nearest dollar. Then perform the indicated operations.

$$\$3.84 + \$16.26 + \$5.14 \rightarrow \$4 + \$16 + \$5 = \$25$$

The estimate for \$3.84 + \$16.26 + \$5.14 is \$25. ■

Determining Whether an Answer Is Reasonable

You can use estimation to determine whether a solution to a problem is reasonable.

> **THINK ABOUT IT**
> If your estimate is close to the answer, then the answer is reasonable.

EXAMPLE 3 Determine whether the answer is reasonable. Explain.

A 398 + 187 + 492

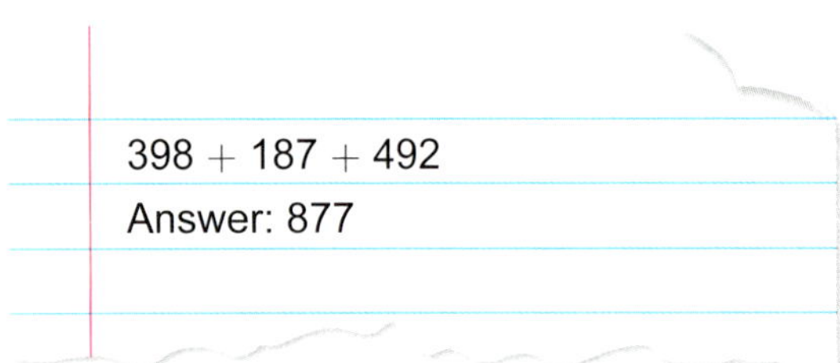

Solution Estimate by rounding to the nearest hundred.

$$398 + 187 + 492 \rightarrow 400 + 200 + 500 = 1100$$

Because the estimate is 1100, the answer 877 is not reasonable. ■

B 4.8×9.2

Solution Estimate by rounding to the nearest unit.

$$4.8 \times 9.2 \rightarrow 5 \times 9 = 45$$

Because the estimate is 45, the answer 470.4 is not reasonable. ■

C $180.96 \div 8.7$

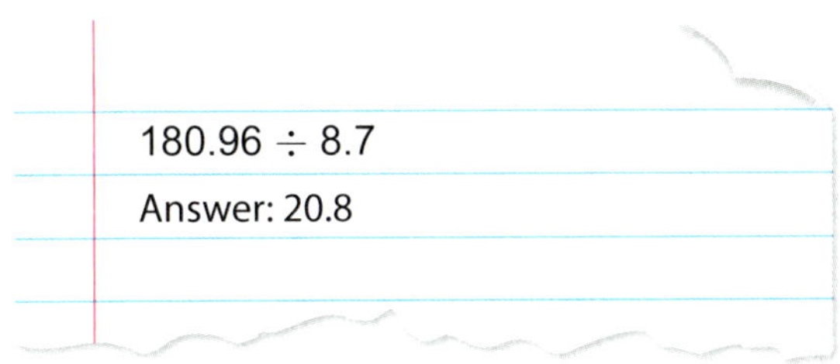

Solution Estimate by rounding to the nearest ten.

$$180.96 \div 8.7 \rightarrow 180 \div 10 = 18$$

Because the estimate is 18, the answer 20.8 is reasonable. ■

> **TIP**
>
> You can use compatible numbers to get a better estimate in Example 3C. Round 8.7 to 9 instead of rounding it to 10.
>
> $$180 \div 9 = 20$$
>
> Twenty is a better estimate than 18.

Application: Estimating Capacity

EXAMPLE 4 An aquarium in the shape of a rectangular prism has dimensions of 3 ft, 2 in.; 2 ft, 1 in.; and 2 ft. Estimate the capacity of the aquarium in gallons.

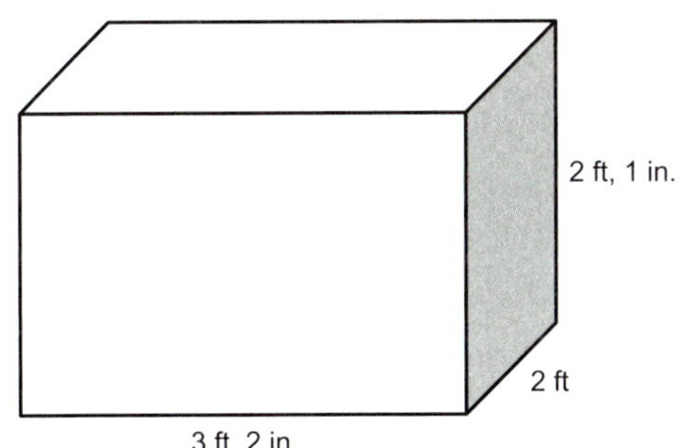

Solution One cubic foot holds approximately 7.48 gal.

Round dimensions to the nearest foot as needed.

$$3 \text{ ft, } 2 \text{ in.} \rightarrow 3 \text{ ft}$$

$$2 \text{ ft, } 1 \text{ in.} \rightarrow 2 \text{ ft}$$

Round 7.48 to 7.5 to get an approximation of the number of gallons in a cubic foot. Multiply the approximate volume in cubic feet by 7.5.

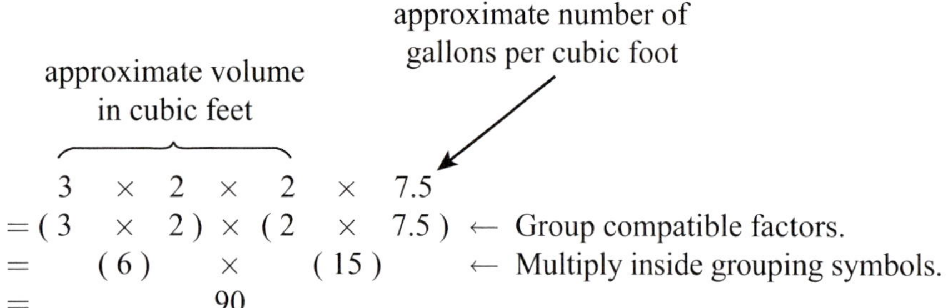

$$\begin{aligned} & 3 \times 2 \times 2 \times 7.5 \\ = & (3 \times 2) \times (2 \times 7.5) \quad \leftarrow \text{Group compatible factors.} \\ = & (6) \times (15) \quad \leftarrow \text{Multiply inside grouping symbols.} \\ = & 90 \end{aligned}$$

The aquarium holds approximately 90 gal. ■

> **TIP**
>
> Capacity and volume are different ways to look at the same concept—the amount of space inside an object. A gallon is a unit of capacity; a cubic foot is a unit of volume.

Application: Using Percent to Estimate

EXAMPLE 5 Based on various studies, from 7% to 11% of people are left handed. Use these results to guess the number of left-handed students in a middle school that has 827 students.

Solution For estimating, it makes sense to use 10% for two reasons: it is between 7% and 11%, and it is easy to compute with. Round 827 to 800.

$$10\% \text{ of } 800 = 0.10 \times 800 = 80$$

Based on the studies, 80 is a good guess of the number of left-handed students in the middle school. ■

> **THINK ABOUT IT**
>
> Ten percent is somewhat more than halfway between 7% and 11% but 800 is somewhat less than 827, so the estimating strategy is sound.

Problem Set

Round the value to the nearest hundredth, tenth, unit, and ten.

1. 6.25

2. 93.548

3. 326.004

4. 62.519

Estimate by rounding each number to the given place and then simplify.

5. Round to the nearest ten.

$$326.5 + 62.48 + 48.62$$

6. Round to the nearest tenth.

$$62.59 - 31.27$$

7. Round to the nearest dollar.

$$\$5.82 + \$13.89 - \$11.09$$

8. Round to the nearest hundred.

$$628 - 85 - 131$$

9. Round to the nearest hundredth.

$$0.026 + 0.041 + 0.52$$

10. Round to the nearest unit.

$$695.324 - 299.67$$

11. Round to the nearest dime.

$$\$58.64 - \$32.19$$

12. Round to the nearest ten.

$$72 + 2.05 - 38.62 + 12.489$$

Choose the most reasonable estimated answer.

13. $62.2 + 48.7$

A. 50

B. 90

C. 110

D. 180

14. $809 \div 78$

A. 4

B. 10

C. 24

D. 30

15. 5.9×32.8

A. 10

B. 70

C. 120

D. 180

16. $9.21 - 3.92$

A. 4

B. 5

C. 6

D. 7

Determine whether the answer is reasonable. Explain.

17. $872 + 94 + 349$

18. 32.5×84.9

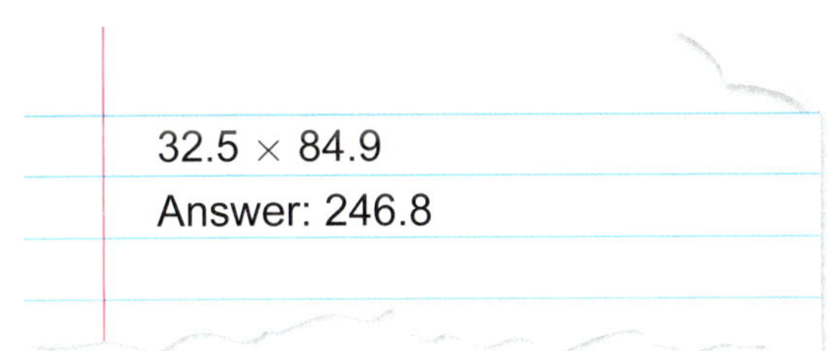

19. $235.98 \div 62.1$

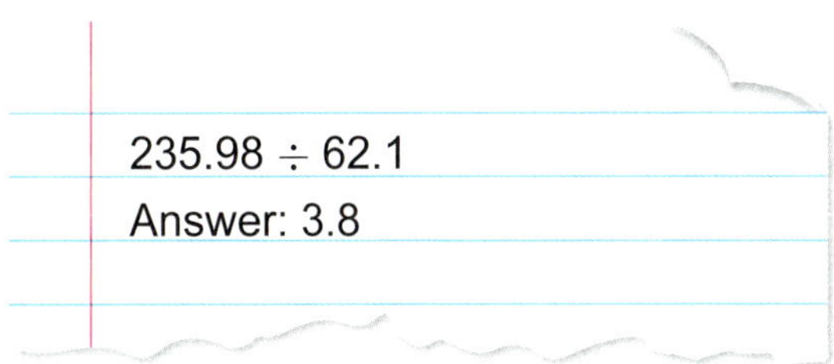

20. $72.518 + 12.84 + 162.7$

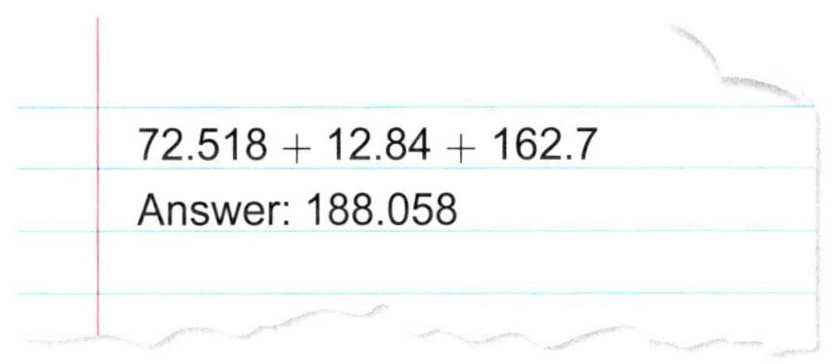

Solve.

21. A brick mold in the shape of a rectangular prism measures 2.25 in. by 3.5 in. by 8 in. What is the approximate volume of the brick?

22. The land for a new playground is in the shape of a triangle with a base of 52.8 m and a height of 178 m. What is the approximate area of the land?

23. A bedroom in the shape of a rectangle measures 11 ft, 3 in. by 15 ft, 8 in. New carpet for the bedroom costs $4.89 per square foot. What is the approximate cost of new carpet for the bedroom?

24. A family's restaurant bill is $42.17. They want to leave a 20% tip for the waiter. About how much should they leave?

25. A political party estimates that its candidate will receive between 28% and 33% of the votes during an election. If 639 people vote, about how many votes can the candidate expect to receive?

26. A room has 4 walls that are each 14 ft, 2 in. long and 8 ft high. If 1 can of paint covers about 325 ft^2, about how many cans of paint will be needed to paint each wall with 2 coats of paint?

Equations Involving Multiplication and Division

If you divide both sides of an equation by the same nonzero number, the equation will still be true. You can use the division property of equality to solve equations.

Using the Division Property of Equality to Solve Equations

You can use the division property of equality to find equivalent equations. The point of this sort of transformation is to find an equation that makes the solution easy to see.

DIVISION PROPERTY OF EQUALITY

For a, b, and n (where $n \neq 0$),

If $a = b$

then $\frac{a}{n} = \frac{b}{n}$

Example

If $2x = 6$

then $\frac{2x}{2} = \frac{6}{2}$

$x = 3$

All three of these are equivalent equations.

REMEMBER

Equivalent equations have the same solution.

EXAMPLE 1 Solve.

A $5 \cdot r = -30$

Solution

$5 \cdot r = -30$

$\frac{5 \cdot r}{5} = \frac{-30}{5}$ Divide both sides of the equation by 5.

$1 \cdot r = -6$ Simplify.

$r = -6$ Identity Property of Multiplication ■

TIP

Check your answer by substituting −6 for r in the original equation. The result should be a true equation.

$5 \cdot r = -30$

$5 \cdot (-6) = -30$

$-30 = -30$ ✓

B $2.1 = -7b$

Solution

$$2.1 = -7b$$

$\frac{2.1}{-7} = \frac{-7b}{-7}$	Divide both sides of the equation by -7.
$-0.3 = 1 \cdot b$	Simplify.
$-0.3 = b$	Identity Property of Multiplication ■

Using the Multiplication Property of Equality to Solve Equations

If you multiply both sides of an equation by the same number, the equation will still be true. You can use the multiplication property of equality to solve equations.

MULTIPLICATION PROPERTY OF EQUALITY

For *a*, *b*, and *n*,	**Example**
If $a = b$	If $\frac{x}{5} = 3$
then $an = bn$	then $\frac{x}{5} \cdot 5 = 3 \cdot 5$
	$x = 15$
	All three of these are equivalent equations.

EXAMPLE 2 Solve.

A $\frac{b}{3} = 10$

Solution

$$\frac{b}{3} = 10$$

$\frac{b}{3} \cdot 3 = 10 \cdot 3$	Multiply both sides of the equation by 3.
$b \cdot 1 = 30$	Simplify.
$b = 30$	Identity Property of Multiplication ■

B $3 = \frac{w}{0.65}$

Solution

$$3 = \frac{w}{0.65}$$

$3 \cdot 0.65 = \frac{w}{0.65} \cdot 0.65$	Multiply both sides of the equation by 0.65.
$1.95 = w \cdot 1$	Simplify.
$1.95 = w$	Identity Property of Multiplication ■

Using the Reciprocal to Solve an Equation

When the variable in an equation is multiplied by a fraction, multiply both sides by the reciprocal of the fraction to solve. Multiplying by the reciprocal is the same as dividing.

EXAMPLE 3 Solve.

$$\frac{2}{3}p = -6$$

Solution

$\frac{2}{3}p = -6$

$\frac{2}{3} \cdot \frac{3}{2} \cdot p = -6 \cdot \frac{3}{2}$ Multiply both sides of the equation by $\frac{3}{2}$.

$1 \cdot p = -9$ Simplify. The product of reciprocals is 1.

$p = -9$ Identity Property of Multiplication ■

> **REMEMBER**
>
> $-6 \cdot \frac{3}{2} = -\frac{6}{1} \cdot \frac{3}{2}$
>
> $= -\frac{\overset{3}{\cancel{6}}}{1} \cdot \frac{3}{\underset{1}{\cancel{2}}}$
>
> $= -\frac{9}{1}$
>
> $= -9$

Application: Science

EXAMPLE 4 Scientists estimate the fish population in a lake every year. In 2008, the estimate was 22,500. The estimate for 2008 was 3 times the estimate for 2005. What was the estimate for 2005?

Solution Use the words to write an equation. The unknown quantity is the estimate for 2005.

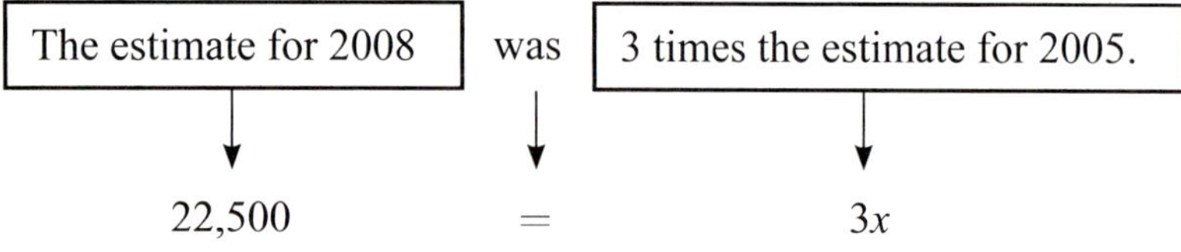

> **TIP**
>
> When modeling a problem, the words *is* and *was* can often be translated to equals signs.

Solve the equation.

$22{,}500 = 3x$

$\frac{22{,}500}{3} = \frac{3x}{3}$ Divide both sides of the equation by 3.

$7500 = x$ Simplify both sides of the equation. ■

Problem Set

Solve.

1. $-2r = 4$
2. $4z = 12$
3. $2b = 10$
4. $6p = -72$
5. $\frac{2}{3}m = -8$
6. $\frac{a}{16} = -20$

7. $-2x = -15$

8. $6x = 42$

9. $\frac{g}{3} = -0.7$

10. $\frac{y}{4} = 3$

11. $-7 = \frac{j}{2}$

12. $\frac{y}{-2} = -6$

13. $-8 = \frac{b}{-3}$

14. $-5x = -30$

15. $-72 = -8x$

16. $\frac{3}{8}t = -27$

17. $\frac{y}{5} = -6$

18. $-\frac{9}{10}b = -18$

19. $\frac{1}{4}z = -2$

20. $12t = 48$

21. $\frac{7}{8}b = 7$

22. $15 = 4x$

23. $\frac{k}{3.2} = -4$

24. $\frac{2}{3}q = -\frac{2}{3}$

25. $-4.5 = 0.9w$

26. $5 = \frac{n}{-0.15}$

27. $\frac{5}{6} = -\frac{10}{13}p$

For each problem:

(a) Write an equation.

(b) Solve the equation.

(c) Answer the question.

28. A carpenter cut a board into 3 pieces of equal length. One of the pieces was 15.2 cm long. What was the length of the board?

29. Mrs. Williams has 24 students in her class this year. The number of students she has this year is 120% of the number she had last year. How many students were in Mrs. Williams's class last year?

30. Raisins make up $\frac{2}{5}$ of Rhonda's trail mix. If she makes a batch of trail mix using $\frac{1}{8}$ lb of raisins, what is the weight of the entire batch?

Multiplication and Division Applications

Many relationships can be described with multiplication or division.

Using Formulas

A **formula** is an equation that defines the relationship between two or more measurable quantities. To use a formula, substitute numbers for all but one of the variables and simplify.

EXAMPLE 1 Solve.

A The formula $P = 4s$ gives the perimeter, P, of a square in which each side measures s units. What is the perimeter of a square with a side length of 13.6 cm?

Solution

$P = 4s$	Write the formula.
$= 4 \cdot 13.6$	Substitute the known value for s.
$= 54.4$	Multiply.

The perimeter of the square is 54.4 cm. ■

TIP

The letters chosen to represent measurements in a formula are often related to the quantities they represent. In Example 1A, ***s*** represents ***s***ide length and ***P*** represents ***P***erimeter.

B A teacher uses the formula $G = 100 \cdot \frac{c}{t}$ to find the grade, G, assigned to a student with c correct answers on a test with t questions. What is the grade assigned to a student with 9 correct answers on a test with 12 questions?

Solution

$G = 100 \cdot \frac{c}{t}$	Write the formula.
$= 100 \cdot \frac{9}{12}$	Substitute the known values for c and t.
$= 100 \cdot 0.75$	Write the fraction as a decimal.
$= 75$	Simplify.

The student's grade is 75. ■

C The percent change, PC, in the price of an item is found using the formula $PC = \frac{n - r}{r}$, where n is the new price and r is the original price. What is the percent change when the price of a gallon of milk goes from \$2.50 to \$2.25?

Solution

$PC = \frac{n - r}{r}$	Write the formula.
$= \frac{\$2.25 - \$2.50}{\$2.50}$	Substitute known values for n and r.
$= \frac{-\$0.25}{\$2.50}$	Simplify the numerator.
$= -0.1$	Simplify.
$= -10\%$	Change decimal to percent.

The percent change is -10%. The price of milk decreased by 10%. ■

THINK ABOUT IT

When the price decreases, the percent change is negative. When the price increases, the percent change is positive.

Using Properties of Equality with Formulas

When you look at a formula, you see that one variable is the output and one or more other variables are the inputs. For example, in the formula $P = 4s$, the perimeter, P, is the output. The side length, s, is the input. This form of the formula is most useful when you know s and want to find P.

What you have learned about solving equations using multiplication and division can help you use formulas when they are not written with the unknown variable as the output.

EXAMPLE 2 Solve.

A The formula $d = rt$ gives the distance, d, traveled in time t at rate r. How long will it take Harry to cycle 39 mi if he maintains a constant speed of 12 mph?

Solution

$d = rt$	Write the formula.
$39 = 12t$	Substitute known values for d and r.
$\frac{39}{12} = \frac{12t}{12}$	Divide both sides by 12.
$3.25 = t$	Simplify.

It will take Harry 3.25 h to cycle 39 mi. ■

B The formula $A = \frac{bh}{2}$ gives the area, A, of a triangle with base length b and height h. What is the height in a triangular garden that has an area of 33.15 m^2 and a base length of 6.5 m?

Solution

$A = \frac{bh}{2}$	Write the formula.
$33.15 = \frac{6.5h}{2}$	Substitute known values for A and b.

$$33.15 \cdot \frac{2}{6.5} = \frac{6.5h}{2} \cdot \frac{2}{6.5}$$ Multiply both sides by the reciprocal of the coefficient of h.

$$10.2 = h$$ Simplify.

The height of the garden is 10.2 m. ■

Solving Literal Equations

A **literal equation** is an equation with one or more variables. A formula is one kind of literal equation. You can use the properties of equality to solve a literal equation for one of its variables.

EXAMPLE 3

A Solve the formula $I = Prt$ for t.

Solution

$$I = Prt$$

$$\frac{I}{Pr} = t$$ Divide both sides by Pr. ■

B Solve the formula $P = 2l + 2w$ for w.

Solution

$$P = 2l + 2w$$

$$P - 2l = 2l - 2l + 2w$$ Subtract $2l$ from both sides to isolate $2w$.

$$P - 2l = 2w$$ Simplify.

$$\frac{P - 2l}{2} = \frac{2w}{2}$$ Divide both sides by 2.

$$\frac{P - 2l}{2} = w$$ Simplify. ■

> **TIP**
>
> When you solve a literal equation for one of its variables, treat the other variables like constants. If the equation $I = Prt$ were $24 = 6 \cdot 2 \cdot t$, how would you solve for t?
>
> Divide both sides by 12.

Problem Set

The formula $A = s \cdot s$ gives the area, A, of a square with side length s. Find the area of the square with the given side length.

1. $s = 7$ in.

2. $s = 14$ m

3. $s = 2.4$ cm

The formula $P = 8s$ gives the perimeter, P, of a regular octagon with side length s. Find the perimeter of the regular octagon with the given side length.

4. $s = 2$ cm

5. $s = 6$ m

6. $s = 3.1$ ft

The formula $A = \frac{bh}{2}$ gives the area, A, of a triangle with base length b and height h. Find the area of the triangle with the given base length and height.

7. $b = 5$ cm; $h = 2$ cm

8. $b = 8$ ft; $h = \frac{3}{4}$ ft

9. $b = 5.2$ m; $h = 3.1$ m

The formula $d = rt$ gives the distance, d, that is traveled in time t at rate r. Find the distance that is traveled in the given time at the given rate.

10. $r = 50$ mph; $t = 3$ h

11. $r = 35$ m/s; $t = 4.3$ s

12. $r = 14$ ft/s; $t = 2.25$ s

13. $r = 80$ kmph; $t = 0.25$ h

The percent change, PC, in the price of an item is found using the formula $PC = \frac{n - r}{r}$, where n is the new price and r is the original price. Find the percent change for the given new and original prices.

14. new price: \$2.40
original price: \$3.00

15. new price: \$820.80
original price: \$720

16. new price: \$14,100
original price: \$15,000

Solve the literal equation for the given variable.

17. Solve for r.

$$d = rt$$

18. Solve for d.

$$C = 3.14d$$

19. Solve for b.

$$A = \frac{bh}{2}$$

20. Solve for y.

$$x = \frac{4}{5}y$$

21. Solve for a.

$$F = ma$$

22. Solve for P.

$$I = Prt$$

23. Solve for V.

$$R = \frac{V}{I}$$

24. **Challenge** Solve for B.

$$S = 2B + ph$$

Solve.

25. The formula $P = 2l + 2w$ gives the perimeter, P, of a rectangle with length l and width w. The perimeter of a rectangle is 24 in. Its length is 3 in. What is its width?

26. The formula $I = Prt$ gives the interest, I, on an investment of P dollars at rate r for time t. If a certain investment yielded \$49 interest when invested at 2% for 7 years, what was the amount of the investment? Hint: Use 0.02 for r.

27. The formula $d = rt$ gives the distance, d, traveled in time t at rate r. A motorcycle traveled 67.2 mi in 1.2 h. What was its average rate of speed?

28. The formula $c = 2.54n$ can be used to convert a measurement of c cm to an equivalent measure of n in. Henry is 170 cm tall. What is his height in inches? Round to the nearest tenth of an inch.

29. **Challenge** The formula $S = 2lw + 2wh + 2lh$ gives the surface area, S, of a rectangular prism with length l, height h, and width w. The surface area of a rectangular prism is 88 in^2. Its length is 6 in. and its height is 2 in. What is its width?

30. **Challenge** The formula $B = \frac{703}{4900}w$ gives the body mass index (BMI), B, for a person 5 ft, 10 in. tall who weighs w pounds. Joe is 5 ft, 10 in. tall and has a BMI of 24. What is his weight? Round your answer to the nearest tenth of a pound.

Core Focus: Modeling with Multiplication and Division

THE CORE CONCEPT

Many real-world problems involve modeling a situation with multiplication or division. The numbers in the model may be rational numbers, not simply whole numbers.

Modeling with Multiplication

Multiplication can model real-world situations involving rates or amounts that are added or subtracted multiple times. The answer to a real-world multiplication problem can be negative as well as positive.

EXAMPLE 1 Solve.

A David bought and sold 40 shares of stock. He earned \$1.67 on each share he sold. How much did David earn altogether, and why would he write this amount as a positive number? Explain.

Solution The amount David earned is the product of the number of shares and the price earned per share.

$$40 \cdot 1.67 = 66.80$$

Since David gained money per share and didn't lose money per share, he would represent the amount earned per share as a positive number. The product of two positive numbers is a positive number. ■

B David bought and sold 35 shares of another stock. He lost 26¢ on each share he sold. How much did David lose altogether, and why would he write this amount as a negative number? Explain.

Solution The amount David lost is the product of the number of shares and the price lost per share.

$$35 \cdot (-0.26) = -9.10$$

Since David lost money on each share (as opposed to gaining money), he would represent the loss per share as a negative number. The product of a positive number and a negative number is a negative number. ■

TIP

Certain words indicate an amount is positive. Here are some examples:

gain
earn
increase
ascend

TIP

Certain words indicate an amount is negative. Here are some examples:

loss
spend
decrease
descend

Modeling with Division

Division can model real-world situations in which a total amount is divided or spread into equal-sized parts. In these problems, you find the quotient of the amount and the number of equal parts into which it is split.

EXAMPLE 2 Steve went hiking in the mountains. He ascended 373.8 m in altitude in 2.8 h.

A Explain why it is reasonable to write the amount that Steve ascended, d, as a positive number. Use the equation $rt = d$ to solve for Steve's average rate of ascent.

Solution Since Steve's change in altitude was an increase of 373.8 m, it is reasonable to write this change as a positive number.

Substitute $t = 2.8$ and $d = 373.8$ into $rt = d$ and solve.

$$2.8r = 373.8$$

$$\frac{2.8r}{2.8} = \frac{373.8}{2.8}$$

$$r = \frac{373.8}{2.8} = 133.5$$

Steve's average rate of ascent is 133.5 m/h. ■

B Steve descended the same distance in 2.1 h. Explain why it is reasonable to write the amount that he descended, d, as a negative number. What is Steve's average rate of descent?

Solution Since Steve's change in altitude was a decrease of 373.8 m, it is reasonable to write this change as a negative number.

Substitute $t = 2.1$ and $d = -373.8$ into $rt = d$ and solve.

$$2.1r = -373.8$$

$$\frac{2.1r}{2.1} = \frac{-373.8}{2.1}$$

$$r = \frac{-373.8}{2.1} = -178$$

Steve's average rate of descent is -178 m/h. ■

REMEMBER

A rate is a ratio of two quantities or measurements.

THINK ABOUT IT

Dividing a distance by a time is spreading the distance evenly over that time. The quotient is a rate, in this case an average speed over that time.

Problem Set

Solve.

1. Cailey has to buy drinks for a party. Seven friends gave her \$3.50 apiece to buy the drinks.

(a) Altogether, how much did Cailey's friends give her to buy drinks for the party? Write an expression to show this amount and simplify it.

(b) Cailey bought 4 bottles of juice at \$4.80 apiece. How does this purchase change the amount of money Cailey has to spend on drinks? Write an expression to show this amount and simplify it.

Solve.

2. Linda had 25.6 m of fencing. She cut 18.2 m of the fencing into 4 equal pieces to make fencing for a square garden. Linda wrote this equation to calculate the amount of fencing, n, she used for each side.

$$4n = 18.2$$

   (a) Explain why Linda wrote the amount of fencing used as 18.2, not 25.6.

   (b) Linda wrote the amount of fencing used as a positive, not negative, number. Is there a situation in which she might want to write this amount as a negative number, not a positive one? Explain.

3. Raj made fruit punch from a recipe. The table shows the ingredients and their amounts in the recipe. The recipe makes 15 servings of fruit punch.

Ingredient	Amount
whole orange	2
lemonade concentrate	6 oz
grape juice concentrate	4 oz
water	64 oz
sugar	2 cups

   (a) Raj wants to make enough fruit punch for only 1 serving instead of 15 servings. Raj uses the formula $a = \frac{1}{15}x$ to calculate the amount, a, of each ingredient he should use. Explain why Raj could use this formula to calculate how much of each of the 5 ingredients he would need.

   (b) Calculate how much of each ingredient Raj would need to make 6 servings. Organize your results in a table.

Core Focus: Decimal Forms of Rational Numbers

THE CORE CONCEPT

Any rational number can be written as a decimal. The digits after the decimal point will either terminate or repeat.

Repeating Decimals

DEFINITION

A decimal is a **repeating decimal** if a digit or a group of digits, other than 0, repeat forever after the decimal point.

Convert a rational number to a decimal by first rewriting the rational number as the ratio of two integers. Use long division to divide the numerator by the denominator. Examine the quotient to see if a digit or group of digits repeats.

EXAMPLE 1 Use long division to show that $\frac{14}{33}$ is a repeating decimal.

Solution

$$\begin{array}{r} 0.4242 \\ 33\overline{)14.0000} \\ \underline{13\,2} \\ 80 \\ \underline{66} \\ 140 \\ \underline{132} \\ 80 \\ \underline{66} \\ 140 \end{array}$$

$\frac{14}{33} = 0.\overline{42}$; The digit pair 42 will repeat forever after the decimal point because the remainder after dividing by 33 will alternate between 14 and 8 without end.

TIP

A shorthand way to write a repeating decimal is to write the repeating digits only once and then draw a line over these digits. For example,

$5.\overline{169} = 5.169169169\ldots$

Terminating Decimals

DEFINITION

A decimal is a **terminating decimal** if it has a finite number of digits.

Convert a fraction to a decimal by using long division to divide the numerator by the denominator. If the quotient eventually goes evenly into the remainder, the decimal terminates.

EXAMPLE 2

A Convert $\frac{29}{40}$ to a decimal.

Solution Divide 29 by 40 using long division.

$$\begin{array}{r} 0.725 \\ 40\overline{)29.000} \\ \underline{280} \\ 100 \\ \underline{80} \\ 200 \\ \underline{200} \\ 0 \end{array}$$

The fraction $\frac{29}{40}$ is equivalent to the decimal 0.725. ■

B Rewrite the quotient you found in Example 2A as a ratio of two integers using a power of 10 for the denominator. Also, explain how this ratio is a fraction equivalent to $\frac{29}{40}$.

Solution First write the quotient as a fraction with the numerator equal to the quotient and the denominator equal to 1. Then convert the numerator to an integer by moving the decimal point three places to the right. To do this, multiply the fraction by 1000 over 1000.

$$\frac{0.725}{1} = \frac{0.725}{1} \cdot \frac{1000}{1000} = \frac{0.725 \cdot 1000}{1 \cdot 1000} = \frac{725}{1000}$$

The fraction $\frac{725}{1000}$ can be simplified by dividing both the numerator and denominator by a common factor of 25.

$$\frac{725}{1000} = \frac{725 \div 25}{1000 \div 25} = \frac{29}{40}$$

Since $\frac{29}{40}$ is a simplified form of $\frac{725}{1000}$, both fractions are equivalent. ■

THINK ABOUT IT

A terminating decimal can be written with an infinite number of zeros after the last nonzero digit. For example,

$$7.8 = 7.800000\ldots$$

Problem Set

Solve.

1. For the fractions $\frac{5}{9}$, $\frac{5}{99}$, and $\frac{5}{999}$:

   (a) Convert each fraction to a decimal.

   (b) What pattern do you observe in these decimals?

   (c) Use this pattern to predict the decimal representation of $\frac{5}{9999}$.

2. The fraction $\frac{2}{40}$ can be used to approximate the value of $\frac{2}{41}$ since $\frac{2}{40}$ equals 0.05, which is a terminating decimal close to $\frac{2}{41}$ in value.

   For each fraction, find a fraction to approximate the given fraction and explain your reasoning.

   (a) $\frac{17}{24}$

   (b) $\frac{23}{98}$

   (c) $\frac{43}{51}$

3. Jamie lists the factors of 100: 1, 2, 5, 10, 20, 25, 50, 100. She claims that any fraction with one of these values as a denominator is represented as a terminating decimal. For example, Jamie claims that the fractions $\frac{1}{25}$, $\frac{2}{25}$, $\frac{3}{25}$, and so on are equivalent to terminating decimals. Jamie says she can show this by finding equivalent fractions with 100 in the denominator. Is Jamie correct? Explain your reasoning.

CHAPTER 4 Review

Choose the answer.

1. What is $-6 \cdot (-2.7)$?
   - A. -162
   - B. -16.2
   - C. 1.62
   - D. 16.2

2. What is the value of ab when $a = -1.3$ and $b = 0.4$?
   - A. -0.52
   - B. -0.052
   - C. 0.52
   - D. 5.2

3. What is $6.4 \div (-0.8)$?
   - A. -80
   - B. -8
   - C. 0.8
   - D. 8

4. What is the value of the expression $\frac{y-6}{3}$ when $y = -1.2$?
   - A. -2.4
   - B. -1.6
   - C. 1.6
   - D. 2.4

5. Which property shows the equation is true?

   $$8 \div (-1) = -8$$

   - A. Identity Property of Division
   - B. Negative One Property of Multiplication
   - C. Negative One Property of Division
   - D. Reciprocal Property of Multiplication

6. What is the value of the expression $\frac{4 \cdot 0}{11 - 12}$?
   - A. -4
   - B. -1
   - C. 0
   - D. 1

7. Which is the best estimate for $12.89 - 6.17$?
   - A. 5
   - B. 6
   - C. 7
   - D. 8

8. Which is the best estimate for 0.39×7.05?
   - A. 0.21
   - B. 0.28
   - C. 2.1
   - D. 2.8

9. What value of p makes the equation true?

   $$-9.3 = 3p$$

   - A. -27.9
   - B. -12.3
   - C. -6.3
   - D. -3.1

10. What value of f makes the equation true?

    $$\frac{2}{3}f = 12$$

    - A. 8
    - B. $11\frac{1}{3}$
    - C. $12\frac{2}{3}$
    - D. 18

11. The formula for the volume of a rectangular prism is $V = lwh$. What equation correctly solves for h?
    - A. $h = \frac{V}{wl}$
    - B. $h = \frac{Vl}{w}$
    - C. $h = \frac{Vw}{l}$
    - D. $h = \frac{wl}{V}$

Solve.

12. Find the sign of the product without calculating it. Write *positive* or *negative*. Explain.

$$(-4) \cdot (17) \cdot (-65) \cdot (-2) \cdot (23) \cdot (-9)$$

13. Find the mean of the set of numbers.

$$\{-4, -23, 7, 6, -11\}$$

14. Solve for h using multiplication and division properties.

$$\frac{h}{4} \cdot \frac{4}{7} = 1$$

15. A salesperson sold a car for a profit of \$4097. She earned a sales commission of 20% of the profit. About how much was the salesperson's commission?

16. Yumi walked 4.8 km around a track this morning. She walked a total of 11 laps around the track. What is the length of each lap?

17. The formula $A = \frac{1}{2}(b_1 + b_2)h$ gives the area, A, of a trapezoid with height h and base lengths of b_1 and b_2. Solve for the height of a trapezoid with an area of 26 cm^2 and base lengths of 6 and 7 cm.

18. Is the set of integers closed under subtraction? If it is, provide at least three examples. If it isn't, provide at least one counterexample as proof.

19. Kara buys coffee in a can holding 28 oz of coffee. She knows that $\frac{1}{8}$ oz of coffee is needed to make 1 cup of coffee.

(a) Write a multiplication equation Kara can use to find the total number, n, of cups of coffee the container can make.

(b) Solve the equation for n.

20. Omar loaded a box with 60 identical cans. He then weighed the box and recorded its weight of 18.1 lb. Omar wrote the expression $\frac{18.1}{60}$ lb to find the weight of 1 can.

(a) Rewrite the expression as a decimal. Is that decimal repeating or terminating?

(b) Omar estimated the weight of 1 can to be $\frac{18}{60}$ lb. Does this fraction overestimate or underestimate the actual weight of 1 can?

Problem	Topic Lookup
1, 2, 12	Multiplying Integers and Decimals
3, 4, 13	Dividing Integers and Decimals
5, 6, 14	Multiplication and Division Properties
18	Core Focus: Closure
7, 8	Rounding and Estimation

Problem	Topic Lookup
9, 10, 15, 16	Equations Involving Multiplication and Division
11, 17	Multiplication and Division Applications
19	Core Focus: Modeling with Multiplication and Division
20	Core Focus: Decimal Forms of Rational Numbers

CHAPTER 5 Fractions

You could do lots of math with only fractions or only decimals, but decimals are used for certain applications just as fractions are used for others. For example, carpenters use fractions and mixed numbers quite a bit. Anybody who builds a house or a deck deals with lots of fractions.

In This Chapter

This chapter covers addition, subtraction, multiplication, and division with fractions. Those topics are also extended to working with mixed numbers and other forms of rational numbers. You'll then apply those skills to solving equations and word problems involving rational numbers.

Topic List

- Foundations for Chapter 5
- Equivalent Fractions
- Multiplying Fractions
- Dividing Fractions
- Core Focus: Rational Numbers
- Common Denominators
- Adding and Subtracting Fractions
- Working with Mixed Numbers
- Multiplying and Dividing with Mixed Numbers
- Equations with Fractions
- Core Focus: Fractions and Mixed Numbers
- Core Focus: Applications with Rational Numbers
- Chapter 5 Review

A carpenter needs to know how to use fractions to make the right cut.

530
1789

Foundations for Chapter 5

Modeling Fractions with Shaded Figures

You can use fractions to compare a part to a whole or a part to a part in a figure.

EXAMPLE A Solve.

A-1 What is the ratio of the shaded portion of the circle to the unshaded portion of the circle?

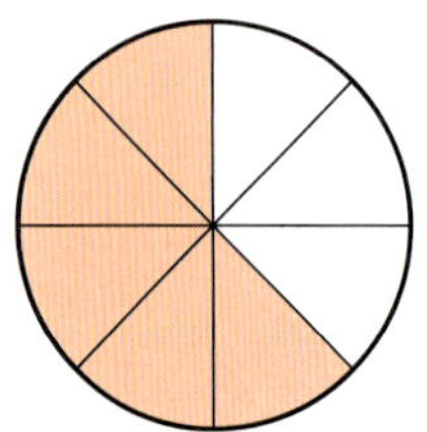

Solution There are 5 shaded sectors and 3 unshaded sectors. The ratio of the shaded to the unshaded portion is $\frac{5}{3}$. ■

A-2 The area shaded represents what portion of the entire grid?

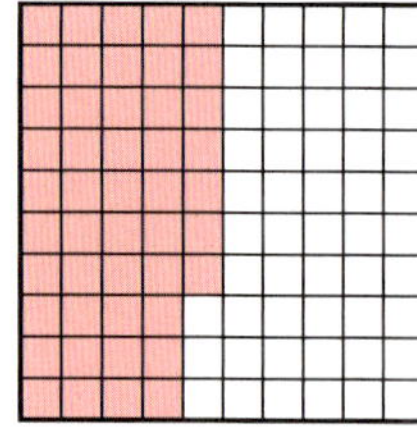

Solution Each row represents $\frac{10}{100}$ of the entire grid. Each small square represents $\frac{1}{100}$ of the entire grid.

There are 4 rows and 7 small squares shaded, so $4 \cdot \frac{10}{100} + 7 \cdot \frac{1}{100} = \frac{40}{100} + \frac{7}{100} = \frac{47}{100}$ of the grid is shaded. ■

Problem Set A

Write the fraction representing the ratio stated. Simplify when possible.

1. shaded region to unshaded region

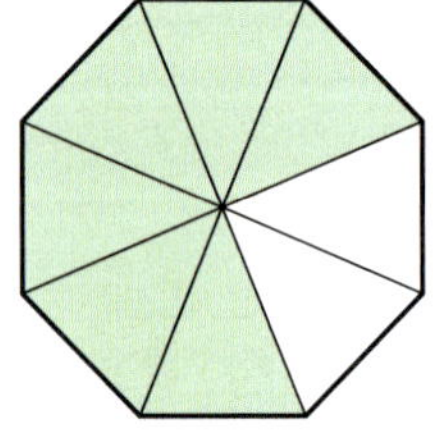

2. shaded region to entire figure

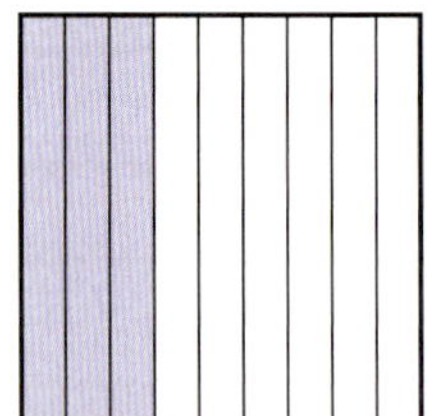

3. unshaded region to entire figure

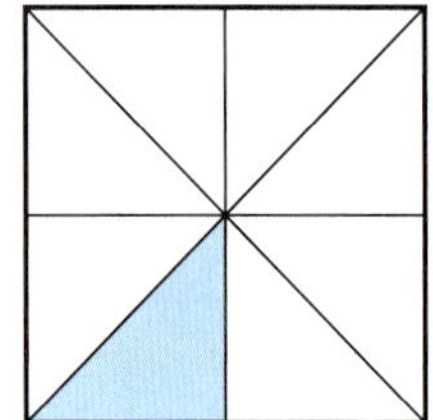

4. unshaded region to shaded region

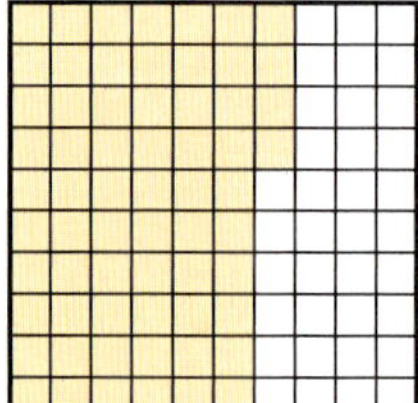

5. shaded region to entire figure

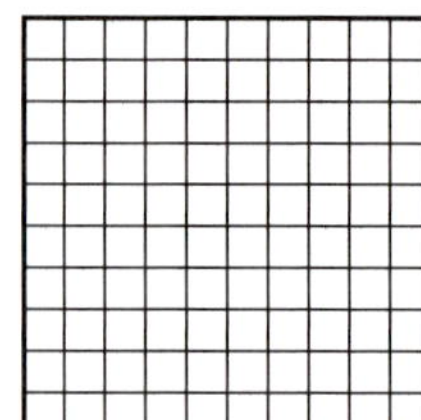

6. shaded region to unshaded region

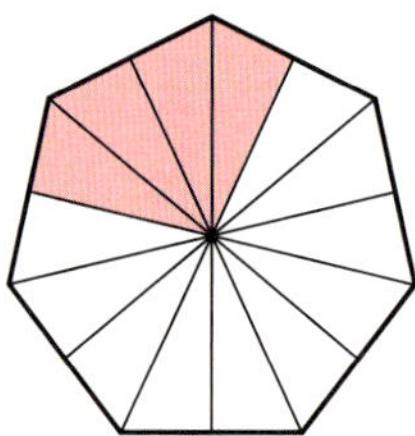

Fractions and Mixed Numbers on a Number Line

DEFINITION

A **coordinate** is a number indicating the location of a point on a number line.

Find the coordinate of a point by starting at zero and counting the number of units to the right or left. Positive numbers are to the right of zero, and negative numbers are to the left of zero. Stop when you reach the point of interest. Be sure to count fractions of a unit correctly.

EXAMPLE B Identify the coordinates of each point shown on the number line.

B-1

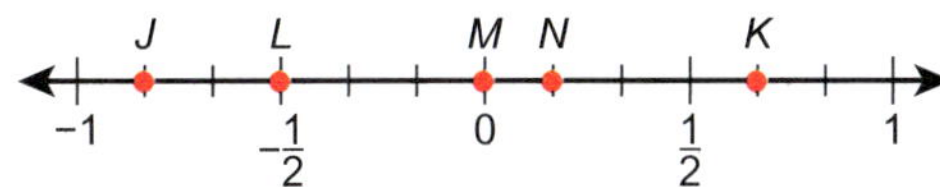

Solution

$$J = -\frac{5}{6}, K = \frac{2}{3}, L = -\frac{1}{2}, M = 0, N = \frac{1}{6}$$

B-2

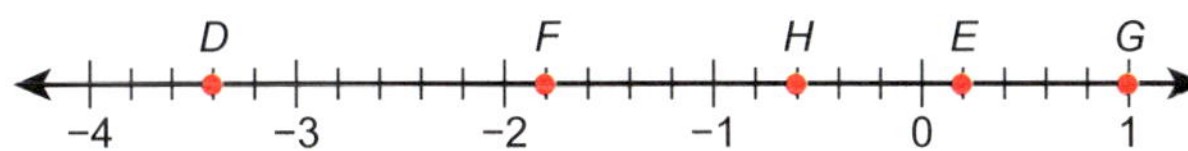

Solution

$$D = -3\frac{2}{5}, E = \frac{1}{5}, F = -1\frac{4}{5}, G = 1, H = -\frac{3}{5}$$

Problem Set B

Identify the coordinates of each point shown on the number line.

1.

2.

Draw and label a number line with all points.

3. $A = \frac{4}{5}, B = -\frac{1}{5}, C = \frac{3}{10}, D = -\frac{1}{2}, E = -\frac{7}{10}$

4. $W = 1\frac{5}{8}, X = -\frac{3}{4}, Y = \frac{1}{2}, Z = -2\frac{1}{8}$

Adding and Subtracting Fractions with Common Denominators

First, make sure both fractions are written with a common denominator. Next, add or subtract the numerators. Simplify the result by putting it in lowest terms.

EXAMPLE C Add or subtract. Express the answer in simplest form.

C-1 $\frac{5}{6} - \frac{3}{6}$

Solution Subtract the numerators and then simplify.

$$\frac{5}{6} - \frac{3}{6} = \frac{2}{6} = \frac{1}{3}$$

C-2 $\frac{4}{15} + \frac{13}{15}$

Solution Add the numerators.

$$\frac{4}{15} + \frac{13}{15} = \frac{17}{15}$$

Convert the improper fraction to a mixed number.

$$\frac{17}{15} = 1\frac{2}{15}$$

Problem Set C

Add or subtract. Express the answer in simplest form.

1. $\frac{7}{8} - \frac{1}{8}$
2. $\frac{3}{6} + \frac{1}{6}$
3. $\frac{1}{7} + \frac{3}{7}$
4. $\frac{15}{16} - \frac{3}{16}$
5. $\frac{8}{9} - \frac{2}{9}$
6. $\frac{4}{14} + \frac{11}{14}$
7. $\frac{7}{12} + \frac{5}{12}$

Equivalent Fractions

A fraction is a number that represents a comparison of two values.

More than one fraction can name the same number.

Equivalent fractions, such as $\frac{1}{3}$ and $\frac{2}{6}$, are fractions with the same value.

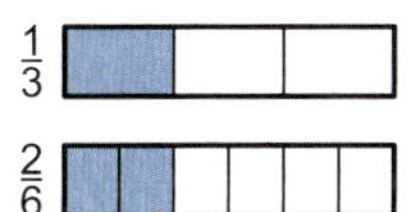

REMEMBER

The numerator is the top number of a fraction. The denominator is the bottom number.

Writing Fractions in Lowest Terms

A fraction is in **lowest terms** when the numerator and denominator have no common factors other than 1. The fraction $\frac{2}{6}$ is not in lowest terms because the numerator and denominator have a common factor of 2.

$$\frac{2}{6} = \frac{1 \cdot 2}{3 \cdot 2}$$

To write a fraction in lowest terms, divide common factors from both the numerator and denominator until no common factors other than 1 remain.

Dividing is the same as multiplying by the reciprocal. When you divide the numerator and denominator by the same value, it is the same as multiplying by a fraction with the same value in the numerator and denominator, which is the same as multiplying by a form of 1.

TIP

The greatest common factor (GCF) is the greatest number that divides evenly into two or more numbers. Use the GCF to reduce the number of times you must divide.

EXAMPLE 1 Write the fraction in lowest terms.

A $\frac{24}{30}$

Solution Divide the numerator and denominator by 6.

$$\frac{24}{30} = \frac{24 \div 6}{30 \div 6}$$
$$= \frac{4}{5}$$

B $\frac{-4}{12}$

Solution Divide the numerator and denominator by 4.

$$\frac{-4}{12} = \frac{-4 \div 4}{12 \div 4}$$
$$= \frac{-1}{3}$$

THINK ABOUT IT

If you use a common factor less than 6 in Example 1A, you will have more than one step to complete.

$$\frac{24 \div 2}{30 \div 2} = \frac{12}{15}$$
$$\frac{12 \div 3}{15 \div 3} = \frac{4}{5}$$

Determining Whether Fractions Are Equivalent

EXAMPLE 2 Determine whether the fractions are equivalent fractions.

> **THINK ABOUT IT**
>
> A negative fraction can be written three different ways.
>
> $\frac{-a}{b} = \frac{a}{-b} = -\frac{a}{b}$

A $\frac{3}{18}$ and $\frac{6}{24}$

Solution Write each fraction in lowest terms.

$$\frac{3}{18} = \frac{3 \div 3}{18 \div 3} = \frac{1}{6} \qquad \frac{6}{24} = \frac{6 \div 6}{24 \div 6} = \frac{1}{4}$$

The fractions are not equivalent fractions. ■

B $\frac{-25}{45}$ and $\frac{10}{-18}$

Solution Write each fraction in lowest terms.

$$\frac{-25}{45} = -\frac{25 \div 5}{45 \div 5} = \frac{5}{9} \qquad \frac{10}{-18} = -\frac{10 \div 2}{18 \div 2} = \frac{5}{9}$$

The fractions are equivalent fractions. ■

Simplifying Algebraic Fractions

To simplify a fraction with a variable, write the numerator and denominator as products of factors and then divide out the factors that appear in each part.

> **TIP**
>
> Simplify a fraction by writing the fraction in lowest terms.

EXAMPLE 3 Simplify the fraction.

 $\frac{5b}{20}$

Solution The numerator and denominator have a common factor of 5. Write each part as a product with a factor of 5.

$$\frac{5b}{20} = \frac{\cancel{5} \cdot b}{\cancel{5} \cdot 4}$$ Divide out the common factor of 5.

$$= \frac{b}{4}$$ ■

> **THINK ABOUT IT**
>
> Simplified algebraic fractions may need to be simplified even further after a value is substituted for the variable.

B $\frac{3}{14d}$

Solution There are no common factors. The fraction is simplified. ■

Application: Entertainment

EXAMPLE 4 Use the chart to determine whether the same fraction of attendees at a movie each day was children.

Attendees	Saturday	Sunday
children	21	15
adults	35	25

Solution Write and compare fractions in which the numerator is the number of children and the denominator is the total number of people.

Saturday: $\frac{21}{21+35} = \frac{21}{56} = \frac{21 \div 7}{56 \div 7}$
$= \frac{3}{8}$

Sunday: $\frac{15}{15+25} = \frac{15}{40} = \frac{15 \div 5}{40 \div 5}$
$= \frac{3}{8}$

The same fraction of attendees each day was children. ■

Problem Set

Write the fraction in lowest terms.

1. $\frac{4}{10}$
2. $\frac{5}{30}$
3. $\frac{7}{28}$
4. $\frac{8}{14}$
5. $\frac{26}{36}$
6. $\frac{-15}{20}$
7. $\frac{18}{-20}$
8. $\frac{36}{63}$
9. $\frac{27}{32}$
10. $-\frac{56}{84}$
11. $\frac{48}{52}$
12. $\frac{72}{120}$

Determine whether the fractions are equivalent fractions.

13. $\frac{1}{3}$ and $\frac{3}{9}$
14. $\frac{3}{6}$ and $\frac{9}{18}$
15. $\frac{4}{10}$ and $\frac{2}{6}$
16. $\frac{15}{40}$ and $\frac{12}{32}$
17. $\frac{10}{35}$ and $\frac{18}{70}$
18. $\frac{12}{15}$ and $\frac{20}{25}$
19. $\frac{35}{45}$ and $\frac{21}{36}$
20. $\frac{6}{27}$ and $\frac{10}{36}$

Simplify the fraction.

21. $\frac{3x}{24}$

22. $\frac{10}{12k}$

23. $\frac{7w}{15}$

24. $\frac{-6a}{-8}$

Solve.

25. A nail is $\frac{14}{16}$ in. long. Write this length in lowest terms.

26. A coin collection consists of 32 pennies and 28 dimes. What fraction of the collection is made up of pennies?

27. A chef used 10 of the 2 dozen eggs that were in the refrigerator. What fraction of the eggs did the chef use? Write the fraction in lowest terms.

28. On Monday, a photographer took 16 portraits and 12 of them were of children. On Tuesday, he took 24 portraits and 20 of them were of children. Determine if the same fraction of portraits taken each day were of children.

29. Of the 135 registered voters who were surveyed in June, 54 said they would vote for Mrs. Mitchell for mayor. In October, 32 of the 80 registered voters surveyed said they would vote for her. Determine if the fraction of voters who said they would vote for Mrs. Mitchell is the same for each survey.

30. **Challenge** Naomi read 200 out of 240 pages in her book. Antonio read the same fraction of pages of his book. If his book has 210 pages, how many pages did he read?

Multiplying Fractions

You can use a diagram to understand what one fraction multiplied by another fraction represents.

This figure illustrates $\frac{1}{3}$ of a whole.

One-half of the shaded square is $\frac{1}{2}$ of $\frac{1}{3}$, or $\frac{1}{2} \cdot \frac{1}{3}$.

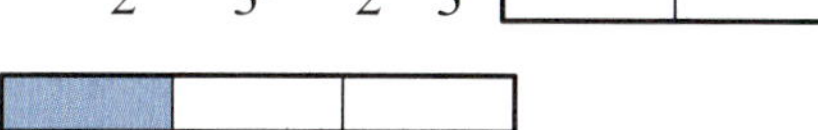

This area is $\frac{1}{6}$ of the whole.

Multiplying Fractions

The example above suggests that when you multiply two fractions, you can multiply the numerators and the denominators. In fact, that's true.

MULTIPLYING FRACTIONS

Property	Example
$\frac{a}{b} \cdot \frac{c}{d} = \frac{ac}{bd}$ $b \neq 0, d \neq 0$	$\frac{2}{3} \cdot \frac{5}{7} = \frac{2 \cdot 5}{3 \cdot 7} = \frac{10}{21}$

EXAMPLE 1 Find the product and simplify.

A $\frac{1}{2} \cdot \frac{4}{5}$

Solution

$\frac{1}{2} \cdot \frac{4}{5} = \frac{1 \cdot 4}{2 \cdot 5}$ Multiply the numerators and the denominators.

$= \frac{4}{10}$

$= \frac{2}{5}$ Write the fraction in lowest terms. ■

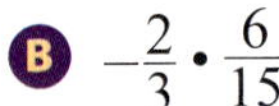

B $-\frac{2}{3} \cdot \frac{6}{15}$

Solution

$$-\frac{2}{3} \cdot \frac{6}{15} = -\frac{2 \cdot 6}{3 \cdot 15}$$ Multiply the numerators and the denominators.

$$= -\frac{12}{45}$$

$$= -\frac{4}{15}$$ Write the fraction in lowest terms. ■

> ▶ **REMEMBER**
> When the signs are different, the product is negative.

C $\frac{5}{8} \cdot \frac{x}{3}$

Solution

$$\frac{5}{8} \cdot \frac{x}{3} = \frac{5x}{8 \cdot 3}$$ Multiply the numerators and the denominators.

$$= \frac{5x}{24}$$ Simplify. The fraction is in lowest terms already. ■

Multiplying by Simplifying First

Common factors in either numerator can be divided out with common factors in either denominator. You can combine the fractions and then simplify, or you can simplify before combining the fractions. It is common practice to simplify first.

EXAMPLE 2 Divide out common factors. Then multiply.

A $\frac{3}{8} \cdot \frac{4}{5}$

Solution

$$\frac{3}{8} \cdot \frac{4}{5} = \frac{3}{\cancel{8}_{2}} \cdot \frac{\cancel{4}^{1}}{5}$$ Divide out the common factor of 4.

$$= \frac{3 \cdot 1}{2 \cdot 5} = \frac{3}{10}$$ Multiply $3 \cdot 1$ and $2 \cdot 5$. ■

> ▶ **TIP**
> To avoid errors, be sure to write the factors that remain after the common factors are divided out.

B $\frac{8}{15} \cdot \left(-\frac{10}{12}\right)$

Solution

$$\frac{8}{15} \cdot \left(-\frac{10}{12}\right) = \frac{\cancel{8}^{2}}{\cancel{15}_{3}} \cdot \left(-\frac{\cancel{10}^{2}}{\cancel{12}_{3}}\right)$$ Divide out the common factor of 4 in 8 and 12 and the common factor of 5 in 10 and 15.

$$= -\frac{2 \cdot 2}{3 \cdot 3} = -\frac{4}{9}$$ Multiply $2 \cdot 2$ and $3 \cdot 3$. ■

Application: Cooking

EXAMPLE 3 Keisha wants to bake 24 soft pretzels, but the recipe she has makes 48 soft pretzels.

A What fraction of each ingredient should she use?

Solution

$$\frac{\text{soft pretzels wanted}}{\text{total recipe makes}} = \frac{24}{48} = \frac{1}{2}$$

Keisha should use $\frac{1}{2}$ of each ingredient.

B The recipe calls for $\frac{3}{4}$ cup of flour. How much flour should Keisha use?

Solution Find $\frac{1}{2}$ of $\frac{3}{4}$.

$$\frac{1}{2} \cdot \frac{3}{4} = \frac{3}{8}$$

Keisha should use $\frac{3}{8}$ cup of flour.

REMEMBER

The word *of* is one way to indicate multiplication.

Problem Set

Find the product and simplify.

1. $\frac{1}{8} \cdot \frac{1}{2}$
2. $\frac{1}{2} \cdot \frac{2}{3}$
3. $-\frac{3}{5} \cdot \frac{3}{4}$
4. $\frac{3}{4} \cdot \frac{1}{4}$
5. $\frac{7}{8} \cdot \frac{3}{4}$
6. $-\frac{5}{11} \cdot \left(-\frac{2}{3}\right)$
7. $\frac{4}{5} \cdot \frac{3}{8}$
8. $\frac{9}{10} \cdot \left(-\frac{5}{6}\right)$
9. $-\frac{4}{7} \cdot \left(-\frac{3}{10}\right)$
10. $\frac{4}{9} \cdot \frac{w}{5}$
11. $\frac{x}{3} \cdot \frac{2}{y}$
12. $\frac{4}{a} \cdot \frac{a}{b}$

Divide out common factors and then multiply.

13. $\frac{2}{5} \cdot \frac{1}{2}$
14. $\frac{3}{6} \cdot \frac{1}{4}$
15. $\frac{3}{5} \cdot \frac{5}{10}$
16. $-\frac{7}{8} \cdot \frac{4}{5}$
17. $\frac{6}{14} \cdot \frac{7}{8}$
18. $-\frac{3}{4} \cdot \left(-\frac{10}{11}\right)$
19. $\frac{12}{15} \cdot \frac{3}{4}$
20. $\frac{6}{7} \cdot \left(-\frac{1}{6}\right)$
21. $-\frac{5}{2} \cdot \left(-\frac{2}{5}\right)$
22. $\frac{15}{20} \cdot \frac{10}{12}$
23. $\frac{8}{9} \cdot \frac{12}{16}$
24. $-\frac{3}{4} \cdot \frac{4}{3}$
25. $\frac{9}{14} \cdot \frac{14}{15}$
26. $\frac{1}{a} \cdot \frac{a}{7}$
27. $\frac{c}{d} \cdot \frac{d}{c}$
28. $\frac{2}{9} \cdot \left(-\frac{b}{6}\right)$
29. $\frac{e}{9} \cdot \frac{3}{f}$
30. $\frac{250c}{25} \cdot \frac{h}{50d}$

Solve.

31. Lydell wants to make 36 granola bars, but the recipe he has makes 60 granola bars.

(a) What fraction of each ingredient should he use?

(b) The recipe calls for $\frac{2}{3}$ cup of brown sugar. How much brown sugar should Lydell use?

32. Victoria needs to make 30 fruit cups for her class party. The recipe she has will make 36 fruit cups.

(a) What fraction of each ingredient should she use?

(b) The recipe she has calls for $\frac{3}{4}$ cup of pears. What amount of pears should Victoria use?

33. So far, Dianne has walked $\frac{1}{4}$ of a trail that is $\frac{7}{8}$ mi long. How far has she walked?

34. This figure illustrates $\frac{2}{5}$ of a whole.

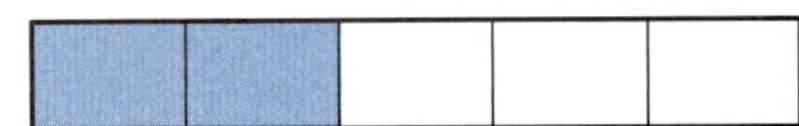

Describe how this figure can be used to illustrate each given fraction.

(a) $\frac{2}{5}$

(b) $\frac{3}{5}$

(c) $\frac{2}{3}$

(d) $\frac{3}{2}$

35. A bottle contains $\frac{1}{2}$ gal of juice. Catalina drank $\frac{1}{5}$ of the juice. How much juice did Catalina drink?

36. Ismael completed $\frac{3}{5}$ of the levels of a video game. His friend Ari completed $\frac{2}{3}$ of the number of levels that Ismael completed. What fraction of the game has Ari completed?

37. Thirty out of 32 students passed the last mathematics test.

(a) What fraction of the students passed the test?

(b) Out of the students who passed the test, $\frac{1}{6}$ earned a grade of A. What fraction of students earned a grade of A?

38. **Challenge** Use a figure to illustrate that $\frac{2}{3}$ of $\frac{2}{3}$ is $\frac{4}{9}$.

Dividing Fractions

Division separates a number into equal groups.

Sometimes the divisor and dividend are fractions.

This figure illustrates $\frac{2}{3}$ of a whole. 

This area is $\frac{1}{6}$ of the whole.

There are four $\frac{1}{6}$s in $\frac{2}{3}$. That is, $\frac{2}{3} \div \frac{1}{6} = 4$.

Finding Reciprocals of Fractions

The reciprocal of $\frac{a}{b} = \frac{1}{\frac{a}{b}}$ — The reciprocal of any number is 1 over the number.

$= \frac{1}{\frac{a}{b}} \cdot \frac{b}{b}$ — Multiply the numerator and denominator by b so there will no longer be a fraction in the bottom.

$= \frac{1 \cdot b}{\frac{a \cdot \cancel{b}}{\cancel{b}}}$

$= \frac{b}{a}$

REMEMBER

The reciprocal is also called the multiplicative inverse.

RECIPROCAL OF A FRACTION

For any nonzero *a* and *b*,	**Example**
The reciprocal of $\frac{a}{b}$ is $\frac{b}{a}$.	The reciprocal of $\frac{2}{3}$ is $\frac{3}{2}$.

EXAMPLE 1 Find the reciprocal of the number.

A $\frac{9}{10}$

Solution The reciprocal is $\frac{10}{9}$. ■

B $\frac{1}{5}$

Solution The reciprocal is $\frac{5}{1}$, or 5. ■

TIP

To find a reciprocal, "flip" the fraction. Check your answer by multiplying.

$$\frac{9}{10} \cdot \frac{10}{9} = \frac{90}{90} = 1$$

To divide fractions, multiply the dividend by the reciprocal of the divisor.

DIVIDING FRACTIONS

Property	Example
$\frac{a}{b} \div \frac{c}{d} = \frac{a}{b} \cdot \frac{d}{c} = \frac{ad}{bc}$ $b \neq 0, c \neq 0, d \neq 0$	$\frac{2}{3} \div \frac{1}{6} = \frac{2}{3} \cdot \frac{6}{1} = \frac{12}{3} = 4$

REMEMBER

In $x \div y$, x is the dividend and y is the divisor.

Dividing Fractions

EXAMPLE 2 Find each quotient and simplify.

A $\frac{1}{2} \div \frac{4}{6}$

Solution

$\frac{1}{2} \div \frac{4}{6} = \frac{1}{2} \cdot \frac{6}{4}$ Multiply by the reciprocal.

$= \frac{1 \cdot 6}{2 \cdot 4}$ Multiply the numerators and the denominators.

$= \frac{6}{8}$

$= \frac{3}{4}$ Write in lowest terms. ■

B $-8 \div \frac{1}{4}$

Solution

$-8 \div \frac{1}{4} = -8 \cdot \frac{4}{1}$ Multiply by the reciprocal.

$= -8 \cdot 4$ Write $\frac{4}{1}$ as 4.

$= -32$ Multiply. ■

TIP

In Example 2B, you can also write $-\frac{8}{1} \cdot \frac{4}{1}$ in the second step.

C $\frac{2}{3} \div 6$

Solution

$\frac{2}{3} \div 6 = \frac{2}{3} \cdot \frac{1}{6}$ Multiply by the reciprocal.

$= \frac{2 \cdot 1}{3 \cdot 6}$ Multiply the numerators and the denominators.

$= \frac{2}{18}$

$= \frac{1}{9}$ Write in lowest terms. ■

D $\frac{5}{x} \div \frac{10}{y}$

Solution

$$\frac{5}{x} \div \frac{10}{y} = \frac{\overset{1}{\cancel{5}}}{x} \cdot \frac{y}{\underset{2}{\cancel{10}}}$$ Multiply by the reciprocal. Divide out the common factor of 5.

$$= \frac{y}{2x}$$ Multiply. ■

Application: Sewing

EXAMPLE 3 Three-fourths of a yard of fabric is divided into 6 sections, each with equal length. How long is each section?

Solution Divide.

$$\frac{3}{4} \div 6 = \frac{\overset{1}{\cancel{3}}}{4} \cdot \frac{1}{\underset{2}{\cancel{6}}}$$ Multiply by the reciprocal. Divide out the common factor of 3.

$$= \frac{1}{8}$$ Multiply.

Each section is $\frac{1}{8}$ yd long.

Check If each section is $\frac{1}{8}$ yd long, then the total length should be

$6 \cdot \frac{1}{8} = \frac{6}{8} = \frac{3}{4}$. ✓

The solution checks. ■

Problem Set

Find the reciprocal of the number.

1. 6
2. $\frac{1}{8}$
3. $-\frac{2}{3}$
4. -15
5. $\frac{8}{9}$
6. $\frac{5}{12}$
7. $\frac{x}{y}$
8. $\frac{3}{h}$

Find the quotient and simplify.

9. $\frac{1}{5} \div \frac{1}{2}$
10. $\frac{5}{6} \div \frac{5}{6}$
11. $3 \div \frac{1}{3}$
12. $\frac{1}{3} \div \frac{4}{5}$
13. $\frac{5}{8} \div 8$
14. $\frac{5}{12} \div 10$
15. $-\frac{1}{8} \div \left(-\frac{3}{4}\right)$
16. $\frac{6}{7} \div 5$

Find the quotient and simplify.

17. $-20 \div \frac{2}{3}$

18. $\frac{1}{a} \div \frac{3}{a}$

19. $1 \div \frac{1}{2}$

20. $-\frac{3}{4} \div \frac{3}{2}$

21. $\frac{4}{9} \div \frac{3}{5}$

22. $\frac{3}{8} \div \frac{6}{11}$

23. $\frac{a}{4} \div a$

24. $\frac{2}{13} \div \frac{1}{13}$

25. $\frac{4}{5} \div (-3)$

26. $2b \div \frac{1}{2}$

27. $\frac{2}{k} \div \frac{m}{k}$

28. $-\frac{15}{32} \div \left(-\frac{1}{2}\right)$

29. $\frac{14}{27} \div \frac{2}{3}$

30. $\frac{5}{a} \div \frac{15}{b}$

31. $\frac{3}{x} \div \frac{4}{x}$

32. $\frac{17}{20} \div (-34)$

33. $3 \div \frac{1}{2} \div \frac{1}{2}$

34. $\frac{3}{4} \bullet \frac{2}{5} \div (-4)$

Solve.

35. A chef cuts a banana in half and sets 1 portion aside. He cuts the remaining half into 4 equal sections. What fraction of the whole banana is each piece?

36. Three girls took turns running equal parts of a relay race. The total length of the race was $\frac{9}{10}$ km. How far did each girl run if each girl ran the same distance?

37. A wire that is $\frac{7}{16}$ ft long is divided into 7 equal sections. How long is each section?

38. A 6 ft long board is divided into sections that are each $\frac{1}{3}$ ft long. How many sections are there?

39. Use a model to show that $3 \div \frac{1}{3} = 9$.

40. **Challenge** Which division problem is illustrated by the model? Explain.

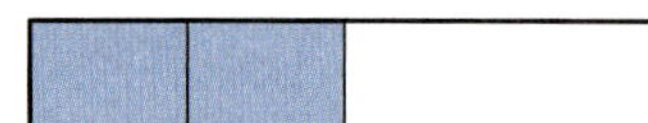

Core Focus: Rational Numbers

THE CORE CONCEPT

Many real-world problems involve finding a fraction or portion of some original amount. The original amount is often not a whole number.

Problem Solving Using Rational Numbers

In real-world problems, you can find the increase or decrease in a quantity directly. Multiply the quantity by a fraction or decimal representing the ratio of the new amount to the old amount.

EXAMPLE 1 Courtney is making taffy-apple dip but wants to make $\frac{1}{3}$ less than called for in the recipe. Courtney says she can multiply the original amount of each ingredient by $\frac{2}{3}$ to get the correct amount she needs. Explain why Courtney is correct.

Use a table similar to the one shown to display the new ingredient amounts. In the table, include a column showing how the new ingredient amounts were determined. (Note: tsp = teaspoon)

Amount	Ingredient
9 oz	cream cheese
$\frac{1}{4}$ cup	white sugar
$\frac{3}{4}$ cup	brown sugar
1 tsp	vanilla
$\frac{1}{2}$ cup	chopped peanuts
6	Granny Smith apples sliced

Solution One-third less of an ingredient is equal to the whole amount of the ingredient minus $\frac{1}{3}$ of that whole amount. This amount is equivalent to $\frac{2}{3}$ of the whole amount of an ingredient, so Courtney is correct to multiply each amount in the table by $\frac{2}{3}$.

THINK ABOUT IT

A decrease or increase can be written as a fraction of the original amount. Here are some examples:

An increase of $\frac{1}{4}$ is equal to

$1 + \frac{1}{4} = \frac{5}{4}$ of the original amount.

A decrease of $\frac{1}{5}$ is equal to

$1 - \frac{1}{5} = \frac{4}{5}$ of the original amount.

Conversion	Amount	Ingredient
$\frac{2}{3} \cdot 9 = \frac{2}{\cancel{3}_1} \cdot \frac{\cancel{9}^3}{1} = 6$	6 oz	cream cheese
$\frac{2}{3} \cdot \frac{1}{4} = \frac{\cancel{2}^1}{3} \cdot \frac{1}{\cancel{4}_2} = \frac{1}{6}$	$\frac{1}{6}$ cup	white sugar
$\frac{2}{3} \cdot \frac{3}{4} = \frac{\cancel{2}^1}{\cancel{3}_1} \cdot \frac{\cancel{3}^1}{\cancel{4}_2} = \frac{1}{2}$	$\frac{1}{2}$ cup	brown sugar
$\frac{2}{3} \cdot 1 = \frac{2}{3}$	$\frac{2}{3}$ tsp	vanilla
$\frac{2}{3} \cdot \frac{1}{2} = \frac{\cancel{2}^1}{3} \cdot \frac{1}{\cancel{2}_1} = \frac{1}{3}$	$\frac{1}{3}$ cup	chopped peanuts
$\frac{2}{3} \cdot 6 = \frac{2}{\cancel{3}_1} \cdot \frac{\cancel{6}^2}{1} = 4$	4	Granny Smith apples sliced

EXAMPLE 2 Mindy, Max, and Sheldon each surveyed 60 13-year-old individuals to see how many of them had a weekend curfew and, if they did, how many of them had to be home by 9:00 p.m. In which person's survey did the greatest number of individuals have a curfew? In which person's survey did the fewest individuals have to be home by 9:00 p.m.?

- Mindy found that $\frac{3}{4}$ of the individuals she surveyed had a curfew, but only $\frac{1}{3}$ of these individuals had to be home by 9:00 p.m.
- Max found that $\frac{2}{3}$ of the individuals he surveyed had a curfew, but only 0.6 of these individuals had to be home by 9:00 p.m.
- Sheldon found that 0.4 of the individuals he surveyed had a curfew, but only $\frac{1}{4}$ of these individuals had to be home by 9:00 p.m.

Solution In each case, start by multiplying the proportion of individuals surveyed by the proportion of these individuals who have a curfew. Next, multiply the number who have a curfew by the proportion that had to be home by 9:00 p.m. If one proportion is a fraction and the other is a decimal, convert the decimal to a fraction.

> **TIP**
> It is often easier to convert a decimal to a fraction than a fraction to a decimal. Converting a decimal to a fraction is as easy as rewriting the decimal as a fraction with a denominator that is a power of 10.

Mindy:

$$\text{curfew: } \frac{3}{4} \cdot 60 = \frac{3}{\cancel{4}_1} \cdot \frac{\cancel{60}^{15}}{1} = 45$$

$$\text{9:00 p.m. curfew: } \frac{1}{3} \cdot 45 = \frac{1}{\cancel{3}_1} \cdot \frac{\cancel{45}^{15}}{1} = 15$$

Max:

$$\text{curfew: } \frac{2}{3} \cdot 60 = \frac{2}{\cancel{3}_1} \cdot \frac{\cancel{60}^{20}}{1} = 40$$

$$\text{9:00 p.m. curfew: } 0.6 \cdot 40 = 24$$

Sheldon:

$$\text{curfew: } 0.4 \cdot 60 = 24$$

$$\text{9:00 p.m. curfew: } \frac{1}{4} \cdot 24 = \frac{1}{\cancel{4}_1} \cdot \frac{\cancel{24}^6}{1} = 6$$

Mindy found that 45 teens had a curfew, which was the greatest number of teens to have a curfew compared to Max's 40 teens and Sheldon's 24 teens.

Sheldon found that 6 teens had a 9:00 p.m. curfew compared to Mindy's 15 teens and Max's 24 teens. Sheldon's group of 6 was the least number of individuals to have a 9:00 p.m. curfew. ■

Problem Set

Solve. Show all work.

1. Nick wants to make 5 servings of caramel popcorn. The recipe makes 15 servings.

Amount	Ingredient
15 cups	popped corn
1 cup	packed brown sugar
$\frac{1}{2}$ cup	margarine or butter
$\frac{3}{8}$ cup	light corn syrup
$\frac{1}{2}$ tsp	salt
$\frac{3}{4}$ tsp	baking soda

(a) Use the table to display the new amount for each ingredient. In the conversion column, show the calculations used to determine the new amounts.

Conversion	Amount	Ingredient
		popped corn
		packed brown sugar
		margarine or butter
		light corn syrup
		salt
		baking soda

(b) Suppose Nick wants to make only 3 servings. What fraction of each ingredient should he use?

2. Roberto completed an endurance race. Three-fourths of the distance in the race was on land and the other $\frac{1}{4}$ was in the water. While racing on land, 0.6 of the distance was completed on a bicycle and the other $\frac{2}{5}$ was completed by running.

(a) What fraction of the distance on land was completed on a bicycle, and what fraction of the distance was completed by running?

(b) In terms of distance, which of the three portions of the race was the longest?

3. Michael works at a paint store. To create a gallon of green paint, he mixes a gallon of white base paint with $\frac{2}{3}$ oz of a yellow dye and $\frac{1}{4}$ oz of a cyan dye.

(a) If a customer wants only 1 qt of green paint, how many ounces of yellow and cyan dye are needed to make this amount of green paint?

(b) Suppose another customer wants 3 qt of green paint. How could Michael use his calculations in Part (a) to help him find the number of ounces of yellow and cyan dye he needs to make 3 qt of green paint?

Common Denominators

A common denominator enables you to compare, add, or subtract fractions.

Some multiples of 4 and 6 are shown. The common multiples are in red.

4: 4, 8, 12, 16, 20, 24, 28, 32, 36, . . .

6: 6, 12, 18, 24, 30, 36, 42, . . .

DEFINITIONS

The **least common multiple (LCM)** is the least number that is a multiple of all numbers in a set. The **least common denominator (LCD)** of a set of fractions is the LCM of the denominators.

TIP

To find the LCM, you can also list multiples of the greater number until you find one that is a multiple of the smaller number.

The LCD of $\frac{3}{4}$ and $\frac{5}{6}$ is 12 because the LCM of 4 and 6 is 12.

Finding the Least Common Denominator

EXAMPLE 1 Find the LCD of the pair of fractions.

A $\frac{2}{5}$ and $\frac{3}{8}$

Solution Find the LCM of 5 and 8.
multiples of 5: 5, 10, 15, 20, 25, 30, 35, 40, . . .
multiples of 8: 8, 16, 24, 32, 40, . . .
The LCD is 40. ■

B $\frac{1}{6}$ and $\frac{5}{9}$

Solution Find the LCM of 6 and 9.
multiples of 6: 6, 12, 18, . . .
multiples of 9: 9, 18, 27, . . .
The LCD is 18. ■

THINK ABOUT IT

The product of the denominators is always a common multiple. It may or may not be the least common multiple.

C $-\frac{5}{84}$ and $-\frac{7}{12}$

Solution Disregard negative signs. Because 84 is a multiple of 12, the LCM of 84 and 12 is 84. The LCD is 84. ■

Expressing Fractions with the Same Denominator

Any fraction can be renamed to an equivalent fraction by multiplying both the numerator and denominator by the same number. When you multiply the numerator and denominator by the same number, you are multiplying the original fraction by a form of 1, resulting in an equivalent fraction.

REMEMBER

Equivalent fractions are fractions with the same value.

EXAMPLE 2 Express the set of fractions using the same denominator.

A $\frac{3}{4}$ and $\frac{2}{3}$

Solution The LCD is 12. Rename both fractions with a denominator of 12.

$$\frac{3}{4} = \frac{3}{4} \cdot \frac{3}{3} = \frac{3 \cdot 3}{4 \cdot 3} = \frac{9}{12} \qquad \frac{2}{3} = \frac{2}{3} \cdot \frac{4}{4} = \frac{2 \cdot 4}{3 \cdot 4} = \frac{8}{12}$$

The fractions are $\frac{9}{12}$ and $\frac{8}{12}$. ■

THINK ABOUT IT

In Example 2, we are using the LCD. Other fractions are possible, such as $\frac{18}{24}$ and $\frac{16}{24}$ for Example 2A.

B $-\frac{1}{6}$ and $\frac{5}{24}$

Solution The LCD is 24. Rename $-\frac{1}{6}$ with a denominator of 24.

$$-\frac{1}{6} = -\frac{1}{6} \cdot \frac{4}{4} = -\frac{1 \cdot 4}{6 \cdot 4} = -\frac{4}{24}$$

The fractions are $-\frac{4}{24}$ and $\frac{5}{24}$. ■

C $\frac{11}{18}$, $\frac{1}{54}$, and $\frac{2}{27}$

Solution The LCD is 54. Rename $\frac{11}{18}$ and $\frac{2}{27}$.

$$\frac{11}{18} = \frac{11}{18} \cdot \frac{3}{3} = \frac{11 \cdot 3}{18 \cdot 3} = \frac{33}{54} \qquad \frac{2}{27} = \frac{2}{27} \cdot \frac{2}{2} = \frac{2 \cdot 2}{27 \cdot 2} = \frac{4}{54}$$

The fractions are $\frac{33}{54}$, $\frac{1}{54}$, and $\frac{4}{54}$. ■

Comparing Fractions

When fractions have a common denominator, you can compare them by comparing the numerators. For example, $\frac{4}{7} > \frac{3}{7}$ because $4 > 3$. When the fractions have unlike denominators, rename one or both fractions so that they have a common denominator. Then compare the numerators.

EXAMPLE 3 Compare the fractions using >, <, or =.

A $\frac{11}{20}$ and $\frac{2}{5}$

Solution Rename $\frac{2}{5}$ with a denominator of 20.

$$\frac{2}{5} = \frac{2 \cdot 4}{5 \cdot 4} \qquad \text{Multiply the numerator and denominator by 4.}$$
$$= \frac{8}{20}$$

Compare $\frac{11}{20}$ and $\frac{8}{20}$. Because $11 > 8$, $\frac{11}{20} > \frac{8}{20}$, and $\frac{11}{20} > \frac{2}{5}$. ■

> **TIP**
> Any common denominator, not necessarily the LCD, can be used to compare fractions.

B $-\frac{3}{7}$ and $-\frac{2}{5}$

Solution Rename both fractions with a denominator of 35.

$$-\frac{3}{7} = -\frac{3 \cdot 5}{7 \cdot 5} = -\frac{15}{35} \qquad -\frac{2}{5} = -\frac{2 \cdot 7}{5 \cdot 7} = -\frac{14}{35}$$

Because $-15 < -14$, $-\frac{15}{35} < -\frac{14}{35}$, and $-\frac{3}{7} < -\frac{2}{5}$. ■

C $\frac{9}{15}$ and $\frac{6}{10}$

Solution Rename both fractions with a denominator of 30.

$$\frac{9}{15} = \frac{9 \cdot 2}{15 \cdot 2} = \frac{18}{30} \qquad \frac{6}{10} = \frac{6 \cdot 3}{10 \cdot 3} = \frac{18}{30}$$

Because $\frac{18}{30} = \frac{18}{30}$, $\frac{9}{15} = \frac{6}{10}$. ■

> **THINK ABOUT IT**
> The fractions in Example 3C can also be compared by simplifying each fraction.
> $\frac{3}{5} = \frac{3}{5}$

Application: Competition

EXAMPLE 4

A Jordan ran $\frac{7}{8}$ mi and Miguel ran $\frac{4}{5}$ mi. Who ran farther?

Solution Compare $\frac{7}{8}$ and $\frac{4}{5}$ using the LCD of 40.

$$\text{Jordan: } \frac{7}{8} = \frac{7 \cdot 5}{8 \cdot 5} = \frac{35}{40} \qquad \text{Miguel: } \frac{4}{5} = \frac{4 \cdot 8}{5 \cdot 8} = \frac{32}{40}$$

Jordan ran farther. ■

B Three neighbors had a tomato-growing contest. The weights of their best tomatoes are shown in the table. List the weights from greatest to least.

Margo	Julie	Hank
$\frac{11}{16}$ lb	$\frac{1}{2}$ lb	$\frac{3}{4}$ lb

Solution Compare the fractions using the LCD of 16.

Margo: $\frac{11}{16}$ Julie: $\frac{1}{2} = \frac{1 \cdot 8}{2 \cdot 8} = \frac{8}{16}$ Hank: $\frac{3}{4} = \frac{3 \cdot 4}{4 \cdot 4} = \frac{12}{16}$

The weights from greatest to least are $\frac{3}{4}$ lb, $\frac{11}{16}$ lb, and $\frac{1}{2}$ lb. ■

Problem Set

Find the LCD of the pair of fractions.

1. $\frac{2}{3}$ and $\frac{1}{2}$
2. $\frac{1}{3}$ and $\frac{1}{4}$
3. $\frac{3}{4}$ and $\frac{7}{9}$
4. $\frac{3}{10}$ and $\frac{1}{2}$
5. $\frac{3}{8}$ and $\frac{2}{7}$
6. $-\frac{4}{9}$ and $\frac{11}{12}$
7. $\frac{3}{5}$ and $\frac{3}{8}$
8. $\frac{1}{18}$ and $\frac{7}{24}$
9. $-\frac{5}{14}$ and $-\frac{1}{3}$
10. $\frac{2}{15}$ and $\frac{5}{6}$

Express the set of fractions using the same denominator.

11. $\frac{1}{2}$ and $\frac{3}{4}$
12. $\frac{2}{5}$ and $\frac{1}{2}$
13. $-\frac{2}{3}$ and $\frac{3}{5}$
14. $\frac{5}{6}$ and $\frac{2}{3}$
15. $\frac{4}{7}$ and $\frac{3}{5}$
16. $-\frac{11}{12}$ and $-\frac{7}{8}$
17. $\frac{1}{8}$ and $\frac{3}{16}$
18. $\frac{4}{15}$ and $\frac{9}{10}$
19. $\frac{1}{2}$, $\frac{1}{3}$, and $\frac{1}{4}$
20. $\frac{5}{6}$, $\frac{9}{10}$, and $\frac{2}{5}$

Compare the fractions using >, <, or =.

21. $\frac{3}{5}$ and $\frac{4}{7}$

22. $\frac{7}{8}$ and $\frac{8}{10}$

23. $\frac{5}{12}$ and $\frac{3}{5}$

24. $\frac{6}{10}$ and $\frac{9}{15}$

25. $-\frac{6}{7}$ and $-\frac{11}{12}$

26. $\frac{13}{20}$ and $\frac{2}{3}$

27. $-\frac{5}{18}$ and $-\frac{3}{10}$

28. $\frac{6}{27}$ and $\frac{10}{36}$

Solve.

29. Johan finished $\frac{3}{4}$ of his math problems and Maria finished $\frac{7}{9}$ of her math problems. Who finished a greater fraction of math problems?

30. The Cherry Tree Trail is $\frac{13}{16}$ mi long and the Weeping Willow Trail is $\frac{7}{10}$ mi long. Which trail is longer?

31. A biologist took the weights of a blue jay and a northern cardinal. The blue jay weighed $\frac{3}{16}$ lb and the cardinal weighed $\frac{3}{32}$ lb Which bird was heavier?

32. The table shows the heights of four plants. List the plants from shortest to tallest.

Plant	A	B	C	D
Height (m)	$\frac{3}{10}$	$\frac{2}{5}$	$\frac{1}{4}$	$\frac{1}{2}$

Adding and Subtracting Fractions

To add and subtract fractions, start by expressing each fraction with the same denominator.

ADDING AND SUBTRACTING FRACTIONS

Like Fractions (same denominator)

- Add or subtract the numerators.
- Keep the same denominator.
- Simplify if possible.

Unlike Fractions (different denominators)

- Write equivalent fractions as needed so that the fractions have the same denominator.
- Add or subtract the like fractions.

Adding and Subtracting Like Fractions

EXAMPLE 1 Find the sum or difference. Write the answer in simplest form.

A $\frac{2}{7}+\frac{4}{7}$

Solution

$\frac{2}{7}+\frac{4}{7}=\frac{2+4}{7}$ Add the numerators. Keep the same denominator.

$=\frac{6}{7}$ Simplify. The fraction is already in lowest terms. ■

B $\frac{5}{8}-\left(-\frac{1}{8}\right)$

Solution

$\frac{5}{8}-\left(-\frac{1}{8}\right)=\frac{5-(-1)}{8}$ Subtract the numerators. Keep the same denominator.

$=\frac{6}{8}$

$=\frac{3}{4}$ Simplify by writing in lowest terms. ■

REMEMBER

To subtract a number, add its opposite.

$5-(-1)=5+1=6$

Adding and Subtracting Unlike Fractions

EXAMPLE 2 Find the sum. Write the answer in simplest form.

$$-\frac{5}{6}+\frac{2}{3}$$

Solution The least common denominator of $-\frac{5}{6}$ and $\frac{2}{3}$ is 6.

$-\frac{5}{6}+\frac{2}{3}=-\frac{5}{6}+\frac{4}{6}$ Write $\frac{2}{3}$ as the equivalent fraction $\frac{4}{6}$ so that the fractions to be added have the same denominator.

$=\frac{-5+4}{6}$

$=\frac{-1}{6}=-\frac{1}{6}$ ■

Working with Improper Fractions and Mixed Numbers

A fraction can represent a number greater than one.

This figure illustrates $\frac{3}{2}$. 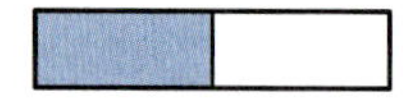

Each shaded area is one-half. There are three one-halves.

Another way to write the number illustrated by the diagram is $1\frac{1}{2}$ because there is one whole and one half rectangle shaded.

DEFINITIONS

An **improper fraction** is a fraction where the numerator is greater than or equal to the denominator. A **mixed number** is a number consisting of both a whole number and a fraction, or the opposite of such a number.

CONVERTING IMPROPER FRACTIONS TO MIXED NUMBERS

Step 1 Divide the numerator by the denominator.
Step 2 Use the quotient as the whole number and the remainder as the numerator.
Step 3 Keep the original denominator.

EXAMPLE 3 Convert the improper fraction to a mixed number.

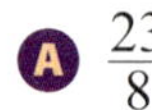 $\frac{23}{8}$

Solution

$8\overline{)23}$ = 2 R 7 Divide the numerator by the denominator.

$2\frac{7}{8}$ Use the quotient as the whole number and the remainder as the numerator. ■

B $-\frac{45}{6}$

Solution

$$-6\overline{)45} \quad \text{quotient } -7 \text{ R } 3$$

Divide the numerator by the denominator.

$$-7\frac{3}{6} = -7\frac{1}{2}$$

Use the quotient as the whole number and the remainder as the numerator. ■

> **TIP**
> Be careful when using a calculator. Most calculators give the quotient as a decimal.
> $23 \div 8 = 2.875$
> $45 \div 6 = 7.5$

Subtracting Unlike Fractions and Converting to a Mixed Number

EXAMPLE 4 Find the difference. Write the answer as a mixed number in simplest form.

$$-\frac{3}{20} - \frac{14}{15}$$

Solution The least common denominator of $-\frac{3}{20}$ and $\frac{14}{15}$ is 60.

$-\frac{3}{20} - \frac{14}{15} = -\frac{9}{60} - \frac{56}{60}$ Write an equivalent fraction for each fraction.

$= \frac{-9 - 56}{60}$ To subtract $\frac{56}{60}$ from $-\frac{9}{60}$, subtract 56 from −9 and keep the same denominator.

$= -\frac{65}{60}$

$= -1\frac{5}{60}$ Write the improper fraction as a mixed number.

$= -1\frac{1}{12}$ Write the fraction part in lowest terms to simplify. ■

Application: Carpentry

EXAMPLE 5 A sheet of plywood is $\frac{4}{3}$ ft wide and $\frac{59}{8}$ ft long. Write each dimension as a mixed number.

Solution

$$3\overline{)4} \;(1 \text{ R } 1) \longrightarrow 1\frac{1}{3} \qquad 8\overline{)59} \;(7 \text{ R } 3) \longrightarrow 7\frac{3}{8}$$

The sheet of plywood is $1\frac{1}{3}$ ft wide and $7\frac{3}{8}$ ft long. ■

Problem Set

Find the sum or difference. Write the answer in simplest form.

1. $\frac{4}{9}+\frac{3}{9}$
2. $\frac{1}{8}+\frac{3}{8}$
3. $\frac{9}{10}-\frac{3}{10}$
4. $-\frac{3}{4}+\frac{1}{4}$
5. $-\frac{7}{20}-\left(-\frac{30}{20}\right)$
6. $-\frac{7}{18}-\frac{13}{18}$
7. $\frac{1}{2}+\frac{1}{4}$
8. $-\frac{1}{6}+\frac{2}{3}$
9. $\frac{3}{8}-\left(-\frac{1}{4}\right)$
10. $-\frac{3}{10}-\left(-\frac{17}{20}\right)$
11. $-\frac{3}{40}-\left(-\frac{2}{10}\right)$
12. $-\frac{7}{16}-\frac{7}{8}$
13. $\frac{7}{30}+\frac{9}{20}$
14. $\frac{7}{8}-\frac{1}{6}$
15. $-\frac{7}{30}-\left(-\frac{1}{25}\right)$
16. $\frac{15}{16}-\left(-\frac{1}{10}\right)$
17. $\frac{4}{9}+\frac{3}{7}$
18. $\frac{4}{5}+\frac{2}{9}$
19. $-\frac{2}{9}-\left(-\frac{2}{3}\right)$
20. $-\frac{7}{12}-\frac{3}{4}$

Convert the improper fraction to an integer or mixed number.

21. $\frac{9}{4}$
22. $\frac{5}{3}$
23. $\frac{4}{3}$
24. $-\frac{5}{5}$
25. $\frac{7}{6}$
26. $\frac{7}{2}$
27. $\frac{25}{5}$
28. $-\frac{8}{7}$
29. $-\frac{16}{5}$
30. $\frac{13}{9}$
31. $\frac{42}{10}$
32. $\frac{35}{12}$
33. $-\frac{54}{8}$
34. $\frac{100}{9}$
35. $\frac{75}{20}$

Choose the answer.

36. Which fraction is **not** an improper fraction?

A. $\frac{4}{3}$

B. $\frac{5}{6}$

C. $\frac{7}{7}$

D. $\frac{9}{2}$

37. Which fraction is equivalent to a whole number?

A. $\frac{3}{6}$

B. $\frac{4}{5}$

C. $\frac{8}{6}$

D. $\frac{10}{5}$

Find the difference. Write the answer as a mixed number in simplest form.

38. $-\frac{1}{10} - \frac{14}{15}$

39. $-\frac{1}{5} - \frac{11}{12}$

40. $-\frac{4}{9} - \frac{8}{11}$

41. $-\frac{3}{8} - \frac{9}{10}$

Solve. Write answers in complete sentences with fractions and mixed numbers in simplest form.

42. One piece of wood measures $\frac{11}{16}$ ft and another piece of wood measures $\frac{5}{16}$ ft. What is the combined length of the two pieces of wood?

43. Ebenezer spent $\frac{3}{8}$ of his allowance on Saturday and $\frac{1}{5}$ on Sunday. What fraction of his allowance did he spend?

44. Kia had $\frac{8}{9}$ yd of ribbon. She used $\frac{2}{3}$ yd for a bow. How much ribbon does Kia have left?

45. **Challenge** Roscoe drank $\frac{1}{4}$ qt of juice for breakfast, $\frac{1}{2}$ qt of water for lunch, and $\frac{1}{2}$ qt of milk for dinner. Between meals, he drank $\frac{5}{8}$ qt of water. How much more water did Roscoe drink than milk and juice combined?

46. **Challenge** Darlene played a video game for 15 min in the morning, $\frac{1}{2}$ h in the afternoon, and 10 min in the evening. What was the total time she spent playing the video game, expressed in hours as a fraction in simplest form?

Working with Mixed Numbers

Sometimes it is easier to work with a value as a mixed number, and sometimes it is better to work with an equivalent improper fraction.

If you keep in mind that a mixed number is the sum of a whole number and a fraction, you can express the mixed number as an improper fraction.

To convert a mixed number to an improper fraction, just use common denominators to add the whole part of the mixed number to the fraction part. If you do the same thing with variables as you work with a specific example, you can see how the general strategy works.

With Numbers	With Variables	
$5\frac{1}{2} = 5 + \frac{1}{2}$	$x\frac{a}{b} = x + \frac{a}{b}$	
$= \frac{5}{1} + \frac{1}{2}$	$= \frac{x}{1} + \frac{a}{b}$	Write the whole as a fraction with denominator 1.
$= \frac{5}{1} \bullet \frac{2}{2} + \frac{1}{2}$	$= \frac{x}{1} \bullet \frac{b}{b} + \frac{a}{b}$	Multiply to get common denominators.
$= \frac{5 \bullet 2}{1 \bullet 2} + \frac{1}{2}$	$= \frac{x \bullet b}{1 \bullet b} + \frac{a}{b}$	Simplify.
$= \frac{5 \bullet 2}{2} + \frac{1}{2}$	$= \frac{x \bullet b}{b} + \frac{a}{b}$	Simplify.
$= \frac{5 \bullet 2 + 1}{2}$	$= \frac{x \bullet b + a}{b}$	Add fractions.
$= \frac{10 + 1}{2} = \frac{11}{2}$		Simplify the number problem.

THINK ABOUT IT

The number $5\frac{1}{2}$ is not the same as $5 \bullet \frac{1}{2}$. It is the same as $5 + \frac{1}{2}$.

Converting Mixed Numbers to Improper Fractions

CONVERTING MIXED NUMBERS TO IMPROPER FRACTIONS

Step 1 Multiply the whole part by the denominator of the fraction part.
Step 2 Add the result to the numerator. Use this as the numerator of the improper fraction.
Step 3 Keep the original denominator.

EXAMPLE 1 Convert the mixed number to an improper fraction.

A $2\frac{3}{5}$

Solution

$2\frac{3}{5} = \frac{2 \cdot 5 + 3}{5}$ Multiply the whole part by the denominator. Add the result to the numerator.

$= \frac{13}{5}$ Simplify. ■

B $-6\frac{7}{8}$

Solution Follow the steps for $6\frac{7}{8}$. Keep the negative sign in front.

$-\left(6\frac{7}{8}\right) = -\left(\frac{6 \cdot 8 + 7}{8}\right)$ Multiply the whole part by the denominator. Add the result to the numerator.

$= -\frac{55}{8}$ Simplify. ■

Adding and Subtracting Mixed Numbers

A mixed number has a whole part and a fraction part.

3 is the whole part $\rightarrow 3\frac{2}{5} \leftarrow \frac{2}{5}$ is the fraction part

ADDING AND SUBTRACTING WITH MIXED NUMBERS

Method 1

- Add or subtract the whole parts and fraction parts separately.
- Simplify if possible.

Method 2

- Write integers and mixed numbers as improper fractions.
- Add or subtract the fractions.
- Simplify if possible.

EXAMPLE 2 Find the value of the expression. Write the answer in simplest form.

A $2\frac{3}{4} + 3\frac{1}{12}$

Solution Use Method 1.

$2\frac{3}{4} + 3\frac{1}{12} = 2\frac{9}{12} + 3\frac{1}{12}$ Write $\frac{3}{4}$ as the equivalent fraction $\frac{9}{12}$.

$= (2 + 3) + \left(\frac{9}{12} + \frac{1}{12}\right)$ Add the whole parts and the fraction parts.

$= 5 + \frac{10}{12} = 5\frac{5}{6}$ Simplify. ■

B $\frac{1}{8} - 1\frac{3}{10}$

Solution Use Method 2.

$\frac{1}{8} - 1\frac{3}{10} = \frac{1}{8} - \frac{13}{10}$	Write the mixed number as an improper fraction.
$= \frac{5}{40} - \frac{52}{40}$	Write each fraction as an equivalent fraction, using the least common denominator 40.
$= -\frac{47}{40}$	Subtract the fractions.
$= -1\frac{7}{40}$	Simplify by writing the improper fraction as a mixed number. ■

C $4 - 2\frac{2}{5} + \frac{1}{2}$

Solution Use Method 2.

$4 - 2\frac{2}{5} + \frac{1}{2} = \frac{4}{1} - \frac{12}{5} + \frac{1}{2}$	Write the integer and mixed number as improper fractions.
$= \frac{40}{10} - \frac{24}{10} + \frac{5}{10}$	Write each fraction as an equivalent fraction, using the least common denominator 10.
$= \frac{40 - 24 + 5}{10}$	
$= \frac{21}{10}$	Subtract and add to simplify the expression in the numerator.
$= 2\frac{1}{10}$	Write the improper fraction as a mixed number to simplify. ■

Application: Carpentry

EXAMPLE 3 A carpenter cuts a board $10\frac{3}{4}$ in. long from a board $33\frac{1}{4}$ in. long. The saw cut is $\frac{1}{8}$ in. wide. What is the length of the remaining piece?

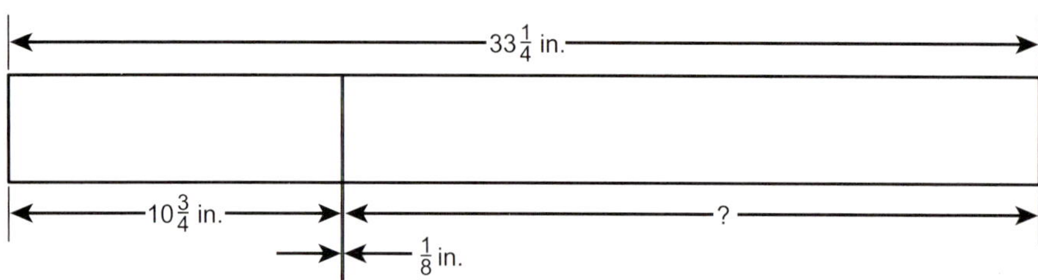

Solution Subtract $10\frac{3}{4}$ and $\frac{1}{8}$ from $33\frac{1}{4}$. Use Method 2.

$$\begin{aligned} 33\frac{1}{4} - 10\frac{3}{4} - \frac{1}{8} &= \frac{133}{4} - \frac{43}{4} - \frac{1}{8} \\ &= \frac{266}{8} - \frac{86}{8} - \frac{1}{8} \\ &= \frac{179}{8} \\ &= 22\frac{3}{8} \end{aligned}$$

The remaining piece is $22\frac{3}{8}$ in. long.

TIP

The expression $33\frac{1}{4} - \left(10\frac{3}{4} + \frac{1}{8}\right)$ can be used in this application. Find the sum $10\frac{3}{4} + \frac{1}{8}$ and then subtract that result from $33\frac{1}{4}$.

Problem Set

Find the value of the expression. Write the answer in simplest form.

1. $6\frac{1}{8} + 1\frac{3}{8}$
2. $6\frac{7}{20} - 2\frac{1}{20}$
3. $-\frac{2}{3} - 3\frac{2}{3}$
4. $1\frac{2}{5} - \left(-\frac{1}{5}\right)$
5. $1\frac{1}{4} + 4\frac{5}{12}$
6. $\frac{11}{12} - 2\frac{5}{6}$
7. $1\frac{5}{6} - \left(-\frac{2}{3}\right)$
8. $5\frac{1}{2} - 3\frac{5}{6}$
9. $4\frac{3}{8} - 2\frac{9}{16}$
10. $-1\frac{9}{10} - \frac{3}{4}$
11. $1\frac{5}{6} - \left(-1\frac{3}{10}\right)$
12. $8 - 3\frac{1}{4} + \frac{7}{8}$
13. $\frac{1}{3} + 3\frac{1}{6} + 3$
14. $-\frac{1}{3} - 2\frac{1}{4} - 1\frac{1}{6}$
15. $4\frac{1}{2} - 1\frac{1}{10} + 6\frac{2}{5}$
16. $\frac{1}{40} - 1\frac{1}{25} - \frac{11}{100}$

Convert the mixed number to an improper fraction.

17. $1\frac{1}{4}$
18. $3\frac{1}{2}$
19. $4\frac{1}{5}$
20. $2\frac{3}{4}$
21. $-1\frac{5}{6}$
22. $6\frac{1}{4}$
23. $-2\frac{3}{5}$
24. $7\frac{1}{3}$
25. $9\frac{7}{8}$
26. $8\frac{3}{10}$
27. $5\frac{8}{9}$
28. $-8\frac{2}{5}$
29. $9\frac{12}{13}$
30. $25\frac{1}{4}$
31. $3\frac{a}{b}$

For each problem:
(a) Write an expression or equation to model the problem.
(b) Answer the question using a mixed number in simplest form.

32. Ed wrote a book report in $1\frac{1}{2}$ h. He spent $\frac{3}{4}$ h studying for a math quiz. How much more time did he spend on the book report?

33. A cafeteria served $5\frac{1}{4}$ lb of beef, $2\frac{5}{8}$ lb of ham, and $4\frac{1}{2}$ lb of turkey 1 day. What was the total amount of meat served that day?

34. The diagram represents a set of stairs. All angles in the diagram are right angles. Two of the treads are each $11\frac{3}{4}$ in. long. What is the length of the bottom tread, labeled x in.?

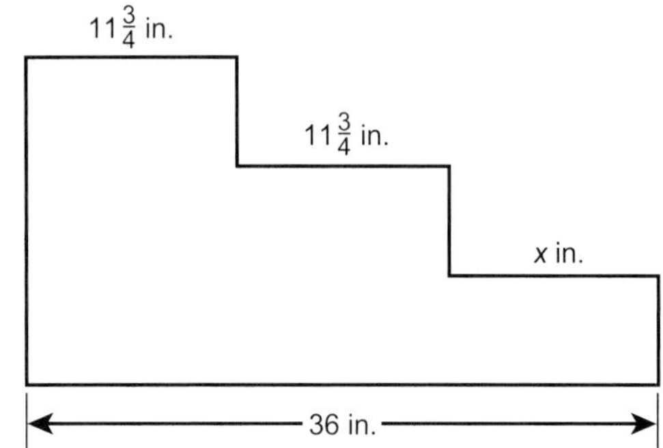

35. A group hiked $2\frac{7}{10}$ mi from their campground to a scenic overlook and then $3\frac{1}{2}$ mi from the overlook to a lake, where they ate lunch. After lunch they hiked $4\frac{3}{4}$ mi directly back to the campground. How much farther did the group hike before lunch than after lunch?

36. A punch recipe calls for $1\frac{1}{3}$ cups of orange juice, $\frac{3}{4}$ cup of grape juice, and $2\frac{1}{2}$ cups of apple juice. How much fruit juice does the recipe call for?

37. **Challenge** A pool manager told three new employees to report the amount of time they worked on their first day of employment. The reported times were $5\frac{1}{2}$ h; 6.75 h; and 5 h, 48 min. What was the total time, expressed in hours as a mixed number?

38. **Challenge** Kristen had a board 8 ft long. She cut these lengths from the board: 1 ft, $2\frac{3}{8}$ in.; $10\frac{5}{8}$ in.; and 2 ft, $6\frac{1}{4}$ in. Allowing $\frac{1}{8}$ in. for each saw cut, what was the length of the remaining piece?

39. **Challenge** Write the fifth term in the number pattern. Then find the sum of all five terms.

$$3, \frac{3}{2}, \frac{3}{4}, \frac{3}{8}, ?$$

Multiplying and Dividing with Mixed Numbers

You will use your skills of multiplying and dividing fractions to multiply and divide mixed numbers.

To multiply mixed numbers, change each mixed number to an improper fraction. Then multiply the numerators, multiply the denominators, and write the product in lowest terms.

Multiplying Mixed Numbers

EXAMPLE 1 Multiply. Write the product as either an integer or a mixed number in lowest terms.

A $3 \cdot 2\frac{1}{2}$

Solution

$3 \cdot 2\frac{1}{2} = \frac{3}{1} \cdot \frac{5}{2}$ Write each factor as an improper fraction.

$= \frac{15}{2}$ Multiply.

$= 7\frac{1}{2}$ Convert the answer to a mixed number. ■

THINK ABOUT IT

Since $3 \geq 1$, $\frac{3}{1}$ is an improper fraction.

B $2\frac{2}{3} \cdot 4\frac{4}{5}$

Solution Write each mixed number as an improper fraction.

$2\frac{2}{3} \cdot 4\frac{4}{5} = \frac{8}{\cancel{3}_1} \cdot \frac{\cancel{24}^8}{5}$ Write each factor as an improper fraction and divide out the common factor of 3.

$= \frac{64}{5}$ Multiply.

$= 12\frac{4}{5}$ Convert the answer to a mixed number. ■

C $6\frac{1}{7} \cdot (-7)$

Solution Write each factor as an improper fraction.

$6\frac{1}{7} \cdot (-7) = \frac{43}{\cancel{7}_1} \cdot \left(-\frac{\cancel{7}^1}{1}\right)$	Divide out the common factor of 7.
$= -\frac{43}{1}$	Multiply.
$= -43$	Simplify.

Dividing Mixed Numbers

Dividing mixed numbers is like multiplying. Start by changing the mixed numbers to improper fractions. Next, change division to multiplying by the reciprocal.

EXAMPLE 2 Divide. Write the quotient as either an integer or a mixed number in lowest terms.

A $-5\frac{2}{3} \div \left(-2\frac{1}{2}\right)$

Solution Write each mixed number as an improper fraction.

$-5\frac{2}{3} \div \left(-2\frac{1}{2}\right) = -\frac{17}{3} \div \left(-\frac{5}{2}\right)$	Write each factor as an improper fraction.
$= -\frac{17}{3} \cdot \left(-\frac{2}{5}\right)$	Multiply by the reciprocal of $-\frac{5}{2}$.
$= \frac{34}{15}$	Multiply. Both factors are negative, so the product is positive.
$= 2\frac{4}{15}$	Convert the answer to a mixed number.

B $6\frac{1}{2} \div 2$

Solution Write each factor as an improper fraction.

$6\frac{1}{2} \div 2 = \frac{13}{2} \div \frac{2}{1}$	Write each factor as an improper fraction.
$= \frac{13}{2} \cdot \frac{1}{2}$	Multiply by the reciprocal of $\frac{2}{1}$.
$= \frac{13}{4}$	Multiply.
$= 3\frac{1}{4}$	Convert the answer to a mixed number.

TIP

Estimate to check your answer for reasonableness. In Example 2B, $6 \div 2 = 3$ and $7 \div 2 = 3\frac{1}{2}$.

C $\frac{a}{b} \div 3\frac{3}{4}$

Solution Write the mixed number as an improper fraction.

$\frac{a}{b} \div 3\frac{3}{4} = \frac{a}{b} \div \frac{15}{4}$	Write the mixed number as an improper fraction.
$= \frac{a}{b} \cdot \frac{4}{15}$	Multiply by the reciprocal of $\frac{15}{4}$.
$= \frac{4a}{15b}$	Commutative Property of Multiplication ■

Application: Catering

EXAMPLE 3

A A recipe serves 6 people. Carla needs to serve 18 people. If the recipe calls for $1\frac{3}{4}$ cups of flour, how much flour will Carla need?

Solution Carla needs to triple every ingredient because 18 people is 3 times the number of people her recipe will serve.

$1\frac{3}{4} \cdot 3 = \frac{7}{4} \cdot \frac{3}{1}$	Write the factors as improper fractions.
$= \frac{21}{4}$	Multiply.
$= 5\frac{1}{4}$	Convert the improper fraction to a mixed number.

She needs $5\frac{1}{4}$ cups of flour. ■

B A recipe that serves 4 people calls for $1\frac{1}{3}$ cups of flour. Carla has $9\frac{1}{3}$ cups of flour. How many people can Carla serve?

Solution Divide to find by how much she can multiply the recipe.

$9\frac{1}{3} \div 1\frac{1}{3} = \frac{28}{3} \div \frac{4}{3}$	Write the mixed numbers as improper fractions.
$= \frac{\overset{7}{\cancel{28}}}{\underset{1}{\cancel{3}}} \cdot \frac{\overset{1}{\cancel{3}}}{\underset{1}{\cancel{4}}}$	Multiply by the reciprocal of $\frac{4}{3}$.
$= \frac{7}{1}$	Multiply.
$= 7$	Simplify.

Carla can multiply the recipe by 7. Multiply to find the maximum number of people Carla can serve.

$$7 \cdot 4 = 28$$

Carla can serve 28 people. ■

Problem Set

Multiply. Write the product as either a whole number or a mixed number in lowest terms.

1. $1\frac{1}{2} \cdot 8$

2. $6 \cdot 4\frac{2}{3}$

3. $10 \cdot 3\frac{1}{4}$

4. $-5 \cdot 2\frac{5}{6}$

5. $3\frac{1}{3} \cdot 2\frac{1}{6}$

6. $4\frac{1}{2} \cdot 4\frac{1}{2}$

7. $-5\frac{2}{3} \cdot 3\frac{3}{4}$

8. $2\frac{3}{7} \cdot 1\frac{3}{4}$

9. $8\frac{1}{3} \cdot (-24)$

10. $4\frac{2}{5} \cdot 3\frac{4}{7}$

11. $3\frac{5}{6} \cdot 4\frac{1}{2} \cdot \left(-\frac{3}{4}\right)$

12. $1\frac{2}{10} \cdot \left(-2\frac{1}{12}\right) \cdot 1\frac{1}{2}$

13. $\frac{x}{2} \cdot 2\frac{4}{5}$

14. $5 \cdot y \cdot \left(-2\frac{4}{13}\right)$

Divide. Write the quotient as either a whole number or a mixed number in lowest terms.

15. $7\frac{1}{2} \div 2\frac{1}{2}$

16. $10 \div 4\frac{1}{4}$

17. $3\frac{1}{2} \div \frac{1}{2}$

18. $5 \div 1\frac{1}{8}$

19. $4\frac{2}{5} \div 1\frac{1}{3}$

20. $6\frac{5}{6} \div 3\frac{2}{3}$

21. $4\frac{4}{5} \div \frac{3}{10}$

22. $2\frac{1}{7} \div 4\frac{2}{7}$

23. $6\frac{2}{3} \div 2\frac{2}{15}$

24. $10\frac{5}{8} \div 3\frac{1}{4}$

25. $\frac{x}{7} \div 1\frac{3}{7}$

26. $-2\frac{1}{2} \div c$

27. $3\frac{2}{5} \cdot 1\frac{1}{2} \div 2\frac{3}{4}$

28. **Challenge** $24\frac{3}{4} \div 2\frac{1}{6} \div 1\frac{2}{3}$

Solve.

29. A carpenter is cutting a board that is $8\frac{1}{2}$ ft long into 6 sections of equal length. What will be the length of each section?

30. A carpenter is cutting a board that is $10\frac{1}{2}$ ft long into as many sections that are $1\frac{7}{8}$ ft long as he can.

(a) How many complete sections will he have?

(b) How much will be left over?

31. A recipe serves 4 people. Andy needs to serve 12 people. If the recipe calls for $1\frac{1}{3}$ cups of sugar, how much sugar will Andy need?

32. A recipe that serves 4 people calls for $2\frac{3}{4}$ cups of nuts. Antonya has $16\frac{1}{2}$ cups of nuts. How many people can she serve?

33. A book weighs $4\frac{7}{16}$ lb. How much does a crate containing 24 of these books weigh if the crate itself weighs $3\frac{1}{4}$ lb?

Equations with Fractions

Use the properties of equality to solve equations with fractions and mixed numbers.

Using Addition and Subtraction to Solve Equations with Fractions

Fractions and mixed numbers are just types of numbers. So addition and subtraction properties of equality that you use to solve equations with integers also work with fractions and mixed numbers.

EXAMPLE 1 Solve.

A $t + \frac{2}{3} = 6$

Solution

$t + \frac{2}{3} - \frac{2}{3} = 6 - \frac{2}{3}$	Subtraction Property of Equality
$t = 6 - \frac{2}{3}$	Simplify on the left.
$t = \frac{18}{3} - \frac{2}{3}$	Rename 6 with a denominator of 3.
$t = \frac{16}{3} = 5\frac{1}{3}$	Subtract and write the answer as a mixed number.

Check $5\frac{1}{3} + \frac{2}{3} = 5 + \frac{3}{3} = 5 + 1 = 6$ ✓ ■

B $1\frac{4}{5} = x - \frac{3}{10}$

Solution

$1\frac{4}{5} = x - \frac{3}{10}$	
$1\frac{4}{5} + \frac{3}{10} = x - \frac{3}{10} + \frac{3}{10}$	Addition Property of Equality
$1\frac{4}{5} + \frac{3}{10} = x$	Simplify on the right.
$1\frac{8}{10} + \frac{3}{10} = x$	Rename $\frac{4}{5}$ with a denominator of 10.

▶ **REMEMBER**

Addition Property of Equality
If $a = b$, then $a + c = b + c$ and $c + a = c + b$.
Subtraction Property of Equality
If $a = b$, then $a - c = b - c$.
Substitution Property of Equality
If $a = b$, then either may replace the other in any expression.

$1\frac{11}{10} = x$ Add.

$1 + 1\frac{1}{10} = x$ Write $\frac{11}{10}$ as a mixed number.

$2\frac{1}{10} = x$ Add. ■

Using Multiplication and Division to Solve Equations with Fractions

Multiplication and division properties of equality that you use to solve equations with integers also work with fractions and mixed numbers.

EXAMPLE 2 Solve.

A $\frac{1}{3}h = \frac{5}{8}$

Solution Use division to isolate the variable h.

$\frac{1}{3}h = \frac{5}{8}$

$\frac{1}{3} \div \frac{1}{3} \cdot h = \frac{5}{8} \div \frac{1}{3}$ Divide each side by $\frac{1}{3}$.

$\frac{1}{3} \cdot \frac{3}{1} \cdot h = \frac{5}{8} \cdot \frac{3}{1}$ Write each division as multiplication by the reciprocal.

$h = \frac{15}{8} = 1\frac{7}{8}$ Multiply and simplfy. ■

B $6 = \frac{2}{3}p$

Solution Multiply by the reciprocal to isolate the variable p.

$6 = \frac{2}{3}p$

$6 \cdot \frac{3}{2} = \frac{2}{3} \cdot \frac{3}{2} \cdot p$ Multiply each side by the reciprocal of $\frac{2}{3}$.

$6 \cdot \frac{3}{2} = p$ Simplify on the right.

$\frac{18}{2} = p$ Multiply.

$9 = p$ Simplify. ■

TIP

If the fraction part is an improper fraction, rewrite the fraction part as a mixed number, and then combine the whole parts.

REMEMBER

Division Property of Equality
For any real numbers a, b, and n (where $n \neq 0$), if $a = b$, then

$$\frac{a}{n} = \frac{b}{n}.$$

Multiplication Property of Equality
For any real numbers a, b, and n, if $a = b$, then $an = bn$.

TIP

Often, the division step is skipped and the first step is to multiply each side by the reciprocal. That method will be shown from now on.

C $3\frac{5}{7}a = 4$

Solution Convert the mixed number to an improper fraction, and then multiply by the reciprocal to isolate a.

$3\frac{5}{7}a = 4$	
$\frac{26}{7}a = 4$	Write $3\frac{5}{7}$ as an improper fraction.
$\frac{26}{7} \cdot \frac{7}{26} \cdot a = 4 \cdot \frac{7}{26}$	Multiply each side by the reciprocal of $\frac{26}{7}$.
$a = 4 \cdot \frac{7}{26}$	Simplify on the left.
$a = \frac{28}{26} = 1\frac{2}{26} = 1\frac{1}{13}$	Multiply and simplify.

Application: Growth

EXAMPLE 3 In June, Richard measured the height of a tree as $2\frac{3}{4}$ ft tall. When he measured it again in October, it was $5\frac{1}{2}$ ft tall. Write and solve an equation to find how much the tree grew between June and October.

Solution

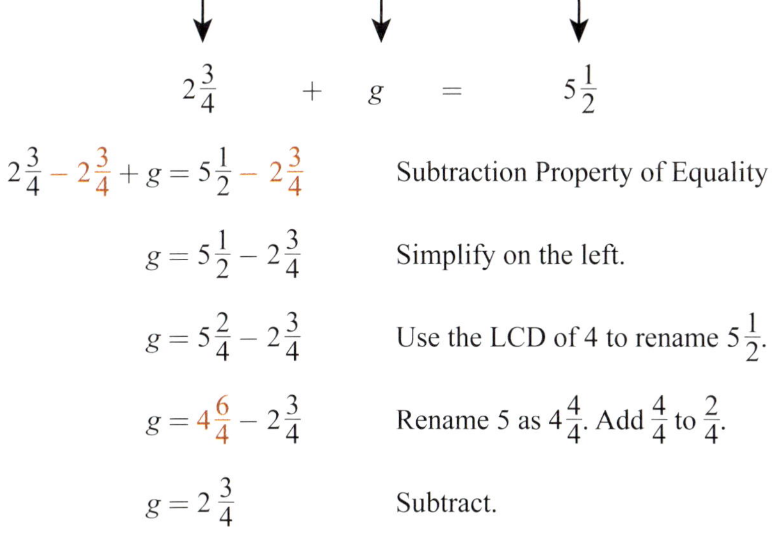

$2\frac{3}{4} - 2\frac{3}{4} + g = 5\frac{1}{2} - 2\frac{3}{4}$	Subtraction Property of Equality
$g = 5\frac{1}{2} - 2\frac{3}{4}$	Simplify on the left.
$g = 5\frac{2}{4} - 2\frac{3}{4}$	Use the LCD of 4 to rename $5\frac{1}{2}$.
$g = 4\frac{6}{4} - 2\frac{3}{4}$	Rename 5 as $4\frac{4}{4}$. Add $\frac{4}{4}$ to $\frac{2}{4}$.
$g = 2\frac{3}{4}$	Subtract.

The tree grew $2\frac{3}{4}$ ft between June and October.

TIP

Renaming $5\frac{2}{4}$ as $4\frac{6}{4}$ is not really necessary, but is one strategy. Instead, we could just break apart the mixed numbers and subtract whole parts from whole parts and fraction parts from fraction parts and then simplify.

Problem Set

Solve.

1. $x + \frac{5}{6} = 3$
2. $\frac{1}{3} + g = 4\frac{1}{2}$
3. $\frac{1}{6}c = 12$
4. $-5\frac{4}{5} + h = 10\frac{1}{5}$
5. $-\frac{7}{10} = k - 6\frac{1}{10}$
6. $2\frac{3}{4} + a = 3\frac{3}{8}$
7. $-\frac{1}{2} + m = -5\frac{3}{7}$
8. $\frac{1}{2} + x + \frac{3}{4} = 5$
9. $\frac{3}{4}a = \frac{2}{5}$
10. $9 = \frac{1}{5}x$
11. $\frac{4}{9} = 2y$
12. $y + 4\frac{1}{3} = -2\frac{1}{2}$
13. $1\frac{1}{5} + d = -6\frac{1}{3}$
14. $-\frac{1}{2}n = 15$
15. $\frac{5}{8}q = -20$
16. $10 = q - 2\frac{1}{8}$
17. $-1\frac{1}{6}b = 5$
18. $21 = 3\frac{1}{2}w$
19. $-2 = -\frac{m}{2}$
20. $t - 4\frac{7}{9} = 16 - \frac{1}{2}$
21. $\frac{1}{8}g + \frac{1}{8}g = 7$
22. $3\frac{1}{8} + p - 1\frac{3}{4} = 10\frac{3}{5}$
23. $3\frac{3}{4} - 2b = 15\frac{7}{8}$
24. $-1\frac{1}{2}f + \frac{7}{10} = 5f$

For each problem:

(a) Write an expression or equation.
(b) Simplify or solve.
(c) Give your answer in a complete sentence with a mixed number in simplest form.

25. Gary ran $5\frac{1}{2}$ mi. That distance is $2\frac{3}{4}$ mi longer than Finn ran. Write and solve an equation to find how far Finn ran.

26. The perimeter of the triangle is $8\frac{5}{8}$ in. Write and solve an equation to find the value of x.

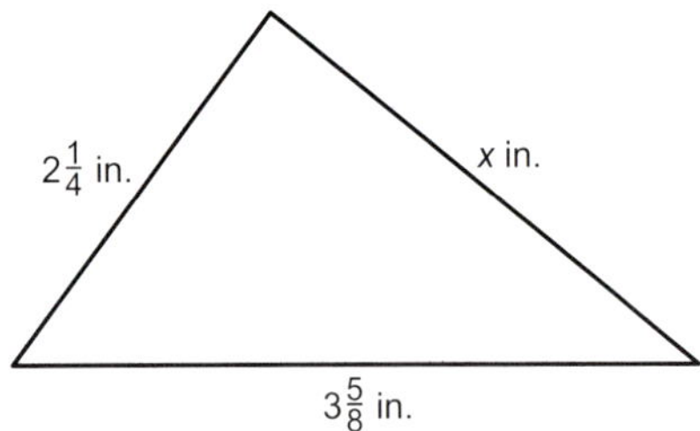

27. A team of runners ran a relay race. Each runner ran $7\frac{1}{2}$ km. The total length of the race was 45 km. Write and solve an equation to find how many runners were on the team.

28. The sum of twice a number and $6\frac{1}{10}$ is $9\frac{2}{5}$. Write and solve an equation to find the number.

29. **Challenge** The mean of a set of values is the quotient of the sum of the values and the number of values. Write and solve an equation to find the value of x in the data set if the mean of the data set is $4\frac{1}{8}$.

$$6\frac{1}{2}, 2\frac{1}{4}, x, 4\frac{3}{4}$$

30. **Challenge** To find the median of a set of values, first arrange the data in order. Then choose the middle values if the number of values is odd, or find the mean of the two middle values if the number of values is even. Write and solve an equation to find the value of y in the data set below if the median of the data set is $3\frac{13}{15}$. (Assume the data are already listed in order.)

$$2\frac{1}{2}, 2\frac{3}{4}, 3\frac{5}{6}, y, 4\frac{5}{8}, 4\frac{3}{4}$$

Core Focus: Fractions and Mixed Numbers

THE CORE CONCEPT

When you estimate the sum or product of mixed numbers, you can tell whether the estimate is an overestimate or underestimate as well as whether it is a close estimate.

Estimating Products

One easy way to estimate the product of two numbers is to round each number to the nearest integer and then multiply them together. For fractions, consider rounding the fraction to either 0, $\frac{1}{2}$, or 1.

EXAMPLE 1 Use rounding to estimate each product.

A $5\frac{1}{8} \cdot 3\frac{2}{3}$

Solution Round $5\frac{1}{8}$ to the nearest integer, 5, and $3\frac{2}{3}$ to the nearest integer, 4. The estimated product of $5\frac{1}{8} \cdot 3\frac{2}{3}$ is $5 \cdot 4 = 20$. ■

B $11\frac{8}{9} \cdot \frac{7}{16}$

Solution Round $11\frac{8}{9}$ to the nearest integer 12 and $\frac{7}{16}$ to $\frac{1}{2}$, since $\frac{8}{16} = \frac{1}{2}$. The estimated product of $11\frac{8}{9} \cdot \frac{7}{16}$ is $12 \cdot \frac{1}{2} = 6$. ■

Accuracy of an Estimated Product

In many real-world situations involving the product of two numbers, estimating the product provides a good enough answer. If one number was rounded up and the other number was rounded down, the estimated product has a good chance of being close to the actual answer.

THINK ABOUT IT

If both factors in an estimated product are rounded up, the product is an overestimate. If both factors in an estimated product are rounded down, the product is an underestimate.

EXAMPLE 2 Burt wants to paint a wall that is $11\frac{2}{3}$ ft wide by $7\frac{1}{4}$ ft long. Estimate the area of the wall. Tell whether your estimate is an underestimate, overestimate, or is likely a close estimate. Explain.

Solution The area of the wall is found by multiplying the length times the width.

$$11\frac{2}{3}\text{ ft} \cdot 7\frac{1}{4}\text{ ft} \approx 12\text{ ft} \cdot 7\text{ ft} = 84\text{ ft}^2$$

The estimated area of the wall is 84 ft^2. This estimate is likely a close estimate because the width was rounded up and the length was rounded down. ■

Accuracy of an Estimated Sum

EXAMPLE 3 Teo drove $107\frac{8}{10}$ mi on Tuesday and $64\frac{7}{10}$ mi on Wednesday. Estimate the number of miles Teo drove altogether. Is your estimate an underestimate or overestimate? Explain.

Solution To estimate the number of miles Teo drove altogether, estimate the sum of the number of miles driven both days.

$$107\frac{8}{10} + 64\frac{7}{10} \approx 108 + 65 = 173$$

Teo drove about 173 mi altogether.

Both numbers were rounded up, so the sum is an overestimate. ■

Q & A

Q How would the sum change if the mileage for each day was rounded to the nearest $\frac{1}{2}$ mi instead?

A $107\frac{8}{10} + 64\frac{7}{10} \approx 108 + 64\frac{1}{2} = 172\frac{1}{2}$

Problem Set

Solve. Show your work.

1. Estimate the value of each expression.
   - **(a)** $-13\frac{1}{8} - \frac{4}{7}$
   - **(b)** $21\frac{11}{12} \cdot \frac{7}{8} \cdot 4\frac{1}{3}$
   - **(c)** $14\frac{2}{5} + \left(-1\frac{1}{7}\right)$
   - **(d)** $41\frac{7}{9} \div 6\frac{1}{10}$
2. Angel can paint $11\frac{1}{5}$ fire hydrants in 1 h.
   - **(a)** Estimate how many fire hydrants he can paint in $3\frac{1}{3}$ h.
   - **(b)** Indicate whether your estimate is an overestimate, underestimate, or likely a close estimate. Explain.
3. Lilly cultivated $395\frac{7}{8}$ rows of corn Monday and $324\frac{1}{4}$ rows on Tuesday.
   - **(a)** Estimate the number of rows of corn Lilly cultivated Monday and Tuesday.
   - **(b)** Indicate whether your estimate is an overestimate, underestimate, or likely a close estimate. Explain.

Core Focus: Applications with Rational Numbers

THE CORE CONCEPT

Calculating the share or portion of a total amount often involves arithmetic using fractions. In these fractions, the numerator or the denominator may be a decimal, not a whole number.

Working with Fractions

EXAMPLE 1 Rod earned \$124.80 last week. He saw there were 4 amounts deducted from his paycheck.

Deduction	Amount
local tax	\$1.62
state tax	\$5.49
SSI (Social Security)	\$7.73
Medicare	\$1.81

A **Take-home pay** is defined as the amount of a paycheck remaining after deductions. What fraction of Rod's paycheck was take-home pay? Write your answer as a fraction rounded to the nearest thousandth, and then convert this number to a percent.

Solution Total deductions are $1.62 + 5.49 + 7.73 + 1.81 = 16.65$.

Take-home pay is the amount earned minus deductions, so Rod's take-home pay was $124.80 - 16.65 = 108.15$.

The fraction of the amount Rod earned that is take-home pay is

$\frac{108.15}{124.80} \approx 0.867$, which is equivalent to $0.867 \cdot 100\% = 86.7\%$. ■

B Use the percentage calculated in Part A to find Rod's take-home pay this week if he earned \$136.74 before deductions.

Solution Rod's take-home pay is 86.7%.of the amount that he earned, so multiply the amount he earned by 0.867.

$$0.867 \cdot 136.74 \approx 118.55$$

Rod's take-home pay this week was \$118.55. ■

DID YOU KNOW?

Four deductions are common on paychecks:

- local tax
- state tax
- SSI (Social Security)
- Medicare

REMEMBER

When calculating an amount of money, always round to the nearest cent (\$0.01).

EXAMPLE 2 Jon has 4 shares in a community farm. There are 81 shares altogether. Each week, Jon gets a portion of the produce harvested based upon his fraction of the total number of shares of the community farm. Last week, the farm harvested the quantities of produce shown in the table.

Produce item	Total harvest (kg)
lettuce	77.1
beets	46.9
cabbage	95.2

A How much of each item should Jon get? Organize your results in a table.

Solution Jon has 4 out of 81 shares, so he should get $\frac{4}{81}$ of each item of produce.

$$\text{lettuce: } \frac{4}{81} \cdot 77.1 = \frac{308.4}{81} \approx 3.8$$

$$\text{beets: } \frac{4}{81} \cdot 46.9 = \frac{187.6}{81} \approx 2.3$$

$$\text{cabbage: } \frac{4}{81} \cdot 77.1 = \frac{380.8}{81} \approx 4.7$$

Produce item	Jon's share (kg)
lettuce	3.8
beets	2.3
cabbage	4.7

B Jon's friend Naomi has double the number of shares that Jon has. How could Naomi estimate the amount of each item she will get? Will this method overestimate or underestimate what Naomi gets?

Solution Naomi has 8 shares, so she gets $\frac{8}{81}$ of each item. The fraction $\frac{8}{81}$ is close to $\frac{8}{80}$, which is equal to $\frac{1}{10}$. Multiplying by $\frac{1}{10}$ is equivalent to dividing by 10, so Naomi could divide each item amount by 10 to estimate how much of each item she will get. Since $\frac{8}{80} > \frac{8}{81}$, this method overestimates the amount of each item Naomi gets.

TIP

Estimate the product of a fraction and number by finding another fraction that is close in value to the original fraction and simplifies easily. For example,

$$\frac{20}{38} \approx \frac{20}{40} = \frac{1}{2}$$

THINK ABOUT IT

If two fractions have the same numerator, then the fraction with the larger denominator is the fraction with the lesser value.

Problem Set

Solve.

1. Students collected donated books for three libraries. The chart shows the number of books given to each of the three libraries.

Library	Number of books
Hillview	37
Summerlin	121
Rockland	56

Each library pays a portion of the cost of collecting and delivering the donated books, based on the number of books it received. The cost of collecting and delivering the books was $15.73. How much should each of the libraries pay? Make a chart to display your results.

2. Peter needs to make enough fruit salad for a graduation party. The recipe he uses requires the following ingredients. The recipe makes 12 servings.

1 cantaloupe $\frac{3}{4}$ lb blueberries

$\frac{1}{4}$ watermelon 4.5 oz honey

$1\frac{1}{2}$ lb strawberries

Peter wants to make 75 servings of the fruit salad. How much of each ingredient does he need? Organize your results in a table.

3. Luisa uses a certain type of computer paper that is 0.097 mm thick. She wants to know how many more pages she can print. Luisa measures the stack of paper loaded in her printer to be $11\frac{1}{2}$ mm high and the stack of paper on her bookshelf to be 23 mm high.

   (a) Calculate the total number of pages she can print based on the heights of the two paper stacks she measured and the thickness of her paper.

   (b) How could Luisa estimate the number of sheets of paper left by rounding? Is this estimate an overestimate, underestimate, or close estimate? Explain.

CHAPTER 5 Review

Choose the answer.

1. What value of z makes the equation true?

$$\frac{18}{45} = \frac{z}{-5}$$

A. -32
B. -2
C. 2
D. 32

2. Which fraction is equivalent to $-\frac{16}{56}$?

A. $-\frac{2}{7}$
B. $-\frac{8}{29}$
C. $-\frac{1}{4}$
D. $-\frac{1}{6}$

3. What is the product of $\frac{7}{10} \bullet \frac{4}{9}$ in lowest terms?

A. $\frac{63}{40}$
B. $\frac{36}{90}$
C. $\frac{14}{45}$
D. $\frac{1}{3}$

4. What is $\frac{1}{3} \div \frac{5}{6}$?

A. $\frac{5}{18}$
B. $\frac{2}{5}$
C. $\frac{5}{2}$
D. $\frac{18}{5}$

5. What is the LCD of $\frac{1}{6}$ and $\frac{3}{4}$?

A. 3
B. 8
C. 12
D. 24

6. What is $\frac{33}{7}$ written as a mixed number?

A. $3\frac{6}{7}$
B. $3\frac{5}{7}$
C. $4\frac{4}{7}$
D. $4\frac{5}{7}$

7. What is $\frac{5}{8} - \frac{11}{12}$?

A. $-\frac{3}{4}$
B. $-\frac{1}{2}$
C. $-\frac{7}{24}$
D. $-\frac{5}{24}$

8. What is the sum of $1\frac{1}{2}$ and $4\frac{2}{3}$?

A. $5\frac{1}{6}$
B. $5\frac{1}{2}$
C. $5\frac{3}{5}$
D. $6\frac{1}{6}$

9. What is $12 \div 1\frac{1}{8}$?

A. $8\frac{7}{11}$

B. $10\frac{2}{3}$

C. $12\frac{1}{8}$

D. $13\frac{1}{2}$

10. For which value of y is the equation true?

$$7\frac{1}{8} = y + 4\frac{7}{8}$$

A. $2\frac{1}{4}$

B. $3\frac{1}{4}$

C. 11

D. 12

Solve.

11. A soccer team has 14 boys and 10 girls. What fraction of the team members are boys? Write your answer in lowest terms.

12. Mira ran $\frac{3}{4}$ of the way around a $\frac{1}{8}$ mi track. How far did Mira run?

13. A loaf of bread 9 in. long is cut into slices $\frac{3}{8}$ in. thick. How many slices of bread are there?

14. Draw a 10×10 grid. Represent the product of $\frac{3}{10} \cdot \frac{7}{10}$ on this grid.

15. Jason made $\frac{10}{13}$ of his free throws, and Alberto made $\frac{4}{5}$ of his free throws. Who made a greater fraction of his free throws?

16. Anya walked $\frac{7}{10}$ km to the bank and then walked $\frac{3}{4}$ km to the flower shop. How far did Anya walk altogether?

17. Kaya had a string $6\frac{1}{8}$ in. long. She cut off a piece $2\frac{3}{4}$ in. long. How long is the original string now?

18. Write each product as either an integer or a mixed number in lowest terms.

(a) $1\frac{2}{7} \cdot 5$

(b) $3\frac{1}{10} \cdot 2\frac{1}{2}$

19. Solve $1\frac{4}{5}h = 12$ for h.

20. Kerri needs wallpaper to cover a wall that is $12\frac{1}{12}$ ft long and $9\frac{1}{6}$ ft high.

(a) Estimate the amount of wallpaper Kerri needs.

(b) Is your estimate an underestimate or overestimate? Explain.

(c) Find the exact amount of wallpaper Kerri needs.

Problem	Topic Lookup	Problem	Topic Lookup
1, 2, 11	Equivalent Fractions	8,17	Working with Mixed Numbers
3, 12	Multiplying Fractions	9, 18	Multiplying and Dividing with Mixed Numbers
4, 13	Dividing Fractions	10,19	Equations with Fractions
14	Core Focus: Rational Numbers	20(a),(b)	Core Focus: Fractions and Mixed Numbers
5, 6, 15	Common Denominators	20(c)	Core Focus: Applications with Rational Numbers
7, 16	Adding and Subtracting Fractions		

CHAPTER 6 Combined Operations

Solving an equation is like a chimpanzee getting delicious ants out of a log. You have to work your way from the outside in to your goal. Tools can help, but persistence is always key.

In This Chapter

The distributive property is a powerful tool for working with expressions and equations that have both multiplication and addition. In this chapter, you'll see how to use the distributive property to work with numerical expressions, variable expressions, and equations. You'll also use inequalities to solve problems.

Topic List

- Foundations for Chapter 6
- The Distributive Property
- Like Terms
- Core Focus: Variable Expressions
- Expressions with Mixed Operations
- Core Focus: Algebraic Expressions
- Equations with Mixed Operations
- Core Focus: Multistep Equations
- Inequalities
- Core Focus: Applications of Inequalities
- Chapter 6 Review

Animals have to be persistent to get to food. ▶

Foundations for Chapter 6

Order of Operations

To simplify a numerical expression, follow the rules for the order of operations, starting at the left of the expression and moving to the right.

EXAMPLE A Simplify the expression.

$$12 \div (-3) + 2 - 3 + 2 \cdot (-2)$$

Solution Use the order of operations.

$12 \div (-3) + 2 - 3 + 2 \cdot (-2)$

$= -4 + 2 - 3 + 2 \cdot (-2)$ Divide.

$= -4 + 2 - 3 + (-4)$ Multiply.

$= -2 - 3 + (-4)$ Add.

$= -5 + (-4)$ Subtract.

$= -9$ Add.

$12 \div (-3) + 2 - 3 + 2 \cdot (-2) = -9$ ■

Problem Set A

Simplify the expression.

1. $5 \cdot 4 + 3 \cdot 2$
2. $3 \cdot (-4) - 10 \cdot 2$
3. $24 \div (-8) + 9 \cdot 3$
4. $-1 + 10 \cdot 8 \div 4$
5. $-2 + (4 + 5) \cdot (-3)$
6. $7 \cdot (-4) + 3 \cdot 2 \div 6$
7. $10 - (-2) + 16 \div (2 + 6)$
8. $12 \div 4 + \frac{6}{3 \cdot 8}$
9. $-12 \cdot (-8) - 10 - (-5)$
10. $\frac{10}{80 \div 4} \cdot 6 - 3$
11. $63 \div 7 + (-2) \cdot 3 - 2 \cdot (-1)$
12. $-32 \div [6 + (-2)] \div 2 - 4 \cdot 3$

One-Step Equations with Addition or Subtraction

Solve an equation that has the sum of a variable and a number by subtracting the number from both sides of the equation. For the difference of a variable and a number, add the number to both sides of the equation.

EXAMPLE B Solve.

$$-7 = 16 + y$$

Solution To isolate y, subtract 16 from each side of the equation. Simplify.

$$\begin{aligned} -7 &= 16 + y \\ -7 - 16 &= 16 - 16 + y \\ -23 &= 0 + y \\ -23 &= y \end{aligned}$$

Check Substitute -23 for y into the original equation.

$$-7 = 16 + (-23) = -7 \checkmark$$

The solution is $y = -23$. ■

Problem Set B

Solve.

1. $-5 = 4 + x$
2. $m + 6 = 8$
3. $-7 + n = 3$
4. $a + 6 = -14$
5. $-9 = -8 + w$
6. $h + (-16) = -10$
7. $-2 = p + 20$
8. $-8 + q = -17$
9. $h + (-5) = 13$
10. $8 = -2 + a$
11. $8 + x = 3$
12. $20 + k = -18$
13. $z + 15 = -15$
14. $22 = b + (-8)$

One-Step Equations with Multiplication or Division

Solve an equation involving the product of a number and a variable by dividing both sides of the equation by the number. For the quotient of a variable and a number, multiply both sides of the equation by the number.

EXAMPLE C Solve.

$$-72 = -18z$$

Solution To isolate z, divide each side of the equation by -18. Simplify.

$$\begin{aligned} -72 &= -18z \\ \frac{-72}{-18} &= \frac{-18z}{-18} \\ 4 &= 1z \\ 4 &= z \end{aligned}$$

Check Substitute $z = 4$ into $-72 = -18z$.

$$-72 = -18(4) = -72 \checkmark$$

The solution is $z = 4$. ■

Problem Set C

Solve.

1. $2x = 12$
2. $45 = 5a$
3. $21 = 3t$
4. $9b = 63$
5. $6h = -18$
6. $-16 = -4z$
7. $8 = -8j$
8. $-7d = 14$
9. $-10m = -30$
10. $5c = 5$
11. $-45 = 15w$
12. $-20r = -20$
13. $90 = 3k$
14. $-46 = -23p$

The Distributive Property

When simplifying an expression involving parentheses, the order of operations tells you to begin inside parentheses and work your way out. There is another way to simplify expressions that have parentheses.

The distributive property combines multiplication with either addition or subtraction.

DISTRIBUTIVE PROPERTY

For all numbers a, b, and c,

$$a(b + c) = ab + ac \text{ and } a(b - c) = ab - ac.$$

Examples $3(5 + 2) = 3 \cdot 5 + 3 \cdot 2$
$6(4 - 10) = 6 \cdot 4 - 6 \cdot 10$

Verifying the Distributive Property

You can use the order of operations to verify the distributive property.

EXAMPLE 1 Verify the distributive property.

A $3(5 + 2) = 3 \cdot 5 + 3 \cdot 2$

Solution

$3(5 + 2) = 3 \cdot 5 + 3 \cdot 2$ On the left side, add inside parentheses first. On the right side, use the distributive property to multiply first.

$3(7) = 15 + 6$

$21 = 21$ ■

TIP

When you use the distributive property, you have distributed the factor through the terms.

B $6(4 - 10) = 6 \cdot 4 - 6 \cdot 10$

Solution

$6(4 - 10) = 6 \cdot 4 - 6 \cdot 10$ On the left side, subtract inside parentheses first. On the right side, use the distributive property to multiply first.

$6(-6) = 24 - 60$

$-36 = -36$ ■

Using the Distributive Property to Rewrite Expressions

You can use the distributive property to change an addition expression without parentheses to one with parentheses (and vice versa).

EXAMPLE 2 Rewrite the expression without grouping symbols.

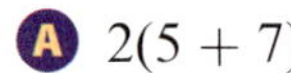

A $2(5 + 7)$

Solution

$$2(5 + 7) = 2 \cdot 5 + 2 \cdot 7$$

B $-3(4 + x)$

Solution

$$-3(4 + x) = -3 \cdot 4 + (-3) \cdot x$$

> **THINK ABOUT IT**
> The parentheses in the expression $-3 \cdot 4 + (-3) \cdot x$ are not grouping symbols. They are there simply to enclose the negative number -3.

EXAMPLE 3 Rewrite the expression with grouping symbols.

A $2 \cdot 3 + 2 \cdot 11$

Solution

$$2 \cdot 3 + 2 \cdot 11 = 2(3 + 11)$$

B $8 \cdot 1 + 8 \cdot (-7)$

Solution

$8 \cdot 1 + 8 \cdot (-7) = 8(1 + (-7))$

$= 8(1 - 7)$ Simplify $1 + (-7)$ by writing $1 - 7$.

C $5r - 5 \cdot 12$

Solution

$$5r - 5 \cdot 12 = 5(r - 12)$$

Using the Distributive Property to Evaluate Expressions

Using the distributive property to combine multiplication with either addition or subtraction gives you a powerful tool for evaluating certain types of expressions.

> **TIP**
> When breaking a factor into a sum, look for numbers that are easier to multiply. For instance, factors of 10 and 5 are usually easy to work with.

EXAMPLE 4 Use properties and mental math to evaluate the expression.

A $6 \cdot 74$

Solution

$6 \cdot 74 = 6(70 + 4)$ Write 74 as a sum.

$= 6 \cdot 70 + 6 \cdot 4$ Apply the distributive property.

$= 420 + 24$ Evaluate the expression.

$= 444$

B $8 \cdot 99$

Solution

$8 \cdot 99 = 8(100 - 1)$	Write 99 as a difference.
$= 8 \cdot 100 - 8 \cdot 1$	Apply the distributive property.
$= 800 - 8$	Evaluate the expression.
$= 792$ ■	

C $7 \cdot 67 + 7 \cdot 3$

Solution

$7 \cdot 67 + 7 \cdot 3 = 7(67 + 3)$	Apply the distributive property.
$= 7(70)$	The sum 70 is easier to multiply.
$= 490$ ■	

> **TIP**
> Use the methods shown in Example 4 to do mental math. In Example 4B, writing 99 as $100 - 1$ gives you numbers that are easy to work with.

Solving Equations by Recognizing the Distributive Property

EXAMPLE 5 Solve.

A $3 \cdot 5 + 3 \cdot a = 3(5 + 7)$

Solution By the distributive property, you know that

$$3 \cdot 5 + 3 \cdot 7 = 3(5 + 7), \text{ so } a = 7.$$ ■

B $b(1.2 + 5.4) = 8 \cdot 1.2 + 8 \cdot 5.4$

Solution By the distributive property, you know that

$$8(1.2 + 5.4) = 8 \cdot 1.2 + 8 \cdot 5.4, \text{ so } b = 8.$$ ■

Application: Perimeter

EXAMPLE 6 Find the perimeter of the rectangle.

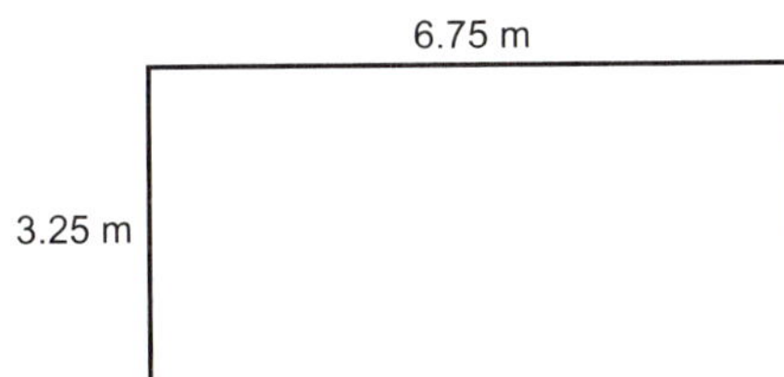

Solution

$P = 2l + 2w$	Write the formula for perimeter of a rectangle.
$= 2 \cdot 6.75 + 2 \cdot 3.25$	Substitute 6.75 for length l and 3.25 for width w.
$= 2(6.75 + 3.25)$	Apply the distributive property, and then add the decimals to get 10, which is easy to multiply.
$= 2(10) = 20$	

The perimeter is 20 m. ■

Problem Set

Verify the distributive property.

1. $2(3 + 6) = 2 \cdot 3 + 2 \cdot 6$
2. $10(5 + 1) = 10 \cdot 5 + 10 \cdot 1$
3. $-1(-3 + 2) = -1 \cdot (-3) + (-1) \cdot 2$
4. $4(6 - 1) = 4 \cdot 6 - 4 \cdot 1$
5. $2(8 - 9) = 2 \cdot 8 - 2 \cdot 9$
6. $-6(1 - 3) = -6 \cdot 1 - (-6) \cdot 3$

Rewrite the expression without grouping symbols.

7. $5(5 + 1)$
8. $2(6 + 6)$
9. $4(v + 7)$
10. $-20(2 + 8)$
11. $-9(1 + y)$
12. $4(-8 + w)$

Rewrite the expression with grouping symbols.

13. $3 \cdot 6 + 3 \cdot 9$
14. $7 \cdot 5 + 7 \cdot (-6)$
15. $4 \cdot 2 - 4 \cdot 11$
16. $3x - 3 \cdot 7$
17. $5 \cdot 8 - 5s$
18. $6n - 6d$
19. $-2x - 2y$
20. $10a - 10 \cdot 1$

Use properties and mental math to evaluate.

21. $2 \cdot 65$
22. $5 \cdot 37$
23. $6 \cdot 99$
24. $5 \cdot 98$
25. $8 \cdot 102$
26. $9 \cdot 34 + 9 \cdot 6$
27. $8 \cdot 87 + 8 \cdot 13$
28. $7 \cdot 248 - 7 \cdot 48$
29. **Challenge** $4.58 \cdot 101$
30. **Challenge** $12.05 \cdot 86 - 12.05 \cdot 75$

Use the distributive property to solve.

31. $2 \cdot 6 + 2 \cdot x = 2(6 + 3)$
32. $5 \cdot a + 5 \cdot 7 = 5(-1 + 7)$
33. $n(4 + 16) = 7 \cdot 4 + 7 \cdot 16$
34. $-2(x + 1) = -2 \cdot 4 + (-2) \cdot 1$
35. $10(-5 + s) = 10 \cdot (-5) + 10 \cdot (-1)$
36. $a(1.5 + 1.5) = -3 \cdot 1.5 + (-3) \cdot 1.5$

Use the distributive property to solve. Show your work.

37. Find the perimeter of the rectangle.

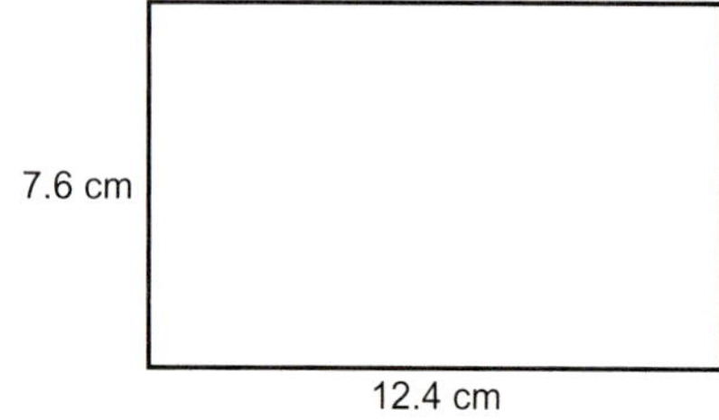

38. Find the perimeter of the equilateral hexagon.

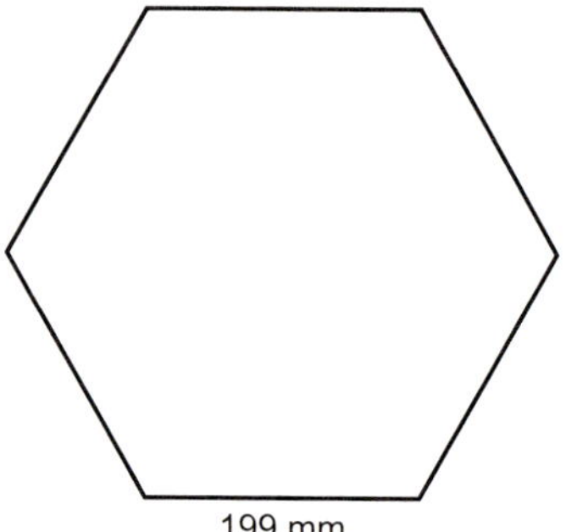

39. The diagram represents a parcel of land formed by two rectangular regions. Find the total area.

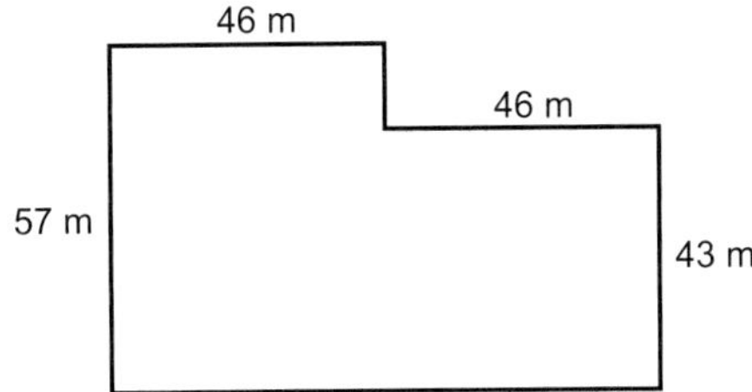

40. Find the total cost of each set of purchases.

(a) 5 gal of milk at \$3.95/gal

(b) 9 yd^2 of carpet at \$29.99/yd^2

(c) 6 boxes of popcorn at \$1.85 per box

(d) 4 bars of soap at \$1.67 each and 4 tubes of toothpaste at \$2.33 each

(e) 15 towels at \$11.25 each and 15 washcloths at \$3.75 each

41. **Challenge** Find the total cost of each set of purchases. Round each answer to the nearest cent.

(a) 8 gal of gasoline at \$2.999/gal

(b) 20 oz of cereal at \$0.241/oz

Like Terms

To simplify some variable expressions, you need to identify and combine like terms.

Identifying Like Terms

A sum or difference expression is made up of terms. **Like terms** have the same variable part or parts. Numbers are considered to be like terms; they can be called numerical terms. Terms are made up of factors that are multiplied together.

THINK ABOUT IT

Like terms can have exponents. For example, the like terms $3x^2$ and $5x^2$ have the exponent 2.

EXAMPLE 1 Identify the like terms.

A $5x, 5y, -2x, 5, -11$

Solution

$\{5x, -2x\}, \{5, -11\}, 5y$ The terms $5x$ and $-2x$ have the same variable. The terms 5 and -11 are numerical terms.

The terms $5x$ and $-2x$ form one pair of like terms, and the terms 5 and -11 form another pair of like terms. ■

B $-3a, 2b, 6ab, 1, a$

Solution The term $6ab$ is the only term that has both variables a and b, so it is not like any of the other terms.

$\{-3a, a\}, 2b, 6ab, 1$ The terms $-3a$ and a have the same variable.

The terms $-3a$ and a are like terms. ■

C $6, 4p, 6p^2, -p, 3pq$

Solution

$6, \{4p, -p\}, 6p^2, 3pq$ The terms $4p$ and $-p$ have the same variables.

The terms $4p$ and $-p$ are like terms. ■

Using the Distributive Property to Combine Like Terms

The distributive property states that $a(b + c) = ab + ac$, which can also be written $ba + ca = (b + c)a$. If you have an expression like $5x - 2x$, you can use the distributive property to write it as $(5 - 2)x$ and simplify it to $3x$ to combine like terms.

EXAMPLE 2 Combine like terms.

A $5x + 2x$

Solution

$5x + 2x = (5 + 2)x$ Apply the distributive property $ba + ca = (b + c)a$.

$= 7x$ Add inside the parentheses. ■

B $3y - y + 6y$

Solution

$3y - y + 6y = 3y - 1y + 6y$ Write $-y$ as $-1y$ so that it has a numerical factor.

$= (3 - 1 + 6)y$ Apply the distributive property.

$= 8y$ Simplify inside the parentheses. ■

Identifying and Combining Like Terms

The numerical factor in a term is called a **coefficient**. To combine like terms, you only need to add or subtract the coefficients.

COMBINING LIKE TERMS

To combine like terms, combine their coefficients. Keep the variable part the same.

Examples $4x + 5x = 9x$

$3ab + 2ab - 1ab = 4ab$

REMEMBER

Combining like terms is based on the distributive property.

$4x + 5x = (4 + 5)x = 9x$

EXAMPLE 3 Combine the like terms in the expression.

A $2a + 3 - 5a + 8b + 3ab$

Solution

$2a + 3 - 5a + 8b + 3ab = 2a - 5a + 3 + 8b + 3ab$ Rewrite so that like terms are together.

$= -3a + 3 + 8b + 3ab$ Combine like terms. ■

B $3s + rs - 4r - 6rs - 8rs$

Solution

$3s + rs - 4r - 6rs - 8rs = 3s - 4r + 1rs - 6rs - 8rs$ Rewrite rs as $1rs$. Write like terms together.

$= 3s - 4r - 13rs$ Combine like terms. ■

Application: Sales Tax

EXAMPLE 4 The sales tax rate in a certain state is 5%. Write a simplified expression for the total cost of an item that has a price of x dollars.

Solution The decimal equivalent of 5% is 0.05. When you pay 5% of x dollars in sales tax, you pay $0.05x$ dollars in sales tax.

$$\text{total cost} = \underbrace{\text{price of item}} + \underbrace{\text{sales tax}}$$

$= x + 0.05x$

$= 1.00x + 0.05x$ Write x as $1.00x$.

$= 1.05x$ Combine like terms.

The total amount paid is $1.05x$ dollars.

Problem Set

Identify the like terms.

1. $4x, 4y, 3y, 5x, -11$
2. $4a, -2b, a, 1, -1$
3. $3c, 3d, 6c, 6, 4a$
4. $-x, y, 6x, -8x, -8, -8z$
5. $4ab, -2b, 4a, 7, -5ab, -5$
6. $12c, d, c, -c, 12, 4d$
7. $-5u, 9v, 6uv, 2v, -uv, -5$
8. $7b, -8ab, 6, 4a, 7, 6bc, -5$
9. $3, 3rs, 3r, 3s, 8rs, 1, -9$
10. $-10, 4xy, 4y, 3y, 5y, -10y$
11. $4w, -9x, 4w, 2wxy, -wy, -wxy$
12. $\frac{1}{2}x, -3x, \frac{1}{2}, 2, -xy, \frac{1}{3}$
13. $1.5s, 1.5w, 2s, 2w, 10sw, 2$
14. $2ab, -2ab, 1.01ab, -b, -a$

Combine like terms.

15. $4a + 3a$
16. $7x + 7x$
17. $-3c + 5c$
18. $\frac{1}{4}x - \frac{1}{8}x$
19. $-5x - 2.2x + x$
20. $6t - \frac{1}{2}t + 8t - \frac{1}{2}t$
21. $5u - 5u + u - u$
22. $x + x + x - 10x$
23. **Challenge** $\frac{2}{3}a - \frac{1}{4}a + \frac{a}{12}$
24. **Challenge** $\frac{2}{5}x + 0.7x + \frac{1}{25}x$

Combine the like terms in the expression.

25. $8a + 5b - 2a$
26. $x + 4x - 6y + 5$
27. $3t + 4t - t + 5$
28. $5xy - 3x + 6y - xy + y$
29. $a - a + 6b - b - 5b + 6$
30. $3ax + 3x - 5ax - x - 5a + 10ax$
31. $z + 4w - (-3w) + 12z - z$
32. $3.5x + 4x - y + 2.5y - 1$

33. $r + rs - 5rs - 5rs + 2r - 6$

34. $4 - cd - 2cd - 3cd + 4 - c + d$

35. $5(x + 3) - 2x$

36. $a + 3(a - 1) - 5a$

37. $-6x + 2.5(x - 1) - 5x$

38. $x + \frac{3}{4}x - y + 5y + 3$

39. $5b + 3(2b + 1) - 5ab - 3$

40. **Challenge** $2.4(2x - 5r) + 3(1.1s + r) - 2x$

Solve.

41. Write a simplified expression for the total cost of each purchase described. Show how you combine like terms to obtain your simplified expression.
    - **(a)** The price of an item is d dollars and the sales tax rate is 6%.
    - **(b)** The price of a meal is m dollars and an 18% tip is added.
    - **(c)** The price of a hotel room is r dollars and there is a hotel tax of 4.5%.

42. Write a simplified expression for the perimeter of each polygon.
    - **(a)** rectangle

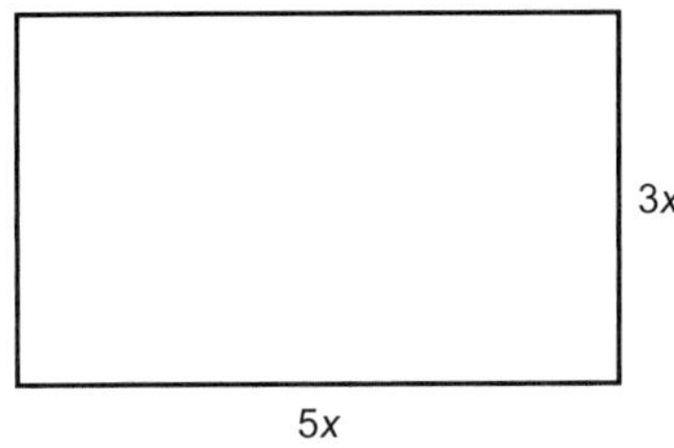

    - **(b)** regular pentagon

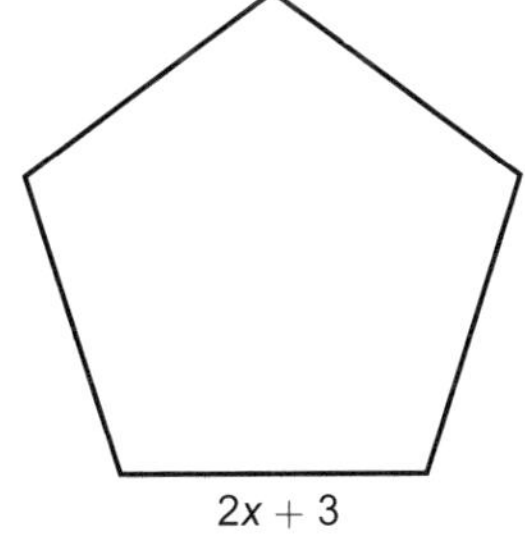

    - **(c)** two rectangles combined

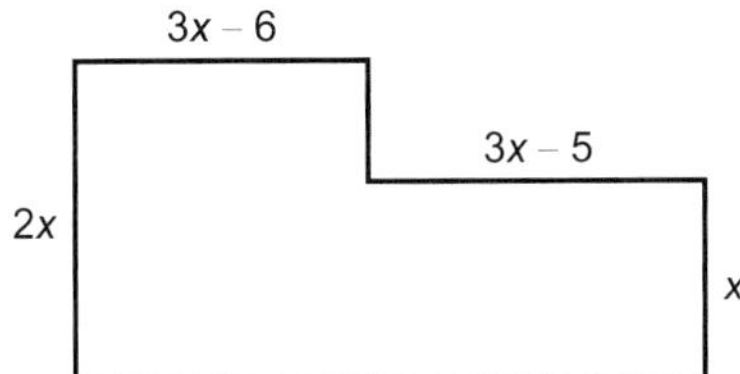

43. **Challenge** Coach Dixon is ordering T-shirts for his players. Each T-shirt costs \$8.85. There is a \$35 setup fee for silk-screening and a screening charge of \$2.15 per shirt.
    - **(a)** Write a simplified expression for the total cost of x T-shirts. Show how you combine like terms to obtain your simplified expression.
    - **(b)** Find the total cost of 12 T-shirts. Show how you evaluate your expression to obtain your answer.
    - **(c)** The T-shirt company offers a 10% discount per shirt for orders of at least 20 shirts. (The discount is applied to both the cost of the shirt and the screening charge.) Explain why 20 shirts cost less than 19 shirts.

44. **Challenge** The diagram consists of a circle with radius r and a square. The circle is tangent to each side of the square, which means that the circle touches each side of the square in exactly 1 point. Write a simplified expression for the sum of the circumference of the circle and perimeter of the square. (Hint: The formula for the circumference of a circle is $C = 2\pi r$.)

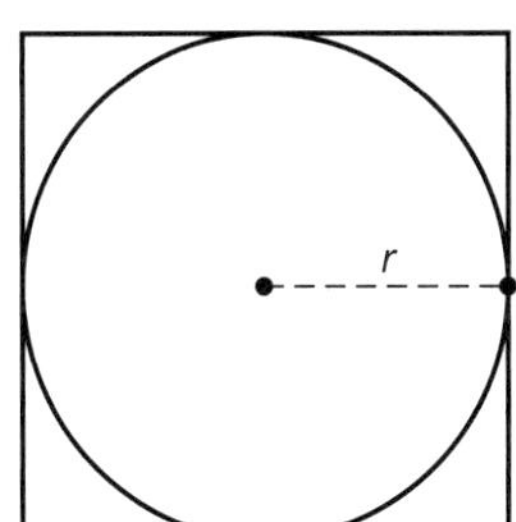

Core Focus: Variable Expressions

THE CORE CONCEPT

Identifying and combining like terms in a math expression helps organize the expression and can make evaluating the expression easier.

Identifying Like Terms

Identify like terms in an expression by finding terms with the same variables and exponents. Start at the left of the expression with the first term, looking for terms similar to it. Continue with each term until all terms have been examined.

EXAMPLE 1 On her pre-algebra test, Lin Yi was asked to identify all of the like terms from the list shown. She answered the question by identifying $-2x$ and $0.6x$ as like terms.

$$5xy,\ 2x,\ \frac{1}{3},\ 0.6x,\ 2y,\ 8$$

A Are the terms $-2x$ and $0.6x$ like terms? Explain.

Solution The terms $-2x$ and $0.6x$ are like terms. They have the same variable, x, raised to the same power, 1. ■

B Identify any other like terms. Explain how the terms are alike.

Solution The terms $\frac{1}{3}$ and 8 are constants, so they are considered to be like terms. No other terms are alike. ■

REMEMBER

Two terms in an expression are **like terms** if the terms have the same variables and the same exponents on those variables.

REMEMBER

A **coefficient** is the number in front of variables in a term. Two like terms do not need to have the same coefficient.

REMEMBER

A numerical term that has no variables is known as a **constant**.

Combining Like Terms

The solution to certain real-world problems involves adding variable expressions. To find the solution, it helps to combine like terms.

EXAMPLE 2 Mia and Jeff plan to meet at the library. The figure details the path and distance (in kilometers) each of them walks to get to the library.

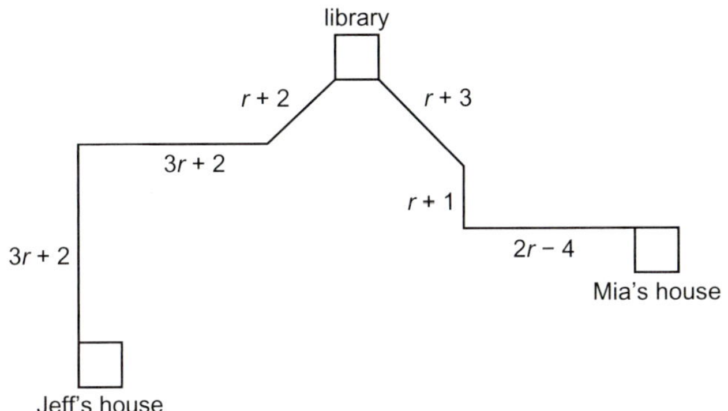

A How far did Mia walk?

Solution

$$\begin{aligned}(2r - 4) + (r + 1) + (r + 3) &= 2r + r + r - 4 + 1 + 3 \\ &= 4r\end{aligned}$$

Mia walked $4r$ kilometers.

B How far did Jeff walk?

Solution

$$\begin{aligned}2(3r + 2) + (r + 2) &= 6r + 4 + r + 2 \\ &= 6r + r + 4 + 2 \\ &= 7r + 6\end{aligned}$$

Jeff walked $(7r + 6)$ kilometers.

C If r is positive, then Jeff walked farther than Mia did. How much farther did he walk?

Solution

$$\begin{aligned}7r + 6 - 4r &= 7r - 4r + 6 \\ &= 3r + 6\end{aligned}$$

Jeff walked $3r + 6$ kilometers farther than Mia.

Problem Set

Solve.

1. Sierra identified $\frac{2}{3}w^2$ and $\frac{1}{2}w$ as like terms from the list shown because each of their coefficients is a proper fraction.

$$\frac{2}{3}w^2, \frac{1}{2}w, 14, 0.7w, -8wy$$

(a) Are the terms $\frac{2}{3}w^2$ and $\frac{1}{2}w$ like terms? Explain.

(b) Are there other like terms in the list? Explain.

2. Vera and her next-door neighbor Mike are putting up a fence around the perimeter of each of their yards. Vera figures that she needs $(2x + 7w - 4)$ feet of fencing and Mike figures he needs $(3w + 8 + 5x)$ feet of fencing. Before going to the store to buy the fencing, they learn that another neighbor, Patty, has $(7x + 10w + 6)$ feet of fencing that she is willing to give them.

(a) How many feet of fencing do both Vera and Mike need? Explain.

(b) Does Patty have enough fencing to fence both of their yards? Explain.

3. In an equilateral triangle, all three side lengths are equal. Suppose you know that the perimeter of equilateral triangle ABC is $(18x - 9)$ meters. Determine which of the given side lengths, if any, represent the side lengths of equilateral triangle ABC. Explain why or why not.

(a) $(6x - 3)$ meters

(b) $(x - 3)$ meters

(c) $3(2x - 1)$ meters

Expressions with Mixed Operations

To simplify an expression that contains negative numbers, fractions, or decimals, use the order of operations.

ORDER OF OPERATIONS

Step 1 Perform operations within grouping symbols.

Step 2 Multiply and divide from left to right.

Step 3 Add and subtract from left to right.

Simplifying Numerical Expressions

EXAMPLE 1 Simplify.

A $5 \cdot 2 - 6(-2)$

Solution

$5 \cdot 2 - 6(-2) = 10 - 6(-2)$	Multiply.
$= 10 - (-12)$	Multiply.
$= 10 + 12$	To subtract −12, add 12.
$= 22$ ■	

B $-5 + 60 \div 5 - 2(-3)$

Solution

$-5 + 60 \div 5 - 2(-3) = -5 + 12 - 2(-3)$	Divide.
$= -5 + 12 - (-6)$	Multiply.
$= -5 + 12 + 6$	To subtract −6, add 6.
$= 7 + 6$	Add from left to right.
$= 13$ ■	

C $-3 - 28 \div (3 + 1)$

Solution

$-3 - 28 \div (3 + 1) = -3 - 28 \div 4$	Add inside the grouping symbols.
$= -3 - 7$	Divide.
$= -10$	Subtract from left to right. ■

D $\dfrac{2 \cdot (7 - 15)}{5 - 10 + 3}$

Solution

$\dfrac{2 \cdot (7 - 15)}{5 - 10 + 3} = \dfrac{2 \cdot (-8)}{5 - 10 + 3}$	In the numerator, subtract inside the parentheses.
$= \dfrac{-16}{-2}$	In the numerator, multiply. In the denominator, subtract then add.
$= 8$	Divide. ■

> **REMEMBER**
>
> A fraction bar represents division. It is also a grouping symbol.

Evaluating Algebraic Expressions

Variables in an algebraic expression can stand for any values. When you need a specific value for the expression, you just need to replace the variables with specific values. To evaluate an algebraic expression, substitute values for the variables and then simplify the resulting numerical expression.

EXAMPLE 2

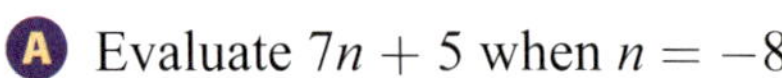

A Evaluate $7n + 5$ when $n = -8$.

Solution

$7n + 5 = 7 \cdot (-8) + 5$	Substitute -8 for n.
$= -56 + 5$	Multiply.
$= -51$	Add. ■

B Evaluate $\frac{c - 5d}{10(2d + 1)}$ when $c = 195$ and $d = -1$.

Solution

$\frac{c - 5d}{10(2d + 1)} = \frac{195 - 5 \cdot (-1)}{10(2 \cdot (-1) + 1)}$ Substitute 195 for c and -1 for d.

$= \frac{195 - (-5)}{10(-2 + 1)}$ Multiply $5 \cdot (-1)$ in the numerator. and $2 \cdot (-1)$ in the denominator.

$= \frac{195 + 5}{10(-1)}$ To subtract -5, add 5 in the numerator. Add $-2 + 1$ in the denominator.

$= \frac{200}{-10}$ Add in the numerator. Multiply in the denominator.

$= -20$ Divide. ■

Simplifying Expressions with Decimals and Fractions

EXAMPLE 3 Simplify.

A $\frac{-2 \cdot 1.5 + 3 \cdot (-2.15)}{0.5}$

Solution

$\frac{-2 \cdot 1.5 + 3 \cdot (-2.15)}{0.5} = \frac{-3.0 + (-6.45)}{0.5}$ Multiply in the numerator.

$= \frac{-9.45}{0.5}$ Add in the numerator.

$= -18.9$ Divide. ■

B $-3 \cdot \frac{2}{5} + \frac{1}{2} \cdot (-6)$

Solution

$-3 \cdot \frac{2}{5} + \frac{1}{2} \cdot (-6) = -\frac{3}{1} \cdot \frac{2}{5} + \left(\frac{1}{2}\right) \cdot \left(-\frac{6}{1}\right)$ Write the integers as fractions.

$= -\frac{6}{5} + (-3)$ Multiply the fractions.

$= -\frac{6}{5} + \left(-\frac{15}{5}\right)$ Write -3 as a fraction with the denominator 5.

$= -\frac{21}{5}$ Add. ■

REMEMBER

You can write an improper fraction as a mixed number.

$-\frac{21}{5} = -4\frac{1}{5}$

Application: Temperature

EXAMPLE 4 The formula to convert a temperature from degrees Celsius to degrees Fahrenheit is $F = \frac{9}{5}C + 32$. What is the Fahrenheit equivalent of $-12°$ Celsius?

Solution Use the formula to convert degrees Celsius to degrees Fahrenheit.

$F = \frac{9}{5}C + 32$	Write the formula.
$= \frac{9}{5} \cdot (-12) + 32$	Substitute -12 for C.
$= \frac{9}{5} \cdot \left(-\frac{12}{1}\right) + 32$	Write -12 as a fraction.
$= -\frac{108}{5} + 32$	Multiply the fractions.
$= -21.6 + 32$	Divide.
$= 10.4$	Add.

$-12°C$ is the Fahrenheit equivalent of $10.4°F$. ■

Problem Set

Simplify.

1. $3 \cdot 5 + 6 \cdot (-1)$
2. $-6 \cdot 5 - 8 \cdot 10$
3. $10 \cdot (-3) - 3 \cdot (-4)$
4. $-6 \cdot (-1) + 6 \cdot 1 - 6 \cdot 2$
5. $-3 + 80 \div 8 - 5 \cdot (-1)$
6. $1 - 6 \cdot 3 + 5 \cdot 2$
7. $12 \div 6 - 10 \cdot 5 - 10 \cdot (-3)$
8. $7 + 2(3 + 7) - 5 \cdot (-3)$
9. $\frac{8}{3 \cdot 4} + 10 \cdot 2$
10. $-5 - (-24) \div 3 + 11$
11. $20 - (-24 - 3) + 16 \div 4$
12. $-1 + 5(100 - 95) + 4 \cdot (-2)$
13. $\frac{(62 - 12) - (4 \cdot 6)}{23 + 5 \cdot (8 - 10)}$
14. $\frac{15 \cdot (12 - 10)}{2 - 3 - 5}$
15. $\frac{2 - 8 \cdot 2 + 20 \div 4}{120 \div 40}$
16. **Challenge** $2 \cdot 12 + 5 \cdot 2 - (1 + 20) + 40 \div (-2)$
17. **Challenge** $\frac{8 - 13}{2 + 3 \cdot (8 - 7)} - 2 + 16 \cdot (14 - 19)$
18. **Challenge** $16 - \frac{18}{9 \cdot 3} \cdot 5$

Evaluate the expression, using the given value(s) of the variable(s).

19. $5a + 10$ when $a = -3$

20. $-2c - 4$ when $c = 5$

21. $22 - 5x - 3x$ when $x = 6$

22. $-6a + a - 3b$ when $a = -5$ and $b = -1$

23. $r \div 3 - 10r + 3(r + 2)$ when $r = 9$

24. $10 + 4(x - 6) - 5(x + 2)$ when $x = 0$

25. $\frac{n}{2} + \frac{6n}{2} + n$ when $n = 10$

26. $\frac{x - 2y}{5(3y + 5)}$ when $x = 1$ and $y = -2$

27. $\frac{-3 \cdot (a - b)}{2 - a + 6}$ when $a = -4$ and $b = -2$

28. $\frac{xy - 2x}{3 + 3(x + y)}$ when $x = 5$ and $y = 4$

29. $\frac{(a - b)(a + b)}{-5 + 3a}$ when $a = 5$ and $b = 7$

30. $\frac{x + 2}{x - 2} \cdot \frac{y + 3}{y - 3}$ when $x = -1$ and $y = 12$

31. **Challenge** $10 - \frac{n}{2} \cdot \frac{n}{4} + n$ when $n = 2.4$

32. **Challenge** $\frac{-4a + b}{a - b} + b$ when $a = 2.5$ and $b = 5$

Simplify.

33. $12 \cdot 1.2 + 3 \cdot (-0.6)$

34. $-4 \cdot \frac{1}{8} + 6 \cdot \frac{2}{3}$

35. $\frac{16.2 - 16}{16}$

36. $\frac{0.25 + 1.75}{40 \cdot 0.2}$

37. $5.6 + 1.05 - 4.4 \div 2$

38. $\frac{1}{4} \cdot \frac{8}{9} + \frac{3}{4} \cdot \frac{4}{9}$

39. $\frac{0.25 \cdot (-4) \cdot (-0.6)}{-6 \cdot 0.02}$

40. **Challenge** $\frac{-6 \cdot 2.5 + 2 \cdot (-1.4)}{0.4}$

Solve. Show your work.

41. The formula to convert degrees Celsius to degrees Fahrenheit is $F = \frac{9}{5}C + 32$. The formula to convert degrees Fahrenheit to degrees Celsius is $C = \frac{5}{9}(F - 32)$.

(a) What is the Fahrenheit equivalent of 5°C?

(b) What is the Celsius equivalent of 5°F?

(c) What is the Celsius equivalent of −40°F?

42. **Challenge** The formula for the area, A, of a trapezoid is $A = \frac{1}{2}(b_1 + b_2)h$, where b_1 and b_2 represent the lengths of the parallel bases and h represents the height. Find the area of the trapezoid.

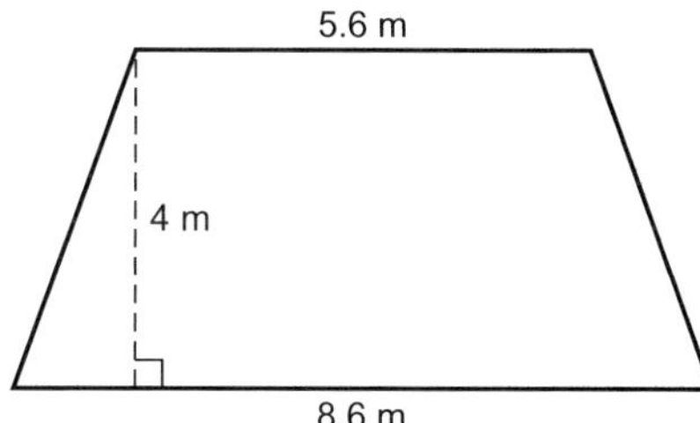

Core Focus: Algebraic Expressions

THE CORE CONCEPT

Follow the order of operations when simplifying an expression containing variables. Treat each variable like any other number.

Order of Operations with Grouping Symbols

Always perform operations within grouping symbols first. Work from the innermost grouping symbols outward.

REMEMBER

Operations are performed from left to right, in the following order:

1. parentheses
2. exponents
3. multiplication/division
4. addition/subtraction

EXAMPLE 1 Lisa and Shari each simplified the expression $-2\,[(-4+5)+0.2\,(-6+8)]$. Which student simplified the expression correctly? Explain.

Lisa

$$\begin{aligned}&-2[(-4+5)+0.2(-6+8)]\\&=-2[1+0.2(2)]\\&=-2(1+0.4)\\&=-2(1.4)\\&=-2.8\end{aligned}$$

Shari

$$\begin{aligned}&-2[(-4+5)+0.2(-6+8)]\\&=-2[1+0.2(-6+8)]\\&=-2[1+(-1.2)+8]\\&=-2(-0.2+8)\\&=-2(7.8)\\&=-15.63\end{aligned}$$

Solution Lisa is correct. When Shari added the -4 and 5 to get 1, she should have also added the -6 and 8 to get 2. The expression $-2[1+0.2(-6+8)]$ simplifies to $-2[1+0.2(-2)]$, not $-2[1+(-1.2)+8]$. ■

Order of Operations in Algebraic Expressions

DEFINITIONS

An **algebraic expression** is an expression containing variables as well as constant values. A **rational expression** is a fraction that includes expressions for the numerator or denominator.

Follow the order of operations when simplifying algebraic expressions. If an algebraic expression is a rational expression, simplify the numerator and the denominator separately, and then divide the numerator by the denominator.

EXAMPLE 2 Shelby and her sister Marlene evenly divide the monthly cost of $88 for their shared cell-phone plan. The only addition to the bill is the $25¢ they are charged for each text message they send during the month.

A Write an expression for each girl's share of the monthly bill when the girls send t text messages during the month

Solution

$$88 + \frac{0.25t}{2}$$ ■

B Last month's bill contained 70 text messages. What was Shelby's portion of the bill? Explain how you use order of operations to solve this problem.

Solution

$$\frac{88 + 0.25t}{2} = \frac{88 + 0.25(70)}{2}$$

The value of the numerator is divided by the denominator, so simplify the numerator first. Perform multiplication before addition, so multiply 0.25 by 70 first, and then add the product to 88. This sum is the value of the numerator, so divide it by 2.

$$\frac{88 + 0.25(70)}{2} = \frac{88 + 17.25}{2}$$
$$= \frac{105.5}{2}$$
$$= 52.75$$

Shelby's portion of the bill is $52.75. ■

REMEMBER

$\frac{5 + 2x}{4}$, $-\frac{1}{3b}$, and $\frac{u + v}{4w}$ are examples of rational expressions.

TIP

Put grouping symbols around any value you substitute for a variable into an algebraic expression.

C This month, the total bill is \$100.50. Describe how you can determine the number of text messages the sisters sent this month.

Solution The total amount of the bill, \$100.50, is equal to the expression $88 + 0.25t$. Subtract the fixed cost of \$88 from both sides.

$$\begin{aligned}100.50 &= 88 + 0.25t\\ 100.50 - 88 &= 88 - 88 + 0.25t\\ 12.50 &= 0.25t\end{aligned}$$

The amount the sisters spent on text messages is \$12.50. Since each text message costs 25¢, divide \$12.50 by 25¢.

$$\begin{aligned}\frac{12.50}{0.25} &= \frac{0.25}{0.25}t\\ 50 &= t\end{aligned}$$

The sisters sent 50 text messages. ■

Q & A

Q What is the minimum amount the sisters will pay each month?

A $88 + 0.25(0) = 88 + 0 = 88$

The minimum amount is \$88 per month.

Problem Set

Solve.

1. Simplify the expression $\frac{-3[4 + 2(-1 + 3)]}{-\frac{1}{3}[0.6 + 2(1.2)]}$. Explain how you used order of operations to simplify.

2. Baseer is charged \$105 per month to ride the train to and from his grandmother's house. Each time he goes, he also has to pay a transfer fee of \$1.20 to ride the bus. To help Baseer with some of his costs, his grandmother shares the cost of these visits equally with Baseer.
   - **(a)** Write an expression for Baseer's share of the monthly cost to visit his grandmother when t transfer fees are paid during the month.
   - **(b)** Last month Baseer paid 5 transfer fees. What was Baseer's share in the cost of visiting his grandmother?
   - **(c)** This month the total cost of Baseer visiting his grandmother was \$113.40. Describe how to determine the number of transfer fees he paid this month.

3. Porsche completed three math exams. Her score on the first exam was 84. She represents her second and third exam scores as x and $x + 8$.
   - **(a)** Porsche writes the expression $\frac{84 + x + (x + 8)}{3}$. What quantity could this expression represent? Explain.
   - **(b)** Find the value of the expression when $x = 89$.
   - **(c)** Solve this equation $\frac{84 + x + (x + 8)}{3} = 86$ for x, and explain what the value of x represents for Porsche's situation.

Equations with Mixed Operations

To solve equations with mixed operations, you need to understand variable terms and indicated operations.

In the equation $5 + 2x = 21$, the variable term is $2x$ and the indicated operations are as follows: The variable is multiplied by 2 and then 5 is added.

In the equation $\frac{t}{3} - 2 = 1$, the variable term is $\frac{t}{3}$ and the indicated operations are as follows: The variable is divided by 3 and then 2 is subtracted.

Solving Simple Equations

To solve an equation, you need to isolate the variable on one side. In $5 + 2x = 21$, subtract 5 from both sides to isolate the terms. The result is $2x = 16$. Similarly, in $\frac{t}{3} - 2 = 1$, add 2 to both sides. The result is then $\frac{t}{3} = 3$.

If an equation has only one variable term and at most one numerical term on each side, use the method described below to isolate the variable. The idea is to peel back the layers one at a time.

SOLVING SIMPLE EQUATIONS IN ONE VARIABLE

Undo indicated operations in reverse order.

EXAMPLE 1 Solve and check.

$$3x - 18 = 39$$

Solution ***Think*:** The variable is multiplied by 3, and then 18 is subtracted. To isolate the variable, add 18 and then divide by 3.

$$3x - 18 = 39$$

$$3x - 18 + 18 = 39 + 18$$ Add 18 to both sides to undo the subtraction.

$$3x = 57$$

$$\frac{3x}{3} = \frac{57}{3}$$ Divide both sides by 3 to undo the multiplication.

$$x = 19$$

TIP

You can show your addition step in this format:

$$\begin{aligned} 3x - 18 &= 39 \\ +18 &\quad +18 \\ 3x \quad &= 57 \end{aligned}$$

Check

$3x - 18 = 39$	Start with the original equation.
$3 \cdot 19 - 18 \stackrel{?}{=} 39$	Substitute 19 for x.
$57 - 18 \stackrel{?}{=} 39$	Multiply.
$39 = 39$ ✓ ■	

EXAMPLE 2 Solve.

A $10 + \frac{a}{2} = 2$

Solution ***Think*:** The variable is divided by 2, and then 10 is added. To isolate the variable, subtract 10 and then multiply by 2.

$10 + \frac{a}{2} = 2$	
$10 - 10 + \frac{a}{2} = 2 - 10$	Subtract 10 from both sides to undo the addition.
$\frac{a}{2} = -8$	
$2 \cdot \frac{a}{2} = 2 \cdot (-8)$	Multiply both sides by 2 to undo the division.
$a = -16$ ■	

B $-6 = \frac{2}{3}c + 1$

Solution ***Think*:** The variable is multiplied by $\frac{2}{3}$, and then 1 is added. To isolate the variable, subtract 1 and then multiply by $\frac{3}{2}$, which is the reciprocal of $\frac{2}{3}$.

$-6 = \frac{2}{3}c + 1$	
$-6 - 1 = \frac{2}{3}c + 1 - 1$	Subtract 1 from both sides to undo the addition.
$-7 = \frac{2}{3}c$	
$\frac{3}{2} \cdot (-7) = \frac{3}{2} \cdot \frac{2}{3}c$	Multiply both sides by $\frac{3}{2}$ to undo the multiplication.
$-\frac{21}{2} = 1 \cdot c$	
$-\frac{21}{2} = c$ ■	

REMEMBER

The solution in Example 1 is 19, not 39.

TIP

In Example 2A, you could start by multiplying by 2, and then you would subtract 20 from each side.

TIP

Check all solutions. Substitute the solution into the original equation and verify that it makes a true statement.

TIP

In Example 2B, you could start by multiplying by $\frac{3}{2}$, and then you would subtract 1 from each side. In general, undoing subtraction or addition first makes the equation neater.

C $\frac{x+1}{3} = -5$

Solution ***Think***: First 1 is added to the variable, and then the result is divided by 3. To isolate the variable, multiply by 3 and then subtract 1.

$$\frac{x+1}{3} = -5$$

$$3 \cdot \frac{x+1}{3} = 3 \cdot (-5)$$ Multiply both sides by 3 to undo the division.

$$x + 1 = -15$$

$$x + 1 - 1 = -15 - 1$$ Subtract 1 from both sides to undo the addition.

$$x = -16$$

THINK ABOUT IT

The equation in Example 2C can be written $\frac{1}{3}(x+1) = -5$. You could solve it the same way as shown here.

Combining Like Terms to Solve Equations

To solve some equations, it helps to simplify expressions by combining like terms. You don't absolutely have to simplify first, but a simpler equation reduces your risk of making mistakes.

EXAMPLE 3 Solve.

A $5x + 5 - 8x - 4 = -29$

Solution

$$5x + 5 - 8x - 4 = -29$$

$$-3x + 1 = -29$$ Combine like terms on the left side.

$$-3x + 1 - 1 = -29 - 1$$ Subtract 1 from both sides to undo the addition.

$$-3x = -30$$

$$\frac{-3x}{-3} = \frac{-30}{-3}$$ Divide both sides by -3 to undo the multiplication.

$$x = 10$$

B $5(n - 2) - n = 14.8$

Solution

$$5(n - 2) - n = 14.8$$

$$5n - 10 - n = 14.8$$ Apply the distributive property to remove parentheses.

$$4n - 10 = 14.8$$ Combine like terms.

$$4n - 10 + 10 = 14.8 + 10$$ Add 10 to both sides to undo the subtraction.

$$4n = 24.8$$

$$\frac{4n}{4} = \frac{24.8}{4}$$ Divide both sides by 4 to undo the multiplication.

$$n = 6.2$$

Solving Equations That Have the Variable on Both Sides

If the variable appears on both sides of the equation, add or subtract a variable term so that the variable appears on only one side.

EXAMPLE 4 Solve.

$$3x + 1 = 5x - 7$$

Solution

$3x + 1 = 5x - 7$

$3x - 3x + 1 = 5x - 3x - 7$ Subtract $3x$ from both sides so that the variable appears on only one side.

$1 = 2x - 7$

$1 + 7 = 2x - 7 + 7$ Add 7 to both sides to undo the subtraction.

$8 = 2x$

$\frac{8}{2} = \frac{2x}{2}$ Divide both sides by 2 to undo the multiplication.

$4 = x$ ■

> **THINK ABOUT IT**
>
> You could begin solving the equation in Example 4 by subtracting $5x$ from both sides, but that would result in a negative coefficient for x. Using positive coefficients helps you avoid mistakes.

Application: Number Problem

EXAMPLE 5 Three more than twice a number is 31. What is the number?

Solution Let n represent the number.

$\underbrace{\text{Three}}_{3}$ $\underbrace{\text{more than}}_{+}$ $\underbrace{\text{twice the number}}_{2n}$ $\underbrace{\text{is 31.}}_{=31}$

$3 + 2n = 31$	Write the equation.
$2n = 28$	Subtract 3 from both sides.
$n = 14$	Divide by 2.

The number is 14. ■

Application: Simple Interest

EXAMPLE 6 Andy deposited some money to open a bank account that paid 8% simple interest. He made no other deposits or withdrawals. At the end of 1 year, the balance was $270. How much did Andy deposit?

Solution Let x represent the amount Andy deposited.

$$\underbrace{\text{amount deposited}} \quad \text{plus} \quad \underbrace{\text{8\% simple interest}} \quad \text{was} \quad \underbrace{\$270}$$

x	$+$	$0.08x$	$=$	270	Write the equation.
$1.00x$	$+$	$0.08x$	$=$	270	Write x as $1.00x$.
		$1.08x$	$=$	270	Combine like terms.
		$\frac{1.08x}{1.08}$	$=$	$\frac{270.00}{1.08}$	Solve the equation.
		x	$=$	250	

Andy deposited $250. ■

Problem Set

Solve and check.

1. $2x - 12 = 14$
2. $5x + 16 = 56$
3. $12.5 + 3x = 20$
4. $18 - 6.3x = 49.5$
5. $-1 + 12x = 29$
6. $10 - 1.4x = 10.84$
7. $-12x + 14 = -34$
8. $-24x - 15 = -27$

Solve.

9. $6 + \frac{x}{3} = 1$
10. $-4 + \frac{a}{5} = 8$
11. $-1 = \frac{x}{9} - 2$
12. $-3 = \frac{3}{4}r + 2$
13. $\frac{2}{9}x - 7 = 9$
14. $6 = \frac{9}{10}a - 1$
15. $\frac{x + 3}{5} = -1$
16. $44 = \frac{n - 6}{2}$
17. $-1 = -\frac{x + 1}{5}$
18. **Challenge** $\frac{3 - x}{9} = \frac{1}{4}$

Collect like terms to solve.

19. $2x + 6 - 7x - 10 = 16$

20. $-x + 11 - 2x - 4x = -24$

21. $0 = 14 - n + 4n - 10$

22. $-15 = 13 - 6c + c + 14.5$

23. $6(x - 1) - 2x = 38$

24. $-9(r - 1) + r = 20$

25. $4(a - 6) - a = 42.3$

26. **Challenge** $4(a - 11) - 7(2a + 1) = -2.28$

Solve.

27. $6b + 27 = -4b - 3$

28. $6x + 2 = 10x - 7$

29. $4(x + 5) = 3(x + 1) - 6$

30. **Challenge** $-2(5 - t) - t = 4(2t + 1) - 6$

31. **Challenge** $s - 0.5(2 - s) - 7.3 = 4.5(2s + 10) - s$

32. **Challenge** $\frac{1}{2}(8 - x) = \frac{1}{5}(x + 10) - x$

Write and solve an equation.
State what your variable represents.

33. Write and solve equations for each word sentence.

(a) Five more than 3 times a number is 38.

(b) Seven less than one-third of a number is 5.

(c) The product of 5 and a number is 18 more than twice the number.

34. At the end of a year, a bank account balance is \$1319.17. The account had earned 6% simple interest during the year, and there had been no deposits or withdrawals. What was the balance at the beginning of the year?

35. Tia paid \$46.28 for a sweater. That amount included a 4% sales tax. What was the price of the sweater?

36. **Challenge** In a week, Ed spent \$12.25 more on entertainment than on all other items combined. During that week, he spent a total of \$34.75. How much did Ed spend on entertainment?

37. **Challenge** There are 4 employees on a building crew: 1 laborer, 2 carpenters who each earn 50% more than the laborer, and 1 supervisor who earns 80% more than the laborer. The total payroll for the crew a week was \$4205. How much did each employee earn that week?

38. **Challenge** The rectangle and triangle have the same perimeter. What is the value of x?

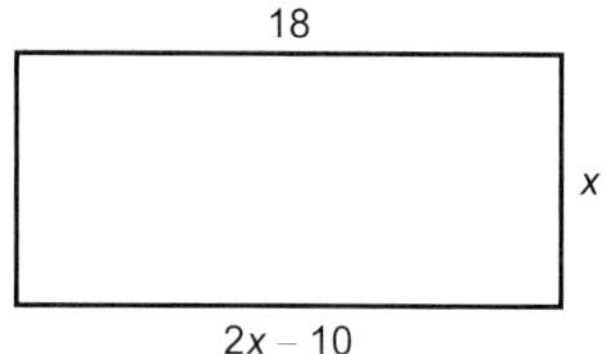

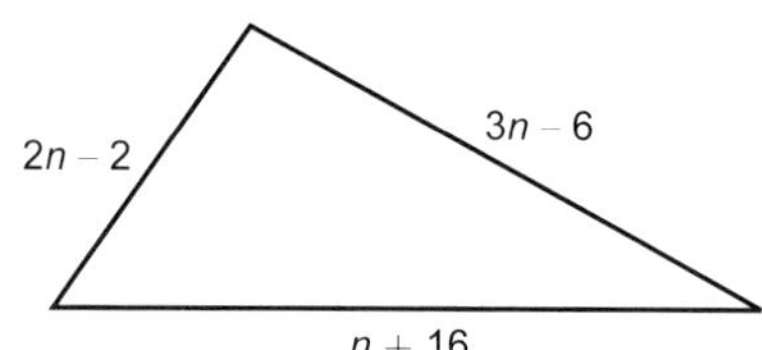

Core Focus: Multistep Equations

THE CORE CONCEPT

Often, you need to perform several steps to solve an equation. With practice, you will develop the ability to solve equations quickly and efficiently.

Solving Multistep Equations Efficiently

Step 1 Simplify both sides of the equation by combining like terms, if needed.

Step 2 Use inverse operations to transform the equation until you have isolated the variable on one side of the equation. When you have isolated the variable, you have solved the equation.

Step 3 Check your answer by substituting the value of the variable into the original equation and simplify to see if you get a true equation.

EXAMPLE 1 Mindy and Phil solved the same problem. Compare Mindy's method of solution to Phil's method of solution. Which method seems simpler? Explain.

Mindy

$$2p - 1 = 15$$
$$\frac{2p - 1}{2} = \frac{15}{2}$$
$$p - \frac{1}{2} = \frac{15}{2}$$
$$p - \frac{1}{2} + \frac{1}{2} = \frac{15}{2} + \frac{1}{2}$$
$$p = \frac{16}{2}$$
$$p = 8$$

Phil

$$2p - 1 = 15$$
$$2p - 1 + 1 = 15 + 1$$
$$2p = 16$$
$$\frac{2p}{2} = \frac{16}{2}$$
$$p = 8$$

Solution Mindy chose to first divide both sides by 2, which created multiple fractions. Phil chose to add 1 to both sides, which did not create fractions. Phil's method is the preferred method because, by not introducing fractions, he was less likely to make a mistake. Using the inverse operations of addition or subtraction first makes the problem easier to solve with less chance of error. ■

THINK ABOUT IT

In some variable equations, it is better to multiply first and then add. Equations with basic rational expressions are a good example.

$$\frac{z + 7}{5} = 2.3$$

NUMBER OF SOLUTIONS TO AN EQUATION

An equation with one variable can have zero, one, or an infinite number of solutions.

EXAMPLE 2 Adele simplified the equation $4x - \frac{2}{3} + 6x = 2\left(5x - \frac{1}{3}\right)$ as shown. What do you observe? What does your observation imply about the solution to the original equation?

$$4x - \frac{2}{3} + 6x = 2\left(5x - \frac{1}{3}\right)$$
$$10x - \frac{2}{3} = 10x - \frac{2}{3}$$

Solution Observe that in the second step the left side of the equation contains the exact same expression as the right side of the equation. This observation implies that the original equation has an infinite number of solutions. Try substituting any number in to confirm this. For example, try $x = -2$.

$$4x - \frac{2}{3} + 6x = 2\left(5x - \frac{1}{3}\right)$$
$$4(-2) - \frac{2}{3} + 6(-2) = 2\left(5(-2) - \frac{1}{3}\right)$$
$$-8 - \frac{2}{3} - 12 = 2\left(-10 - \frac{1}{3}\right)$$
$$-20\frac{2}{3} = 2\left(-10\frac{1}{3}\right)$$
$$-20\frac{2}{3} = -20\frac{2}{3}$$

This is a true statement, so -2 is a solution. ■

EXAMPLE 3 DeShawn solved the equation $3.1x + 7.5 + 0.9x = \frac{1}{2}(8x + 20)$ as shown. What do you observe? What does this imply about the solution to the original equation?

$$3.1x + 7.5 + 0.9x = \frac{1}{2}(8x + 20)$$
$$4x + 7.5 = 4x + 10$$
$$4x - 4x + 7.5 = 4x - 4x + 10$$
$$7.5 = 10$$

Solution Observe that in the last step you obtain a false statement because $7.5 \neq 10$. The original equation does not have a solution. ■

TIP

Any time you simplify an equation and wind up with a false statement, check your work before you conclude that the equation has no solutions.

Problem Set

Solve.

1. Julie solved each of the equations. To solve the first equation, she added first and then multiplied. To solve the second equation, she multiplied first and then added. Why did Julie add and multiply in a different order each time? Explain your thinking.

$$\frac{1}{8}a - \frac{3}{4} = \frac{1}{2}$$

$$\frac{a-5}{9} = \frac{1}{3}$$

2. Emilia simplified the equation $\frac{a-3}{2} = \frac{1}{6}(3a - 9)$ as shown. What do you observe? What does this imply about the solution to the original equation?

$$\frac{a-3}{2} = \frac{1}{6}(3a - 9)$$

$$\frac{a-3}{2} = \frac{3a}{6} - \frac{9}{6}$$

$$\frac{a-3}{2} = \left(\frac{a}{2} - \frac{3}{2}\right)$$

$$\frac{a-3}{2} = \frac{a-3}{2}$$

3. Without actually solving, describe the number of solutions for each equation. Explain your reasoning.

(a) $\frac{2}{3}(x + 6) = \frac{2}{3}x$

(b) $\frac{2}{3}(x + 6) = \frac{2}{3}x + 4$

(c) $\frac{2}{3}(x + 6) = 4$

Inequalities

Working with inequalities is similar to working with equations.

Identifying Solutions of Inequalities

DEFINITIONS

An **inequality** is a mathematical sentence that compares numbers or expressions using one of the symbols $<$, $>$, $\leq$, or $\geq$.

A **solution** of a one-variable inequality is a value for the variable that makes the inequality true.

The set of all solutions of an inequality is the **solution set** of the inequality.

EXAMPLE 1 Identify the solution set of the inequality $x > -3$, using the replacement set $\{-5, -3.5, -3, -2, 0, 1\}$.

Solution Determine which of the numbers are to the right of -3 on a number line.

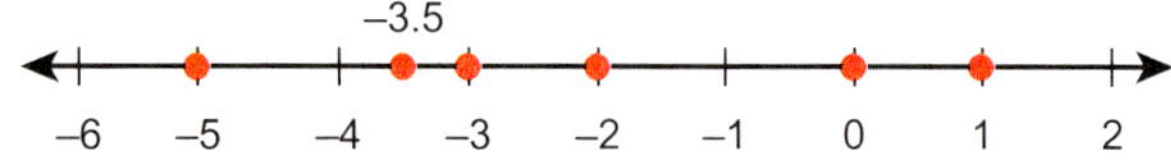

Using the replacement set, only the numbers -2, 0, and 1 are to the right of -3. The solution set is $\{-2, 0, 1\}$. ■

THINK ABOUT IT

These statements are all false:

$-5 > -3$, $-3.5 > -3$, and $-3 > -3$.

These statements are all true:

$-2 > -3$, $0 > -3$, and $1 > -3$.

Graphing Simple Inequalities

Most inequalities that have a solution have an infinite number of solutions.

The **graph of a one-variable inequality** is the set of points on a number line that represents all the solutions of the inequality.

When graphing a one-variable inequality, draw an open dot if the endpoint is not a solution and draw a solid dot if the endpoint is a solution. Draw a shaded arrow on one side of the endpoint to show the solutions. The following table shows some simple one-variable inequalities and their graphs.

Inequality	Words	Graph
$x < 2$	x is less than 2.	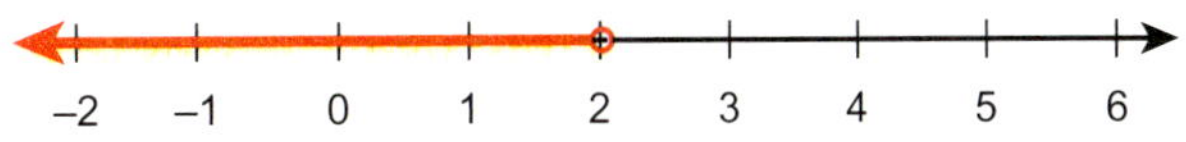
$n > -1$	n is greater than -1.	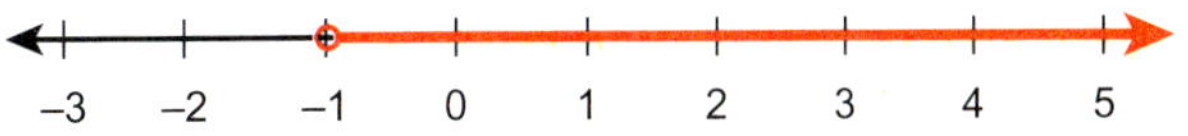
$s \leq 0$	s is less than or equal to 0.	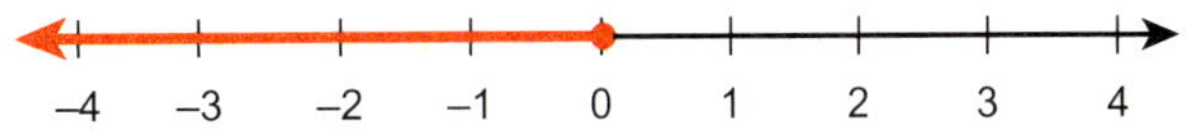
$a \geq 4.35$	a is greater than or equal to 4.35.	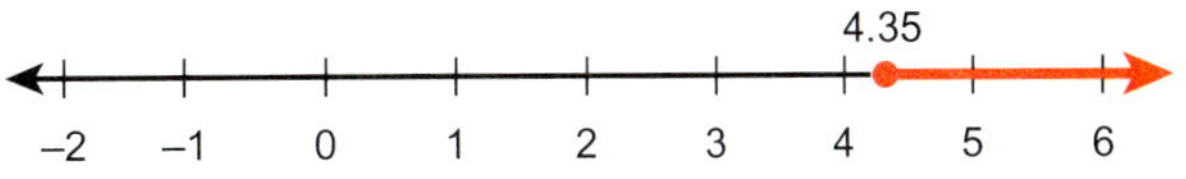

Solving and Graphing Inequalities

Equivalent inequalities are inequalities that have the same solution set. The properties of order tell you how to obtain equivalent inequalities by adding, subtracting, multiplying, and dividing.

PROPERTIES OF ORDER

Property	Symbols	Examples
Addition and Subtraction Properties of Order Adding or subtracting the same number on both sides of an inequality produces an equivalent inequality.	If $a > b$, then $a + c > b + c$. If $a < b$, then $a + c < b + c$. If $a \geq b$, then $a + c \geq b + c$. If $a \leq b$, then $a + c \leq b + c$. If $a > b$, then $a - c > b - c$. If $a < b$, then $a - c < b - c$. If $a \geq b$, then $a - c \geq b - c$. If $a \leq b$, then $a - c \leq b - c$.	If $5 > 2$, then $5 + 6 > 2 + 6$. If $x > 3$, then $x + 4 > 3 + 4$. If $u + 5 \leq 11$, then $u + 5 - 5 \leq 11 - 5$.
Multiplication and Division Properties of Order (Positive Multiplier/Divisor) Multiplying or dividing both sides of an inequality by a positive number produces an equivalent inequality.	For any $c > 0$, If $a > b$, then $a \cdot c > b \cdot c$. If $a < b$, then $a \cdot c < b \cdot c$. If $a \geq b$, then $a \cdot c \geq b \cdot c$. If $a \leq b$, then $a \cdot c \leq b \cdot c$. If $a > b$, then $\frac{a}{c} > \frac{b}{c}$. If $a < b$, then $\frac{a}{c} < \frac{b}{c}$. If $a \geq b$, then $\frac{a}{c} \geq \frac{b}{c}$. If $a \leq b$, then $\frac{a}{c} \leq \frac{b}{c}$.	If $2 < 3$, then $4 \cdot 2 < 4 \cdot 3$. If $2x \geq 6$, then $\frac{2x}{2} \geq \frac{6}{2}$.

continued

PROPERTIES OF ORDER (*continued*)

Property	Symbols	Examples
Multiplication and Division Properties of Order (Negative Multiplier/Divisor) Multiplying or dividing both sides of an inequality by a negative number and reversing the direction of the inequality symbol produces an equivalent inequality.	For any $c < 0$, If $a > b$, then $a \cdot c < b \cdot c$. If $a < b$, then $a \cdot c > b \cdot c$. If $a \geq b$, then $a \cdot c \leq b \cdot c$. If $a \leq b$, then $a \cdot c \geq b \cdot c$. If $a > b$, then $\frac{a}{c} < \frac{b}{c}$. If $a < b$, then $\frac{a}{c} > \frac{b}{c}$. If $a \geq b$, then $\frac{a}{c} \leq \frac{b}{c}$. If $a \leq b$, then $\frac{a}{c} \geq \frac{b}{c}$.	If $\frac{a}{-3} < 5$, then $-3\left(\frac{a}{-3}\right) > -3 \cdot 5$. If $12 > 8$, then $\frac{12}{-4} < \frac{8}{-4}$.

Multiply both sides by −2 and see what happens.

$$5 > 2$$
$$5 \cdot (-2) \overset{?}{>} 2 \cdot (-2)$$
$$-10 < -4$$

THINK ABOUT IT

Note that the inequality symbol changes when you multiply through by a negative number.

The method of solving an inequality is similar to the method of solving an equation. Use inverse operations along with the properties of order to obtain simpler inequalities that are equivalent. When you have the simplest equivalent inequality, you have the statement that best describes the solution set. When you have that statement, graph it.

EXAMPLE 2 Solve and graph the inequality.

 $5x - 10 < 60$

Solution

$5x - 10 < 60$

$5x - 10 + 10 < 60 + 10$ Add 10 to both sides.

$5x < 70$

$\frac{5x}{5} < \frac{70}{5}$ Divide both sides by 5.

$x < 14$

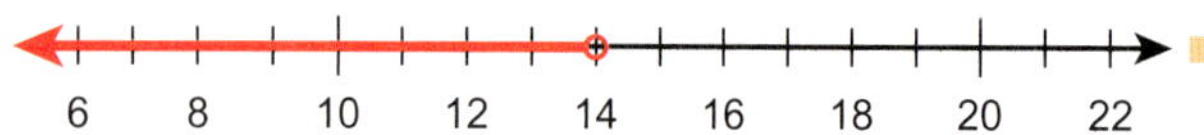

THINK ABOUT IT

The graph represents all the inequalities in Example 2A because they are all equivalent. The simplest inequality, $x < 14$, is the statement that best describes the graph or the solution set.

B $\frac{-t}{3} \geq 2$

Solution

$$\frac{-t}{3} \geq 2$$

$-3 \cdot \left(\frac{-t}{3}\right) \leq -3 \cdot 2$ Multiply both sides by -3. Reverse the inequality symbol.

$$t \leq -6$$

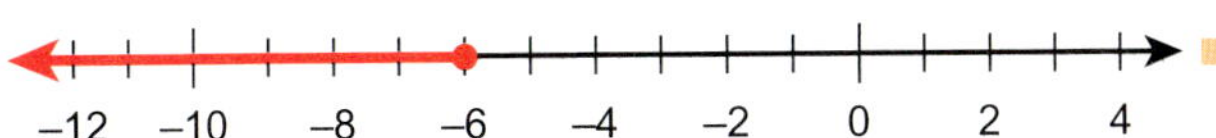

C $2(a + 2) - a > 0$

Solution

$2(a + 2) - a > 0$

$2a + 4 - a > 0$ Apply the distributive property.

$a + 4 > 0$ Combine like terms.

$a + 4 - 4 > 0 - 4$ Subtract 4 from both sides.

$a > -4$

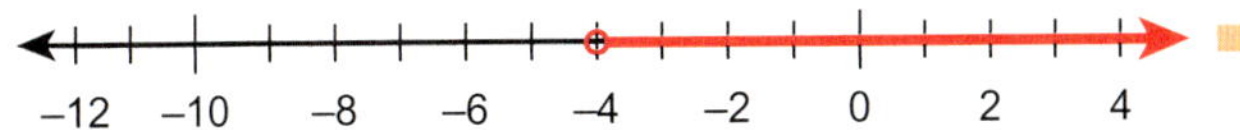

D $3 > -\frac{5x + 1}{2}$

Solution

$$3 > -\frac{5x + 1}{2}$$

$3 > -\frac{1}{2}(5x + 1)$ Write $-\frac{5x + 1}{2}$ as $-\frac{1}{2}(5x + 1)$.

$-2 \cdot 3 < -2 \cdot \left(-\frac{1}{2}\right)(5x + 1)$ Multiply both sides by -2. Reverse the inequality symbol.

$-6 < 5x + 1$

$-6 - 1 < 5x + 1 - 1$ Subtract 1 from both sides.

$-7 < 5x$

$\frac{-7}{5} < \frac{5x}{5}$ Divide both sides by 5.

$-\frac{7}{5} < x$

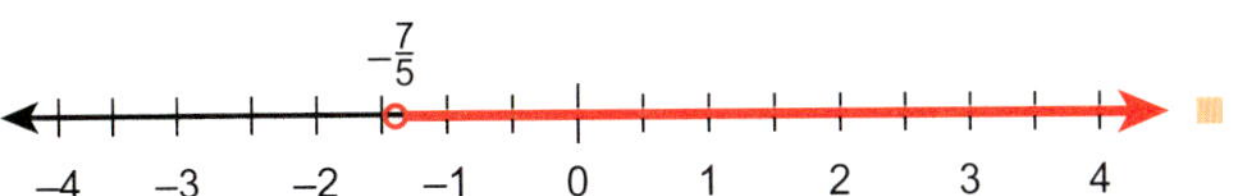

▶ REMEMBER

When graphing, draw an open dot for the symbols $<$ and $>$. Draw a solid dot for the symbols $\leq$ and $\geq$.

▶ REMEMBER

In general, $a < b$ is equivalent to $b > a$. In Example 2D, $-\frac{7}{5} < x$ is equivalent to $x > -\frac{7}{5}$.

Application: Comparing Membership Fees

EXAMPLE 3 Eli is deciding whether to join Gym A or Gym B. Gym A costs \$50 to join and \$31.50 per month. Gym B costs \$170 to join and \$24 per month. For what length of time will it cost less to belong to Gym A?

Solution Let x represent the number of months Eli has a gym membership.

cost of Gym A < cost of Gym B

$50 + 31.50x < 170 + 24x$ — Write an inequality to represent the situation.

$50 + 31.50x - 24x < 170 + 24x - 24x$ — Subtract $24x$ from both sides so that the variable appears on only one side.

$50 + 7.50x < 170$

$50 - 50 + 7.50x < 170 - 50$ — Subtract 50 from both sides.

$7.50x < 120$

$\frac{7.50x}{7.50} < \frac{120}{7.50}$ — Divide both sides by 7.50.

$x < 16$

It will cost less to belong to Gym A for any number of months less than 16 months. ■

Problem Set

Identify the solution set of the inequality, using the given replacement set.

1. $x > -5$; $\{-8, -5.01, -5, -4.8, 0, 4\}$
2. $x < -1$; $\{-2, -1.6, -1, 0, 0.5\}$
3. $x \geq 4$; $\{-4, -3, 0, 3.8, 4, 4.2, 5\}$
4. $x \leq -3.5$; $\{-3.55, -3.5, -3.4, -3, 0, 1, 5\}$
5. $x > -1$; $\left\{-4, -1.5, -1\frac{1}{4}, -\frac{3}{5}, 0, \frac{1}{10}\right\}$
6. **Challenge** $x < -3.2$; $\left\{-4, -3\frac{1}{4}; -3.21, -3\frac{3}{20}, -3\frac{1}{8}, -3, 0\right\}$

Solve and graph the inequality.

7. $4x - 15 < 17$
8. $\frac{b}{2} \leq 4$
9. $-8 < 2x + 4$
10. $7x + 9 \geq 2$
11. $-\frac{v}{6} \geq -2$
12. $-5x - 25 > 30$
13. $1 - x \leq -6$
14. $6 - 3r - 25 > r + 1$
15. $\frac{x}{4} - 5 < -1$
16. $1 - \frac{t}{2} < -1$
17. $3(d + 5) > 30$
18. $2(x + 3) - 1 > 3$
19. $1 < \frac{4k + 3}{2}$
20. $-\frac{x + 3}{2} \leq -9$

21. $1 < -\frac{x-1}{5}$

22. $x - 3(x + 1) - 7 > -x$

23. **Challenge** $4(a - 4) - 5(2a + 3) > 1 + a$

24. **Challenge** $\frac{1}{2}(w + 6) - 1 < \frac{1}{3}w$

25. **Challenge** $-10 < 3 + \frac{2x - 7}{2}$

26. **Challenge** $r - 5 > 3 - \frac{4r - 1}{3}$

Write and solve an inequality.
State what your variable represents.

27. Carlos wants to send a gift basket to his grandmother. Deliver Quick charges \$4.15 plus 85¢/lb. Ship Fast charges \$2.75 plus \$1.05/lb.

    (a) For what weights will it cost less to use Ship Fast than Deliver Quick?

    (b) For what weight do the two companies charge the same amount? What is that charge?

28. Kathleen is a sales associate in a jewelry store. She earns \$560/wk plus an 8% commission on sales. How much does she need to sell in a week to earn at least \$700 that week?

29. The cost to ride a Sedan Service taxicab is \$2.90 plus \$1.80/mi. The cost to ride a Green taxicab is \$2.15 plus \$1.95/mi.

    (a) For what distances does it cost less to ride a Green taxicab than a Sedan Service taxicab?

    (b) For what distance is the cost the same? What is that cost?

30. **Challenge** The Golden Rectangle has been used in art and architecture since ancient times. It is a rectangle whose length is approximately 1.618 times its width. An artist has 1000 cm of framing material. He wants to frame a painting in the shape of a Golden Rectangle. Describe the dimensions he can use for the painting. Round dimensions to the nearest centimeter.

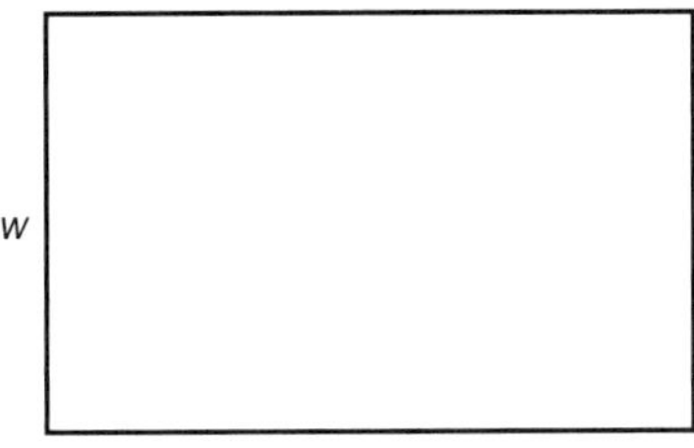

Core Focus: Applications of Inequalities

THE CORE CONCEPT

Many real-world situations involve a quantity that has a minimum or maximum possible value. An inequality can represent a quantity that is at least or no more than some value.

Representing Inequalities

Translate a problem statement into an inequality by translating words and phrases into variables, operators ($+$, $-$, $\times$, $\div$), and inequality symbols ($<$, $\leq$, $>$, $\geq$), just as you would for any problem involving an equation.

EXAMPLE 1 Adele is swimming laps at swim practice. To prevent injury, Adele's coach tells her to swim no more than 2400 m that day. Each lap is 50 m. Adele has swum 600 m so far.

A Write an inequality that expresses how many more laps Adele can swim at practice. Explain your reasoning.

Solution Let n represent the number of laps Adele can swim without exceeding her coach's recommendation. This distance, in meters, is the product of the number of laps and the length of 1 lap, equal to $50n$.

The sum of the distance Adele has already swum, 600 m, and the remaining distance she can swim, $50n$ meters, can be no more than 2400 m. Written as an inequality, this is

$$600 + 50n \leq 2400.$$

B Solve the inequality in Example 1A.

Solution

$$600 + 50n \leq 2400$$

$$600 - 600 + 50n \leq 2400 - 600$$

$$50n \leq 1800$$

$$\frac{50n}{50} \leq \frac{1800}{50}$$

$$n \leq 36$$

Adele can swim no more than 36 more laps.

REMEMBER

A lap in a swimming pool is down the length of the pool and back. If a pool is 25 m long, one lap is

$2 \times 25\text{ m} = 50\text{ m}.$

TIP

Certain phrases suggest representing a real-world situation as an inequality with a $\leq$ sign:

- *at most*
- *maximum*
- *no more than*

EXAMPLE 2 Ibrahim wants to buy a new pair of basketball shoes. He has \$55 right now. New basketball shoes cost \$133 or more. Ibrahim earns \$12/h tutoring.

A Write an inequality that expresses the minimum number of hours Ibrahim needs to work to earn enough money to buy new basketball shoes. Explain your reasoning.

Solution Let h represent the number of hours Ibrahim must work to earn enough additional money. This amount, in dollars, is the product of his hourly wage and the number of hours he works at this rate, or $12h$.

The sum of the amount of money Ibrahim already has, \$55, and the amount of money he still needs, $12h$ dollars, must be at least \$133. Written as an inequality, this is

$$55 + 12h \geq 133.$$ ■

TIP

Certain phrases suggest representing a real-world situation as an inequality with a $\geq$ sign:

- *at least*
- *minimum*
- *no less than*

B Solve the inequality in Example 2A.

Solution

$$55 + 12h \geq 133$$

$$55 - 55 + 12h \geq 133 - 55$$

$$12h \geq 78$$

$$\frac{12h}{12} \geq \frac{78}{12}$$

$$h \geq 6\frac{1}{2} \text{ or } h \geq 6.5$$

Ibrahim needs to work at least another 6.5 h to have enough money for new basketball shoes. ■

Problem Set

Solve.

1. Leanna washes dogs to raise money for a local animal shelter. She has already raised \$48. Her goal is to raise at least \$250. She charges \$12 to wash a dog.

(a) Write an inequality to represent how many more dogs Leanna must wash to reach her goal.

(b) Solve the inequality in Part (a).

(c) Does it make sense for the minimum number of dogs Leanna needs to wash to be a decimal? Explain your thinking.

2. Joe is loading a duffel bag with baseballs. He has loaded 24 baseballs into the bag. Each baseball has a mass of 0.15 kg. Joe believes that he can carry at most 12 kg of baseballs in the duffel bag.

(a) Joe wrote the inequality $0.15(24 + b) \leq 12$ to represent how many more kilograms, b, of baseballs he can load into the duffel bag. Explain why Joe's inequality is correct.

(b) Use the distributive property to simplify the inequality and then solve it.

(c) Graph the solution to the inequality on a number line.

3. Write a real-world problem that could represent each inequality. Solve the problem and graph the solution on a number line.

(a) $35 + 12n \geq 265$

(b) $62 + 25p \leq 138$

(c) $5 + \frac{1}{2}d \leq 8$

CHAPTER 6 Review

Choose the answer.

1. Which expression is equivalent to $-7(y - 12)$?

   A. $-7y - 12$
   B. $7y + 12$
   C. $7y - 84$
   D. $-7y + 84$

2. What is the solution to the equation?

   $$7 \cdot z + 7 \cdot 9 = 7(10 + 9)$$

   A. 7
   C. 10
   B. 9
   D. 19

3. Which term is like $12ab$?

   A. 12
   C. $6b$
   B. $2a$
   D. $9ab$

4. Which expression is equivalent to the expression simplified?

   $$uv - v + 7uv - 4v + 9 - 2uv$$

   A. $-8uv - 5v + 9$
   B. $6uv - 5v + 9$
   C. $6uv - 3v + 9$
   D. $uv + 9$

5. What is the value of the expression?

   $$12 - 5 \cdot 4 + 7 \cdot 2$$

   A. 6
   C. 70
   B. 42
   D. 154

6. What is the value of the expression when $x = 3$ and $y = 1$?

   $$\frac{4 \cdot (x - y)}{2 - x + 6}$$

   A. $-\frac{11}{7}$
   B. $-\frac{8}{7}$
   C. $\frac{8}{5}$
   D. $\frac{11}{5}$

7. What is the solution to the equation?

   $$-6x + 3 = -27$$

   A. $x = -5$
   B. $x = -4$
   C. $x = 4$
   D. $x = 5$

8. What is the solution to the equation?

   $$7 - \frac{h}{4} = 5$$

   A. $h = -48$
   B. $h = -3$
   C. $h = \frac{1}{2}$
   D. $h = 8$

9. Which elements of the replacement set $\{-7.5, -5.2, -1.6, 0, 3.7, 4.8\}$ are solutions to the inequality?

   $$q \geq -4$$

   A. $\{-7.5, -5.2\}$
   B. $\{-7.5, -5.2, 4.8\}$
   C. $\{-1.6, 0, 3.7, 4.8\}$
   D. $\{4.8\}$

10. What is the solution to the inequality?

    $$2(w - 5) < -8$$

    A. $w < -21$
    B. $w < -16$
    C. $w < 1$
    D. $w < -11$

Solve.

11. Use the distributive property to evaluate the expression.

$$9 \cdot 99 + 9 \cdot 101$$

12. Write and simplify an expression for the total perimeter of each figure described. Show how you combine like terms to obtain your simplified expression.

(a) a rectangle with length $2x$ and width $x - 3$

(b) an isosceles triangle with 2 sides with length $3a - 1$ and a third side with length $2a + 4$

13. The perimeter of a rectangle is $6z - 14$. Which of the following could represent the length and width of the rectangle?

A. length $= 4z - 5$, width $= 2z - 9$

B. length $= 2z + 3$, width $= z - 10$

C. length $= z - 6$, width $= 2z - 1$

14. Evaluate the expression for the values given.

$$\frac{(u - 2v)(u + v)}{4u - v}$$

(a) $u = -1, v = -5$

(b) $u = 2, v = 6$

15. Simplify the expression. Explain how you used the order of operations to simplify.

$$\frac{-2\,[6(4 - 3.6) + 0.9]}{\frac{1}{4}[7.8 + 2(2.1)]}$$

16. Kendra earned \$275 for selling a house plus a commission of 3% of the sale price of the house. She earned a total of \$7775. What was the sales price of the house?

17. Describe the solution to each of the equations. Explain your thinking.

(a) $6k - 30 = 4(k - 5)$

(b) $\frac{2p + 14}{2} = p - 5$

(c) $d + 3 = \frac{d - 2}{4}$

18. Ye-jun is loading fruit into a cargo van. He has already loaded 44 kg of apples. Ye-jun then wants to load as many crates of oranges into the van as he can. Each crate of oranges has a mass of 12 kg. The maximum amount the van can hold is 300 kg.

(a) Ye-jun wrote the inequality $44 + 12n \geq 300$ to represent the maximum number, n, of crates of oranges he can load. Explain why the inequality incorrectly represents the situation.

(b) Write an inequality to correctly represent this situation.

(c) Solve this inequality for n and graph the solution on a number line.

Problem	Topic Lookup
1, 2, 11	The Distributive Property
3, 4, 12	Like Terms
13	Core Focus: Variable Expressions
5, 6, 14	Expressions with Mixed Operations
15	Core Focus: Algebraic Expressions

Problem	Topic Lookup
7, 8, 16	Equations with Mixed Operations
17	Core Focus: Multistep Equations
9, 10	Inequalities
18	Core Focus: Applications of Inequalities

CHAPTER 7 Ratio, Proportion, and Percent

Automobile and aircraft engines mix air and fuel so they can have the perfect combustible mixture. Each mixture can be described with a ratio that represents the mix of fuel and air it contains. Using the correct ratio to get the mix right is important for an engine's performance and efficiency.

In This Chapter

In this chapter, you will work with ratios and proportions. You'll learn to calculate and convert ratios. You'll also solve proportions and use ratios, proportions, and percents to solve real-world problems.

Topic List

Automobile engines use a ratio of fuel and air to create the perfect explosive mix.

MADE IN JAPAN

Foundations for Chapter 7

Simplifying Fractions

To simplify a fraction, divide both the numerator and the denominator by the same factor.

EXAMPLE A Simplify. Leave improper fractions in improper form.

 $\frac{12}{20}$

Divide both the numerator and the denominator by the greatest common factor, which is 4.

Solution

$$\frac{12}{20} = \frac{12 \div 4}{20 \div 4} = \frac{3}{5}$$

In simplest form $\frac{12}{20}$ is $\frac{3}{5}$. ■

 $\frac{84}{48}$

Divide both the numerator and the denominator by the greatest common factor, which is 12.

Solution

$$\frac{84}{48} = \frac{84 \div 12}{48 \div 12} = \frac{7}{4}$$

In simplest form $\frac{84}{48}$ is $\frac{7}{4}$. ■

Problem Set A

Simplify. Leave improper fractions in improper form.

1. $\frac{6}{10}$
2. $\frac{12}{14}$
3. $\frac{25}{35}$
4. $\frac{14}{6}$
5. $\frac{90}{60}$
6. $\frac{28}{21}$
7. $\frac{45}{63}$
8. $\frac{42}{18}$
9. $\frac{55}{100}$
10. $\frac{13}{65}$
11. $\frac{70}{14}$
12. $\frac{200}{80}$

Converting Between Fractions and Decimals

To convert a fraction to a decimal, divide the numerator by the denominator.

To convert a decimal to a fraction with integer numerator and denominator, write the decimal as a fraction with a denominator of 1. Multiply both the numerator and the denominator by a power of 10 that changes the decimal to an integer. Simplify.

EXAMPLE B Solve.

B-1 Write $\frac{5}{8}$ as a decimal.

Solution

$$\begin{array}{r} 0.625 \\ 8\overline{)5.0} \\ \underline{4\,8} \\ 20 \\ \underline{16} \\ 40 \\ \underline{40} \\ 0 \end{array}$$

Divide 5 by 8 using long division.

So $\frac{5}{8}$ is equivalent to 0.625. ■

B-2 Write 3.15 as a fraction in simplest form.

Solution There are two digits after the decimal point, so multiply the numerator and the denominator by $10^2 = 100$.

$$\frac{3.15}{1} = \frac{3.15 \bullet 100}{1 \bullet 100} = \frac{315}{100}$$

Divide the numerator and denominator by the greatest common factor to simplify.

$$\frac{315}{100} = \frac{315 \div 5}{100 \div 5} = \frac{63}{20}$$

So 3.15 is equivalent to $\frac{63}{20}$. ■

Problem Set B

Write the fraction as a decimal.

1. $\frac{2}{5}$
2. $\frac{7}{20}$
3. $\frac{21}{6}$
4. $\frac{18}{8}$
5. $\frac{5}{6}$
6. $\frac{17}{9}$

Write the decimal as a fraction in simplest form.

7. 0.2
8. 0.35
9. 2.7
10. 0.76
11. 10.8
12. 1.12

Multiplying and Dividing Fractions

Multiply two fractions by first multiplying the two numerators to get the numerator of the product. Next multiply the two denominators to get the denominator of the product. Simplify.

Divide two fractions by first flipping the divisor and then multiplying the two fractions. Simplify.

EXAMPLE C Multiply or divide.

 $\frac{5}{6} \bullet \frac{3}{4}$

Solution

$\frac{5}{6} \bullet \frac{3}{4} = \frac{15}{24}$ Multiply.

$= \frac{15 \div 3}{24 \div 3} = \frac{5}{8}$ Simplify. ■

C-2 $\frac{7}{12} \div \frac{3}{4}$

Solution

$\frac{7}{12} \div \frac{3}{4} = \frac{7}{12} \bullet \frac{4}{3}$

$= \frac{28}{36}$ Flip the divisor, then multiply.

$= \frac{28 \div 4}{36 \div 4} = \frac{7}{9}$ Simplify. ■

Problem Set C

Multiply or divide.

1. $\frac{1}{2} \bullet \frac{5}{7}$

2. $\frac{1}{3} \bullet \frac{3}{11}$

3. $\frac{5}{4} \bullet \frac{3}{20}$

4. $\frac{1}{5} \div \frac{1}{3}$

5. $\frac{1}{6} \div \frac{2}{3}$

6. $\frac{1}{35} \bullet \frac{10}{7}$

7. $\frac{3}{16} \div \frac{1}{8}$

8. $\frac{9}{5} \div \frac{1}{10}$

9. $\frac{3}{2} \bullet \frac{14}{9}$

10. $\frac{6}{7} \div 8$

11. $\frac{3}{10} \bullet \frac{8}{21}$

12. $\frac{9}{11} \div \frac{3}{22}$

Ratios

A ratio shows how one quantity compares in value to another, related quantity.

Writing Ratios

DEFINITION

A **ratio** is a comparison of two quantities by division.

A ratio can be written as a fraction, with a colon, or with the word *to*.

$\frac{2}{3}$ $\quad$ 2 : 3 $\quad$ 2 to 3

TIP

All these ratios are read as "2 to 3."

Simplifying Ratios

To write a ratio in simplest form, write it as a fraction in simplest form.

EXAMPLE 1 Simplify the ratio. Write your answer in all three forms.

 $\frac{8}{10}$

Solution Simplify the fraction.

$\frac{8 \div 2}{10 \div 2} = \frac{4}{5}$ $\quad$ Divide the numerator and the denominator by the greatest common factor.

$\frac{4}{5}$ or 4 : 5 or 4 to 5 ■

B 28 to 4

Solution Write the ratio as a fraction, and then simplify it.

$$\frac{28}{4} = \frac{28 \div 4}{4 \div 4} = \frac{7}{1}$$

$\frac{7}{1}$ or 7 : 1 or 7 to 1 ■

C 63 to 27

Solution Write the ratio as a fraction, and then simplify it.

$\frac{63}{27} = \frac{63 \div 9}{27 \div 9} = \frac{7}{3}$ $\quad$ Don't write a ratio as a mixed number. Write the improper fraction $\frac{7}{3}$.

$\frac{7}{3}$ or 7 : 3 or 7 to 3 ■

Comparing Parts and Wholes

You can use a ratio to compare a part to a part, a part to a whole, or a whole to a part.

EXAMPLE 2 A jar contains 21 marbles: 8 white, 3 green, and 10 red. Write the described ratio in simplest form.

A number of white marbles to number of green marbles

Solution There are 8 white marbles and 3 green marbles.

The ratio is $\frac{8}{3}$ or 8 : 3 or 8 to 3. ■

B number of green marbles to total number of marbles

Solution There are 3 green marbles and 21 marbles in all.

Since $\frac{3}{21} = \frac{1}{7}$, the ratio is $\frac{1}{7}$ or 1 : 7 or 1 to 7. ■

C total number of marbles to number of white marbles

Solution There are 21 marbles in all and 8 white marbles.

The ratio is $\frac{21}{8}$ or 21 : 8 or 21 to 8. ■

TIP

Example 2A compares a part to a part. Example 2B compares a part to a whole. Example 2C compares a whole to a part.

EXAMPLE 3 The table shows the number of sandwiches sold at a lunch truck on 1 day. Write each ratio in simplest form.

Sandwich	Number sold
veggie sub	13
hamburger	8
hot dog	15

A number of veggie subs sold to hamburgers sold

Solution There were 13 veggie subs and 8 hamburgers sold.

The ratio is $\frac{13}{8}$ or 13 : 8 or 13 to 8. ■

B number of hot dogs sold to total number of sandwiches sold

Solution There were 15 hot dogs sold. The total number of sandwiches sold was $13 + 8 + 15 = 36$.

The ratio is $\frac{15}{36} = \frac{5}{12}$ or 5 : 12 or 5 to 12. ■

C total number of sandwiches sold to hamburgers sold

Solution There were 8 hamburgers sold. The total number of sandwiches sold was $13 + 8 + 15 = 36$.

The ratio is $\frac{36}{8} = \frac{9}{2}$ or 9 : 2 or 9 to 2. ■

REMEMBER

Sometimes you will need to find the sum of all items in order to find a part-to-a-whole ratio or a whole-to-a-part ratio.

Application: Win-Loss Ratio

EXAMPLE 4 A softball team wins 12 of its 22 games and loses the rest. What is the ratio of wins to losses in simplest form?

Solution Since $22 - 12 = 10$, the team loses 10 games.

$$\frac{\text{number of wins}}{\text{number of losses}} = \frac{12}{10}$$

$$= \frac{12 \div 2}{10 \div 2} = \frac{6}{5}$$ Divide by the greatest common factor to simplify the fraction.

The ratio of wins to losses is $\frac{6}{5}$ or 6 : 5 or 6 to 5.

REMEMBER

A ratio is not usually written as a mixed number or a decimal, but a ratio can contain a mixed number or a decimal.

Problem Set

Simplify the ratio. Write your answer in all three forms.

1. $\frac{10}{12}$
2. 8 to 64
3. 20 : 30
4. $\frac{18}{9}$
5. 16 to 56
6. 32 : 72
7. $\frac{18}{54}$
8. 35 to 14
9. 30 : 42
10. $\frac{48}{16}$
11. 35 to 7
12. 88 : 11
13. $\frac{64}{24}$
14. 14 to 21
15. 30 : 18
16. $\frac{50}{140}$

An aquarium has a total of 24 freshwater creatures in it: 9 angelfish, 6 koi, 4 snails, 3 mini crabs, and 2 frogs. Write a simplified ratio in all three forms for the situation.

17. number of mini crabs to number of angelfish
18. number of koi to number of frogs
19. number of snails to number of all creatures
20. number of all creatures to number of snails
21. number of mini crabs to number of fish (angelfish and koi)

The table shows the number of students in each school club. Write a simplified ratio in all three forms for the situation.

Club	Students
drama	20
chess	10
environmental	12
music	18

22. number of students in drama club to number of students in chess club

23. number of students in music club to number of students in drama club

24. number of students in environmental club to number of students in drama and chess clubs combined

25. number of students in chess club to number of students in all clubs combined

The bar graph shows the points scored and the number of rebounds for three players in a basketball game. Write a simplified ratio as a fraction for the situation.

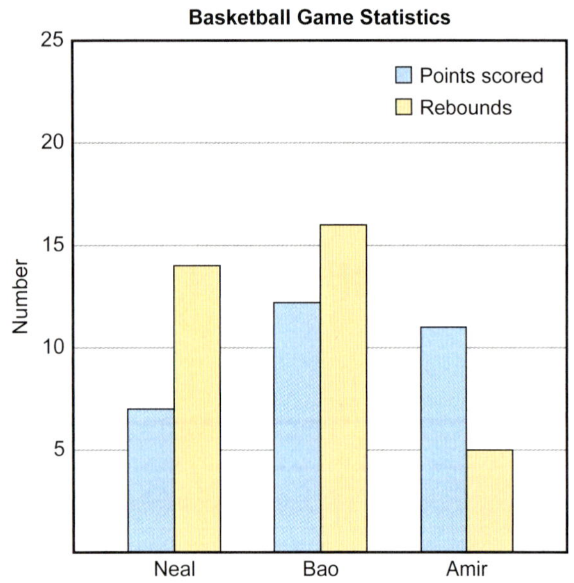

26. Neal's points scored to his number of rebounds

27. Bao's number of rebounds to Neal's number of rebounds

28. Amir's points scored to total points scored by all three players

29. total number of rebounds by all three players to Bao's number of rebounds

30. **Challenge** total points scored by all three players to total number of rebounds by all three players

Rates

A rate indicates how two related quantities, measured in different units, compare in value.

Writing Rates

DEFINITION

A **rate** is a ratio of quantities that have different units.

To write a rate, write a fraction with the first quantity as the numerator and the second quantity as the denominator. Keep the units with each quantity as you write it.

EXAMPLE 1 Write a rate to represent the situation.

A It costs \$3 for a 5 min phone call.

Solution $\frac{\$3}{5 \text{ min}}$ ■

B A car travels 85 mi on 4 gal of gasoline.

Solution $\frac{85 \text{ mi}}{4 \text{ gal}}$ ■

TIP

It is also correct, in some contexts, to use the reciprocal as the ratio as well. You could write the ratio $\frac{4 \text{ gal}}{85 \text{ mi}}$ for Example 1B.

C Three T-shirts cost \$17.50.

Solution $\frac{\$17.50}{3 \text{ shirts}}$ ■

D Two cups of flour are needed to make 14 pancakes.

Solution $\frac{2 \text{ cups}}{14 \text{ pancakes}}$ ■

Finding Unit Rates

DEFINITION

A **unit rate** is a rate in which the second quantity is 1.

To find a unit rate,

Step 1 Separate the units from the number part of the fraction.

Step 2 Simplify the number part of the fraction.

EXAMPLE 2 Write a unit rate for the situation.

A Mr. Beck drives 120 mi in 3 h.

Solution Write a ratio. Divide the numerator and the denominator by 3.

$\frac{120}{3} \cdot \frac{\text{miles}}{\text{hours}} = \frac{120 \div 3}{3 \div 3} \cdot \frac{\text{miles}}{\text{hours}} = \frac{40}{1} \cdot \frac{\text{miles}}{\text{hour}}$, or 40 mph ■

> **THINK ABOUT IT**
> The abbreviation mph means miles per hour.

B There are 36 servings in 4 bags.

Solution Write a ratio. Divide the numerator and the denominator by 4.

$\frac{36}{4} \cdot \frac{\text{servings}}{\text{bags}} = \frac{36 \div 4}{4 \div 4} \cdot \frac{\text{servings}}{\text{bags}} = \frac{9}{1} \cdot \frac{\text{servings}}{\text{bag}}$, or 9 servings/bag ■

C Ella types 474 words in 6 min.

Solution Write a ratio. Divide the numerator and the denominator by 6.

$\frac{474}{6} \cdot \frac{\text{words}}{\text{minutes}} = \frac{474 \div 6}{6 \div 6} \cdot \frac{\text{words}}{\text{minutes}} = \frac{79}{1} \cdot \frac{\text{words}}{\text{minute}}$, or

79 words/min ■

D Sana earns $104 in 8 h.

Solution Write a ratio. Divide the numerator and the denominator by 8.

$\frac{104}{8} \cdot \frac{\text{dollars}}{\text{hours}} = \frac{104 \div 8}{8 \div 8} \cdot \frac{\text{dollars}}{\text{hours}} = \frac{13}{1} \cdot \frac{\text{dollars}}{\text{hour}}$, or

$13/hour ■

Application: Fuel Economy

EXAMPLE 3 A car travels 255 mi and uses 8.5 gal of gasoline. Write the unit rate that describes the car's fuel economy.

Solution Write a rate, and then convert it to a unit rate.

$\frac{255}{8.5} \cdot \frac{\text{miles}}{\text{gallons}} = \frac{255 \div 8.5}{8.5 \div 8.5} \cdot \frac{\text{miles}}{\text{gallons}} = \frac{30}{1} \cdot \frac{\text{miles}}{\text{gallon}}$

The car's fuel economy is described by the unit rate 30 mpg. ■

> **THINK ABOUT IT**
> The abbreviation mpg means miles per gallon.

Application: Ticket Sales

EXAMPLE 4 The table shows the number of tickets sold at a movie theater and the total sales for each ticket type. Find the unit rate that describes each ticket price.

Ticket type	Number sold	Total sales ($)
adult	12	108.00
senior	15	90.00
youth	7	24.50

Solution Write a rate for each ticket price, and then simplify the rate to find the unit rate representing the ticket price.

adult: $\frac{108}{12} \cdot \frac{\text{dollars}}{\text{tickets}} = \frac{108 \div 12}{12 \div 12} \cdot \frac{\text{dollars}}{\text{tickets}} = \frac{9}{1} \cdot \frac{\text{dollars}}{\text{ticket}}$, or \$9/ticket

senior: $\frac{90}{15} \cdot \frac{\text{dollars}}{\text{tickets}} = \frac{90 \div 15}{15 \div 15} \cdot \frac{\text{dollars}}{\text{tickets}} = \frac{6}{1} \cdot \frac{\text{dollars}}{\text{ticket}}$, or \$6/ticket

youth: $\frac{24.5}{7} \cdot \frac{\text{dollars}}{\text{tickets}} = \frac{24.5 \div 7}{7 \div 7} \cdot \frac{\text{dollars}}{\text{tickets}} = \frac{3.5}{1} \cdot \frac{\text{dollars}}{\text{ticket}}$,

or \$3.50/ticket ■

THINK ABOUT IT

Rates with money are often written like \$9/ticket, which is the same as 9 dollars per ticket.

Problem Set

Write a rate to represent the situation.

1. A squirrel ate 7 acorns in 4 h.
2. A scale displayed a weight of 45 g for 40 jelly beans.
3. A tank holding 120 L of water drained in 14 min.
4. David paid \$17 for 5 lb of avocados.
5. A car wash washed 4 cars in 22 min.
6. Ana drove 1600 km in 3 days.

Write a rate to represent the situation. Then write the unit rate.

7. Emile paid \$3.96 for 4 songs.
8. The bakery set a price of 30¢ for 3 cookies.
9. It took a boy 20 min to walk 2 mi.
10. A car travels 120 mi on 6 gal of gasoline.
11. The manager paid \$37.50 for 5 movie tickets.
12. Michele loaded 33 boxes onto a truck in 12 min.
13. A cheetah ran 200 m in 8 s.
14. The winner of an egg-eating contest ate 117 eggs in 10 min.

The table shows the number of points scored by three football teams during the playoffs.

Team	Points scored	Number of games played
Badgers	117	5
Senators	63	3
Thunder	96	4

15. For each team, write a unit rate representing the points scored per number of games played.
16. Which team had the highest number of points scored per game played?
17. **Challenge** Write a unit rate representing the total number of points scored by all three teams per total number of games played.

For each problem:

(a) Write a unit rate or a ratio.

(b) Write your answer in a complete sentence.

18. Luc shelled 18 oysters in 3 min. Write a unit rate that describes the number of oysters Luc shelled per minute.

19. Fencing costs $65 for 10 ft. Write a unit rate that describes the cost of fencing per foot.

20. A bike rider travels 68 mi in 5 h. Write the unit rate that describes the bike rider's speed in miles per hour.

21. A type of bamboo grew 30 cm in 5 h. Write the unit rate that describes the bamboo's rate of growth in centimeters per hour.

Solve.

22. **Challenge** A tortoise travels 0.875 mi in 0.25 h.

(a) Write the unit rate that describes the tortoise's speed in miles per hour.

(b) Calculate the distance the tortoise will travel in 2.75 h.

23. **Challenge** Two restaurants are selling hamburgers at different prices. Burger Barn sells 5 hamburgers for $4.50. Bargain Burger sells 8 hamburgers for $6.00.

(a) What is the unit rate for Burger Barn?

(b) What is the unit rate for Bargain Burger?

(c) Which restaurant has the better deal? Explain.

Core Focus: Unit Rates

THE CORE CONCEPT

Calculating a unit rate sometimes involves finding the ratio of noninteger values.

Solving Unit Rates Involving Complex Fractions

DEFINITION

A **complex fraction** is a fraction that has fractions in the numerator and/or the denominator.

When either of the quantities in a rate is a fraction or a mixed number, write the rate of the two quantities as a complex fraction. Then simplify the complex fraction to find the unit rate.

EXAMPLE 1 Suppose $2\frac{1}{2}$ lb of apples cost \$6. Write a unit rate representing the amount of apples per dollar.

Solution First convert the mixed number to an improper fraction. Then write the rate comparing the two quantities as a fraction and simplify.

$$\frac{2\frac{1}{2}\text{ lb}}{\$6} = \frac{\frac{5}{2}}{6} \cdot \frac{\text{pounds}}{\text{dollars}}$$

$$= \left(\frac{5}{2} \div 6\right) \cdot \frac{\text{pounds}}{\text{dollars}}$$

$$= \left(\frac{5}{2} \cdot \frac{1}{6}\right) \cdot \frac{\text{pounds}}{\text{dollars}}$$

$$= \frac{5}{12} \cdot \frac{\text{pounds}}{\text{dollars}}$$

The unit rate is $\frac{5}{12}$ lb/dollar. ■

TIP

To simplify a complex fraction, rewrite the fraction as a division problem, and then find the quotient.

EXAMPLE 2 A gazelle took 14 s to run $\frac{1}{4}$ mi. Write a unit rate representing the time it would take the gazelle to run 1 mi.

Solution Write a rate comparing the time the gazelle ran to the distance covered as a fraction and simplify.

$$\frac{14 \text{ s}}{\frac{1}{4} \text{ mi}} = \left(14 \div \frac{1}{4}\right) \cdot \frac{\text{seconds}}{\text{miles}}$$
$$= \left(14 \cdot \frac{4}{1}\right) \cdot \frac{\text{seconds}}{\text{miles}}$$
$$= 56 \cdot \frac{\text{seconds}}{\text{mile}}$$

The unit rate is 56 s/mi. ■

REMEMBER

Either of the two quantities in a rate may have a fractional amount.

EXAMPLE 3 David used $\frac{2}{3}$ gal of paint to cover $\frac{1}{12}$ of a large floor.

A Write a unit rate comparing the amount of paint David used to the portion of the floor covered.

Solution

$$\frac{\frac{2}{3} \text{ gal}}{\frac{1}{12} \text{ floor}} = \left(\frac{2}{3} \div \frac{1}{12}\right) \cdot \frac{\text{gallons}}{\text{floor}}$$
$$= \left(\frac{2}{3} \cdot \frac{12}{1}\right) \cdot \frac{\text{gallons}}{\text{floor}}$$
$$= \left(\frac{24}{3}\right) \cdot \frac{\text{gallons}}{\text{floor}}$$
$$= 8 \cdot \frac{\text{gallons}}{\text{floor}}$$

The unit rate is 8 gal/floor. ■

B How much paint is needed to cover the entire floor? Explain your reasoning.

Solution The unit rate of 8 gal per floor is equivalent to $\frac{8}{1} \cdot \frac{\text{gallons}}{\text{floor}}$, indicating that 8 gal of paint is needed to cover an area equal to the size of 1 whole floor.

Therefore, 8 gal of paint is needed to cover the entire floor. ■

Problem Set

Solve.

1. Sarah bikes $\frac{4}{5}$ km in 2 min. Write and simplify a unit rate that represents the distance Sarah bikes in 1 min.

2. A crate of oranges weighs 9 kg and is $\frac{3}{4}$ full.

   Write and simplify a unit rate that represents the weight of 1 full orange crate.

3. $2\frac{1}{3}$ cups of flour is needed for $\frac{1}{2}$ of a batch of cookies.

   (a) Write a unit rate comparing the amount of flour needed to the portion of a batch of cookies made.

   (b) How many cups of flour are needed to make 1 batch of cookies? Explain your reasoning.

Proportion

Ratios that describe the same numerical relationship are **equivalent ratios**.

Finding Equivalent Ratios

Multiplying or dividing the numerator and the denominator of a fraction by the same value is the same as multiplying the fraction by a form of 1. Multiplying by 1 does not change the value, so it's a good way to find equivalent ratios.

EXAMPLE 1 Find two ratios that are equivalent to the given ratio.

A 20 : 25

Solution Write the ratio as a fraction. Then multiply or divide the numerator and the denominator by the same nonzero number.

$$\frac{20}{25} = \frac{20 \div 5}{25 \div 5} = \frac{4}{5}$$

$$\frac{20}{25} = \frac{20 \cdot 3}{25 \cdot 3} = \frac{60}{75} \blacksquare$$

B 3 : 4

Solution This ratio is already in simplest form, so you can only multiply the numerator and the denominator by the same nonzero number.

$$\frac{3}{4} = \frac{3 \cdot 2}{4 \cdot 2} = \frac{6}{8}$$

$$\frac{3}{4} = \frac{3 \cdot 10}{4 \cdot 10} = \frac{30}{40} \blacksquare$$

THINK ABOUT IT

Saying that a ratio is $\frac{1.5}{2}$ is okay, but for convenience, generally try to use integer values for the numerator and denominator and write the ratio as $\frac{3}{4}$.

THINK ABOUT IT

Any given ratio has infinite equivalent ratios because there are infinite versions of 1 to multiply by.

Determining Whether Ratios Are Proportional

A **proportion** is an equation stating that two ratios are equal. In the proportion $\frac{a}{b} = \frac{c}{d}$, a and d are called the **extremes** and b and c are called the **means**. These definitions are easier to remember when you write the proportion with colons, because the extremes are on the exterior and the means are in the middle.

$$a : b = c : d$$

TIP

Read the proportion $\frac{a}{b} = \frac{c}{d}$ as "*a* is to *b* as *c* is to *d*."

Two ratios form a proportion if and only if the product of the means is equal to the product of the extremes.

MEANS-EXTREMES PRODUCT PROPERTY

For any *a* and *c* and nonzero *b* and *d*,

$\frac{a}{b} = \frac{c}{d}$ if and only if $ad = bc$.

Examples

$\frac{3}{5} = \frac{9}{15}$ because $3 \cdot 15 = 5 \cdot 9$

$\frac{7}{10} \neq \frac{2}{3}$ because $7 \cdot 3 \neq 10 \cdot 2$

If two ratios form a proportion, those ratios are called proportional, or in proportion.

When you write the product of the means and the product of the extremes, it is sometimes called **cross multiplying**.

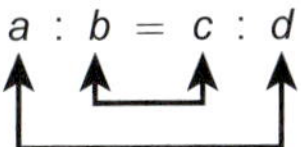

ad is the product of the extremes.
bc is the product of the means.

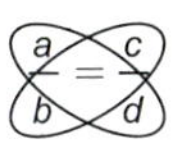

ad and *bc* are called cross products.

TIP

These all mean the same thing:

equal ratios
equivalent ratios
proportional ratios
ratios in proportion

You could also simplify each ratio to determine whether they are proportional, but cross multiplying is generally quicker.

EXAMPLE 2 Determine whether the ratios are proportional.

A $\frac{4}{6}$ and $\frac{10}{15}$

Solution

Method A Use the means-extremes product property.

$4 \cdot 15 \stackrel{?}{=} 6 \cdot 10$

$60 = 60$

The cross products are equal, so $\frac{4}{6}$ and $\frac{10}{15}$ are proportional.

Method B Simplify the ratios and then compare them.

$\frac{4}{6} = \frac{4 \div 2}{6 \div 2} = \frac{2}{3}$

$\frac{10}{15} = \frac{10 \div 5}{15 \div 5} = \frac{2}{3}$

The simplified ratios are identical, so $\frac{4}{6}$ and $\frac{10}{15}$ are proportional. ■

B $\frac{8}{12}$ and $\frac{24}{30}$

Solution

Method A Use the means-extremes product property.

$8 \cdot 30 \stackrel{?}{=} 12 \cdot 24$

$240 \neq 288$

The products are not equal, so $\frac{8}{12}$ and $\frac{24}{30}$ are not proportional.

Method B Simplify the ratios and then compare them.

$\frac{8}{12} = \frac{8 \div 4}{12 \div 4} = \frac{2}{3}$

$\frac{24}{30} = \frac{24 \div 6}{30 \div 6} = \frac{4}{5}$

The simplified ratios are not identical, so $\frac{8}{12}$ and $\frac{24}{30}$ are not proportional. ■

Solving Proportions

You can use the means-extremes product property to solve proportions.

EXAMPLE 3 Solve the proportion.

A $\frac{n}{15} = \frac{6}{20}$

Solution

$$\frac{n}{15} = \frac{6}{20}$$

$20n = 90$ Multiply means and extremes (cross multiply).

$\frac{20n}{20} = \frac{90}{20}$ Divide each side by 20.

$n = 4.5$ ■

B $\frac{5.6}{14} = \frac{x}{8}$

Solution

$$\frac{5.6}{14} = \frac{x}{8}$$

$8 \cdot 5.6 = 14x$ Multiply means and extremes (cross multiply).

$44.8 = 14x$

$\frac{44.8}{14} = \frac{14x}{14}$ Divide each side by 14.

$3.2 = x$ ■

Application: Travel

You can apply proportions to many real-world situations.

EXAMPLE 4 A train traveled 234 mi in 4 h. If the train continues at the same rate, how many miles will it travel in 10 h?

Solution Write and solve a proportion.

$\frac{234 \text{ mi}}{4 \text{ h}} = \frac{x \text{ miles}}{10 \text{ h}}$ The train continues at the same rate, so the rate for 4 h equals the rate for 10 h.

$\frac{234}{4} = \frac{x}{10}$ Write the proportion without units.

$2340 = 4x$ Cross multiply.

$\frac{2340}{4} = \frac{4x}{4}$ Divide both sides by 4.

$585 = x$ Simplify.

The train will travel 585 mi in 10 h. ■

TIP

When you set up a proportion, include the units so that you can see whether you have put everything in the right place.

THINK ABOUT IT

In Example 4, the proportion could have been set up as $\frac{4 \text{ h}}{234 \text{ mi}} = \frac{10 \text{ h}}{x \text{ miles}}$.

Problem Set

Find two ratios that are equivalent to the given ratio.

1. $8 : 16$
2. $6 : 10$
3. $7 : 3$
4. $50 : 75$
5. $8 : 24$
6. $72 : 36$
7. $1 : 5$
8. $45 : 63$
9. $12 : 4$
10. $10 : 8$

Determine whether the ratios are proportional.

11. $\frac{6}{36}$ and $\frac{1}{6}$
12. $\frac{3}{18}$ and $\frac{2}{9}$
13. $\frac{10}{22}$ and $\frac{5}{11}$
14. $\frac{2}{4}$ and $\frac{20}{36}$
15. $\frac{15}{18}$ and $\frac{5}{6}$
16. $\frac{7}{35}$ and $\frac{35}{70}$
17. $\frac{11.9}{42}$ and $\frac{1.7}{6}$
18. $\frac{3.4}{8}$ and $\frac{34}{80}$

Solve the proportion.

19. $\frac{6}{18} = \frac{m}{3}$
20. $\frac{x}{8} = \frac{1}{2}$
21. $\frac{3}{b} = \frac{15}{20}$
22. $\frac{2.5}{8} = \frac{t}{12}$
23. $\frac{3.2}{y} = \frac{6}{12}$
24. $\frac{x}{4.8} = \frac{10}{15}$
25. $\frac{32.5}{50} = \frac{x}{20}$
26. $\frac{25}{75} = \frac{8.2}{a}$
27. $\frac{17}{b} = \frac{25.5}{33}$
28. $\frac{9.5}{6} = \frac{g}{18}$
29. $\frac{16}{5} = \frac{3}{n}$
30. **Challenge** $\frac{x}{16} = \frac{4}{x}$
31. **Challenge** $\frac{2}{a} = \frac{a}{50}$
32. **Challenge** $\frac{x+1}{32} = \frac{3}{4}$

For each problem:

(a) Write a proportion.

(b) Solve the proportion.

(c) Write your answer in a complete sentence.

33. A car traveled 93 mi in $1\frac{1}{2}$ h. If the car continues at the same rate, how many miles will it travel in $3\frac{1}{2}$ h?

34. A machine is wrapping 18 boxes in 5 min. If the machine continues at the same rate, how many boxes will it wrap in 1 h?

35. An employee made $27 in 3 h. If the employee continues to earn at the same rate, how much will the employee make in 8 h?

36. A grocery store is selling 5 lb of oranges for $4.45. How much will 12 lb of oranges cost?

37. A student reads 40 pages of a book in 60 min. If the student continues to read at the same rate, how long will it take to read 220 pages?

38. A printer can print 30 pages in 2.8 min. If the printer prints at the same rate, how long will it take to print 120 pages?

Solve.

39. **Challenge** A swimming pool is filling at the rate of 40 gal every 2 min.

(a) If the pool continues to fill at the same rate, how many gallons will be in the pool after 3 h?

(b) The pool will hold about 88,000 gal of water. How long will it take to fill the pool?

Percents, Fractions, and Decimals

Every fraction can be written as an equivalent decimal and as a percent.

A **percent** is a ratio that compares a number to 100. Every percent can be written as a fraction and as a decimal. The table shows a few examples.

Fraction	Decimal	Percent
$\frac{1}{10}$	0.1	10%
$\frac{1}{4}$	0.25	25%
$\frac{1}{2}$	0.5	50%

Converting Fractions to Decimals

A fraction bar can be thought of as a division symbol.

HOW TO CONVERT A FRACTION TO A DECIMAL

For any b and nonzero a,

$\frac{b}{a}$ is equivalent to $b \div a$.

Example

$\frac{1}{5} = 1 \div 5 = 0.2$

$$\begin{array}{r} 0.2 \\ 5\overline{)1.0} \\ \underline{1\,0} \\ 0 \end{array}$$

EXAMPLE 1 Convert the fraction to a decimal.

A $\frac{3}{8}$

Solution

$\frac{3}{8} = 3 \div 8 = 0.375$

$$\begin{array}{r} 0.375 \\ 8\overline{)3.000} \\ \underline{2\,4} \\ 60 \\ \underline{56} \\ 40 \\ \underline{40} \\ 0 \end{array}$$

B $\frac{2}{3}$

Solution Divide.

$\frac{2}{3} = 2 \div 3 = 0.\overline{6}$

Place a bar over a digit or group of digits to indicate a repeating pattern.

$$\begin{array}{r} 0.666\ldots \\ 3\overline{)2.000} \\ \underline{1\,8} \\ 20 \\ \underline{18} \\ 20 \\ \underline{18} \\ \vdots \end{array}$$

THINK ABOUT IT

You could go on forever with this division problem and always end up with another 6.

Converting Decimals to Fractions

Every decimal represents a fraction or a mixed number whose denominator is 10, 100, 1000, or some other power of 10.

HOW TO CONVERT A DECIMAL TO A SIMPLIFIED FRACTION

Write the decimal as a fraction or a mixed number, and then simplify.

Example

$0.36 = \frac{36}{100} = \frac{36 \div 4}{100 \div 4} = \frac{9}{25}$

EXAMPLE 2 Convert the decimal to a fraction or a mixed number. Simplify.

A 0.8

Solution

$0.8 = \frac{8}{10} = \frac{8 \div 2}{10 \div 2} = \frac{4}{5}$

B 7.405

Solution

$7.405 = 7\frac{405}{1000} = 7\frac{405 \div 5}{1000 \div 5} = 7\frac{81}{200}$

Converting Decimals to Percents

To write a decimal as a percent, write a fraction with a denominator of 100. The numerator is the percent. For example, $0.35 = \frac{35}{100} = 35\%$. Notice that you can obtain the answer by just moving the decimal point two places to the right.

HOW TO CONVERT A DECIMAL TO A PERCENT

Move the decimal point two places to the right and write a percent sign (%).

Example

$0.35 = 035.\%$

$= 35\%$

THINK ABOUT IT

You can write any decimal as a fraction with a denominator of 100 and then a percent.

$$\begin{aligned} 0.625 &= \frac{625}{1000} \\ &= \frac{625 \div 10}{1000 \div 10} \\ &= \frac{62.5}{100} \\ &= 62.5\% \end{aligned}$$

EXAMPLE 3 Convert the decimal to a percent.

A 0.72

Solution $0.72 = 072.\%$

$= 72\%$ ■

B 5.43

Solution $5.43 = 543.\%$

$= 543\%$ ■

C 0.0005

Solution $0.0005 = 000.05\%$

$= 0.05\%$ ■

Converting Percents to Decimals

Because a percent is a ratio with 100 in the denominator, converting a percent to a decimal is the same as dividing by 100.

CONVERTING A PERCENT TO A DECIMAL

Move the decimal point two places to the left and remove the percent sign (%).	**Example** $68\% = 0.68$ $= 0.68$

EXAMPLE 4 Convert the percent to a decimal.

A 4%

Solution $4\% = 0.04$

$= 0.04$ ■

B 127%

Solution $127\ \% = 1.27$

$= 1.27$ ■

C 0.6%

Solution $0.6\% = 0.006$

$= 0.006$ ■

Converting Fractions to Percents

HOW TO CONVERT A FRACTION TO A PERCENT

Convert the fraction to a decimal, and then convert the decimal to a percent.

Example

$\frac{4}{5} = 4 \div 5 = 0.8 = 80\%$

EXAMPLE 5 Convert the fraction or mixed number to a percent. Round your answer to the nearest percent if rounding is necessary.

A $\frac{3}{40}$

Solution $\frac{3}{40} = 3 \div 40 = 0.075 = 7.5\%$ ■

B $2\frac{4}{13}$

Solution $2\frac{4}{13} = \frac{30}{13} = 30 \div 13 \approx 2.308 = 230.8\% \approx 231\%$ ■

THINK ABOUT IT

You can convert a fraction to a percent by solving a proportion.

$$\frac{3}{40} = \frac{n}{100\%}$$
$$300\% = 40n$$
$$\frac{300}{40}\% = n$$
$$7.5\% = n$$

So $\frac{3}{40} = 7.5\%$.

Converting Percents to Fractions

HOW TO CONVERT A PERCENT TO A SIMPLIFIED FRACTION

Write the percent as a fraction with a denominator of 100, and then simplify.

Example

$45\% = \frac{45}{100} = \frac{45 \div 5}{100 \div 5} = \frac{9}{20}$

EXAMPLE 6 Convert the percent to a fraction or mixed number. Simplify.

A 320%

Solution $320\% = \frac{320}{100} = \frac{320 \div 20}{100 \div 20} = \frac{16}{5} = 3\frac{1}{5}$ ■

B 8.7%

Solution $8.7\% = \frac{8.7}{100} = \frac{8.7 \times 10}{100 \times 10} = \frac{87}{1000}$ ■

TIP

In Example 6B, you must multiply to eliminate the decimal in the numerator.

Application: Marketing

EXAMPLE 7 A marketing survey indicates that 18 of 64 people plan to purchase a video game in the next year. To the nearest tenth of a percent, what percent of those surveyed plan to purchase the video game?

Solution $\frac{18}{64} = 18 \div 64 = 0.28125 = 28.125\%$

About 28.1% of those surveyed plan to purchase the video game. ■

Problem Set

Convert the fraction to a decimal.

1. $\frac{7}{10}$
2. $\frac{4}{12}$
3. $\frac{3}{5}$
4. $\frac{11}{20}$
5. $\frac{19}{25}$
6. $\frac{3}{8}$

Convert the decimal to a fraction or mixed number. Simplify.

7. 0.75
8. 0.6
9. 1.5
10. 6.05
11. 0.34
12. 10.8

Convert the decimal or whole to a percent.

13. 7.21
14. 6
15. 0.03
16. 65.4
17. 1.004
18. 62.01

Convert the percent to a decimal.

19. 7.8%
20. 23%
21. 0.5%
22. 0.007%
23. 10.85%
24. 50.6%

Convert the fraction or mixed number to a percent. Round your answer to the nearest percent if rounding is necessary.

25. $\frac{8}{50}$
26. $\frac{7}{25}$
27. $5\frac{3}{5}$
28. $10\frac{2}{3}$
29. $\frac{5}{12}$
30. $\frac{8}{9}$

Convert the percent to a fraction or mixed number. Simplify.

31. 60%
32. 22%
33. 5%
34. 175%
35. 84%
36. 23%

Solve. Simplify all fractions.

37. A survey showed that $\frac{4}{5}$ of moviegoers think tickets are too expensive. What percent of those surveyed think tickets are too expensive?
38. Bob has completed 65% of the levels on a video game. What fraction of the levels has Bob completed?
39. A bank paid 3.4% interest on a savings account. What is 3.4% in decimal form?
40. A restaurant found that 80% of employees liked working on Mondays. What fraction of the employees liked working on Mondays?
41. Doug has finished reading 220 pages of a 500-page book. What percent of the book has Doug read so far?
42. A scientist found that 12 of 18 birds had a red spot on their heads. What fraction of the birds had a red spot on their head?
43. **Challenge** Order the following sets of numbers from least to greatest.
    - **(a)** $\frac{1}{4}$, 0.32, 28%
    - **(b)** 0.05, 0.5%, $\frac{1}{5}$

Working with Percent

You can use percent to solve problems that involve parts of whole amounts.

Using the Percent Proportion

You can use the following proportion to solve percent problems:

$$\frac{\text{part}}{\text{whole}} = \frac{\text{percent}}{100}$$

For example,

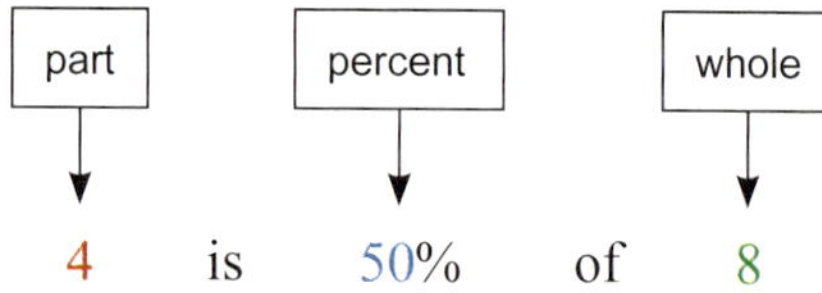

4 is 50% of 8

can be rewritten as

$$\frac{4}{8} = \frac{50}{100}.$$

EXAMPLE 1 What is 20% of 250?

Solution Write the percent proportion and fill in the known information. Use x for the unknown.

$$\frac{\text{part}}{\text{whole}} = \frac{\text{percent}}{100}$$

$\frac{x}{250} = \frac{20}{100}$ The part is the unknown.

$100x = 250 \cdot 20$ Cross multiply.

$100x = 5000$ Multiply.

$\frac{100x}{100} = \frac{5000}{100}$ Divide each side by 100.

$x = 50$ Simplify.

Twenty percent of 250 is 50.

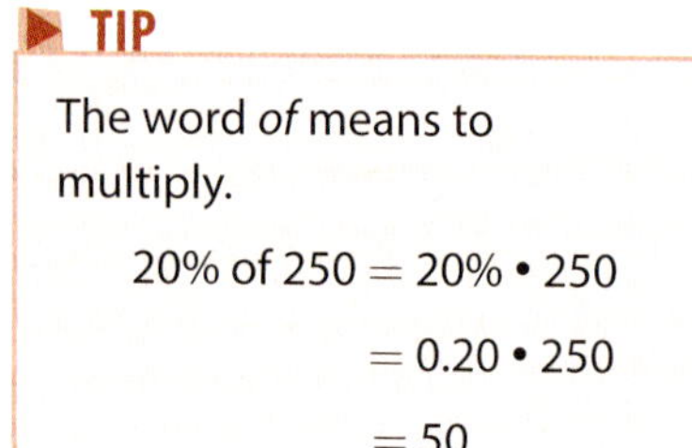

TIP

The word *of* means to multiply.

20% of $250 = 20\% \cdot 250$
$= 0.20 \cdot 250$
$= 50$

EXAMPLE 2 Eighteen is what percent of 72?

Solution Write and solve a percent proportion.

$$\frac{\text{part}}{\text{whole}} = \frac{\text{percent}}{100}$$

$\frac{18}{72} = \frac{x}{100}$ The percent is the unknown.

$18 \cdot 100 = 72x$ Cross multiply.

$1800 = 72x$ Multiply.

$\frac{1800}{72} = \frac{72x}{72}$ Divide each side by 72.

$25 = x$ Simplify.

Eighteen is 25% of 72. ■

EXAMPLE 3 One hundred nineteen is 70% of what number?

Solution Write and solve a percent proportion.

$$\frac{\text{part}}{\text{whole}} = \frac{\text{percent}}{100}$$

$\frac{119}{x} = \frac{70}{100}$ The whole is the unknown.

$119 \cdot 100 = 70x$ Cross multiply.

$11{,}900 = 70x$ Multiply.

$\frac{11{,}900}{70} = \frac{70x}{70}$ Divide each side by 70.

$170 = x$ Simplify.

One hundred nineteen is 70% of 170. ■

Application: Biology

EXAMPLE 4 At birth, an elephant weighs about 2.5% of its adult weight. If an elephant weighs 8000 lb as an adult, about how many pounds did the elephant weigh at birth?

Solution Write and solve a percent proportion.

$$\frac{\text{part}}{\text{whole}} = \frac{\text{percent}}{100}$$

$\frac{x}{8000} = \frac{2.5}{100}$ The part is unknown.

$100x = 8000 \cdot 2.5$ Means-Extremes Product Property

$100x = 20{,}000$ Multiply.

$\frac{100x}{100} = \frac{20{,}000}{100}$ Divide each side by 100.

$x = 200$ Simplify.

The elephant weighed about 200 lb at birth. ■

Problem Set

Write a proportion to solve the problem. Then solve the proportion.

1. What is 76% of 30?
2. Seven is 20% of what number?
3. Thirteen is what percent of 15?
4. What is 85% of 81?
5. Twenty is 10% of what number?
6. What is 34% of 57?
7. Seventeen is 20% of what number?
8. What is 72% of 29?
9. Fifteen is what percent of 30?
10. What is 44% of 55?
11. One hundred thirty-three is 35% of what number?
12. What is 105% of 380?
13. Ninety-nine is what percent of 150?
14. What is 15% of 260?
15. Seventeen is what percent of 85?
16. Thirty-five is what percent of 7?
17. What is 34% of 50?
18. Twenty is 150% of what number?
19. Twenty-one is what percent of 28?
20. What is 44% of 325?
21. Seven is 14% of what number?
22. What is 42% of 25?
23. One hundred forty-seven is what percent of 210?
24. Ninety-five is what percent of 57?
25. What is 150% of 65?
26. Fifteen is 108% of what number?
27. **Challenge** What is 6% of 3.5?
28. **Challenge** Twenty-two and seventy-seven hundredths is 46% of what number?
29. **Challenge** Five and seven hundredths is what percent of 65?
30. **Challenge** What is 82.5% of 145.8?

Solve.

31. A cell phone costs $170 and has a tax rate of 7%. Write and solve a proportion to find how much tax is paid on the cell phone.
32. Maureen spent $48 on books, which is 70% of her savings. Write and solve a proportion to find the total amount of Maureen's savings.
33. There are 260 students in grade 6, which accounts for 40% of the school population. Write and solve a proportion to find the total number of students at the school.
34. A window measures 45 in. long. The wall is 210 in. long. Write and solve a proportion to find the percent of the wall's length that is taken up by the window.
35. A music player has 1230 songs. Three hundred of the songs are hip-hop style. Write and solve a proportion to find the percent of songs that are hip-hop.
36. The music club spent $400 on snacks for an after-concert party. That expenditure was 25% of the total budget. Write and solve a proportion to find the total budget for the music club.
37. Mia received 420 text messages last month, of which 140 were from Shannon. Write and solve a proportion to find the percent of text messages that were sent by Shannon.
38. A used bookstore sold 150 fiction books in 1 wk. That number accounted for 75% of all books sold that week. Write and solve a proportion to find the total number of books sold.

Core Focus: Identifying Proportions

THE CORE CONCEPT

The relationship between two quantities is proportional if the ratio of each data pair equals the same value.

Determining Proportional Relationships from Table Data

HOW TO DETERMINE WHETHER THE DATA IN A TABLE DEFINE A PROPORTIONAL RELATIONSHIP

For each pair of values in a table,

Step 1 Calculate the ratio of the two values.

Step 2 Compare the ratios for all pairs.

If the ratios are all the same value, the two quantities are proportional.

EXAMPLE 1 A gardener uses a table to determine how much organic fertilizer is needed for a given number of tomato plants.

Number of tomato plants	Fertilizer (g)
5	150
10	300
20	600
30	900

Is there a proportional relationship between the number of tomato plants and the amount of fertilizer needed? Show your reasoning.

Solution Write a ratio comparing fertilizer amount to number of tomato plants for each row in the table. Then simplify each ratio.

$$\frac{150}{5} = 30$$
$$\frac{300}{10} = 30$$
$$\frac{600}{20} = 30$$
$$\frac{900}{30} = 30$$

All four ratios have the same value of 30, so the relationship between the number of tomato plants and the amount of fertilizer needed is proportional. ■

 **TIP**

It does not matter whether you choose the values in the first column to be the numerators or the denominators of the fractions. You must, however, be consistent in your choice.

EXAMPLE 2 A clothing store offers a coupon, good for the next purchase, proportional to the amount of today's purchase. The table shows the coupon amount for several purchase amounts.

Today's purchase amount ($)	Coupon amount ($)
20	3
40	6
100	15
200	?

A What is the coupon amount if today's purchase amount is $200? Show your reasoning.

Solution Because the coupon amount is proportional to today's purchase amount, set up a means-extremes proportion equation and solve.

$$\frac{x}{200} = \frac{3}{20}$$
$$20x = 600$$
$$x = 30$$

If today's purchase amount is $200, the coupon amount is $30. ■

B What is today's purchase amount if the coupon amount is $24? Show your reasoning.

Solution Set up a means-extremes proportion equation and solve.

$$\frac{3}{20} = \frac{24}{x}$$
$$3x = 480$$
$$x = 160$$

For a coupon amount of $24, today's purchase amount is $160. ■

EXAMPLE 3 Billon is an alloy of silver used in ancient Greece to make coins. Billon is made by combining 3 parts of copper for every 2 parts of silver.

A Make a table indicating how much copper should be added to 2, 5, 10, and 15 g of silver to make billon.

Solution The ratio of silver to copper is 2 : 3, so set up a means-extremes proportion equation for each amount of silver given and solve.

5 g

$$\frac{x}{5} = \frac{3}{2}$$
$$2x = 15$$
$$x = 7.5$$

10 g

$$\frac{x}{10} = \frac{3}{2}$$
$$2x = 30$$
$$x = 15$$

15 g

$$\frac{x}{15} = \frac{3}{2}$$
$$2x = 45$$
$$x = 22.5$$

Silver (g)	2	5	10	15
Copper (g)	3	7.5	15	22.5

B Is the relationship between the amounts of silver and copper proportional? Explain your reasoning.

Solution The ratio of silver to copper is 2 : 3. It is constant, regardless of the actual amounts of silver and copper used to make the billon, so the amounts of silver and copper in billon are proportional.

BY THE WAY

An alloy is a mixture of two or more metals made by heating and then cooling the mixture.

Problem Set

Solve.

1. Tom records his distance and time traveled at several points on a bike ride.

Distance (km)	2	4	6	8
Time (min)	5	10	15	20

Is there a proportional relationship between the distance traveled and the time recorded? Show your reasoning.

2. A pizzeria puts 5 slices of pepperoni on every piece of pepperoni pizza made.
   - **(a)** Make a table showing the total number of slices of pepperoni added to 2, 4, 8, and 12 pieces of pizza.
   - **(b)** Is the number of pieces of pizza proportional to the total number of slices of pepperoni? Explain your thinking.

3. The amount of bleach needed to make a cleaning solution is proportional to the quantity of cleaning solution made.

Bleach (mL)	Solution (L)
30	1.2
60	2.4
90	?
120	4.8
?	6.0

   - **(a)** How much solution does 90 mL of bleach make? Show your reasoning.
   - **(b)** How much bleach is needed to make 6.0 L of the solution? Show your reasoning.

CHAPTER 7 Review

Choose the answer.

1. What is the ratio in simplified form?

40 : 32

A. 20 : 16

B. 10 : 8

C. 8 : 4

D. 5 : 4

2. A sock drawer has 6 blue socks, 8 black socks, 4 green socks, and 2 gray socks. What is the ratio of green socks to the total number of socks, in simplified form?

A. $\frac{1}{5}$

B. $\frac{1}{4}$

C. $\frac{4}{20}$

D. $\frac{20}{4}$

3. A biologist counted 12 robin's nests in an area. The nests contained a total of 40 eggs. What rate represents the number of nests compared to the number of eggs?

A. $\frac{2 \text{ nests}}{7 \text{ eggs}}$

B. $\frac{3 \text{ nests}}{7 \text{ eggs}}$

C. $\frac{3 \text{ nests}}{10 \text{ eggs}}$

D. $\frac{3 \text{ nests}}{13 \text{ eggs}}$

4. What value of k makes the equation true?

$$\frac{9}{10} = \frac{4.5}{k}$$

A. 4.05

B. 5

C. 5.5

D. 20

5. What value of y makes the equation true?

$$\frac{y}{24} = \frac{8}{6}$$

A. 2

B. 18

C. 26

D. 32

6. What is 4.6 written as a mixed number?

A. $4\frac{3}{50}$

B. $4\frac{3}{5}$

C. $6\frac{2}{50}$

D. $6\frac{2}{5}$

7. What is $\frac{8}{25}$ written as a percent?

A. 0.32%

B. 0.8%

C. 32%

D. 312.5%

8. Twenty-eight is what percent of 50?

A. 1.4%

B. 14%

C. 28%

D. 56%

Solve.

9. The table shows the number of players on an ice-hockey team, by position. Write a simplified ratio for each situation described.

Position	Number
center	4
wing	10
defense	9
goalie	2

   (a) goalies to wing

   (b) centers to goalies

   (c) defense to all players

   (d) all players to wings

10. Pete drove 138 km in 3 h.

   (a) Write a rate to represent the situation.

   (b) Express this rate as a unit rate.

11. Saul used $3\frac{7}{10}$ m of fencing to enclose $\frac{1}{4}$ of a patio.

   (a) Write a unit rate comparing the amount of fencing Saul used to the portion of the patio enclosed.

   (b) How much fencing is needed to enclose the whole patio? Explain your reasoning.

12. Are $\frac{2}{9}$ and $\frac{8}{34}$ proportional? Show your reasoning.

13. A machine can seal 10 envelopes in 3.2 s. If the machine works at the same rate, how long will it take to seal 120 envelopes?

14. What is 64% written as a simplified fraction?

15. The price of a stock rose 152% over 1 year. Write a mixed number representing the rise in the price of the stock. Simplify.

16. Twelve is 40% of what number?

17. Fifty-one adult tickets were sold for a circus performance, accounting for 30% of the total number of tickets sold. Write and solve a proportion to find the total number of tickets sold.

18. A cost of a certain dressmaking fabric is proportional to the length of fabric purchased. The table shows the cost of the fabric for several lengths.

Length (yd)	Cost ($)
2	13
3	19.50
4	?
6	39

   (a) What is the cost of 4 yd of the fabric? Show your reasoning.

   (b) Kiya paid $22.75 for a length of the fabric. How much fabric did she buy? Show your reasoning.

Problem	Topic Lookup
1, 2, 9	Ratios
3, 10	Rates
11	Core Focus: Unit Rates
4, 5, 12, 13	Proportion

Problem	Topic Lookup
6, 7, 14, 15	Percents, Fractions, and Decimals
8, 16, 17	Working with Percent
18	Core Focus: Identifying Proportions

CHAPTER 8 Proportion Applications

Model builders use proportions to figure out the length of every item in their models. For the model to be accurate, every length needs to be in the same proportion to the original object.

In This Chapter

Proportional thinking is important in many real-world applications. In this chapter, you will focus on many applications of proportions. Applications include markup and discount, percent problems, simple interest, and problems from science.

Topic List

- Foundations for Chapter 8
- Proportion Problems
- Similarity and Scale
- Proportional Relationships
- Core Focus: Graphing Proportions
- Percent Problems
- Percent of Increase or Decrease
- Core Focus: Percent Error
- Simple Interest
- Core Focus: Multistep Ratio and Percent Problems
- Core Focus: Constant of Proportionality
- Chapter 8 Review

Model builders make sure that every person, car, and building is in scale.

Foundations for Chapter 8

Plotting Points

To plot a point (x, y) on a coordinate grid, use the x-coordinate to move left or right, and use the y-coordinate to move up or down.

EXAMPLE A Solve.

A-1 Plot and label the points on a coordinate grid.

$A(5, -8), B(-6, 2)$

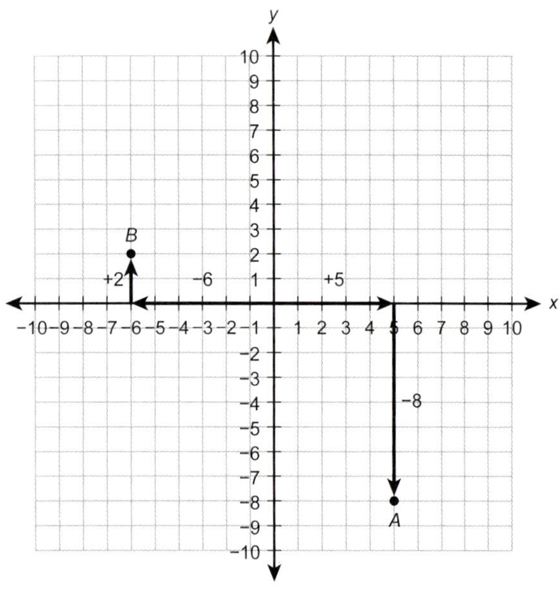

Solution To plot point A, start at the origin, move 5 units to the right, and then move 8 units down.

To plot point B, start at the origin, move 6 units to the left, and then move 2 units up. ■

A-2 Plot and label the points on a coordinate grid. Draw segments between the points to form a square.

$W(-2, 4), X(5, 4), Y(5, -3), Z(-2, -3)$

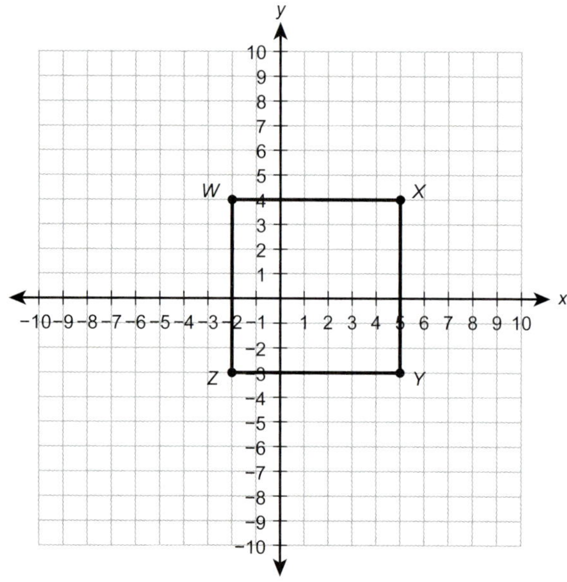

Solution Plot each of the four points. Each point represents a vertex of the square, so connect adjacent points with a line segment to form a square. ■

Problem Set A

Plot and label the points on a coordinate grid.

1. $D(4, -3), E(1, 5), F(-2, -6)$
2. $J(0, -7), K(-9, -3), L(-6, 5)$
3. $U(2, 0), V(6, 4), W(2, -5)$
4. $P(-8, 1), Q(2, 5), R(0, 0)$

Plot and label the points on a coordinate grid. Draw segments between the points to form the figure indicated.

5. $A(-5, 0), B(4, 0), C(4, 6)$; right triangle
6. $K(1, -5), L(1, 2), M(6, 2), N(6, -5)$; rectangle
7. $S(-6, -7), T(-9, -7), U(-9, -4), V(-6, -4)$; square
8. $C(0, -6), D(0, 2), E(3, -4), F(3, 0)$; trapezoid

Solving Multiplication Equations with Decimals and Fractions

To solve a multiplication equation, use the multiplication or division property of equality to isolate the variable. Be sure to simplify your answer.

EXAMPLE B Solve.

B-1 $2.5x = 12$

Solution

$\frac{2.5x}{2.5} = \frac{12}{2.5}$ Divide both sides by 2.5.

$x = 12 \div 2.5$

$x = 4.8$ ■

B-2 $\frac{2}{3}z = 14$

Solution

$3\left(\frac{2}{3}\right)z = 3 \cdot 14$ Multiply both sides by 3.

$\frac{6}{3}z = 42$

$2z = 42$

$\frac{2z}{2} = \frac{42}{2}$ Divide both sides by 2.

$z = 21$ ■

Problem Set B

Solve.

1. $3a = 16.5$
2. $1.2h = 30$
3. $\frac{1}{4}f = 7$
4. $7y = \frac{2}{3}$
5. $0.4m = 5$
6. $\frac{3}{5}y = 9$
7. $\frac{1}{2}p = 1\frac{3}{10}$
8. $6w = 13.5$
9. $4.2q = 44.1$
10. $\frac{4}{7}b = \frac{5}{8}$
11. $0.9c = 0.7$
12. $1\frac{1}{3}b = 8$

Converting Between Fraction, Decimal, and Percent Representations

A percent can be written as a fraction because *percent* means "per hundred." A fraction can be turned into a decimal using long division.

EXAMPLE C Find the equivalent representations.

C-1 Convert $\frac{19}{25}$ to its decimal and percent representations.

Solution Convert $\frac{19}{25}$ to a decimal by dividing 19 by 25.

$$\begin{array}{r} 0.76 \\ 25\overline{)19.0} \\ -175 \\ \hline 150 \\ -150 \\ \hline 0 \end{array}$$

Convert 0.76 to a percent.

$$0.76 \cdot 100\% = 76\%$$

The value $\frac{19}{25}$ is equivalent to 0.76 and 76%.

C-2 Convert 55% to its decimal and fraction representations.

Solution Convert 55% to a decimal.

$$\frac{55\%}{100\%} = \frac{55}{100} = 0.55$$

Convert 0.55 to a fraction, and then simplify.

$$\begin{aligned} \frac{0.55}{1} &= \frac{0.55 \cdot 100}{1 \cdot 100} \\ &= \frac{55}{100} \\ &= \frac{55 \div 5}{100 \div 5} \\ &= \frac{11}{20} \end{aligned}$$

The value 55% is equivalent to 0.55 and $\frac{11}{20}$.

Problem Set C

Find the equivalent representations.

1. $\frac{9}{10}$ as a decimal and a percent
2. 60% as a decimal and a fraction
3. $\frac{23}{40}$ as a decimal and a percent
4. 92% as a decimal and a fraction
5. 0.32 as a percent and a fraction
6. 2.8 as a percent and a fraction
7. 62.5% as a decimal and a fraction
8. $\frac{66}{8}$ as a decimal and a percent
9. 0.048 as a percent and a fraction
10. 2.03 as a percent and a fraction
11. 245% as a decimal and a fraction
12. $1\frac{4}{9}$ as a decimal and a percent

Proportion Problems

You can join two equivalent ratios together to form an equation called a **proportion**.

The ratio of 24 to 15 is equivalent to the ratio of 8 to 5, so the equation $\frac{24}{15} = \frac{8}{5}$ is a proportion. Proportions can be represented by $\frac{a}{b} = \frac{c}{d}$, where a and d are called the **extremes** and b and c are called the **means**. You can use the following properties to write proportions in equivalent forms.

TIP

The proportion $\frac{a}{b} = \frac{c}{d}$ can also be written as $a:b = c:d$.

MEANS-EXTREMES PRODUCT PROPERTY

If $\frac{a}{b} = \frac{c}{d}$, then $ad = bc$, as long as b and d are not 0.

In other words, the product of the extremes equals the product of the means. This property is often called cross multiplying.

Using the Means-Extremes Product Property

EXAMPLE 1 Solve the proportion.

$$\frac{1}{2} = \frac{x+1}{6}$$

Solution

$\frac{1}{2} = \frac{x+1}{6}$	
$1 \cdot 6 = 2(x+1)$	Means-Extremes Product Property
$6 = 2x + 2$	Multiply on the left; distribute 2 on the right.
$4 = 2x$	Subtract 2 from each side.
$2 = x$	Divide each side by 2. ■

Solving Application Problems

When solving an application problem involving proportions, it is important to set up the proportion correctly.

There are different strategies you can use to set up a proportion problem, but in every case you must identify the unknown quantity before writing the proportion. If the unknown quantity is a rate, define the variable you will use, and then set up the proportion, making sure you compare units the same way on each side of the proportion. For example, if a problem states that there are 200 electronic devices manufactured every 2 h and asks how many will be manufactured in 8 h, you can define the variable x as the number of items that will be manufactured in 8 h. When writing the proportion, make sure the hours are both listed in the numerators of the fractions or both listed in the denominators. In this example, two possible proportions that will give you a correct answer are $\frac{x}{8} = \frac{200}{2}$ and $\frac{8}{x} = \frac{2}{200}$.

Predicting an Outcome

EXAMPLE 2 A town has 6420 registered voters. A survey of the people in the town found that 3 of 4 people would vote for Ms. Chang for mayor. Predict the number of people who would vote for Ms. Chang if all 6420 registered voters voted.

Solution Write and solve a proportion with one ratio for the survey and one ratio for the number of voters. Let x represent the number of people who would vote for Ms. Chang.

$$\frac{3}{4} = \frac{x}{6420}$$

$3 \cdot 6420 = 4x$ Means-Extremes Product Property.

$19{,}260 = 4x$ Multiply.

$4815 = x$ Divide each side by 4.

Of the 6420 voters, about 4815 would vote for Ms. Chang. ■

Using Scale

EXAMPLE 3 On a map, the distance between two cities is 7.5 in. Find the actual distance in miles between the two cities if the scale on the map is 1 in. to 35 mi.

Solution Let x represent the actual distance. Then write and solve a proportion.

$$\frac{1}{35} = \frac{7.5}{x}$$

$1x = 35 \cdot 7.5$ Means-Extremes Product Property.

$x = 262.5$ Multiply.

The actual distance between the two cities is 262.5 mi. ■

Application: Gas Mileage

EXAMPLE 4 Julio used 5 gal of gas to drive 187 mi. How far can he drive on a full tank if his gas tank holds 12 gal of gas?

Solution Let x represent the distance on a full tank. Then write and solve a proportion.

$$\frac{187}{5} = \frac{x}{12}$$

$187 \cdot 12 = 5x$ Means-Extremes Product Property

$2244 = 5x$ Multiply.

$448.8 = x$ Divide each side by 5.

Julio can drive 448.8 mi using a full tank of gas. ■

Application: Cost

EXAMPLE 5 Kim bought 12 bottles of juice for \$16.68. How much will it cost her to buy 30 bottles of the same juice?

Solution Let x represent the cost of 30 bottles of juice. Then write and solve a proportion.

$$\frac{12}{16.68} = \frac{30}{x}$$

$12x = 16.68 \cdot 30$ Means-Extremes Product Property

$12x = 500.4$ Multiply.

$x = 41.7$ Divide each side by 12.

It will cost Kim \$41.70 to buy 30 bottles of juice. ■

Problem Set

Solve.

1. $\frac{x+2}{8} = \frac{1}{2}$
2. $\frac{x-2}{5} = \frac{1}{5}$
3. $\frac{3x+1}{10} = \frac{x-1}{7}$
4. $x + 1 = \frac{x-2}{4}$
5. $\frac{1}{7} = \frac{x-3}{14}$
6. $\frac{x-10}{3} = \frac{1}{15}$
7. $x - 6 = \frac{2x+1}{3}$
8. $\frac{1}{9} = \frac{x+3}{2}$
9. $\frac{5x+2}{11} = \frac{x}{3}$
10. $\frac{x}{6} = \frac{7}{12}$
11. $2x + 12 = \frac{3(x-1)}{4}$

For each problem:

(a) Define variables for the unknowns.
(b) Write a proportion to model the problem.
(c) Solve.
(d) Give your answer in a complete sentence.

12. Quaid buys 3 ft^2 of grass sod for \$11. If Quaid wants to buy 50 ft^2, how much will he pay?

13. In a survey, 6 of 10 customers preferred Cleanbiz laundry detergent over Zapout. If 150 customers participated in the survey, how many people preferred Cleanbiz?

14. Abraham bought 3 bottles of floor cleaner for \$12.05. How much will Abraham pay for 15 bottles?

15. A realtor earns a \$25,000 commission for selling a \$300,000 house. At the same rate, what commission would the realtor make when selling a \$250,000 house?

16. The ratio of perimeters of two triangles is 2 to 7. If the perimeter of the smaller triangle is 24 in., what is the perimeter of the larger triangle?

17. A fourth-grade class is going on a treasure hunt. If the map scale is 1 in. to 3 ft and the treasure is 8.5 in. away from the class on the map, what is the actual distance between the class and the treasure?

18. In a television survey, 4 of 5 people liked comedy shows more than reality shows. If 6000 people were surveyed, how many people preferred comedy shows?

19. Samir paid \$15.50 in shipping charges on a package that weighed 20 lb. If shipping costs a certain set amount per pound, what shipping charges would Samir pay on a 50 lb package?

20. The ratio of the areas of two rectangles is 2 to 3. If the area of the larger rectangle is 600 ft^2, what is the area of the smaller rectangle?

21. On a map, a housing development is represented by a rectangle with a width of 5 cm and a length of 10 cm. If the development is 2 mi wide, how long is it?

22. **Challenge** At SaveRite, a 4 oz carton of juice costs 85¢ and a 16 oz carton costs \$2.70. Which size carton would you buy to pay the least amount per ounce?

On a game show, 4 of 7 people in the 434-person audience chose the correct answer to the geography question and 1 of 2 people chose the incorrect answer to the trivia question.

23. **Challenge** How many people answered the geography question correctly?

24. **Challenge** How many people answered the trivia question incorrectly?

Similarity and Scale

Similar figures are figures that have the exact same shape but not necessarily the same size.

> **REMEMBER**
> Congruent angles are angles having equal measures.

Figures are similar if corresponding angles are congruent and corresponding sides are proportional.

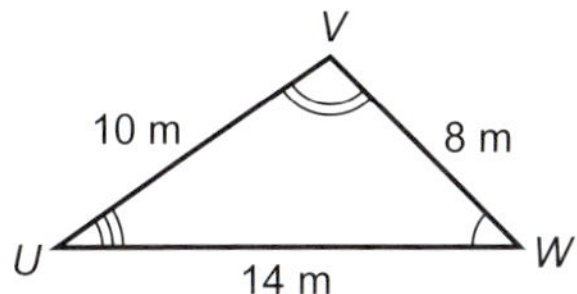

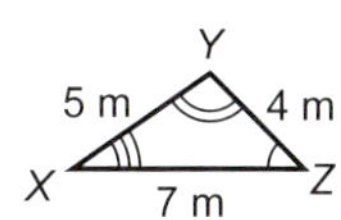

ΔUVW is similar to ΔXYZ so

$$\angle U \cong \angle X, \quad \angle V \cong \angle Y, \quad \angle W \cong \angle Z$$

$$\frac{UV}{XY} = \frac{VW}{YZ}; \frac{UV}{XY} = \frac{WU}{ZX}; \frac{VW}{YZ} = \frac{WU}{ZX}$$

> **TIP**
> UV means the length of $\overline{UV}$.

Cross multiply to see if the fractions are equal.

$\frac{10}{5} \stackrel{?}{=} \frac{8}{4}$	$\frac{10}{5} \stackrel{?}{=} \frac{14}{7}$	$\frac{8}{4} \stackrel{?}{=} \frac{14}{7}$
$10 \cdot 4 \stackrel{?}{=} 5 \cdot 8$	$10 \cdot 7 \stackrel{?}{=} 5 \cdot 14$	$8 \cdot 7 \stackrel{?}{=} 4 \cdot 14$
$40 = 40$ ✓	$70 = 70$ ✓	$56 = 56$ ✓

Determining Whether Two Figures Are Similar

EXAMPLE 1 Determine whether rectangles $ABCD$ and $EFGH$ are similar.

Solution

Step 1 Check corresponding angles.

Because both figures are rectangles, all angles measure 90°.
Thus, $\angle A \cong \angle E$; $\angle B \cong \angle F$; $\angle C \cong \angle G$; $\angle D \cong \angle H$.

Therefore, corresponding angles are congruent.

Step 2 Check corresponding sides.

If corresponding sides are proportional, then $\frac{AD}{EH} = \frac{AB}{EF}$.

$\frac{2}{8} \stackrel{?}{=} \frac{5}{20}$	Write the measures of the side lengths as a proportion and check to see if the proportion is true.
$2 \cdot 20 \stackrel{?}{=} 8 \cdot 5$	Cross multiply to see if the fractions are equal.
$40 = 40$	

Because corresponding angles are congruent and corresponding sides are proportional, the rectangles are similar. ■

Using Similarity to Find Missing Side Lengths

You can use the properties of similar figures to find a missing side.

EXAMPLE 2 ΔGHI and ΔJKL are similar. What is the length of $\overline{JK}$?

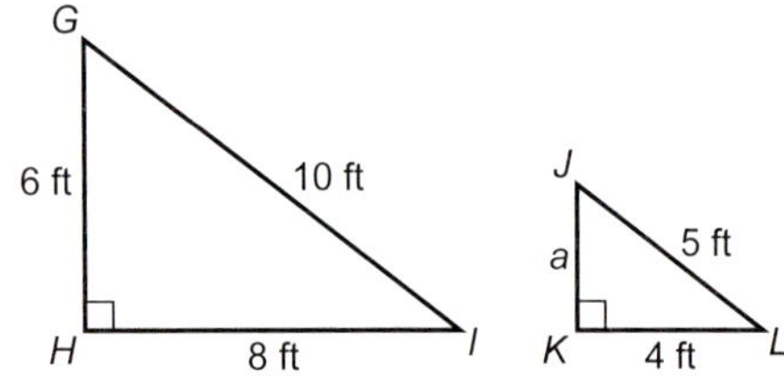

Solution $\overline{GH}$ corresponds to $\overline{JK}$. $\overline{HI}$ corresponds to $\overline{KL}$. Set up the corresponding sides as a proportion. Then solve for a.

$\frac{6}{a} = \frac{8}{4}$	Write a proportion.
$6 \cdot 4 = 8a$	Cross multiply.
$\frac{24}{8} = \frac{8a}{8}$	Divide both sides by 8.
$3 = a$	Simplify.

The length of $\overline{JK}$ is 3 ft. ■

▶ REMEMBER

In the proportion $\frac{a}{b} = \frac{c}{d}$, a and d are the extremes, and b and c are the means. The product of the means equals the product of the extremes.

Determining Scale

A **scale factor** is a ratio of one measure to another. You can find a scale factor of a figure by using the ratio of corresponding parts.

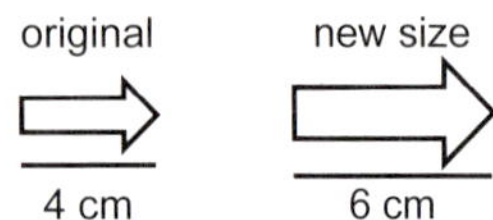

The new size is an enlargement and therefore is similar to the original figure. To find the scale factor, write a ratio comparing corresponding sides.

$\frac{\text{new size}}{\text{original size}} = \frac{6 \text{ cm}}{4 \text{ cm}} = \frac{3}{2}$ The scale factor for the arrows is 3 : 2 or 1.5.

EXAMPLE 3 The regular pentagons shown are similar. What is the scale factor?

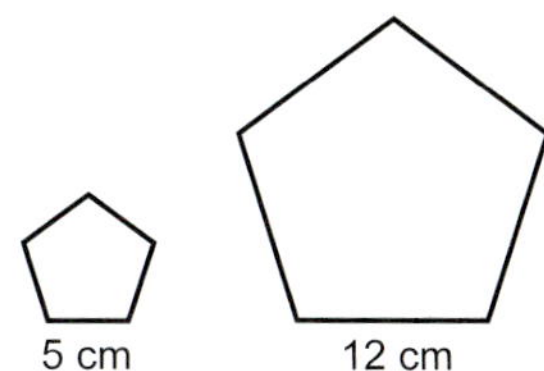

Solution These figures show an enlargement, so the scale factor is greater than 1.

The scale factor is $\frac{12}{5}$. ■

> **THINK ABOUT IT**
> All regular pentagons are similar to each other.

Using a Scale Factor

A scale factor greater than 1 indicates an enlargement. A scale factor less than 1 indicates a reduction. A scale factor equal to 1 means there is no change in size.

EXAMPLE 4 An equilateral triangle with a side length of 8 cm is multiplied by the scale factors below. State whether the new triangle is an enlargement or a reduction. Then find the side length of the new size.

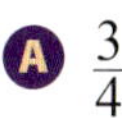

$\frac{3}{4}$

Solution This triangle is a reduction because the scale factor is less than 1.

Multiplying by the scale factor, you have $\frac{3}{4} \cdot 8 = 6$. The new side measure is 6 cm. ■

B 2.2

Solution This triangle is an enlargement because the scale factor is greater than 1. Multiplying by the scale factor, you have $2.2 \cdot 8 = 17.6$. The new side measure is 17.6 cm. ■

Application: Photography

EXAMPLE 5 A rectangular picture is 2.5 in. wide and 4 in. long. If the picture is enlarged so that it is 10 in. long, what is the new width?

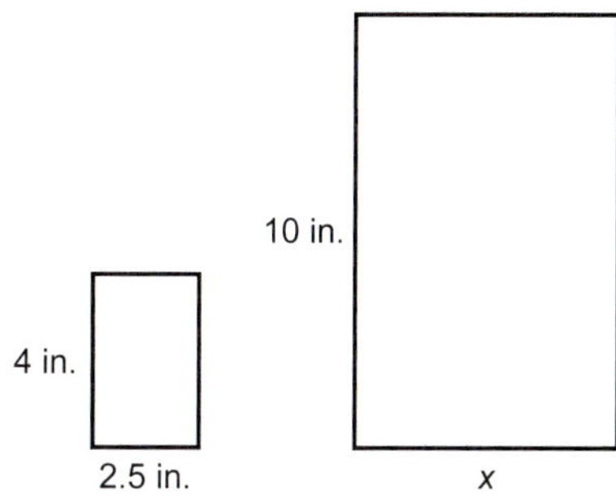

Solution Because the figures show an enlargement, the pictures will be similar.

$\frac{2.5}{x} = \frac{4}{10}$ Set up a proportion using corresponding sides.

$2.5 \cdot 10 = 4x$ Cross multiply.

$\frac{25}{4} = \frac{4x}{4}$ Divide both sides by 4.

$6.25 = x$ Simplify.

The width of the enlarged picture is 6.25 in. ■

Problem Set

Solve.

1. Determine whether *GHIJ* and *KLMN* are similar.

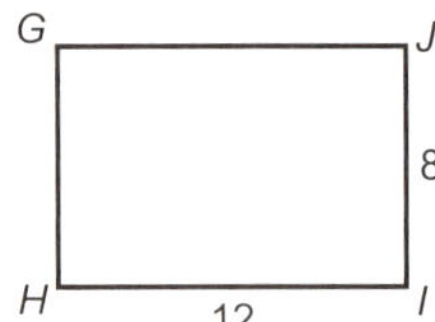

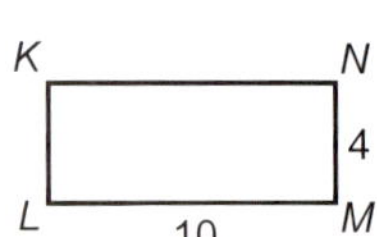

2. The corresponding angles of the triangles are congruent. Determine whether ΔABC and ΔDEF are similar.

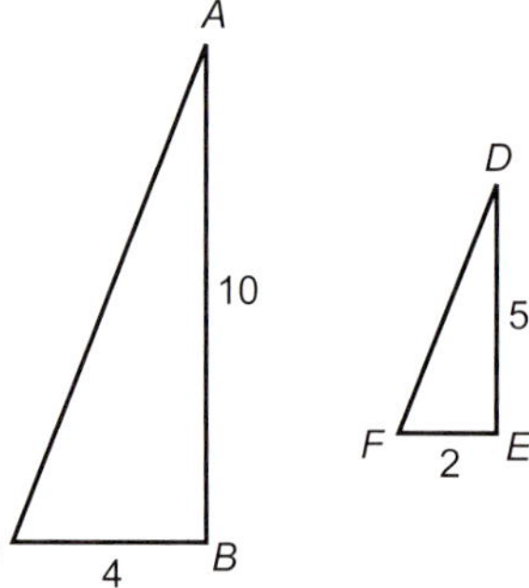

The paired figures are similar. Find the value of *x*.

3.

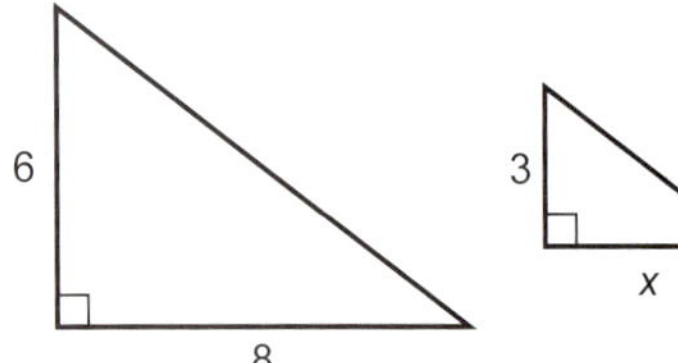

4.

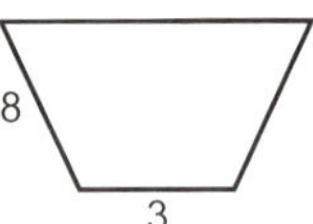

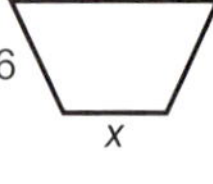

5.

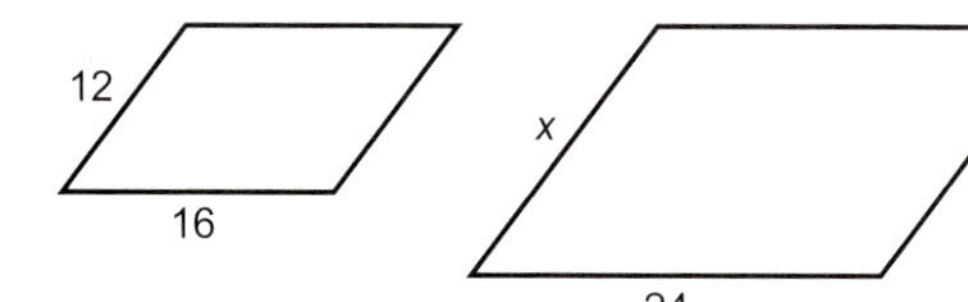

6.

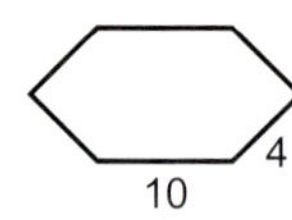

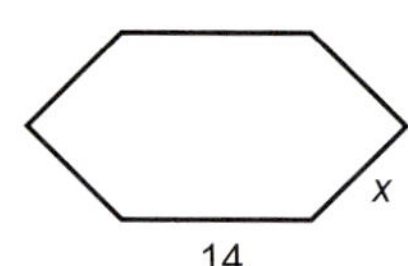

The two figures are similar. State the scale factor.
Determine whether the scale factor is an enlargement or a reduction.

7.

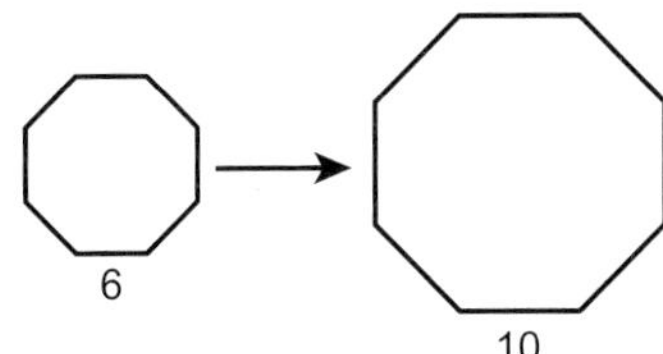

8.

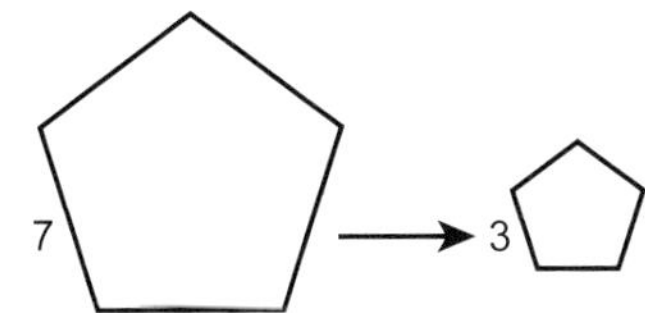

9.

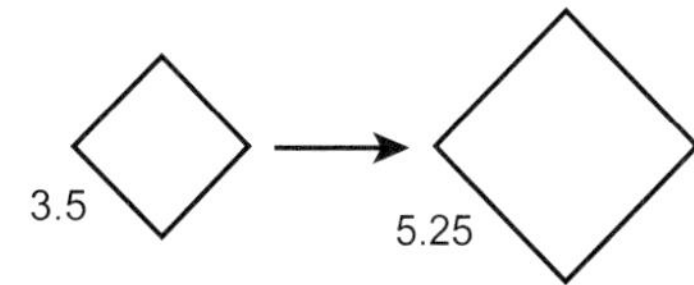

10.

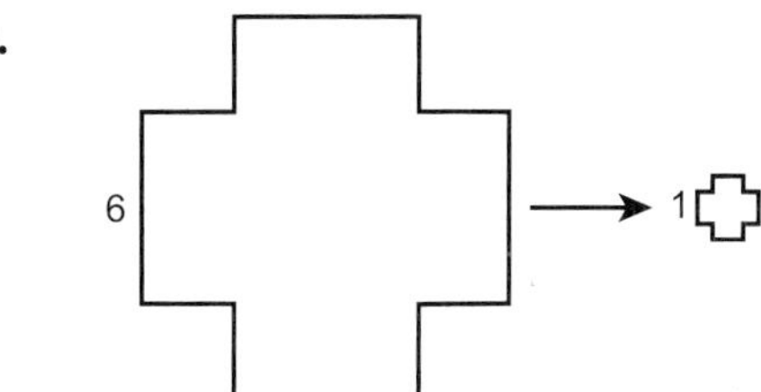

Solve.

11. A regular pentagon has sides measuring 5 cm. The pentagon is enlarged using a scale factor of $\frac{3}{2}$. What are the lengths of each side of the enlarged pentagon?

12. A photograph measures 10 in. wide by 18 in. long. If the picture is reduced so that the length is 6 in. what is the new width?

13. **Challenge** An equilateral triangle has a perimeter of 33 cm. If the triangle is enlarged using a scale factor of 4, what is the length of one side of the triangle?

14. **Challenge** A square with side lengths of 12 cm is multiplied by a scale factor of $\frac{3}{4}$.

(a) State whether the new square is an enlargement or a reduction.

(b) Find the side lengths of the new square.

(c) How did the perimeter of the square change after the scale factor was applied? Explain.

(d) How did the area of the square change after the scale factor was applied? Explain.

Proportional Relationships

You can use equations and tables to describe proportional relationships.

DEFINITIONS

A relationship between x and y is a **proportional relationship** if you can write the relationship between the two variables in a form of the **general equation**, $y = kx$, where k is the **constant of variation**.

Identifying Proportional Relationships and the Constant of Variation

If $y = kx$, then $k = \frac{y}{x}$. If $\frac{y}{x}$ is the same value k for every ordered pair (x, y), then x and y have a proportional relationship.

EXAMPLE 1 Determine whether the relationship is proportional. If so, state the constant of variation.

A

x	2	4	6	8	10
y	5	10	15	20	25

Solution Divide each value of y by its corresponding x-value.

$$\frac{5}{2} = 2.5, \frac{10}{4} = 2.5, \frac{15}{6} = 2.5, \frac{20}{8} = 2.5, \frac{25}{10} = 2.5$$

The relationship is proportional with a constant of variation of 2.5. ■

B $y - 4 = -2x$

Solution Solve for y to see if the specific equation fits the form of the general equation $y = kx$.

$y - 4 = -2x$

$y = -2x + 4$ Add 4 to each side.

The equation does not fit the form of the general equation because it has a constant term 4. The relationship is not proportional. ■

Writing and Using Equations for Proportional Relationships

You can write an equation for a proportional relationship if you know a pair of values.

EXAMPLE 2 If y and x have a proportional relationship, and $y = -12$ when $x = 18$, find the value of y when $x = 15$.

Solution

Step 1 Find k.

$y = kx$	General form of equation
$k = \frac{y}{x}$	Solve the general equation for k.
$k = \frac{-12}{18}$	Substitute -12 for y and 18 for x.
$k = -\frac{2}{3}$	Simplify.

Step 2 Substitute the value of k found in Step 1 into the general equation.

$y = kx$	General form of equation
$y = -\frac{2}{3}x$	Substitute $-\frac{2}{3}$ for k to obtain the specific equation.

Step 3 Use the specific equation $y = -\frac{2}{3}x$ to find y when $x = 15$.

$y = -\frac{2}{3}x$	Specific equation
$= -\frac{2}{3} \cdot 15$	Substitute 15 for x.
$= -10$	Simplify.

So $y = -10$ when $x = 15$.

TIP

The equation for a proportional relationship is $y = kx$. Once you find the constant of variation and substitute that value for k in the general equation, you get the specific equation for a particular problem.

Application: Cost

EXAMPLE 3 The cost of grapes is proportional to the weight. If 3.5 lb of grapes costs \$4.55, write an equation that represents the relationship. Then determine the number of pounds of grapes that can be purchased for \$10.14, before tax.

Solution

Step 1 Find the equation. Let w represent the weight and c represent the cost.

The cost is proportional to the number of pounds, so $c = 4.55$ when $w = 3.5$. Find k.

$$k = \frac{c}{w} = \frac{4.55}{3.5} = 1.3$$

The specific equation is $c = 1.3w$.

Step 2 Substitute 10.14 for c and solve for w.

$c = 1.3w$	
$10.14 = 1.3w$	Substitute 10.14 for c.
$7.8 = w$	Divide each side by 1.3.

So 7.8 lb of grapes can be purchased for \$10.14, before tax.

Problem Set

Determine whether the relationship is proportional. If so, state the constant of variation.

1.

x	3	6	9	12	15
y	6	12	18	24	30

2.

x	1	3	5	7	9
y	4	10	16	22	28

3. $y = 10x$

4. $y = x - 12$

5. $y = \frac{9}{x}$

6. $y = \frac{1}{7}x$

7.

a	2	4	6	8	10
b	8	16	24	32	40

8.

t	1	2	3	4	5
h	3	5	7	9	11

Write an equation for the relationship and find the missing value.

9. If y varies directly with x, and $y = 6$ when $x = 9$, what is the value of x when $y = 7$?

10. If y varies directly with x, and $y = 20$ when $x = -4$, what is the value of y when $x = 2$?

11. If h varies directly with d, and $h = 30$ when $d = -10$, what is the value of d when $h = 4$?

12. If g varies directly with a, and $g = 3$ when $a = 9$, what is the value of g when $a = 6$?

13. If g varies directly with t, and $g = 5$ when $t = 20$, what is the value of t when $g = 9$?

14. If y varies directly with x, and $y = 49$ when $x = 7$, what is the value of y when $x = 12$?

15. If y varies directly with x, and $y = 1$ when $x = -4$, what is the value of y when $x = 10$?

16. If h varies directly with z, and $h = 6$ when $z = -20$, what is the value of z when $h = 11$?

Write an equation for the proportional relationship.

17. $y = 4$ when $x = 12$

18. $y = 30$ when $x = 3$

19. $b = -5$ when $a = 2$

20. $y = 8$ when $x = -16$

21. $y = 2$ when $x = -8$

22. $n = 6$ when $m = 3$

Write an equation for the relationship and solve.

23. The total cost of gas varies directly with the price paid per gallon. If 5 gal of gas costs \$13.35, determine the number of gallons of gas purchased if the total cost is \$34.71.

24. The acceleration of an object varies directly with the force acting on it. If a force of 70 newtons (N) causes an acceleration of 6.5 m/s^2, what force will cause an acceleration of 8 m/s^2?

25. The time Oni spends running varies directly with the miles he runs. If he runs 4 mi in 1 h at a steady pace, determine how long it will take Oni to run 5.7 mi.

26. The circumference of a circle varies directly with its radius. If the circumference of a circle with a radius of 1.5 in. is 9.42 in., what is the circumference of a circle with a radius of 9 in.?

27. The stretch of a loaded spring varies directly with the load it supports. If a load of 7 kg stretches a certain spring 2.5 cm, what load would stretch the spring 5 cm?

28. Paula's pay varies directly with the number of hours that she works. If she earned \$52.50 for 6 h of work, how much will she earn for 11 h of work?

Core Focus: Graphing Proportions

THE CORE CONCEPT

You can use the graph of a proportional relationship to find the ratio of the two quantities.

Rates

Each point on the graph of a proportional relationship represents a rate. You can find the rate by calculating the ratio of the y-coordinate to the x-coordinate.

REMEMBER

A **rate** is a ratio of two quantities measured in different units.

EXAMPLE 1 The number of loaves of bread baked is proportional to the amount of sugar used. The graph shows this relationship.

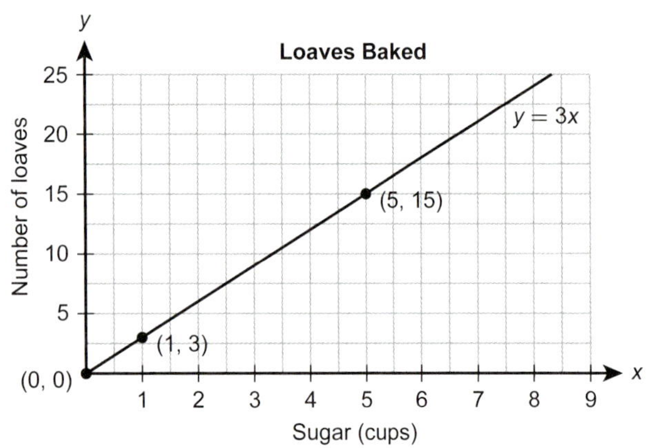

A What rate does the point (5, 15) on the graph represent?

Solution The x-coordinate represents 5 cups of sugar, and the y-coordinate represents 15 loaves baked. So the ratio of loaves of bread baked to sugar used is $\frac{y}{x}$, equal to the rate of $\frac{15 \text{ loaves}}{5 \text{ cups}}$. ■

B What does the point (0, 0) represent?

Solution The x-coordinate represents 0 cups of sugar, and the y-coordinate represents 0 loaves baked. So for every 0 cups of sugar used, 0 loaves of bread are baked.

The point (0, 0) does **not** represent a rate, since the ratio of loaves baked to sugar used is $\frac{0}{0}$, which is undefined because the denominator is 0. ■

C Why does the point (1, 3) represent a unit rate?

Solution The x-coordinate represents 1 cup of sugar, and the y-coordinate represents 3 loaves baked. Thus, the ratio of loaves of bread baked to sugar used is $\frac{y}{x}$, equal to the rate of $\frac{3 \text{ loaves}}{1 \text{ cup}}$, which is the unit rate of 3 loaves/cup. ■

EXAMPLE 2 The graph shows the price of silver in relation to the amount of silver purchased.

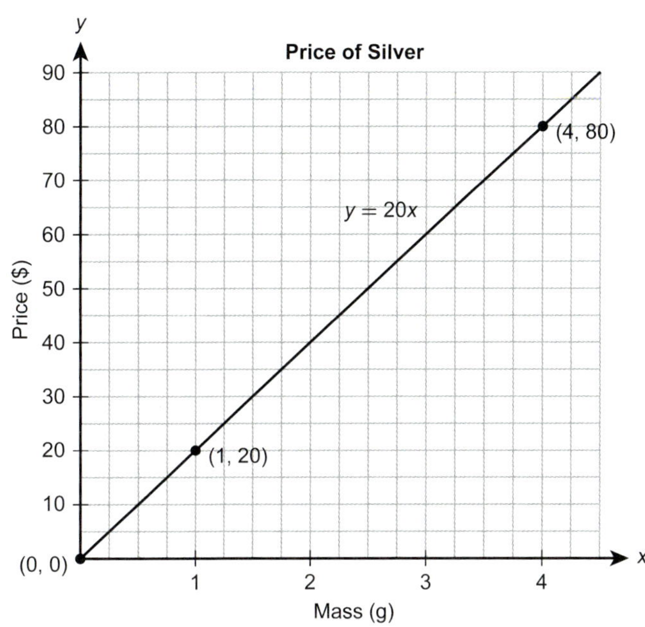

A How does the point (4, 80) represent a rate?

Solution The x-coordinate represents a mass of 4 g, and the y-coordinate represents a price of $80. The ratio of the price of silver to the amount purchased is $\frac{y}{x}$, equal to the rate $\frac{\$80}{4 \text{ g}}$. ■

B How does the point (1, 20) represent a unit rate?

Solution The x-coordinate represents a mass of 1 g, and the y-coordinate represents a price of $20. The ratio of the price of silver to the amount purchased is $\frac{y}{x}$, equal to the unit rate of $20/g. ■

C Explain why the points (4, 80) and (1, 20) show that the price of silver varies directly with the amount purchased.

Solution For both points, the ratio of $\frac{y}{x}$ is equal to 20.

point (4, 80): $\frac{80}{4} = 20$ point (1, 20): $\frac{20}{1} = 20$

Because the ratio of y to x is constant, at 20, the price of silver varies directly with the amount purchased, with a constant of variation of $20. ■

DID YOU KNOW?

The price of precious metals such as silver is often given in dollars per gram.

Q & A

Q According to the graph, how much would 2 g of silver cost?

A $40

Problem Set

Solve.

1. The amount of salt, in grams, in a solution is proportional to the volume, in liters, of the solution. The graph shows this relationship.

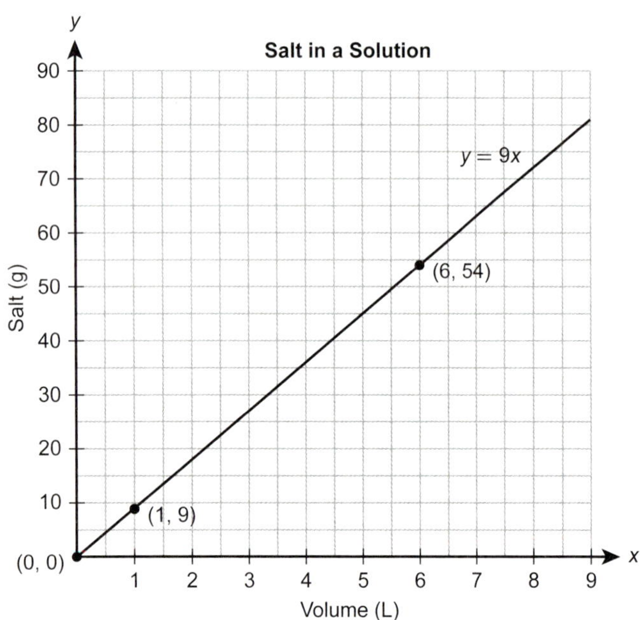

(a) What rate does the point (6, 54) on the graph represent? Explain.

(b) What does the point (0, 0) represent? Does it represent a rate? Explain.

(c) Why does the point (1, 9) represent a unit rate? Explain.

2. The graph shows the distance traveled by a turtle over time.

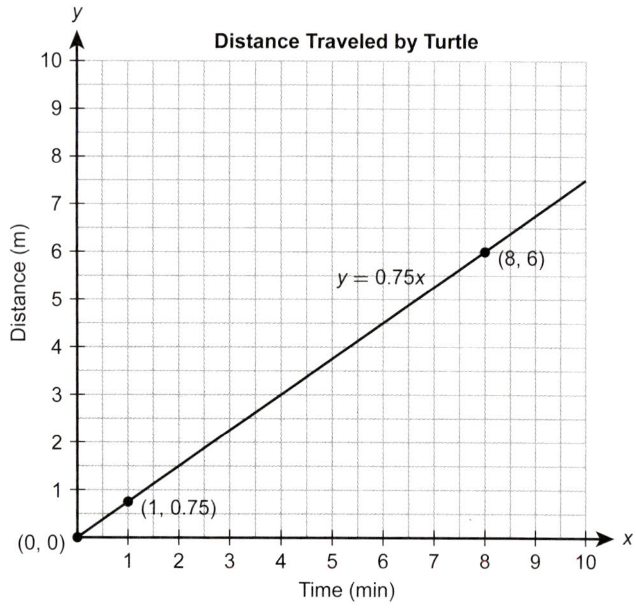

(a) How does the point (8, 6) represent a rate? Explain.

(b) How does the point (1, 0.75) represent a unit rate? Explain.

(c) Explain how the points (8, 6) and (1, 0.75) show that the distance the turtle travels varies directly with the passage of time.

Percent Problems

Percent means "parts per hundred."

Because you can write every ratio as a fraction or decimal, you can also write every percent as a fraction or decimal.

Converting Between Fraction, Decimal, and Percent

Use the following rules to make conversions involving percents.

PROPERTIES

Percent to Fraction To write a percent as a fraction, remove the percent sign, and then write the number with a denominator of 100. Simplify the fraction if necessary.

Fraction to Percent To write a fraction as a percent, divide the numerator by the denominator and multiply by 100%.

Percent to Decimal To write a percent as a decimal, remove the percent sign, and then divide by 100.

Decimal to Percent To write a decimal as a percent, multiply by 100%.

REMEMBER

To multiply by 100, move the decimal point two places to the right. To divide by 100, move the decimal point two places to the left.

EXAMPLE 1 Write the percent as a decimal.

A 145%

Solution Remove the percent sign and divide by 100.

$$\begin{aligned} 145\% &= 145 \div 100 \\ &= 1.45 \end{aligned}$$

B 0.38%

Solution Remove the percent sign and divide by 100.

$$\begin{aligned} 0.38\% &= 0.38 \div 100 \\ &= 0.0038 \end{aligned}$$

EXAMPLE 2 Write the decimal as a percent.

A 0.003

Solution Multiply by 100%.

$$\begin{aligned} 0.003 &= 0.003 \cdot 100\% \\ &= 0.3\% \end{aligned}$$

B 6.5

Solution Multiply by 100%.

$$\begin{aligned} 6.5 &= 6.5 \cdot 100\% \\ &= 650\% \end{aligned}$$

EXAMPLE 3 Write the fraction as a percent.

A $\frac{5}{8}$

Solution Divide the numerator by the denominator and multiply by 100%.

$$\begin{aligned} \frac{5}{8} &= (5 \div 8) \cdot 100\% \\ &= 0.625 \cdot 100\% \\ &= 62.5\% \end{aligned}$$

B $\frac{7}{20}$

Solution Divide the numerator by the denominator and multiply by 100%.

$$\begin{aligned} \frac{7}{20} &= (7 \div 20) \cdot 100\% \\ &= 0.35 \cdot 100\% \\ &= 35\% \end{aligned}$$

Using the Percent Proportion

You can use the following proportion to solve percent problems.

$$\frac{\text{part}}{\text{whole}} = \frac{\text{percent}}{100}$$

EXAMPLE 4 Solve.

A What percent is 13 of 25?

Solution Write the percent proportion and fill in the known information.

$$\frac{\text{part}}{\text{whole}} = \frac{\text{percent}}{100}$$

$\frac{13}{25} = \frac{x}{100}$ Use x for the unknown percent.

$13 \cdot 100 = 25x$ Means-Extremes Product Property

$1300 = 25x$ Multiply.

$52 = x$ Divide each side by 25.

Thus, 13 is 52% of 25.

B What is 215% of 212?

Solution Write and solve a percent proportion.

$$\frac{\text{part}}{\text{whole}} = \frac{\text{percent}}{100}$$

$\frac{x}{212} = \frac{215}{100}$ Use x for the unknown part.

$100x = 212 \cdot 215$ Means-Extremes Product Property

$100x = 45{,}580$ Multiply.

$x = 455.8$ Divide each side by 100.

Thus, 455.8 is 215% of 212. ■

C Find the number of which 122 is 40%.

Solution

$$\frac{\text{part}}{\text{whole}} = \frac{\text{percent}}{100}$$

$\frac{122}{x} = \frac{40}{100}$ Use x for the unknown whole.

$122 \cdot 100 = x \cdot 40$ Means-Extremes Product Property

$12{,}200 = 40x$ Multiply.

$305 = x$ Divide each side by 40.

Therefore, 122 is 40% of 305. ■

Application: Recycling

EXAMPLE 5 During a recycling drive, the Green Club collected 125 cans and bottles. If 72% of the collected items were cans, how many bottles were collected?

Solution Let x equal the number of bottles collected. If 72% were cans, then 28% (100% − 72% = 28%) were bottles. Use this information to write and solve a percent proportion.

$$\frac{\text{part}}{\text{whole}} = \frac{\text{percent}}{100}$$

$\frac{x}{125} = \frac{28}{100}$ Note that x (the number of bottles) is an unknown part.

$x \cdot 100 = 125 \cdot 28$ Means-Extremes Product Property

$100x = 3500$ Multiply.

$x = 35$ Divide each side by 100.

A total of 35 bottles were collected during the recycling drive. ■

Problem Set

Write the percent as a decimal.

1. 8.4%
2. 215%
3. 147.3%
4. 0.09%

Write the number as a percent.

5. 2.7
6. 0.05
7. $\frac{4}{5}$
8. $\frac{3}{8}$
9. 0.7
10. 1.325
11. $\frac{27}{40}$
12. **Challenge** $2\frac{2}{5}$

Solve. Use the percent proportion and show your work.

13. What percent is 24 of 60?
14. What percent is 17 of 20?
15. What is 48% of 180?
16. What is 160% of 94?
17. Twelve is 30% of what number?
18. Eighty is 125% of what number?
19. Thirty-six is 40% of what number?
20. What percent is 18 of 15?
21. What is 74% of 325?
22. What percent is 65 of 81.25?
23. What is 30% of 25?
24. **Challenge** Find the number of which 41.76 is 43.5%.

Set up an equation and solve it to answer the question.

25. Yoshi spent $28.80 at the supermarket, which was 36% of the cash he had in his wallet.
    - **(a)** How much cash did Yoshi have before he paid his supermarket bill?
    - **(b)** After shopping, Yoshi bought dinner for his family for $16.50. He gave the server a 16% tip. How much money did Yoshi have left?
26. Julia has two memory cards for her digital camera. She has used 332.8 MB of the 512 MB card, and 22.4 MB of the 32 MB card. Which card has the highest percent used, and what is the difference between the percents?
27. Marisol scored 80% on her math test. The test had 45 questions, and each question was worth 1 point. How many questions did Marisol answer correctly?
28. Last softball season, Tai was at bat 75 times and got 24 hits. Show Tai's batting average as a percent and as a decimal to the thousandths place.
29. Three candidates were running for class president. Of the 250 students eligible to vote, 75 voted for Carlos and 32% of the students voted for LaToya. Of those who didn't vote for Carlos or LaToya, 60% voted for Stephanie and the rest of the students chose not to vote.
    - **(a)** What percent of the eligible students voted for Carlos?
    - **(b)** How many votes did LaToya receive?
    - **(c)** How many votes did Stephanie receive?
    - **(d)** Who won the election?
30. In Alan's survey of his classmates, he asked if they preferred swimming, skating, or skiing. In the survey, 27.5% of Alan's classmates chose swimming.
    - **(a)** If 11 classmates chose swimming, how many classmates does Alan have?
    - **(b)** Seventeen classmates chose skiing. What percent was that?

Percent of Increase or Decrease

Percent change is the the extent to which a quantity increases or decreases, expressed as a percent.

DETERMINING PERCENT OF CHANGE

amount of change = new amount − original amount

percent of change $= \frac{\text{amount of change}}{\text{original amount}} \cdot 100\%$

Finding Percent Increase and Decrease

EXAMPLE 1

A Find the percent increase from 10 to 15.

Solution

amount of change = new amount − original amount	Find the amount of change.
$= 15 - 10$	Substitute.
$= 5$	
percent of change $= \frac{\text{amount of change}}{\text{original amount}} \cdot 100\%$	
$= \frac{5}{10} \cdot 100\%$	Substitute.
$= 0.5 \cdot 100\%$	Multiply.
$= 50\%$	

The percent increase is 50%. ■

B Find the percent decrease from 15 to 10.

Solution

amount of change = new amount − original amount	Find the amount of change.
$= 10 - 15$	Substitute.
$= -5$	Subtract.

$$\text{percent of change} = \frac{\text{amount of change}}{\text{original amount}} \cdot 100\%$$

$= -\frac{5}{15} \cdot 100\%$ Substitute.

$= -\frac{500}{15}\%$ Simplify.

$= -33\frac{1}{3}\%$

The percent decrease is $33\frac{1}{3}\%$. ■

THINK ABOUT IT

A percent increase is not offset by the same percent decrease. For example, if an item that costs \$10 is marked up to \$15, the percent increase is 50%. If that item that costs \$15 is discounted to \$10, the percent decrease is $33\frac{1}{3}\%$.

EXAMPLE 2

A The population of Smalltown changed from 125 to 150. What was the percent increase?

Solution

$$\text{percent of change} = \frac{\text{amount of change}}{\text{original amount}} \cdot 100\%$$

$$= \frac{150 - 125}{125} \cdot 100\% = \frac{25}{125} \cdot 100\% = 0.2 \cdot 100\% = 20\%$$

The percent increase was 20%. ■

B Juan bought a new car for \$16,000. A year later, its value was \$13,600. What was the percent decrease in the value of the car in 1 year?

Solution

$$\text{percent of change} = \frac{\text{amount of change}}{\text{original amount}} \cdot 100\%$$

$$= \frac{13{,}600 - 16{,}000}{16{,}000} \cdot 100\% = \frac{-2400}{16{,}000} \cdot 100\% = -0.15 \cdot 100\% = -15\%$$

The percent decrease was 15%. ■

Using Percent Increase and Decrease

You can use a known percent of change to find a new value.

EXAMPLE 3

A A worker's salary is increased by 5%. If the old salary was \$12,500/year, what is the worker's new salary?

Solution Find the amount of increase, and then add that amount to the original amount.

increase $= 5\%$ of $12{,}500$ Find the increase.

$= 0.05 \times 12{,}500$

$= 625$

original amount + increase = new amount

$12{,}500 + 625 = 13{,}125$ Add the increase to the original amount.

The worker's new salary is \$13,125. ■

B Nathan weighed 180 lb. He went on a diet and lost 10% of his weight. What was Nathan's new weight?

Solution Find the amount of decrease, and then subtract this amount from the original amount.

decrease $= 10\%$ of 180	Find the decrease.
$= 0.10 \times 180$	
$= 18$	
original amount $-$ decrease $=$ new amount	
$180 - 18 = 162$	Subtract the decrease from the original amount.

Nathan's new weight was 162 lb.

TIP

For problems that involve percent of change, be careful to answer the question. If asked for a new value, do not answer with the amount of change.

Application: Zoology

EXAMPLE 4 Camels can go for a week without drinking water. A camel can survive a 40% weight loss due to lack of water. If a camel starts off weighing 1200 lb, how much will the camel weigh after a 40% weight loss?

Solution

decrease $= 40\%$ of 1200	Find the decrease.
$= 0.40 \times 1200$	
$= 480$	
original amount $-$ decrease $=$ new amount	
$1200 - 480 = 720$	Subtract the decrease from the original amount.

After a 40% weight loss, a camel originally weighing 1200 lb would weigh 720 lb.

Application: Real Estate

EXAMPLE 5 Mariah's house has appreciated in value over the last 3 years. It has gone from being worth \$125,000 to being worth \$175,000. What is the percent increase in the value of Mariah's house?

Solution

$$\text{percent of change} = \frac{\text{amount of change}}{\text{original amount}} \bullet 100\%$$

$$= \frac{175{,}000 - 125{,}000}{125{,}000} \bullet 100\% = \frac{50{,}000}{125{,}000} \bullet 100\% = 0.4 \bullet 100\% = 40\%$$

There has been a 40% percent increase in the value of Mariah's house.

Application: Sports

EXAMPLE 6

A The chart shows Nathan's bowling scores. What was the percent increase in his score from Game 1 to Game 2?

Game	Score
1	180
2	200
3	180

Solution

$$\text{percent of change} = \frac{\text{amount of change}}{\text{original amount}} \cdot 100\%$$

$$= \frac{200 - 180}{180} \cdot 100\% = \frac{20}{180} \cdot 100\% \approx 0.11 \cdot 100\% = 11\%$$

Nathan's score increased about 11% percent from Game 1 to Game 2. ■

B What was the percent decrease in Nathan's score from Game 2 to Game 3?

Solution

$$\text{percent of change} = \frac{\text{amount of change}}{\text{original amount}} \cdot 100\%$$

$$= \frac{180 - 200}{200} \cdot 100\% = \frac{-20}{200} \cdot 100\% = -0.1 \cdot 100\% = -10\%$$

Nathan's score decreased 10% percent from Game 2 to Game 3. ■

Problem Set

Find the percent increase or decrease. Round the percent to the nearest tenth, if necessary.

1. 25 to 15
2. 20 to 45
3. 95 to 60
4. 3 to 40
5. 150 to 230
6. 110 to 40
7. 250 to 100
8. 35 to 90
9. **Challenge** 23.5 to 119
10. **Challenge** 0.05 to 1.5

The chart shows the population each year for a small town. Use the chart to find the percent increase or decrease in population.

11. Year 1 to Year 2
12. Year 2 to Year 3
13. Year 3 to Year 4
14. Year 4 to Year 5
15. Year 1 to Year 5

Year	Population
1	2150
2	2500
3	2240
4	3200
5	3650

The chart shows the average temperature in degrees Fahrenheit for each month for a certain city. Use the information to find the percent increase or decrease in temperature.

Month	Jan.	Feb.	Mar.	Apr.	May	June	July	Aug.	Sept.	Oct.	Nov.	Dec.
Temp (°F)	24	28	33	40	47	54	56	55	50	42	33	28

16. January to February

17. January to June

18. March to August

19. November to April

20. December to July

21. April to October

22. **Challenge** Between which two consecutive months is there about a 9% decrease in temperature? Explain.

23. **Challenge** Between which two consecutive months is there about a 15% decrease in temperature? Explain.

Solve.

24. An e-waste collection drive gathered 3500 lb of e-waste last year. This year the collection drive gathered 5200 lb of e-waste. What is the percent of increase?

25. A cell phone plan allows 500 min of calling each month. The new plan will increase the number of minutes by 150%. What is the number of minutes allowed on the new plan?

26. Last year Dale mowed the lawn in 45 min. This year, it took Dale 38 min to mow the lawn. What is the percent decrease?

27. Ten years ago, a movie ticket sold for \$6.50. Now a movie ticket costs \$9.50. What is the percent increase?

28. An airplane was at an altitude of 33,000 ft. The plane decreased its altitude by 5%. What was the new altitude of the plane?

29. The temperature at one point during the day was 73°F. During the next hour it dropped to 68°F. What was the percent decrease?

30. Patrick reached a score of 1750 on a computer game. The next day he reached a score of 2300. What was the percent increase?

31. **Challenge** Doug's height was 5 ft. The next year Doug was 5 ft 4 in. tall. What was the percent increase?

Core Focus: Percent Error

THE CORE CONCEPT

The **percent error** of a quantity's measurement indicates how close the measurement is to the quantity's actual value.

Calculating Percent Error

PERCENT ERROR FORMULA

$$\text{percent error} = \frac{|\text{measured value} - \text{actual value}|}{\text{actual value}} \cdot 100\%$$

EXAMPLE 1 The measured width of a small bookcase is 90.6 cm. Its actual width is 90 cm. Find the percent error of the measurement. Round your answer to the nearest tenth of a percent.

Solution Use the percent error formula to calculate the percent error of the measured value.

$$\frac{|90.6 - 90|}{90} \cdot 100\% = \frac{|0.6|}{90} \cdot 100\% = \left(\frac{0.6}{90} \cdot 100\right)\% = \left(\frac{60}{90}\right)\% \approx 0.7\%$$

The percent error in the measured value is 0.7%.

DID YOU KNOW?

The absolute value of the difference between the measured value and the actual value is known as the **absolute error**.

Calculating Percent Error in an Estimate

Calculate the percent error in an estimate by substituting the estimated value in the percent error formula for the measured value. Then calculate the percent error as you would normally.

THINK ABOUT IT

Percent error is always greater than or equal to 0%. Its value is never negative.

EXAMPLE 2 Gunther estimates a mountain is 3000 m high. He later learns its actual height is 2876 m. What is the percent error in his estimate? Round your answer to the nearest tenth of a percent.

Solution Substitute the estimated and actual values into the percent error formula, and then calculate the percent error.

$$\frac{|2876 - 3000|}{3000} \cdot 100\% = \frac{|-124|}{3000} \cdot 100\% = \left(\frac{124}{3000} \cdot 100\right)\%$$

$$= \left(\frac{12{,}400}{3000}\right)\% \approx 4.1\%$$

The percent error in the estimated value is about 4.1%.

EXAMPLE 3 A scale is 10% off in measuring mass. The actual mass of a bracelet is 30 g. What masses might the scale show?

Solution Substitute known values into the percent error formula, and then solve for the bracelet's measured mass. The percent error is 10%, and the actual mass is 30 g. Let m represent the measured mass.

$$\frac{|\text{measured mass} - \text{actual mass}|}{\text{actual mass}} \bullet 100\% = \text{percent error}$$

$$\frac{|m - 30|}{30} \bullet 100\% = 10\%$$

$$\frac{|m - 30|}{30} \bullet \frac{100\%}{100\%} = \frac{10\%}{100\%}$$

$$\frac{|m - 30|}{30} = 0.1$$

$$30 \bullet \frac{|m - 30|}{30} = 30 \bullet 0.1$$

$$|m - 30| = 3$$

The equation $|m - 30| = 3$ is a distance equation indicating that the distance between m and 30 is 3. There are two values that are a distance of 3 units from 30: 27 and 33.

The scale is likely to show that the bracelet's mass is between 27 g and 33 g. ■

Problem Set

Find the percent error. Round to the nearest tenth of a percent.

1. Danni counted 48 apples in a basket of apples. The basket really contained 46 apples.
2. The measurement of the side length of a square piece of land is 215 m. Its actual length is 209.8 m.

Calculate the percent error in the estimate. Round to the nearest tenth of a percent.

3. Lina estimates that a bottle contains 500 mL of water, but it actually contains 473 mL of water.
4. A runner guesses that his time in a 400 m race was 56 s. His actual time was 54.7 s.
5. Frank thinks there were about 130 space shuttle missions. In reality, there were exactly 135 missions.

Solve.

6. According to a car's speedometer, the car is traveling at a speed of 47 mph. The speedometer's reading has a 5% error. What could the actual speed of the car be?

Simple Interest

If you borrow money from a bank, you have to pay interest. But if you deposit money into a savings account, the bank will pay you interest.

Interest is the cost to borrow money. **Principal** is money that earns interest at a given rate over time. The **interest rate** is the percentage of the original amount of money that the interest is based on. **Simple interest** is interest earned at a fixed percent of the initial deposit, or principal amount.

SIMPLE INTEREST FORMULA

When principal P is invested at annual interest rate r for t years, then the simple interest I earned is

$$I = Prt.$$

Borrowing Money

EXAMPLE 1

A Laura borrowed $48,000 at a 6% interest rate for 7 years. What was the total interest?

Solution

$I = Prt$

$= \$48{,}000 \cdot 0.06 \cdot 7$ Substitute.

$= \$20{,}160$ Multiply.

The total interest was $20,160. ■

B Bryan borrowed $12,800 at a 4.8% interest rate for 6 years. What was the total interest?

Solution

$I = Prt$

$= \$12{,}800 \cdot 0.048 \cdot 6$ Substitute.

$= \$3686.40$ Multiply.

The total interest was $3686.40. ■

REMEMBER

To write a percent as a decimal, move the decimal point two places to the left.

Saving Money

EXAMPLE 2 Cecil deposited \$5600 in a savings account earning 2.5% interest over 8 years. What was the total interest earned after 8 years?

Solution

$I = Prt$

$= \$5600 \cdot 0.025 \cdot 8$ Substitute.

$= \$1120$ Multiply.

Cecil's account earned \$1120 in interest. ■

Using the Simple Interest Formula to Calculate Other Values

EXAMPLE 3

A Fritz borrowed \$8000 at an interest rate of 6%. He paid \$1440 interest. Fritz borrowed the money for how much time?

Solution

$I = Prt$

$\$1400 = \$8000 \cdot 0.06 \cdot t$ Substitute.

$\$1440 = \$480t$ Multiply.

$\frac{\$1440}{\$480} = \frac{\$480t}{\$480}$ Divide each side by \$480.

$3 = t$

Fritz borrowed the money for 3 years. ■

B Hillary borrowed \$1500 for 5 years. She paid \$435 in interest. What was the interest rate?

Solution

$I = Prt$

$\$435 = \$1500 \cdot r \cdot 5$ Substitute.

$\$435 = \$7500r$ Multiply.

$\frac{\$435}{\$7500} = \frac{\$7500r}{\$7500}$ Divide each side by \$7500.

$0.058 = r$

$5.8\% = r$

The interest rate was 5.8%. ■

C Sue earned \$99.75 in interest from her savings account. If the interest rate is 2.5% over 7 years, what amount did Sue deposit?

Solution

$I = Prt$

$\$99.75 = P \cdot 0.025 \cdot 7$ Substitute and solve for P.

$\$99.75 = 0.175P$ Multiply.

$\frac{\$99.75}{0.175} = \frac{0.175P}{0.175}$ Divide each side by 0.175.

$\$570 = P$

Sue deposited \$570.

Problem Set

Use the simple interest formula $I = Prt$ to solve.

1. Find the interest if the principal is \$500, the interest rate is 3%, and the time is 5 years.
2. Find the interest if the principal is \$2300, the interest rate is 4%, and the time is 3 years.
3. Find the interest if the principal is \$10,000, the interest rate is 2%, and the time is 8 years.
4. Find the principal if the interest is \$264, the interest rate is 5.5%, and the time is 6 years.
5. Find the principal if the interest is \$857.50, the interest rate is 3.5%, and the time is 7 years.
6. Find the interest rate if the principal is \$8900, the interest is \$4272, and the time is 10 years.
7. Find the interest rate if the principal is \$25,000, the interest is \$10,875, and the time is 15 years.
8. Find the time if the principal is \$32,500, the interest is \$12,870, and the interest rate is 3.3%.
9. Find the time if the principal is \$5300, the interest is \$1335.60, and the interest rate is 7.2%.
10. Find the interest if the principal is \$8400, the interest rate is 6.3%, and the time is $6\frac{3}{4}$ years.

Solve.

11. Mark deposited \$750 in a savings account earning 3% interest over 9 years. What was the total interest earned after 9 years?
12. Taylor borrowed \$14,000 at a 6% interest rate for 5 years. What was the total interest?
13. You borrow \$5000 at an interest rate of 4%. The interest paid is \$1800. For how long did you borrow the money?
14. Jerry borrows \$6200 for 8 years. The interest paid is \$2579.20. What was the interest rate?
15. Ryan earned \$212 in interest from his savings account. If the interest rate is 3% over 8 years, what amount did Ryan deposit?
16. Morgan borrowed \$28,000 at an 8% interest rate for 10 years. What was the total interest?
17. Milo borrows \$15,000 for 12 years. The interest paid is \$7200. What was the interest rate?
18. Casey borrowed \$10,000 at a 5.5% interest rate for 7 years. What was the total interest?
19. Bella earned \$85.60 in interest from her savings account. If the interest rate is 2% over 6 years, what amount did Bella deposit?
20. Alfredo deposited \$3500 in a savings account earning 5% interest over 7 years. What was the total interest earned after 7 years?

21. Rita borrowed \$7500 at an interest rate of 3%. The interest paid is \$1462.50. For how long did she borrow the money?

22. Corinne deposited \$15,000 in a savings account earning 3.5% interest over 6 years. What was the total interest earned after 6 years?

23. Christa earned \$1400 in interest from her savings account. If the interest rate is 3.5% over 10 years, what amount did Christa deposit?

24. You borrow \$11,000 for 6 years. The interest paid is \$1800. What is the interest rate?

25. Francesca deposited \$920 in a savings account earning 2% interest over 12 years. What was the total interest earned after 12 years?

26. Carrie borrows \$2600 at an interest rate of 2.5%. The interest paid is \$536.25. For how long did she borrow money?

27. Sam borrowed \$7000 at a 5% interest rate for 12 years. What is the total amount Sam must pay?

28. Carson deposited \$2350 in a savings account at a 4.5% interest rate for 15 years. What is the total amount Carson will have in the savings account at the end of 15 years?

29. **Challenge** Allison deposited \$5000 in a savings account that pays 3% interest.

    (a) What is the total amount Allison will have after 1 year? 2 years? 3 years?

    (b) Allison's savings will double after how many years?

Core Focus: Multistep Ratio and Percent Problems

THE CORE CONCEPT

It often takes several steps to solve a real-world percent problem.

Application: Percent of Total Cost

Some real-world problems involve finding the percent that an individual cost is of the total cost. To find the percent of a total cost, first add all of the individual costs to find the total cost. Then find the ratio of the individual cost to the total cost and multiply this ratio by 100%.

$$\text{percent of total cost} = \frac{\text{individual cost}}{\text{total cost}} \cdot 100\%$$

EXAMPLE 1 Membership at a health club costs \$35/month plus a one-time initial fee of \$50. For a 1-year membership, what percent of the total cost is the initial fee? Round to the nearest tenth of a percent.

Solution The total cost is the sum of the initial fee and the total monthly charges. The total monthly charges equal the product of the monthly fee and 12, the number of months in 1 year.

$$\$50 + \$35 \cdot 12 = \$50 + \$420 = \$470$$

Find the percent that the initial fee is of the total cost.

$$\frac{\$50}{\$470} \cdot 100\% \approx 10.6\%$$

The initial fee is about 10.6% of the total cost for 1 year.

DID YOU KNOW?

Many contracts for a monthly service, such as for a cell phone or a club membership, include a one-time initial fee as well as a monthly charge.

Application: Pre-Tax Price from a Final Price

FINAL PRICE FORMULA

The final price of an item is the sum of the pre-tax price and the amount of tax on the item.

final price = pre-tax price + tax paid

The tax paid is often a percent of the item's pre-tax price. You find the tax paid by converting the tax rate, expressed as a percent, to a decimal. Then multiply the decimal by the pre-tax price to find the tax paid.

EXAMPLE 2 Jenn bought a sweater for $41.73. The price she paid included 7% sales tax. What was the price of the sweater before the tax was added?

Solution The price Jenn paid for the sweater is equal to the sum of the price before tax and the amount of tax paid.

$$\text{final price} = \text{pre-tax price} + \text{tax paid}$$

Let p be the pre-tax price. The tax paid is 7% of the pre-tax price, represented by $0.07p$.

$$41.73 = p + 0.07p$$

$$41.73 = 1.07p$$

$$\frac{41.73}{1.07} = \frac{1.07p}{1.07}$$

$$39 = p$$

The price of the sweater before the tax was $39.

DID YOU KNOW?

The sales tax rate changes from state to state and, in some cases, from county to county within a state.

REMEMBER

The amount of tax paid is the product of the sales tax rate, as a decimal, and the pre-tax price.

Problem Set

Solve.

1. Juliana's cell phone bill includes a fixed monthly charge of $59/month plus a data charge of $6/GB downloaded. In August, Juliana downloaded 4 GB of data. What percent of Juliana's cell phone bill for August was from the data charge? Round your answer to the nearest tenth of a percent.

2. Eddie bought a used car for a total of $4792.50. The total amount that Eddie paid included 6.5% sales tax. What was the price of the car before the sales tax was added?

3. Naila had dinner delivered to her home from a restaurant. The check for her meal included three charges: the menu price of the meal, a delivery charge of 10% on the menu price of her meal, and sales tax of 5% on the sum of the menu price of her meal and the delivery charge. The total check amount was $32.34.

   (a) Let m represent the menu price of the meal. Write an equation that can be used to find the menu price of the meal.

   (b) What was the menu price for the meal?

Core Focus: Constant of Proportionality

THE CORE CONCEPT

You can determine the constant of proportionality between two quantities from a table of values, an equation, or a graph.

Finding the Constant of Proportionality

DEFINITIONS

Two quantities that vary directly with each other are also said to be **directly proportional**. The **constant of proportionality** is equal to the ratio of the two directly proportional quantities.

DID YOU KNOW?

The constant of proportionality is just another term for the constant of variation.

You find the constant of proportionality k between two proportional quantities x and y as you would find the constant of variation between two quantities that vary directly with each other. Find the ratio between the quantities: $k = \frac{y}{k}$.

EXAMPLE Tami makes salsa at a restaurant. The amount of salsa made is proportional to the amount of lime juice used.

Lime juice (tbsp)	2	4	6
Salsa (cups)	5	10	15

A Find the constant of proportionality.

Solution The constant of proportionality is the ratio of the amount of salsa made to the amount of lime juice used.

$$\frac{5}{2} = 2.5, \frac{10}{4} = 2.5, \frac{15}{6} = 2.5$$

The constant of proportionality is 2.5. ■

B Write an equation expressing the relationship between the two quantities. Graph the equation along with the values from the table.

Solution Let S be the amount of salsa made and L be the amount of lime juice used.

If $\frac{S}{L} = 2.5$, then $S = 2.5L$.

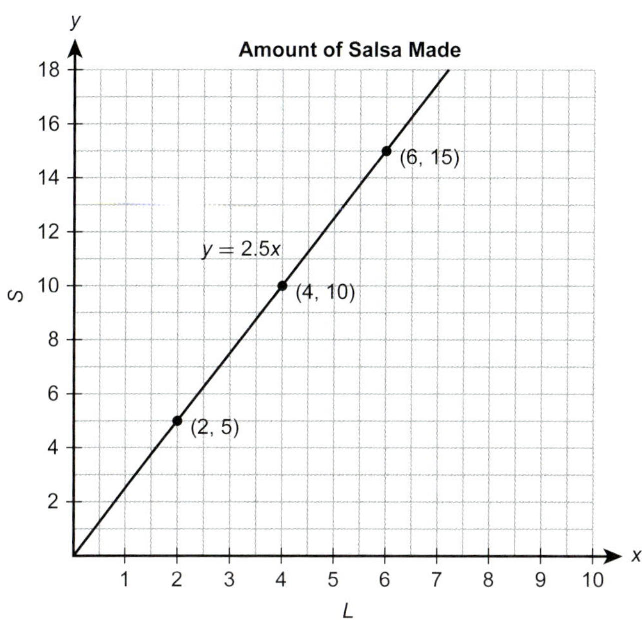

Problem Set

Solve.

1. Tami works as a lifeguard at a swimming pool. She works a 4, 6, or 8 hr shift. The table shows the pay Tami receives for the number of hours worked.

Hours worked	4	6	8
Pay ($)	46	69	92

(a) Find the constant of proportionality.

(b) Write an equation expressing the relationship between the number of hours Tami worked and her pay.

(c) Graph the equation and graph the values in the table.

(d) How much would Tami earn for 7 h of work?

2. The speed s, measured in meters per second, of a ball dropped from a tower is $s = 9.8t$, where t is the time elapsed, in seconds, after the ball was dropped.

(a) What is the constant of proportionality? Show your reasoning.

(b) How are the unit rate and the constant of proportionality related? Explain.

3. The table shows the cost of printing travel brochures.

Quantity	100	200	500	1000
Cost ($)	5	10	24	46

Is the cost of printing the brochures proportional to the quantity printed? Show your reasoning using ratios.

CHAPTER 8 Review

Choose the answer.

1. The two figures are similar. What is the value of x?

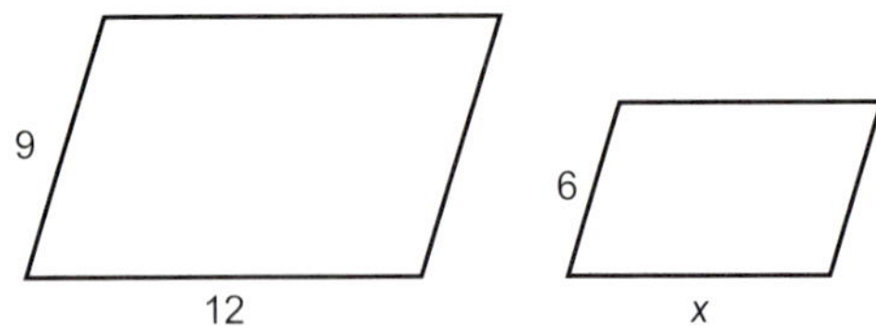

A. 4.5

B. 8

C. 9

D. 18

2. What value of z makes the equation true?

$$\frac{1}{8} = \frac{z - 5}{16}$$

A. −3

B. 4

C. 7

D. 14

3. Avishai sold 4 identical pillows for \$39. For how much would Avishai sell 10 of the same pillow?

A. \$9.75

B. \$87.50

C. \$97.50

D. \$390

4. If y is proportional to x and $y = -10$ when $x = 15$, what is the value of x when $y = 12$?

A. −18

B. −8

C. 17

D. 37

5. What percent is 40 of 25?

A. 10%

B. 62.5%

C. 115%

D. 160%

6. What is the percent of increase from 40 to 100?

A. 40%

B. 60%

C. 150%

D. 250%

7. Keiko estimated that she would get an 85 on her next math quiz. Her actual score was a 93. What was the percent error in her estimate, rounded to the nearest tenth of a percent?

A. 8.0%

B. 8.6%

C. 9.4%

D. 15.0%

8. Gaby deposited \$200 in a savings account earning 5% simple interest over 7 years. What was the total interest Gaby earned?

A. \$10

B. \$14

C. \$35

D. \$70

9. Are x and y proportional? $y = 2.4x$

A. No, because the ratio of x to y is not a constant

B. No, because the ratio of y to x is not an integer

C. Yes, because the ratio of x to y is a constant, equal to 2.4

D. Yes, because the ratio of y to x is a constant, equal to 2.4

Solve.

10. The polygons are similar. State the scale factor. Determine whether the scale factor is an enlargement or a reduction.

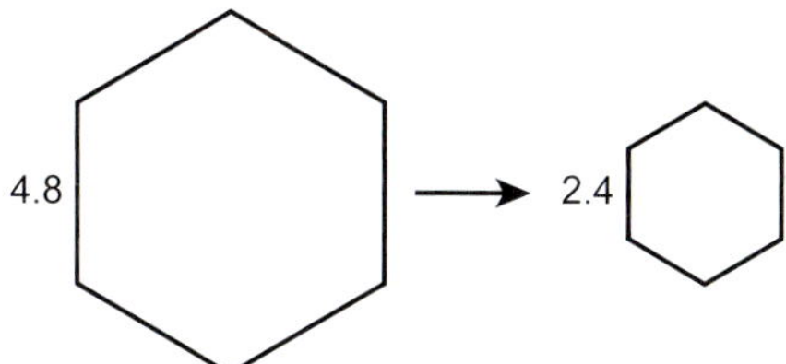

11. The tension in a spring is proportional to the distance the spring is stretched. If the tension is 10 newtons (N) for a spring stretched 0.2 m, what is the tension in the spring if it is stretched 0.35 m?

12. Jeremy made 65% of the free throws he attempted in one basketball season. He made 26 free throws. How many free throws did Jeremy attempt?

13. An eagle was at an altitude of 1450 m. The eagle increased its altitude to 1600 m. What was the percent increase in the altitude? Round to the nearest percent.

14. John guessed that a jar held 475 pennies. The actual number of pennies in the jar was 537. What is the percent error of John's guess?

15. Linda borrowed $12,000 for 6 years. The simple interest Linda paid was $2520. What was the interest rate?

16. DeSean paid $15.08 to buy a book online. The amount he paid included the price of the book plus 4% sales tax. What was the price of the book before the sales tax was added? Show your reasoning.

17. The graph compares numbers of peanuts and almonds in a nut mixture.

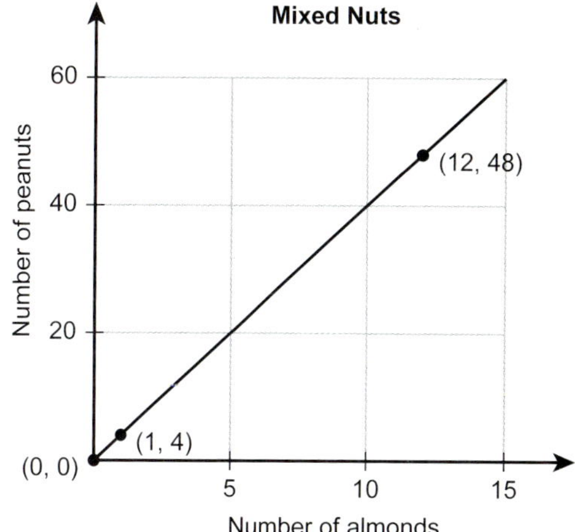

(a) How does the point (12, 48) represent a rate? Explain.

(b) How does the point (1, 4) represent a unit rate? Explain.

(c) Explain how the points (12, 48) and (1, 4) show that number of peanuts varies directly with the number of almonds.

18. The table shows the amount of lemon juice needed to make lemonade.

Lemon juice (cups)	5	10	20
Servings	35	70	140

(a) Are the two quantities proportional?

(b) If so, what is the constant of proportionality?

Problem	Topic Lookup	Problem	Topic Lookup
2, 3	Proportion Problems	6, 13	Percent of Increase or Decrease
1, 10	Similarity and Scale	7, 14	Core Focus: Percent Error
4, 11	Proportional Relationships	8, 15	Simple Interest
17	Core Focus: Graphing Proportions	16	Core Focus: Multistep Ratio and Percent Problems
5, 12	Percent Problems	9, 18	Core Focus: Constant of Proportionality

CHAPTER 9 Plane Figures

You can find geometric shapes in art. Artists need to understand angles and areas to create beautiful objects and to solve practical problems.

In This Chapter

In this chapter, you'll focus on geometry, including angles, triangles, and quadrilaterals. The chapter devotes special attention to constructing triangles and calculating the areas of triangles, quadrilaterals, and other polygons.

Topic List

- Foundations for Chapter 9
- Parallel Lines and Transversals
- Triangles
- Constructing Triangles
- Areas of Rectangles and Triangles
- Areas of Special Quadrilaterals
- Areas of Polygons
- Core Focus: How Many Triangles?
- Chapter 9 Review

An artist uses area to determine the amount of glass needed to create a piece like this. ▶

Foundations for Chapter 9

Naming Points and Lines

A point is named with a capital letter. Point M: •M

You can identify a line in two ways: (1) you can name any two points that are on the line (in any order); or (2) you can use a lowercase letter that might appear near the line.

EXAMPLE A List all the ways the line can be named.

Solution There is no lowercase letter near the line. Therefore, you can only name the line by using two points. It can be named line XY, line YX, line XZ, line ZX, line YZ, or line ZY. ■

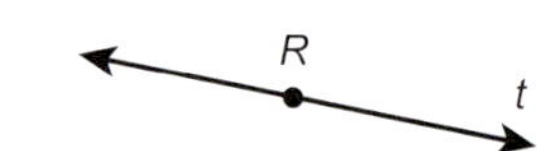

Solution Because only one point on the line is named, the line cannot be named by using points. The only name possible is line t. ■

Problem Set A

List all the ways the line can be named.

1.

2.

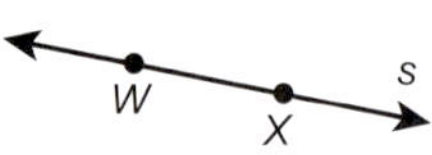

3. P C

4.

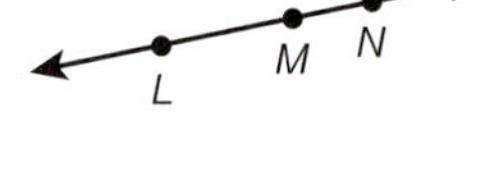

5.

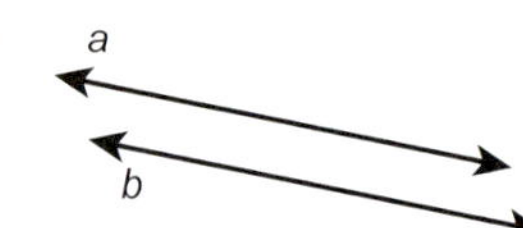

Name the lines drawn in the figure.

6.

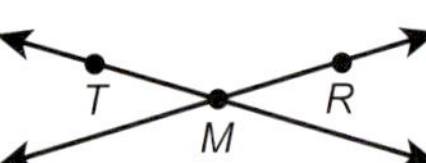

7.

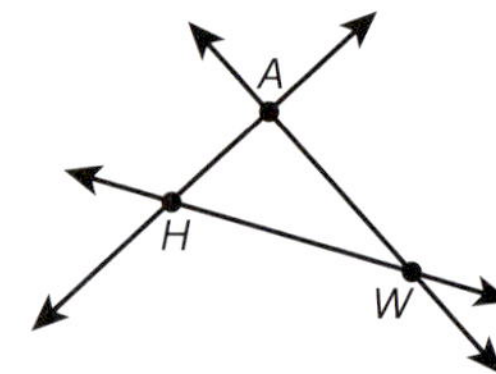

Naming Angles

There are three ways to name an angle: (1) you can use three points by naming a point on one side, the vertex, and then a point on the other side; (2) you can use just the vertex point; or (3) you can use the number that may appear near the vertex of the angle, between the sides.

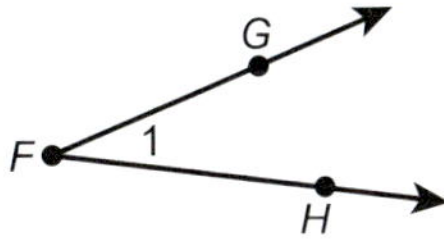

This angle can be named as angle *GFH*, angle *HFG*, $\angle GFH$, $\angle HFG$, angle *F*, $\angle F$, angle 1, or $\angle 1$

EXAMPLE B List all the ways the angle can be named.

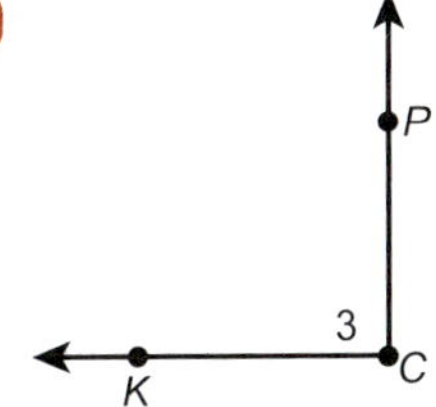

Solution The vertex is *C* so one possible name is $\angle C$. Other possible names are $\angle KCP$, $\angle PCK$, and $\angle 3$. ■

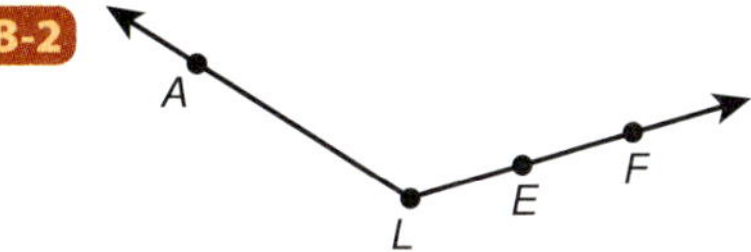

Solution The vertex is *L* so one possible name is $\angle L$. Other possible names are $\angle ALE$, $\angle ALF$, $\angle FLA$, and $\angle ELA$. ■

Problem Set B

List all the ways the angle can be named.

1.

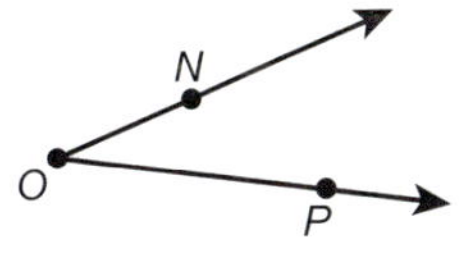

2.

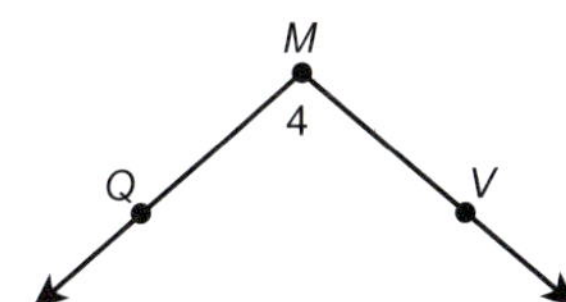

3.

4.

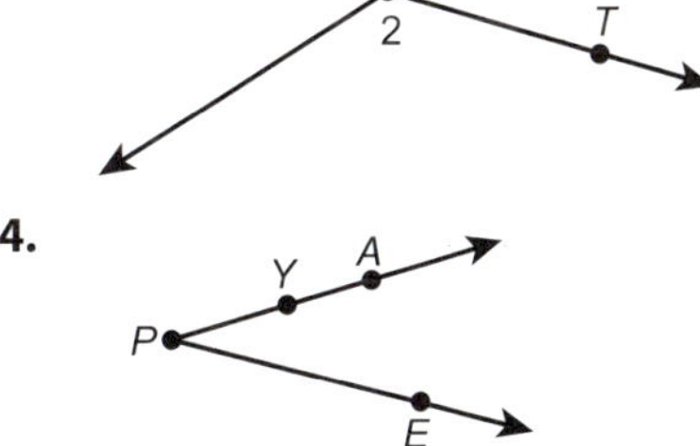

Describing Polygons by Side and Angle Congruence

DEFINITIONS

Two segments or angles are **congruent** if they have the same measure.

A polygon is **equiangular** if all of its angles are congruent.

A polygon is **equilateral** if all of its sides are congruent.

A polygon is **regular** if it is both equiangular and equilateral.

Tick marks indicate congruent sides, and arcs or ticks in arcs indicate congruent angles. Use these markings to determine whether a polygon is equiangular, equilateral, regular, or none of these.

EXAMPLE C Determine whether the polygon is equiangular, equilateral, regular, or none of these.

Solution equiangular ■

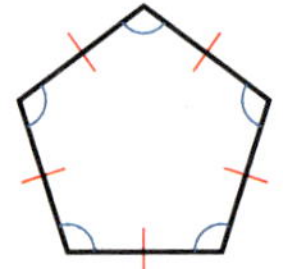

Solution regular ■

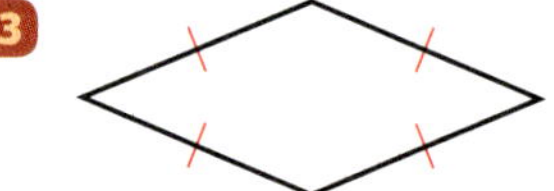

Solution equilateral ■

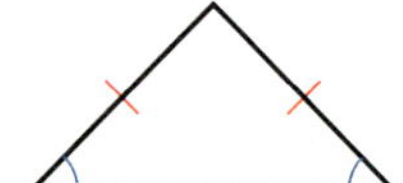

Solution none of these ■

Problem Set C

Determine whether the polygon is equiangular, equilateral, regular, or none of these.

1.
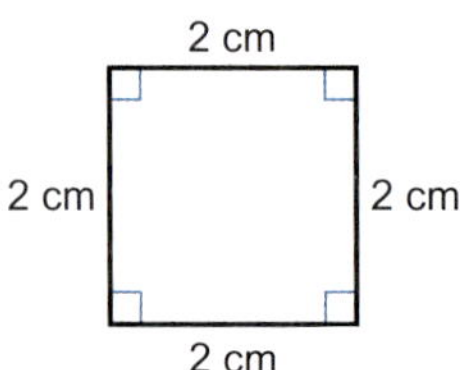

2.
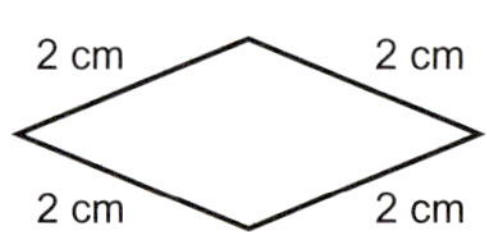

3.
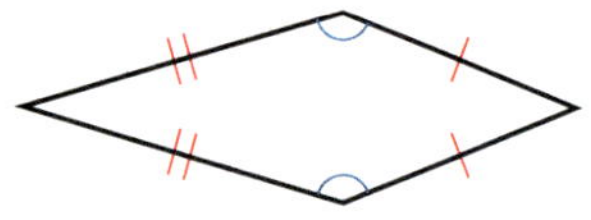

4.
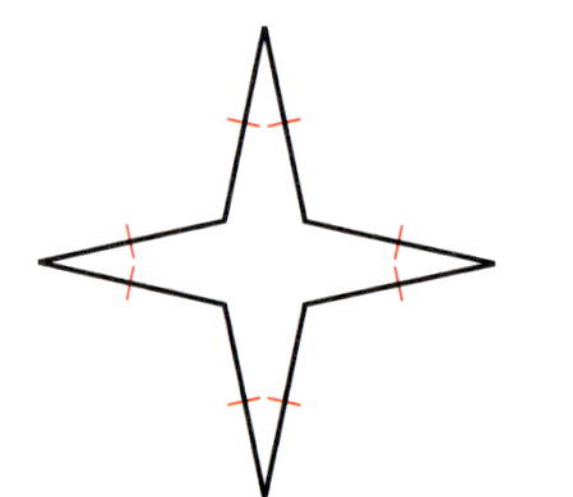

5.
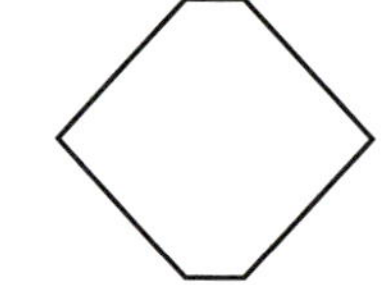

6.
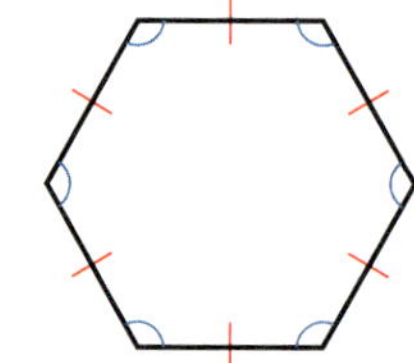

Parallel Lines and Transversals

Two lines either intersect or do not intersect each other.

Parallel lines are lines on the same plane that never intersect. The symbol for parallel is $\parallel$.

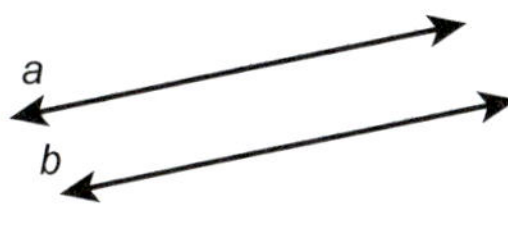

$a \parallel b$ is read "line a is parallel to line b."

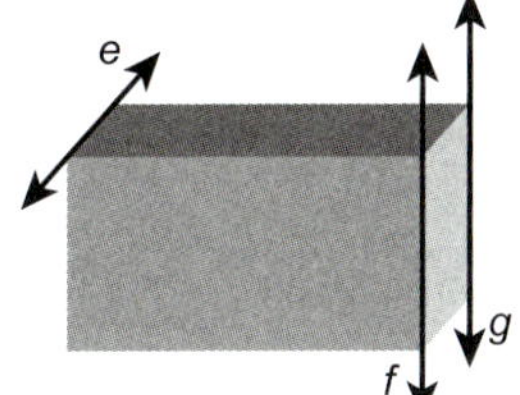

line $f \parallel$ line g

Line $e \nparallel$ line f and line $e \nparallel g$ because line e and the other lines are not on the same plane.

A **transversal** is a line that intersects two or more lines in a plane.

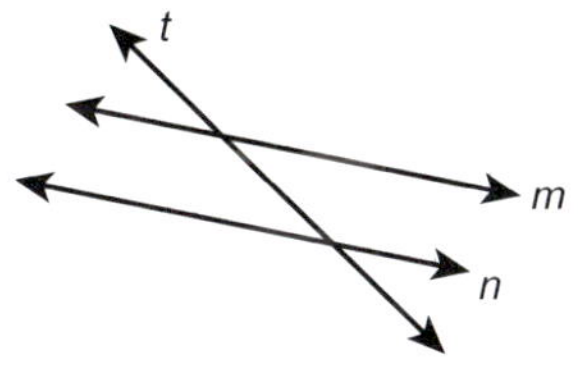

Line t is a transversal to lines m and n.

▶ **THINK ABOUT IT**

Like roads at an intersection, lines can intersect or cross one another.

▶ **TIP**

The symbol $\nparallel$ is read "is not parallel to."

Pairs of Angles

Notice that eight angles are formed when a transversal crosses two lines.

Corresponding angles are angles that lie in the same position or match up with respect to the transversal when the transversal crosses two lines. Pairs of corresponding angles in this figure are $\angle 1$ and $\angle 5$, $\angle 2$ and $\angle 6$, $\angle 3$ and $\angle 7$, and $\angle 4$ and $\angle 8$.

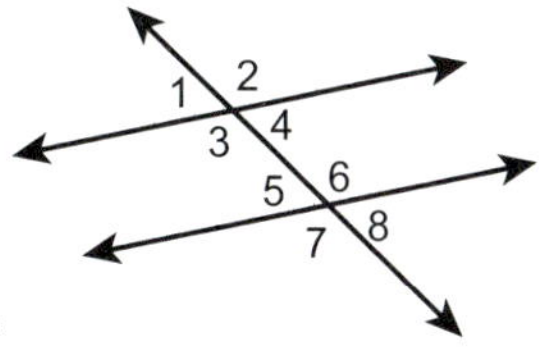

Alternate interior angles are the inside angles that do not share the same vertex and are on opposite sides of a transversal crossing two lines. Pairs of alternate interior angles in this figure are $\angle 3$ and $\angle 6$, as well as $\angle 4$ and $\angle 5$.

TIP

interior = **in**side
exterior = outside

Alternate exterior angles are the outside angles that do not share the same vertex and are on opposite sides of a transversal crossing two lines. In the figure on the previous page, the alternate exterior angles are the angle pair $\angle 1$ and $\angle 8$ and the angle pair $\angle 2$ and $\angle 7$.

Adjacent angles are angle pairs with a common side and a common vertex that do not overlap. There are several adjacent angles in the figure on the previous page, including $\angle 1$ and $\angle 2$, $\angle 1$ and $\angle 3$, $\angle 3$ and $\angle 4$, $\angle 5$ and $\angle 7$, $\angle 5$ and $\angle 6$, and $\angle 7$ and $\angle 8$.

TIP

$\angle ABD$ and $\angle CBD$ are adjacent angles.
common side: $\overrightarrow{BD}$
common vertex: B

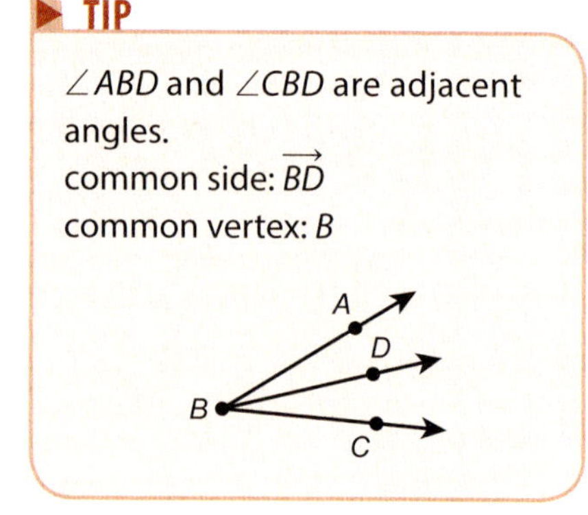

EXAMPLE 1 Identify the pair of angles as corresponding, alternate interior, alternate exterior, adjacent, or none of these.

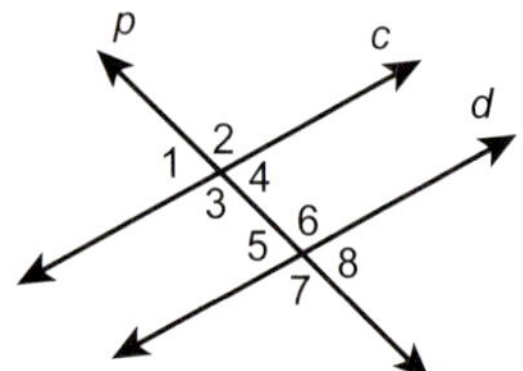

A $\angle 3$ and $\angle 6$

Solution $\angle 3$ and $\angle 6$ are on opposite sides of the transversal, line p, and they do not share a vertex. They are in between lines c and d, so they are alternate interior angles. ■

B $\angle 2$ and $\angle 7$

Solution $\angle 2$ and $\angle 7$ are on opposite sides of the transversal, line p, and they do not share the same vertex. They are outside of lines c and d, so they are alternate exterior angles. ■

C $\angle 5$ and $\angle 6$

Solution $\angle 5$ and $\angle 6$ share a common side and a common vertex. They are adjacent angles. ■

D $\angle 4$ and $\angle 8$

Solution $\angle 4$ and $\angle 8$ are in the same position within their group of four angles. They are corresponding angles. ■

Finding Angle Measures

The letter m is used to represent the word measure. So $m\angle 1$ is read as "the measure of angle 1."

The sum of the measures of two adjacent angles equals the measure of the angle formed by the sides that are not common.

In the figure, $m\angle ABD + m\angle DBC = m\angle ABC$.

If $m\angle ABD = 20°$ and $m\angle DBC = 17°$, then $m\angle ABC = 37°$.

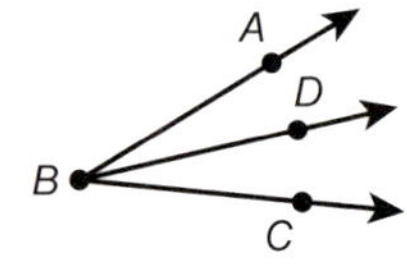

PROPERTIES OF SPECIAL ANGLE PAIRS

When two lines are crossed by a transversal, the sum of the measures of any two adjacent angles is 180°.

When the two lines crossed by the transversal are parallel, the following statements are also true:

The measures of any pair of corresponding angles are equal.
The measures of any pair of alternate interior angles are equal.
The measures of any pair of alternate exterior angles are equal.

EXAMPLE 2 Find the measure of the angle if $j \parallel k$.

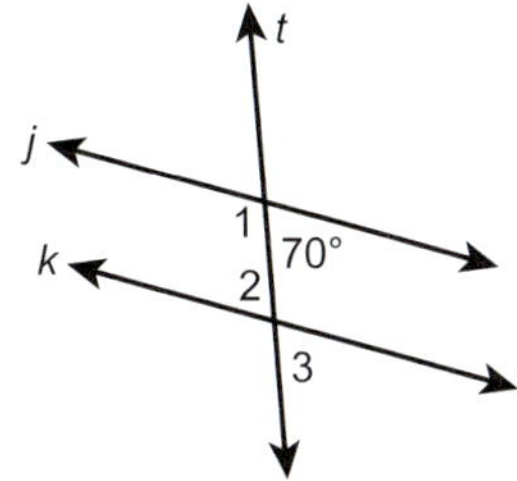

A $m\angle 1$

Solution $\angle 1$ is adjacent to the 70° angle. Because the sum of these angles is 180°, $m\angle 1 = 180° - 70° = 110°$. ■

B $m\angle 2$

Solution $\angle 2$ and the 70° angle are alternate interior angles, so they have the same measure: $m\angle 2 = 70°$. ■

C $m\angle 3$

Solution $\angle 3$ and the 70° angle are corresponding angles, so they have the same measure: $m\angle 3 = 70°$. ■

EXAMPLE 3 Find the measure of the angle if $m\angle 1 = 45°$ and $m \parallel n$.

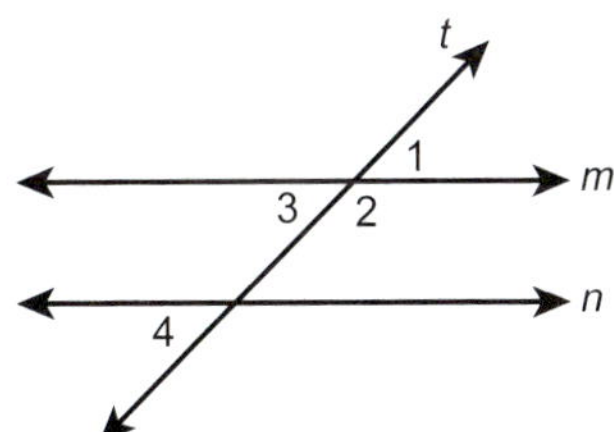

A $m\angle 2$

Solution $\angle 2$ is adjacent to $\angle 1$, so $m\angle 2 = 180° - 45° = 135°$. ■

B $m\angle 3$

Solution $\angle 3$ is adjacent to $\angle 2$, so $m\angle 3 = 180° - 135° = 45°$. ■

C $m\angle 4$

Solution $\angle 4$ and $\angle 1$ are alternate exterior angles, so they have the same measure: $m\angle 4 = 45°$. ■

Problem Set

Identify the pair of angles as corresponding, alternate interior, alternate exterior, adjacent, or none of these.

1. $\angle 3$ and $\angle 7$
2. $\angle 6$ and $\angle 7$
3. $\angle 3$ and $\angle 4$
4. $\angle 5$ and $\angle 7$
5. $\angle 4$ and $\angle 8$

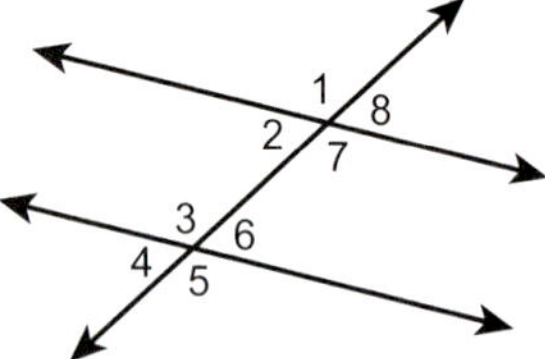

6. $\angle 2$ and $\angle 6$
7. $\angle 2$ and $\angle 7$
8. $\angle 3$ and $\angle 8$
9. $\angle 2$ and $\angle 5$
10. $\angle 4$ and $\angle 6$

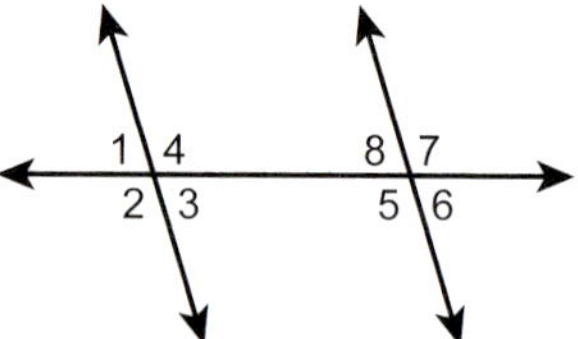

Find the unknown angle measure.

11. Find the measure of each angle if $c \parallel d$.

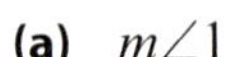

(a) $m\angle 1$
(b) $m\angle 2$
(c) $m\angle 3$
(d) $m\angle 4$

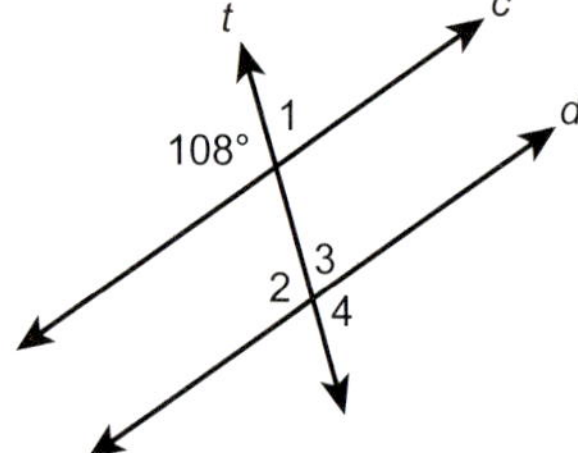

12. Find the measure of each angle if $g \parallel h$.

(a) $m\angle 1$
(b) $m\angle 2$
(c) $m\angle 3$
(d) $m\angle 4$

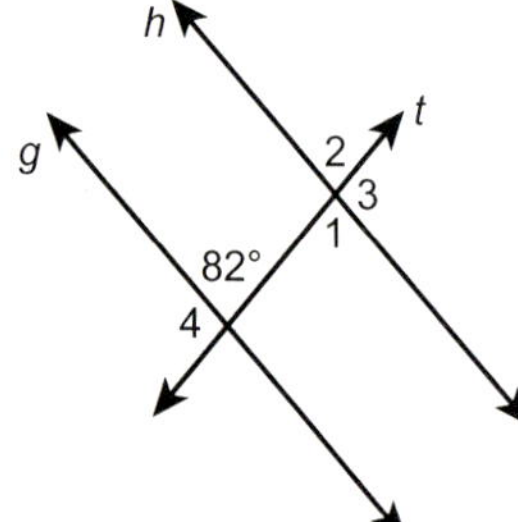

13. Find the measure of each angle if $m\angle 1 = 38°$ and $s \parallel t$.

(a) $m\angle 2$
(b) $m\angle 3$
(c) $m\angle 4$
(d) $m\angle 5$

14. Find the measure of each angle if $m\angle 1 = 53°$ and $a \parallel b \parallel c$.

(a) $m\angle 2$
(b) $m\angle 3$
(c) $m\angle 4$
(d) $m\angle 5$

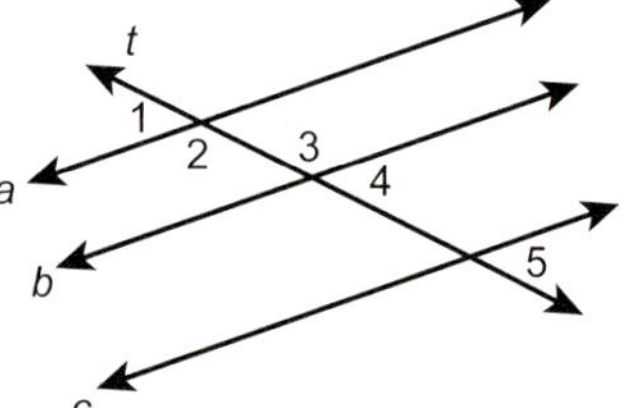

Solve.

15. Describe two ways to find $m\angle 1$ if $m \parallel n$.

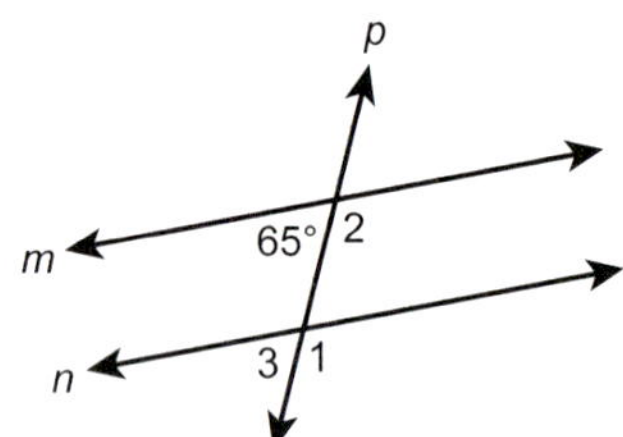

16. Two parallel lines are intersected by a transversal and one of the angles formed measures 27°. What are the measures of the other seven angles?

17. For each pair of angles, state whether they are alternate interior, alternate exterior, or corresponding. Then state which line is used as the transversal.

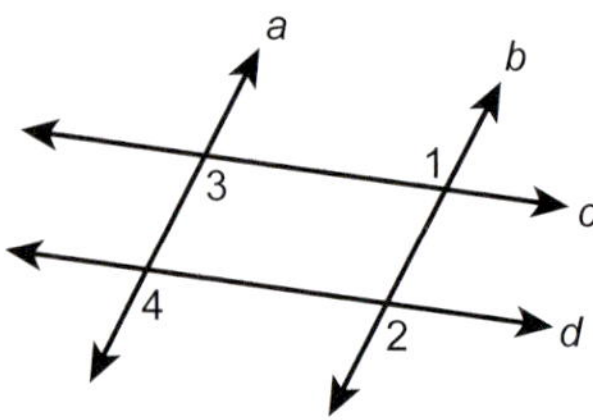

(a) $\angle 1$ and $\angle 2$
(b) $\angle 1$ and $\angle 3$
(c) $\angle 3$ and $\angle 4$
(d) $\angle 2$ and $\angle 4$

18. **Challenge** For each pair of angles, state whether they are alternate interior, alternate exterior, or corresponding. Then state which line is used as the transversal.

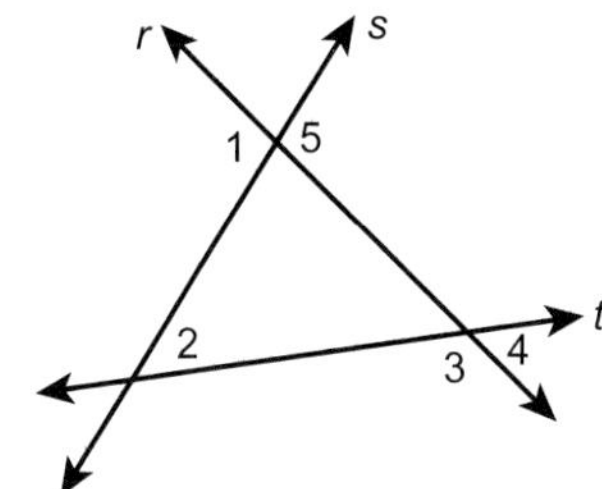

(a) $\angle 1$ and $\angle 2$

(b) $\angle 2$ and $\angle 3$

(c) $\angle 1$ and $\angle 4$

(d) $\angle 2$ and $\angle 5$

19. **Challenge** Skew lines are sometimes defined as lines that are not in the same plane and do not intersect. Or they may simply be defined as lines that are not in the same plane. Explain why the definitions are equivalent. Explain why any two lines can be classified in exactly one of the following ways: intersecting, parallel, or skew.

Triangles

Many figures can be formed when parts of lines, rather than lines, are used.

DEFINITION

A **line segment** is part of a line. It includes any two points on the line and all the points between those points.

A line segment is named by its endpoints. The points can be written in any order.

segment *ST*, segment *TS*, $\overline{ST}$, or $\overline{TS}$

TIP

A line segment is often more simply called a segment.

DEFINITION

A **triangle** is a figure made up of three segments joined at their end-points. Each endpoint is a vertex.

To name a triangle, use all three vertices. They can be listed in any order.

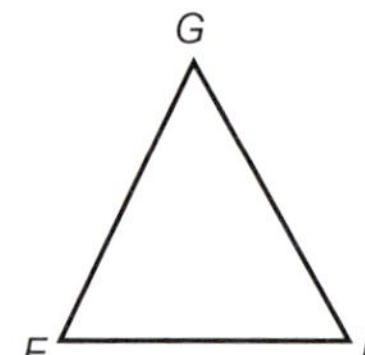

Two possible names for this triangle are $\triangle FGH$ or $\triangle GHF$.

TIP

The plural of *vertex* is *vertices*.

Classifying Triangles by Angle Measures

Every triangle can be classified according to its angle measures.

DEFINITIONS

An **acute triangle** is a triangle with three acute angles.

A **right triangle** is a triangle with a right angle.

An **obtuse triangle** is a triangle with an obtuse angle.

EXAMPLE 1 Classify the triangle as acute, right, or obtuse.

A

Solution Because $m\angle C > 90°$, $\angle C$ is an obtuse angle, so the triangle is an obtuse triangle. ■

B

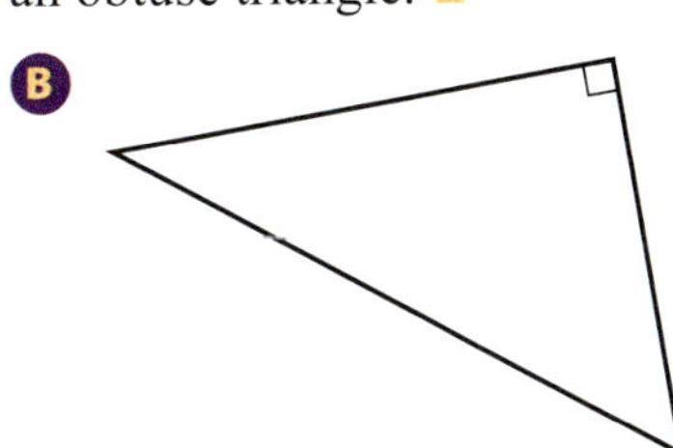

Solution Because one of the angles is a right angle, the triangle is a right triangle. ■

Using the Triangle Angle Sum Property

TRIANGLE ANGLE SUM PROPERTY

The sum of the measures of the angles of any triangle is 180°.

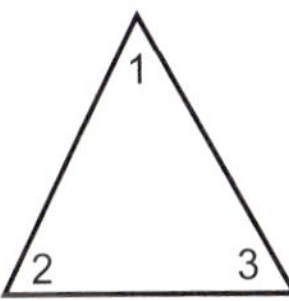

$$m\angle 1 + m\angle 2 + m\angle 3 = 180°$$

> **THINK ABOUT IT**
>
> It is not possible for a triangle to have more than one right angle or more than one obtuse angle.

EXAMPLE 2 Find the value of x in the triangle.

A

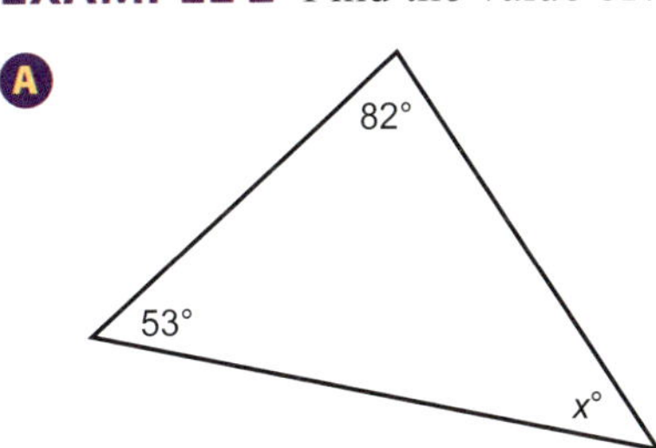

Solution Find the sum of the measures of the two known angles: $82° + 53° = 135°$. Subtract this sum from 180°: $180° - 135° = 45°$.

$$x = 45$$ ■

> **THINK ABOUT IT**
>
> In Example 2A, you can also solve the equation $x + 82 + 53 = 180$.

B

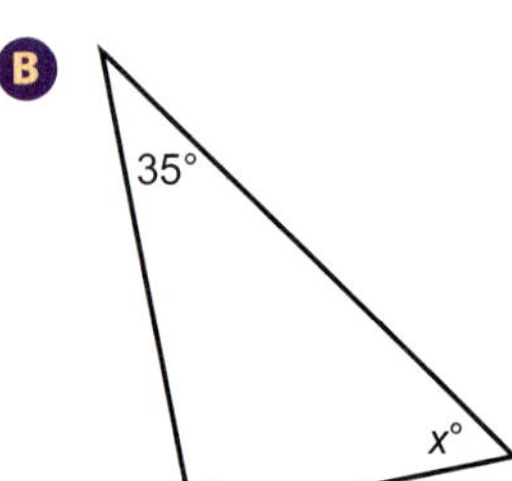

Solution Because the triangle is a right triangle, the sum of the measures of the two acute angles must be 90°.

$$x + 35 = 90$$
$$x + 35 - 35 = 90 - 35$$
$$x = 55$$

Application: Home Improvement

EXAMPLE 3 A homeowner leans a ladder against her house so that the bottom of the ladder makes a 62° angle with the ground. What angle does the top of the ladder make with the building?

Solution Draw a model. Assume that the ground is perpendicular to the building. The ladder, ground, and building form a right triangle.

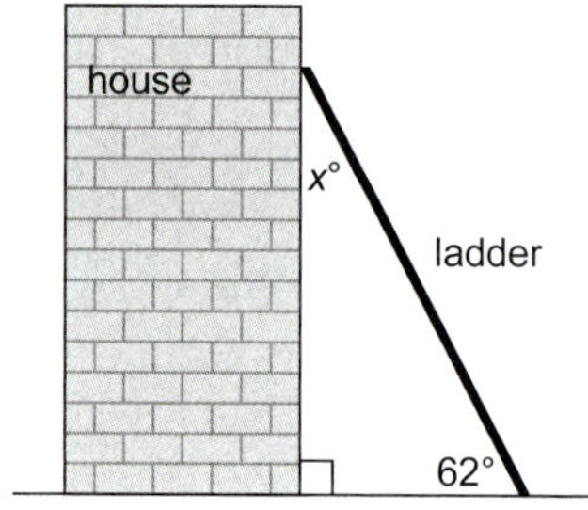

$$x + 62 = 90$$
$$x = 90 - 62$$
$$x = 28$$

Check $28 + 62 + 90 = 180$ ✓

The top of the ladder makes a 28° angle with the building.

TIP

Two lines, or segments, that form right angles are perpendicular to each other.

Problem Set

Classify the triangle as acute, right, or obtuse.

1. 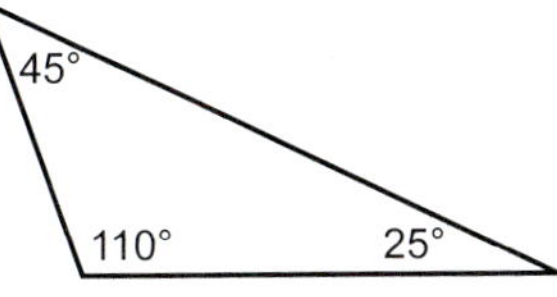

2. 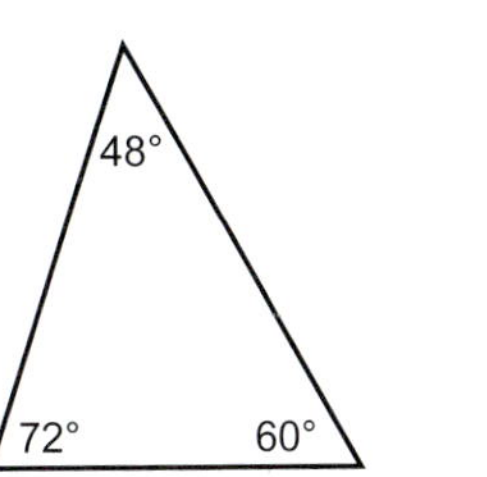

3. 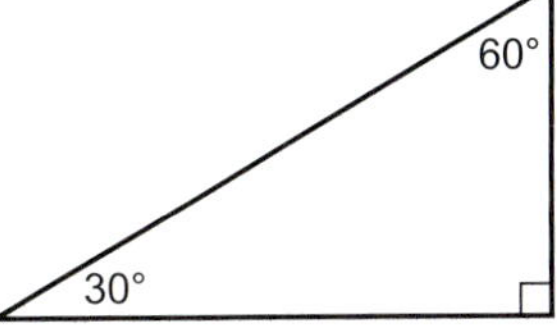

4. 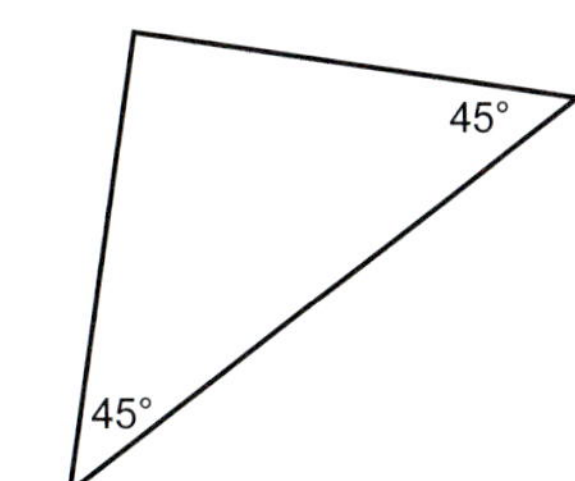

5. 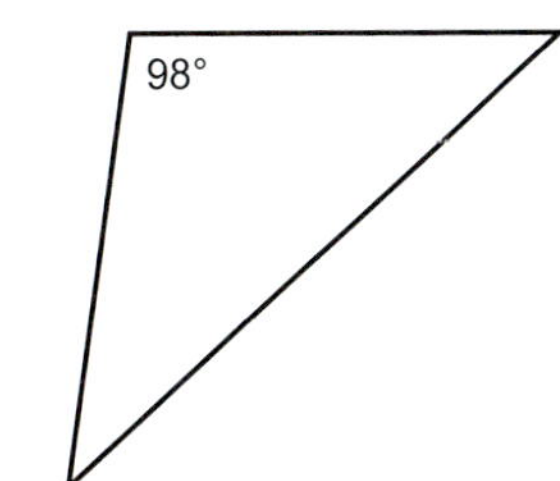

6. 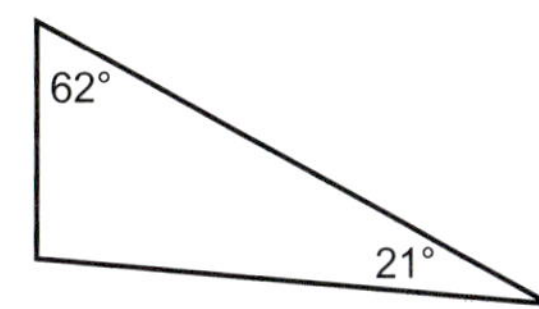

Find the value of *x* in the triangle.

7. 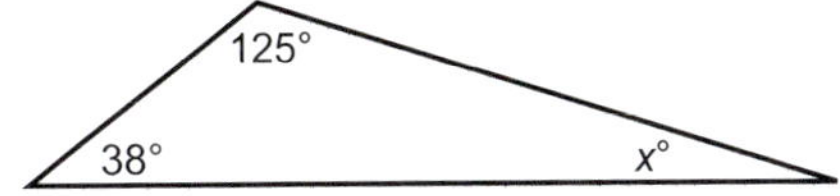

8. 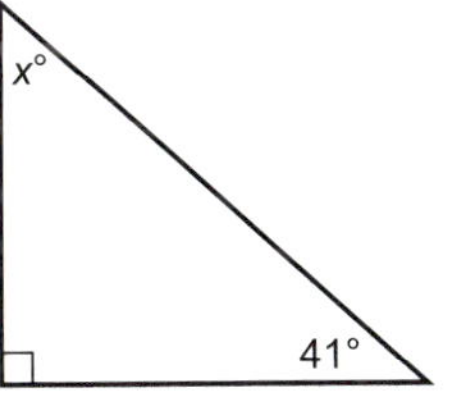

9. 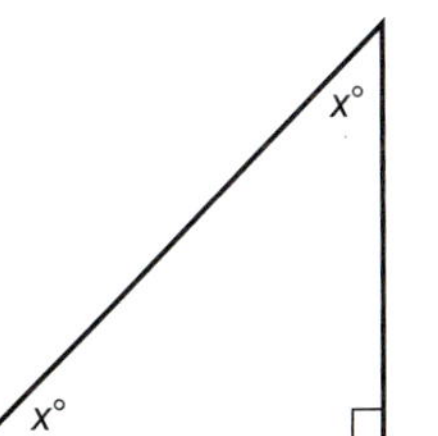

10. 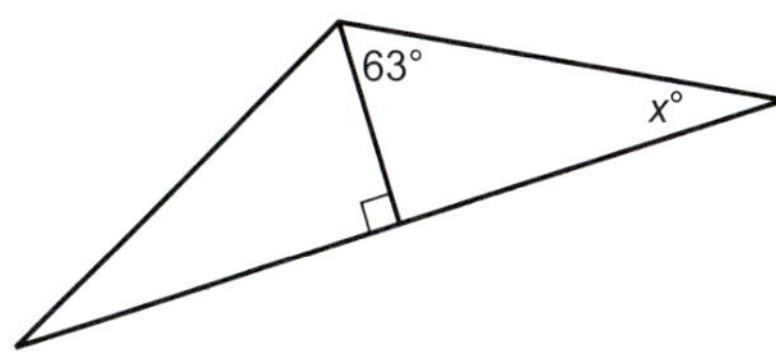

11. 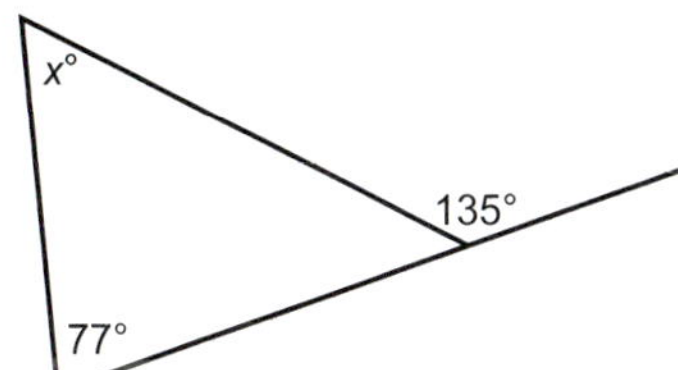

12. 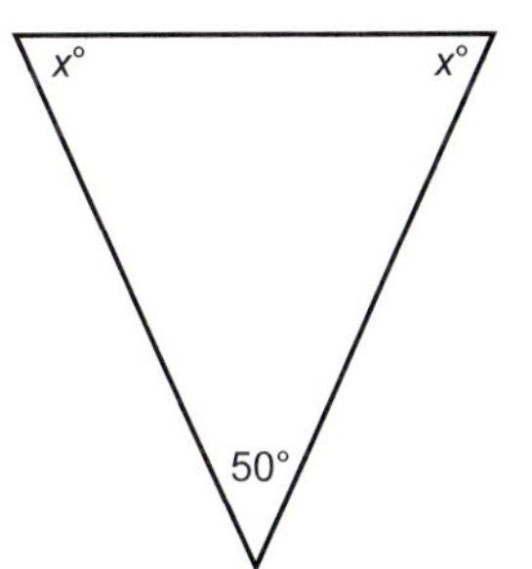

13. 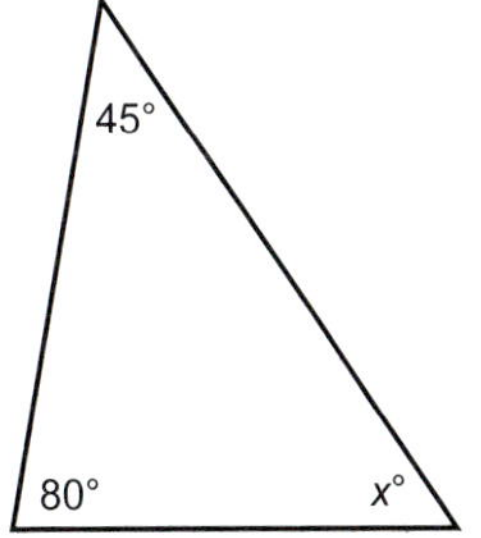

Find the value of *x* in the triangle.

14. a

15. b

16. c

17. d

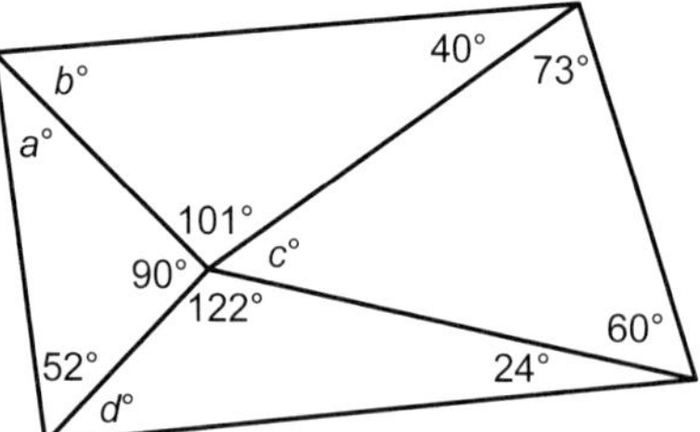

Solve.

18. A homeowner leans a ladder against his house so that the top of the ladder makes a 31° angle with the house.

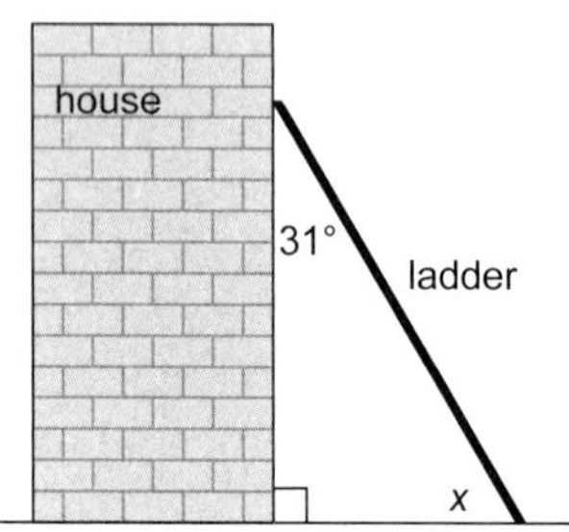

(a) What angle does the bottom of the ladder make with the ground?

(b) Classify the triangle formed by the ladder, the ground, and the building by angle measure.

Constructing Triangles

You can use a ruler and a protractor to construct the sides and the angles that define a triangle.

Constructing Angles

To construct an angle with a given measure:

Step 1 Use a ruler to draw a line segment.

Step 2 Place the protractor along the drawn line segment so it lies along the 0° base of the protractor and one endpoint is at the protractor's vertex.

Step 3 Make a mark at the degree measure of the angle.

Step 4 Draw the second segment from the mark to the endpoint of the first line segment that lies at the protractor's vertex.

Step 5 If the line segments forming the angle are to be a given length, place the ruler at the vertex of the angle and then mark each segment at the desired length.

EXAMPLE 1 Construct an angle with the given measure.

A 90° (right angle)

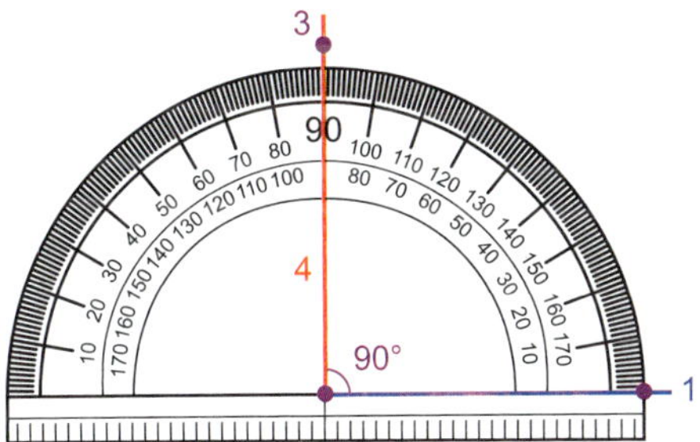

Solution

Step 1 Place the ruler on the paper and draw a horizontal line segment forming one side of the angle.

Step 2 Place the protractor on the paper so that the crossbar lines up with the left endpoint of the line segment drawn.

Step 3 Make a mark at the desired degree measure, 90°.

Step 4 Remove the protractor and draw a line segment connecting the mark to the left endpoint of the first line segment. ■

THINK ABOUT IT

Knowing the measures of the three angles in a triangle is not enough to determine the triangle's size. You need to know at least one side length.

B 45°, with side lengths of 3 cm

Solution

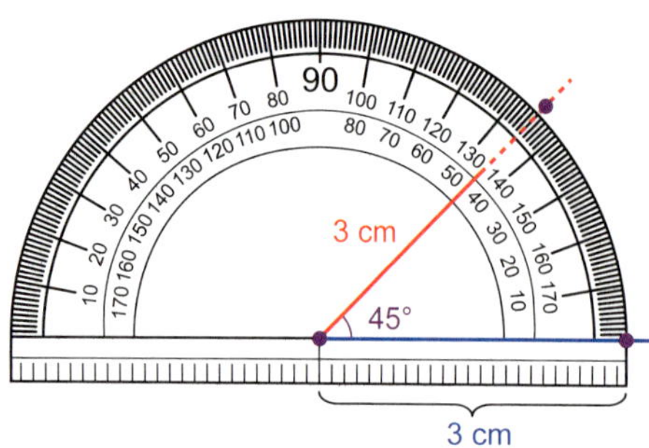

Step 1 Place the ruler on the paper and draw a horizontal line segment 3 cm long.

Step 2 Place the protractor on the paper so that the crossbar lines up with the left endpoint of the line segment drawn.

Step 3 Make a mark at the desired degree measure, 45°.

Step 4 Remove the protractor and draw a line segment connecting the mark to the left endpoint of the first line segment.

Step 5 Mark a length of 3 cm on the second segment. ■

> **TIP**
> Use a pencil instead of a pen to draw the line segments. You may need to erase part of a line segment to make it the correct length.

Constructing Triangles

You can construct a triangle if you know the measures of all three angles or are given enough information to find the measures of all three angles. Use a ruler to draw the line segments forming the angle, and use a protractor to construct angles with the given measures.

EXAMPLE 2 Construct an equilateral triangle with side lengths of 2 cm.

Solution

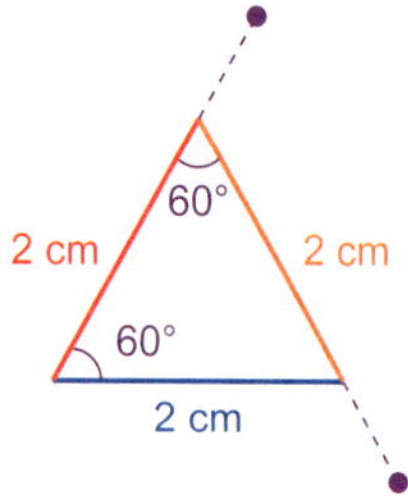

Step 1 Place the ruler on the paper and draw a horizontal line segment 2 cm long.

Step 2 Place the protractor on the paper so that the crossbar lines up with the left endpoint of the line segment drawn.

Step 3 Make a mark at the 60° measure.

Step 4 Remove the protractor and draw a line segment connecting the mark to the left endpoint of the first line segment. Adjust the length of the line segment so that it is 2 cm long.

Step 5 Repeat Step 2 for the apex (top) angle.

Step 6 Repeat Step 3, connecting the second line segment to the right endpoint of the first line segment, forming an equilateral triangle. ■

You can measure the angles of the triangle with the protractor to verify that each angle measures 60°.

EXAMPLE 3 Construct an isosceles triangle with two sides equal to 3 cm and an included angle of 40°.

Solution

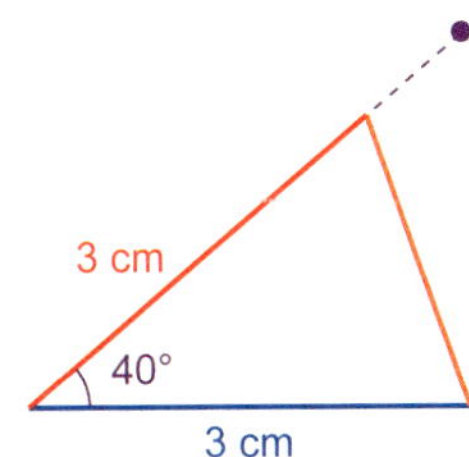

Step 1 Place the ruler on the paper and draw a horizontal line segment 3 cm long.

Step 2 Use the protractor to construct a 40° angle.

Step 3 Remove the protractor and draw a line segment connecting the mark to the left endpoint of the first line segment. Adjust the length of the line segment so that it is 3 cm long.

Step 4 Connect the second line segment to the right endpoint of the first line segment, forming an isosceles triangle. ■

Constructing Right Triangles

You can construct a right triangle given only its side lengths. First draw the two shorter sides of the triangle with the right angle between them. Then draw the hypotenuse by connecting the endpoints of the other two sides, thus completing the triangle.

REMEMBER

The hypotenuse is the longest side in a right triangle. Also, it is always opposite the right angle.

BY THE WAY

The 2 shorter sides that form the right angle in a right triangle are also known as the **legs** of the right triangle.

EXAMPLE 4 Construct a right triangle with side lengths equal to 3, 4, and 5 cm. The base of the triangle is the 3 cm side.

Solution

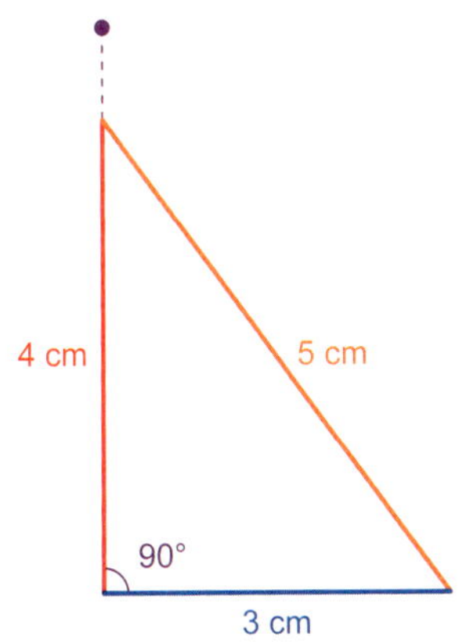

Step 1 Place the ruler on the paper and draw a horizontal line segment 3 cm long.

Step 2 Use the protractor to construct a 90° (right) angle.

Step 3 Draw a line segment connecting the mark to the left endpoint of the first line segment. Adjust the length of the line segment so that it is 4 cm long.

Step 4 Connect the top endpoint of the second line segment to the right endpoint of the first line segment, forming a hypotenuse 5 cm long. ■

Problem Set

Construct an angle with the given measure and, if specified, with given segment lengths.

1. 45°
2. 30°
3. 120°
4. 90°
5. 135°, with line segments 4 cm long
6. 75°, with line segments 3 in. long
7. 150°, with line segments 3.5 cm long
8. 10°, with line segments 2 in. long

Construct a triangle with the given characteristics.

9. all three side lengths of 3 cm
10. with two sides with length 4 cm and an included angle of 30°
11. with two sides with length 2 in. and an included angle of 120°
12. with angles of 40°, 60°, and 80°
13. with a base length of 1 in. and a pair of congruent angles, each equal to 65°
14. with one angle equal to 20° and another equal to 140°
15. right, with side lengths of 1.5 in., 2 in., and 2.5 in.
16. right, with side lengths of 7 mm, 24 mm, and 25 mm
17. **Challenge** with base length of 5 cm and two base angles equal to 25° and 75°

Solve.

18. Sasha wants to make a pendant in the shape of a triangle with two 50° angles and an included side length of 4 cm. Make a sketch, with the correct scale, of Sasha's pendant, using a ruler and a protractor.

Areas of Rectangles and Triangles

Every closed figure has an interior.

The interior of the rectangle is the space enclosed by the sides of the rectangle. The interior of this rectangle is shaded.

DEFINITION

The **area** of a figure is the number of square units in the interior of the figure.

This rectangle has an area of 32 units^2. Notice that 32 is the product of the number of rows, 4, and number of columns, 8.

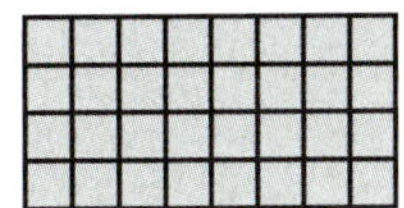

THINK ABOUT IT

Area is expressed using square units, such as square feet (ft^2). When no units are provided, use square units (units^2).

Finding the Area of a Rectangle

AREA OF A RECTANGLE

The area of a rectangle with length l and width w is

$$A = lw.$$

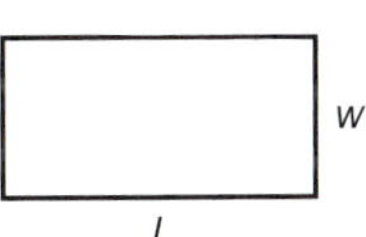

EXAMPLE 1 Find the area of the rectangle.

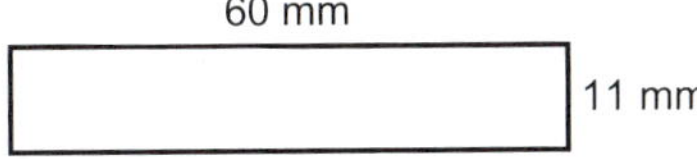

Solution Use the formula. The calculation may be performed with or without the units.

Method 1

$A = lw$

$= 60 \cdot 11$ Substitute 60 for l and 11 for w.

$= 660$ Multiply.

Method 2

$A = lw$

$= (60 \text{ mm}) \cdot (11 \text{ mm})$

$= 60 \cdot 11 \cdot \text{mm} \cdot \text{mm}$

$= 660 \text{ mm}^2$

The area is 660 mm^2. ■

TIP

Generally use the first method because it is simpler.

Finding the Area of a Triangle

The formula for the area of a triangle is half the formula for the rectangle.

AREA OF A TRIANGLE

The area of a triangle with base b and height h is

$$A = \frac{1}{2}bh.$$

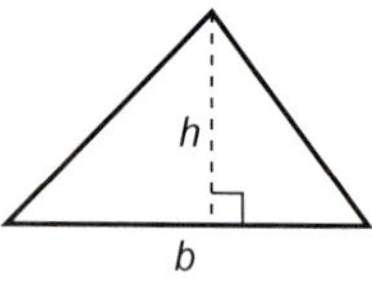

The base of a triangle always forms a right angle with the height of the triangle.

For acute triangles, the height is always shown inside the triangle.
For obtuse triangles, height can be shown in the exterior of the triangle.
In a right triangle, the height can be one of the sides of the triangle.

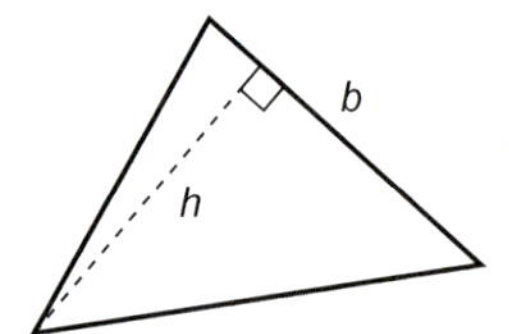

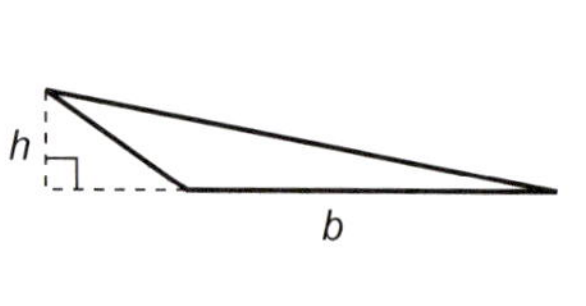

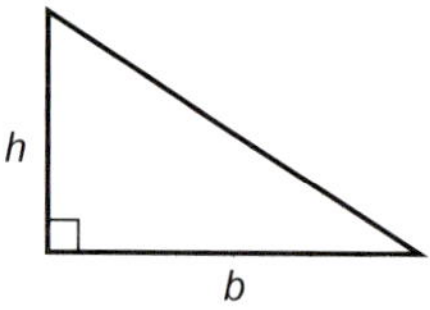

TIP

Any side can be used as the base. The height will change accordingly.

EXAMPLE 2 Find the area of the triangle.

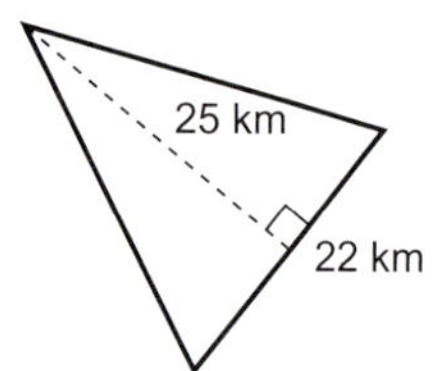

Solution Use the formula.

$A = \frac{1}{2}bh$

$= \frac{1}{2} \cdot 22 \cdot 25$ Substitute 22 for b and 25 for h.

$= 11 \cdot 25$ Multiply.

$= 275$ Multiply.

The area is 275 km^2.

Finding Missing Lengths

EXAMPLE 3

A The area of the triangle is 54 cm^2. What is the height of the triangle?

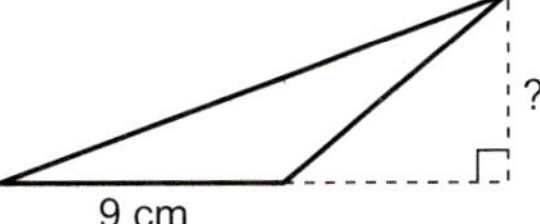

Solution Substitute the known information into $A = \frac{1}{2}bh$. Solve for h.

$A = \frac{1}{2}bh$	Write the formula.
$54 = \frac{1}{2} \cdot 9 \cdot h$	Substitute 54 for A and 9 for b.
$54 = 4.5h$	Simplify.
$12 = h$	Divide both sides by 4.5.

The height is 12 cm. ■

B The area of a rectangle is 231 in^2. What is the length of the rectangle if the width is 42 in.?

Solution Substitute the known information into $A = lw$. Solve for l.

$A = lw$	Write the formula.
$231 = l \cdot 42$	Substitute 231 for A and 42 for w.
$5.5 = l$	Divide both sides by 42.

The length is 5.5 in. ■

Finding Areas of Combination Figures

EXAMPLE 4 Find the area of the figure.

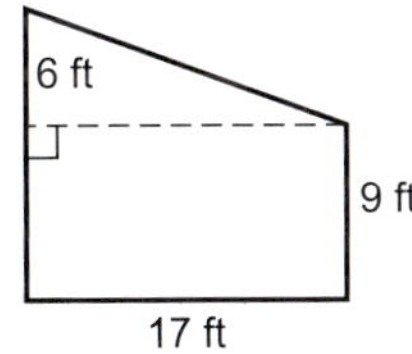

Solution Add the area of the triangle to the area of the rectangle. The base of the right triangle is the length of the rectangle, 17 ft.

$A = \frac{1}{2}bh + lw$	Use the formulas for area of a triangle and area of a rectangle.
$= \frac{1}{2} \cdot 17 \cdot 6 + 17 \cdot 9$	Substitute 17 for b and l, 6 for h, and 9 for w.
$= 51 + 153$	Multiply.
$= 204$	Add.

The area is 204 ft^2. ■

Finding the Difference of Areas

EXAMPLE 5 Find the area of the shaded portion of the square.

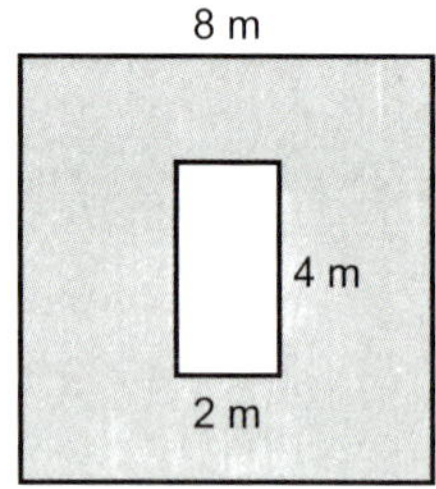

Solution Subtract the area of the rectangle from the area of the square.

$A = s^2 - lw$	Use the formulas for area of a square and area of a rectangle.
$= 8^2 - 2 \cdot 4$	Substitute 8 for s, 2 for l, and 4 for w.
$= 64 - 8$	Simplify.
$= 56$	Subtract.

The area of the shaded region is 56 m^2. ■

> **REMEMBER**
> The formula for the area of a square is s^2.

Problem Set

Find the area of the figure.

1.

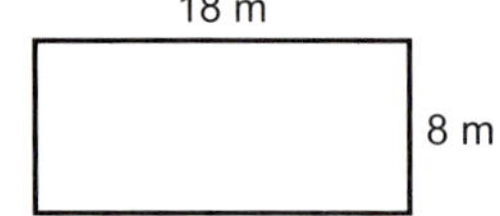

2.

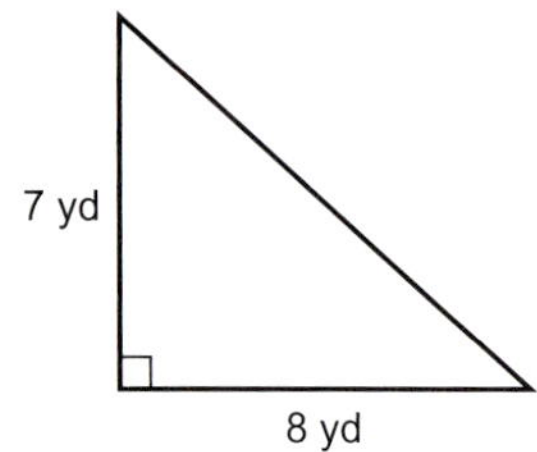

3.

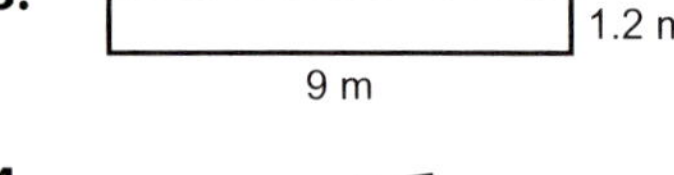

4.

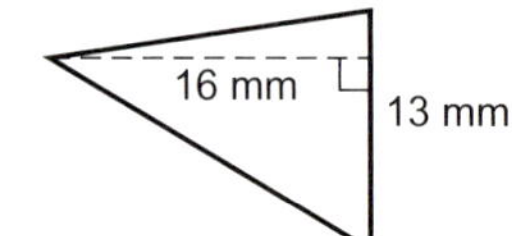

5.

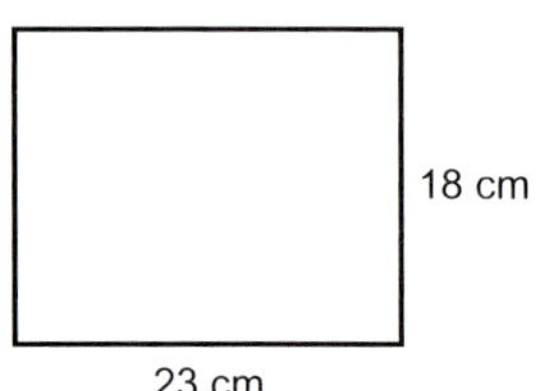

6.

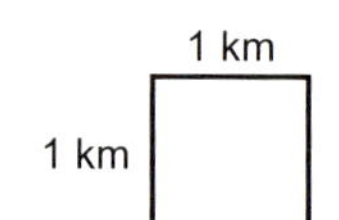

7.

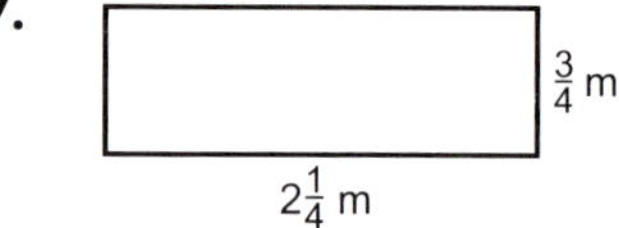

8.

9.

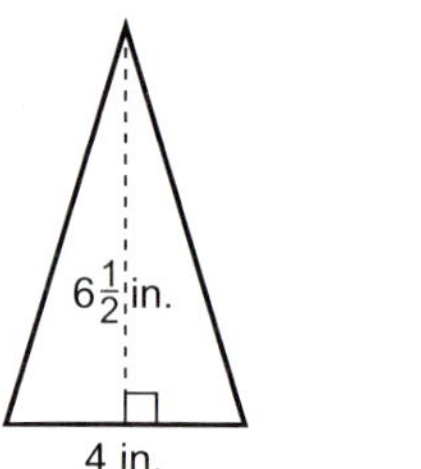

10.

3.9 ft
3 ft
3.5 ft

Solve.

11. The area of the rectangle is 114 units^2. What is the width of the rectangle?

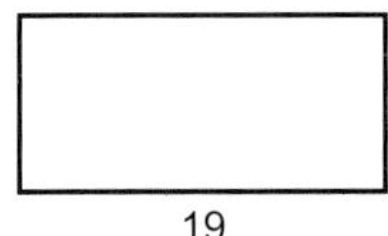

12. The area of the triangle is 52.5 units^2. What is the base of the triangle?

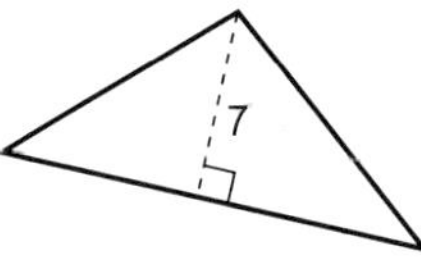

13. What is the length of a rectangle if its width is 7 m and its area is 63 m^2?

14. The area of the triangle is 384 in^2. What is the height of the triangle?

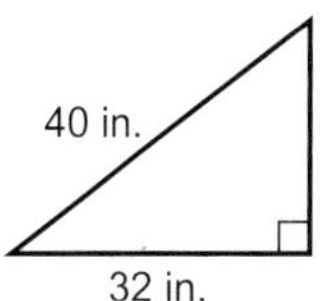

15. What is the height of a triangle if its area is 192 ft^2 and its base is 16 ft?

16. The area of a square is 9 m^2. What is the length of each side of the square?

17. The area of a square is 49 m^2. What is the perimeter of the square?

Find the area of the figure.

18.

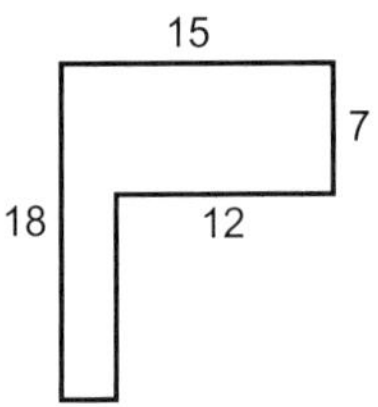

19.

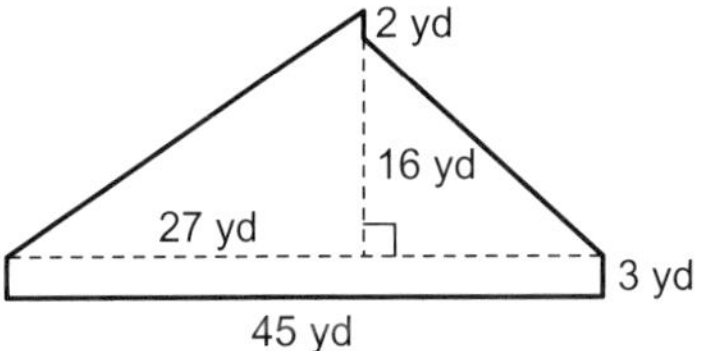

20.

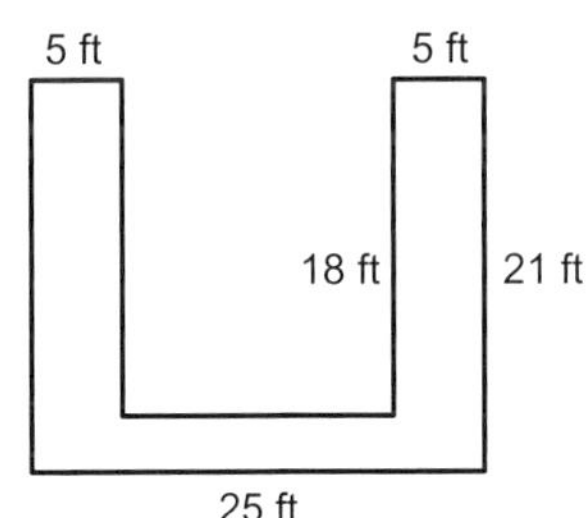

21.

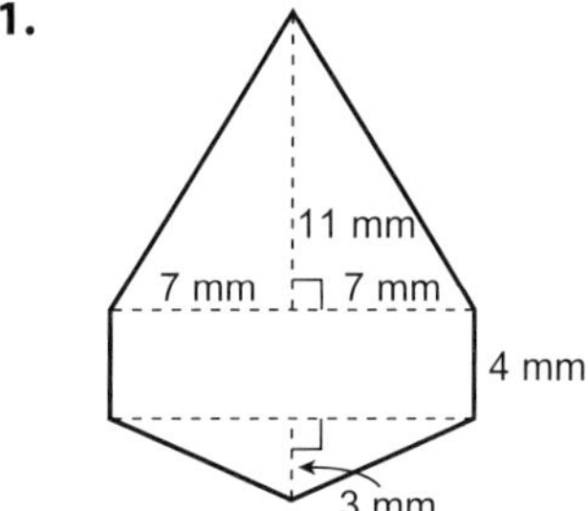

22.

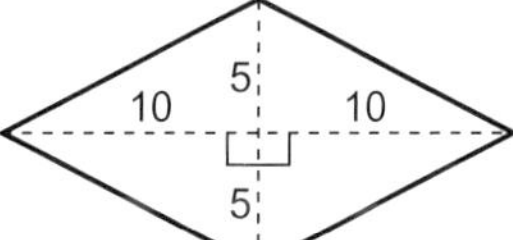

23.

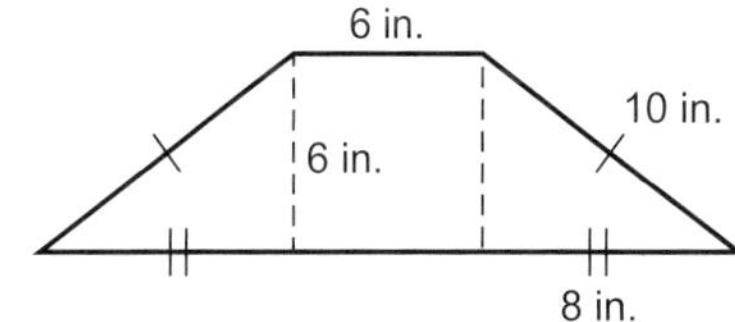

Find the area of the shaded region.

24.

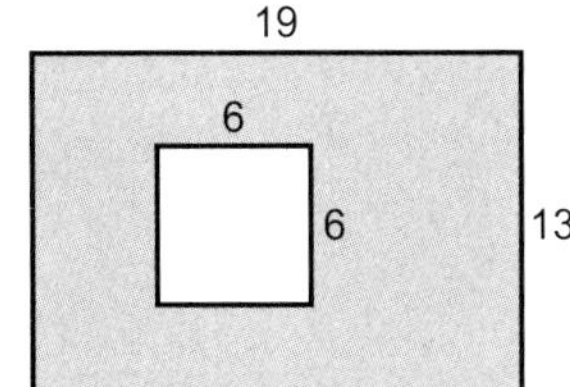

25.

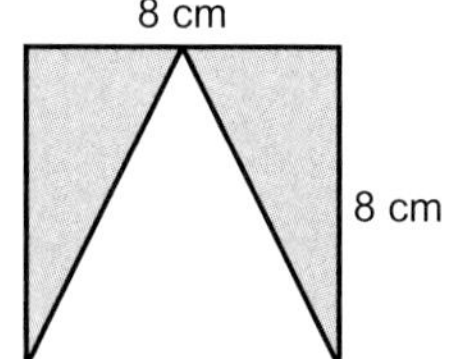

Solve. Write your answer in a complete sentence.

26. A basketball court is 94 ft long and 50 ft wide. What is the area of the basketball court?

27. Mr. Nunez has a backyard that is shaped like a right triangle with a base of 84 m and a height of 60 m. How much will it cost him to fertilize the yard at 3¢/m^2?

28. **Challenge** Show that the area of the triangle is the same regardless of which side is used as the base.

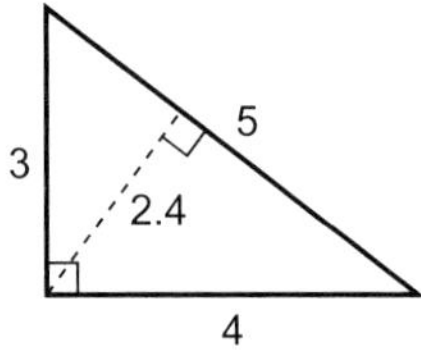

29. **Challenge** Tell how the formula for the area of a triangle is related to the formula for the area of a rectangle.

30. **Challenge** Find the area of a triangle with length of 12 cm and width of 55 mm.

Areas of Special Quadrilaterals

Two types of special quadrilaterals are parallelograms and trapezoids. In a parallelogram, both pairs of sides are parallel; in a trapezoid, only one pair of sides is parallel.

Parallelograms and trapezoids have bases and heights. A **base** is defined to be the bottom side of a geometric figure. The **height** is perpendicular to the base. It is the length of the segment that extends from the base to the opposite side.

Finding the Area of a Parallelogram

Every parallelogram has four bases; each side can be a base. The height depends on which side is used as the base. Heights are sometimes shown outside the parallelogram.

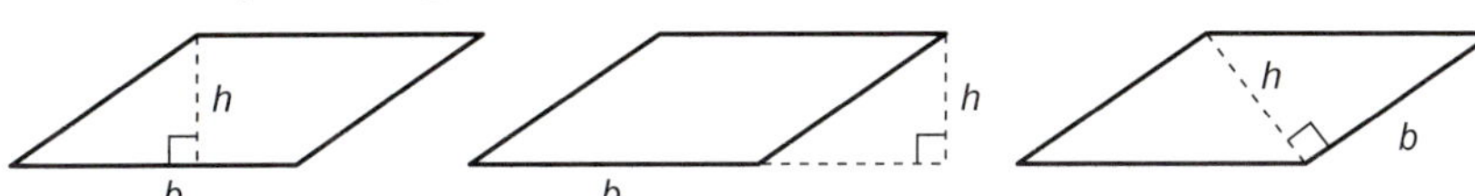

> **THINK ABOUT IT**
>
> Any side of a parallelogram can be the base because the parallelogram can be rotated so that any side is on the bottom.

AREA OF A PARALLELOGRAM

The area of a parallelogram with base b and height h is

$$A = bh.$$

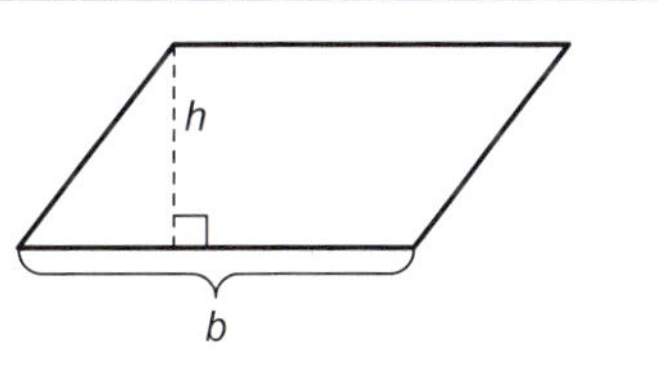

EXAMPLE 1 Find the area of the parallelogram.

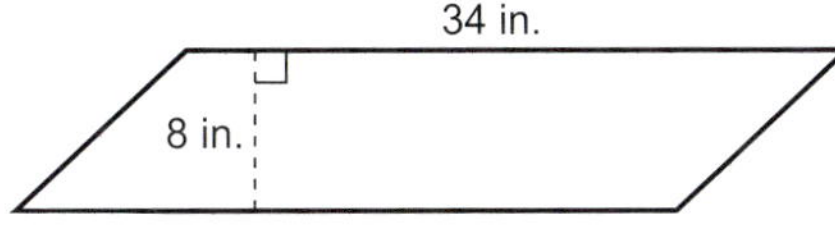

Solution $A = bh$ Write the formula.

$= 34 \cdot 8$ Substitute 34 for b and 8 for h.

$= 272$ Multiply.

The area is 272 in^2. ■

Finding the Area of a Trapezoid

A trapezoid has two bases: b_1 and b_2. The parallel sides are always the bases. The height is the length of a segment that joins the bases and forms right angles with them.

AREA OF A TRAPEZOID

The area of a trapezoid with bases b_1 and b_2 and height h is

$$A = \frac{1}{2}h(b_1 + b_2).$$

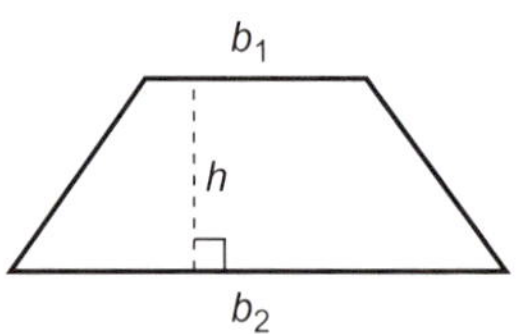

EXAMPLE 2 Find the area of the trapezoid.

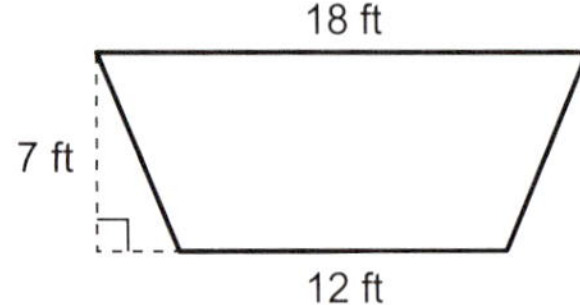

Solution

$A = \frac{1}{2}h(b_1 + b_2)$	Write the formula.
$= \frac{1}{2} \cdot 7 \cdot (18 + 12)$	Substitute 18 for b_1, 12 for b_2, and 7 for h.
$= \frac{1}{2} \cdot 7 \cdot 30$	Simplify inside the parentheses.
$= 105$	Multiply.

The area is 105 ft^2. ■

THINK ABOUT IT

It does not matter which base is used for b_1 and which is used for b_2.

Finding Missing Lengths

With a known area and some algebra, you can find missing side lengths.

EXAMPLE 3 Find the missing side length.

A The area of a parallelogram is 675 cm^2. What is the height of the parallelogram if its base is 45 cm long?

Solution Substitute the known information into $A = bh$. Solve for h.

$A = bh$	Write the formula.
$675 = 45 \cdot h$	Substitute 675 for A and 45 for b.
$15 = h$	Divide both sides by 45.

The height is 15 cm. ■

B The area of the trapezoid is 54 m. What is the base length?

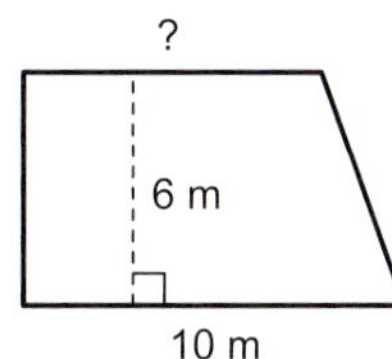

Solution	$A = \frac{1}{2}h(b_1 + b_2)$	Write the formula.
	$54 = \frac{1}{2} \cdot 6 \cdot (b_1 + 10)$	Substitute 54 for A, 6 for h, and 10 for one of the bases.
	$54 = 3 \cdot (b_1 + 10)$	Multiply on the right.
	$18 = b_1 + 10$	Divide both sides by 3.
	$8 = b_1$	Subtract 10 from both sides.

Check $A = \frac{1}{2}h(b_1 + b_2) = \frac{1}{2} \cdot 6 \cdot (8 + 10) = 3 \cdot 18 = 54$ ✓

The length of the unknown base is 8 m.

Application: Painting

EXAMPLE 4 Each wall of a 4-sided garden shed is 10 ft long and 8 ft high and has one rhombus-shaped window. The windows are congruent and each has a base of 2 ft and a height of 1.5 ft. The gardener wants to paint the inside of the walls. A can of the paint covers about 350 ft^2/gal. How many cans of paint will she need for 2 coats?

Solution Find the area to be painted.

First find the area that is covered with 1 coat.

$A = 4lw - 4bh$	Subtract the area of the windows from the area of the walls.
$= 4 \cdot 10 \cdot 8 - 4 \cdot 2 \cdot 1.5$	Substitute values for the variables.
$= 320 - 12$	Multiply.
$= 308$	Subtract.

She has to cover 308 ft^2 with 1 coat.

Next double that amount to find the area covered in 2 coats.

$2 \times 308 = 616$	Multiply the area covered by 1 coat by 2.

Divide by 350 to find how many cans of paint she needs.

$616 \div 350 = 1.76$	Divide by 350.

The gardener will need 2 cans of paint.

TIP

A rhombus is a parallelogram with 4 equal sides. A square is one example of a rhombus.

THINK ABOUT IT

You can also use $A = 4(lw - bh)$.

Problem Set

Find the area of the figure.

1.

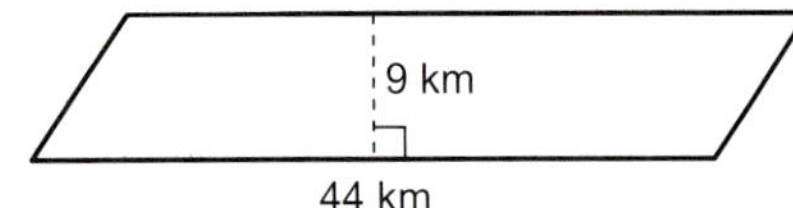

2.

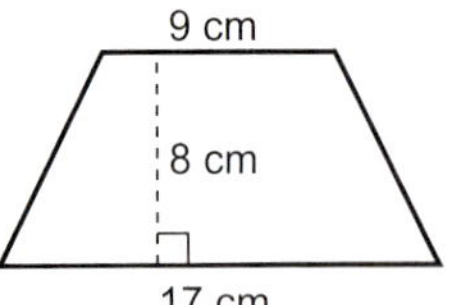

3.

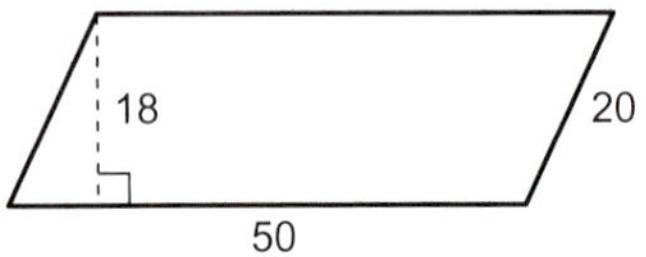

4.

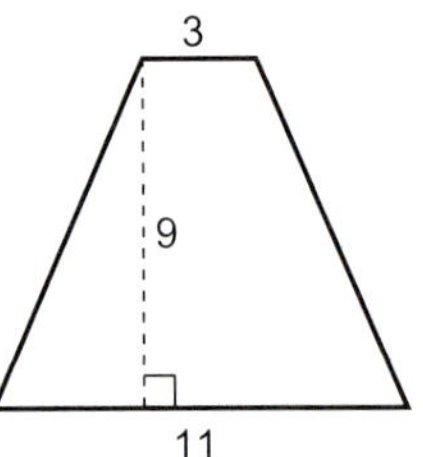

5.

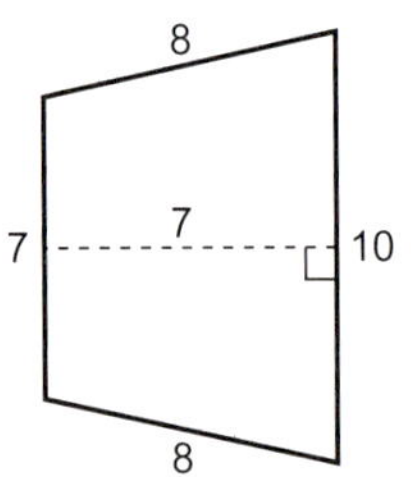

6.

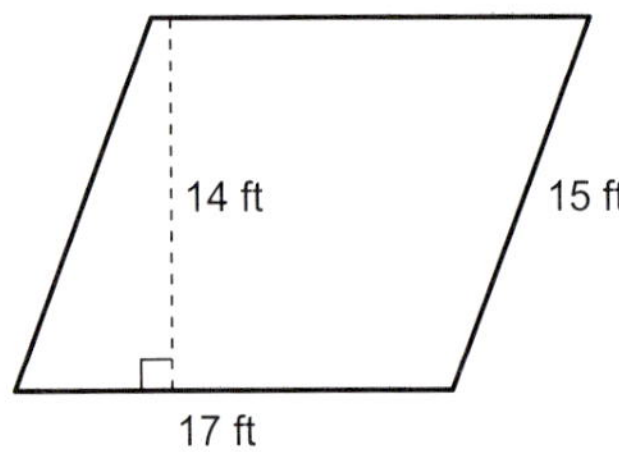

7.

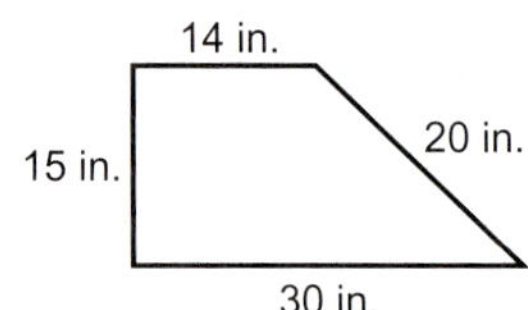

8.

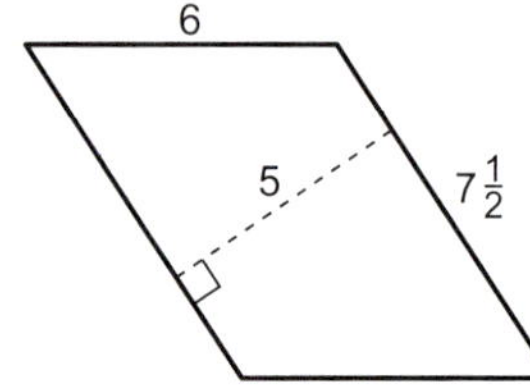

9.

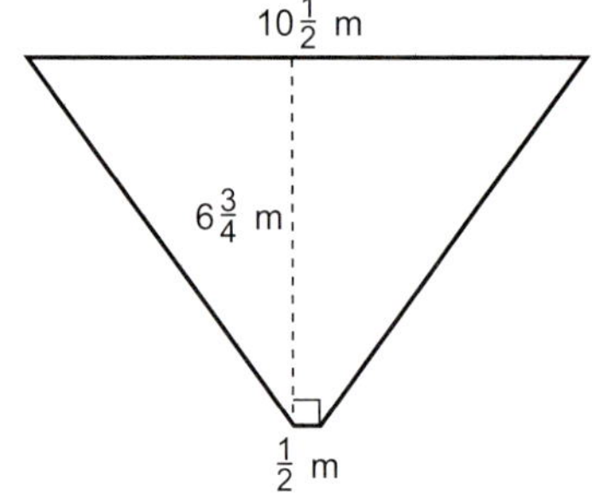

10.

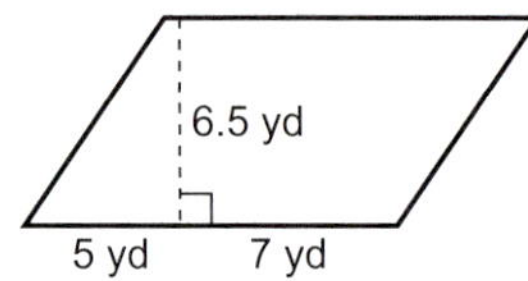

11.

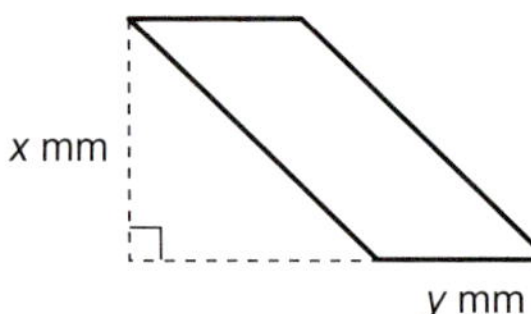

12.

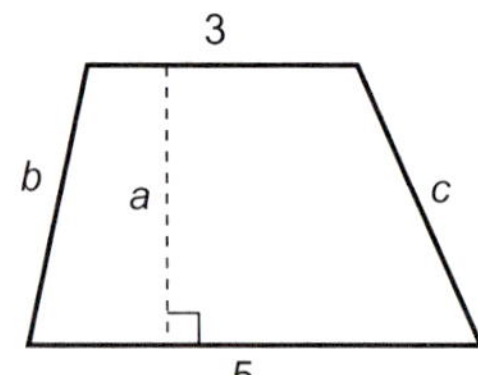

Solve.

13. The area of the parallelogram is 126 units^2. What is the height of the parallelogram?

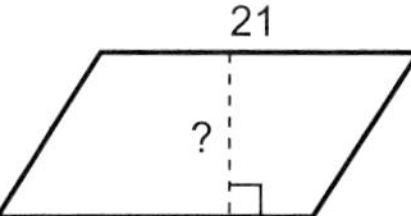

14. The area of the trapezoid is 56 units^2. What is the height of the trapezoid?

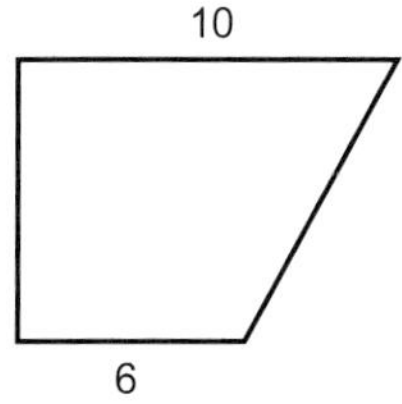

15. How long is the base of a parallelogram if its area is 100 m^2 and its height is 5 m?

16. What is the height of a parallelogram with base length of 16 m and area of 136 m^2?

17. What is the height of a trapezoid with base lengths of 9 cm and 12 cm, and area of 52.5 cm^2?

18. The area of a trapezoid is 65 ft^2. The height is 10 ft, and the length of one of the bases is $9\frac{1}{2}$ ft. Find the length of the other base.

Find the area of the figure.

19.

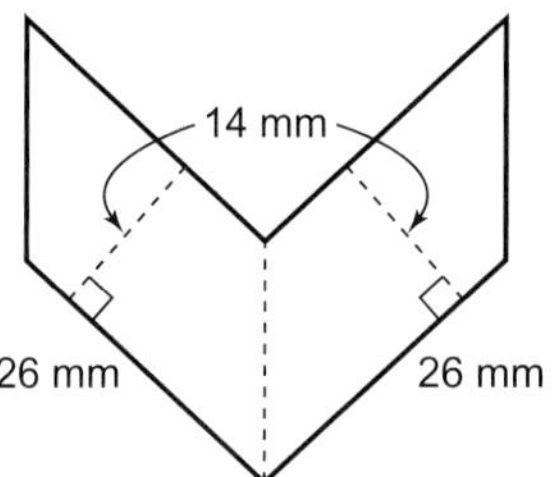

20.

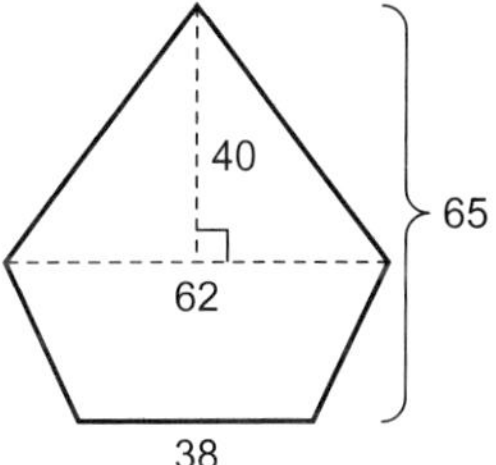

21.

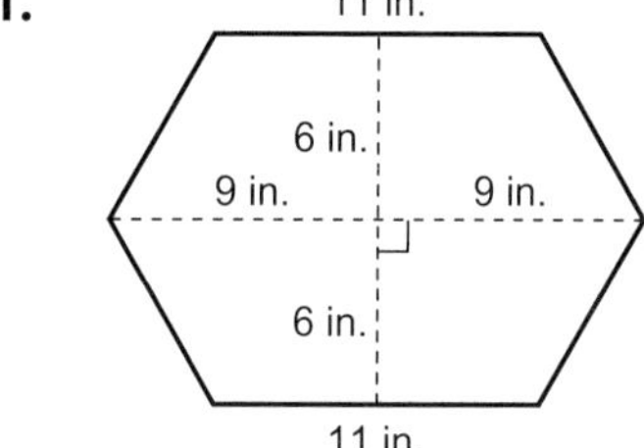

22.

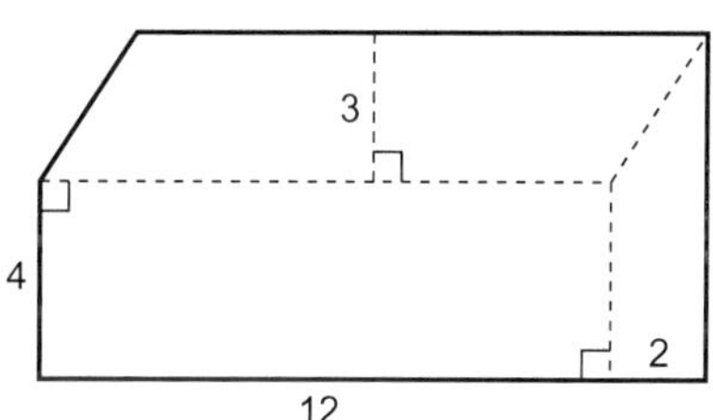

Solve.

23. Find the area of a parallelogram with vertices located at (−1, 1), (5, 1), (3, −2), and (−3, −2).

24. Find the area of a trapezoid with vertices located at (0, 4), (9, 4), (5, 2), and (2, 2).

25. Joey will both mow and rake a yard for a fee of 5¢/m^2. How much will Joey charge to mow and rake a front yard that is shaped like a trapezoid with bases of 30 m and 35 m and with a height of 48 m?

26. Lee is making a rock garden in the shape of a rhombus. He wants the area of the garden to be exactly 50 ft^2. Give two possible sets of dimensions Lee could use.

27. **Challenge** Find the area of a trapezoid with base lengths of 1 ft and 2 yd, and height of 18 in.

Areas of Polygons

You can find the area of a complex figure by breaking it down into polygons whose areas are easily found.

Finding the Area of a Regular Polygon

REGULAR POLYGONS AND CONGRUENT TRIANGLES

An *n*-sided regular polygon can be divided into *n* congruent triangles.

The **apothem** of a regular polygon is a line segment that joins the center of the polygon to the midpoint of one of its sides.

REMEMBER

Congruent triangles are identical to each other.

To find the area of a regular polygon, first divide it into congruent triangles. Find the area of one triangle, using the apothem length as the height of the triangle. Then multiply the area of this one triangle by n, the number of congruent triangles, to find the area of the entire polygon.

EXAMPLE 1 Find the area of the regular polygon.

A a regular pentagon with an apothem length of 11 units and a side length of 16 units

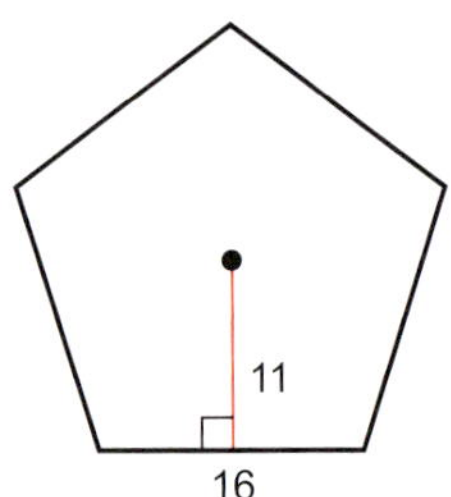

Solution Divide the pentagon into five congruent triangles.

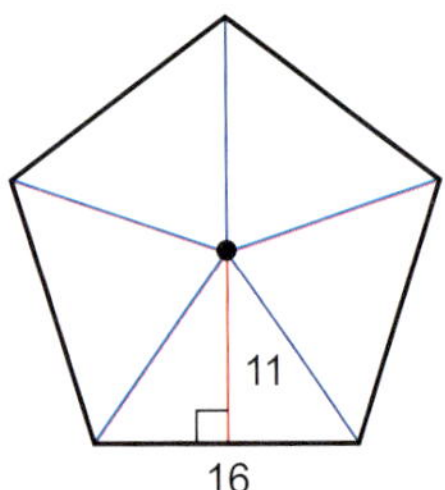

The area of one triangle is $A = \frac{1}{2}(b \bullet h) = \frac{1}{2}(16 \bullet 11) = \frac{176}{2} = 88$.

Multiply by 5 to find the area of the entire pentagon: $88 \bullet 5 = 440$.

The area of the regular pentagon is 440 units^2. ■

TIP

You know that a polygon is a many-sided figure (the prefix *poly–* means many). But did you know that the name of a particular polygon can tell you exactly how many sides the figure has? For instance, *penta–* means five, and a *pentagon* has 5 sides.

octagon: *octa–* = eight;
An octagon has 8 sides.

hexagon: *hexa–* = six;
A hexagon has 6 sides.

decagon: *deca–* = ten;
A decagon has 10 sides.

B a regular octagon with an apothem length of 7 cm and a perimeter of 46.4 cm

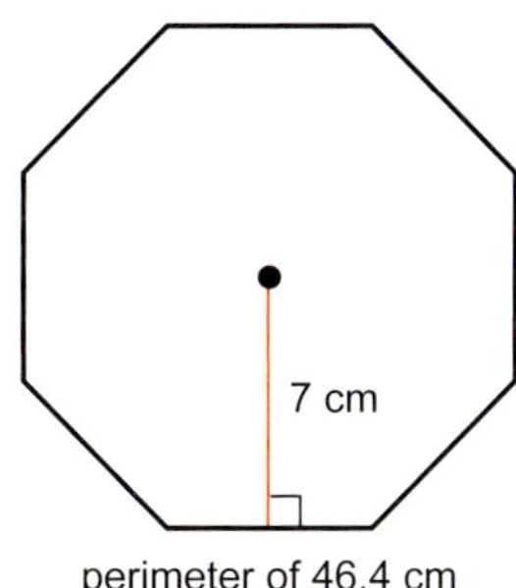

Solution All 8 sides of the octagon are the same length, so the length of each side is the perimeter divided by 8: $\frac{46.4}{8} = 5.8$.

Divide the octagon into eight congruent triangles.

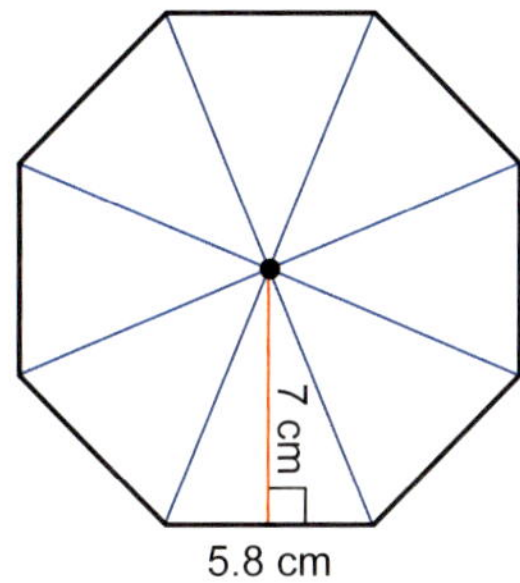

The area of one triangle is $A = \frac{1}{2}(b \cdot h) = \frac{1}{2}(7 \cdot 5.8) = \frac{40.6}{2} = 20.3$.

Multiply by 8 to find the area of the entire octagon: $20.3 \cdot 8 = 162.4$.

The area of the regular octagon is 162.4 cm^2. ■

Finding the Area of an Irregular Polygon

You can find the area of an irregular polygon if you can represent the polygon either as a combination of familiar polygons or as a polygon with one or more familiar polygons removed.

> **REMEMBER**
> Irregular polygons do not have equal side lengths and angles like regular polygons do.

EXAMPLE 2 Find the area of the figure.

A

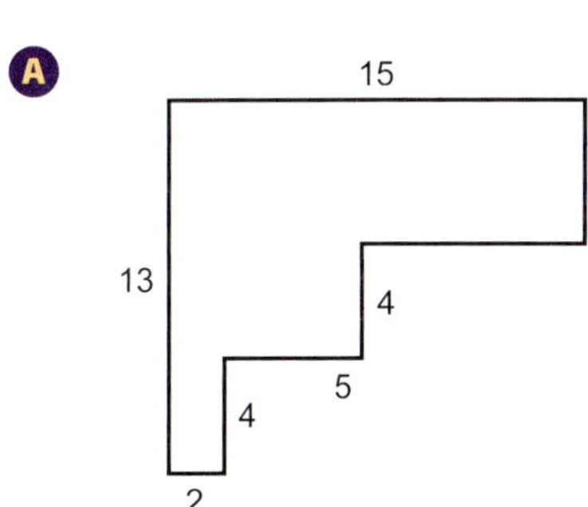

Solution Break the figure into three rectangles.

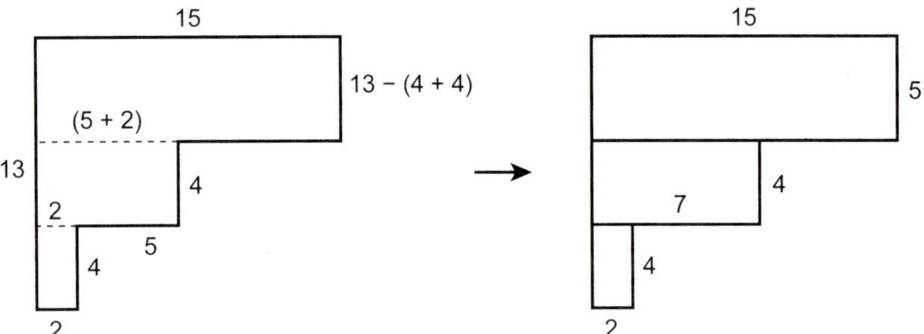

Write an expression for the area of each rectangle, and sum the expressions to find the area of the entire figure.

$$(15 \bullet 5) + (7 \bullet 4) + (2 \bullet 4) = 75 + 28 + 8 = 111$$

The area of the figure is 111 units^2. ■

B

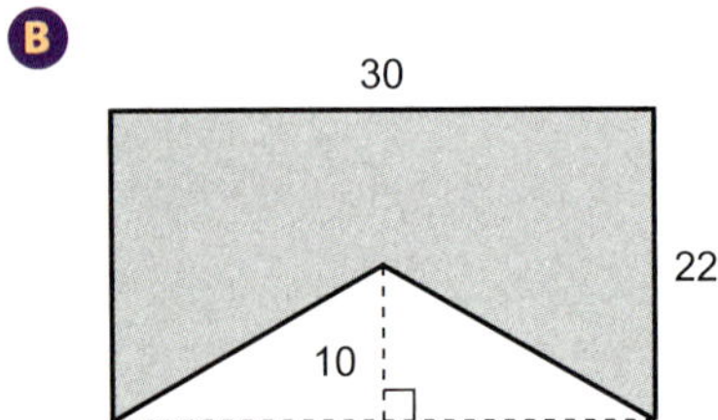

Solution The figure is equivalent to a rectangle with a triangle removed.

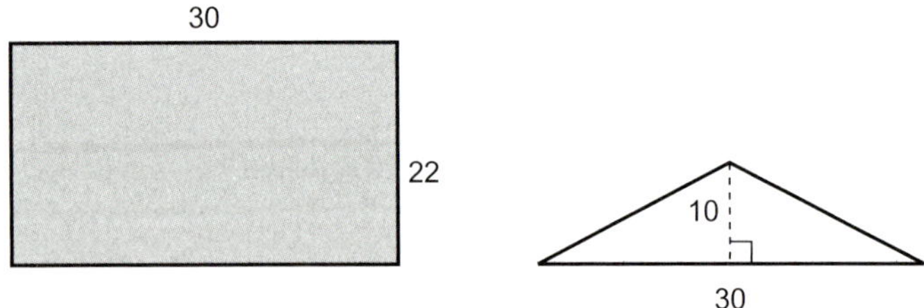

Find the areas of the rectangle and the triangle. The area of the entire figure is the area of the rectangle minus the area of the triangle.

$$(30 \bullet 22) - \frac{1}{2}(30 \bullet 10) = 660 - \frac{300}{2} = 660 - 150 = 510$$

The area of the figure is 510 units^2. ■

EXAMPLE 3 Find the area of the figure in two different ways. Show that both ways yield the same answer for the area.

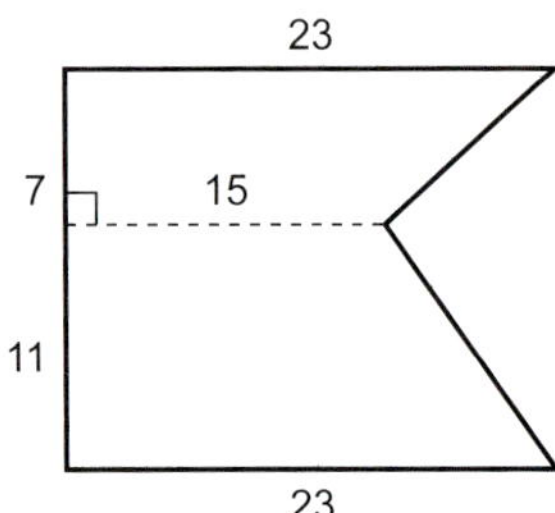

Solution One way is to split the figure into two separate trapezoids along the dashed line segment. The area of the figure is the sum of the two trapezoids' areas.

$$\frac{1}{2}[(23 + 15) \cdot 7] + \frac{1}{2}[(23 + 15) \cdot 11] = \frac{1}{2}[38 \cdot 7] + \frac{1}{2}[38 \cdot 11]$$

$$= \frac{266}{2} + \frac{418}{2} = \frac{684}{2} = 342$$

A second way is to represent the figure as a rectangle with a triangle removed from the right side.

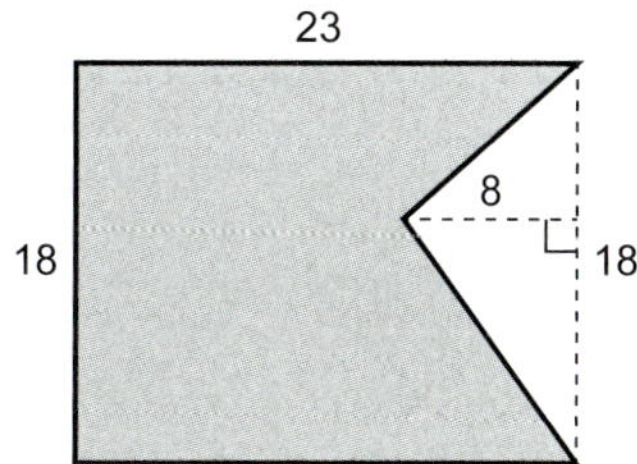

The area of the figure is the difference between the area of the rectangle and the area of the triangle.

$$(23 \cdot 18) + \frac{1}{2}(8 \cdot 18) = 414 + \frac{144}{2} = 414 - 72 = 342$$

In both cases, the area is equal to 342 units^2. ■

Problem Set

Find the area of the regular polygon.

1.

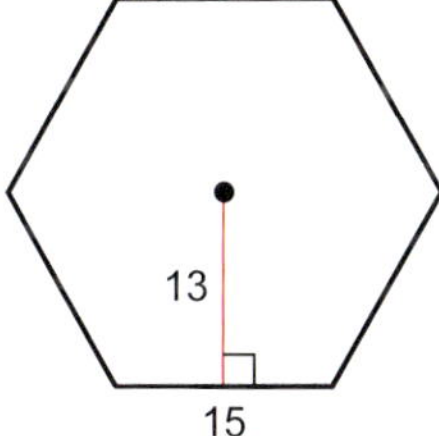

2.

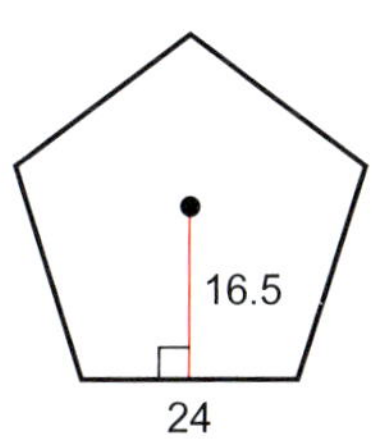

3. a hexagon with apothem 7.9 cm and perimeter 54 cm

4. a heptagon (7 sides) with an apothem length of 26 m and perimeter 175 m

5. an octagon (8 sides) with an apothem length of 1.8 m and a side length of 1.5 m

6. a dodecagon (12 sides) with an apothem length of 14 in. and a side length of 7.5 in.

Find the area of the figure.

7.

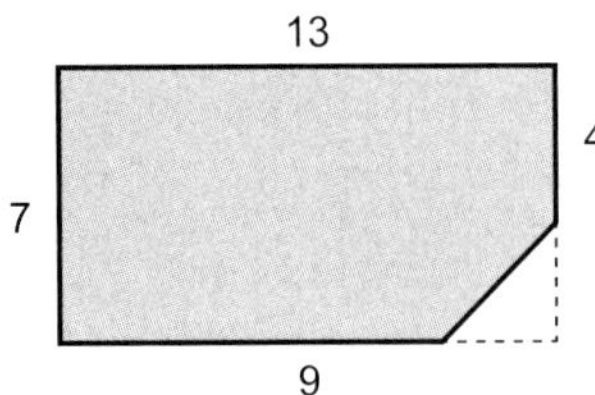

8.

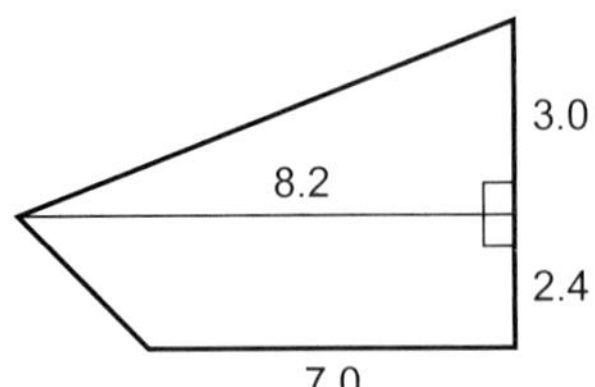

9.

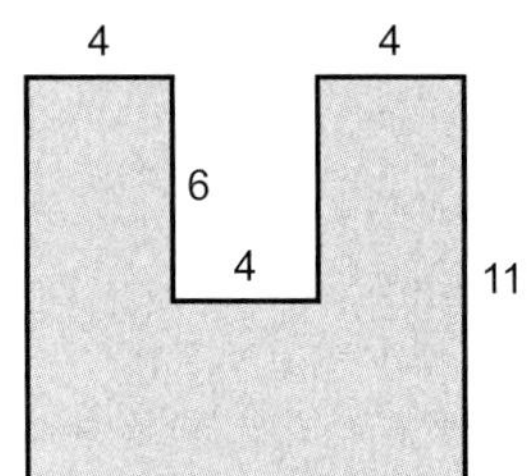

10.

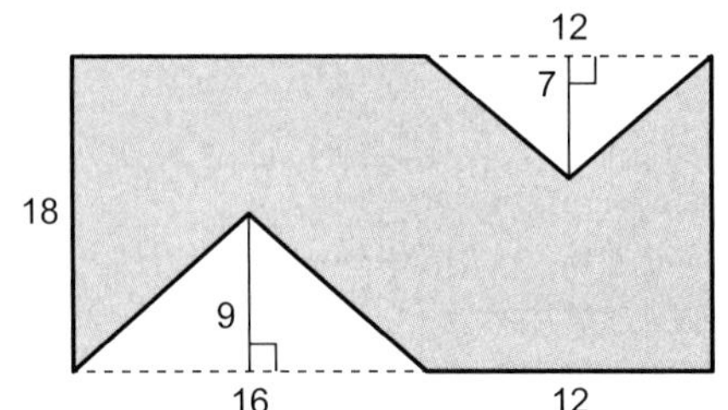

Solve.

11. A stop sign is a regular octagon with an apothem length of 39.5 cm and a side length of 32.7 cm. Find the area of the stop sign. Round your answer to the nearest tenth.

12. **Challenge** Find the area of a regular pentagon with an apothem of 2.2 m and a perimeter of 32 m. Round your answer to the nearest tenth.

13. **Challenge** Show that the area of shaded region is equal to the area of the nonshaded region.

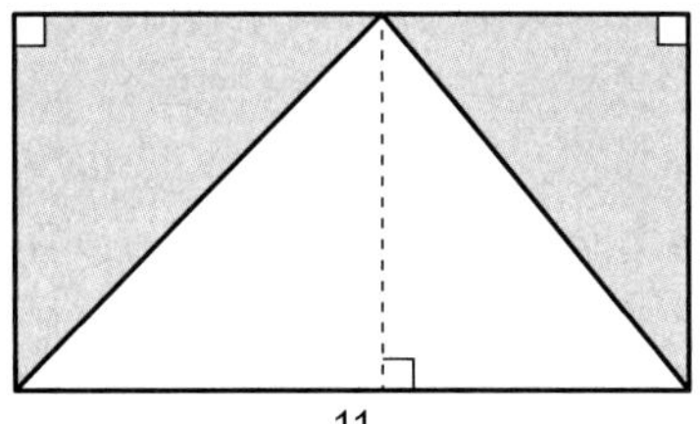

Core Focus: How Many Triangles?

THE CORE CONCEPT

You can determine how many triangles fit a given description by applying triangle math facts.

Finding How Many Triangles Are Possible, Given Angle Measures

SUM OF THE INTERIOR ANGLE MEASURES OF A TRIANGLE

The sum of the measures of a triangle's three interior angles is always equal to 180°.

To find how many triangles fit a given description, first use triangle math facts to determine whether it is possible to construct even one triangle fitting that description. If at least one triangle is possible, use any side length information you have to work through different possibilities for triangle shapes.

Q & A

Q How many equilateral triangles are possible?

A an infinite number; Although all three angles measure 60°, there is an infinite number of possible side lengths.

EXAMPLE 1 How many triangles are possible with the given characteristics: zero, one, or more than one? Explain your reasoning.

A angles whose measures are 50°, 50°, and 80°

Solution The sum of the measures of the three angles is $50° + 50° + 80° = 180°$. The triangle is an isosceles triangle, but you don't know any of the side lengths. Therefore, you can construct infinitely many similar triangles, all with angle measures of 50°, 50°, and 80°. More than one triangle is possible.

B two angles whose measures are 30° and 50°, and one side 4 cm in length

Solution Because two of the angle measures are 30° and 50°, the measure of the third angle must be $180° - (30° + 50°) = 180° - 80° = 100°$. However, any of the three sides could be 4 cm in length. You can confirm this by setting each of the sides equal to 4 cm and then measuring the lengths of the other two sides.

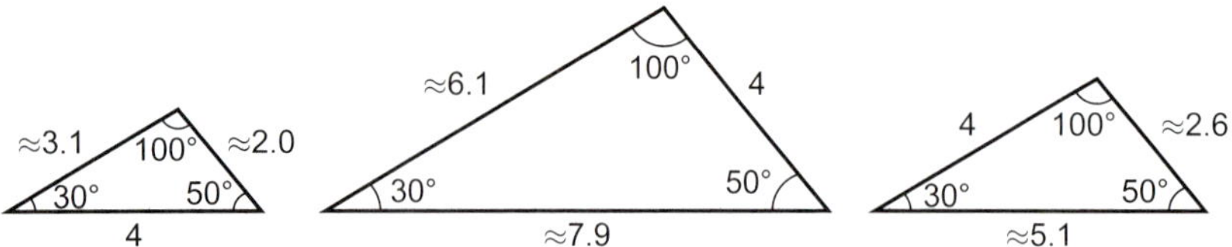

More than one triangle is possible. ■

THINK ABOUT IT

Knowing the measure of two of a triangle's interior angles is enough to determine the measure of the third interior angle.

Finding How Many Triangles Are Possible, Given Only Side Lengths

TRIANGLE SIDE LENGTHS

The length of any side of a triangle is always shorter than the sum of the lengths of the other two sides.

To determine how many triangles are possible based on side length, find the sum of the lengths of the two shorter sides and compare that to the length of the longest side. If the longest side is shorter than the two other sides combined, then exactly one triangle is possible. If the longest side is longer than or equal to the sum of the two other sides, then no triangle is possible.

EXAMPLE 2 How many triangles are possible with the given characteristics: zero, one, or more than one? Use a sketch to illustrate your reasoning.

A side lengths of 4, 6, and 12 units

Solution The sum of the lengths of the two shorter sides is $4 + 6 = 10$ units. If the longest side were equal to 10 (the sum of the other two sides), then the angle included between these two sides would have to equal 180°, and no triangle could exist.

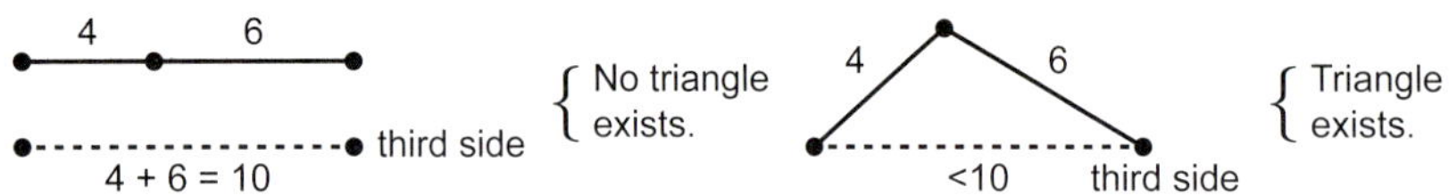

Therefore, to make an angle of less than 180° between the two shorter sides, the longest side must be less than 10.

In this case, the longest side is 12 units (i.e., greater than 10), so no triangle is possible. ■

REMEMBER

An angle that measures 180° is known as a **straight angle**.

B side lengths of 2, 4, and 5 cm

Solution The sum of the lengths of the two shorter sides is $2 + 4 = 6$ cm. The longest side is 5 cm, which is less than the sum of the two shorter sides, so exactly one triangle exists.

A right triangle with legs 2 and 4 has a hypotenuse that is too short.

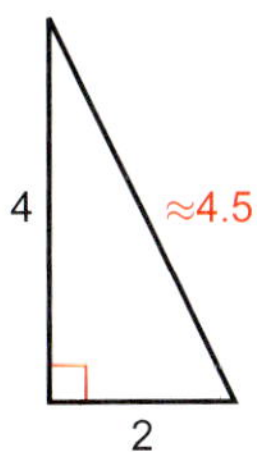

With some trial-and-error, you can find that an angle of 110° is about right.

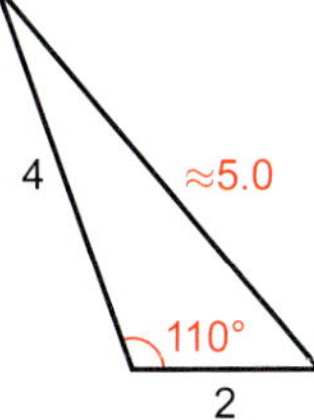

Using a ruler, you can draw a right triangle with legs of 2 and 4 cm. If you measure the hypotenuse, you see that it is shorter than 5 cm. If you increase the angle between the two shorter sides, you see that a measure of about 110° makes a triangle with the given side lengths of 2, 4, and 5 cm. ■

Problem Set

Solve.

1. How many triangles are possible with the given characteristics: zero, one, or more than one? Explain your reasoning.

(a) angles measuring 45°, 45°, and 90°

(b) angles measuring 65°, 65°, and 65°

(c) two angles measuring 65° and 100°, and one side 5 cm in length

(d) two angles, each measuring 50°, and at least one side 3 in. in length

2. How many triangles are possible with the given characteristics: zero, one, or more than one? Use a sketch to illustrate your reasoning.

(a) side lengths of 7.2 cm, 6.9 cm, and 12.8 cm

(b) side lengths of 13 cm, 5 cm, and 8 cm

(c) side lengths of 1.5 in, 1.5 in, and 1.5 in.

3. Danny designed a storefront sign in the shape of an isosceles triangle. The two congruent sides were 70 cm long and at least one of the angles was 50°.

(a) How many possible shapes are there for the triangular sign? Use a sketch to show your reasoning.

(b) Do all of the possible shapes have the same perimeter? Explain your answer.

CHAPTER 9 Review

Choose the answer.

1. Which pair of angles are alternate interior angles?

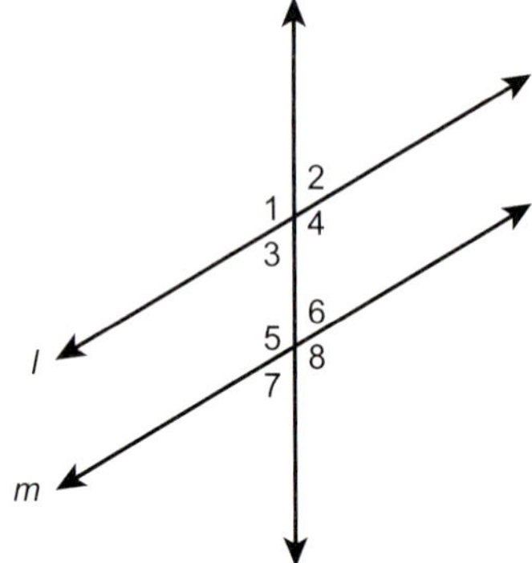

A. $\angle 1$ and $\angle 6$

B. $\angle 2$ and $\angle 8$

C. $\angle 3$ and $\angle 7$

D. $\angle 4$ and $\angle 5$

2. What is the value of x?

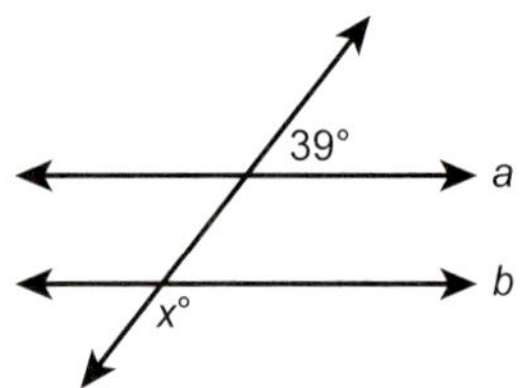

A. 39 **C.** 141

B. 51 **D.** 161

3. What is the value of z?

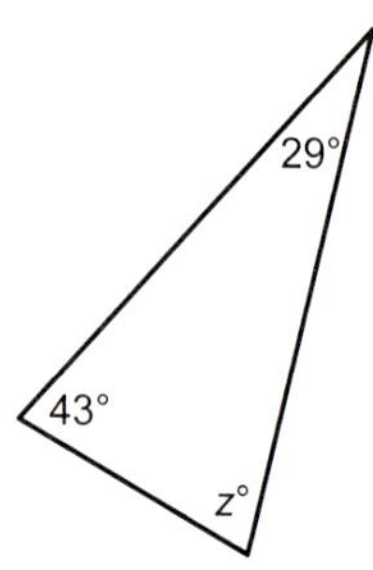

A. 72 **C.** 108

B. 98 **D.** 288

4. What is the height of a triangle if its area is 27 m^2 and its base is 9 m?

A. 3 m **C.** 12 m

B. 6 m **D.** 18 m

5. Which is the area of the figure?

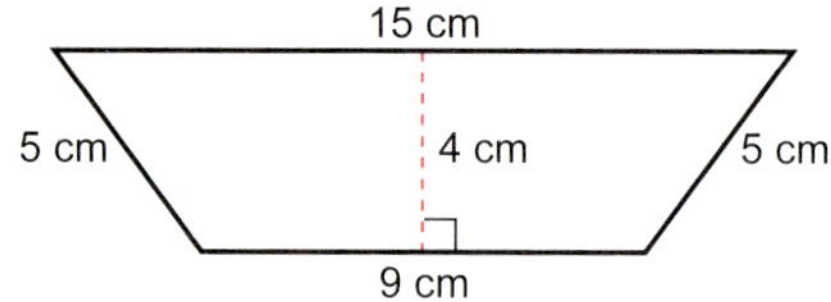

A. 34 cm^2

B. 48 cm^2

C. 60 cm^2

D. 96 cm^2

6. What is the area of the regular heptagon?

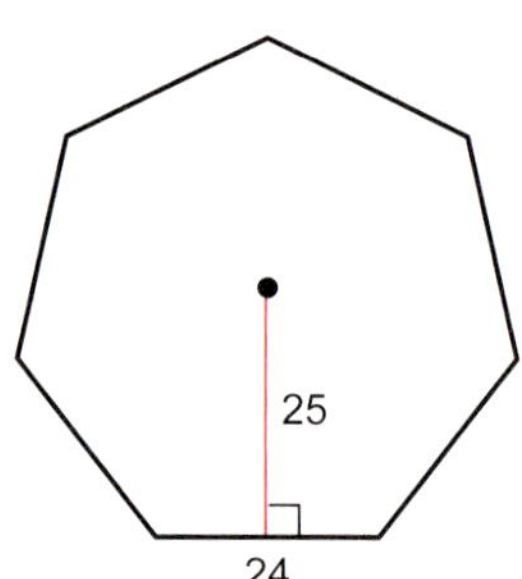

A. 300 units^2 **C.** 2100 units^2

B. 600 units^2 **D.** 4200 units^2

7. How many triangles have interior angles whose measures are 110°, 38°, and 32°?

A. 0

B. 1

C. 2

D. infinitely many

Solve.

8. For each pair of angles, state whether they are alternate interior, alternate exterior, or corresponding. Then state which line is the transversal forming the pair.

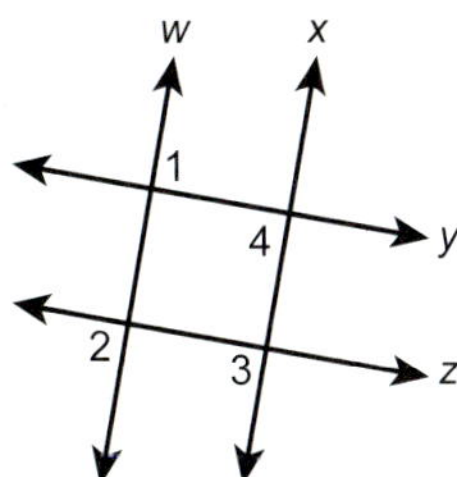

(a) $\angle 1$ and $\angle 2$

(b) $\angle 1$ and $\angle 3$

(c) $\angle 1$ and $\angle 4$

(d) $\angle 2$ and $\angle 3$

(e) $\angle 2$ and $\angle 4$

(f) $\angle 3$ and $\angle 4$

9. Use a ruler and a protractor to construct a triangle with two side lengths equal to 2.5 cm and an included angle of 20°.

10. What is the area of a regular decagon (10 sides) with an apothem length of 8 cm and a side length of 5.2 cm? Round your answer to the nearest tenth.

11. The shaded region is enclosed in a rectangle with a length of 10 units and a width of 12 units. Find the area of the shaded region.

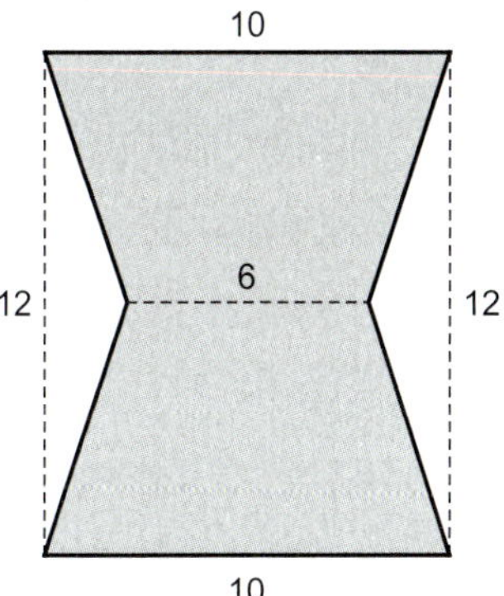

12. Find the area of the entire region.

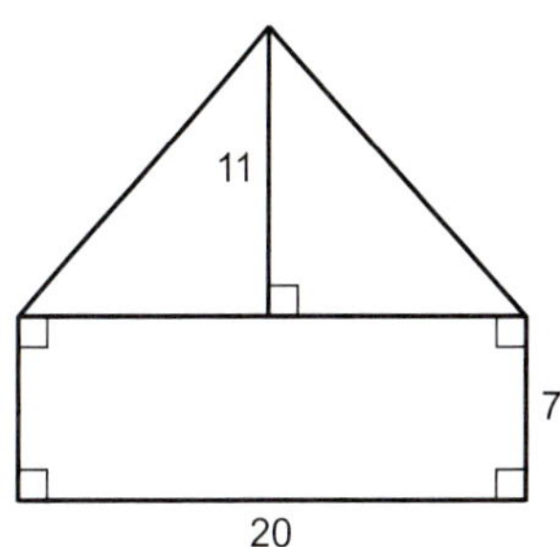

13. A triangle has at least two congruent sides with a length of 5 in. and at least one angle whose measure is 40°.

(a) How many triangles can you construct that fit this description? Explain.

(b) Use a protractor and a ruler to construct the triangles that fit this description.

Problem	Topic Lookup	Problem	Topic Lookup
1, 2, 8	Parallel Lines and Transversals	5	Areas of Special Quadrilaterals
3	Triangles	6, 10, 11	Areas of Polygons
9	Constructing Triangles	7, 13	Core Focus: How Many Triangles?
4, 12	Areas of Rectangles and Triangles		

CHAPTER 10 Circles and Measurement

Some creative, ambitious people use properties of circles to create large designs in crops such as wheat, barley, or corn. It's hard to tell what's going on with a crop circle design if you are on the ground, standing on the design. But if you are a few dozen meters in the air above it, you can see its impressive geometric patterns.

In This Chapter

Circles are some of the most useful geometric shapes. In this chapter, you will learn how to compute the circumference and area of a circle, and how to use circles to solve real-world problems.

Topic List

- Foundations for Chapter 10
- Circles
- Circumference
- Areas of Circles
- Core Focus: Circumference and Area
- Chapter 10 Review

Crop circles are large designs in crops. ▶

Foundations for Chapter 10

Simplifying Expressions with π

THE NUMBER π

Pi is a number represented by the Greek letter π. When written as a decimal, the digits of π start with 3.14159. . ., but they go on forever without repeating. You can find π in the formulas for the circumference and area of a circle.

When simplifying expressions involving π, substitute an approximation for π, such as 3.14 or $\frac{22}{7}$, into the expression. Then perform any necessary operations, such as addition or multiplication, to find the value of the expression.

EXAMPLE A Simplify the expression using the indicated value of π. Write improper fractions as mixed numbers.

A-1 12π, using 3.14 for π

Solution Use a calculator to multiply 12 and 3.14.

$$12\pi \approx 12 \cdot 3.14$$
$$\approx 37.7$$

Using 3.14 for π, 12π is approximately equal to 37.7. ■

A-2 12π, using $\frac{22}{7}$ for π

Solution $12\pi \approx 12 \cdot \frac{22}{7}$

$$= \frac{264}{7}$$
$$= 37\frac{5}{7}$$

Using $\frac{22}{7}$ for π, 12π is approximately equal to $37\frac{5}{7}$. ■

Problem Set A

Simplify the expression using the indicated value of π. Write improper fractions as mixed numbers.

1. 14π, using both 3.14 and $\frac{22}{7}$ for π
2. 9π, using both 3.14 and $\frac{22}{7}$ for π
3. $\frac{1}{4}\pi$, using both 3.14 and $\frac{22}{7}$ for π
4. 8.4π, using 3.14 for π
5. $\frac{5}{2}\pi$, using $\frac{22}{7}$ for π
6. $\frac{1}{2} + \pi$, using $\frac{22}{7}$ for π
7. $7\pi + 2$, using both 3.14 and $\frac{22}{7}$ for π
8. $11.2\pi + 4.9$, using 3.14 for π
9. $14\pi - 5$, using both 3.14 and $\frac{22}{7}$ for π
10. $3\frac{5}{6}\pi$, using $\frac{22}{7}$ for π

Evaluating Variable Expressions with π

Evaluate expressions involving a variable and π by substituting both the value of the variable and a close approximation for π, such as 3.14 or $\frac{22}{7}$, into the expression. Then perform all operations to find the value of the expression.

EXAMPLE B Simplify the expression using the value of the variable and the indicated value of π. Write improper fractions as mixed numbers.

B-1 $2x\pi$, where $x = 4$ and $\pi \approx 3.14$

Solution Substitute 4 for x. Use a calculator to find the product of the numbers.

$$\begin{aligned} 2x\pi &\approx 2 \cdot (4) \cdot 3.14 \\ &= 8 \cdot 3.14 \\ &\approx 25.1 \end{aligned}$$

When $x = 4$, $2x\pi$ is approximately equal to 25.1. ■

B-2 $2x\pi$, where $x = 4$ and $\pi \approx \frac{22}{7}$

Solution Substitute 4 for x.

$$\begin{aligned} 2x\pi &\approx 2 \cdot (4) \cdot \frac{22}{7} \\ &= \frac{2 \cdot 4 \cdot 22}{7} \\ &= \frac{176}{7} \\ &= 25\frac{1}{7} \end{aligned}$$

When $x = 4$, $2x\pi$ is approximately equal to $25\frac{1}{7}$. ■

Problem Set B

Simplify the expression using the value of the variable and the indicated value of π. Write improper fractions as mixed numbers.

1. $5z\pi$, where $z = 3$ and $\pi \approx 3.14$
2. $7b\pi$, where $b = 8$ and $\pi \approx \frac{22}{7}$
3. $\frac{1}{10}x\pi$, where $x = 5$ and $\pi \approx \frac{22}{7}$
4. $3.5d\pi$, where $d = 4$ and $\pi \approx 3.14$
5. $15w\pi$, where $w = \frac{1}{6}$ and $\pi \approx \frac{22}{7}$
6. $1\frac{2}{3}(y\pi)$, where $y = 9$ and $\pi \approx \frac{22}{7}$
7. $3k\pi - 15$, where $k = 2$ and $\pi \approx 3.14$
8. $5.2p\pi + 2.7$, where $p = 4$ and $\pi \approx 3.14$
9. $6h\pi - \frac{3}{7}$, where $h = \frac{1}{2}$ and $\pi \approx \frac{22}{7}$
10. $0.9s\pi + 2.7$, where $s = 4.4$ and $\pi \approx 3.14$

Evaluating Complex Variable Expressions with π

Evaluate expressions involving a variable and π by substituting both the value of the variable and a close approximation for π, such as 3.14 or $\frac{22}{7}$, into the expression. Then perform all operations to find the value of the expression. Follow the rules for the order of operations.

EXAMPLE C Simplify the expression using the value of the variable and the indicated value of π. Write improper fractions as mixed numbers.

C-1 $x^2\pi$, where $x = 3$ and $\pi \approx 3.14$

Solution Substitute 3 for x. Use a calculator to find the product of the numbers.

$$x^2\pi \approx (3)^2 \cdot 3.14$$
$$= 9 \cdot 3.14$$
$$\approx 28.3$$

When $x = 3$, $x^2\pi$ is approximately equal to 28.3. ■

C-2 $x^2\pi$, where $x = 3$ and $\pi \approx \frac{22}{7}$

Solution Substitute 3 for x.

$$x^2\pi \approx (3)^2 \cdot \frac{22}{7}$$
$$= 9 \cdot \frac{22}{7}$$
$$= \frac{198}{7}$$
$$\approx 28\frac{2}{7}$$

When $x = 3$, $x^2\pi$ is approximately equal to $28\frac{2}{7}$. ■

Problem Set C

Simplify the expression using the value of the variable and the indicated value of π. Write improper fractions as mixed numbers.

1. $m^2\pi$, where $m = 5$ and $\pi \approx 3.14$
2. $q^2\pi$, where $q = 7$ and $\pi \approx \frac{22}{7}$
3. $r^2\pi$, where $r = \frac{1}{4}$ and $\pi \approx \frac{22}{7}$
4. $y^2\pi$, where $y = 2.7$ and $\pi \approx 3.14$
5. $x^2\pi$, where $x = \frac{2}{3}$ and $\pi \approx \frac{22}{7}$
6. $4a^2\pi$, where $a = 3$ and $\pi \approx 3.14$
7. $\left(\frac{d}{2}\right)^2\pi$, where $d = 6$ and $\pi \approx \frac{22}{7}$
8. $\left(\frac{n}{2}\right)^2\pi$, where $n = 9$ and $\pi \approx 3.14$
9. $w^2\pi + 19$, where $w = \frac{7}{8}$ and $\pi \approx \frac{22}{7}$
10. $2t^2\pi - 8.2$, where $t = 3.8$ and $\pi \approx 3.14$

Circles

The circle is a common and useful shape.

DEFINITIONS

A **circle** is the set of all points in a plane that are equidistant from a given point called the **center**.

▶ **TIP**

Equidistant means "the same distance."

Remember that the side of a polygon is a line segment. A circle does not have any sides, so circles are not polygons.

The center of a circle is not part of the circle. It is used to determine which points form the circle. The center point can be used to name the circle.

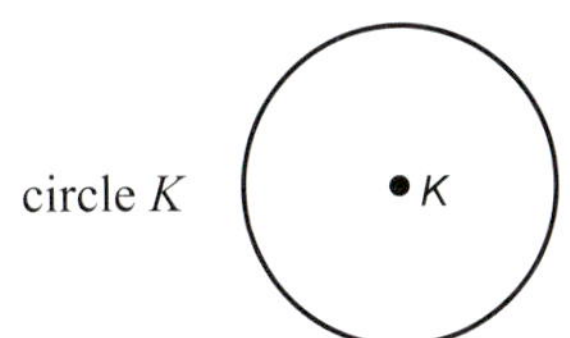

Identifying Radii

DEFINITIONS

A **radius** of a circle is a segment that connects the center to a point on the circle. The plural of *radius* is **radii**.

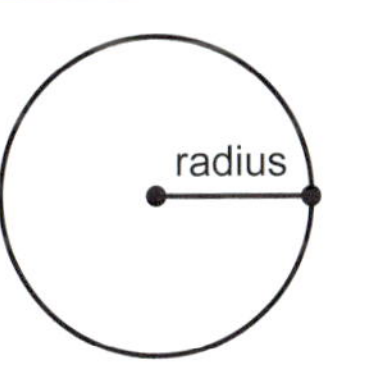

EXAMPLE 1

A Name the radii shown for circle P.

Solution The radii are $\overline{PR}$, $\overline{PQ}$, and $\overline{PT}$. ■

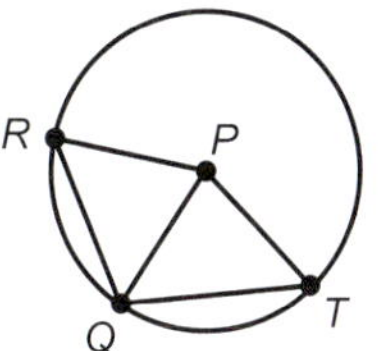

▶ **TIP**

Every circle has an infinite number of radii.

B Name the radii shown for circle A.

Solution Because A is the center of the circle, $\overline{AG}$ is the only radius shown. ■

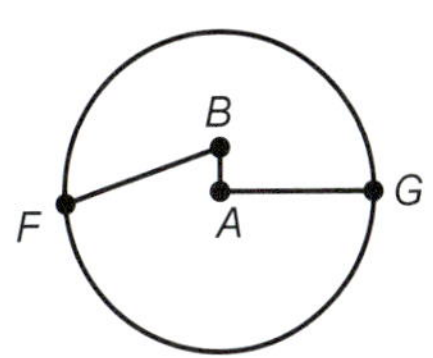

Identifying Chords and Diameters

DEFINITIONS

A **chord** is a line segment that connects any two points on a circle. A **diameter** is a chord that contains the center of the circle.

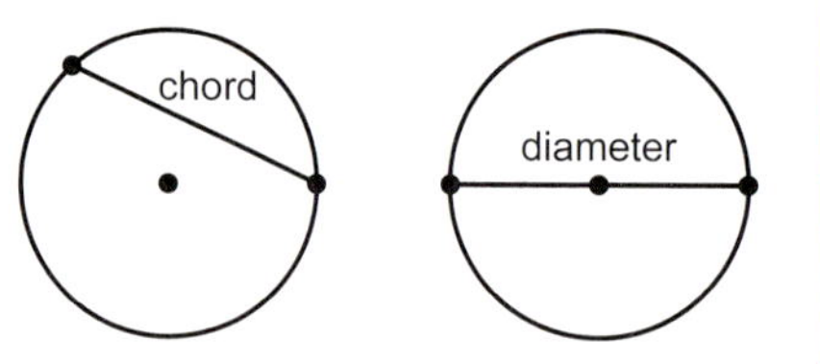

EXAMPLE 2

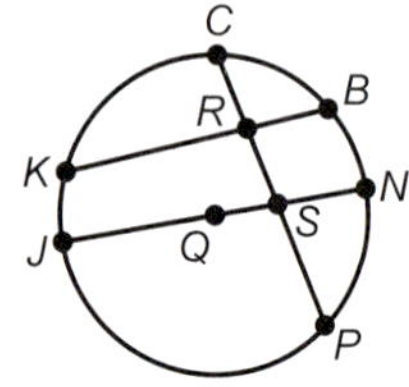

A Name the chords of circle Q.

Solution Look for segments whose endpoints are on the circle. The chords are $\overline{KB}$, $\overline{JN}$, and $\overline{CP}$. ■

B Name the diameters of circle Q.

Solution The only chord that passes through the center of the circle is $\overline{JN}$, so $\overline{JN}$ is a diameter of the circle. ■

TIP

Every circle has an infinite number of diameters and an infinite number of chords.

THINK ABOUT IT

Every diameter is a chord, but not every chord is a diameter.

Calculating a Radius or Diameter

Look again at circle Q in Example 2. Point Q separates the diameter $\overline{JN}$ into two segments of equal length: $\overline{QJ}$ and $\overline{QN}$, which are both radii.

RADIUS AND DIAMETER PROPERTY

Let d be the diameter of a circle and r be the radius. The diameter d of a circle is twice the radius r of the circle.

$$d = 2r$$

TIP

Diameter and radius can each refer to the segment or to the length of the segment. The radius refers to the length. A radius refers to a segment.

EXAMPLE 3

A What is the diameter of circle M?

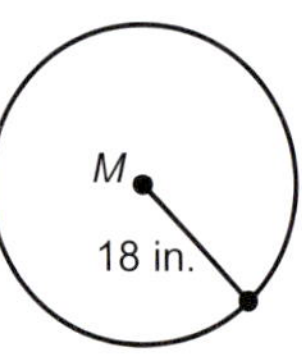

Solution The radius r is 18 in.

$d = 2r$

$= 2 \cdot 18$ Substitute 18 for r.

$= 36$ Multiply.

The diameter is 36 in. ■

B Find the radius of a circle that has a diameter of 15 cm.

Solution Substitute 15 for d and solve for r.

$d = 2r$	
$15 = 2r$	Substitute 15 for d.
$\frac{15}{2} = r$	Divide both sides by 2.
$7.5 = r$	Simplify.

The radius is 7.5 cm. ■

Application: Boating

EXAMPLE 4 A lake is approximately circular and has an average diameter of 3265 ft. A small island is located so the dock is at the center of the lake. A tour boat takes people to and from the island several times a day. If the boat travels about 26,120 ft every day, how many one-way trips does the boat make every day?

Solution The distance from the side of the lake to the island is the radius of the lake. Find the average radius of the lake.

$d = 2r$	
$3265 = 2r$	Substitute 3265 for d.
$\frac{3265}{2} = r$	Divide both sides by 2.
$1632.5 = r$	Simplify.

Divide the total distance the boat travels by the radius to determine how many one-way trips the boat makes.

$$26{,}120 \div 1632.5 = 16$$

The boat makes 16 one-way trips every day. ■

Problem Set

For each circle:

(a) Name all the radii.

(b) Name all the chords.

(c) Name all the diameters.

1.

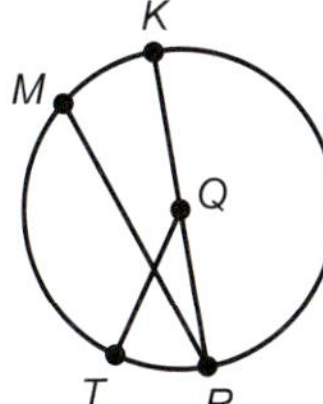

2.

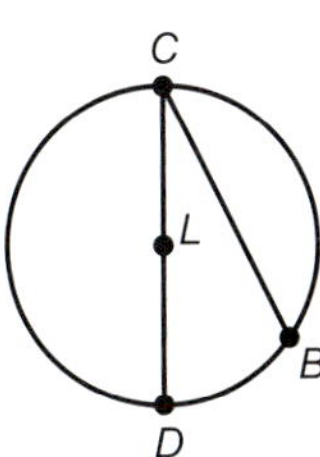

3.

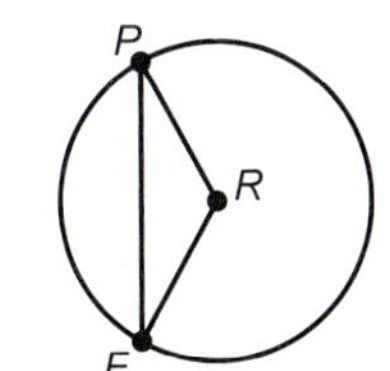

4.

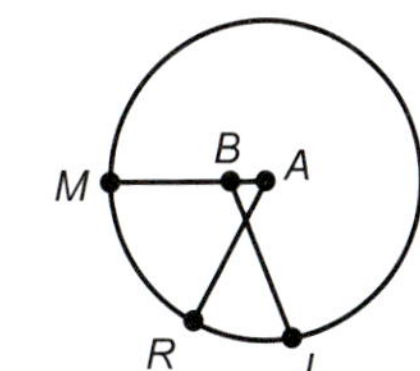

5.

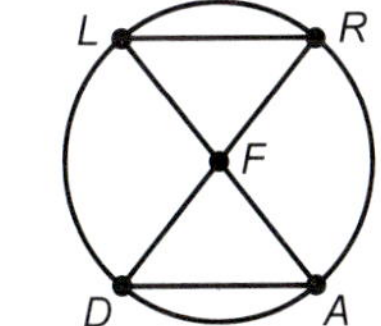

6.

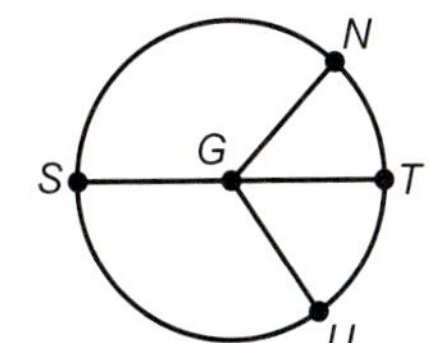

Determine whether the statement is *True* or *False*.

7. All the radii of the same circle have the same length.

8. All the diameters of the same circle have the same length.

9. All the chords of the same circle have the same length.

10. A radius of a circle is shorter than any chord of the circle.

11. A diameter is the longest chord in a circle.

Solve.

12. What is the radius of circle S?

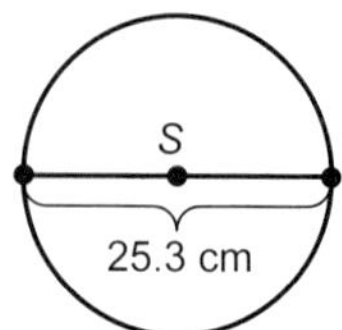

13. What is the diameter of circle X?

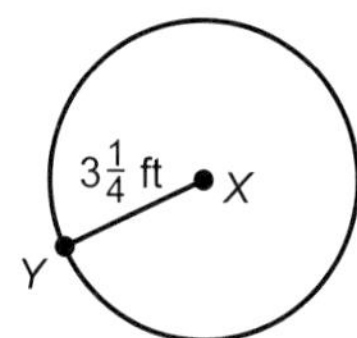

14. Find the radius of a circle if its diameter is $2\frac{1}{2}$ in.

15. Find the diameter of a circle if its radius is 34.5 cm.

16. Explain why a circle is not a polygon.

17. What must be true about $\overline{KR}$ if the circle is named circle E? Why?

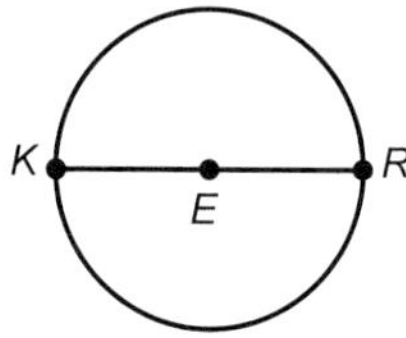

18. A circular swimming pool has a radius of 15 ft. What is the least number of times you can swim across the pool so that you swim 1 mi? (Hint: 1 mi = 5280 ft)

19. A town center has a circular lake with a diameter of 450 ft. A ferry boat takes visitors to and from the dock of a floating restaurant located in the center of the lake. If the boat travels about 3375 ft every day, how many one-way trips does the boat make every day?

20. **Challenge** Ricardo is building a feeding station for his three cats. As the diagram illustrates, each cat will have its own bowl, and all the bowls will be the same size. There will be 2 in. between the bowls, as well as between the bowls and the edges of the feeder. Find the length and width of the feeding station.

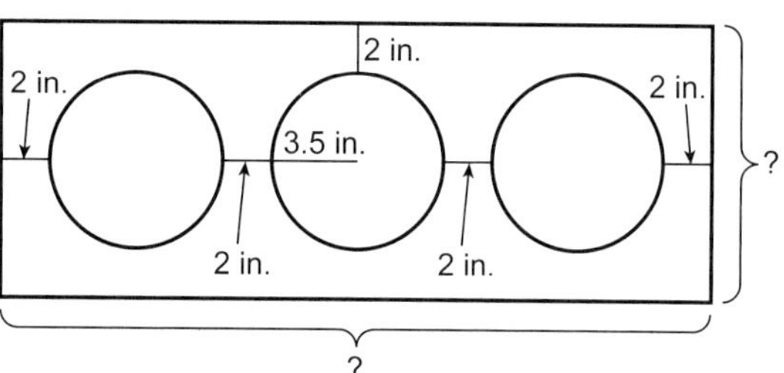

21. **Challenge** In the diagram, points A, B, C, D, E, and F are on the circle.

    (a) Name all the chords.

    (b) Given that $\overline{AB} \parallel \overline{CD} \parallel \overline{EF}$, find $m\angle 1$, $m\angle 2$, $m\angle 3$. Justify your answers.

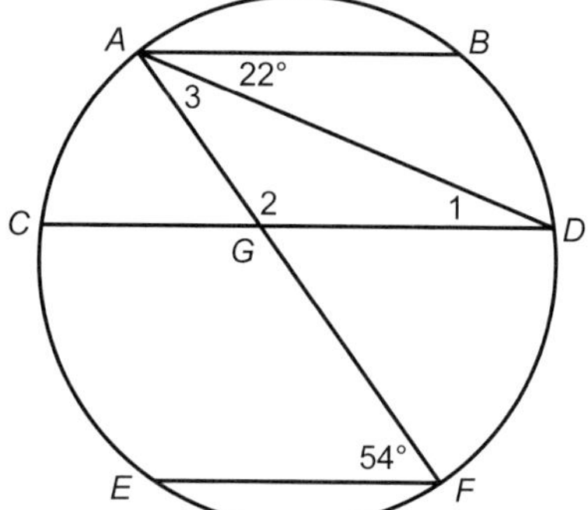

Circumference

The distance around a polygon is called its perimeter, and the distance around a circle is called its circumference.

DEFINITION

The **circumference** of a circle is the distance around the circle.

Finding the Circumference of a Circle

Since ancient times, people have known that the ratio of the circumference to the diameter of any circle is a constant that is just a bit more than 3. This constant is called π (pi), which is a decimal number that never repeats and never ends. In calculations, it is often approximated as 3.14.

CIRCUMFERENCE OF A CIRCLE

The circumference of a circle with diameter d and radius r is

$$C = \pi d \text{ or } C = 2\pi r.$$

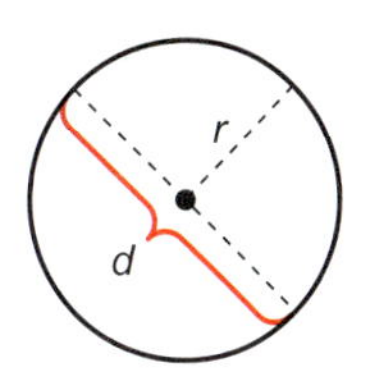

THINK ABOUT IT

In a given circle, the diameter is twice the radius, so $C = \pi d = \pi 2r = 2\pi r$.

Answers that are found by substituting 3.14 for π are estimates and should include the approximately equal to ($\approx$) symbol. Answers that use the symbol π are exact answers.

EXAMPLE 1 Find the circumference of the circle. Give both exact and approximate answers.

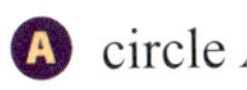

circle A

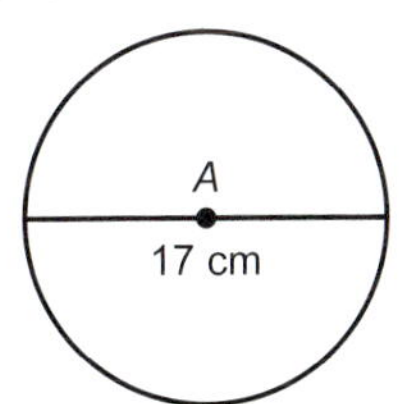

Solution Because the diameter is given, use $C = \pi d$.

$C = \pi d$	Write the formula.
$= \pi \bullet 17$	Substitute 17 for d.
$\approx 3.14 \bullet 17$	Substitute 3.14 for π.
≈ 53.4	Multiply.

The circumference is exactly 17π cm, or about 53.4 cm. ■

TIP

When using 3.14 for π, use three digits when writing the circumference.

B circle with radius of 5 m

Solution Because the radius is given, use $C = 2\pi r$.

$C = 2\pi r$	Write the formula.
$= 2 \cdot \pi \cdot 5$	Substitute 5 for r.
$= 10\pi$	Multiply.
$\approx 10 \cdot 3.14$	Substitute 3.14 for π.
≈ 31.4	Multiply.

The circumference is exactly 10π m, or about 31.4 m.

TIP

Find the exact answer in terms of π first, and then substitute a value of π to find an approximation.

Finding Missing Lengths

EXAMPLE 2

A The circumference of a circle is 18π ft. What is the radius?

Solution Substitute the known information into $C = 2\pi r$. Solve for r.

$C = 2\pi r$	Write the formula.
$18\pi = 2 \cdot \pi \cdot r$	Substitute 18π for C.
$18 = 2r$	Divide both sides by π.
$9 = r$	Divide both sides by 2.

The radius is 9 ft.

B The circumference of a circle is 40 yd. What is the diameter?

Solution Substitute the known information into $C = \pi d$. Solve for d.

$C = \pi d$	Write the formula.
$40 = \pi d$	Substitute 40 for C.
$\frac{40}{\pi} = d$	Divide both sides by π.
$\frac{40}{3.14} \approx d$	Substitute 3.14 for π.
$12.7 \approx d$	Divide both sides by 3.14.

The diameter is about 12.7 yd.

Finding Perimeters of Partial and Combination Figures

A semicircle is half a circle. To find the circumference of a semicircle, divide by 2: $C = \frac{\pi d}{2}$ or $C = \frac{^{1}\cancel{2}\pi r}{\cancel{2}_{1}} = \pi r$. A quarter circle is one-fourth of a circle. To find the circumference of a quarter circle, divide by 4: $C = \frac{\pi d}{4}$ or $C = \frac{^{1}\cancel{2}\pi r}{\cancel{4}_{2}} = \frac{\pi r}{2}$.

EXAMPLE 3

A Find the exact circumference of a semicircle with radius 5 cm.

Solution Use the formula $C = \pi r$.

$C = \pi r$ Use the formula for circumference of a semicircle.

$C = \pi \cdot 5$ Substitute 5 for r.

$C = 5\pi$ Simplify.

The exact circumference is 5π cm. ■

B Find the circumference of a quarter circle with diameter 6 in. Use 3.14 to approximate π.

Solution Use the formula $C = \frac{\pi d}{4}$.

$C = \frac{\pi \cdot 6}{4}$ Subtitute 6 for d.

$C = 1.5\pi$ Simplify.

$C \approx 1.5 \cdot 3.14$ Substitute 3.14 for π.

$C \approx 4.71$ Multiply.

The circumference is exactly 1.5π cm, or about 4.71 cm. ■

EXAMPLE 4

A The figure is made up of two semicircles and a rectangle. Find the perimeter of the figure.

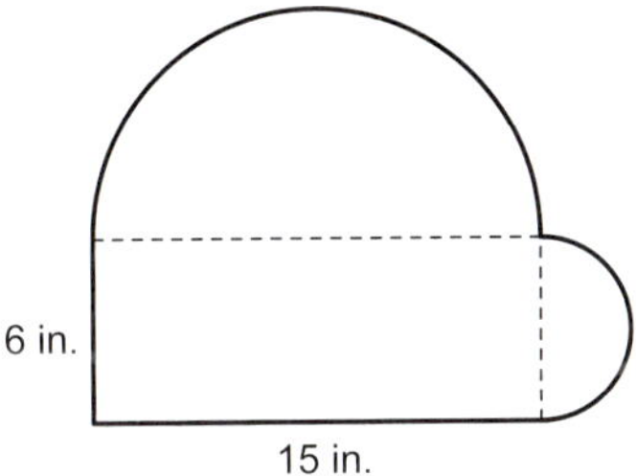

Solution

$P = \frac{\pi d_1}{2} + \frac{\pi d_2}{2} + 6 + 15$ Add the circumference of the semicircles to the 2 sides of the rectangle.

$= \frac{\pi \cdot 15}{2} + \frac{\pi \cdot 6}{2} + 6 + 15$ The diameters are 15 and 6.

$= 10.5\pi + 21$ Simplify.

$\approx 10.5 \cdot 3.14 + 21$ Substitute 3.14 for π.

≈ 54.0 Simplify.

The perimeter is about 54 in. ■

B The figure is made up of two congruent squares and a quarter circle. Find the perimeter of the figure to the nearest tenth.

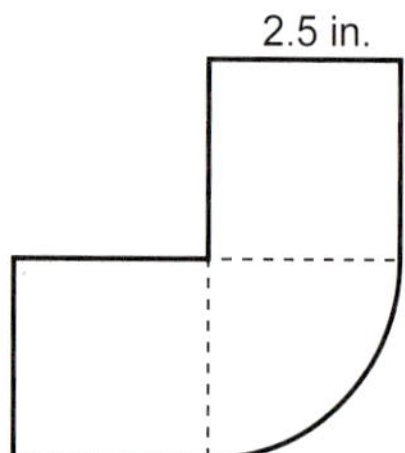

Solution The side of each square is the radius of the quarter circle.

$P = 6s + \frac{\pi r}{2}$	Add the 6 sides of the square to the circumference of the quarter circle.
$= 6 \cdot 2.5 + \frac{\pi \cdot 2.5}{2}$	Substitute 2.5 for s and r.
$= 15 + 1.25\pi$	Simplify.
$\approx 15 + 1.25 \cdot 3.14$	Substitute 3.14 for π.
$\approx 15 + 3.93$	Multiply.
≈ 18.9	Add.

The perimeter is about 18.9 in. ■

Application: Sports

EXAMPLE 5 A bicycle wheel has a radius of 16 in. It is rolled on the ground for one complete revolution. How far did the wheel travel?

Solution The distance traveled equals the circumference of the wheel.

$C = 2\pi r$	Write the formula.
$= 2 \cdot \pi \cdot 16$	Substitute 16 for r.
$= 32\pi$	Multiply.
$\approx 32 \cdot 3.14$	Substitute 3.14 for π.
≈ 100	Multiply.

The wheel traveled about 100 in. ■

Problem Set

The center of the circle is shown. Find the circumference of the circle. Give both exact and approximate answers.

1.

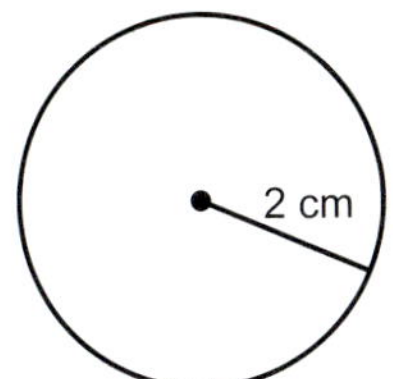

2.

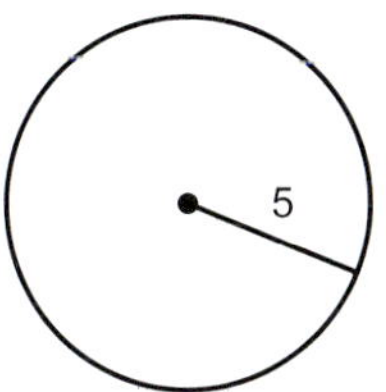

3.

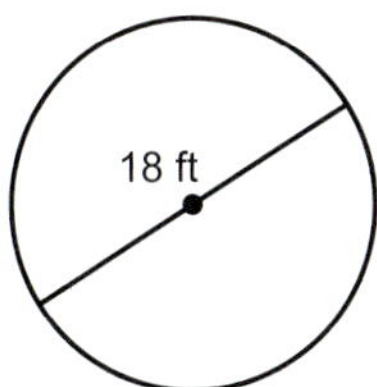

4.

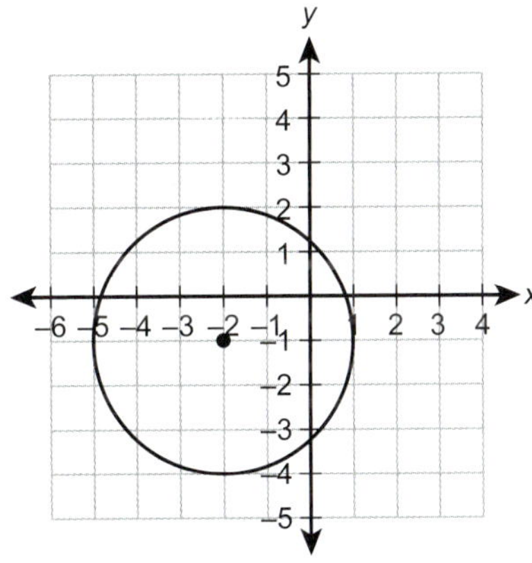

5.

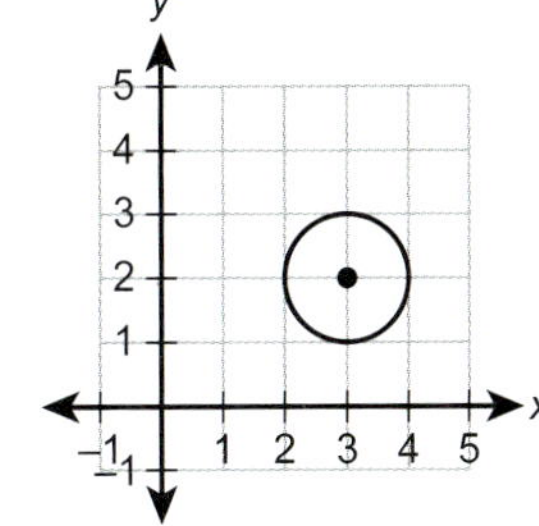

6.

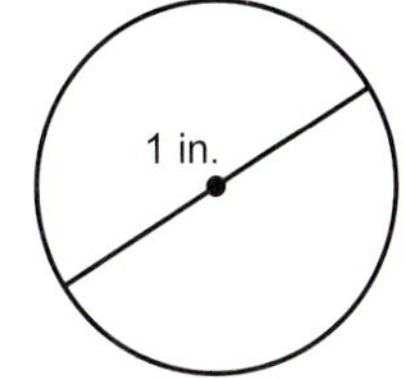

7.

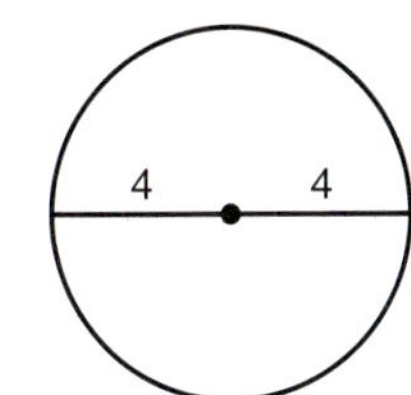

8.

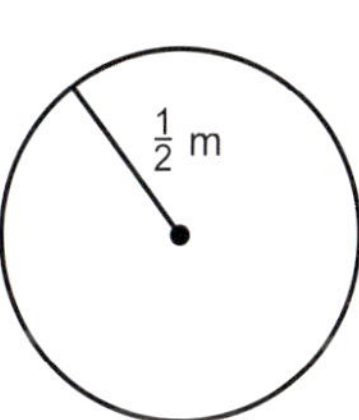

Solve.

9. The circumference of a circle is 19π in. What is the radius of the circle?

10. The circumference of a circle is 76 cm. What is the diameter of the circle?

Estimate the circumference of the circle using $\pi \approx \frac{22}{7}$.

11.

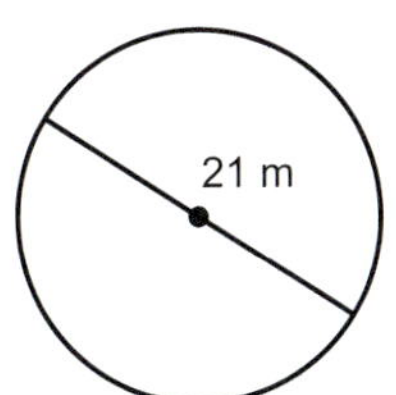

12.

Find the perimeter of the figure. Use $\pi \approx 3.14$.

13. 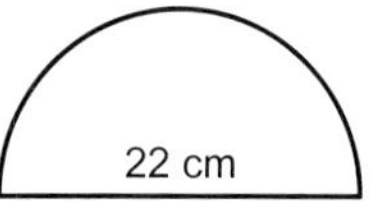

14. 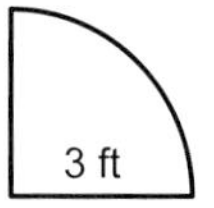

15. 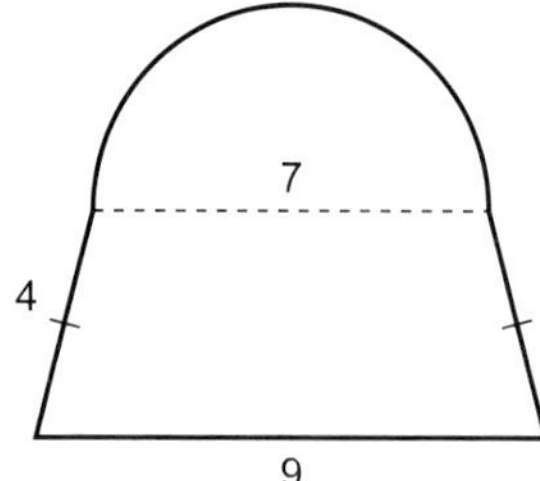

16. 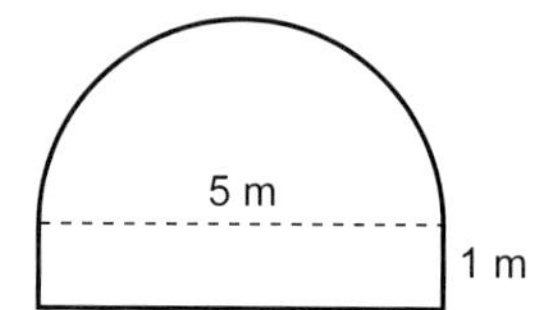

17. 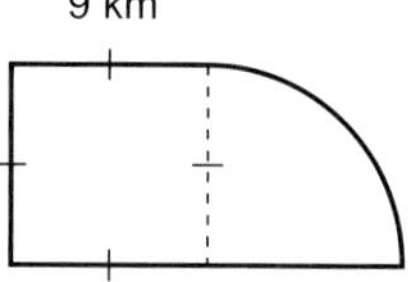

18. 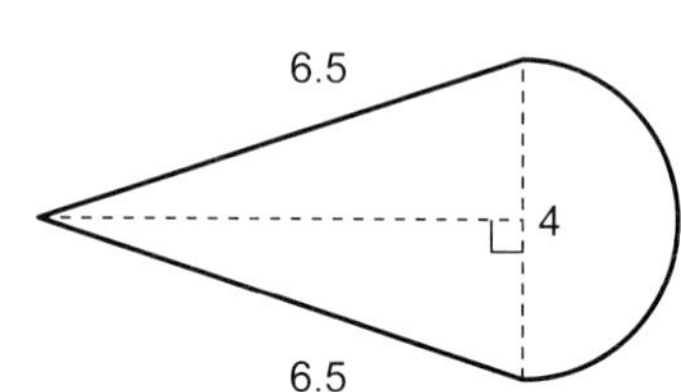

Solve. Round your answer to the nearest tenth, if necessary.

19. What is the circumference of a swimming pool if its diameter is 8.5 m?

20. The bottom of a lamp shade has a circumference of about 60 in. Estimate the diameter to the nearest tenth.

21. A ring has a diameter of 1.6 cm. Estimate the circumference of the ring.

22. A tire has a radius of 15 in. How far does it travel in 5 revolutions?

23. Joseph is making a plant holder so that the pot sits partly above and partly below a wooden board. To cut the hole in the board, he needs to know the diameter of the circle, but because a plant is already in the pot, he cannot measure it directly. Instead, he measures how much string can be wrapped around the pot at the desired height. What will be the diameter of the circle he cuts in the board if he used 35 mm of string?

24. A pitcher's mound on a baseball field has a diameter of 18 ft. What is its circumference?

25. A gardener has 48 km of fencing material. If she makes a circular garden and uses all her fencing material, what will be the radius of her garden?

26. At the center of a basketball court, the inner circle has a radius of 2 ft and the outer circle has a radius of 6 ft. What is the difference of the circumferences of the circles?

27. Suri's circular ornament has a diameter of 2.75 in., and Ada's circular ornament has a diameter of 1.25 in. How much greater is the circumference of Suri's ornament than Ada's ornament?

28. **Challenge** A wheel has a diameter of 14 in. How many revolutions will it make after rolling 20 ft?

Find the length of the darkened part of the circle.

29. **Challenge**

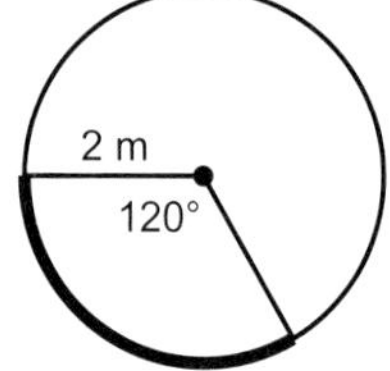

30. **Challenge**

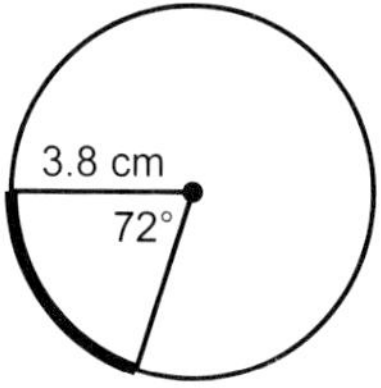

Areas of Circles

In addition to its use in the formula for circumference, π can help you calculate the area of a circle.

Finding the Area of a Circle

AREA OF A CIRCLE

The area of a circle with radius r is

$$A = \pi r^2.$$

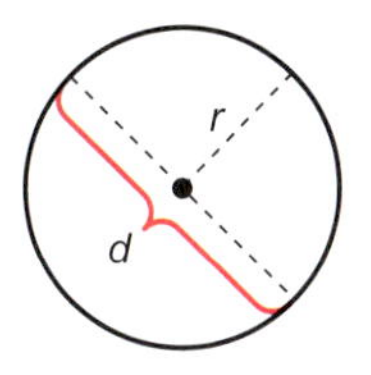

TIP

r^2 is read "r squared" and means $r \cdot r$.

EXAMPLE 1 Find the area of the circle. Give both exact and approximate answers.

A circle C

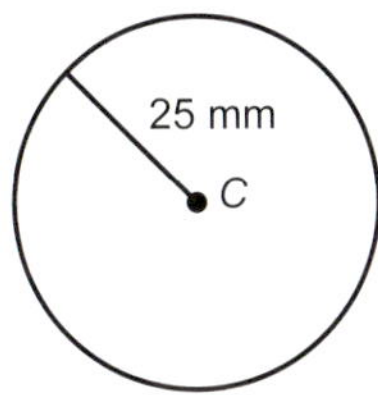

Solution Use the formula with $r = 25$.

$A = \pi r^2$	Write the formula.
$= \pi \cdot 25^2$	Substitute 25 for r.
$= 625\pi$	$25^2 = 625$
$\approx 625 \cdot 3.14$	Substitute 3.14 for π.
≈ 1960	Multiply.

The area is exactly 625π mm^2, or about 1960 mm^2. ■

TIP

In the area formula, the order of operations tells you that only the radius is squared. Do not square π.

B circle D

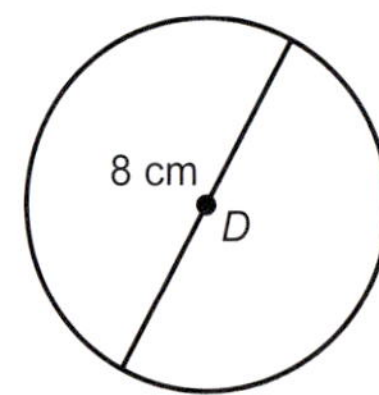

Solution The diameter is given. Divide to find the radius: $8 \div 2 = 4$.

$A = \pi r^2$	Write the formula.
$= \pi \cdot 4^2$	Substitute 4 for r.
$= 16\pi$	Simplify.
$\approx 16 \cdot 3.14$	Substitute 3.14 for π.
≈ 50.2	Multiply.

The area is exactly 16π cm², or about 50.2 cm².

Finding Missing Lengths

EXAMPLE 2

A The area of a circle is 100π m². What is the radius?

Solution Substitute the known information into $A = \pi r^2$. Solve for r.

$A = \pi r^2$	Write the formula.
$100\pi = \pi r^2$	Substitute 100π for A.
$100 = r^2$	Divide both sides by π.
$10 = r$	***Think:*** What number times itself is 100?

The radius is 10 m.

B The area of a circle is 50 in². What is the diameter?

Solution After solving for r, multiply by 2 to find d.

$A = \pi r^2$	Write the formula.
$50 = \pi \cdot r^2$	Substitute 50 for A.
$\frac{50}{\pi} = r^2$	Divide both sides by π.
$\frac{50}{3.14} \approx r^2$	Substitute 3.14 for π.
$15.9 \approx r^2$	Divide.
$4 \approx r$	***Think:*** $16 = 4 \cdot 4$.

Because the radius is about 4 in., the diameter is about 8 in.

Finding Areas of Partial and Combination Figures

To find the area of a semicircle, divide the formula for the area of a circle by 2: $A = \frac{\pi r^2}{2}$. To find the area of a quarter circle, divide by 4: $A = \frac{\pi r^2}{4}$.

EXAMPLE 3 The radius of the semicircle and height of the triangle are shown. Find the area of the figure.

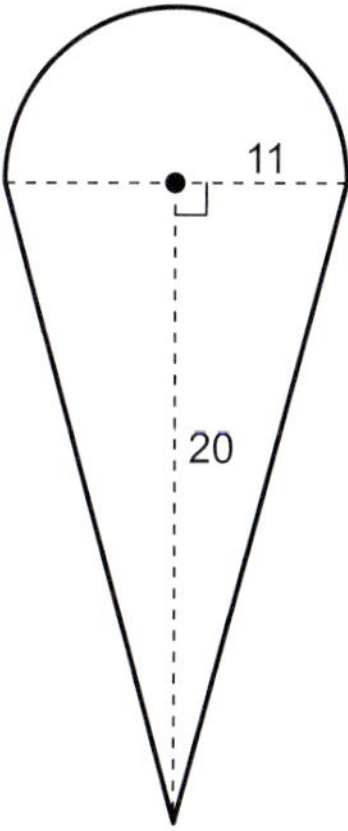

Solution

$A = \frac{\pi r^2}{2} + \frac{1}{2}bh$	Add the area of the semicircle to the area of the triangle.
$= \frac{\pi \cdot 11^2}{2} + \frac{1}{2} \cdot 22 \cdot 20$	The base of the triangle is $11 + 11 = 22$.
$= 60.5\pi + 220$	Simplify.
$\approx 60.5 \cdot 3.14 + 220$	Substitute 3.14 for π.
$\approx 190 + 220$	Multiply.
≈ 410	Add.

The area is about 410 units^2.

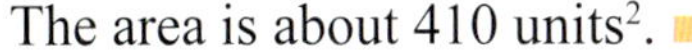

Application: Food

EXAMPLE 4 A small pizza has a diameter of 10 in., a medium pizza has a diameter of 13 in., and a large pizza has a diameter of 16 in.

A Estimate the difference in the areas of a medium and large pizza.

Solution Find the area of each pizza.

medium:	large:
$A = \pi r^2$	$A = \pi r^2$
$= \pi \cdot 6.5^2$	$= \pi \cdot 8^2$
$= \pi \cdot 42.25$	$= \pi \cdot 64$
$\approx 3.14 \cdot 42.25$	$\approx 3.14 \cdot 64$
≈ 133	≈ 201

> **REMEMBER**
> Divide each diameter by 2 to find each radius.

Subtract to find the difference: $201 - 133 = 68$.

The difference is about 68 in^2.

B Angie ate one-fourth of a small pizza. About how many square inches of pizza did she eat?

Solution Find the area of a quarter circle with a radius of 5 in.

$A = \frac{\pi r^2}{4}$	Write the formula.
$= \frac{\pi \cdot 5^2}{4}$	Substitute 5 for r.
$= 6.25\pi$	Simplify.
$\approx 6.25 \cdot 3.14$	Substitute 3.14 for π.
≈ 19.6	Multiply.

Angie ate about 19.6 in^2 of pizza.

C A pizza with a 14 in. diameter costs \$12.95 while a 12 in. pizza costs \$10.95. Which pizza is a better deal?

Solution Find the unit price of each pizza by dividing the cost of the pizza by the area.

14 in. diameter

$$\begin{aligned} A &= \pi r^2 \\ &= \pi \cdot 7^2 \\ &\approx 3.14 \cdot 49 \\ &\approx 154 \end{aligned}$$

$$\text{unit price} \approx \frac{\$12.95}{154 \text{ in}^2} \approx \$0.084 \text{ per square inch}$$

12 in. diameter

$$\begin{aligned} A &= \pi r^2 \\ &= \pi \cdot 6^2 \\ &\approx 3.14 \cdot 36 \\ &\approx 113 \end{aligned}$$

$$\text{unit price} \approx \frac{\$10.95}{113 \text{ in}^2} \approx \$0.097 \text{ per square inch}$$

The 14 in. pizza is the better deal.

Finding Areas by Subtraction

EXAMPLE 5 Find the area of the shaded region.

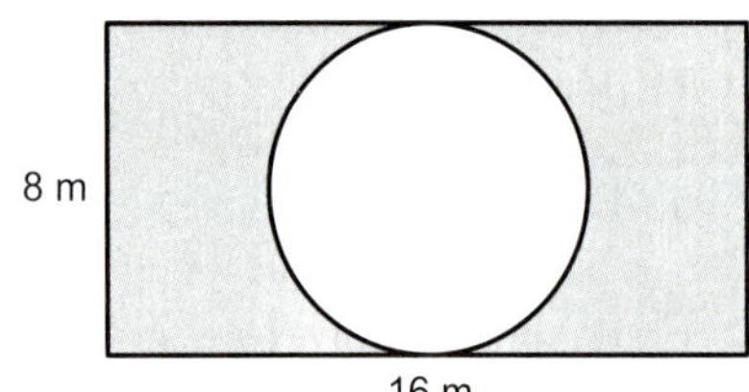

Solution

$A = lw - \pi r^2$	Subtract the area of the circle from the area of the rectangle.
$= 16 \cdot 8 - \pi \cdot 4^2$	Substitute 16 for l, 8 for w, and 4 for r.
$= 128 - 16\pi$	Simplify.
$\approx 128 - 16 \cdot 3.14$	Substitute 3.14 for π.
$\approx 128 - 50.2$	Multiply.
≈ 77.8	Subtract.

The area of the shaded region is about 77.8 ft^2.

Problem Set

The center of the circle is shown. Find the area of the circle. Give both exact and approximate answers.

1.

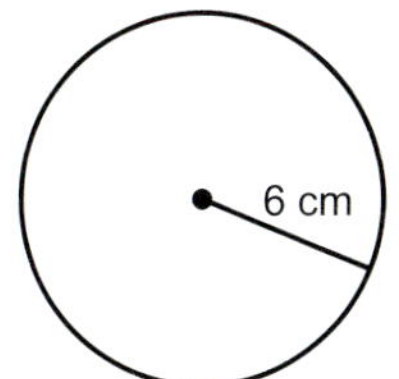

2.

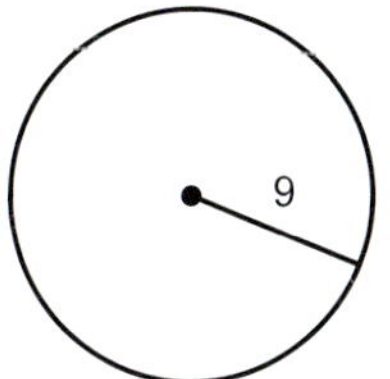

3.

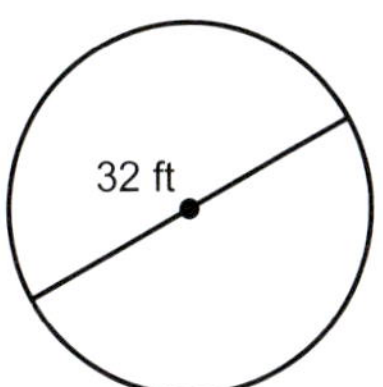

4.

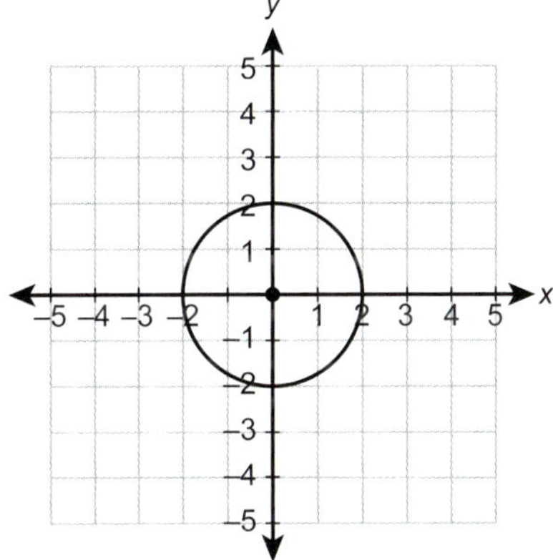

5.

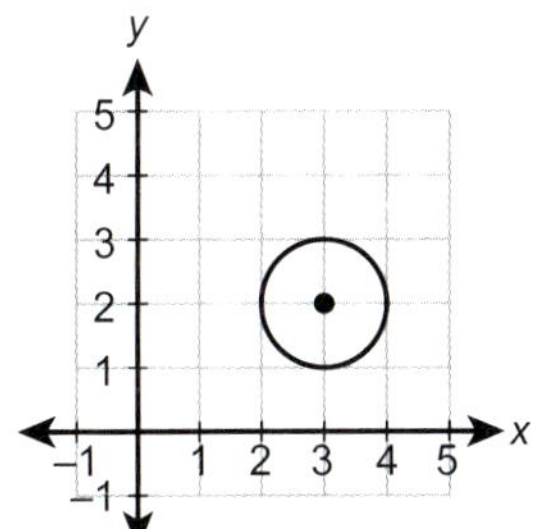

6.

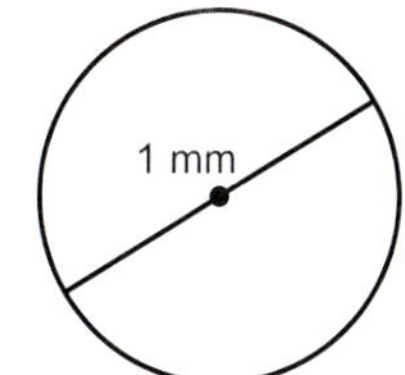

7.

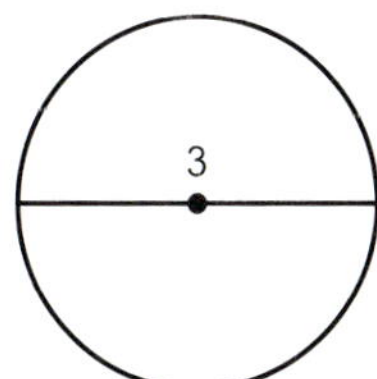

8.

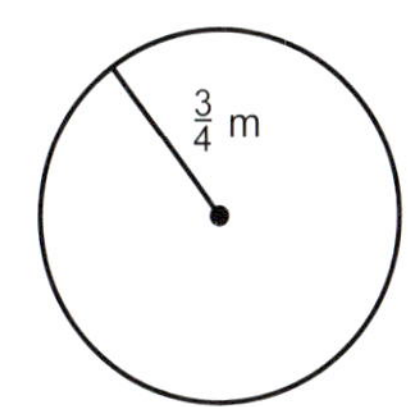

9.

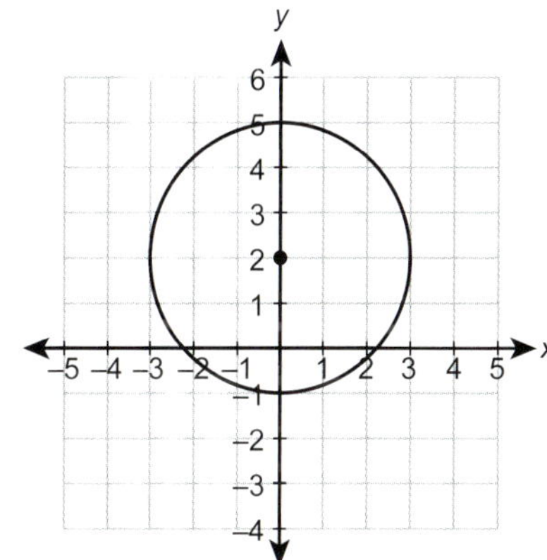

10.

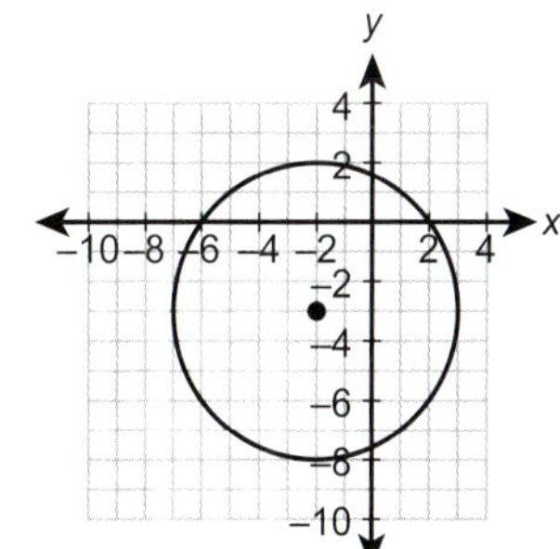

Solve.

11. The area of a circle is 16π m^2. What is the radius of the circle?

12. The area of a circle is 36π ft^2. What is the diameter of the circle?

13. The area of a circle is 12.5 cm^2. What is the diameter of the circle?

14. The area of a circle is 154 mm^2. What is the radius of the circle?

Find the area of the figure.

15. 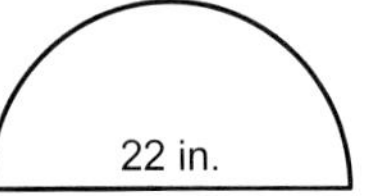

16. 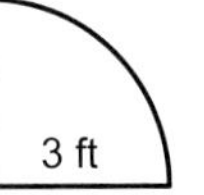

17. 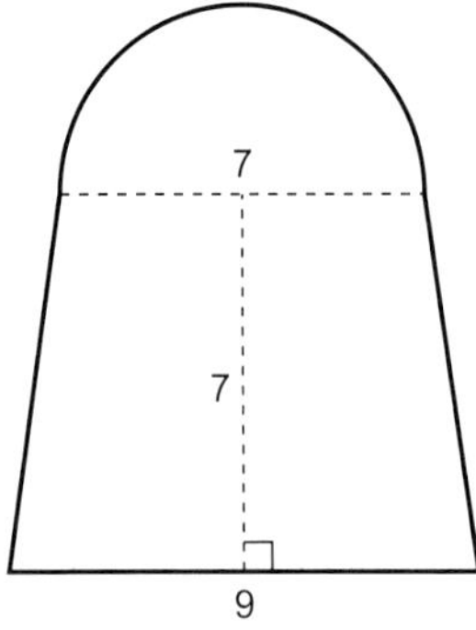

18. 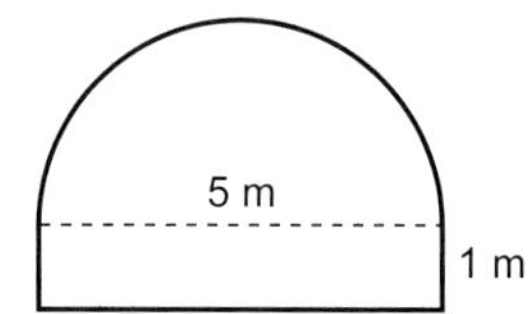

19. 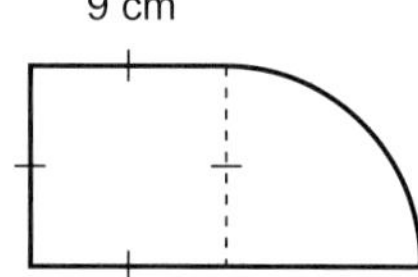

20. 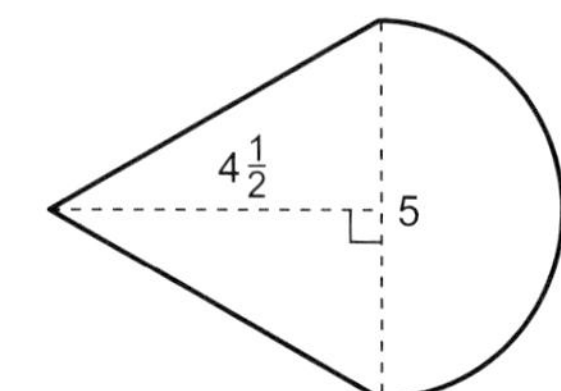

Find the area of the shaded region.

21. 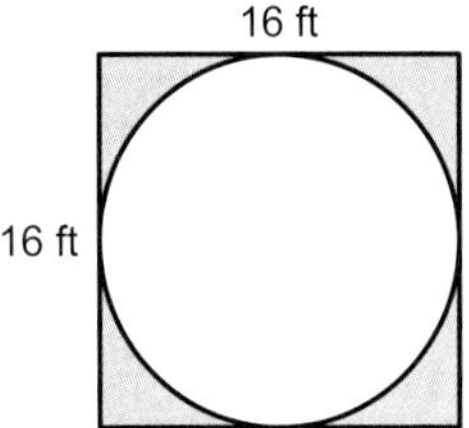

22. 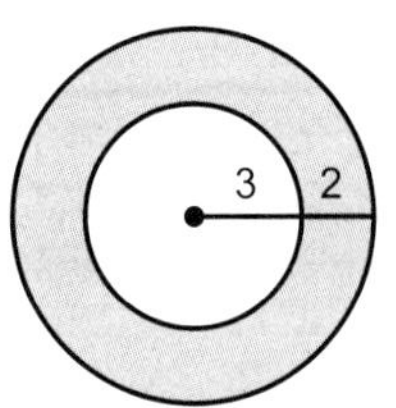

23. 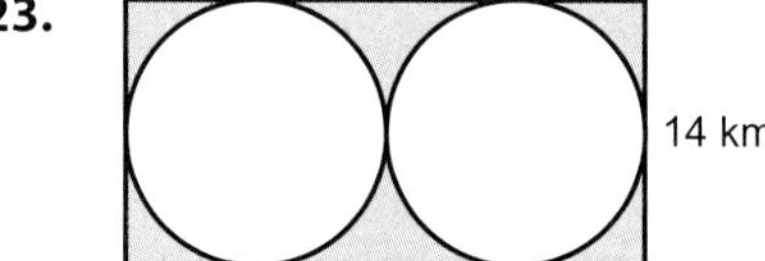

24. 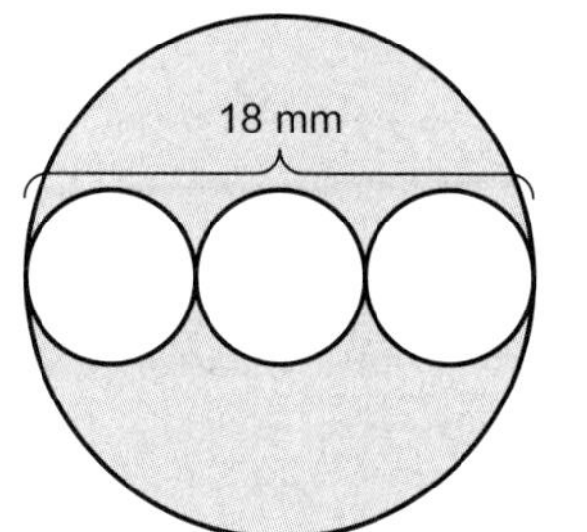

Solve.

25. What is the area of a swimming pool if its diameter is 12 m?

26. A pizza with a 14 in. diameter costs $12.99, while a 12 in. pizza costs $9.99. Which pizza is a better deal?

27. An 18 in. pizza costs $22.99, while a 16 in. pizza costs $18.99. Which pizza is a better deal?

28. The center circle on a soccer field has an area of 100π m². Find the circumference of the center circle.

29. Which area is greater: a circle with a diameter of 10 km or a square with a side length of 10 km?

30. Ms. Brady's old waffle maker made circular waffles with a diameter of 17 cm. Her new waffle maker makes rectangular waffles that are 22 cm long and 13 cm wide. Which makes waffles with a greater area? How much greater?

31. **Challenge** Explain how you would find the area of a figure with this shape.

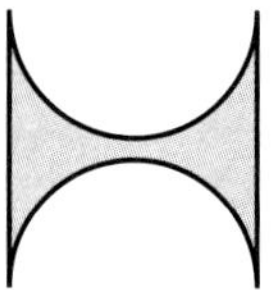

Core Focus: Circumference and Area

THE CORE CONCEPT

If you know the circumference of a circle, you can calculate its area.

Finding Area from Circumference

Given the circumference of a circle, you can find the circle's area by solving the circumference formula for the radius. Substitute the value of the radius into the formula for the area of the circle and simplify.

EXAMPLE 1 Ricki wants to show that the area of a circle with circumference C and radius r is equal to the area of a rectangle with length $\frac{C}{2}$ and width r. How could she show this using a diagram?

Solution Ricki could draw a circle divided into many equal sectors, and then divide the circle into two equal halves.

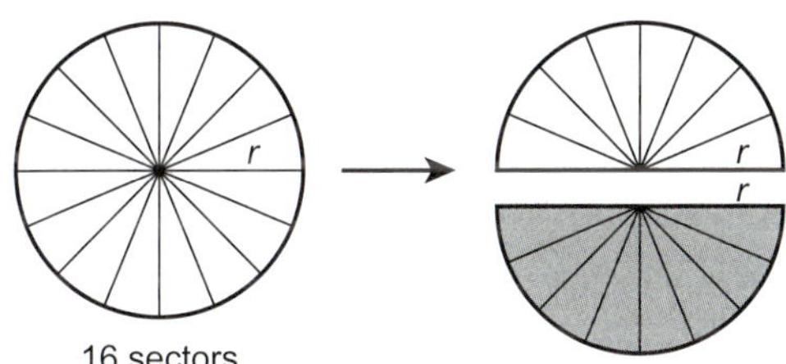

The sectors could be pulled apart and then put back together so that sectors alternate. One sector could be cut in half, and then one of the halves could be moved to form a figure close to the shape of a rectangle.

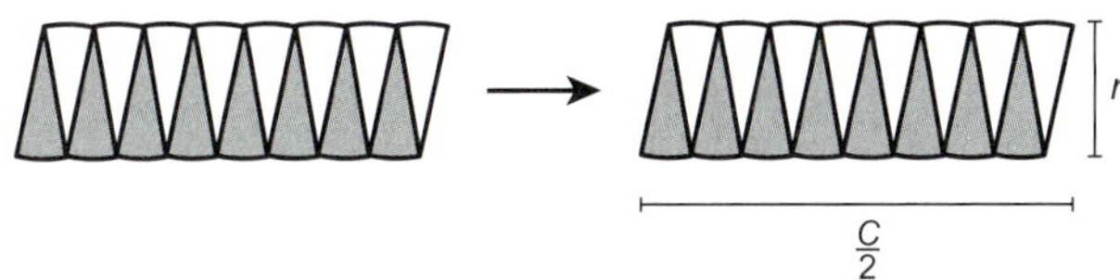

The rectangle has a length of $\frac{C}{2}$ and a width of r, so the area of the rectangle is $A = \frac{C}{2} \cdot r$.

Substituting $C = 2\pi r$ for C into this equation, you get

$A = \frac{2\pi r}{2} \cdot r = \pi r \cdot r = \pi r^2$.

Therefore, the area of a rectangle with length $\frac{C}{2}$ and width r is equal to the area of a circle with radius r. ■

REMEMBER

The formula for the circumference of a circle with radius r is $C = 2\pi r$.
The formula for the area of a circle with radius r is $A = \pi r^2$.

THINK ABOUT IT

If you know the area of a circle, you can find its circumference.

Application: Tiling

EXAMPLE 2 Jaime creates a tiling pattern from 8 blank square tiles, each with a perimeter of 12 cm. He draws circular arcs to define the border of the pattern, then colors in the pattern. What is the area of the colored pattern Jaime created, to the nearest tenth? Explain.

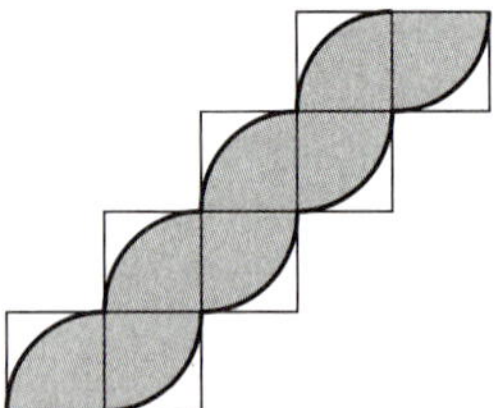

Solution The circular arc in one tile forms a sector that is one-fourth of a circle with radius 2. The area of this sector is one-fourth of the area A of the complete circle.

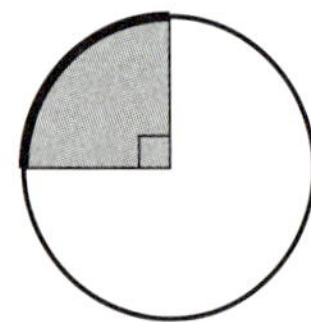

The radius of this complete circle is equal to the side length s of the square. You know the perimeter of the square, so you can find s and then solve for A.

Since $4s = 12$, $s = 3$.

$$A = \pi r^2 = \pi(3)^2 = 9\pi$$

The sector area is one-fourth the area of the circle, or $\frac{A}{4}$, which is equal to $\frac{9\pi}{4}$.

If $\frac{9\pi}{4}$ is the colored-pattern area in one tile and there are 8 tiles in all, then the total colored-pattern area for all 8 tiles is

$$8 \cdot \frac{9\pi}{4} = \frac{8 \cdot 9\pi}{4} = \frac{72\pi}{4} = 18\pi \approx 18 \cdot 3.14 \approx 56.5.$$

The colored-pattern area is about 56.5 cm^2.

TIP

When simplifying expressions containing π, perform all operations before substituting a numeric value such as 3.14 or $\frac{22}{7}$ for π.

Problem Set

Solve. Round your answer to the nearest tenth, if necessary.

1. Reshma draws a circle with a circumference of 26π. How can Reshma prove that the area of the circle is equivalent to the area of a rectangle with length 13π and width 13? Use a diagram to show your reasoning.

2. A rectangle has length of 9π cm and width of 9 cm. What is the radius of the circle whose area is equivalent to the area of the rectangle? Explain.

3. A square and a semicircle were combined to make the figure shown. The perimeter of the square is 48 m. What is the area of the entire figure?

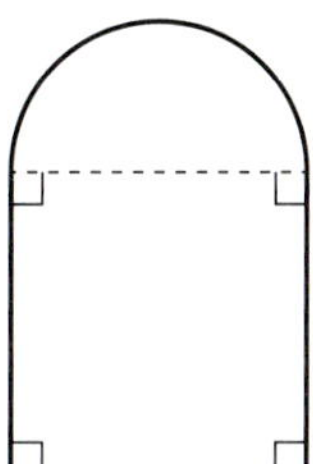

4. Imelda traced a circular arc on a metal square that was 8 mm on each side. She cut along the arc and kept the portion of the square represented by the shaded region. Imelda traced and cut 4 squares in all, then combined the 4 cut pieces to form a metal pendant. What is the area of the metal pendant (the shaded area)?

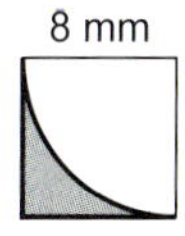

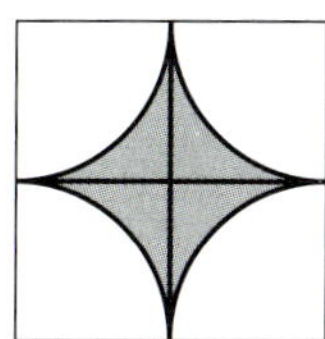

CHAPTER 10 Review

Choose the answer.

1. Which line segments are diameters of circle V?

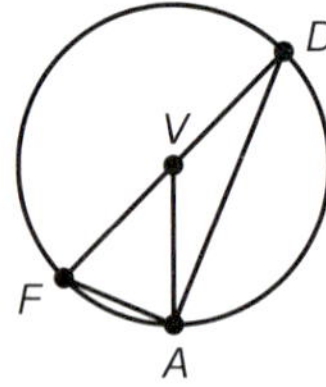

   A. $\overline{AD}$
   B. $\overline{DF}$
   C. $\overline{AV}$ and $\overline{DV}$
   D. $\overline{AD}$, $\overline{AF}$, $\overline{AV}$ and $\overline{DF}$

2. Which statement is true?
   A. All chords of a circle are also radii of the circle.
   B. All chords of a circle are also diameters of the circle.
   C. All diameters of a circle are also chords of the circle.
   D. All radii of a circle are also diameters of the circle.

3. The length of $\overline{DF}$ is 7.6 cm. What is the approximate circumference of the circle?

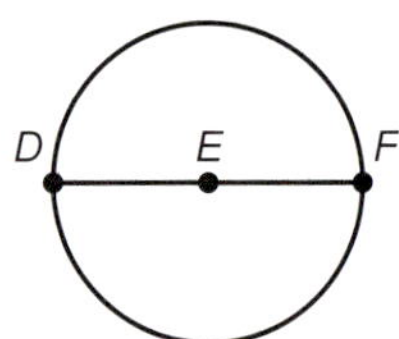

   A. 7.6 cm
   B. 11.9 cm
   C. 15.2 cm
   D. 23.9 cm

4. The circumference of a circle is 14π. What is the radius of the circle?
   A. 7
   B. 14
   C. 7π
   D. 28π

5. Using $\pi \approx \frac{22}{7}$, what is the area of the circle?

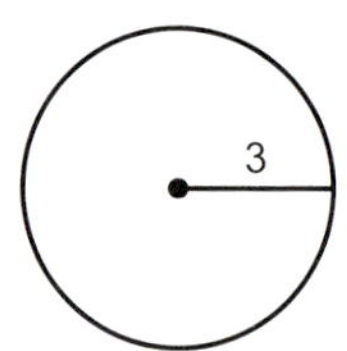

   A. $18\frac{6}{7}$
   B. $28\frac{2}{7}$
   C. $37\frac{5}{7}$
   D. $75\frac{3}{7}$

6. The diameter of a circle is 1.8 m. What is the best approximation of the area of the circle?
   A. 2.54 m^2
   B. 5.65 m^2
   C. 10.2 m^2
   D. 40.7 m^2

7. The circumference of a circle is 10π in. What is the area of the circle?
   A. 20π in^2
   B. 25π in^2
   C. 100π in^2
   D. 400π in^2

Solve.

8. The length of $\overline{WY}$ is 4.6 cm.

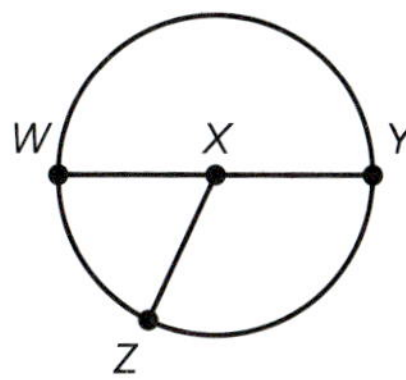

(a) Name all line segments that are radii of the circle.

(b) What is the length of the radius of the circle?

9. Izzy has a strip of paper that is 12 in. long by 1.5 in. wide. She wants to cut circles out of the paper.

(a) What is the diameter of the largest circle Izzy can cut out of the paper strip?

(b) How many of these circles can Izzy cut out of the strip?

10. A bicycle tire travels 6.59 m along the ground in three revolutions. Find the radius of the bicycle tire. Round your answer to the nearest hundredth.

11. What is the perimeter of the figure?

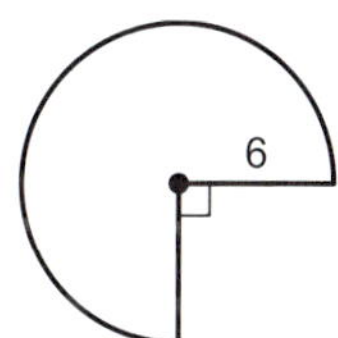

12. A cell phone tower can receive calls from within a 62 km radius. What is the area covered by the tower? Round your answer to the nearest tenth.

13. Two semicircles are removed from the rectangle to form the shaded region. Find this shaded region's area.

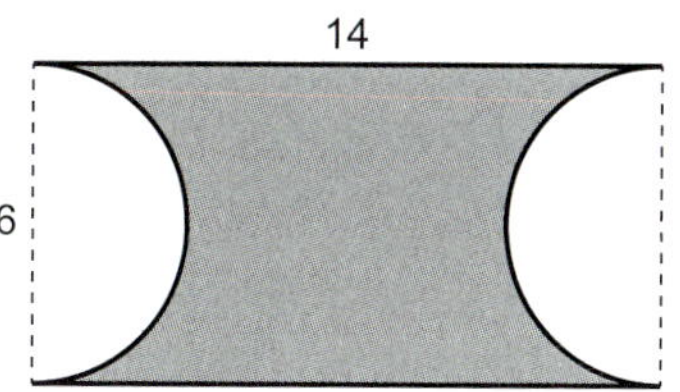

14. The shaded region is made up of four semicircles with equal diameters.

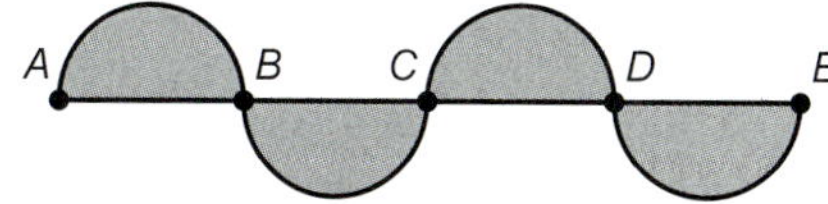

$AB = BC = CD = DE$

$AE = 25$

What is the area of the shaded region? Use $\pi \approx \frac{22}{7}$.

15. The semicircular shape has a perimeter of $10\pi + 10$.

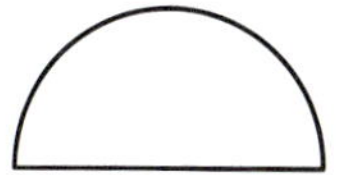

(a) What is the radius of the semicircle? Explain your reasoning with a diagram.

(b) What is the area of the semicircle?

Problem	Topic Lookup	Problem	Topic Lookup
1, 2, 8, 9	Circles	5, 6, 12, 13	Areas of Circles
3, 4, 10, 11	Circumference	7, 14, 15	Core Focus: Circumference and Area

CHAPTER 11 Solid Figures

Many shipping containers are shaped like boxes (rectangular prisms) with consistent volume and surface area. People who have to fill, move, or even paint these containers need to understand volume and surface area.

In This Chapter

In this chapter, you'll start with finding volumes of prisms, and then you'll learn about cross sections of solid figures. Next you'll learn about surface area and use properties of volume and surface area to solve problems.

Topic List

- Foundations for Chapter 11
- Volume
- Volumes of Prisms
- Slicing Solids
- Surface Area
- Surface Areas of Prisms
- Properties of Volume and Surface Area
- Core Focus: Applications of Volume and Surface Area
- Chapter 11 Review

Shipping containers help transport goods all around the world. ▶

Foundations for Chapter 11

Converting Area Units

To convert area expressed in one unit to a different unit, write an equation expressing the area in the new units as the product of the area in the original units and a conversion factor. Choose the conversion factor so that the original units divide out.

EXAMPLE A Convert the area to the units indicated.

A-1 A wall has an area of 16 yd^2. What is the area in square feet?

Solution Write the area as the product of 16 yd^2 and a conversion factor.

$$16 \text{ yd}^2 \bullet (\text{conversion factor})$$

Because 1 $yd^2 = 9$ ft^2, the conversion factor is

$$\frac{9 \text{ ft}^2}{1 \text{ yd}^2}.$$

Multiply the area in the original units by the conversion factor and simplify.

$$16 \cancel{\text{yd}^2} \bullet \frac{9 \text{ ft}^2}{1 \cancel{\text{yd}^2}} = \frac{144}{1} \text{ ft}^2$$
$$= 144 \text{ ft}^2$$

The wall has an area of 144 ft^2. ■

A-2 A box top has an area of 1200 cm^2. What is the area in square meters?

Solution Write the area in units of square meters as the product of 1200 cm^2 and a conversion factor.

$$1200 \text{ cm}^2 \bullet (\text{conversion factor})$$

Because 1 $m^2 = 10{,}000$ cm^2, the conversion factor is

$$\frac{1 \text{ m}^2}{10{,}000 \text{ cm}^2}.$$

Multiply the area in the original units by the conversion factor and simplify.

$$1200 \cancel{\text{cm}^2} \bullet \frac{1 \text{ m}^2}{10{,}000 \cancel{\text{cm}^2}} = \frac{1200}{10{,}000} \text{ m}^2$$
$$= 0.12 \text{ m}^2$$

The box top has an area of 0.12 m^2. ■

Problem Set A

Convert the area to the units indicated.

1. 3 ft^2 to square inches
2. 7.1 m^2 to square centimeters
3. 4685 m^2 to square kilometers
4. 26.5 yd^2 to square feet
5. 320.7 ft^2 to square yards
6. 0.89 km^2 to square meters
7. 0.042 m^2 to square millimeters
8. 4 yd^2 to square inches

Converting Units for Capacity or Volume

To convert volume or capacity expressed in one unit to a different unit, write the new unit as the product of the original unit and one or more conversion factors. Choose the conversion factor so that the original units divide out.

EXAMPLE B Convert the volume or capacity to the units indicated.

B-1 A bottle contains 354 mL of juice. What is the volume of the juice in liters?

Solution Write the volume in liters as the product of 354 mL and a conversion factor.

$$354 \text{ mL} \bullet (\text{conversion factor})$$

Because 1 L = 1000 mL, the conversion factor is

$$\frac{1\text{L}}{1000 \text{ mL}}.$$

Multiply 354 mL by the conversion factor and simplify.

$$\begin{aligned} 354 \cancel{\text{mL}} \bullet \frac{1 \text{ L}}{1000 \cancel{\text{mL}}} &= \frac{354}{1000} \text{ L} \\ &= 0.354 \text{ L} \end{aligned}$$

The bottle has 0.354 L of juice. ■

B-2 A gas can holds 5 gal of gas. What is the capacity of the gas can in pints?

Solution Write the capacity in gallons as the product of 5 gal and a conversion factor.

$$5 \text{ gal} \bullet (\text{conversion factor})$$

Because 1 gal = 4 qt and 1 qt = 4 pt, the conversion factors are

$$\frac{4 \text{ qt}}{1 \text{ gal}} \text{ and } \frac{4 \text{ pt}}{1 \text{ qt}}.$$

Multiply 5 gal by the conversion factors and simplify.

$$\begin{aligned} 5 \cancel{\text{gal}} \bullet \frac{4 \cancel{\text{qt}}}{1 \cancel{\text{gal}}} \bullet \frac{4 \text{ pt}}{1 \cancel{\text{qt}}} &= \frac{80}{1} \text{ pt} \\ &= 80 \text{ pt} \end{aligned}$$

The gas can holds 80 pt of gasoline. ■

Problem Set B

Convert the volume or capacity to the units indicated.

1. 8 qt to gallons
2. 5.1 L to milliliters
3. 470 cm^3 to cubic meters
4. 3 yd^3 to cubic inches
5. 64 oz to pints
6. 68 pt to gallons
7. 65.4 m^3 to cubic centimeters
8. 17 gal to ounces

Counting Cubes to Determine Volume

Find the volume of a solid made up of equal-sized cubes by first counting the number of cubes and then multiplying the number of cubes by the volume of each cube. Split the solid into smaller pieces, if needed, to count the number of cubes more easily.

EXAMPLE C Find the volume of the solid. Each cube is $\frac{2}{3}$ cm^3.

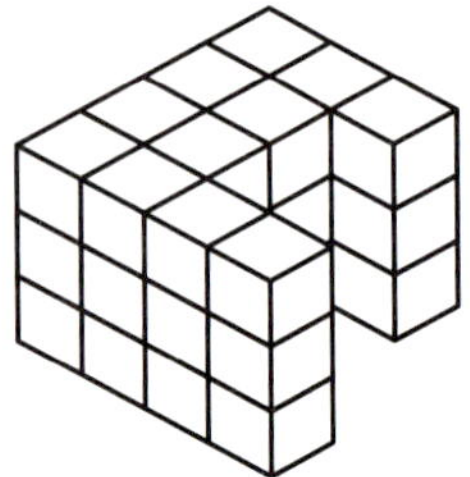

Solution Split the solid into three pieces that can be easily counted.

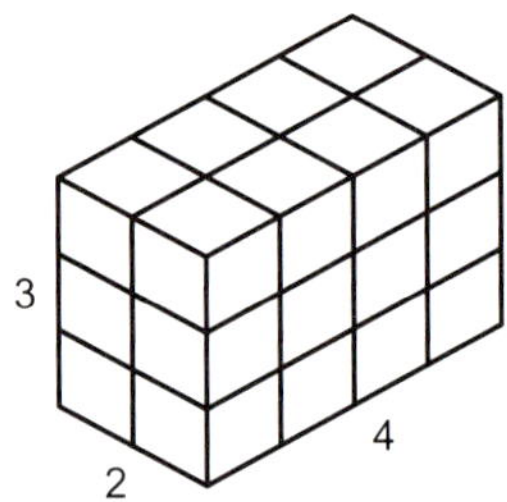

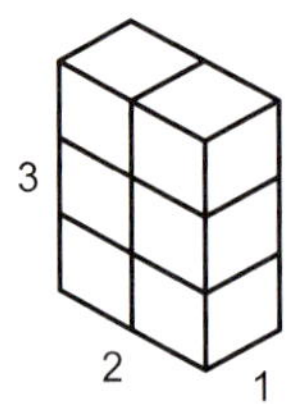

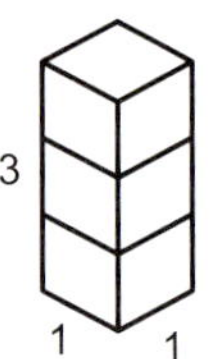

The left piece has $3 \cdot 2 \cdot 4 = 24$ cubes. The center piece has $3 \cdot 2 \cdot 1 = 6$ cubes. The right piece has $3 \cdot 1 \cdot 1 = 3$ cubes. There are $24 + 6 + 3 = 33$ cubes in all.

Multiply the number of cubes by the volume of each cube.

$$33 \cdot \frac{2}{3}\text{ cm}^3 = \frac{33 \cdot 2}{3}\text{ cm}^3 = \frac{66}{3}\text{ cm}^3 = 22\text{ cm}^3$$

The volume of the solid is 22 cm^3. ■

Problem Set C

Find the volume of the solid.

1.

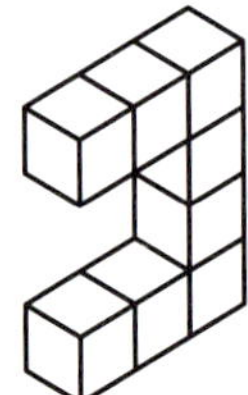

Each cube is 1 cm^3.

2.

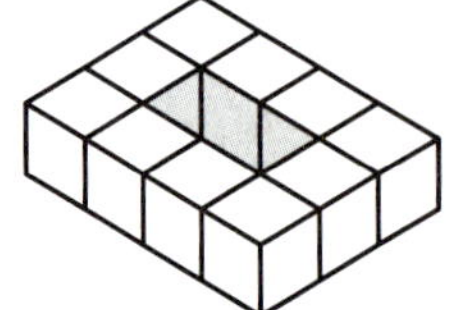

Each cube is 8 mm^3.

3.

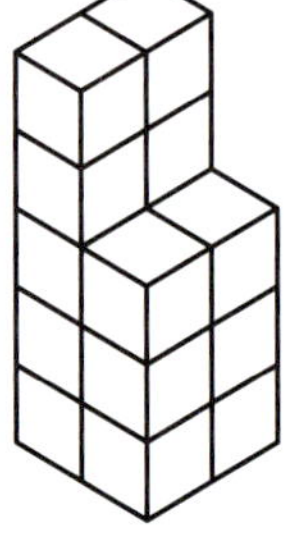

Each cube is 0.5 ft^3.

Volume

Volume is a way to measure a three-dimensional object.

A **cube** is a solid figure made up of 6 square faces that meet each other at right angles. A cube has 8 vertices and 12 edges. The length, width, and height of a cube are equal.

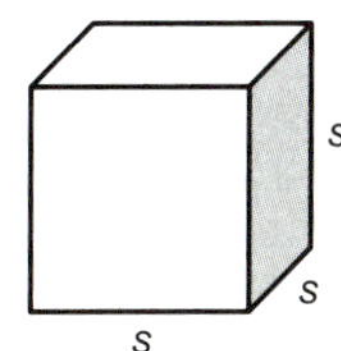

Counting to Find the Volume of a Cube

The **volume** of a three-dimensional figure is a measure of the space inside the figure. You find volume by determining the number of cubes needed to fill a figure. Volume is measured in **cubic units**.

EXAMPLE 1 Find the volume of the cube.

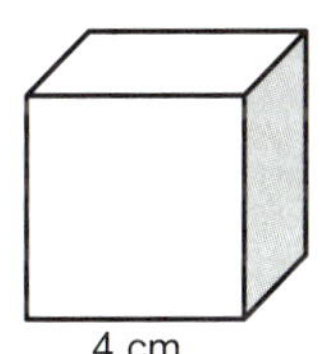

Solution Fill the cube with centimeter cubes.

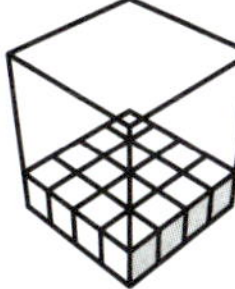

Place 4 rows of 4 cubes on the bottom.

$4 \times 4 = 16$

The first layer holds 16 centimeter cubes.

Make 4 layers of 16 cubes.

$4 \times 16 = 64$

The figure holds 64 centimeter cubes.

The volume of the cube is 64 cubic centimeters, or 64 cm^3. ■

Using a Formula to Find the Volume of a Cube

You can use a formula to find the volume of a cube.

VOLUME OF A CUBE FORMULA

The formula for the volume of a cube with side s is

$$V = s \cdot s \cdot s = s^3.$$

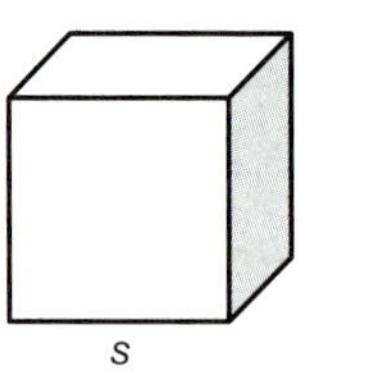

EXAMPLE 2 Find the volume of the cube.

A

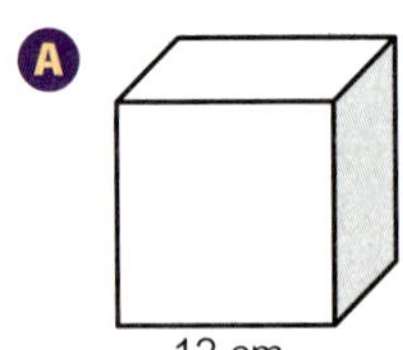

Solution

$V = s^3$	Write the volume formula.
$= 12^3$	Substitute 12 for s.
$= 1728$	Evaluate the power.

The volume is 1728 cm^3. ■

B

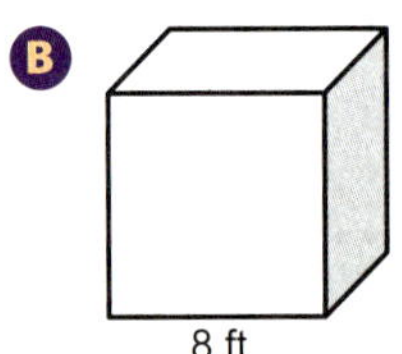

Solution

$V = s^3$	Write the volume formula.
$= 8^3$	Substitute 8 for s.
$= 512$	Evaluate the power.

The volume is 512 ft^3. ■

TIP

When calculating volume, it is easier to calculate without the units, then add them in the final answer. But you can certainly include the units in your calculations. However you do it, be careful with your units.

Problem Set

Find the volume of the cube with the given side length.

1. $s = 4$ in.
2. $s = 8$ m
3. $s = 11$ ft
4. $s = 3.2$ cm

Find the volume of the cube.

5.

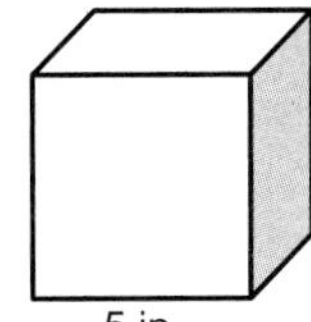

5 in.

6.

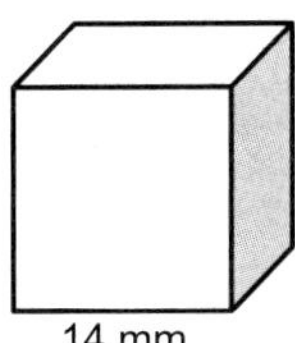

14 mm

7.

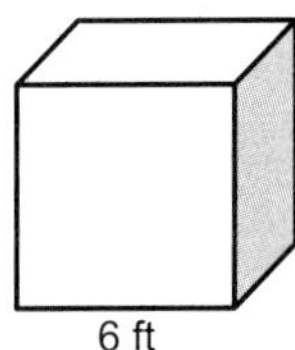

6 ft

8.

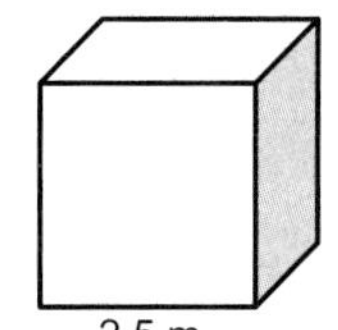

2.5 m

9.

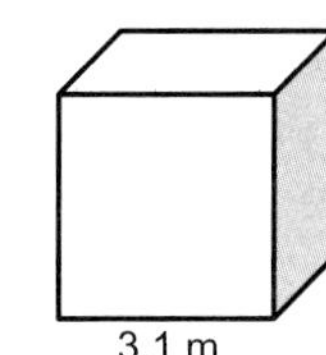

3.1 m

10.

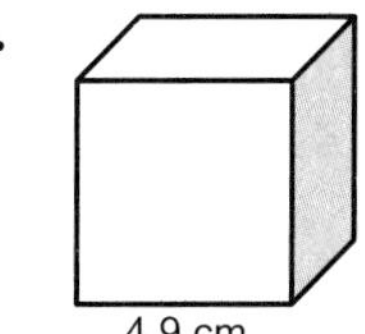

4.9 cm

Solve.

11. A gift box has the shape of a cube. The box is 75 cm tall. What is the volume of the box?

12. Molly is filling a serving dish with sugar cubes. Each sugar cube measures 1 cm on each side. The serving dish has the shape of a cube and measures 4 cm on each side. What is the greatest number of sugar cubes Molly can fit in the serving dish?

13. **Challenge** Each side of a cube is 2 ft long. What is the volume of the cube in cubic inches?

14. **Challenge** The volume of a cube is 27 cm^3. What is the length of each side of the cube?

Volumes of Prisms

Many real-world containers have the shape of a prism. Calculating the capacity tells you how much the container can hold.

Identifying Parts of Prisms

A **prism** is a solid figure with parallel congruent **bases** that are both polygons. The **lateral faces** are all parallelograms. The name of a prism comes from the shape of its bases.

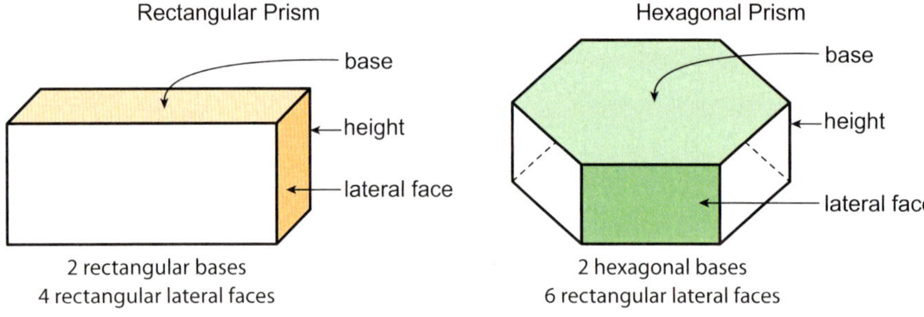

EXAMPLE 1 Name the prism. Give the shape of its bases and the number of lateral faces.

A

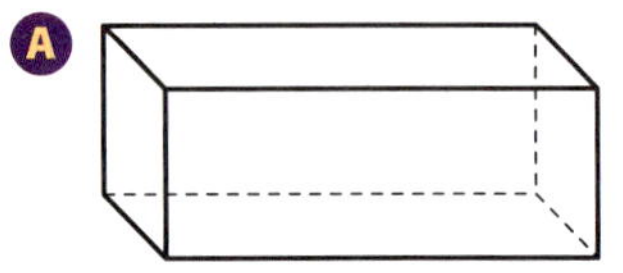

Solution The bases are rectangles. There are 4 lateral faces. The figure is a rectangular prism. ■

B

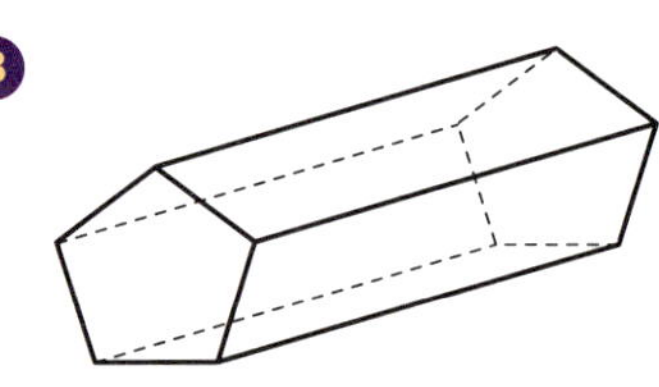

Solution The bases are pentagons. There are 5 lateral faces. The figure is a pentagonal prism. ■

C

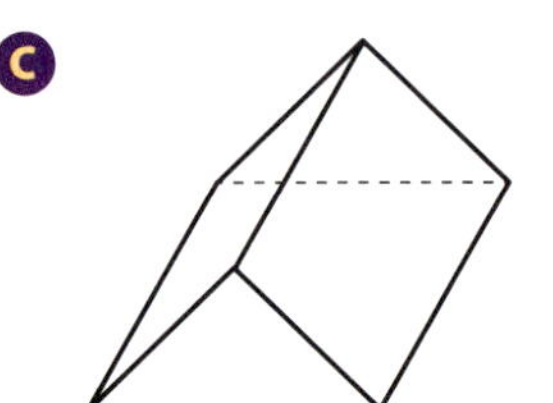

Solution The bases are triangles. There are 3 lateral faces. The figure is a triangular prism. ■

TIP

Think of the bases of a prism as its floor and ceiling. Think of the lateral faces as walls. But watch out! A prism does not always sit on one of its bases. Sometimes it sits on a lateral face, as in Examples 1B and 1C.

Computing the Volume of a Prism

VOLUME OF A PRISM FORMULA

The formula for the volume of a prism with base area B and height h is

$$V = Bh.$$

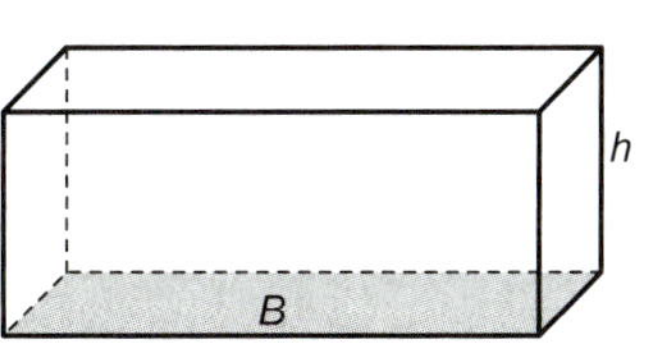

EXAMPLE 2 Find the volume of the prism.

A

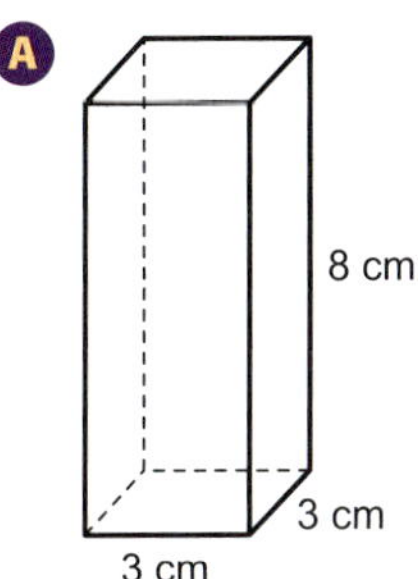

Solution The figure is a square prism.

Step 1 Find B.

$B = s^2$ Write the area of a square formula.

$= 3^2$ Substitute the side length of the square.

$= 9$ Simplify.

The area B of the base of the square prism is 9 cm^2.

Step 2 Find V. The area of the base is 9 cm^2. Use the value for B in the formula.

$V = Bh$ Write the volume formula.

$= 9 \bullet 8$ Substitute the base area for B and the prism height for h.

$= 72$ Multiply.

The volume of the square prism is 72 cm^3.

THINK ABOUT IT

For a rectangular prism, $B = lw$, so $V = Bh = lwh$. Another way to find the volume is to use the formula $V = lwh$.

$V = lwh$
$= 3 \times 3 \times 8$
$= 72$

B

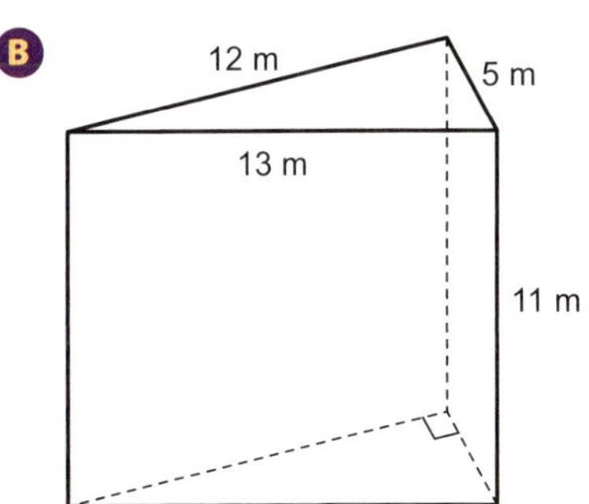

Solution The figure is a triangular prism. Use the formula $A = \frac{1}{2}bh$ to find the area of base B.

TIP

Do a separate calculation to find B, using the appropriate area formula.

Step 1 Find B.

$B = \frac{1}{2}bh$ Write the area of a triangle formula.

$= \frac{1}{2} \cdot 5 \cdot 12$ Substitute the base and height of the triangle.

$= 30$ Multiply.

The area B of the base of the triangular prism is 30 m^2.

Step 2 Find V. Use the value for B in the formula $V = Bh$.

$V = Bh$ Write the volume formula.

$= 30 \cdot 11$ Substitute the base area for B and the prism height for h.

$= 330$ Multiply.

The volume of the triangular prism is 330 m^3.

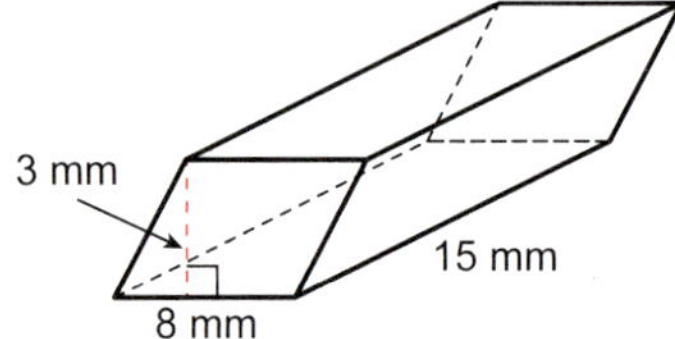

Solution The figure is a prism with parallelograms as bases. Use the formula $A = bh$ to find the area of base B.

Step 1 Find B.

$B = bh$ Write the area of a parallelogram formula.

$= 8 \cdot 3$ Substitute the base and height of the parallelogram.

$= 24$ Multiply.

The area B of the base of the prism is 24 mm^2.

Step 2 Find V. Use the value for B in the formula $V = Bh$.

$V = Bh$ Write the volume formula.

$= 24 \cdot 15$ Substitute the base area for B and the prism height for h.

$= 360$ Multiply.

The volume of the prism is 360 mm^3.

Problem Set

Find the volume of the prism.

1. $B = 12\text{ in}^2$
   $h = 3\text{ in.}$

2. $B = 4\text{ mm}^2$
   $h = 3\text{ mm}$

3. $B = 200\text{ ft}^2$
   $h = 60\text{ ft}$

4. $B = 3.5\text{ cm}^2$
   $h = 2.5\text{ cm}$

5. $l = 6\text{ in.}$
   $w = 5\text{ in.}$
   $h = 11\text{ in.}$

6. $l = 0.5\text{ m}$
   $w = 0.4\text{ m}$
   $h = 8.2\text{ m}$

7.
10 in.
6 in.
6 in.

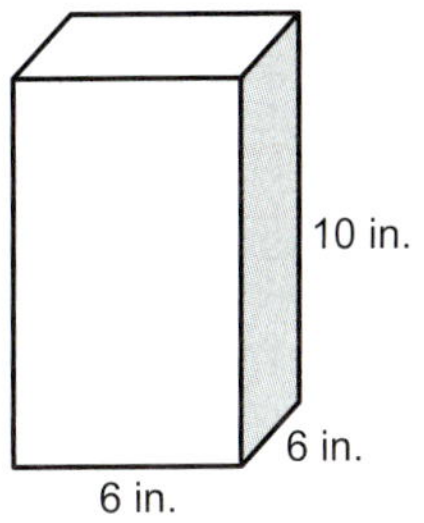

8.
7 cm
6 cm
15 cm

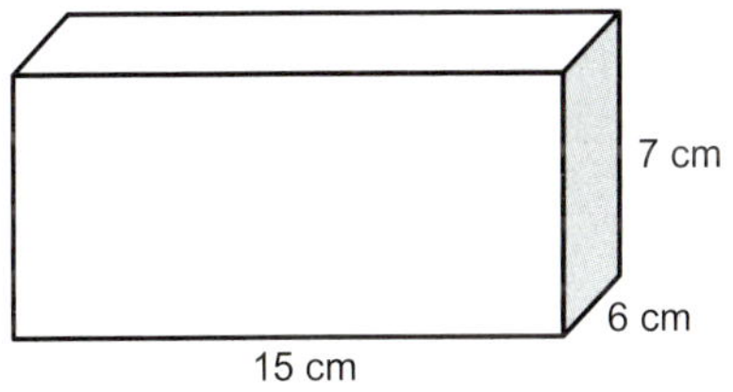

9.

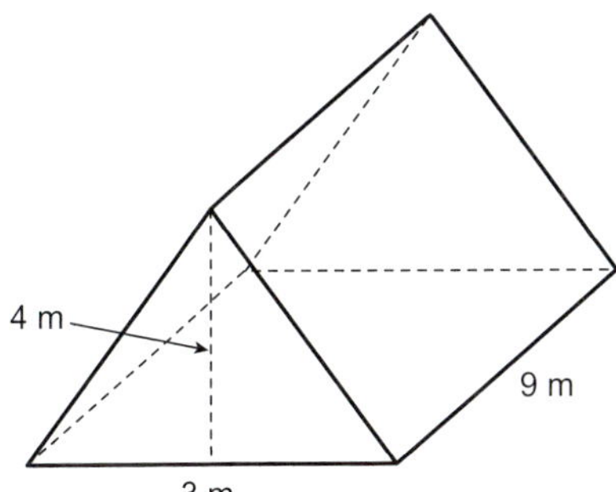

10.
8 in.
6 in.
10 in.

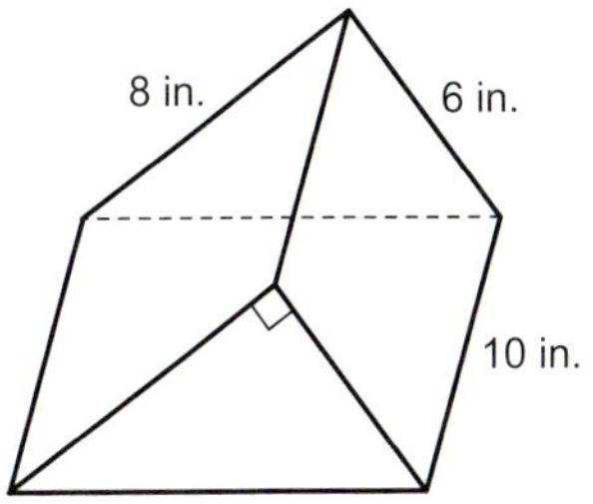

11.
10 m
8 m
2 m
4 m

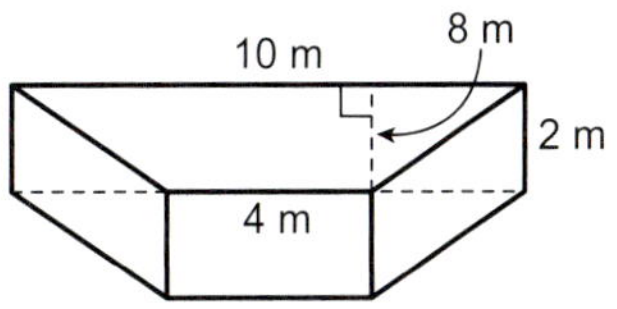

12.
24 ft
7 ft
18 ft
25 ft

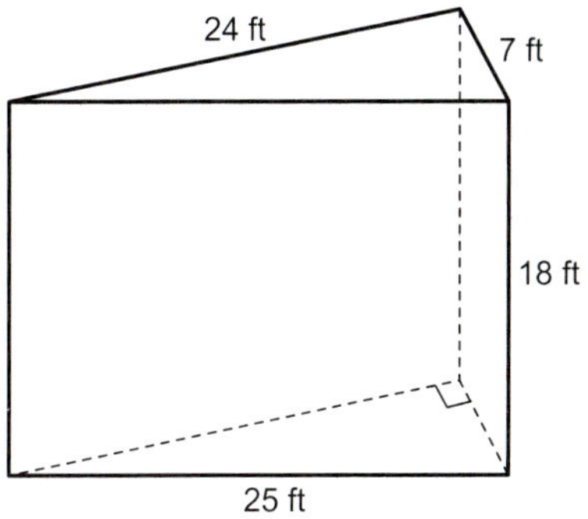

13.
11 cm
2 cm
7 cm

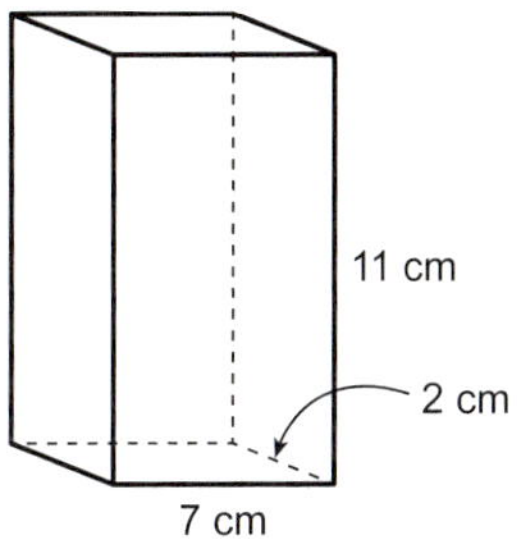

14.
10 in.
12 in.
4 in.

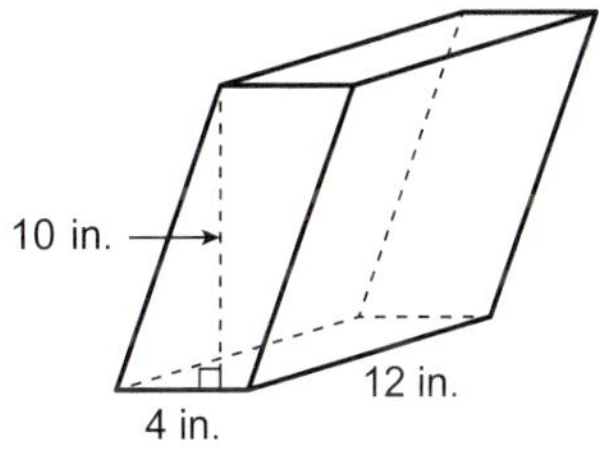

15. **Challenge**
18 cm
8 cm

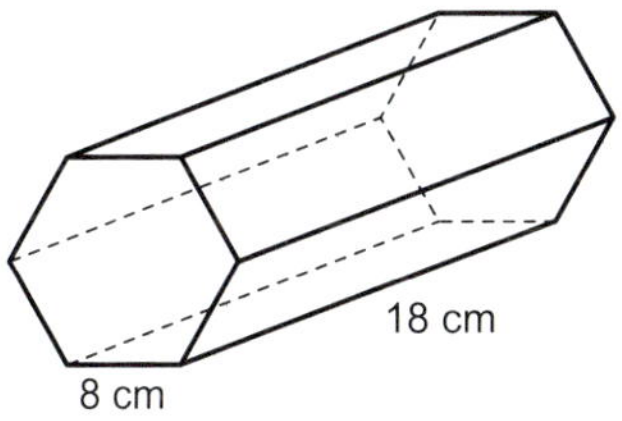

Hint: The area of a regular hexagon with side s is $\frac{3\sqrt{3}}{2}s^2$.

16.
8 cm
8 cm
4 cm
4 cm
18 cm

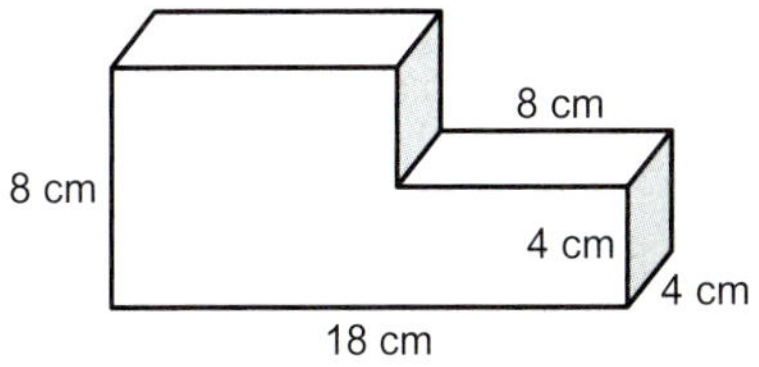

Slicing Solids

The intersection of a plane and a solid often creates a recognizable two-dimensional shape.

Finding Cross Sections

DEFINITION

A **cross section** is a plane figure that results from the intersection of a plane and a solid.

The shape of a cross section depends on the shape of the solid and the angle of the slice.

EXAMPLE 1 Find the cross section of the right rectangular prism and a plane parallel to its base.

Solution The plane slices through the right rectangular prism horizontally, creating a rectangle parallel to the base. This rectangle is congruent to the base of the prism.

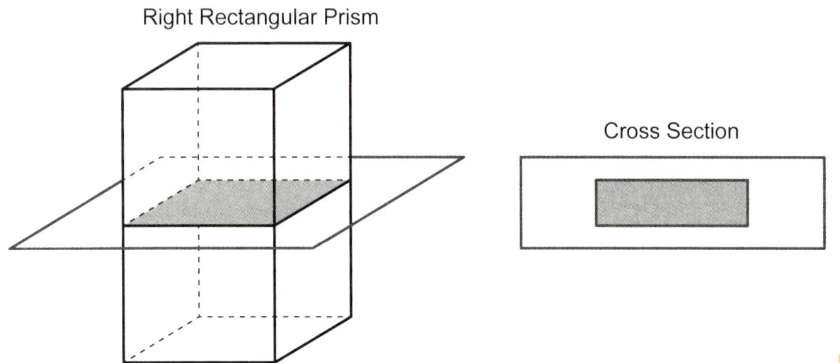

REMEMBER

The base of a right rectangular prism is a rectangle.

EXAMPLE 2 Find the cross section of the right rectangular pyramid and a plane perpendicular to its base. The plane passes through the pyramid's vertex.

Solution The plane slices through the right rectangular pyramid vertically, creating a triangle perpendicular to the base of the pyramid. The triangle is isosceles, with height equal to the height of the pyramid.

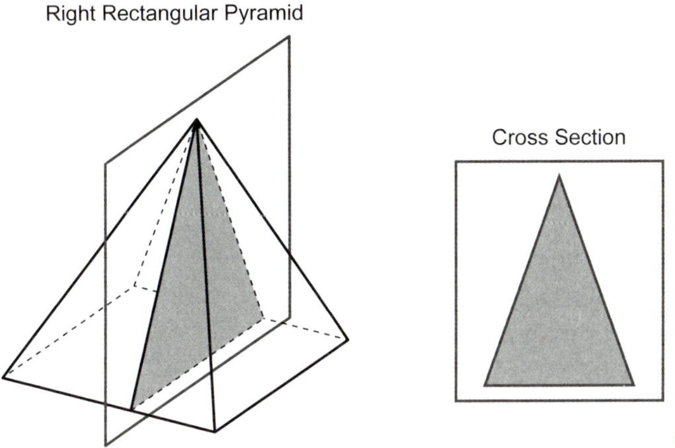

EXAMPLE 3 Find the cross section of the cone and a plane parallel to its base.

Solution The plane slices through the cone horizontally, creating a circle parallel to the base of the cone. The closer the plane is to the base, the larger the diameter of the circular cross section.

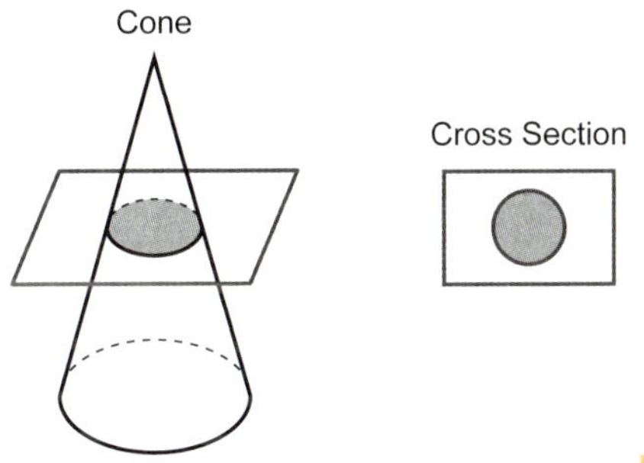

EXAMPLE 4 Find the cross section of the right cylinder and the plane. The plane is neither parallel nor perpendicular to the cylinder's base.

Solution If the plane slicing the cylinder were parallel to the base, the cross section would be a circle. However, the plane slicing the cylinder is not parallel to the base and does not intersect either base. So the cross section is in the shape of an ellipse.

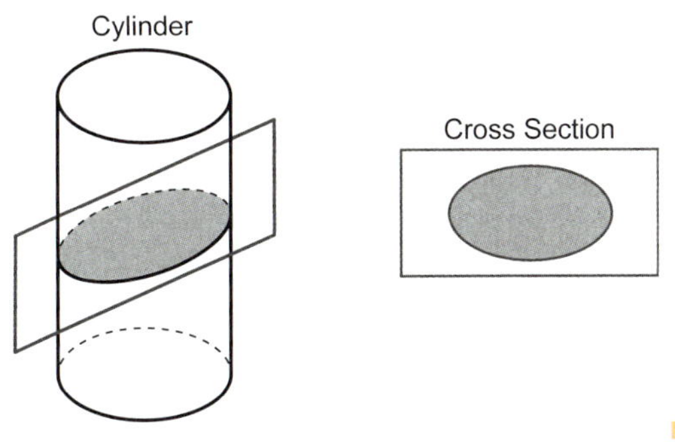

REMEMBER

An **ellipse** looks like a circle that is stretched, or **elongated**, either vertically or horizontally.

Problem Set

Identify the resulting two-dimensional cross section.

1. A slice is made perpendicular to the base of a right rectangular pyramid but doesn't pass through the vertex.

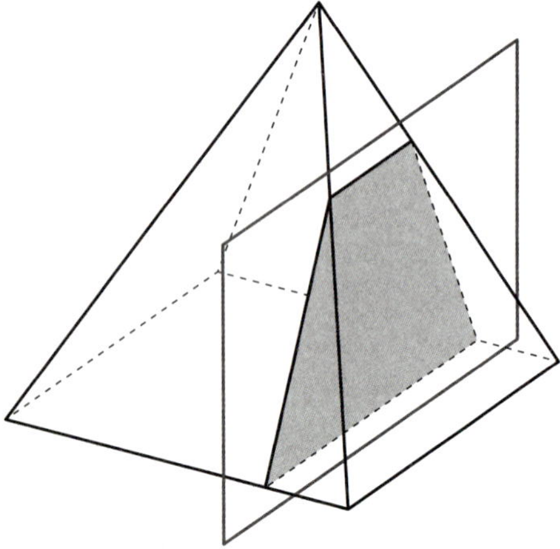

2. A slice is made perpendicular to the base of a cube and passes through the two pairs of vertices opposite each other.

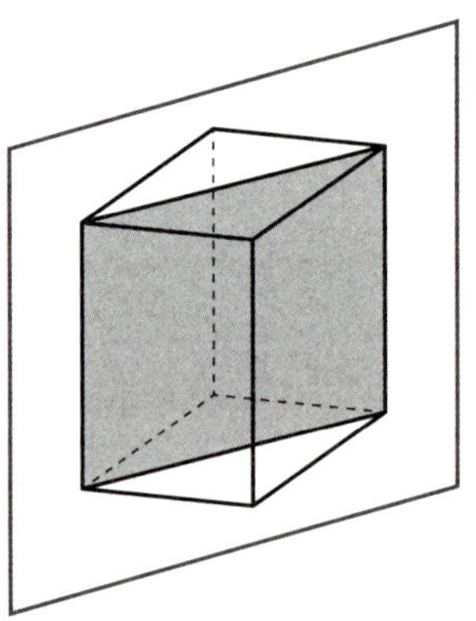

3. A slice is made through a cone but tilted at an angle relative to the base.

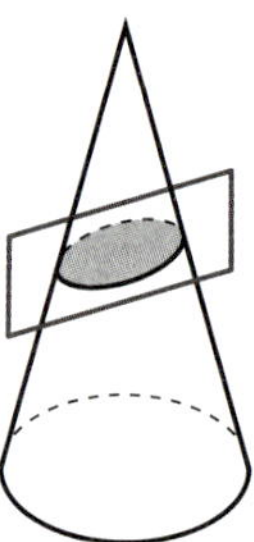

4. A slice is made through the center of a sphere.
5. A slice is made parallel to the base of a right rectangular pyramid.
6. A slice is made parallel to the two bases of a cylinder.
7. A slice is made perpendicular to the base of a cone passing through the vertex of the cone.
8. A slice is made parallel to the base of a triangular pyramid whose base is an equilateral triangle.

Surface Area

The surface area of a figure is the sum of the areas of each of its faces (including bases).

Finding the Surface Area of a Cube

A cube has 6 congruent square faces. If each square face has side length s, then the area of each one is s^2. The surface area of a cube with side length s is $6 \cdot s^2$.

SURFACE AREA OF A CUBE FORMULA

The formula for the surface area of a cube with side s is

$$SA = 6s^2.$$

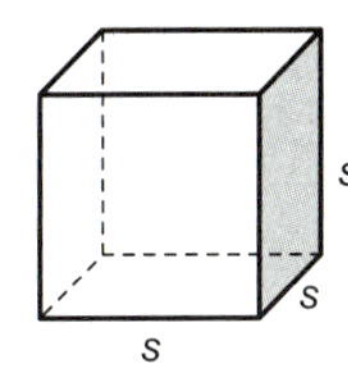

EXAMPLE 1 Find the surface area of the cube.

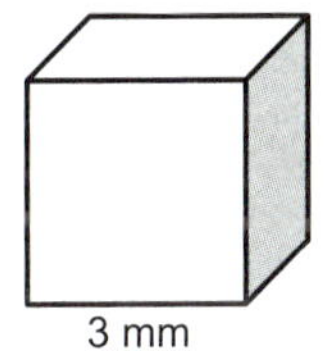

Solution The length s of each side is 3 mm.

$SA = 6s^2$	Write the surface area formula.
$= 6 \cdot 3^2$	Substitute for s.
$= 6 \cdot 9$	Evaluate the power.
$= 54$	Multiply.

The surface area of the cube is 54 mm^2. ■

REMEMBER

Area is measured in square units.

Finding the Lateral Area of a Prism

The **lateral area** of a figure is the sum of the areas of its lateral faces only. One way to find the lateral area is to find the area of each lateral face, and then add. Or you can use a formula.

LATERAL AREA OF A PRISM FORMULA

The formula for the lateral area of a prism with perimeter P and height h is

$$LA = ph.$$

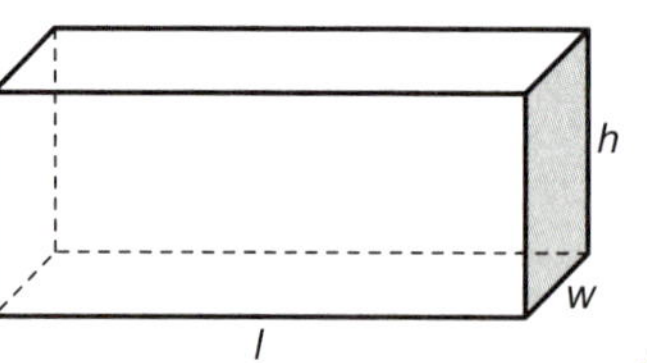

EXAMPLE 2

A Find the lateral area of the rectangular prism by adding the areas of its lateral faces. Assume the figure is resting on its base.

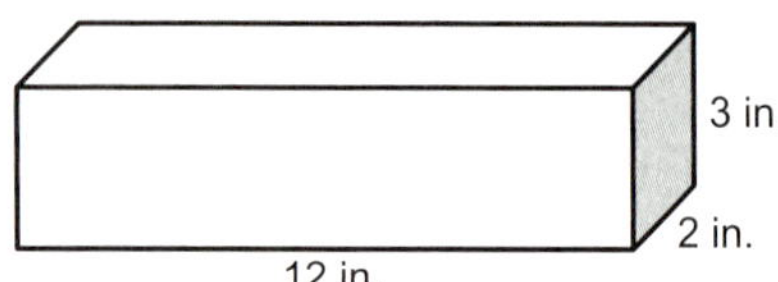

> **TIP**
> With a rectangular prism, any of the faces could be the base.

Solution The 4 lateral faces are the front, right side, back, and left sides of the prism.

area of front: $12 \times 3 = 36$ area of back: $12 \times 3 = 36$

area of right side: $2 \times 3 = 6$ area of left side: $2 \times 3 = 6$

lateral area $= 36 \text{ in}^2 + 36 \text{ in}^2 + 6 \text{ in}^2 + 6 \text{ in}^2 = 84 \text{ in}^2$ ■

B Find the lateral area of the rectangular prism using the formula. Assume the figure is resting on its base.

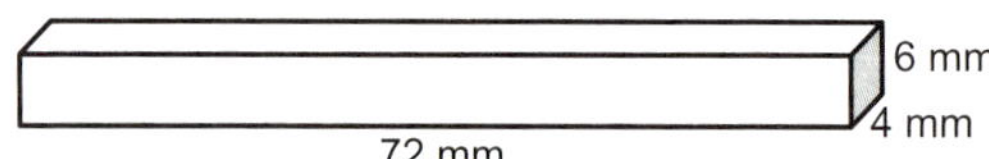

Solution Find the perimeter P of the base.

$P = 2l + 2w$	Write the perimeter of a rectangle formula.
$= 2 \cdot 72 + 2 \cdot 4$	Substitute 72 for l and 4 for w.
$= 144 + 8$	Multiply.
$= 152$	Add.

> **REMEMBER**
> The perimeter of a rectangle with length l and width w is
> $2l + 2w$.

Substitute P and h in the formula for lateral area.

$LA = Ph$	Write the lateral area formula.
$= 152 \cdot 6$	Substitute for P and h.
$= 912$	Multiply.

The lateral area of the figure is 912 mm^2. ■

One way to find the **surface area of a rectangular prism** is to find the lateral area and the area of each base, and then add. Or you can use a formula.

SURFACE AREA OF A RECTANGULAR PRISM FORMULA

The formula for the surface area of a rectangular prism with base area B, perimeter of the base P, and height h is

$$SA = 2B + LA = 2B + Ph$$
$$= 2lh + 2hw + 2lw.$$

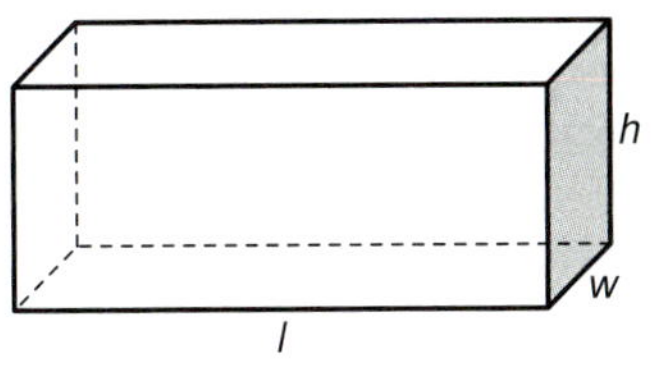

Finding the Surface Area of a Prism

EXAMPLE 3

A Find the surface area of the rectangular prism by adding the areas of its lateral faces and bases.

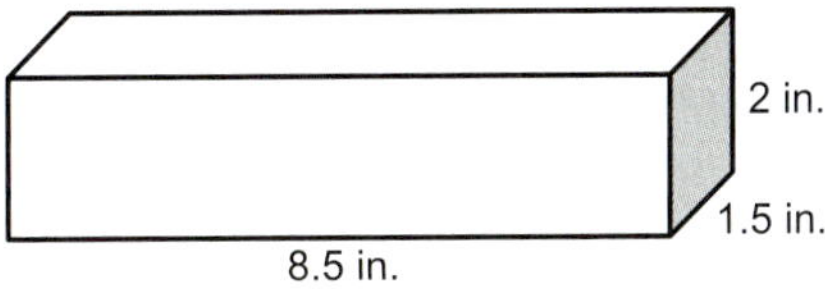

Solution The 4 lateral faces are the front, right side, back, and left side of the prism.

area of front: $8.5 \times 2 = 17$ area of back: $8.5 \times 2 = 17$

area of right side: $1.5 \times 2 = 3$ area of left side: $1.5 \times 2 = 3$

area of top: $8.5 \times 1.5 = 12.75$ area of bottom: $8.5 \times 1.5 = 12.75$

surface area $= 2 \cdot (17 \text{ in}^2) + 2 \cdot (3 \text{ in}^2) + 2 \cdot (12.75 \text{ in}^2)$

$= 34 \text{ in}^2 + 6 \text{ in}^2 + 25.5 \text{ in}^2 = 65.5 \text{ in}^2$ ■

B Find the surface area of the rectangular prism using the formula.

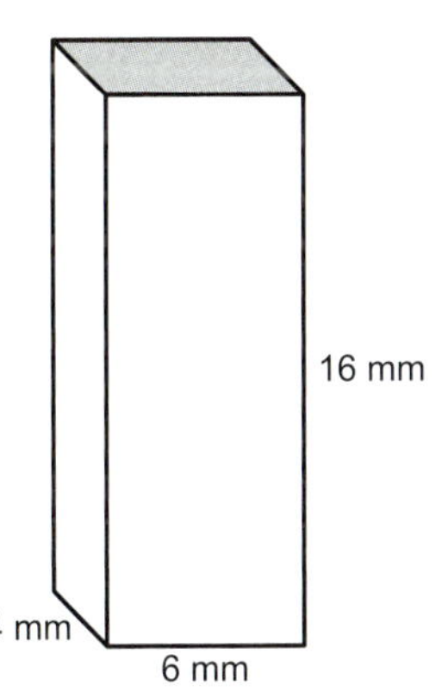

Solution Find the base area.

$B = lw$	Write the area of a rectangle formula.
$= 4 \cdot 6$	Substitute 4 for l and 6 for w.
$= 24$	Simplify.

Find the perimeter of the base.

$P = 2l + 2w$	Write the perimeter of a rectangle formula.
$= 2 \cdot 4 + 2 \cdot 6$	Substitute 4 for l and 6 for w.
$= 8 + 12$	Multiply.
$= 20$	Add.

Plug B, P, and h into the formula for surface area.

$SA = 2B + Ph$	Write the surface area formula.
$= 2 \cdot 24 + 20 \cdot 16$	Substitute for B, P, and h.
$= 48 + 320$	Multiply.
$= 368$	Add.

The surface area of the figure is 368 mm^2. ■

TIP

Finding B, P, and h before substituting into the surface area formula can help you avoid mistakes.

Finding the Surface Area of a Complex Figure

EXAMPLE 4 Find the surface area of the figure.

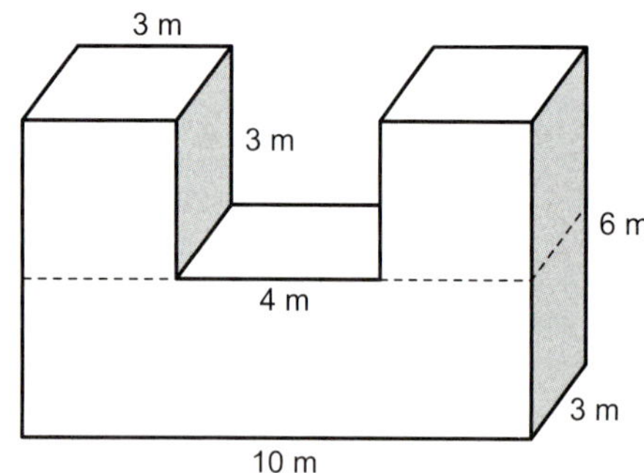

Solution The figure is a rectangular prism topped with two congruent cubes. Find the sum of the surface areas of the three figures, then subtract the area where the figures meet.

> **THINK ABOUT IT**
> You could also find the surface area of the figure by adding the areas of each face.

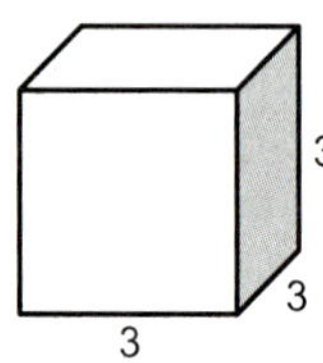

$SA = 6s^2$
$= 6 \cdot 3^2$
$= 6 \cdot 9$
$= 54$

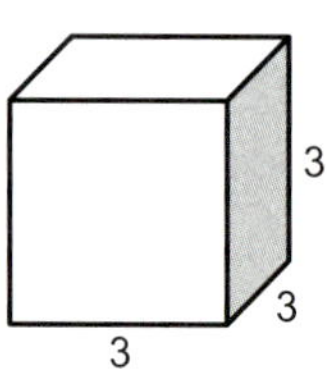

$SA = 6s^2$
$= 6 \cdot 3^2$
$= 6 \cdot 9$
$= 54$

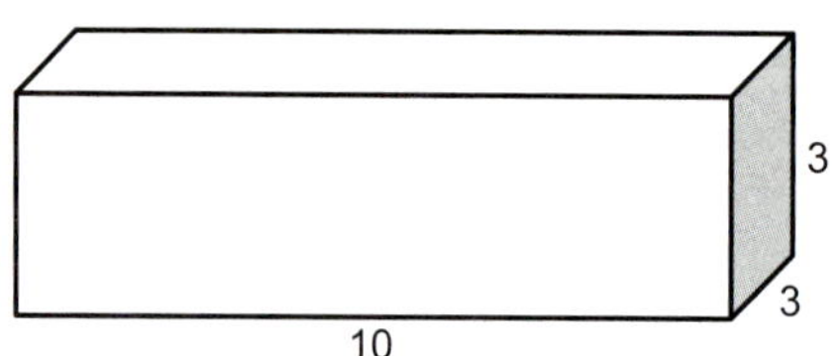

$SA = 2B + Ph$
$= 2 \cdot (10 \cdot 3) + (2 \cdot 10 + 2 \cdot 3) \cdot 3$
$= 2 \cdot 30 + 26 \cdot 3$
$= 60 + 78$
$= 138$

The total surface area of the figures is 54 m^2 + 54 m^2 + 138 m^2 = 246 m^2.

Subtract the area of the bottom face of each cube and the areas on the top of the rectangular prism where the figures meet.

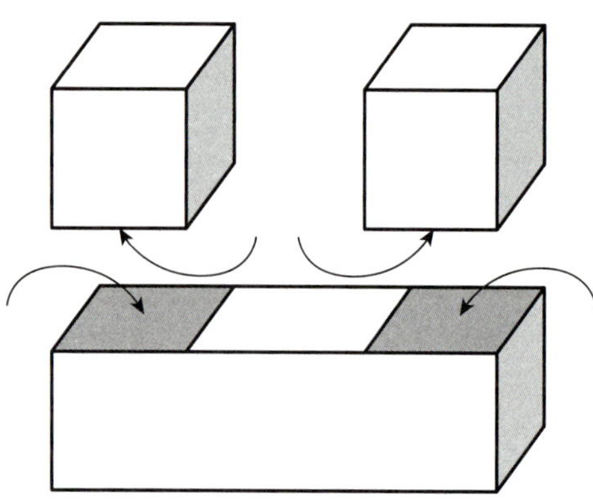

$246 - 4 \cdot 3^2 = 246 - 4 \cdot 9$	For each square surface, use $s = 3$ m.
$= 246 - 36$	Multiply.
$= 210$	Subtract.

The surface area of the figure is 210 m^2.

Problem Set

Find the surface area of the cube with the given side length.

1. $s = 2$ m

2. $s = 5$ cm

3. $s = 3.5$ mm

Find the surface area of the cube.

4.

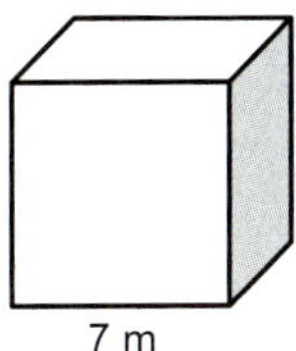

5.

6.

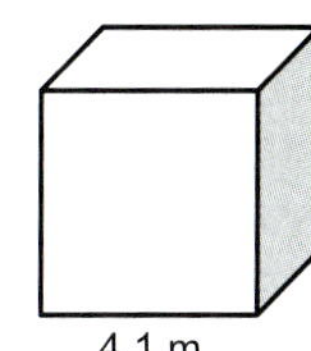

Find the lateral area of the rectangular prism.

7.

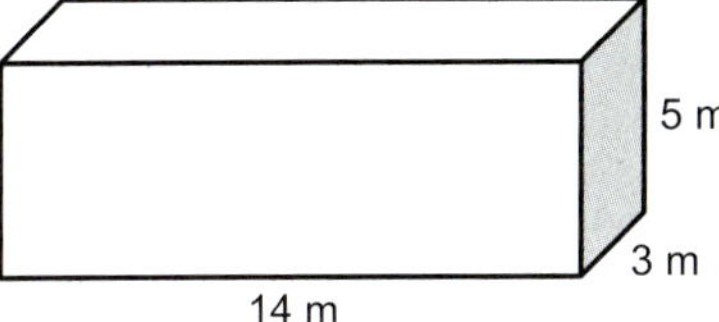

8.

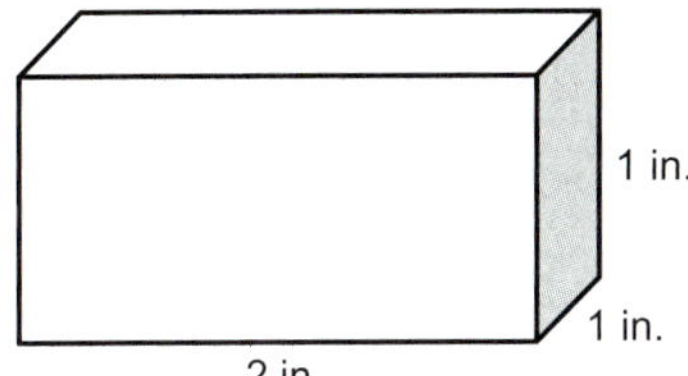

9.

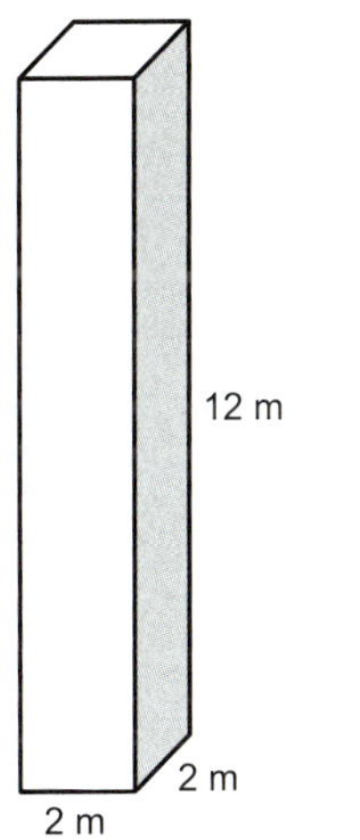

10.

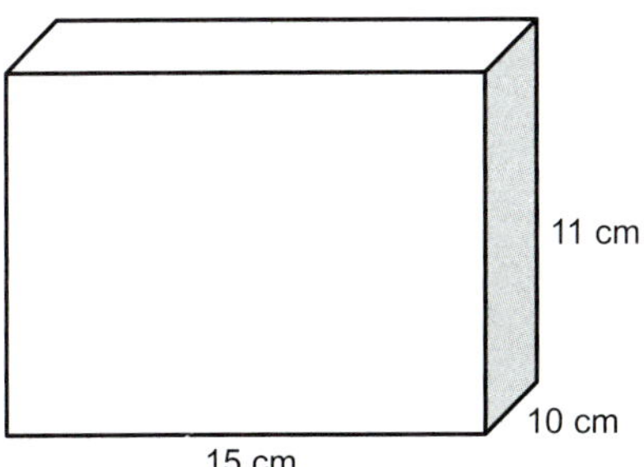

11.

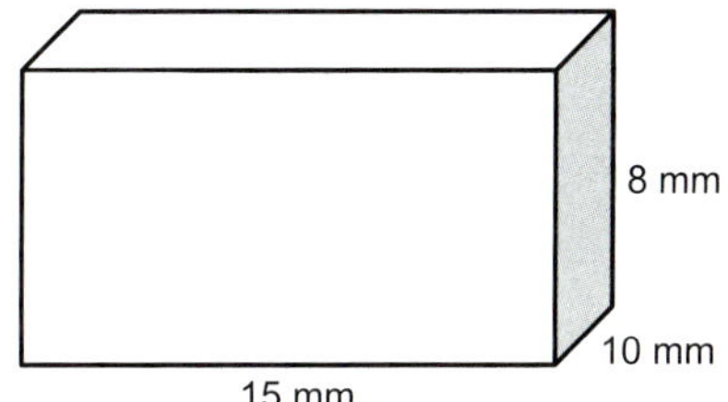

12.

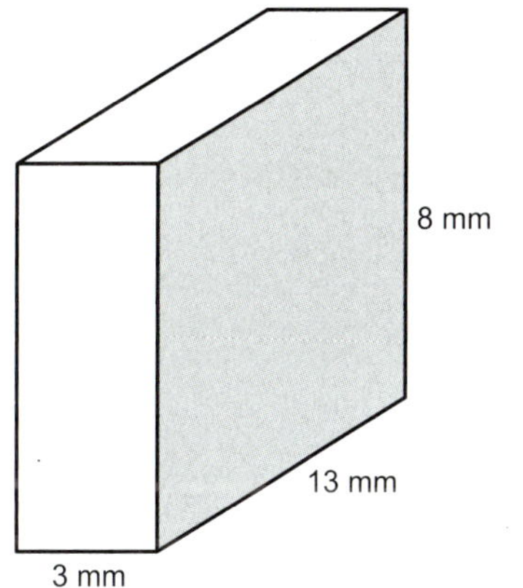

13.

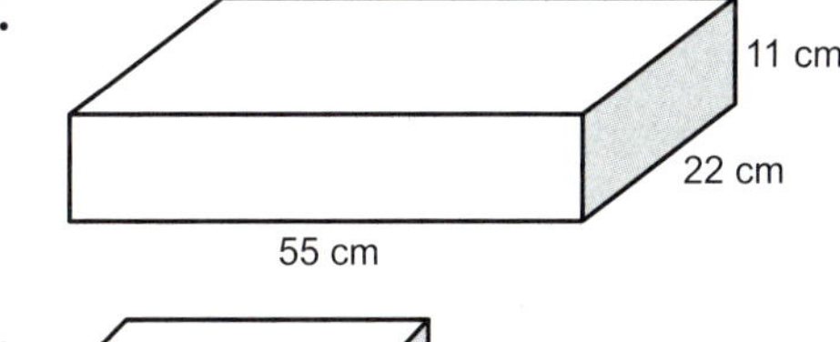

14.

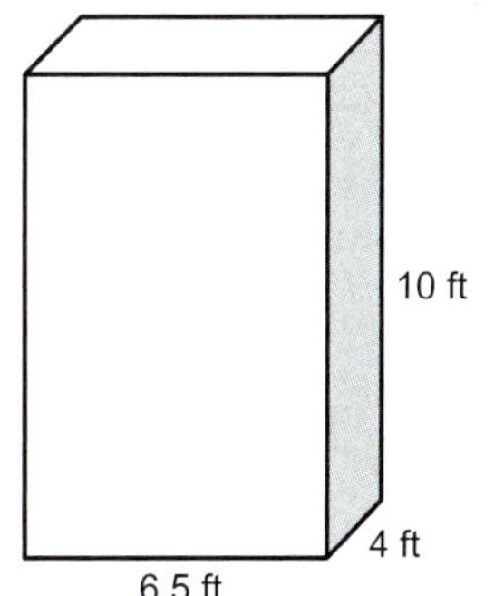

Find the lateral area of the rectangular prism. For each figure, *l* and *w* are the length and width of the base and *h* is the height of the rectangular prism.

15. $l = 7$ m
$w = 12$ m
$h = 4$ m

16. $l = 3$ cm
$w = 6$ cm
$h = 12$ cm

17. $l = 15$ mm
$w = 22$ mm
$h = 48$ mm

18. $l = 5$ ft
$w = 2.5$ ft
$h = 7.5$ ft

Find the surface area of the rectangular prism.

19.

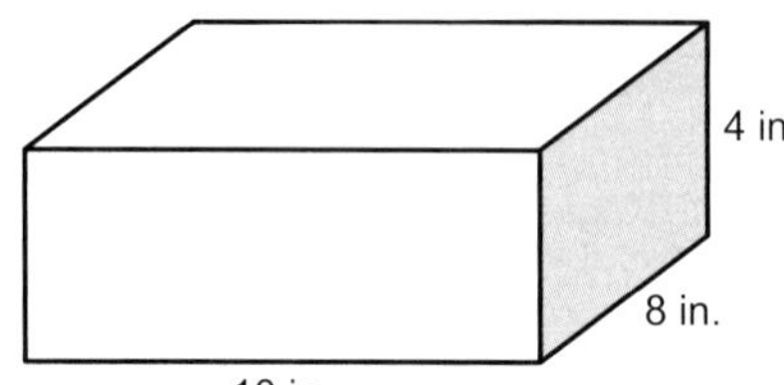

20.

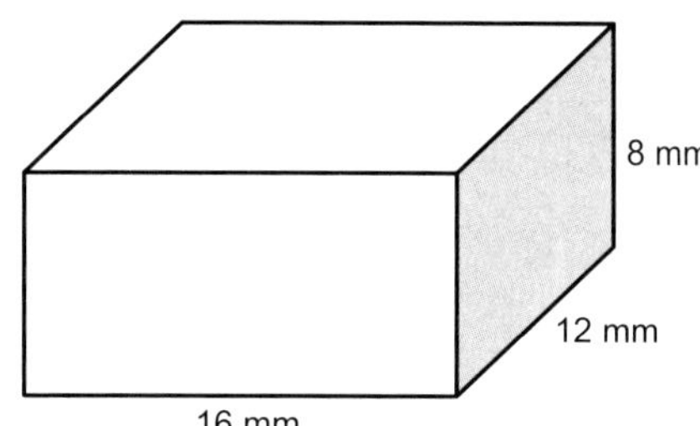

21.

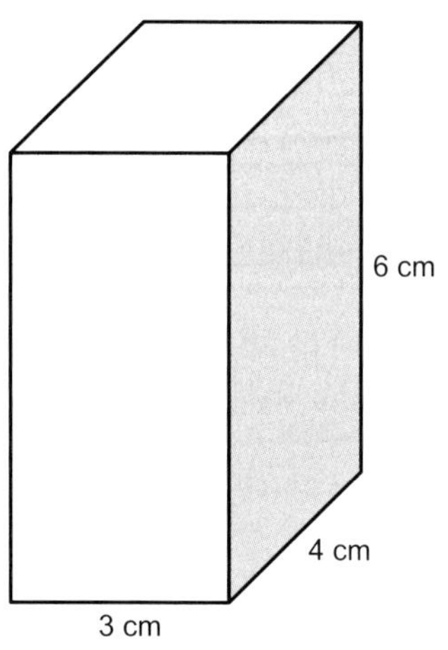

22.

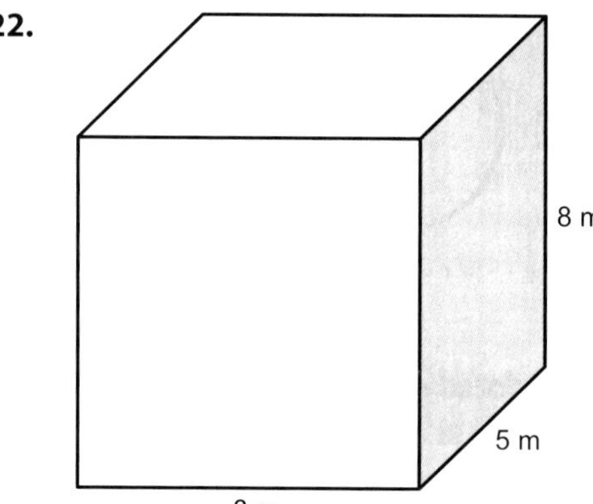

23.

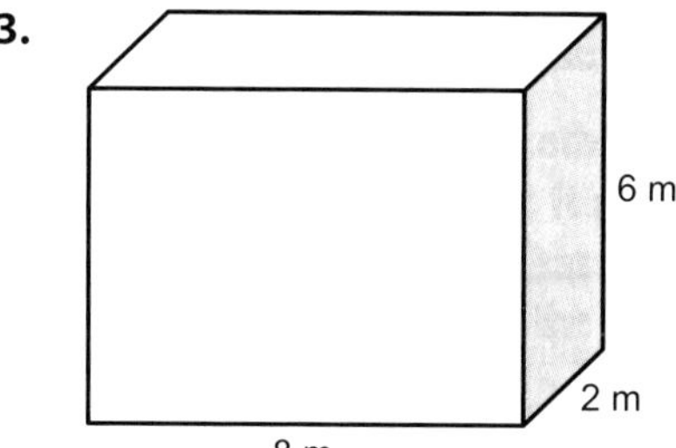

24.

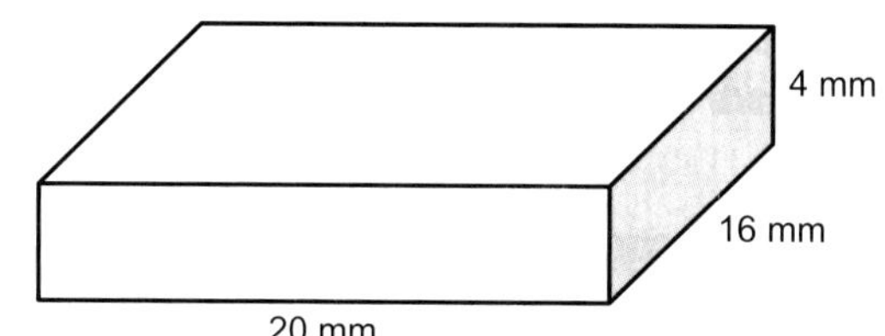

Find the surface area of the figure.

25.

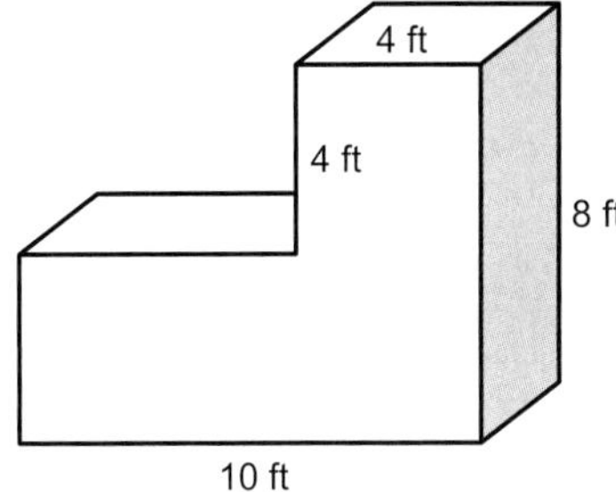

26.

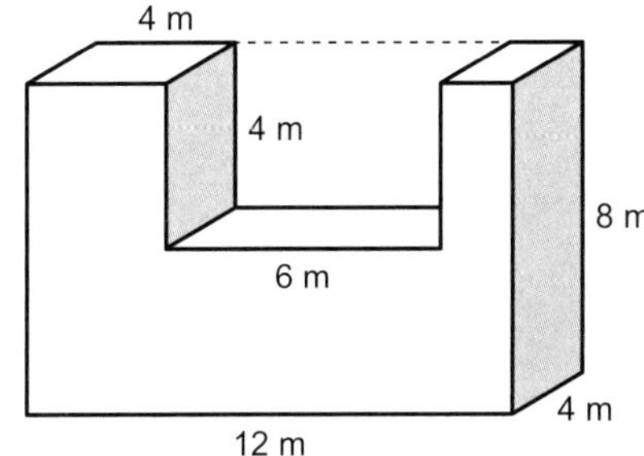

27. Challenge

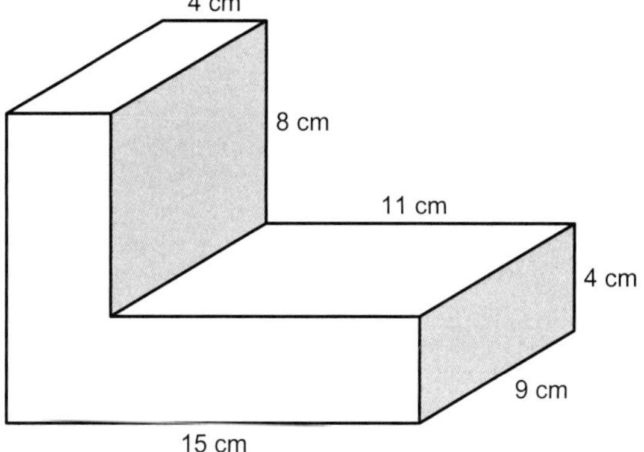

28. Challenge

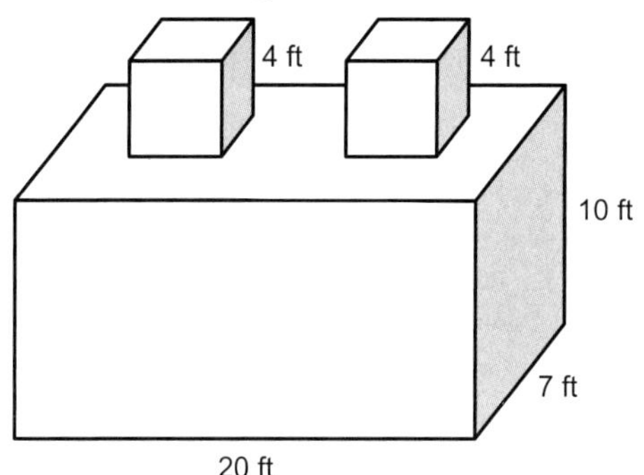

Surface Areas of Prisms

You can find the surface area of any prism using the same formula you used to find the surface area of a rectangular prism.

Finding the Surface Area of a Prism

SURFACE AREA OF A PRISM FORMULA

The formula for the surface area of a prism with base area B, perimeter of the base P, and height h is

$$SA = 2B + LA = 2B + Ph.$$

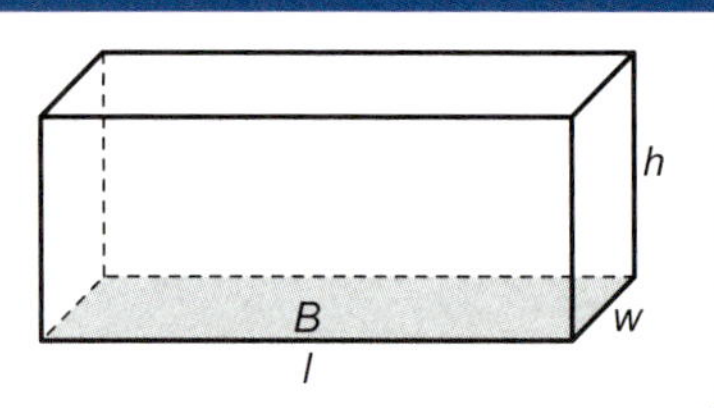

EXAMPLE 1 Find the surface area of the triangular prism.

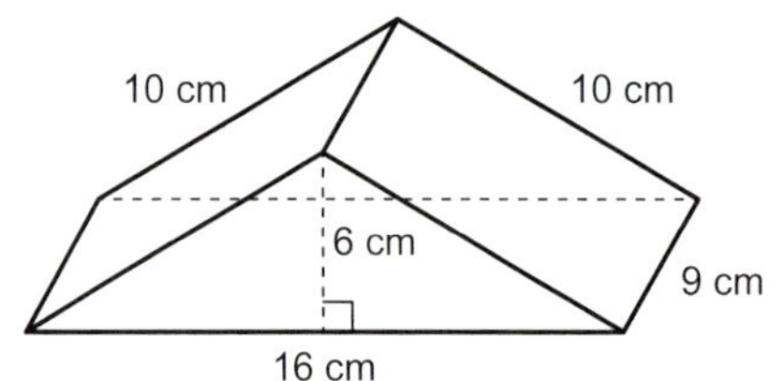

REMEMBER

The bases of the prism are the parallel triangles. The lateral faces are rectangles.

Solution The height h of the prism is 9 cm. Find B and P, then use B, P, and h in the surface area formula.

$B = \frac{1}{2}bh_{\text{triangle}}$	Write the area of a triangle formula.
$= \frac{1}{2} \cdot 16 \cdot 6$	Substitute 16 for b and 6 for h_{triangle}.
$= 48$	Multiply.

Find the perimeter of the base.

$P = 10 + 10 + 16$	Add the side lengths.
$= 36$	Add.

Substitute B, P, and h into the surface area formula.

$SA = 2B + Ph_{\text{prism}}$	Write the surface area formula.
$= 2 \cdot 48 + 36 \cdot 9$	Substitute 48 for B, 36 for P, and 9 for h_{prism}.
$= 96 + 324$	Multiply.
$= 420$	Add.

The surface area of the triangular prism is 420 cm^2.

TIP

Use subscripts to distinguish between the height of the triangle h_{triangle} and the height of the prism h_{prism}.

EXAMPLE 2 The base of the prism is a regular hexagon. Find the surface area of the prism.

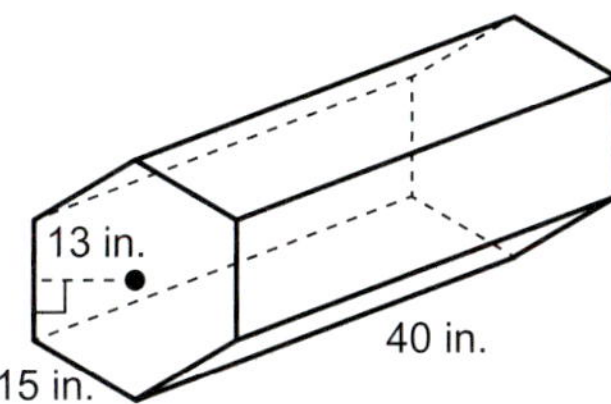

> **REMEMBER**
>
> The area A of an n-sided regular polygon is
>
> $$A = n \cdot \left(\frac{1}{2}bh\right)$$
>
> where b is the side length and h is the apothem length.

Solution The apothem of the hexagon is 15 in. Find B and P, and then use B, P, and h_{hexagon} in the surface area formula.

Find B.

$B = 6\left(\frac{1}{2}bh_{\text{hexagon}}\right)$	Write the area of a regular hexagon formula.
$= 6\left(\frac{1}{2} \cdot 15 \cdot 13\right)$	Substitute 15 for b and 13 for h.
$= 6\left(\frac{195}{2}\right)$	Multiply.
$= \frac{1170}{2}$	
$= 585$	

Find the perimeter of the base.

$P = 6(15)$	Find the perimeter of the base.
$= 90$	

Substitute B, P, and h into the surface area formula.

$SA = 2B + Ph_{\text{prism}}$	Write the surface area formula.
$= 2 \cdot 585 + 90 \cdot 40$	Substitute 585 for B, 90 for P, and 40 for h.
$= 1170 + 3600$	Multiply.
$= 4770$	Add.

The volume of the hexagonal prism is 4770 in^3. ■

Using the Surface Area to Volume Ratio

Scientists and business people often need to figure out how an object's surface area compares to its volume. For instance, biologists study organisms that have more surface area to increase their drag in the water environment. Any business that needs to store or ship products cares about how surface area compares to the volume or capacity.

One way to compare the surface area of a figure to its volume is the **surface area to volume ratio**. This ratio can help you compare figures.

EXAMPLE 3 A company is purchasing boxes to ship its product. The price of a box depends on the amount of material used to make it, and the company wants to pack as much product in the box as possible. So the company wants to minimize surface area while maximizing volume. The company's suppliers have presented the two options shown.

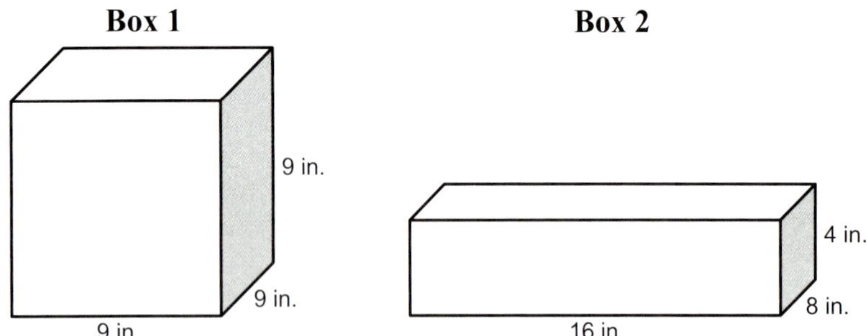

A Find the surface area to volume ratio for each figure.

Solution Calculate the surface area and volume for each figure.

Box 1

$$SA = 6s^2$$
$$= 6 \bullet 9^2$$
$$= 6 \bullet 81$$
$$= 486$$
$$V = s^3 = 9^3 = 729$$

The surface area is 486 in^2.

The volume is 729 in^3.

Box 2

$$B = 16 \bullet 8 = 128$$
$$P = 2 \bullet 16 + 2 \bullet 8 = 48$$
$$SA = 2B + Ph$$
$$= 2 \bullet 128 + 48 \bullet 4$$
$$= 256 + 192$$
$$= 448$$
$$V = Bh = 128 \bullet 4 = 512$$

The surface area is 448 in^2.

The volume is 512 in^3.

Find the surface area to volume ratios.

Box 1

$$\frac{486}{729} \approx \frac{0.67}{1}$$

Box 2

$$\frac{448}{512} = \frac{0.875}{1}$$ ■

B Analyze the ratios. Which package is the better choice?

Solution Compare the ratios $\frac{0.67}{1}$ and $\frac{0.875}{1}$. The second ratio shows a greater surface area to volume ratio. So Box 2 uses more material per unit of volume than Box 1 does. To save on materials, the company should choose Box 1, the cube. ■

Problem Set

Find the surface area of the prism with area of the base *B*, perimeter of the base *P*, and height *h*.

1. $B = 8\text{ m}^2$
$P = 12\text{ m}$
$h = 3\text{ m}$

2. $B = 20\text{ ft}^2$
$P = 18\text{ ft}$
$h = 2\text{ ft}$

3. $B = 40\text{ cm}^2$
$P = 28\text{ cm}$
$h = 10\text{ cm}$

4.

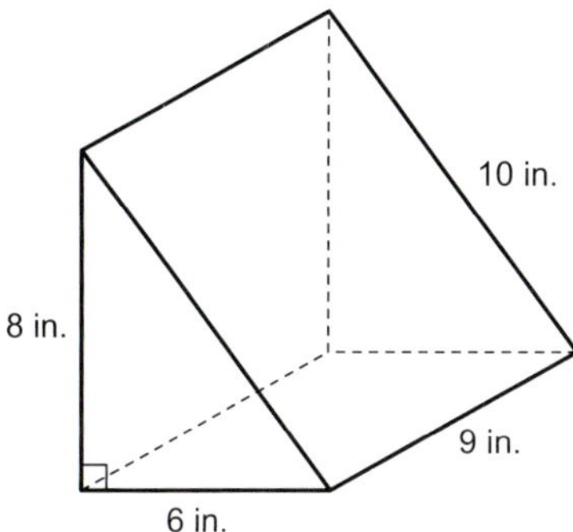

5.

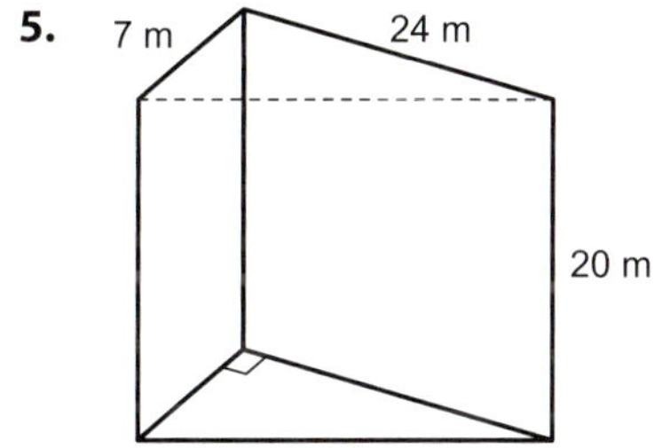

6. $B = 3\frac{2}{3}\text{ cm}^2$
$P = 5\frac{1}{3}\text{ cm}$
$h = 2\text{ cm}$

7. $B = 48\text{ in}^2$
$P = 28\text{ in.}$
$h = 12.4\text{ in.}$

8. **Challenge** Find *SA* in cubic centimeters.
$B = 325\text{ mm}$
$P = 40\text{ m}$
$h = 120\text{ cm}$

9.

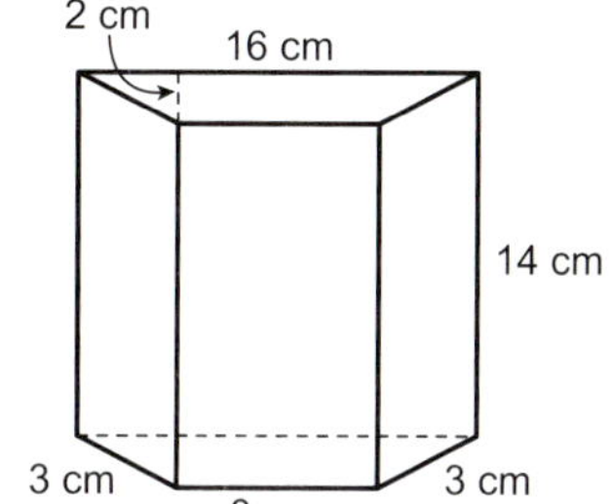

10.

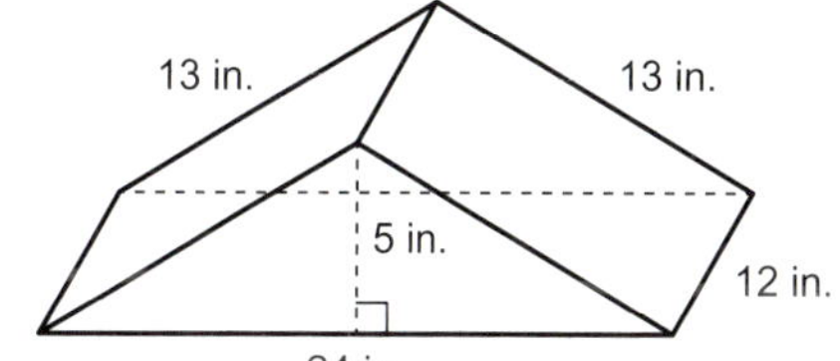

Find the surface area to volume ratio for the figure.

11. a cube with $s = 1$ cm

12. a cube with $s = 5$ cm

13. a cube with $s = 10$ cm

14. a rectangular prism with $l = 5$ cm, $w = 4$ cm, and $h = 2$ cm

15. a rectangular prism with $l = 1$ cm, $w = 5$ cm, and $h = 10$ cm

16. **Challenge** a regular pentagonal prism with side length of 17 cm, apothem length of 25 cm, and height of 50 cm

Solve.

17. **Challenge** What is the surface area to volume ratio for any cube? Give your answer in terms of *s*, the length of one side of the cube.

Properties of Volume and Surface Area

A solid figure's surface area and volume change when the figure's dimensions change.

Measuring Figures with Different Units

EXAMPLE 1 The surface area of a cube is 150 cm^2. What would change if the surface area of the cube were measured in square meters?

Solution The surface area does not change. A square meter is larger than a square centimeter, so the number would decrease.

The number representing the surface area would decrease. ■

EXAMPLE 2 The volume of a cube is 125 cm^3. What would change if the volume of the cube were measured in cubic millimeters?

Solution The volume does not change. A cubic millimeter is smaller than a cubic centimeter, so the number would increase.

The number representing the volume would increase. ■

THINK ABOUT IT

The length of a rope does not change when the length is measured with different units. But the number does change. A rope 1 m long also is 100 cm long.

1 m = 100 cm

Finding Surface Area with Scaled Figures

If you know the surface area or volume of a figure and the scale factor between it and its scaled image, you can use a formula to find the surface area or volume of the scaled image.

TIP

A scaled image is an enlarged or a reduced image of a figure.

DEFINITION

A **scale factor** is a ratio of one measure to another. A scale factor greater than 1 enlarges a figure, and a scale factor less than 1 reduces a figure.

SCALE FACTOR FORMULA

If SA_F is the surface area of a figure that is enlarged or reduced with a scale factor, then the surface area of the scaled image SA_I is

$$SA_I = (\text{scale factor})^2 \cdot SA_F.$$

TIP

The capital I in SA_I is a subscript. SA_I is read "*SA* sub I."

SA_F is read "*SA* sub F."

V_I is read "*V* sub I."

V_F is read "*V* sub F."

EXAMPLE 3 Find the surface area of a figure that is an enlargement of a prism with surface area of 160 cm². Use a scale factor of 2.

Solution

$SA_I = (\text{scale factor})^2 \cdot SA_F$	Write the scale factor formula.
$= 2^2 \cdot 160$	Replace scale factor with 2 and SA_F with 160.
$= 640$	Simplify.

Check The figure is an enlargement. The figure's surface area should be greater than the original prism's surface area.

$$640 > 160 \checkmark$$

The surface area of the enlargement is 640 cm².

Finding Figures with the Same Volume but Different Surface Areas

You can use factoring and multiplication properties to find figures that have the same volume but different surface areas.

REMEMBER

The volume of a rectangular prism with dimensions *l*, *w*, and *h* is

$V = lwh.$

The surface area of a rectangular prism is the sum of the areas of the faces.

EXAMPLE 4 Find the dimensions of two rectangular prisms, each with a volume of 48 m³, but each with a different surface area.

Solution Write the volume 48 as the product of three numbers two different ways. Use the factors as dimensions of the prisms.

$V = 48 = 6 \cdot 4 \cdot 2 \qquad V = 48 = 2 \cdot 3 \cdot 8$

$= l_1 w_1 h_1 \qquad = l_2 w_2 h_2$

Find the surface area of each prism.

$SA_1 = (6 \cdot 2) + (4 \cdot 2) + (6 \cdot 4) + (6 \cdot 2) + (4 \cdot 2) + (6 \cdot 4)$

$= 12 + 8 + 24 + 12 + 8 + 24$

$= 88$

$SA_2 = (2 \cdot 8) + (3 \cdot 8) + (2 \cdot 3) + (2 \cdot 8) + (3 \cdot 8) + (2 \cdot 3)$

$= 16 + 24 + 6 + 16 + 24 + 6$

$= 92$

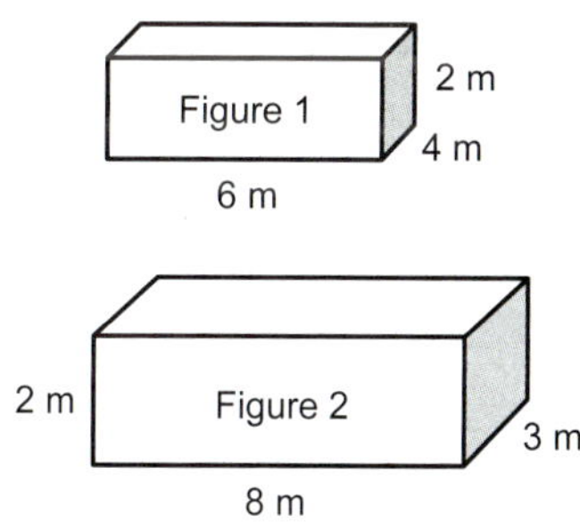

Rectangular prisms with dimensions of 6 m × 4 m × 2 m and 2 m × 3 m × 8 m have the same volume of 48 m³ but different surface areas.

Problem Set

Solve.

1. The surface area of a prism is 1400 mm^2. What would change if the surface area of the prism were measured in square centimeters?

2. The volume of a prism is 45 yd^3. What would change if the volume of the prism were measured in cubic feet?

3. The surface area of a triangular pyramid is 375.2 m^2. What would change if the surface area were measured in square centimeters?

4. The volume of a cube is 512 cm^3. What would change if the volume of the cube were measured in cubic meters?

Find the surface area of the scaled image by using the original figure's measurement and the given scale factor.

5. prism with $SA = 108$ in^2; scale factor $= 3$

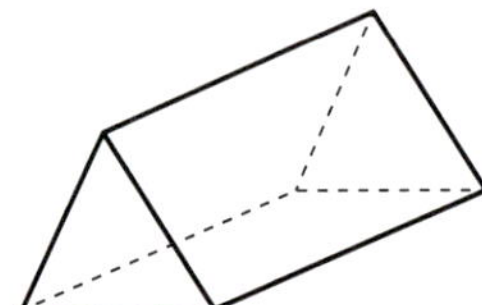

6. prism with $SA = 288$ cm^2; scale factor $= 2$

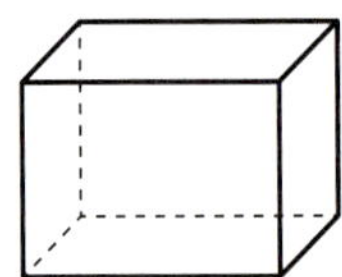

7. pyramid with $SA = 300$ yd^2; scale factor $= 5$

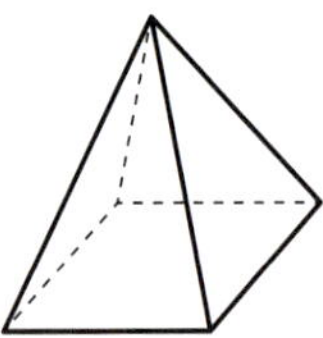

8. pyramid with $SA = 648$ m^2; scale factor $= 3$

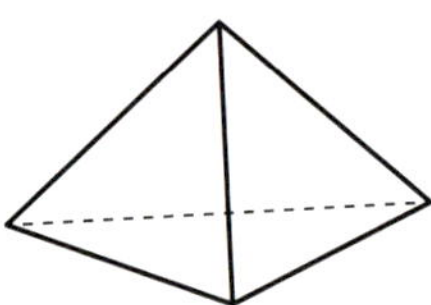

9. prism with $SA = 2592$ ft^2; scale factor $= \frac{1}{6}$

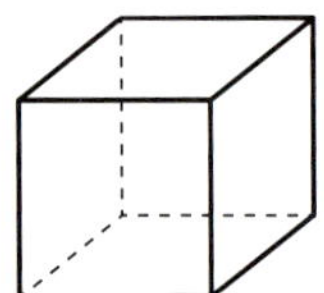

10. prism with $SA = 3375$ cm^2; scale factor $= \frac{1}{5}$

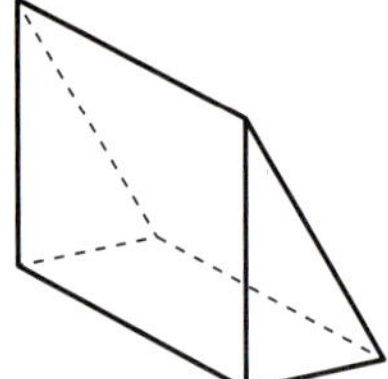

11. prism with $SA = 1104$ m^2; scale factor $= 4$

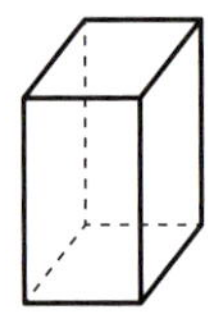

Solve.

12. **Challenge** The entrance to the Louvre Museum in Paris, France, is a large square pyramid with a surface area of 1950 m^2. Regina bought a $\frac{1}{300}$ scale model of the museum entrance. To the nearest tenth, what is the surface area of the scale model Regina bought?

Find the dimensions of two rectangular prisms that have the given volume but have different surface areas.

13. $V = 24 \text{ m}^3$

14. $V = 36 \text{ cm}^3$

15. $V = 32 \text{ mm}^3$

16. $V = 60 \text{ m}^3$

17. $V = 80 \text{ ft}^3$

18. $V = 72 \text{ in}^3$

19. $V = 40 \text{ m}^3$

20. $V = 64 \text{ cm}^3$

21. $V = 54 \text{ cm}^3$

22. $V = 56 \text{ mm}^3$

23. $V = 162 \text{ m}^3$

24. $V = 250 \text{ in}^3$

25. $V = 225 \text{ cm}^3$

26. **Challenge** $V = 189 \text{ mm}^3$

27. **Challenge** $V = 536 \text{ cm}^3$

Choose the answer.

28. A prism has a surface area of 100 cm^2. Which sentence describes the effect of measuring the surface area in square millimeters?

A. The surface area increases.

B. The surface area decreases.

C. The surface area stays the same, but the number representing the surface area increases.

D. The surface area stays the same, but the number representing the surface area decreases.

29. An image is created of a triangular prism using a scale factor of 3. What is the surface area of the scaled image if the surface area of the original triangular prism is 45 cm^2?

A. 9 cm^2

B. 15 cm^2

C. 135 cm^2

D. 405 cm^2

30. Which dimensions of two rectangular prisms have volumes of 100 m^3 but different surface areas?

A. $25 \text{ m} \times 2 \text{ m} \times 2 \text{ m}$; $4 \text{ m} \times 2 \text{ m} \times 5 \text{ m}$

B. $5 \text{ m} \times 5 \text{ m} \times 2 \text{ m}$; $2 \text{ m} \times 10 \text{ m} \times 5 \text{ m}$

C. $2 \text{ m} \times 2 \text{ m} \times 25 \text{ m}$; $2 \text{ m} \times 2 \text{ m} \times 5 \text{ m}$

D. $2 \text{ m} \times 10 \text{ m} \times 5 \text{ m}$; $4 \text{ m} \times 5 \text{ m} \times 5 \text{ m}$

Core Focus: Applications of Volume and Surface Area

THE CORE CONCEPT

The solution of many real-world problems involves finding the volume or surface area of everyday objects.

Application: Shipping

Many real-world objects are modeled by prisms. Find the capacity of a real-world object by finding the volume of the prism representing the object.

EXAMPLE 1 The dimensions of a cardboard shipping box are 7.6 cm, 7.6 cm, 10.8 cm, and 91.4 cm.

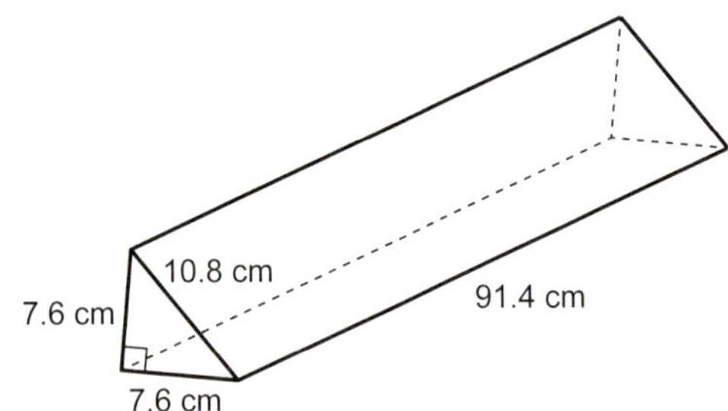

A What is the volume of the box? Round to the nearest cubic centimeter.

Solution The box is a triangular prism, so use the formula $V = Bh_{\text{prism}}$. The base is a right triangle, so $B = \frac{1}{2}bh_{\text{triangle}}$ where $b = 7.6$ cm and $h_{\text{triangle}} = 7.6$ cm.

$$B = \frac{1}{2}bh_{\text{triangle}}$$

$$= \frac{1}{2} \cdot (7.6) \cdot (7.6) = \frac{57.76}{2} = 28.88$$

$$V = Bh_{\text{prism}}$$

$$= (28.88) \cdot 91.4$$

$$= 2639.632$$

$$\approx 2640$$

The volume of the box is about 2640 cm^3.

REMEMBER

The formula for the volume of a prism is

$$V = Bh_{\text{prism}}$$

where B is the area of the base of the prism and h_{prism} is the prism's height.

B How much cardboard is used to make the box? Round to the nearest square centimeter.

Solution Find the surface area of the box. The box is a prism with a triangular base. Use the formula $SA = 2B + Ph_{prism}$.

$$P = 7.6 + 7.6 + 10.8 = 26$$

B was previously calculated and is equal to 28.8 cm².

$$\begin{aligned} SA &= 2B + Ph_{prism} \\ &= 2(28.88) + 26 \cdot (91.4) \\ &= 57.76 + 2376.4 \\ &= 2434.16 \\ &\approx 2434 \end{aligned}$$

About 2434 cm² of cardboard is needed to make the box. ■

REMEMBER

The formula for the surface area of a prism is

$$SA = 2B + Ph_{prism}$$

where B is the area of the base, P is the perimeter of the base, and h_{prism} is the height of the prism.

Application: Capacity of a Feed Bag

In some real-world situations, you want to estimate how many objects a container can hold.

EXAMPLE 2 A chicken feed container in the shape of a rectangular box is 60 cm long, 32 cm wide, and 6 cm high. Each feed pellet is 0.12 cm³. About how many chicken feed pellets will fit in the box?

Solution Find the volume of the box.

$$\begin{aligned} V &= lwh \\ &= 60 \cdot 32 \cdot 6 = 11{,}520 \end{aligned}$$

The volume of the box is 11,520 cm³. Multiply this amount by the unit rate.

$$\begin{aligned} 11{,}520 \text{ cm}^3 \cdot \frac{1 \text{ pellet}}{0.12 \text{ cm}^3} &= 11{,}520 \cancel{\text{cm}^3} \cdot \frac{1 \text{ pellet}}{0.12 \cancel{\text{cm}^3}} \\ &= \frac{11{,}520}{0.12} \text{ pellets} \\ &= 96{,}000 \text{ pellets} \end{aligned}$$

About 96,000 feed pellets will fit in the box. ■

Application: Painting a Room

Surface area is used to determine how much material is needed to cover an entire object.

EXAMPLE 3 Dean wants to paint a room with a door. The room has 9 ft ceilings and is 12 ft long by 14 ft wide. A single can of paint covers 350 ft^2. How many cans of paint does Dean need to cover the 4 walls with 2 coats of paint?

Solution Find the combined area of all 4 walls.

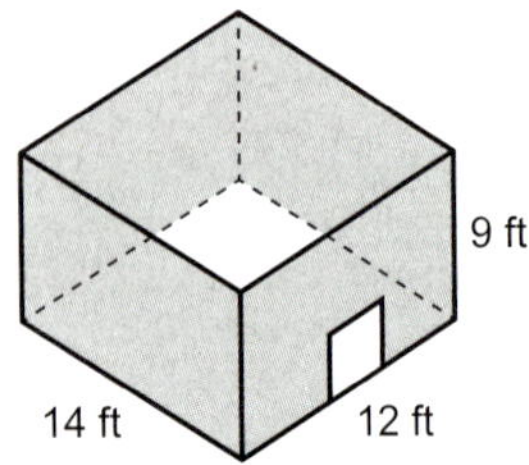

$$\begin{aligned} LA = Ph &= (2l + 2w) \cdot h \\ &= (2 \cdot 12 + 2 \cdot 14) \cdot 9 \\ &= (24 + 28) \cdot 9 \\ &= 52 \cdot 9 \\ &= 468 \text{ ft}^2 \end{aligned}$$

The area of all 4 walls is 468 ft^2. Two coats of paint will require $2 \cdot 468 \text{ ft}^2 = 936 \text{ ft}^2$ of paint.

Multiply the total area of 936 ft^2 by the unit rate of 1 can/350 ft^2 to find the number of cans of paint Dean needs.

$$\begin{aligned} 936 \text{ ft}^2 \cdot \frac{1 \text{ can}}{350 \text{ ft}^2} &= 936 \cancel{\text{ft}^2} \cdot \frac{1 \text{ can}}{350 \cancel{\text{ft}^2}} \\ &= \frac{936}{350} \text{ cans} \\ &\approx 2.7 \text{ cans} \end{aligned}$$

Dean needs 3 cans of paint to cover the 4 walls and the door with 2 coats of paint. ■

BY THE WAY

Not all real-world area problems involve finding the total surface area. Sometimes you only need to find the area of some faces of the shape, then add those areas.

Problem Set

Solve.

1. An aquarium has glass sides and a glass bottom, but no top.

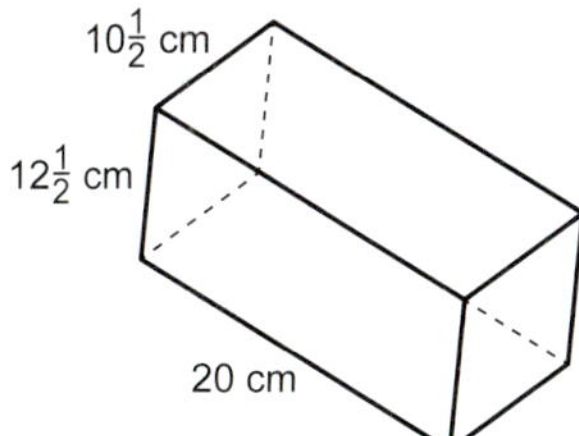

   (a) How many square centimeters of glass were used to make the aquarium?

   (b) What is the maximum amount of water the aquarium can hold?

2. The bottom floor of a barn is in the shape of a rectangular prism. The top floor is in the shape of a triangular prism.

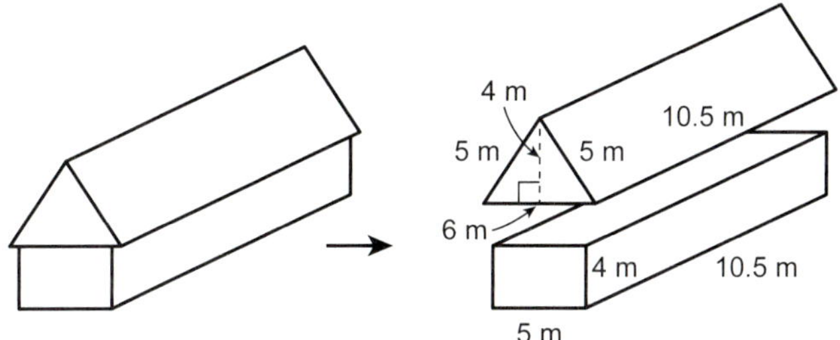

   (a) Find the volume of the bottom floor.

   (b) Find the volume of the top floor.

   (c) A farmer wants to cover the bottom floor of the barn with a layer of sawdust 2 cm high. How many cubic meters of sawdust should the farmer buy? Explain your reasoning.

3. Liu-Qin wants to cover a floor with tiles. The floor is 4 m long and $3\frac{1}{4}$ m wide. Each tile is a square with an area of $\frac{1}{12}$ m^2. What is the maximum number of tiles needed to cover the floor?

4. Molly is filling a serving dish with sugar cubes. Each cube measures 1 cm on a side. The serving dish has the shape of a cube and measures 8 cm on a side. What is the greatest number of sugar cubes Molly can fit into the serving dish? Explain your reasoning.

5. A packaging company needs to design a rectangular box with volume 240 in^3 and a height of 20 in.

   (a) Find the dimensions of two different boxes that the packaging company could design.

   (b) Sketch each box and label the dimensions.

   (c) Find the surface area of each box. Which box uses less material to make?

CHAPTER 11 Review

Choose the answer.

1. What is the volume of the solid?

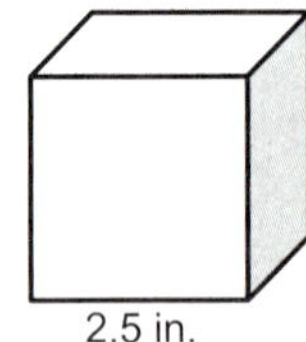

   A. 6.25 in^2
   B. 20 in^3
   C. 15.625 in^3
   D. 37.5 in^3

2. What is the volume of a cube with a side length of 4 cm?
   A. 16 cm^3
   B. 64 cm^3
   C. 96 cm^3
   D. 256 cm^3

3. A triangular prism has a base area of 22 cm^2 and a height of 8 cm. What is the volume of the prism?
   A. 88 cm^3
   B. 176 cm^3
   C. 352 cm^3
   D. 704 cm^3

4. A slice is made perpendicular to the base of a right circular cone, through the cone's apex. What two-dimensional cross section results?
   A. circle
   B. cone
   C. rectangle
   D. triangle

5. What is the surface area of the solid?

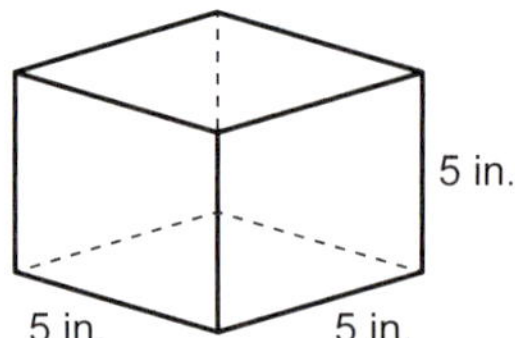

   A. 100 in^2
   B. 125 in^2
   C. 150 in^2
   D. 200 in^2

6. What is the surface area of a rectangular prism with base $B = 15 \text{ mm}^2$, perimeter $P = 20$ mm, and height $h = 4$ mm?
   A. 95 mm^2
   B. 110 mm^2
   C. 880 mm^2
   D. 1200 mm^2

7. The prism has a volume $V = 80 \text{ ft}^3$. The prism is changed by a scale factor of $\frac{1}{2}$. What is the volume of the new prism?

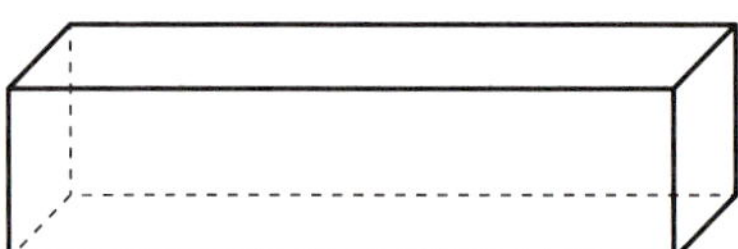

   A. 10 ft^3
   B. 40 ft^3
   C. 160 ft^3
   D. 640 ft^3

8. A wooden box for road salt is 2 m long, 0.8 m wide, and 0.6 m high. The salt box is about a third full. About how much salt is in the salt box?
   A. 0.32 m^3
   B. 0.64 m^3
   C. 0.96 m^3
   D. 2.88 m^3

Solve.

9. What is the volume of the trapezoidal prism?

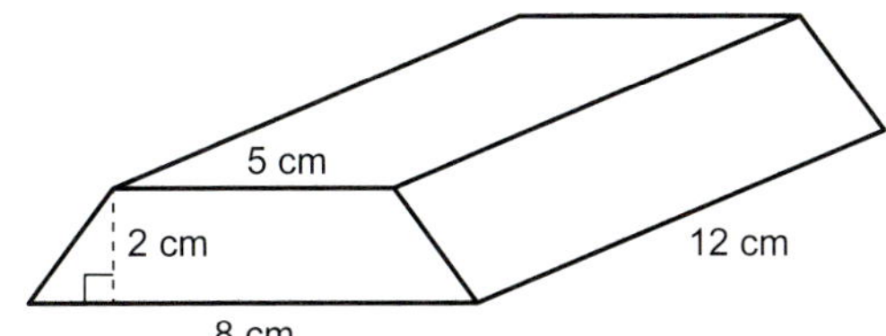

10. A plane slices a triangular pyramid whose base is an equilateral triangle. The slice is parallel to the triangle's base.

(a) Make a sketch of the plane slicing the triangular pyramid, showing the resulting cross section.

(b) Describe the shape of the cross section.

11. Find the lateral area of the rectangular prism.

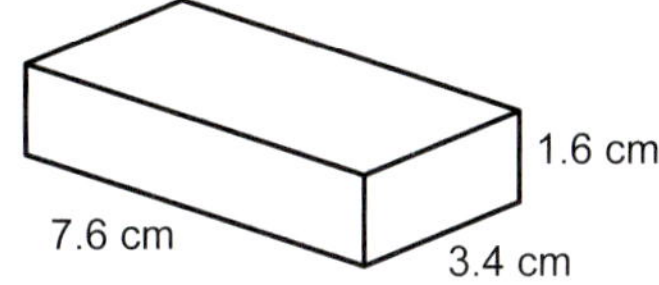

12. The base of the prism is a right triangle.

(a) Find the surface area of the prism.

(b) Calculate the ratio of the surface area to volume.

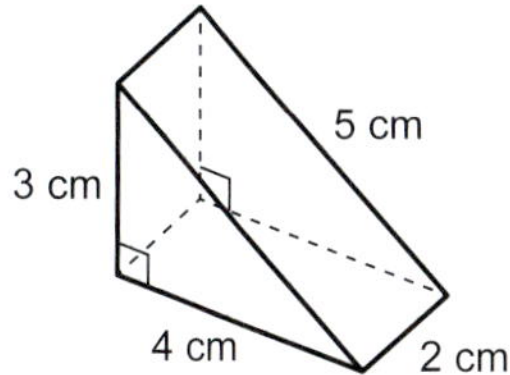

13. Find the dimensions of two rectangular prisms with a volume of 40 m^3 but with different surface areas.

14. The dimensions of a cardboard pizza box are 16 in., 16 in., and 1.5 in. The lower part of the box is the bottom, which has 4 sides. The upper part of the box is the lid plus 3 additional flaps, each the same size as one of the sides. How much cardboard is used to make the entire box?

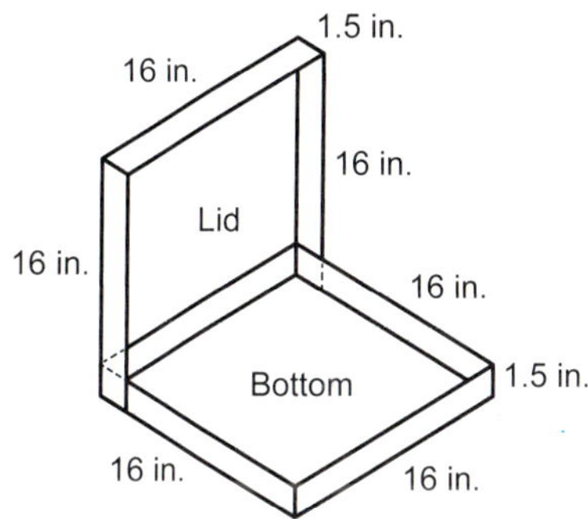

Problem	Topic Lookup	Problem	Topic Lookup
1, 2	Volume	6, 12	Surface Areas of Prisms
3, 9	Volumes of Prisms	7, 13	Properties of Volume and Surface Area
4, 10	Slicing Solids	8, 14	Core Focus: Applications of Volume and Surface Area
5, 11	Surface Area		

CHAPTER 12 Probability and Statistics

Data are everywhere. When you look at a group of people, you could use many numbers to describe them. How tall are they? How long is their hair? How old are they? What is their gender? What color are their eyes? Statistics helps you make sense of data.

In This Chapter

In this chapter, you'll use statistical graphs and measures of center and spread to compare populations. Next you will use statistics and samples to make predictions. Finally you'll learn about simple probability and probability of compound events.

Topic List

- Foundations for Chapter 12
- Measures of Center
- Measures of Variability
- Samples and Prediction
- Drawing Inferences
- Comparing Distributions
- Using Statistical Measures
- Probability
- Relative Frequency
- Combined Probability
- Core Focus: Probability Models
- Chapter 12 Review

You can find lots of data in any group of people. ▶

ST. MARK'S
SOCCER

Foundations for Chapter 12

Finding the Average of Two Numbers

To find the average of two numbers, divide their sum by 2.

EXAMPLE A Find the average of the two numbers.

 39, 46

Solution

$$\frac{39 + 46}{2} = \frac{85}{2} = 42.5$$

The average of 39 and 46 is 42.5.

Check

$$42.5 \cdot 2 = 85 \checkmark$$

Twice the average is equal to the sum of the two numbers. ■

A-2 10.9, 12.3

Solution

$$\frac{10.9 + 12.3}{2} = \frac{23.2}{2} = 11.6$$

The average of 39 and 46 is 11.6.

Check

$$11.6 \cdot 2 = 23.2 \checkmark$$

Twice the average is equal to the sum of the two numbers. ■

A-3 $\frac{1}{2}, \frac{7}{8}$

Solution

$$\frac{1}{2} = \frac{4}{8}$$

$$\left(\frac{4}{8} + \frac{7}{8}\right) \div 2 = \frac{11}{8} \div 2$$

$$= \frac{11}{8} \cdot \frac{1}{2} = \frac{11}{16}$$

The average of $\frac{1}{2}$ and $\frac{7}{8}$ is $\frac{11}{16}$.

Check

$$\frac{11}{16} \cdot 2 = \frac{22}{16} = \frac{11}{8} \checkmark$$

Twice the average is equal to the sum of the two numbers. ■

Problem Set A

Find the average of the two numbers.

1. 5, 9
2. 18, 24
3. 4.5, 6.3
4. 53.8, 57.6
5. 17, 41
6. $\frac{1}{6}, \frac{5}{6}$
7. 6.71, 6.87
8. $\frac{1}{4}, \frac{7}{12}$
9. 168, 193
10. 13.04, 13.6
11. 3.7, 3.802
12. $2\frac{3}{5}, 4\frac{1}{5}$

Converting a Decimal to a Percent

To convert a decimal to a percent, multiply by 100%. Expand a repeating decimal to several digits before multiplying by 100%. Then round to the desired place value.

EXAMPLE B Convert the decimal to a percent. Round your answer to the nearest tenth, if necessary.

 0.825

Solution Multiply 0.825 by 100%.

$$0.825 \cdot 100\% = 82.5\%$$

Check

$$\frac{82.5\%}{100\%} = 0.825 \checkmark$$

The decimal 0.825 is equal to 82.5%. ■

B-2 $0.\overline{15}$

Solution Expand the repeating decimal.

$$0.\overline{15} = 0.151515\ldots \approx 0.1515$$

Multiply 0.1515 by 100%.

$$0.1515 \cdot 100\% = 15.15\% \approx 15.2\%$$

Check

$$\frac{15.2\%}{100\%} = 0.152 \approx 0.\overline{15} \checkmark$$

The decimal $0.\overline{15}$ is equal to about 15.2%. ■

Problem Set B

Convert the decimal to a percent. Round your answer to the nearest tenth, if necessary.

1. 0.6
2. 0.38
3. $0.\overline{2}$
4. 0.136
5. $0.\overline{6}$
6. 0.507
7. $0.2\overline{3}$
8. $0.\overline{45}$
9. 0.053
10. 0.0972
11. 0.0028
12. $0.61\overline{8}$
13. 0.0106
14. 0.0007
15. $0.60\overline{13}$
16. 0.598
17. 0.0996

Converting a Fraction to a Percent

First convert the fraction to a decimal by dividing the numerator by the denominator. Next convert the decimal as you would normally, by multiplying by 100%. Then round to the desired place value.

EXAMPLE C Convert the fraction to a percent. Round your answer to the nearest tenth, if necessary.

 $\frac{17}{40}$

Solution Divide 17 by 40.

$$\begin{array}{r} 0.425 \\ 40\overline{)17.0} \\ \underline{16\,0} \\ 1\,00 \\ \underline{80} \\ 200 \\ \underline{200} \\ 0 \end{array}$$

$0.425 \cdot 100\% = 42.5\%$

The fraction $\frac{17}{40}$ is equal to 42.5%. ■

C-2 $\frac{11}{18}$

Solution Divide 11 by 18.

$$\begin{array}{r} 0.611 \\ 18\overline{)11.0} \\ \underline{10\,8} \\ 20 \\ \underline{18} \\ 20 \\ \underline{18} \\ 20 \end{array}$$

$0.611\ldots = 0.6\overline{1} \approx 0.611$

$0.611 \cdot 100\% = 61.1\%$

The fraction $\frac{11}{18}$ is equal to about 61.1%. ■

Problem Set C

Convert the fraction to a percent. Round your answer to the nearest tenth, if necessary.

1. $\frac{9}{10}$

2. $\frac{2}{5}$

3. $\frac{13}{20}$

4. $\frac{4}{9}$

5. $\frac{5}{12}$

6. $\frac{8}{11}$

7. $\frac{41}{50}$

8. $\frac{1}{16}$

9. $\frac{5}{14}$

10. $\frac{16}{45}$

Measures of Center

A measure of center is one number used to describe the typical value in a data set.

There are three types of measures of center: mean, median, and mode. They are measures of center because they describe what the "center" or middle of the data looks like.

Mean

The mean is the average of the data. It is found by dividing the sum of the values by the number of values. The mean is often denoted by $\bar{x}$.

DEFINITION

The **mean** is the sum of the values in a data set divided by the number of values.

$$\bar{x} = \frac{x_1 + x_2 + \ldots + x_n}{n}$$

NOTATION

The symbol $\bar{x}$ is pronounced "x bar."

EXAMPLE 1 Find the mean of the data set. Round to the nearest tenth.

A $\{8, 9, 2, 3, 0, 6\}$

Solution

$\bar{x} = \frac{8 + 9 + 2 + 3 + 0 + 6}{6}$ Use the formula for mean.

$= \frac{28}{6} \approx 4.7$ Add the data values and divide by the number of data values.

The mean is about 4.7. ■

THINK ABOUT IT

Although a value of 0 does not increase the sum of the values in the numerator, it is still counted as a data value in the denominator.

B $\{100, 125, 111, 132, 151\}$

Solution

$\bar{x} = \frac{100 + 125 + 111 + 132 + 151}{5}$ Use the formula for mean.

$= \frac{619}{5} = 123.8$ Add the data values and divide by the number of data values.

The mean is 123.8. ■

C $\{-3, -3, -2, 0, 4, 6\}$

Solution

$\bar{x} = \frac{-3 + (-3) + (-2) + 0 + 4 + 6}{6}$ Use the formula for mean.

$= \frac{2}{6} \approx 0.3$ Add the data values and divide by the number of data values.

The mean is about 0.3. ■

Median

DEFINITION

The **median** is the middle value of a data set after the values have been ordered from least to greatest.

- In a set of data ordered from least to greatest with an odd number of values, the median is the center value.
- In a set of data ordered from least to greatest with an even number of values, the median is the average of the two center values.

To find the median for an odd number of values, such as 22, 42, 13, 12, and 8, do the following:

Step 1 Arrange the data in order from least to greatest.

8, 12, (13), 22, 42

Step 2 Find the middle number. The number 13 is in the middle. The median is 13.

To find the median for an even number of values, such as 6, 2, 0, 4, 7, and 12, do the following:

Step 1 Arrange the data in order from least to greatest.

0, 2, (4, 6), 7, 12

Step 2 Find the middle numbers. Both 4 and 6 are in the middle.

Step 3 Find the mean of 4 and 6.

$\frac{4 + 6}{2} = \frac{10}{2} = 5$ The median is 5.

THINK ABOUT IT

Both the mean and the median can be values that do not appear in the data set.

EXAMPLE 2 Find the median of the set of data.

A hourly wages: \$8.50, \$7.25, \$6.75, \$10.00, \$9.80

Solution Arrange the data in order.

\$6.75, \$7.25, \$8.50, \$9.80, \$10.00

There are five values, so the median is the third one.

The median wage is \$8.50. ■

B height of plant after 2 wk (in centimeters): 1.7, 1.0, 1.7, 2.4, 3.2, 1.8

Solution Arrange the data in order.

1.0, 1.7, 1.7, 1.8, 2.4, 3.2

$\frac{1.7 + 1.8}{2} = 1.75$ There are six values, so the median is the average of the third and fourth values.

The median height is 1.75 cm. ■

Mode

DEFINITION

The **mode** is the data value that occurs the most. If all values occur the same number of times, there is no mode. If two values appear the same number of times, there are two modes.

EXAMPLE 3 Find the mode.

A Find the mode of the values: 7, 4, 2, 2, 4, 7, 9, 7.

Solution The number 2 occurs twice, 4 occurs twice, 9 occurs once, and 7 occurs 3 times. The mode is 7. ■

B Test scores are 78, 65, 23, 78, and 42. What is the mode?

Solution The value 78 occurs twice. All other values occur once. The mode is 78. ■

Identifying the Best Measure of Center

The mean, median, and mode can all be used to describe a data set. Sometimes one measure of center might be a better description than another. For example, the mean, median, and mode of 22, 31, 40, 210, and 31 are as follows:

The mean is 66.8. The median is 31. The mode is 31.

Notice the mean is much different from the median and mode. When extreme values occur in a data set, they can pull the mean far away from most of the data values in the set. An extreme value is called an outlier. An **outlier** is a value that is far from the rest of the data.

EXAMPLE 4 Find the mean, median, and mode of the data set. State which measure or measures of center best represent the data.

$$\{2.8, 1.2, 1.5, 2.0, 2.4, 1.8\}$$

Solution

mean: $\frac{2.8 + 1.2 + 1.5 + 2.0 + 2.4 + 1.8}{6} = \frac{11.7}{6} = 1.95$

median: 1.2, 1.5, (1.8, 2.0), 2.4, 2.8; $\frac{1.8 + 2.0}{2} = 1.9$

Each value appears once. There is no mode.

The best measures of center are the mean and the median. ■

Application: Management

EXAMPLE 5 A manager is writing a report describing the salaries of the workers at the store. The salaries are listed.

{$20,000; $35,000; $28,000; $180,000; $20,000}

Find the mean, median, and mode of the data. Which measure or measures best represent the data? Explain your reasoning.

Solution The mean is $\frac{\$283{,}000}{5} = \$56{,}600$

The data in order are $20,000; $20,000; $28,000; $35,000; $180,000.

The median is $28,000.

The mode is $20,000.

The measure that best represents the data is the median. The mean is not a good measure because the outlier of $180,000 makes the mean a much greater number than the median. The mode is not a good measure because it is also the minimum value of the set. ■

Problem Set

Find the mean, median, and mode for the data set.

1. {96, 84, 92, 96, 100}
2. {74, 88, 79, 70, 74}
3. {4, 8, 9, 2, 7, 2}
4. {32, 29, 35, 25, 32, 22, 30}
5. {106, 106, 92, 96, 92, 104}
6. {50, 80, 60, 70, 60}
7. {48, 46, 44, 40, 42, 50}
8. {5, 3, 4, 2, 6}
9. {102, 102, 100, 94, 102}
10. $\{-6, -7, -2, -4, -1\}$
11. {1, 1, 0, 2, 1, 0}
12. {1.4, 1.6, 1.0, 2.3, 1.4}
13. $\{-5, -2, 3, 7, 2, -4, -1, 0\}$
14. {422, 350, 401, 376}
15. **Challenge** $\left\{\frac{1}{2}, \frac{1}{4}, \frac{3}{4}, \frac{5}{8}, \frac{1}{2}\right\}$
16. **Challenge** $\left\{3\frac{1}{3}, 2\frac{1}{4}, \frac{5}{12}, 5\frac{1}{6}, 1\frac{1}{4}\right\}$

State the best measure or measures of center to use for the data set. Explain your reasoning.

17. {4, 8, 6, 5, 32, 1}

18. {1, 1, 3, 3, 4, 1, 3, 4}

19. {22, 27, 32, 45, 36, 25}

20. {102, 105, 233, 100, 110}

21. {1, 1, 7, 1, 1, 1, 1, 1, 1}

22. {14, 19, 20, 28, 13, 10, 25}

23. {0, 0, 4, 2, 0, 1, 3, 2, 4}

24. {2, 6, 1, 9, 11, 67}

25. {5, 5, 15, 20, 14, 21}

26. {62, 75, 53, 81}

27. {5.6, 4.2, 3.1, 4.8, 4.2, 3.0}

28. {2.3, 0.1, 3.8, 1.7, 2.9}

Quiz scores for several classes are shown in the table.

29. Which class has the highest mean?

30. Which class has the highest median?

31. Which class has the highest mode?

Class A	Class B	Class C
15	10	13
18	15	14
19	19	20
16	19	19
16	20	12

Solve.

32. A weather forecaster kept track of the low temperature for five consecutive days. The temperatures (in degrees Celsius) are −5, 3, −3, 0, and −1. What is the mean low temperature?

33. A biologist listed the weights of several beetles. The weights are shown in the table. What is the median weight of the beetles?

Weight (oz)	2.1	2.8	1.7	1.5	3.0
	2.0	1.9	1.2	1.8	1.1

34. Students conducted a survey of the cost of shoes at different stores. They noticed that one pair of shoes cost a lot more than the other pairs. The data are shown.

cost of shoes with outlier: $28, $30, $240, $27, $24

cost of shoes without outlier: $28, $30, $27, $24

(a) Find the mean and median of the data for both sets of data.

(b) For which set were the mean and median close together? For which set were the mean and median far apart?

(c) What can be said if the mean and median of a set of data are far apart?

35. The test scores for Class A have a mean of 85 and a median of 85. Class B test scores have a mean of 63 and a median of 85. Which class most likely has an outlier? Explain.

36. **Challenge** Julie kept track of her test scores. The first four tests had scores of 82, 95, 88, and 79. What was the score on the fifth test if Julie had a mean test score of 87?

37. **Challenge** Write a set of five different numbers that have a mean and median of 3.

38. **Challenge** John needs a mean test score of 90 or above to get an A in a class. There are six tests total. The maximum score on any test is 100. The scores on the first five tests are 85, 100, 75, 82, and 90. Is it possible for John to get an A in the class? Show your work.

Measures of Variability

Measures of variation show the spread in a set of data.

DEFINITIONS

An **absolute deviation** is the absolute value of the difference between a data value and the mean. The **mean absolute deviation**, or MAD, is the mean of all the absolute deviations.

DID YOU KNOW?

There are other measures of variability besides the mean absolute deviation, but they often involve more complex calculations than the MAD.

To find the MAD of a set of data, first calculate the absolute deviation of each data value in the data set. Then add all the absolute deviations and divide by the number of data values.

EXAMPLE 1 Find the mean absolute deviation of the data.

A $\{6, 8, 11, 13, 17\}$

Solution Find the mean of the data.

$$\frac{6 + 8 + 11 + 13 + 17}{5} = \frac{55}{5} = 11$$

Calculate the absolute deviation for each data value and add.

$$\begin{aligned}&|6 - 11| + |8 - 11| + |11 - 11| + |13 - 11| + |17 - 11|\\&= |-5| + |-3| + |0| + |2| + |6|\\&= 5 + 3 + 0 + 2 + 6\\&= 16\end{aligned}$$

Divide the sum by the number of data values.

$$\frac{16}{5} = 3.2$$

The mean absolute deviation of the data set is 3.2. ■

B $\{3.1, 14.6, 19.7, 31.5, 37.8, 43.2\}$

Solution Find the mean of the data.

$$\frac{3.1 + 14.6 + 19.7 + 31.5 + 37.8 + 43.2}{6} = \frac{149.9}{6} = 24.9833\ldots \approx 25$$

Calculate the absolute deviation for each data value and add.

$$\begin{aligned}&|3.1 - 25| + |14.6 - 25| + |19.7 - 25| + |31.5 - 25| + |37.8 - 25| \\ &\quad + |43.2 - 25| \\ &= |-21.9| + |-10.4| + |-5.3| + |6.5| + |12.8| + |18.2| \\ &= 21.9 + 10.4 + 5.3 + 6.5 + 12.8 + 18.2 \\ &= 75.1\end{aligned}$$

Divide the sum by the number of data values.

$$\frac{75.1}{6} = 12.51666\ldots \approx 12.5$$

The mean absolute deviation of the data set is about 12.5. ■

> **TIP**
>
> For large data sets, you should use a calculator to find the mean absolute deviation.

Application: Quiz Scores

EXAMPLE 2 A teacher divided a group of 16 students into two groups of 8 students each. She recorded each student's score on a quiz.

Group 1: 87, 88, 96, 91, 78, 90, 83, 95

Group 2: 95, 80, 87, 76, 89, 91, 82, 96

A Calculate the MAD of each group's quiz scores.

Solution

Group 1 Calculate the mean of the quiz scores.

$$\frac{87 + 88 + 96 + 91 + 78 + 90 + 83 + 95}{8} = \frac{708}{8} = 88.5$$

Add the absolute deviations and divide the sum by the number of data items.

$$\begin{aligned}&|87 - 88.5| + |88 - 88.5| + |96 - 88.5| + |91 - 88.5| + |78 - 88.5| \\ &\quad + |90 - 88.5| + |83 - 88.5| + |95 - 88.5| \\ &= |-1.5| + |-0.5| + |7.5| + |2.5| + |-10.5| + |1.5| + |-5.5| + |6.5| \\ &= 1.5 + 0.5 + 7.5 + 2.5 + 10.5 + 1.5 + 5.5 + 6.5 = 36\end{aligned}$$

$$\frac{36}{8} = 4.5$$

> **THINK ABOUT IT**
>
> A data set is not always ordered from least to greatest. However, the mean absolute deviation is the same whether the data are ordered or unordered.

Group 2 Calculate the mean of the quiz scores.

$$\frac{95 + 80 + 87 + 76 + 89 + 91 + 82 + 96}{8} = \frac{696}{8} = 87$$

Add the absolute deviations and divide the sum by the number of data items.

$$\begin{aligned}&|95 - 87| + |80 - 87| + |87 - 87| + |76 - 87| + |89 - 87| + |91 - 87| \\ &\qquad + |82 - 87| + |96 - 87| \\ &= |8| + |-7| + |0| + |-11| + |2| + |4| + |-5| + |9| \\ &= 8 + 7 + 0 + 11 + 2 + 4 + 5 + 9 = 46\end{aligned}$$

$$\frac{46}{8} = 5.75$$

The MAD of Group 1's quiz scores is 4.5. The MAD of Group 2's quiz scores is 5.75. ■

B Which group has the larger variation in their quiz scores? Explain your reasoning.

Solution Group 2 has the larger variation in their quiz scores. The MAD is a measure of the variation, or spread, of a set of data. Because the MAD of Group 2's scores, 5.75, is larger than the MAD of Group 1's scores, 4.5, Group 2 has the larger variation in their quiz scores. ■

Application: Manufacturing

EXAMPLE 3 A hardware manufacturer selects 9 bolts from a batch of newly made bolts. The bolt widths are 5.7, 5.8, 5.8, 5.9, 6, 6, 6, 6, and 6.1 mm.

A Find the MAD of the bolt widths. Round to the nearest hundredth.

Solution Determine the mean bolt width.

$$\frac{5.7 + 5.8 + 5.8 + 5.9 + 6 + 6 + 6 + 6 + 6.1}{9} = \frac{53.3}{9} = 5.9222\ldots \approx 5.9$$

Calculate the MAD.

$$\begin{aligned}&|5.7 - 5.9| + |5.8 - 5.9| + |5.8 - 5.9| + |5.9 - 5.9| + |6 - 5.9| \\ &\qquad + |6 - 5.9| + |6 - 5.9| + |6 - 5.9| + |6.1 - 5.9| \\ &= |-0.2| + |-0.1| + |-0.1| + |0| + |0.1| + |0.1| + |0.1| + |0.1| + |0.2| \\ &= 0.2 + 0.1 + 0.1 + 0 + 0.1 + 0.1 + 0.1 + 0.1 + 0.2 = 1.0\end{aligned}$$

$$\frac{1.0}{9} = 0.111\ldots \approx 0.11$$

The MAD of the bolt widths is 0.11 mm. ■

B Explain what the value of the MAD represents.

Solution The MAD is a measure of the variation in bolt widths about their mean value of 5.9 mm. The larger the MAD, the more variation there would be in the width of the bolts manufactured. ■

Problem Set

Find the mean absolute deviation (MAD) of the data set. Round to the nearest tenth, if necessary.

1. $\{8, 11, 12, 17\}$
2. $\{3, 4, 9, 13, 16\}$
3. $\{21.5, 26.6, 25.8, 23.1, 20.1, 32.9\}$
4. $\{-4, 3, -2, 0, -7\}$
5. $\{4.2, 16.8, 25.6, 31.4, 36, 48.2, 53.6, 61\}$
6. $\left\{0, \frac{1}{4}, \frac{1}{4}, \frac{1}{4}, \frac{1}{2}, \frac{3}{4}, 1, 1\right\}$

Find the mean absolute deviation of the data set. Round to the nearest tenth, if necessary.

7. Manny kept track of the number of home runs he hit every year in high school.

   $\{11, 10, 17, 18\}$

8. Jayden's report card shows the points he received in each subject for the autumn term.

Subject	Total points
English	95
history	91
math	97
science	96
Spanish	91

9. A coach records the 100 m finish times, in seconds, for 8 runners in a race.

   $\{10.9, 11, 11, 11.2, 11.5, 11.6, 11.7, 12.3\}$

10. A scuba diver's watch shows his depth, in meters, every 5 min from the beginning to the end of his dive.

    $\{12, 17, 23, 24, 17, 15, 8, 0\}$

11. The temperature at noon was recorded over 1 wk.

Day	Temperature (°C)
Sunday	3
Monday	0
Tuesday	−4
Wednesday	−1
Thursday	2
Friday	5
Saturday	4

12. **Challenge** A biologist measured the length of a species of caterpillars. She organized the data in a stem-and-leaf plot.

3	6 6 7 9
4	1 4 5 8
5	2 2

Key: 3 | 6 = 3.6 cm

Solve.

13. The table shows the altitude of the four highest mountain peaks in Ecuador.

Peak	Altitude (m)
Chimborazo	6267
Cotopaxi	5897
Cayambe	5790
Antisana	5758

Juan estimates that the mean absolute deviation of the peaks' altitudes is 200 m. Calculate the mean absolute deviation and compare it to Juan's estimate.

14. Ingrid earned money over 6 wk for walking dogs. For each of the 6 wk, she earned \$66, \$68, \$59, \$74, \$70, and \$68.

    (a) What was the mean absolute deviation in the amount Ingrid earned over the 6 wk?

    (b) What does the value of the mean absolute deviation represent? Explain.

15. **Challenge** A set of data has a mean of 1 and MAD of 0. What can you conclude about the values of the data set?

Samples and Prediction

You can use information about part of a group to make predictions about the entire group. The way you choose a part of a group affects how useful your prediction about the whole group will be.

If a population is small, you can survey, or question, the entire population. However, if a population is large, such as every citizen in a certain state, it is more practical to survey a sample of the population.

DEFINITIONS

A **population** is a group of individuals or objects that you want information about. A **sample** is part of the population.

Identifying Bias and Possible Sources of Bias

For a sample to be useful, it must be representative of the population. A representative sample generally has the same characteristics as the population. For example, if most of a population is female, then most of the sample should be female.

DEFINITIONS

An **unbiased sample** is representative of the population. A **biased sample** is not representative of the population.

EXAMPLE 1 State whether the sample is likely to be biased. Identify possible sources of bias.

A Claire wants to know if the people in her neighborhood think that the speed limit on their street should be reduced. She asks the parents of the children she babysits.

Solution It is unlikely that everyone in the neighborhood is a parent, so the sample is probably not representative of the population. Parents are likely to think of their children's safety and request lower speed limits. The sample is likely to be biased. ■

B A boss wants to know if his employees would be interested in a company picnic. He prints an alphabetical list of all the employee names and asks every 10th person on the list.

Solution This sample is likely to be representative of all the employees, so it is likely to be unbiased. ■

C A reporter wants to know how many people in a town are interested in rock climbing. She goes to a sporting-goods store and asks every 10th person who exits.

Solution People who shop in a sporting-goods store are more likely to be interested in sports, such as rock climbing. The sample is likely to be biased. ■

D On a TV news program, viewers are asked to go to the program's website and tell whether they are opposed to a recent tax increase.

Solution People opposed to the tax increase are more likely to make the effort to record their opinions than people who are not opposed. Also, not all viewers will have access to the Internet. For these reasons, the sample is likely to be biased. ■

THINK ABOUT IT

Bias depends on the population you are working with. For instance, in Example 1C, if the reporter wanted to know how many patrons of that store are interested in rock climbing, this sampling method would not be bad.

Making Predictions About a Population

A prediction is an educated guess, or estimate. It is important to keep in mind the following points when making a prediction about a population:

- Estimates tend to become more accurate as the size of the sample increases. For example, an estimate based on a sample of 100 is likely to be better than an estimate based on a sample of 50.
- An estimate based on an unbiased sample is likely to be better than an estimate based on a biased sample.

REMEMBER

A biased sample does not represent the population well.

EXAMPLE 2 In a sample of 100 people at a stadium, 72 preferred Brand A mustard to Brand B mustard. Predict about how many of the estimated 62,000 people in the stadium would prefer Brand A mustard.

Solution Write and solve a proportion.

$\frac{x}{62{,}000} = \frac{72}{100}$ Write a proportion.

$100x = 4{,}464{,}000$ Cross multiply.

$x = 44{,}640$ Divide both sides by 100.

Based on the sample, about 44,640 people in the stadium would prefer Brand A. ■

TIP

In Example 2, you could simplify the fraction before cross multiplying.

EXAMPLE 3 A study showed that 14% of the plants randomly sampled in a field were damaged by pests. Predict how many of the 750 plants from that field will show damage by pests.

Solution Find 14% of 750.

$14\% \text{ of } 750 = 14\% \cdot 750$ The word *of* indicates multiplication.

$= 0.14 \cdot 750$ Write the percent as a decimal.

$= 105$ Multiply.

Based on the study, about 105 plants will show damage by pests. ■

Problem Set

State whether the sample is likely to be biased. Identify possible sources of bias.

1. A magazine editor wants to know what percent of people ski. She chooses people randomly on a winter weekend and calls them at home to ask them.
2. To find out what percent of people approve of plans to convert a meadow into a shopping mall, a reporter goes to a nearby mall and asks every fifth person he sees.
3. An apartment manager is giving away coupons for $50 off a month's rent. He writes each apartment number on a slip of paper, puts the paper slips into a box, mixes them up, and picks 10 slips of paper without looking.
4. The question, "About how many hours per week do you spend on the Internet?" appears on a website. People respond by clicking the link and typing their answer.
5. At a voting site, a surveyor asks every 15th voter who exits the building whether he or she voted *Yes* or *No* on a proposed bill.
6. To find out if people think a new traffic light is needed at a certain intersection in a small town, surveys are mailed to 100 homes distributed randomly throughout the town. People are asked to mark *Yes* or *No* and send the survey back within 1 wk.
7. At a baseball game, seat numbers are randomly chosen. People sitting in those seats are surveyed about raising ticket prices 10% to make improvements to the stadium.
8. At a soccer game, people sitting in the first 15 rows are surveyed about raising all ticket prices by $2 to make improvements to the stadium.
9. The manager at the new radio station in town wants to know what kind of music is popular in the area. She surveys people at random as they exit a supermarket between noon and 2 p.m. on a Monday.
10. A quality control worker needs to check samples of the items being produced on an assembly line to see if the machines are working properly. She checks the first 10 items produced on the assembly line every morning.
11. A quality control worker checks 5 randomly selected items produced during each hour on an assembly line.
12. To learn about opinions of people living in the United States, a reporter randomly chooses 10 cross-country airplane flights and questions people sitting in every 10th seat.

Solve.

13. In an unbiased sample of 320 state residents, 115 answered *Yes* when asked if they like the current design on the state's license plate.
    - **(a)** Predict how many people in a town of 14,280 people in that state would like the current design on the license plate.
    - **(b)** Predict how many people in a city of 245,600 people in that state would not like the current design on the license plate.
14. A study showed that 3% of the potatoes randomly sampled did not meet standards for making potato chips. Any potato that does not meet standards will not be used.
    - **(a)** A load of potatoes contains approximately 1600 potatoes. About how many of those will not be used to make potato chips?
    - **(b)** A quality control manager discarded about 75 potatoes from a load. Predict how many potatoes were in the load.

15. In a survey, approximately 2 out of every 3 people said the current mayor was doing a good job.

(a) If 400 people were surveyed, about how many said the mayor was doing a good job?

(b) Predict how many of 2000 people would say the mayor is doing a good job.

16. A drink vendor at a flea market knows that about 20% of his customers in the past have preferred no ice in their drinks.

(a) On a certain weekend, about 15,000 customers are expected at the market. Past experience shows that about 8% of the customers will stop at the vendor's stall for a drink. About how many of those people will prefer ice in their drinks?

(b) The vendor uses about one-fifth pound of ice per drink. Use your answer for Part (a) to find how many pounds of ice the vendor should have on hand that weekend.

17. **Challenge** Identify a potential source of bias and suggest a change that can be made to minimize that bias.

(a) A restaurant owner wants to know what percent of her customers like a new hot and spicy sauce. One evening, she asks all the customers who order entrées with that sauce.

(b) An insulation contractor wants to know how much energy is used by residents in a town. He selects random odd-numbered houses on random streets in the town to survey.

(c) A biologist collects samples of lake water by standing at one spot of the lake and filling test tubes.

18. **Challenge** To estimate a population under certain conditions, you can use the following proportion:

$$\frac{\text{number tagged on 2nd visit}}{\text{number found on 2nd visit}} = \frac{\text{number tagged on 1st visit}}{\text{total number in population}}$$

(a) A biologist visits a lake and tags 45 fish. A week later, he visits the same lake and finds 30 fish, of which 12 are tagged. Estimate the total number of fish in the lake.

(b) A researcher visits a park and tags 12 deer. Two weeks later, she visits the same park and finds 8 deer, of which 3 are tagged. Estimate the number of deer in the park.

Drawing Inferences

You can draw inferences about a population from a random sample.

Drawing Inferences from a Single Sample

You can draw inferences from a single random sample of a population. Perform calculations on the sample data and then assume that the results of the calculation extend to the whole population. For example, to estimate the mean of a population, calculate the mean of the randomly sampled data.

DID YOU KNOW?

An **inference** is a conclusion reached from facts, evidence, and reasoning.

EXAMPLE 1 A survey was taken of Belleville's 6741 voters. Two hundred voters were selected at random and asked which candidate for mayor they preferred.

Candidate	Baker	Jimenez	Washington
Number of voters	33	59	108

A candidate with more than 50% of the vote will win the election for mayor. What can you infer about who will win the election?

REMEMBER

Estimates tend to become more accurate as the size of the sample increases.

Solution In the survey, voters preferred Washington (108 voters out of 200 surveyed). The percent equivalent of this ratio is

$$\frac{108}{200} \cdot 100\% = 0.54 \cdot 100\% = 54\%.$$

Because the survey was a random sample, its results represent the preference of the entire population of Belleville's voters. Therefore, you can infer that Washington will win with about 54% of the vote. ■

EXAMPLE 2 In a school population of 568 students, Janelle selected 20 students at random. She asked each of them how many pets he or she had at home. Janelle recorded the results in a table.

Number of pets	Number of Students
0	5
1	7
2	4
3	2
4	1
5	1

A Estimate the mean number of pets in the 568 students' homes.

Solution Calculate the mean using the sample data.

$$\frac{\overbrace{(0 + \ldots + 0)}^{5} + \overbrace{(1 + \ldots + 1)}^{7} + \overbrace{(2 + \ldots + 2)}^{4} + (3 + 3) + 4 + 5}{20}$$

$$= \frac{5(0) + 7(1) + 4(2) + 6 + 4 + 5}{20}$$

$$= \frac{0 + 7 + 8 + 6 + 4 + 5}{20} = \frac{30}{20} = 1.5$$

The estimated mean number of pets in students' homes is 1.5. ■

B Estimate the mean absolute deviation in the number of pets in the 568 students' homes.

Solution Calculate the mean absolute deviation using the sample data.

$$\frac{5|0 - 1.5| + 7|1 - 1.5| + 4|2 - 1.5| + 2|3 - 1.5| + |4 - 1.5| + |5 - 1.5|}{20}$$

$$= \frac{5|-1.5| + 7|-0.5| + 4|0.5| + 2|1.5| + |2.5| + |3.5|}{20}$$

$$= \frac{5(1.5) + 7(0.5) + 4(0.5) + 2(1.5) + 2.5 + 3.5}{20}$$

$$= \frac{7.5 + 3.5 + 2 + 3 + 2.5 + 3.5}{20} = \frac{22}{20} = 1.1$$

The estimated mean absolute deviation of pets in students' homes is 1.1. ■

REMEMBER

A frequency table shows the number of times a data value occurs.

Q & A

Q What are the median and mode of the data set?

A median = 1.5, mode = 1

Drawing Inferences from Multiple Samples

You can draw multiple random samples from a population to check whether the sample selection process is biased. The samples whose results agree are more likely to be representative of the population. The sample whose results differ from the other samples is likely to be biased and thus not representative of the population.

REMEMBER

A sample is biased if some items or individuals in a population are favored over others.

BY THE WAY

Businesses often conduct surveys of their customers to better understand their customers' favorite products and services.

EXAMPLE 3 A restaurant took four separate samples of its customers to find out which kind of salad they preferred. In each sample, 50 customers were selected at random and their salad preference recorded.

Sample	Caesar	fruit	house
1	14	14	22
2	26	18	6
3	13	16	21
4	16	14	20

A According to each sample, what can the restaurant infer about which salad customers prefer?

Solution According to Samples 1, 3, and 4, the restaurant can infer that its customers prefer the house salad over either the Caesar salad or the fruit salad. However, according to Sample 2, the customers seem to prefer the Caesar salad over either the fruit salad or the house salad. ■

B What could explain why the results from Sample 2 differ from the other samples? What could the restaurant do to handle this discrepancy?

Solution The sampling process used to collect Sample 2 could be different from the sampling process used to collect Samples 1, 3, and 4. Sample 2 could be biased due to a poor sampling technique.

Because the results from Samples 1, 3, and 4 agree, the restaurant could infer that those results represent customers' salad preference. The restaurant could also infer that the results from Sample 2 are not representative, so Sample 2 could be ignored. ■

Problem Set

Each data set is a random sample drawn from a larger population. For each sample:

(a) Create a frequency table.

(b) Estimate the mean of the population.

(c) Estimate the MAD (mean absolute deviation) of the population.

1. $\{50, 50, 51, 51, 51, 51, 52, 52\}$
2. $\{3, 4, 4, 5, 5, 6, 6, 6, 7, 8, 8, 10\}$
3. $\{76, 77, 80, 83, 79, 79, 76, 76, 82, 82\}$
4. $\{1, 2, -2, -1, 0, 3, -2, 1, 2, -1, 1, 4, 3, 3, 1\}$
5. $\{92, 96, 96, 94, 96, 94, 94, 95, 95, 93, 95, 93, 94, 96\}$
6. **Challenge** $\left\{0, \frac{1}{4}, \frac{1}{2}, 0, \frac{1}{4}, \frac{1}{2}, \frac{1}{4}, \frac{1}{4}, 0, \frac{1}{2}\right\}$

Each study has multiple samples from a population. For each study:

(a) State whether one or more samples are likely to be biased.

(b) If a sample is biased, list two possible sources for the bias.

7. A farmer took four samples of 20 cornstalks per sample. He counted the ears of corn on each stalk and recorded the results in a table.

Number of ears/ stalk	Sample			
	1	2	3	4
0	1	2	1	2
1	17	15	11	16
2	2	3	8	2

8. Dr. Gomes selected 50 of her patients at random and asked each one whether he or she had ever had an operation. She repeated this survey 2 more times.

Ever had an operation?	Survey		
	1	2	3
Yes	37	34	35
No	13	16	15

9. Deepika selected 25 classmates at random and recorded their heights in a frequency table. She conducted five such surveys in all.

Height (m)	Survey				
	1	2	3	4	5
1.50 ≤	2	6	2	3	1
1.51–1.60	6	13	7	6	3
1.61–1.70	10	4	9	9	5
1.71–1.80	5	1	4	5	10
≥1.81	2	1	3	2	6

10. **Challenge** An animal shelter chose 75 people who had adopted a pet and recorded each adopter's age. The shelter calculated the mean and MAD of each sample. There were four samples in all.

Sample 1: mean = 36.7, MAD = 11.3

Sample 2: mean = 28.9, MAD = 10.6

Sample 3: mean = 30.1, MAD = 11.2

Sample 4: mean = 29.4, MAD = 9.8

Solve.

11. On Monday, over 500 people attended a county fair. Fifteen of the people who attended the fair that day were selected at random and asked how many rides they went on that day. The line plot shows the results of the survey.

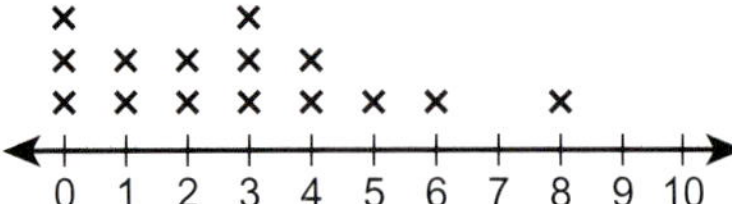

Estimate the mean number of rides that a person who attended the fair went on that day.

12. An athletic shoe company selected 80 of its customers at random and asked each person which brand of athletic shoe he or she preferred.

Brand	Fleet	Winner's Circle	Agora
Number of customers	17	25	38

(a) For each brand, calculate the percent of customers sampled who prefer that brand.

(b) Which brand of athletic shoe is most likely preferred by all of the store's customers? Explain.

13. A mail carrier delivered mail to 327 houses a day. The mail carrier picked 12 houses at random, and then counted and recorded the number of pieces of mail delivered to each of those 12 houses.

{7, 6, 4, 5, 7, 0, 4, 2, 10, 5, 4, 7}

(a) Which is a better measure of the number of pieces of mail received by a house that day—the mean, median, or mode?

(b) What is the number of pieces of mail received by a house that day? Why?

14. **Challenge** A store sells three models of digital music players. In one year, more than 1000 digital music players were purchased. The store selected 20 of these purchases at random and recorded the sale price.

Model	**Number sold**	**Sale price**
Basic	6	$60
Sport	10	$90
Ultimate	4	$110

(a) Calculate the mean and MAD of the sample. Round to the nearest whole dollar.

(b) Estimate the average price and the variation in this price that the store's customers paid for a digital music player. Explain.

Comparing Distributions

You can describe the overlap between two data sets visually and numerically.

Using Distributions to Determine Data Set Overlap

DEFINITION

The **distribution** of a data set is the shape of the plotted data over the range of the data set's values.

SIMILAR DISTRIBUTIONS

Two data sets' distributions are similar if both their central values are approximately equal and their spreads are approximately equal.

You can compare two data sets by

- Inspecting their distributions visually, looking for the amount they overlap.
- Calculating the difference in their means and comparing this difference to the mean absolute deviation.

EXAMPLE 1 Two teams of 12 people each played golf. Each team's scores were recorded and displayed in a line plot.

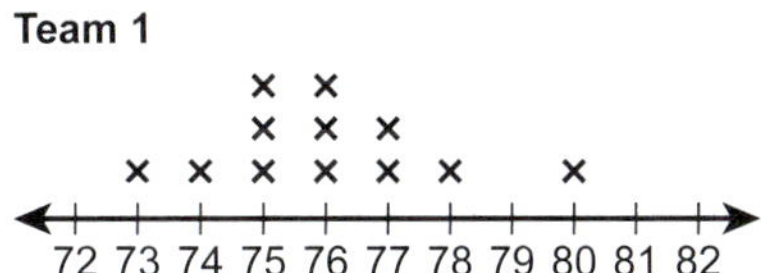

Team 2

72 73 74 75 76 77 78 79 80 81 82

A Estimate the center of each data set visually.

Solution The center of Team 1's score distribution is about 76. The center of Team 2's score distribution is about 77. ■

> **TIP**
> To compare the overlap of two distributions best, line the plots up vertically so that their labels match.

B Describe the degree of overlap of the two data sets in terms of their centers and variability.

Solution Both teams have about the same mean score, around 76 to 77. The spread of the data is about the same for both data sets. The degree of overlap of the two data sets is high. ■

EXAMPLE 2 After a hailstorm, a meteorologist recorded the diameters, in millimeters, of hailstones at two different sites.

Site 1: $\{4, 6, 7, 5, 7, 5, 5, 6, 6, 9\}$

Site 2: $\{8, 11, 9, 10, 14, 8, 11, 10, 9, 10\}$

A Create a line plot for each data set. Estimate the center of each data set visually.

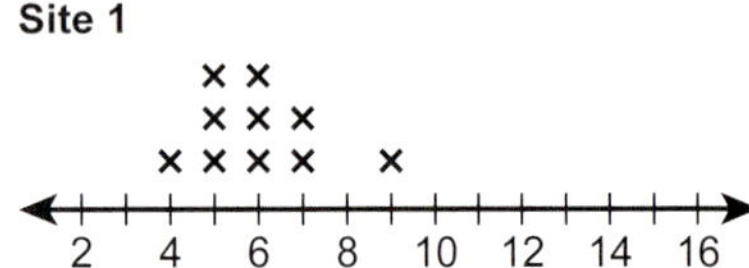

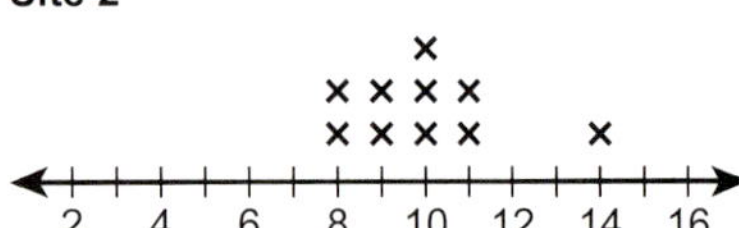

Solution The center of Site 1's score distribution is about 6 mm. The center of Site 2's score distribution is about 10 mm. ■

B Calculate the mean and MAD of each data set.

Solution

Site 1

mean: $\frac{4 + 3(5) + 3(6) + 2(7) + 9}{10} = \frac{4 + 15 + 18 + 14 + 9}{10} = \frac{60}{10} = 6$

MAD: $\frac{|4 - 6| + 3|5 - 6| + 3|6 - 6| + 2|7 - 6| + |9 - 6|}{10}$

$= \frac{|-2| + 3|-1| + 3|0| + 2|1| + |3|}{10} = \frac{10}{10} = 1$

The mean diameter is 6 mm, and the mean absolute deviation is 1 mm.

Q & A

Q What is the median of each distribution?

A Site 1: median $= 6$

Site 2: median $= 10$

Site 2

mean: $\dfrac{2(8) + 2(9) + 3(10) + 2(11) + 14}{10} = \dfrac{16 + 18 + 30 + 22 + 14}{10} = \dfrac{100}{10} = 10$

MAD: $\dfrac{2|8 - 10| + 2|9 - 10| + 3|10 - 10| + 2|11 - 10| + |14 - 10|}{10}$

$= \dfrac{2|-2| + 2|-1| + 3|0| + 2|1| + |4|}{10} = \dfrac{12}{10} = 1.2$

The mean diameter is 10 mm, and the mean absolute deviation is 1.2 mm. ■

C Compare the estimated mean and the MAD of the two data sets. What does this comparison say about the degree of overlap of the two data sets' distributions?

Solution The difference in the two means is $10 - 6 = 4$. This difference is much larger than the spread of hailstone diameters at either site, at least 3 times larger than either of the MAD values. The degree of overlap between the two distributions is low. ■

Problem Set

For each pair of line plots:

(a) Estimate the center of each data set visually.

(b) Describe the overlap of the two data sets as high, moderate, low, or none.

1. **Data Set 1**

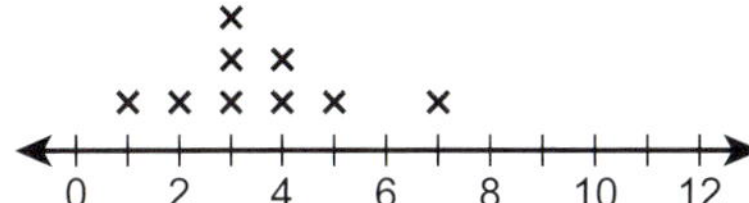

Data Set 2

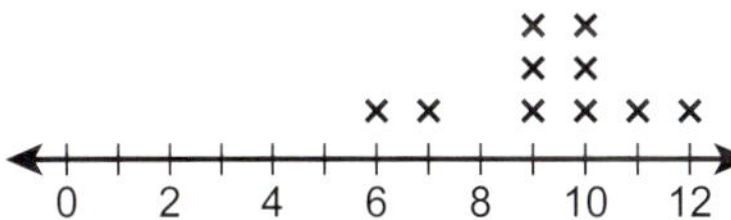

2. **Data Set 1**

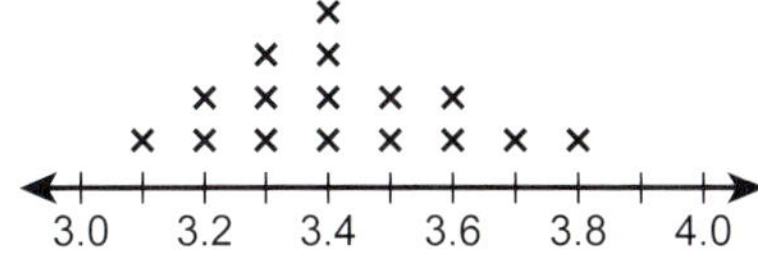

Data Set 2

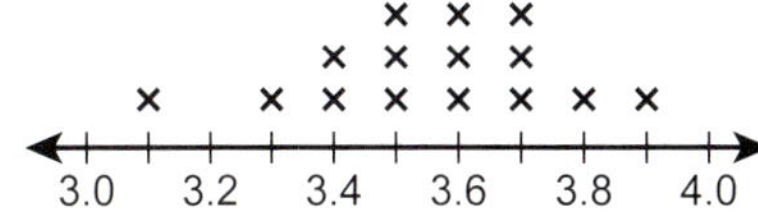

3. **Data Set 1**

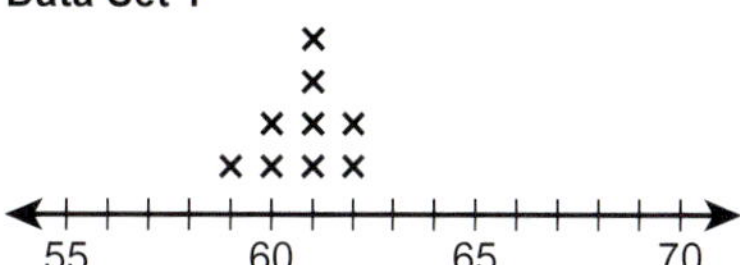

Data Set 2

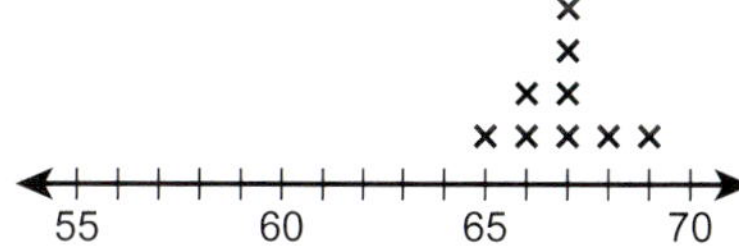

4. **Data Set 1**

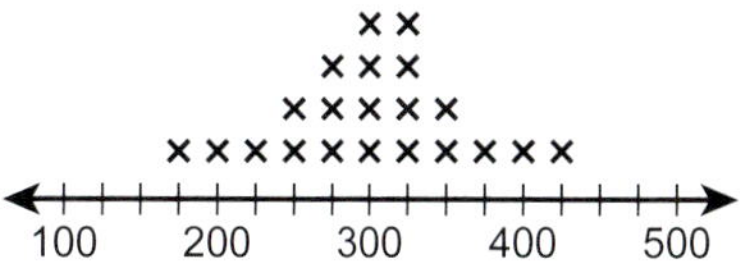

Data Set 2

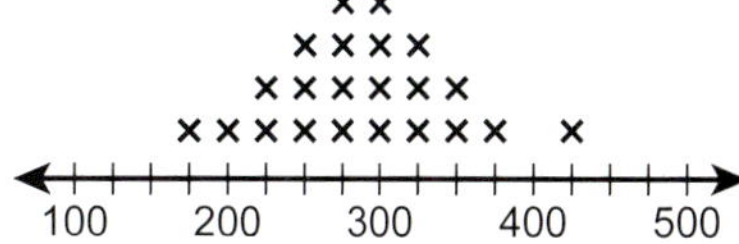

For each pair of data sets:

(a) Create a line plot for each data set.
(b) Calculate the mean of each data set.
(c) Calculate the MAD of each data set.
(d) Use the mean and MAD to describe the degree of overlap between the data sets.

5. the noon temperature in degrees Celsius at various locations around each of two cities

Rockville: {12, 14, 16, 16, 17, 17, 20}

Center City: {16, 16, 17, 17, 19, 20, 21}

6. the number of points scored by each player on two basketball teams

Jaguars: {2, 2, 3, 5, 7, 9, 9, 10, 11, 12}

Bears: {2, 3, 6, 7, 11, 11, 13, 14, 15, 18}

7. the number of times two different songs were downloaded in 1 h, in six 1 h periods

Song 1: {140, 127, 129, 124, 111, 125}

Song 2: {117, 102, 107, 105, 109, 90}

8. the number of pieces of fruit filling a 1 pt container

grapes: {29, 34, 36, 33, 34, 31, 35, 32}

raspberries: {37, 45, 43, 41, 41, 40, 43, 38}

9. a random sample of the number of puppies in a litter for two different breeds of dog

beagle: {4, 4, 6, 6, 7, 7, 8, 8, 9, 11}

border collie: {2, 2, 4, 4, 5, 6, 6, 7, 9, 10}

10. twelve words chosen at random from each of two poems and the word lengths recorded

Poem 1: {3, 4, 3, 3, 2, 5, 6, 7, 5, 1, 7, 8}

Poem 2: {6, 4, 5, 5, 6, 2, 3, 3, 8, 2, 6, 10}

Solve.

11. Kevin measured the diameter of sand grains, in millimeters, at two beaches.

Sandy Cay: {0.2, 0.5, 0.6, 0.4, 0.5, 0.3, 0.4, 0.3}

Crab Beach: {0.2, 0.3, 0.4, 0.3, 0.2, 0.3, 0.3, 0.4}

(a) Create a line plot for each data set.

(b) Find the mean and MAD of each data set.

(c) Compare the difference between the two means to the MAD of the data sets. What does this say about the degree of overlap of the two data sets' distributions?

12. **Challenge** Create three different data sets of 5 items, each with a mean of 2.

(a) Plot each data set.

(b) Describe the overlap of the two data sets in terms of their centers and variability.

(c) Calculate the mean and MAD of each data set.

Using Statistical Measures

You can determine whether two distributions are similar by comparing their means numerically.

Comparing Two Distributions

MEANS-TO-MAD RATIO

$$\frac{|\overline{X}_1 - \overline{X}_2|}{\text{MAD}_{\text{larger}}}$$

You can use the means-to-MAD ratio to describe the similarity of two distributions. Divide the positive difference in the means by the larger of the two MAD values. If this ratio is 1or less, the two distributions are similar. If this ratio is between 1 and 2.5, the two distributions are somewhat similar. If this ratio is greater than 2.5, the two distributions are different.

EXAMPLE 1 Kim and Lisa had a friendly competition to determine who is better at a card game. They played 10 games of cards and recorded their scores. The person with the highest score wins.

Game	1	2	3	4	5	6	7	8	9	10
Kim	−2	0	2	−1	0	3	0	1	8	−1
Lisa	−2	7	−1	2	0	1	3	−1	0	1

A Create a line plot for each data set.

Solution

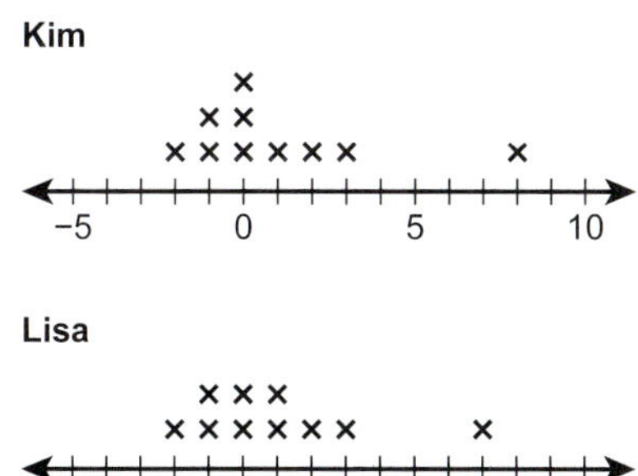

TIP

When creating a line plot, put the data in order first, and then plot the data. Check the correctness of your plot by comparing the ordered data values against the plot.

B Find the mean and MAD of each data set.

Solution

Kim

mean: $\frac{(-2) + 2(-1) + 3(0) + 1 + 2 + 3 + 8}{10} = \frac{10}{10} = 1$

MAD: $\frac{|-2 - 1| + 2|-1 - 1| + 3|0 - 1| + |1 - 1| + |2 - 1| + |3 - 1| + |8 - 1|}{10}$

$= \frac{|-3| + 2|-2| + 3|-1| + |0| + |1| + |2| + |7|}{10} = \frac{20}{10} = 2$

Kim's mean score is 1, with a MAD of 2.

Lisa

mean: $\frac{(-2) + 2(-1) + 2(0) + 2(1) + 2 + 3 + 7}{10} = \frac{10}{10} = 1$

MAD: $\frac{|-2 - 1| + 2|-1 - 1| + 2|0 - 1| + 2|1 - 1| + |2 - 1| + |3 - 1| + |7 - 1|}{10}$

$= \frac{|-3| + 2|-2| + 2|-1| + 2|0| + |1| + |2| + |6|}{10} = \frac{18}{10} = 1.8$

Lisa's mean score is 1, with a MAD of 2. ■

C Can you infer that one player is better than the other? Why or why not?

Solution The difference in the two data sets' means is $1 - 1 = 0$. The difference in their mean scores is less than 1. With a means-to-MAD ratio of $\frac{0}{2} = 0$, you can conclude that both data sets have similar distributions. Therefore, you cannot infer that Kim or Lisa is the better player. ■

Comparing Two Populations from Samples

In some situations, it is not easy or even possible to collect data on every member in a population. Instead, you can compare two populations by obtaining samples from the populations and calculating the means-to-MAD ratio from the sample data.

REMEMBER

The larger the sample size, the better the sample represents the entire population.

EXAMPLE 2 An orchard has two types of red apples. The orchard owner wants to know which variety of red apple produces bigger fruit. The farmer selects 9 apples at random from each variety and measures the circumference, in centimeters, of each apple.

Variety A: {24, 26, 24, 25, 23, 23, 25, 24, 22}

Variety B: {26, 27, 28, 30, 24, 26, 27, 27, 28}

A Create a line plot for each data set.

Solution

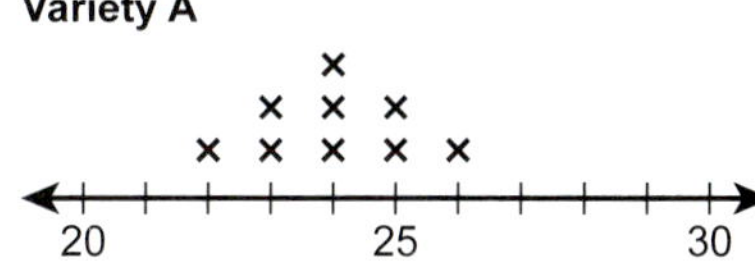

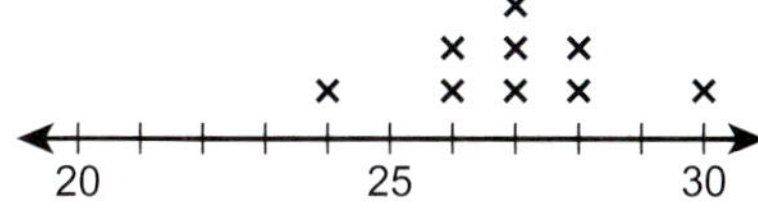

DID YOU KNOW?

To calculate the mean and MAD of a large data set, you can use computer software such as a spreadsheet or database program.

B Find the mean and MAD of each data set.

Solution

Variety A

mean: $\frac{22 + 2(23) + 3(24) + 2(25) + 26}{9} = \frac{216}{9} = 24$

MAD: $\frac{|22 - 24| + 2|23 - 24| + 3|24 - 24| + 2|25 - 24| + |26 - 24|}{9}$

$= \frac{|-2| + 2|-1| + 3|0| + 2|1| + |2|}{9} = \frac{8}{9} \approx 0.9$

Variety A's mean circumference is 24 cm, with a MAD of 0.9 cm.

Variety B

mean: $\frac{24 + 2(26) + 3(27) + 2(28) + 30}{9} = \frac{243}{9} = 27$

MAD: $\frac{|24 - 27| + 2|26 - 27| + 3|27 - 27| + 2|28 - 27| + |30 - 27|}{9}$

$= \frac{|-3| + 2|-1| + 3|0| + 2|1| + |3|}{9} = \frac{10}{9} \approx 1.1$

Variety B's mean circumference is 27 cm, with a MAD of 1.1 cm.

C Can you infer that one variety of apples is larger than the other? Why or why not?

Solution Variety A's mean circumference is 24 cm, and Variety B's mean circumference is 27 cm, 3 cm larger. The positive difference in the means is $27 - 24 = 3$. With a means-to-MAD ratio of $\frac{3}{1.1} \approx 3$, you can conclude that their distributions are different. You can infer that Variety B apples are larger than Variety A apples.

Problem Set

For each problem:

(a) Calculate the mean and MAD of each data set. Round to the nearest tenth, if necessary.

(b) Calculate the means-to-MAD ratio. Round to the nearest tenth, if necessary.

1. {0, 2, 4, 6, 8, 10}

   {1, 3, 5, 7, 9, 11}

2. {4, 4, 4, 6, 7, 7, 8, 8}

   {6, 8, 8, 8, 8, 8, 8, 10}

3. {25, 26, 27, 27, 25, 27, 28, 26, 29, 30}

   {20, 28, 26, 26, 30, 24, 25, 26, 28, 27}

4. {4, −2, 0, 5, −3, −6, 2}

   {−10, 2, 7, 9, −5, −3, 0}

5. {63, 64, 59, 66, 64, 63, 62, 65, 61}

   {74, 72, 74, 74, 75, 77, 74, 74, 72}

6. {18, 19, 20, 20.5, 21, 21.5, 21.5, 22.5}

   {27, 28.5, 31, 32.5, 34, 35.5, 37, 38.5}

For each problem:

(a) Create a line plot for each data set.

(b) Calculate the means-to-MAD ratio.

(c) Use the value of the ratio to answer the question.

7. At lunchtime, Alyssa selected 10 second-year and 10 third-year students at random and asked each how many basketball games he or she had attended that season. Can Alyssa conclude that second-year students were more likely than third-year students to attend a basketball game?

   Second year: {6, 4, 6, 7, 0, 1, 8, 2, 6, 8}

   Third year: {0, 6, 1, 7, 0, 4, 8, 1, 4, 9}

8. Mr. Higgins recorded the temperature, in degrees Celsius, at six locations in a city at noon on Thursday and the same six locations at noon on Friday. Can Mr. Higgins say that the noon temperature in the city was higher on Thursday or Friday?

   Thursday: {18, 19, 20, 19, 19, 19}

   Friday: {22, 24, 23, 23, 24, 22}

9. A traffic camera registered the speed of passing cars at two different intersections. Nine cars' speeds were selected from each of the two locations. Can you infer that cars passed through Intersection 2 faster than through Intersection 1?

   Intersection 1: {34, 29, 32, 32, 33, 27, 33, 34, 34}

   Intersection 2: {33, 33, 29, 35, 37, 31, 37, 34, 35}

10. A bank teller selected ten \$1 bills and recorded each bill's series date. The bank teller repeated the same process for ten \$5 bills. The results were organized in a frequency table. Do the \$1 and \$5 sets of bills have about the same mean series date?

Series date	2003	2006	2009	2013
Number of \$1 bills	1	4	3	2
Number of \$5 bills	0	4	3	3

11. Demi and Renae compared the number of text messages they sent to each other for 1 wk. On average, who sent more text messages?

    Demi to Renae: {6, 7, 11, 8, 4, 6, 7}

    Renae to Demi: {8, 4, 3, 7, 8, 6, 6}

12. Omar measured the depth of a stream, in centimeters, at six different times on January 1. He measured the depth of the same stream a month later, on February 1. Can Omar conclude that the stream was deeper on February 1 than on January 1?

    January 1: {16, 17, 17, 17, 17, 17, 18}

    February 1: {14, 16, 17, 17, 18, 18, 19}

Solve.

13. A state fair holds a hot dog-eating contest each year. Each contestant tries to eat as many hot dogs as possible in 10 min. The table shows the results for the top five finishers for 2010 and 2011.

Finisher	Number of hot dogs eaten	
	2010	**2011**
1	45	48
2	37	41
3	31	32
4	30	25
5	28	24

(a) Calculate the mean and MAD of the top five finishers for each year.

(b) On average, did the top five finishers in 2011 perform better than in 2010? Use the means-to-MAD ratio in your explanation.

14. **Challenge** Jacob, Rennie, and Wes deliver pizzas for the same pizzeria. Each person recorded the number of pizzas he delivered each work day for 1 wk.

Jacob: {14, 15, 12, 16, 10, 17}

Rennie: {18, 12, 10, 17, 12, 15}

Wes: {18, 19, 14, 23, 20, 17}

(a) Calculate the mean and MAD for each person.

(b) Calculate the means-to-MAD ratio for each pair of people.

(c) Did anyone deliver more pizzas, on average, than the others? Explain.

Probability

Probability is a measure of how likely it is that something will happen.

In the study of probability, some terms have different meanings from what you might be used to. For instance, you might think that an experiment is something that scientists do, an event is some sort of social gathering, and a trial involves a judge.

Understanding Basic Concepts of Probability

DEFINITIONS

Statement	Example
An **experiment** is any process or action that has a result.	Roll a 6-sided number cube.
A result is called an **outcome**.	A possible outcome is 4.
The set of all possible outcomes of an experiment is the **sample space**.	{1, 2, 3, 4, 5, 6}
An **event** is a set of one or more outcomes. An event is a subset of the sample space. Events are sometimes described as actions.	Roll a 4. {4} Roll an even number. {2, 4, 6} Roll a number less than 3. {1, 2}

If an experiment is performed more than once, each performance can be called a **trial**. For example, 100 rolls of a number cube can be described as 100 trials of an experiment.

Calculating Probability

PROBABILITY OF AN EVENT (THEORETICAL PROBABILITY)

The **probability** of an event E, written $P(E)$, is a number from 0 to 1 that describes how likely event E is to occur. If all outcomes in the sample space S are equally likely, then

$$P(E) = \frac{\text{number of outcomes in event } E}{\text{total number of outcomes in sample space } S} = \frac{n(E)}{n(S)}.$$

TIP

Unless otherwise noted, *probability* means theoretical probability. You will learn about experimental probability later in this chapter.

You can write a probability as a fraction, decimal, or percent.

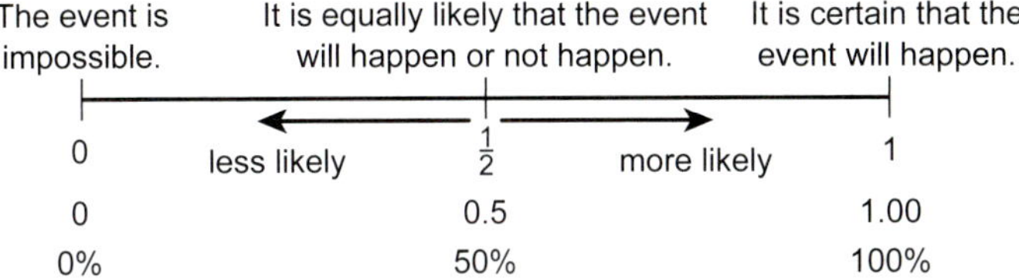

EXAMPLE 1 A 6-sided number cube is rolled.

A Find $n(S)$.

Solution The sample space S is $\{1, 2, 3, 4, 5, 6\}$, so there are 6 outcomes.

$$n(S) = 6$$ ■

B Find $P(4)$.

Solution $P(4)$ represents the probability of rolling a 4. There is only 1 outcome that is a 4, so $n(4) = 1$.

$$P(4) = \frac{n(4)}{n(S)} = \frac{1}{6} \approx 0.17, \text{ or about } 17\%$$ ■

C Find $P(\text{odd number})$.

Solution The event "roll an odd number" contains 3 outcomes: 1, 3, and 5.

$$P(\text{odd number}) = \frac{n(\text{odd number})}{n(S)} = \frac{3}{6} = \frac{1}{2} = 0.5 = 50\%$$ ■

EXAMPLE 2 The integers 1 through 10 are written on 10 index cards, with a different integer on each card. The cards are placed in a bag. One card is chosen without looking.

A Find $n(S)$.

Solution There are 10 cards, so $n(S) = 10$. ■

B Find $P(\text{integer} > 7)$.

Solution $P(\text{integer} > 7)$ represents the probability of choosing an integer greater than 7. There are 3 outcomes in this event: 8, 9, and 10. So $n(\text{integer} > 7) = 3$.

$$P(\text{integer} > 7) = \frac{n(\text{integer} > 7)}{n(S)} = \frac{3}{10} = 0.3 = 30\%$$ ■

C Find $P(12)$.

Solution There is no card with 12 written on it, so $n(12) = 0$.

$$P(12) = \frac{n(12)}{n(S)} = \frac{0}{10} = 0 = 0\%$$ ■

D Find $P(\text{integer} < 12)$.

Solution Every integer in the bag is less than 12, so choosing an integer less than 12 is certain to happen.

$$P(\text{integer} < 12) = 1 = 100\%$$ ■

Calculating Probability Involving Complementary Events

If one of two events must occur, but both cannot occur at the same time, then those events are **complementary**. When two events are complementary, the sum of their probabilities is 1.

EXAMPLE 3 A bag contains 3 green marbles, 7 white marbles, and 5 red marbles (and no other marbles). One marble is chosen without looking.

A Find $n(S)$.

Solution Since $3 + 7 + 5 = 15$, there are 15 outcomes in the sample space.

$$n(S) = 15$$

B Find $P(\text{green})$.

Solution $P(\text{green})$ represents the probability of choosing a green marble. There are 3 outcomes in this event, so $n(\text{green}) = 3$.

$$P(\text{green}) = \frac{n(\text{green})}{n(S)} = \frac{3}{15} = \frac{1}{5} = 0.2 = 20\%$$

C Find $P(\text{not green})$.

Solution

Method 1 The outcomes that are *not green* are the outcomes *white* and *red*, so $n(\text{not green}) = n(\text{white}) + n(\text{red}) = 7 + 5 = 12$.

$$P(\text{not green}) = \frac{n(\text{not green})}{n(S)} = \frac{n(\text{white}) + n(\text{red})}{n(S)} = \frac{12}{15} = \frac{4}{5} = 0.8 = 80\%$$

Method 2 The outcomes *green* and *not green* are complementary because one of them must occur, but both cannot occur at the same time.

$$P(\text{green}) + P(\text{not green}) = 1$$

$$\frac{1}{5} + P(\text{not green}) = 1$$

$$P(\text{not green}) = 1 - \frac{1}{5} = \frac{4}{5} = 0.8 = 80\%$$

THINK ABOUT IT

The definition of *probability* requires that all outcomes in the sample space are equally likely, so think of each marble as an outcome, not each color.

Application: Weather

EXAMPLE 4 A meteorologist forecasts that the probability of snow is 70%. What is the probability that it will not snow?

Solution The outcomes *snow* and *no snow* are complementary, so $P(\text{snow}) + P(\text{no snow}) = 100\%$.

$$100\% - 70\% = 30\%$$

The probability that it will not snow is 30%.

Problem Set

List the sample space for the experiment.

1. Toss 1 coin.

2. Toss 2 coins.

3 Toss 3 coins.

4. Roll a number cube.

5. Toss a coin and then roll a number cube.

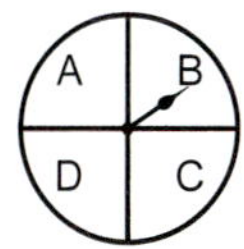

6. Spin the spinner once.

7. Spin the spinner twice.

Solve.

8. A number cube is rolled. Write each answer as a fraction, decimal, and percent.

(a) Find $P(2)$.

(b) Find $P(\text{number} < 4)$.

(c) Find $P(\text{not } 5)$.

9. A bag contains 7 white marbles, 3 blue marbles, and 15 red marbles (and no other marbles). One marble is chosen without looking.

(a) Find $n(S)$.

(b) Find $P(\text{white})$.

(c) Find $P(\text{red})$.

(d) Find $P(\text{green})$.

(e) Find $P(\text{not red})$.

10. The numbers 1 through 12 are written on 12 slips of paper, with a different number on each paper slip, and placed in a bag. One slip of paper is chosen without looking.

(a) Find $n(S)$.

(b) Find $P(5)$.

(c) Find $P(\text{multiple of } 4)$.

(d) Find $P(\text{multiple of } 2)$.

(e) Find $P(\text{number} < 13)$.

11. A coin is tossed, and then a number cube is rolled.

(a) Find $n(S)$.

(b) Find $P(\text{heads and } 4)$.

(c) Find $P(\text{tails and even number})$.

(d) Find $P(\text{heads and number} > 2)$.

12. The letters A through M are written on slips of paper so that each letter is written once and a different letter is on each paper slip. The slips of paper are placed in a bag, and a slip of paper is chosen without looking.

(a) Find $n(S)$.

(b) Find $P(\text{vowel})$.

(c) Find $P(\text{consonant})$.

13. A volunteer called 280 homes to ask questions about an upcoming election. Of these calls, 92 were not answered. Based on those results, what is the probability that the next call the volunteer makes is not answered?

14. **Challenge** The odds in favor of an event is the ratio $n(E)$ to $n(\text{not } E)$. A number cube is rolled.

(a) Find the odds in favor of rolling a 2.

(b) Find the odds in favor of rolling an even number.

15. **Challenge** Adam, Bob, Cathy, Dan, and Eric line up in a row for a photo. What is the probability that they line up in alphabetical order from left to right?

Relative Frequency

Increasing the number of trials improves the accuracy of the experiment.

Calculating Relative Frequency

Theoretical probability is based on the assumption that all outcomes in a sample space are equally likely. Relative frequency is based on actual observations or results of an experiment.

RELATIVE FREQUENCY OF AN EVENT (EXPERIMENTAL PROBABILITY)

If n is the number of trials of an experiment or number of observations in a study, then the relative frequency of an event E is

$$P(E) = \frac{\text{number of times event } E \text{ has occurred}}{n}.$$

BY THE WAY

Experimental probability is another term for relative frequency.

EXAMPLE 1 Alicia rolls a number cube 50 times. The results are shown.

Outcome	1	2	3	4	5	6
Frequency	10	8	12	8	7	5

Based on the results, what is the relative frequency that the next roll will be a 3?

Solution The outcome 3 has occurred 12 times in 50 trials. Based on the results in the table, $P(3) = \frac{12}{50} = \frac{6}{25} = 0.24 = 24\%$. ■

THINK ABOUT IT

Relative frequency might not equal theoretical probability. The theoretical probability of rolling a 3 is $\frac{1}{6}$, or about 17%.

EXAMPLE 2 Ramon chooses a marble from a bag without looking and then replaces it. He does this 75 times. The results are shown.

Outcome	red	white	blue
Frequency	7	40	28

Based on the results, what is the relative frequency of choosing a red marble?

Solution The outcome *red* has occurred 7 times out of 75 trials. Based on the results in the table, $P(\text{red}) = \frac{7}{75} \approx 0.093$, which is 9.3%. ■

THINK ABOUT IT

There is no way to calculate theoretical probability for the experiment in Example 2 because the contents of the bag are unknown.

Application: Surveys

EXAMPLE 3 A survey shows that 171 out of 460 students play a team sport. Based on the survey, what is the relative frequency that a student chosen at random plays a team sport?

Solution Based on the survey, the relative frequency that a student chosen at random plays a team sport is $\frac{171}{460}$, or about 0.372, which is 37.2%. ■

Relative Frequency and Theoretical Probability

LAW OF LARGE NUMBERS

The **law of large numbers** states that the relative frequency of an event becomes closer to the theoretical probability of the event as the number of trials increases.

THINK ABOUT IT

The law of large numbers is another way of saying that increasing the sample size of a survey increases the survey's accuracy.

EXAMPLE 4 A coin was tossed 10 times, 100 times, and then 1000 times. The number of heads was recorded in a frequency table.

Number of tosses	10	100	1000
Heads	6	44	483

A Calculate the relative frequency of tossing heads for each sample size. Organize the results in a table.

Solution

Number of tosses	10	100	1000
Relative frequency of heads	$\frac{6}{10} = 0.6 = 60\%$	$\frac{44}{100} = 0.44 = 44\%$	$\frac{483}{1000} = 0.483 = 48.3\%$

■

B The coin is a fair coin. What is the theoretical probability $P(\text{heads})$?

Solution The sample space S is {heads, tails}, so there are two equally probable outcomes.

$$P(\text{heads}) = \frac{1}{2} = 0.5 = 50\%$$ ■

C Based on the theoretical probability, predict how many of 1000 coin flips will be heads.

Solution Multiply $P(\text{heads})$ by n, the number of coin flips.

$$P(\text{heads}) \bullet n = 0.50 \bullet 1000 = 500$$

Out of 1000 coin flips, is it expected that 500 will be heads. ■

D As the number n of trials increases from 10 to 1000, how does the value of the relative frequency change? Is this result expected?

Solution As n increases from 10 to 1000, the relative frequency gets closer to 50%. This result is expected according to the law of large numbers, which states that the relative frequency of an event becomes closer to its theoretical probability as the number of trials increases. ■

EXAMPLE 5 Jalisa has a bag that contains 10 marbles: some green, some red, and some blue. Jalisa randomly chooses a marble out of the bag, records the color, and then places that marble back in the bag. She repeats this experiment 3 times, increasing the number of trials from 10 to 50 and then to 200.

Outcome	Number of trials		
	10	50	200
green	7	28	104
red	3	18	78
blue	2	4	18

A Calculate the relative frequencies for each sample size and organize the results in a table.

Solution

Outcome	Number of trials		
	10	50	200
green	$\frac{7}{10} = 0.7 = 70\%$	$\frac{28}{50} = 0.56 = 56\%$	$\frac{104}{200} = 0.52 = 52\%$
red	$\frac{3}{10} = 0.3 = 30\%$	$\frac{18}{50} = 0.36 = 36\%$	$\frac{78}{200} = 0.39 = 39\%$
blue	$\frac{2}{10} = 0.2 = 20\%$	$\frac{4}{50} = 0.08 = 8\%$	$\frac{18}{200} = 0.09 = 9\%$

■

B Can Jalisa calculate the theoretical probability that a green marble will be chosen? Why or why not?

Solution Jalisa does not know how many of each marble—green, red, or blue—is actually in the bag, so she cannot calculate the theoretical probability that a green marble will be chosen. ■

C Predict how many green, red, and blue marbles are actually in the bag. Explain your thinking.

Solution According the law of large numbers, the relative frequency of an event is close to the theoretical probability of the event for a large number of trials.

For each marble type, multiply the relative frequency after 200 trials by 10, the actual number of marbles in the jar. Then round the product to the nearest whole number.

green: $10 \cdot 52\% = 10 \cdot 0.52 = 5.2 \approx 5$
red: $10 \cdot 39\% = 10 \cdot 0.39 = 3.9 \approx 4$
blue: $10 \cdot 9\% = 10 \cdot 0.09 = 0.9 \approx 1$

It is likely that there are 5 green marbles, 4 red marbles, and 1 blue marble in the bag.

TIP

When rounding, check that the sum of the rounded numbers equals the total.

$5 + 4 + 1 = 10$

Problem Set

A card was selected at random from a standard deck. The suit of the card was recorded, and then the card was replaced. The table shows the results after 52 trials. Find the relative frequency of each event. Round to the nearest percent.

Outcome	club	diamond	heart	spade
Number of times	12	16	10	14

1. A diamond was selected.
2. A spade was selected.
3. A club or a heart was selected.
4. A heart was not selected.
5. A club or a heart or a spade was selected.
6. **Challenge** Neither a club nor a spade was selected.

Frank opens 40 pea pods and counts the number of peas in each pod. He records the number. Round to the nearest tenth.

Peas per pod	7	8	9	10	11
Number of times	1	4	18	15	2

7. Calculate the relative frequency of each outcome and organize the results in a table.
8. Find the experimental probability that the next pea pod opened has 9 or 10 peas in it.
9. Find the experimental probability that the next pea pod opened has fewer than 9 peas in it.
10. Find the experimental probability that the next pea pod opened does not have 11 peas in it.

Solve.

11. Denise rolled a number cube 30 times. The results are shown.

Outcome	1	2	3	4	5	6
Frequency	4	4	7	3	7	5

Write each answer as a percent rounded to the nearest tenth.

(a) With what relative frequency was a 5 rolled?

(b) With what relative frequency was a number less than 4 rolled?

(c) What is theoretical probability $P(2)$?

(d) Explain why the relative frequency and theoretical probability of rolling a 2 differ.

12. A board game uses a number spinner that is divided into four equal sections. A game tester spins the dial 20 times, 100 times, and then 500 times. She records the results in a frequency table.

Outcome	Number of trials		
	20	100	500
1	4	19	120
2	6	32	127
3	7	28	132
4	3	21	121

(a) Calculate the relative frequencies for all three sample sizes and organize the results in a table.

(b) Calculate the theoretical probability $P(4)$.

(c) Based on the theoretical probability, predict how many of 500 spins will be 4.

(d) As n, the number of trials, increases from 20 to 500, how does the relative frequency of spinning a 4 change? Explain how this relates to the value of $P(4)$.

13. Each day, a student is randomly selected to read a school's morning announcements. The school records whether the student is a boy or a girl. The results after 10, 25, and 100 days are displayed in the table.

Outcome	Number of days		
	10	25	100
boy	4	11	47
girl	6	14	53

(a) Calculate the relative frequencies for each sample size and organize the results in a table.

(b) Is it possible to calculate the theoretical probability that a boy will be chosen to read the morning announcements? Explain.

(c) Use the table to predict what percentage of the school's population is made up of girls. Explain your reasoning.

14. **Challenge** A spinner is divided into 10 equal sections. Each section is labeled with a number from 1 to 5. The dial was spun repeatedly and the results recorded in the frequency table.

Outcome	Number of trials		
	10	25	100
1	2	5	22
2	1	2	9
3	3	8	33
4	3	7	28
5	1	3	8

Predict the how many of the 10 sections are labeled with each of the 5 numbers.

Combined Probability

For events A and B, you can find $P(A \text{ or } B)$ and $P(A \text{ and } B)$.

Events of an experiment may share outcomes.

Determining Whether Events Are Mutually Exclusive

If events do not share outcomes, they are mutually exclusive.

DEFINITION

Mutually exclusive events cannot happen at the same time.

THINK ABOUT IT

Complementary events are mutually exclusive events.

EXAMPLE 1 A number cube is rolled. Determine whether the events are mutually exclusive.

A roll an even number, roll a prime number

Solution You roll an even number and a prime number at the same time when you roll a 2.

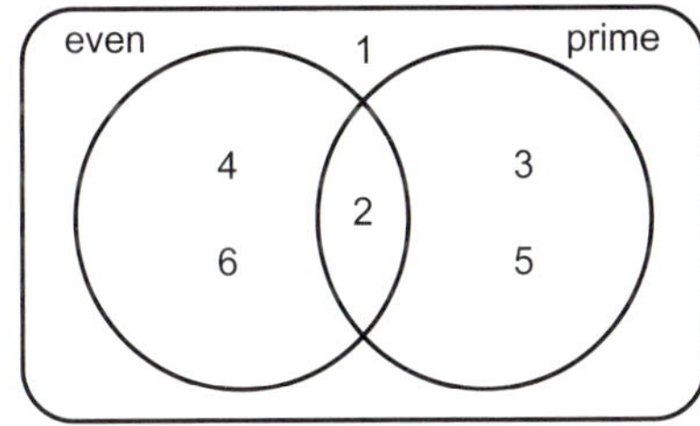

TIP

A Venn diagram can help when you are analyzing sets of events.

The events are not mutually exclusive. ■

B roll a 1, roll an even number

Solution You cannot roll a 1 and an even number at the same time.

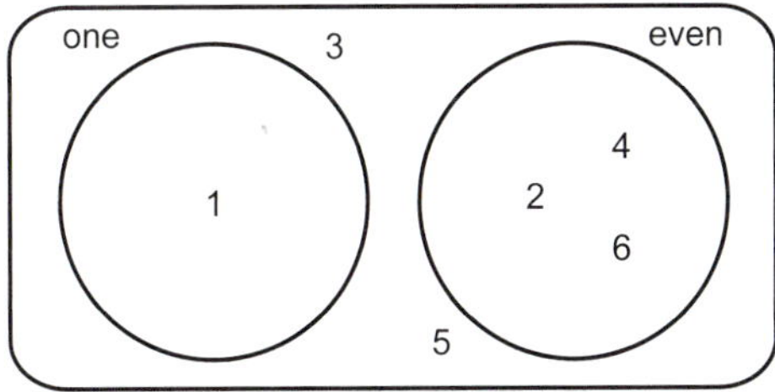

The events are mutually exclusive. ■

Finding the Probability of Mutually Exclusive Events

PROBABILITY OF MUTUALLY EXCLUSIVE EVENTS

For mutually exclusive events A and B,

$$P(A \text{ or } B) = P(A) + P(B).$$

TIP

The rule extends to three or more mutually exclusive events.

EXAMPLE 2 The whole numbers from 1 to 20 are each written on a slip of paper and placed into a bag. A volunteer selects a slip of paper without looking.

A Find $P(3 \text{ or number} > 15)$.

Solution The events are mutually exclusive because you cannot select a 3 and a number greater than 15 at the same time.

$P(3 \text{ or number} > 15) = P(3) + P(\text{number} > 15)$

$= \frac{1}{20} + \frac{5}{20}$ There is 1 outcome in the first event $\{3\}$ and 5 outcomes in the second event $\{16, 17, 18, 19, \text{ and } 20\}$.

$= \frac{6}{20}$

$= \frac{3}{10}$ ■

B Find $P(\text{multiple of 7 or multiple of 10})$.

Solution The events are mutually exclusive because you cannot select a multiple of 7 and a multiple of 10 at the same time.

$P(\text{multiple of 7 or multiple of 10}) = P(\text{multiple of 7}) + P(\text{multiple of 10})$

$= \frac{2}{20} + \frac{2}{20}$ There are 2 outcomes in the first event $\{7, 14\}$ and 2 outcomes in the second event $\{10, 20\}$.

$= \frac{4}{20}$

$= \frac{1}{5}$ ■

Determining Whether Events Are Independent or Dependent

DEFINITIONS

Two events are **independent events** if they are related in such a way that one event's occurrence has no effect on the probability of the other event.

Two events are **dependent events** if they are related in such a way that knowing about one event's occurrence has an effect on the probability of the other event.

EXAMPLE 3 Determine whether the events are independent or dependent.

A Select a red marble from a bag, keep it out of the bag, and then select another red marble from the bag containing 10 red marbles and 10 yellow marbles.

Solution For the first selection, $P(\text{red}) = \frac{10}{20} = \frac{1}{2}$ because there are 10 red marbles and 20 marbles in all. Knowing that a red marble was selected and not replaced changes $P(\text{red})$ to $\frac{9}{19}$ for the second selection, because there are only 9 red marbles and a total of 19 marbles left in the bag. The events are dependent. ■

THINK ABOUT IT

When a situation involves selection without replacement, the sample space changes.

B Select a red marble from a bag, put it back in the bag, and then select a yellow marble from the bag containing 10 red marbles and 10 yellow marbles.

Solution For the second selection, $P(\text{yellow}) = \frac{10}{20} = \frac{1}{2}$ because there are 10 yellow marbles and 20 marbles in all. Because the first marble is replaced before the second selection, the probability is $\frac{1}{2}$ regardless of which color is chosen first. The events are independent. ■

C Roll a 3 on a number cube 3 times in a row.

Solution $P(3)$ on each roll is $\frac{1}{6}$. The probabilities do not change for the second and third rolls because $n(E)$ and $n(S)$ remain 1 and 6, respectively. The events are independent. ■

Finding the Probability of Independent Events

PROBABILITY OF INDEPENDENT EVENTS

For independent events A and B,

$$P(A \text{ and } B) = P(A) \cdot P(B).$$

TIP

The rule extends to three or more independent events.

EXAMPLE 4 Find the probability.

A A coin is tossed and a number cube is rolled. Find P(tails and even number).

Solution The events are independent because the probability of rolling an even number is not affected by the outcome of the coin toss.

$$\begin{aligned} P(\text{tails and even number}) &= P(\text{tails}) \cdot P(\text{even number}) \\ &= \frac{1}{2} \cdot \frac{3}{6} \\ &= \frac{3}{12} \\ &= \frac{1}{4} \end{aligned}$$

THINK ABOUT IT

There are 12 outcomes in the experiment of tossing a coin and rolling a number cube. Three of the outcomes contain both tails and an even number: {T2, T4, T6}.

B A bowl contains 3 pennies, 5 dimes, and 2 quarters. A coin is selected and replaced 3 times. Find P(penny then a penny then a quarter).

Solution The events are independent because each selection is replaced before the next selection.

$$\begin{aligned} P(\text{penny then a penny then a quarter}) &= P(\text{penny}) \cdot P(\text{penny}) \cdot P(\text{quarter}) \\ &= \frac{3}{10} \cdot \frac{3}{10} \cdot \frac{2}{10} \\ &= \frac{18}{1000} \\ &= \frac{9}{500} \end{aligned}$$

Finding the Probability of Dependent Events

PROBABILITY OF DEPENDENT EVENTS

For dependent events A and B,

$$P(A \text{ and } B) = P(A) \cdot P(B \text{ after } A)$$

where $P(B$ after $A)$ is the probability of B knowing that event A has already occurred.

TIP

The rule extends to three or more dependent events.

EXAMPLE 5 A bag contains 8 white potatoes and 4 red potatoes. A cook selects a potato, puts it on the counter, and then selects another potato without looking.

A Find P(white and white).

Solution The probability of selecting a white potato on the second selection is different from selecting a white potato on the first selection because the sample space is different.

$P(\text{white and white}) = P(\text{white}) \cdot P(\text{white after white})$

$= \frac{8}{12} \cdot \frac{7}{11}$ For the first selection, there are 8 white potatoes and 12 total potatoes. For the second selection, there are 7 white potatoes and 11 total potatoes.

$= \frac{56}{132}$

$= \frac{14}{33} \approx 42\%$ ■

B Find $P(\text{white and red})$.

Solution

$P(\text{white and red}) = P(\text{white}) \cdot P(\text{red after white})$

$= \frac{8}{12} \cdot \frac{4}{11}$ For the second selection, there are 4 red potatoes and 11 total potatoes.

$= \frac{32}{132}$

$= \frac{8}{33} \approx 24\%$ ■

THINK ABOUT IT

For events involving selection without replacement, $n(S)$ will always change for the second probability. $n(E)$ may or may not change.

Problem Set

Determine whether the events are mutually exclusive.

When rolling a number cube:

1. rolling an even number and rolling an odd number
2. rolling an odd number and rolling a number greater than 3
3. rolling a multiple of 2 and rolling a multiple of 5

When selecting a card from a standard deck:

4. selecting a queen and selecting an ace
5. selecting a queen and selecting a black card
6. selecting a red card and selecting a heart

Each side of a 12-sided number cube has a number from 1 to 12. The number cube is rolled. Find the probability.

7. $P(1 \text{ or } 12)$
8. $P(\text{number} < 4 \text{ or number} \geq 10)$
9. $P(\text{multiple of 4 or multiple of 5})$
10. $P(\text{even number or } 11)$

The table shows how many cans of each paint color are on the top shelf in a paint warehouse. One can is selected at random. Find the probability.

Whites	Blues	Greens
7 off white	4 baby blue	2 emerald
3 pure white	10 sea blue	3 moss
	1 deep blue	

11. P(baby blue or deep blue)

12. P(pure white or moss)

13. P(any blue or off white)

14. P(any blue or any green)

Determine whether the events are independent or dependent.

15. Select an ace, keep it, and then select another ace from a standard deck of cards.

16. Select the king of spades, return it, and then select the king of clubs from a standard deck of cards.

17. Toss heads 2 times on 2 tosses of a coin.

18. Roll an even number on a number cube and toss tails on the toss of a coin.

19. Select a volunteer from a group, bring her on stage, and then select another volunteer.

20. Select a volunteer from a group, have him assist and return to his seat, and then select a volunteer from the group again.

Find the probability.

21. A coin is tossed 2 times. Find P(heads and heads).

22. A coin is tossed 4 times. Find P(tails and tails and tails and tails).

23. A coin is tossed and a number cube is rolled. Find P(heads and odd number).

24. A number cube is rolled 2 times. Find P(not 1 and not 1).

25. A number cube is rolled and the spinner is spun. Find P(6 on roll and 2 on spinner).

26. The spinner is spun 2 times. Find P(4 and odd number).

Find the probability.

27. Two hundred raffle tickets, numbered 001 to 200, are in a basket. Four tickets are selected without replacement. Find the probability that 001 is selected first, 002 is selected second, 003 is selected third, and 004 is selected fourth.

28. Suppose you take a 3-question multiple choice quiz. Each question has 4 options. You guess the answer to each question. What is the probability that you answer all the questions incorrectly?

29. Suppose you take a 3-question true-false quiz. You guess the answer to each question. What is the probability that you answer all the questions correctly?

30. **Challenge** There are 10 red and 4 black checkers in a bag. A checker is chosen, and then another checker is chosen without replacing the first checker. What is the probability of choosing one of each color?

Core Focus: Probability Models

THE CORE CONCEPT

The theoretical probability of an event, calculated from a probability model, often differs from the event's relative frequency.

Application: Geometric Probability Model

FORMULA

In a **geometric probability** model, the probability of an event (E) is

$$P(E) = \frac{\text{area of region of success}}{\text{area of entire region}}.$$

In a geometric probability model, a region representing successful outcomes is part of an entire region representing the sample space. Find the probability of an event by dividing the area of the region of success by the area of the entire region.

EXAMPLE 1 Nigel creates a circular dartboard. The radius of the dartboard is 10 in. At the center of the dartboard is a shaded circular region with a radius of 3 in. A player gets triple points if the dart lands in the shaded region.

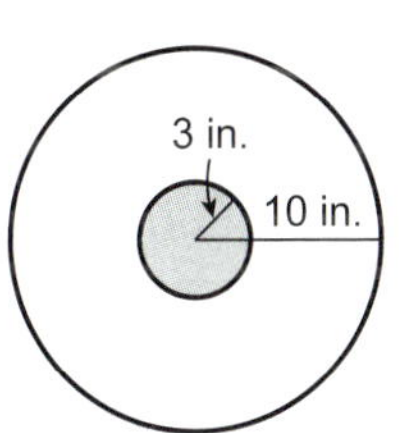

A Nigel throws a dart at the dartboard. Suppose the dart hits any spot on the dartboard at random. What is the probability that Nigel's throw earned triple points?

Solution In this situation,

$$\frac{\text{are of region of success}}{\text{area of entire region}} = \frac{\text{area of shaded region}}{\text{area of whole dartboard}}.$$

The shaded region and the whole dartboard are circles, so use the formula for the area of a circle, $A = \pi r^2$, to calculate the areas.

$$\frac{\text{area of shaded region}}{\text{area of whole dartboard}} = \frac{\pi(3)^2}{\pi(10)^2} = \frac{\pi \cdot 9}{\pi \cdot 100} = 0.09 = 9\%$$

The probability that Nigel's throw earned triple points is 9%. ■

B Nigel lands 100 throws on the dartboard. He earns triple points 11 times. Nigel says that the probability that the 101st throw earns triple points is 11%. Is Nigel correct? Explain.

Solution Nigel is not correct. He did calculate the relative frequency of 11% correctly. Nigel should use the geometric model to calculate the probability. In this model, the theoretical probability of a throw landing in the shaded region is 9%. It does not depend upon the results from previous throws. ■

REMEMBER

Variation between experimental results and probabilities from a model is to be expected.

Application: Uniform Probability Model

In a uniform probability model, all outcomes are equally likely. Examples of processes following a uniform probability model include flipping a fair coin, tossing an unbiased number cube, and selecting a student from a class at random.

EXAMPLE 2 Chad has a fair number cube that he uses for a game. The number cube has the shape of a triangular pyramid, with 4 faces numbered 1 to 4. Chad rolled the number cube 100 times and recorded the results in a table.

Value	1	2	3	4
Number of rolls	22	29	26	23

BY THE WAY

Not all number cubes have 6 sides. Some games use number cubes with 4, 8, and 20 sides.

A With what relative frequency did Chad roll an odd number?

Solution The relative frequency was

$$\frac{\text{number of rolls with 1 or 3}}{\text{total number of rolls}} = \frac{22 + 26}{100} = \frac{48}{100} = 0.48 = 48\%.$$

Chad rolled an odd number 48% of the time. ■

Q & A

Q What is the probability that Chad rolls a prime number?

A $\frac{29 + 26}{100} = \frac{55}{100} = 0.55 = 55\%$

B What is the theoretical probability of Chad rolling an odd number?

Solution The number cube is fair, thus each roll would be equally probable. There are 4 possible rolls, so the probability of rolling an odd number is

$$\frac{\text{number of rolls with 1 or 3}}{\text{total number of rolls}} = \frac{2}{4} = \frac{1}{2} = 0.50 = 50\%.$$

The probability of Chad rolling an odd number is 50%. ■

C Because the theoretical probability of rolling an odd number differs from relative frequency observed, Chad says the number cube cannot be fair. Is Chad right? Explain your thinking with an example.

Solution Chad is not right. Often, relative frequencies do not exactly match the theoretical probabilities calculated from a model. For example, when a fair coin is tossed 100 times, heads should come up, on average, 50 times. However, the actual number of heads flipped would likely be a number close to 50, not 50 every time. ■

Problem Set

Solve.

1. A board game uses a spinner with 12 equal sectors.

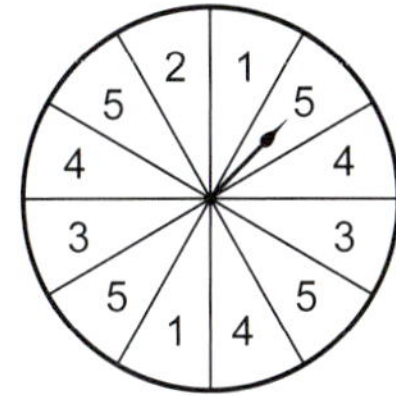

(a) What is the theoretical probability that the dial will land on the number 5?

(b) In one game, the dial was spun 86 times and landed on the number 5 a total of 31 times. Calculate the relative frequency that the number 5 was observed.

(c) While playing the game, a player wishes to know what her chances are of spinning a 5. What would you tell her? Why?

2. A point is chosen at random inside the outer square region. The number of times a point is drawn from the shaded square is recorded. The results after 10, 100, and 1000 trials are recorded in the table.

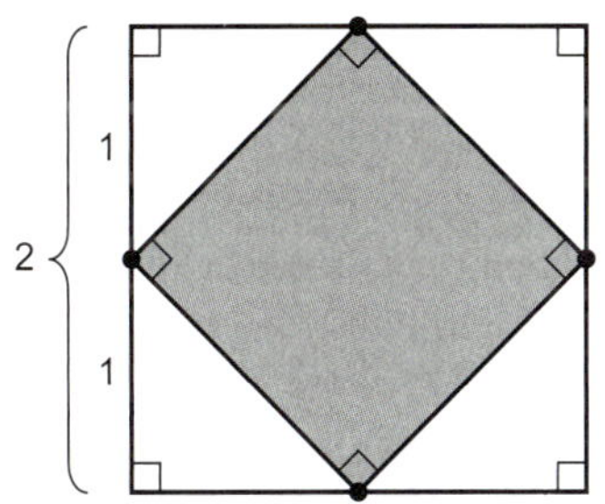

Number of trials	10	100	1000
Number in shaded area	4	56	511

(a) What is the theoretical probability that the point is chosen from the shaded region?

(b) Calculate the relative frequency observed for each set of trials.

(c) What trend do you notice in the relative frequency as the number of trials increases?

(d) What is the probability that the 1001st time a point is chosen, the point is selected from the shaded region? Explain.

3. A college football team has 57 players. Each player's year in college is recorded in the table.

Year	first	second	third	fourth
Number of players	6	10	18	23

During each game, a TV station selected players at random to be interviewed.

(a) For each year, calculate the probability that a player from that year is selected to be interviewed. Round to the nearest tenth of a percent. Organize the results in a table.

(b) Over the entire football season, the TV station conducted 40 interviews. How many third-year players do you predict were interviewed?

(c) At the end of the season, the actual number of third-year players interviewed was 11. What accounts for the difference in the actual and predicted number of third-year players interviewed?

CHAPTER 12 Review

Choose the answer.

1. What is the mode of the data set?

   $\{4, 6, 5, 8, 4, 1, 3, 9, 5, 4\}$

   A. 4

   B. 4.5

   C. 4.9

   D. 5

2. What is the MAD of the data set?

   $\{3, 5, 10, 14\}$

   A. 0

   B. 4

   C. 8

   D. 16

3. A survey of 50 homes in a town showed that 9 of the homes have an aquarium. If the town has 2650 homes in all, about how many of these homes have an aquarium?

   A. 9

   B. 477

   C. 2173

   D. 2609

4. What can you infer about the distributions of two data sets?

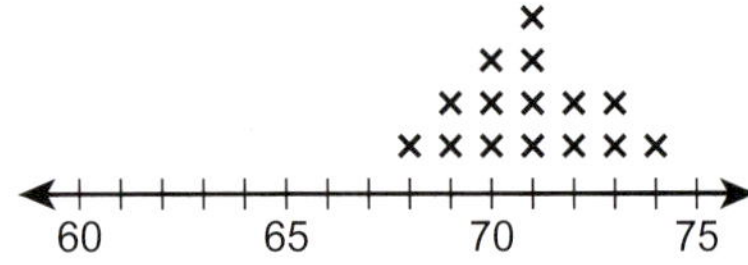

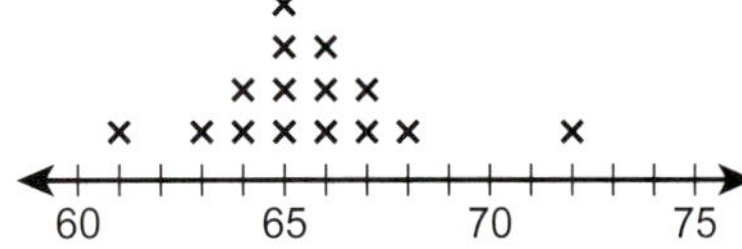

   A. Both distributions have the same mean.

   B. Neither distribution has outliers.

   C. The overlap of the distributions is low.

   D. The overlap of the distributions is high.

5. Six motels were selected at random from all the motels in a town. The number of ice machines and the number of swimming pools at each of the six motels were recorded. Which statement about the sample means is true?

   ice machines: 2, 3, 2, 1, 2, 2

   swimming pools: 1, 0, 1, 1, 1, 2

   A. $\overline{x}_{\text{pools}} > \overline{x}_{\text{ice machines}}$

   B. $\overline{x}_{\text{pools}} < \overline{x}_{\text{ice machines}}$

   C. $\overline{x}_{\text{pools}} \approx \overline{x}_{\text{ice machines}}$

   D. none of the above

6. An amusement park asked 80 visitors which ride they enjoyed most. With what relative frequency did visitors say they enjoyed the water slide the most?

Ride	roller coaster	Ferris wheel	water slide
Number of visitors	25	11	44

   A. 8%

   B. 36%

   C. 44%

   D. 55%

7. A coin is tossed and then a number cube is rolled. What is $P(\text{tails and number} > 3)$?

   A. $\frac{1}{4}$

   B. $\frac{1}{3}$

   C. $\frac{1}{2}$

   D. 1

Solve.

8. The table shows the percentage of free throws made for the starting players on three basketball teams.

Sonics	Badgers	Warriors
52	79	52
76	68	68
72	58	89
81	57	84
64	88	77

(a) Which team has the lowest mean?

(b) Which team has the lowest median?

9. A music website tracked the number of new users per day over 1 wk. The number of new users for each of the 7 days was 40, 45, 47, 52, 53, 58, and 69.

(a) What was the MAD of the number of new users per day? Round to the nearest tenth.

(b) What does the value of the MAD represent? Explain.

10. A food company randomly selected 60 pistachios from a recent shipment. The company found that 3 pistachios should be discarded. A large bag of pistachios holds about 380 pistachios. Predict how many of the 380 pistachios should be discarded.

11. A card is drawn from a deck of 52 cards. Find the probability that the card is a red, even-numbered card.

12. Four students each surveyed 40 shoppers at a supermarket to find out which brand of coffee they preferred.

Brand	A	B	C
Kira	12	11	17
Mary	13	9	18
Chuck	17	14	9
Sven	11	11	18

Which student most likely conducted a biased survey? Why?

13. A: {2, 1, 3, 1, 2, 3, 2, 2}

B: {1, 1, 1, 1, 0, 2, 2, 0}

(a) Create a line plot for each data set, and estimate the center of each data set visually.

(b) Describe the overlap of the two data sets as high, moderate, low, or none.

14. Julian rolled a fair number cube 10, 100, and then 1000 times. He recorded the number of times the number 4 was rolled.

Number of trials	10	100	1000
Rolled a 4	2	18	172

(a) What is the theoretical probability $P(4)$?

(b) Calculate the relative frequency observed for each set of trials.

(c) If Julian rolls the number cube 1 more time, what is the probability that he will roll a 4? Explain.

Problem	Topic Lookup	Problem	Topic Lookup
1, 8	Measures of Center	5	Using Statistical Measures
2, 9	Measures of Variability	11	Probability
3, 10	Samples and Prediction	6	Relative Frequency
12	Drawing Inferences	7	Combined Probability
4, 13	Comparing Distributions	14	Core Focus: Probability Models

Pronunciation Guide

The table below provides sample words to explain the sounds associated with specific letters and letter combinations used in the respellings in this book. For example, *a* represents the short "a" sound in *cat*, while *ay* represents the long "a" sound in *day*.

Letter combinations are used to approximate certain more complex sounds. For example, in the respelling of *trapezoid*—TRA-puh-zoyd—the letters *uh* represent the vowel sound you hear in *shut* and *other*.

Vowels

a	short a: **a**pple, c**a**t
ay	long a: c**a**ne, d**ay**
e, eh	short e: h**e**n, b**e**d
ee	long e: f**ee**d, t**ea**m
i, ih	short i: l**i**p, act**i**ve
iy	long i: tr**y**, m**igh**t
ah	short o: h**o**t, f**a**ther
oh	long o: h**o**me, thr**ow**
uh	short u: sh**u**t, **o**ther
yoo	long u: **u**nion, c**u**te

Letter Combinations

ch	**ch**in, an**ci**ent
sh	**sh**ow, mi**ss**ion
zh	vi**s**ion, a**z**ure
th	**th**in, heal**th**
th	**th**en, hea**th**er
ur	b**ir**d, f**ur**ther, w**or**d
us	b**us**, cr**us**t
or	c**our**t, f**or**mal
ehr	**err**or, c**are**
oo	c**oo**l, tr**ue**, r**u**le
ow	n**ow**, **ou**t
ou	l**oo**k, p**u**ll, w**ou**ld
oy	c**oi**n, t**oy**
aw	s**aw**, m**au**l, f**a**ll
ng	so**ng**, fi**ng**er
air	**Ar**istotle, b**arr**ister
ahr	c**ar**t, m**ar**tyr

Consonants

b	**b**utter, ba**b**y
d	**d**og, cra**d**le
f	**f**un, **ph**one
g	**g**rade, an**g**le
h	**h**at, a**h**ead
j	**j**u**dg**e, gor**g**e
k	**k**ite, **c**ar, bla**ck**
l	**l**i**l**y, mi**l**e
m	**m**o**m**, ca**m**el
n	**n**ext, ca**n**did
p	**p**rice, co**pp**er
r	**r**ubber, f**r**ee
s	**s**mall, **c**ircle, ha**ss**le
t	**t**on, po**tt**ery
v	**v**ase, **v**i**v**id
w	**w**all, a**w**ay
y	**y**ellow, ka**y**ak
z	**z**ebra, ha**z**e

Glossary

abscissa the first number in an ordered pair of numbers; also called the *x*-coordinate

absolute deviation the absolute value of the difference between a data value and the mean

absolute value a number's distance from zero

acute angle an angle that measures greater than 0° and less than 90°

acute triangle a triangle with 3 acute angles

addends numbers that are added

additive identity a number whose sum with any given number is the given number; The additive identity for the real numbers is 0.

additive inverses two numbers whose sum, when added together, is zero; A number's additive inverse is its opposite.

adjacent angles angles in the same plane that share a vertex and a side but do not share any interior points

algebraic expression an expression containing variables as well as constant values

alternate exterior angles the outside angles that do not share the same vertex and are on opposite sides of a transversal crossing two lines

alternate interior angles the inside angles that do not share the same vertex and are on opposite sides of a transversal crossing two lines

altitude a line segment that extends from a figure's vertex and intersects the opposite side at a right angle

angle of rotation the number of degrees a figure is rotated

apothem a line segment that joins the center of a polygon to the midpoint of one of its sides

area the number of square units in the interior of a figure

base a number or variable that is raised to a given power; For example, in 5^2, 5 is the base.

base of a prism one of two parallel congruent faces in a prism

biased sample a sample that is not representative of the population

Cartesian coordinate system method of locating points in a plane in which the coordinates of the points are their distances from two intersecting perpendicular lines called axes

categorical variable a variable that has two or more categories

center of rotation the point about which a figure is rotated

chord a segment with endpoints that are points on a circle

circle the set of all points in a plane that are equidistant from a given point called the center

circumference distance around a circle

closed a set is closed under an operation if the operation performed on any two numbers in the set produces another number in the set

cluster a group of points that are close together in comparison to other points

coefficient the numerical factor in a term in a variable term

coincident system of linear equations consistent system of linear equations with infinitely many solutions; also called a consistent dependent system

collinear points points that lie on the same line

common factor a factor that two or more given numbers have in common; For example, 9 and 12 have a common factor of 3.

complementary angles a pair of angles for which the sum of their measures is 90°

complementary events two events such that one must occur, but both cannot occur at the same time

complex fraction a fraction that has a fraction in the numerator or the denominator (or both)

cone a three-dimensional figure with one base that is a circle, a curved lateral surface, and a point called a vertex

congruent having exactly the same size and shape, even though orientation may vary

congruent polygons polygons that have the same size and shape

congruent triangles triangles that are identical to each other

consistent dependent system of linear equations a system of linear equations with infinitely many solutions; also called a coincident system

consistent independent system of linear equations a system of linear equations with exactly one solution

consistent system of linear equations a system having exactly one solution or infinitely many solutions

constant a numerical term that has no variables

constant function a function that neither rises nor falls as the input variable increases

constant of variation the ratio of two directly proportional quantities; also the nonzero constant k defined by $y = kx$ in a direct variation; also called the constant of proportionality

contradiction an equation that is true for no values of the variable

coordinate a number that indicates the location of a point on a number line

corresponding angles angles that lie in the same position or match up with respect to the transversal when the transversal crosses two lines

cross section a plane figure that results from the intersection of a plane and a solid

cube a solid figure made up of 6 square faces that meet at right angles

cubic unit a cube that is 1 unit on each side; a measure of volume

cylinder a three-dimensional figure with 2 congruent, parallel bases that are circles and a curved lateral surface that joins them

decreasing function a function whose output values decrease as the input values increase

denominator the bottom number of a fraction

dependent events two events that are related in such a way that knowing about one event's occurrence has an effect on the probability of the other event

dependent variable the output variable

diameter a chord that passes through the center of a circle

diameter of a sphere a line segment passing through the center of a sphere that joins two points on the sphere

direct linear variation a function where y varies directly with x following the equation $y = kx$ where k is a nonzero constant

directly proportional a relationship in which two quantities vary directly with each other

distribution of a data set the shape of the plotted data over the range of the data set's values

domain the set of allowable inputs of a relation

equiangular polygon a polygon with all angles congruent

equivalent equations equations with the same solution or solutions

equivalent fractions fractions with the same value

equivalent inequalities inequalities that have the same solution set

equivalent ratios ratios that describe the same numerical relationship

evaluate a variable expression to replace all the variables in the expression with numbers and simplify

event a set of one or more outcomes; a subset of the sample space; also called actions

experiment any process or action that has a result

experimental probability probability based on actual observations or results of an experiment

exponent a number or variable attached to the base to show how many times the base will be a factor; For example, in 5^2, the exponent is 2.

expression a group of mathematical symbols that represents a numerical value; Most expressions contain numerals as well as operation signs or grouping symbols or a combination of these elements. An expression containing one or more variables is a variable expression or an algebraic expression.

exterior angle of a triangle an angle formed by two sides of a triangle, one of which extends outside the triangle; Each interior angle of a triangle forms a linear pair with an exterior angle.

extremes the values a and d in the proportion $\frac{a}{b} = \frac{c}{d}$

factors numbers that are multiplied

formula an equation that defines the relationship between two or more measurable quantities

function a relation in which every element of the domain is assigned to exactly one element of the range

geometric probability the probability of an event equal to the ratio of the area of success to the area of the entire region

graph (n.) a diagram that shows the relationship between quantities

graph (v.) to draw a visual representation of data

graph of a one-variable inequality the set of points on a number line that represents all the solutions of the inequality

greatest common factor (GCF) the greatest number that divides evenly into two or more numbers

grouping symbols symbols such as parentheses, brackets, and fraction bars used to set apart an expression that should be simplified before other operations are performed

horizontal intercept the value of the variable on the horizontal axis at the point where a graph crosses the horizontal axis

hypotenuse the side opposite the right angle in a right triangle

identity an equation that is true for every value of the variable

image the new figure that results from a transformation

improper fraction a fraction in which the numerator is greater than or equal to the denominator

inconsistent system of linear equations a system with no solution

increasing function a function whose output values increase as input values increase

independent events two events that are related in such a way that one event's occurrence has no effect on the probability of the other event

independent variable the input variable

inequality a mathematical sentence that compares numbers or expressions using one of the symbols $<$, $>$, $\leq$, or $\geq$

inference a conclusion reached from facts, evidence, and reasoning

integers the set of whole numbers and their opposites

interest the cost to borrow money or the amount earned by lending money

interest rate the percentage of the original amount of money on which the interest will be calculated

irrational number a real number that cannot be written in the form $\frac{a}{b}$, for integers a and b, with $b \neq 0$

lateral area the sum of the areas of a figure's lateral faces only

lateral face one of the parallelograms that form a prism and is not a base

law of large numbers a law that states that the relative frequency of an event becomes closer to the theoretical probability of the event as the number of trials increases

least common denominator (LCD) in a set of fractions, the least common multiple of the denominators

least common multiple (LCM) the least number that is a multiple of all numbers in a set

legs the two sides of a right triangle that form the right angle

like fractions fractions with the same denominator

like terms terms that have the same variable part(s) raised to the same powers; Constants (numbers without variables) are also like terms.

line a collection of points arranged in a straight path

line segment part of a line including two points on the line and all the points between those points

linear association in a scatter plot, points following a pattern that resembles a line

linear function a function whose graph is a straight line

linear pair two angles that have a common side and whose other sides point in opposite directions

literal equation an equation with two or more variables; Formulas are common examples of literal equations.

lowest terms when the numerator and the denominator of a fraction have no common factors other than 1

mean the sum of the values in a data set divided by the number of values

mean absolute deviation (MAD) the mean of all the absolute deviations of a data set

means the values b and c in the proportion $\frac{a}{b} = \frac{c}{d}$

median the middle value when the data are ordered; If there is an even number of data values, the median is the average of the two middle values.

mixed number a number consisting of both a whole number and a fraction, or the opposite of such a number

mode the most common value; A data set can have no mode, one mode, or more than one mode.

multiplicative identity the number 1

multiplicative inverse the reciprocal of a number

mutually exclusive events events that cannot happen at the same time

negative association in a scatter plot, a relationship between two variables for which an increase in one variable corresponds to a decrease in the other variable

no association in a scatter plot, a relationship between two variables for which an increase in one variable doesn't correspond to any particular pattern for the other variable

nonlinear association in a scatter plot, points following a pattern that does not resemble a line

nonlinear function a function whose graph is not a straight line

nonrepeating decimal a nonterminating decimal that has no repeating pattern of digits

nonterminating decimal a decimal that does not terminate or end

nonzero opposites two numbers that are the same distance from zero on a number line

***n*th root** any number x such that x raised to the n power equals some given number a for a whole number $n > 1$

number line a line that has equally spaced intervals labeled with coordinates

numerator the top number of a fraction

numerical expression an expression consisting of numbers and one or more operations

obtuse angle an angle that measures greater than 90° and less than 180°

obtuse triangle a triangle with an obtuse angle

open sentence an equation or inequality that contains one or more variables

ordered pair a pair of numbers in which the first number is the x-coordinate, or abscissa, and the second number is the y-coordinate, or ordinate, of a point's location in the coordinate plane

order of operations mathematical order that should be followed to simplify an expression when there is more than one operation

order-of-magnitude estimate an estimate expressed as a power of 10

ordinate the second number in an ordered pair of numbers; the y-coordinate

origin on a number line, the point with coordinate zero; on a coordinate plane, the point where the x-axis and the y-axis intersect; The ordered pair at the origin is (0, 0).

outcome a result of an experiment

outlier a point that is far from other points in a data set

parallel lines lines on the same plane that never intersect

percent error the ratio of the absolute error of a measurement to the actual value, written as a percent

perfect square a rational number with a rational square root

point a location in space with no length, width, or depth

point-slope form of a linear equation $y - y_1 = m(x - x_1)$ where m is the slope of the line and x_1 and y_1 are the coordinates of a point through which the line passes

polygon a closed figure formed by 3 or more line segments in a plane, such that each line segment intersects 2 other line segments at their endpoints only

population a group of individuals or objects about which information is wanted

positive association in a scatter plot, a relationship between two variables for which an increase in one variable corresponds to an increase in the other variable

power the product that results when a number, called the base, is multiplied by itself the number of times indicated by its exponent

pre-image the original figure in a transformation

prism a three-dimensional figure whose surfaces, called faces, are polygons; At least 2 faces are parallel and congruent and are called bases, and all other faces are parallelograms. (In a right prism, all other faces are rectangles.)

probability a number from 0 to 1 that describes how likely an event is to occur

product the result of multiplying two or more factors together

proper fraction a fraction in which the numerator is less than the denominator

proportion an equation stating that two ratios are equal

proportional relationship a relationship that can be described by an equation of the form $y = kx$ where k is the constant of proportionality

quadratic variation a relationship between x and y in which you can write the function describing the relationship in a form of the general equation, $f(x) = kx^2$ where k is a nonzero constant

quotient the result of division

radius (of a circle) a segment whose endpoints are the center of the circle and a point on the circle (plural: radii)

radius (of a sphere) a line segment joining the center of the sphere and a point on the surface of the sphere (plural: radii)

range the set of allowable outputs of a relation

rate a ratio of two quantities measured in different units

rate of change the ratio of a change in one quantity to a change in a second quantity

ratio a comparison of two quantities by division

rational expression a fraction that includes expressions for the numerator or the denominator

rational number a number that can be expressed as a ratio $\frac{a}{b}$ where a and b are integers and $b \neq 0$; A rational number can be written as a fraction, a decimal, or a percent.

rational square root a square root that is a rational number

reciprocal a number by which a given number must be multiplied to get a result of 1; also called the multiplicative inverse

reflection a transformation of a figure by flipping it across a line or line segment, creating a mirror image of the figure

regular polygon a polygon with all its sides congruent and all it angles congruent

relation a mapping from a set of inputs to a set of outputs

repeating decimal a decimal in which a digit, or a group of digits, other than 0 repeats forever after the decimal point

right angle an angle that measures 90°

right triangle a triangle with a right angle

rigid transformations transformations that do not change the size or shape of a figure

rise the vertical change between two selected points on a line

rotation the turning of a figure around a given point

run the horizontal change between two selected points on a line

sample part of a population

sample space the set of all possible outcomes of an experiment

scale factor the ratio of two corresponding sides in two similar figures

scatter plot a graph that displays data as points

scientific notation a system of writing numbers as the product of a number that is greater than or equal to 1 but less than 10 and an integer power of 10

sides of a polygon the segments forming a polygon

similar figures two figures in which each pair of corresponding angles is congruent and the ratio of the lengths of corresponding sides is constant

simple interest interest earned at a fixed percent of the initial deposit, or principal amount

simplest form of a fraction a fraction in which the numerator and the denominator have no common factor other than 1 or -1

simplify a numerical expression to find the value of a numerical expression

slope of a line the ratio of the vertical change, or rise, between any two points on the line to the horizontal change, or run, between the same two points

slope-intercept form of a linear equation $y = mx + b$ where m is the slope of the line and b is the y-intercept

solution a value for the variable that makes the equation or inequality a true statement

solution set of an inequality the set of all solutions of the inequality

solution of an open sentence a number that makes the open sentence true

solutions values of the variables in an equation that make the equation true

solve to find the value(s) of the variable(s) that make an equation true

sphere the set of all points in space that are a given distance from a point called the center

square of a number the product of a number and itself

square root of a number a factor that can be multiplied by itself to produce the number

standard form of a linear equation $Ax + By = C$ where A, B, and C are integers, and A and B are both nonzero

standard form of a number a number expressed using digits and place values

straight angle an angle that measures 180°

subtrahend a number that is subtracted from another number

supplement one of two supplementary angles

supplementary angles a pair of angles for which the sum of their measures is 180°

surface area of a rectangular prism the sum of the areas of a prism's lateral faces and two bases

system of linear equations two or more linear equations using the same variables

terminating decimal a decimal that has a finite number of nonzero digits to the right of the decimal point

transformation a change in the position, orientation, or size of a figure

translation a sliding of a figure in a straight path without rotation or reflection

transversal a line that intersects two or more lines in a plane

triangle a figure made up of 3 segments joined at their endpoints; Each endpoint is a vertex.

two-way relative frequency table a table that shows the relative frequencies of each data value in a two-way table

two-way table a frequency table for two categorical variables

unbiased sample a sample that is representative of the population

unit rate a rate in which the second quantity in the ratio is 1

variable a symbol that represents a value

variable expression an expression consisting of one or more variables, one or more operations, and possibly one or more numbers; also called an algebraic expression

vertical angles two nonadjacent angles that share a vertex and are formed by two intersecting lines

vertical intercept the value of the variable on the vertical axis at the point where a graph crosses the vertical axis

vertex a point where two sides of a polygon meet (plural: vertices)

volume a measure of space inside a figure

whole number any member of the set $\{0, 1, 2, 3, 4, \ldots\}$

***x*-axis** in a coordinate plane, the horizontal line, or axis

***x*-coordinate** the first number in an ordered pair of numbers; also called the abscissa

***x*-intercept of a graph** the x-coordinate of the point where the graph intersects the x-axis; also called the horizontal intercept

***y*-axis** in a coordinate plane, the vertical line, or axis

***y*-coordinate** the second number in an ordered pair of numbers; also called the ordinate

***y*-intercept of a graph** the y-coordinate of the point where the graph intersects the y-axis; also called the vertical intercept

Symbols

$\mid$	such that
$\in$	is an element of
$\varnothing$ or $\{\}$	null or empty set
$\sqrt{a}$	principal square root of a
π	pi
$\approx$	is approximately equal to
$=$	is equal to
$\neq$	is not equal to
$\cong$	is congruent to; is similar to
$<$	is less than
$>$	is greater than
$\leq$	is less than or equal to
$\geq$	is greater than or equal to
$\lvert x \rvert$	absolute value of x
$-a$	the opposite of a
a^n	a to the nth power
$\{\ldots\}$	description or list of all elements in a set; roster notation
$\%$	percent
$\overline{}$	placed over a digit or a block of digits in a decimal to show that the digit or block of digits repeats
$\pm$	plus or minus
$a : b$	ratio of a to b
$\circ$	degree
$\overline{AB}$	line segment AB
AB	length of line segment AB
$\overrightarrow{AB}$	ray AB
$\overleftrightarrow{AB}$	line AB
$\triangle ABC$	triangle ABC
$\angle ABC$	angle ABC
$m\angle ABC$	measure of angle ABC
⌟	right angle
$\parallel$	is parallel to
$\perp$	is perpendicular to

Properties

Real Number Properties

Let a, b, and c be any real numbers.

Addition Property of Equality	If $a = b$, then $a + c = b + c$ and $c + a = c + b$.	
Addition Property: Addends with Like Signs	For all $a > 0$ and $b > 0$, $a + b = \|a\| + \|b\|$. For all $a < 0$ and $b < 0$, $a + b = -\|a\| + \|b\|$.	
Addition Property: Addends with Unlike Signs	For all $a > 0$ and $b < 0$, If $\|a\| > \|b\|$, then $a + b = \|a\| - \|b\|$. If $\|a\| < \|b\|$, then $a + b = -\|b\| - \|a\|$.	
Subtraction Property of Equality	If $a = b$, then $a - c = b - c$.	
Substitution Property of Equality	If $a = b$, then a may be replaced with b in any expression or equation.	
Multiplication Property of Equality	If $a = b$, then $c \bullet a = c \bullet b$ and $a \bullet c = b \bullet c$.	
Division Property of Equality	If $a = b$ and $c \neq 0$, then $\frac{a}{c} = \frac{b}{c}$.	
Distributive Property	$a(b + c) = ab + ac$	
	Addition	**Multiplication**
Commutative Properties	$a + b = b + a$	$a \bullet b = b \bullet a$
Associative Properties	$(a + b) + c = a + (b + c)$	$(a \bullet b) \bullet c = a \bullet (b \bullet c)$
Inverse Properties	$a + (-a) = 0$ and $(-a) + a = 0$	$a \bullet \frac{1}{a} = 1$ and $\frac{1}{a} \bullet a = 1, a \neq 0$
Identity Properties	$a + 0 = a$ and $0 + a = a$	$a \bullet 1 = a$ and $1 \bullet a = a$

Absolute Value Equations

If $|x| = a$ for some positive number a, then $x = a$ or $x = -a$.

Properties of Exponents

Let a and b be nonzero real numbers. Let m and n be integers.

If n is a positive integer, then $a^n = a \bullet a \bullet a \bullet \ldots \bullet a$ (n factors).

Zero Exponent Property	$a^0 = 1, a \neq 0$
Negative Exponent Property	$a^{-m} = \frac{1}{a^m}, a \neq 0$
Product of Powers Property	$a^m \bullet a^n = a^{m+n}$

Square Root Properties

For nonnegative values of m, n, and p, if $m < n < p$, then $\sqrt{m} < \sqrt{n} < \sqrt{p}$.

Product Property	For real numbers a and b, $\sqrt{ab} = \sqrt{a} \bullet \sqrt{b}$ and $\sqrt{a} \bullet \sqrt{b} = \sqrt{ab}$.
Quotient Property	For real numbers a and b with $b \neq 0$, $\sqrt{\frac{a}{b}} = \frac{\sqrt{a}}{\sqrt{b}}$.

Reciprocal Properties

Reciprocal Property of Multiplication	For any nonzero real number a, $a \bullet \frac{1}{a} = 1$.

For all nonzero real numbers a and b, the reciprocal of $\frac{a}{b}$ is $\frac{b}{a}$.

For any nonzero real number a, $\frac{1}{-a} = \frac{-1}{a} = -\frac{1}{a}$.

For all nonzero real numbers a and b, $\frac{1}{ab} = \frac{1}{a} \bullet \frac{1}{b}$.

Division Properties

For any real number a and nonzero real number b, $a \div b = a \bullet \frac{1}{b}$.

For all real numbers a and b and nonzero real number c, $a + \frac{b}{c} = \frac{a}{c} + \frac{b}{c}$.

For all $a > 0$ and $b > 0$, $a \div b > 0$.

For all $a < 0$ and $b < 0$, $a \div b > 0$.

For all $a < 0$ and $b > 0$, $a \div b < 0$.

Properties of Order

Comparison Property of Order	If $a > b$, then $b < a$. If $a < b$, then $b > a$.
Transitive Property of Order	If $a > b$ and $b > c$, then $a > c$. If $a < b$ and $b < c$, then $a < c$.
Addition Property of Order	If $a > b$, then $a + c > b + c$. If $a < b$, then $a + c < b + c$.
Subtraction Property of Order	If $a > b$, then $a - c > b - c$. If $a < b$, then $a - c < b - c$.
Multiplication Property of Order, Positive Multiplier	If $a > b$ and $c > 0$, then $ca > cb$ and $ac > bc$. If $a < b$ and $c > 0$, then $ca < cb$ and $ac < bc$.
Multiplication Property of Order, Negative Multiplier	If $a > b$ and $c < 0$, then $ca < cb$ and $ac < bc$. If $a < b$ and $c < 0$, then $ca > cb$ and $ac > bc$.
Division Property of Order, Positive Multiplier	If $a > b$ and $c > 0$, then $\frac{a}{c} > \frac{b}{c}$. If $a < b$ and $c > 0$, then $\frac{a}{c} < \frac{b}{c}$.
Division Property of Order, Negative Multiplier	If $a > b$ and $c < 0$, then $\frac{a}{c} < \frac{b}{c}$. If $a < b$ and $c < 0$, then $\frac{a}{c} > \frac{b}{c}$.

Comparison Property of Rational Numbers

For nonzero integers a and c and positive integers b and d,

$\frac{a}{b} > \frac{c}{d}$ if, and only if, $ad > bc$.

$\frac{a}{b} < \frac{c}{d}$ if, and only if, $ad < bc$.

Properties of Proportions

Let a, b, c, and d be real numbers.

Means-Extremes Product Property	$\frac{a}{b} = \frac{c}{d}$ if, and only if, $ad = bc$, given that b and d are not 0.
Reciprocal Property	If $\frac{a}{b} = \frac{c}{d}$, then $\frac{b}{a} = \frac{d}{c}$, given that a, b, c, and d are all nonzero.

Formulary

Geometry

Circle

circumference $C = \pi d = 2\pi r$

area $A = \pi r^2$

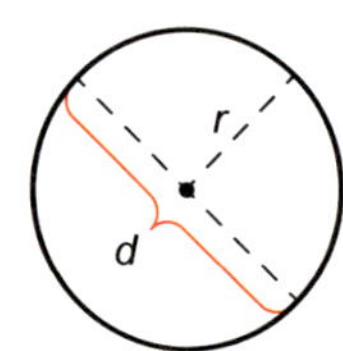

Cone

volume $V = \frac{1}{3}Bh = \frac{1}{3}\pi r^2 h$

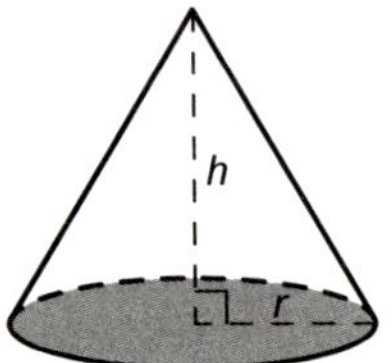

Cylinder

volume $V = Bh = \pi r^2 h$

surface area $S = 2\pi r^2 + 2\pi rh$

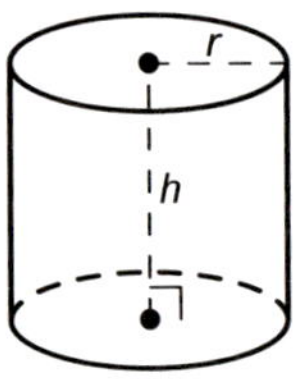

Regular Polygon with *n* Sides

perimeter of regular polygon $P = ns$

area of regular polygon $A = \frac{1}{2}aP$

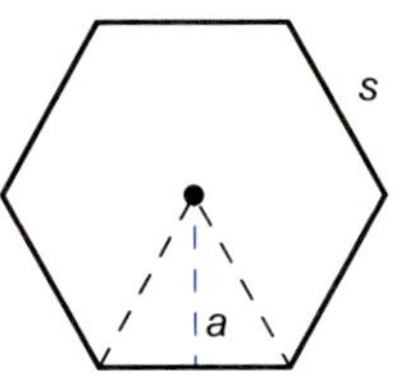

Parallogram

area $A = bh$

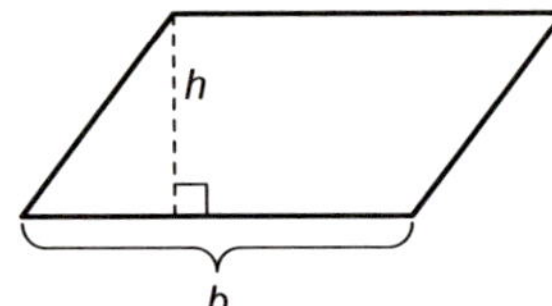

Prism: Cube

volume $V = s^3$

surface area $S = 6s^2$

lateral area of a prism $L = Ph$

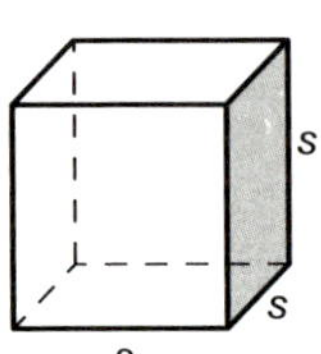

Prism: Right Rectangular

volume $V = lwh$

surface area $S = 2lw + 2lh + 2wh$

length of diagonal $d = \sqrt{l^2 + w^2 + h^2}$

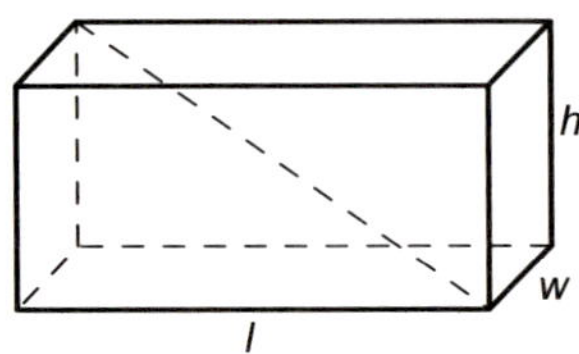

Pyramid

volume $V = \frac{1}{3}Bh$

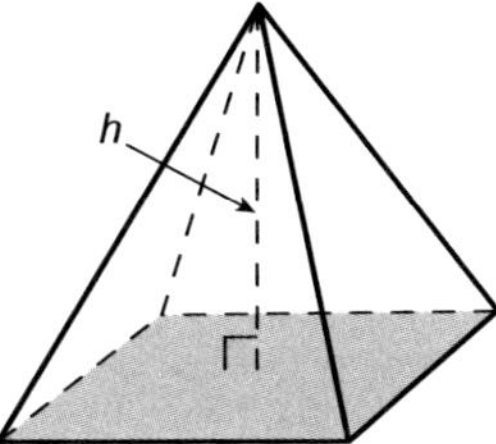

Sphere

volume $V = \frac{4}{3}\pi r^3$

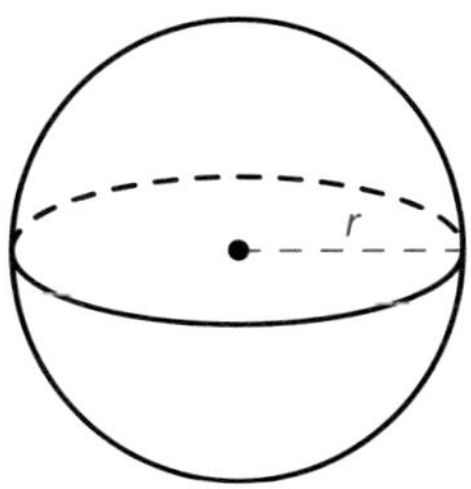

Surface Area Scale Factor Formula

$$SA_1 = (\text{scale factor})^2 \bullet SA_F$$

Rectangle

area $A = lw$

perimeter $P = 2l + 2w$

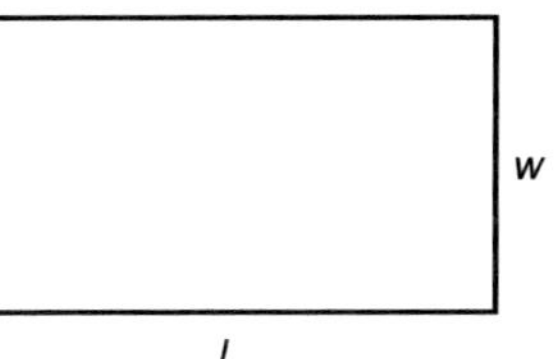

Square

area $A = s^2$

perimeter $P = 4s$

Trapezoid

area $A = \frac{1}{2}h\left(b_1 + b_2\right)$

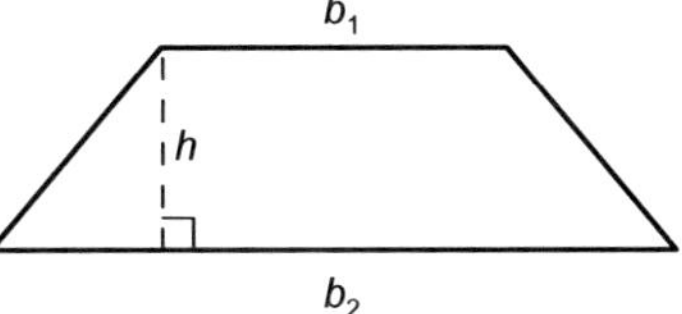

Triangle: General

area $A = \frac{1}{2}bh$

perimeter $P = a + b + c$

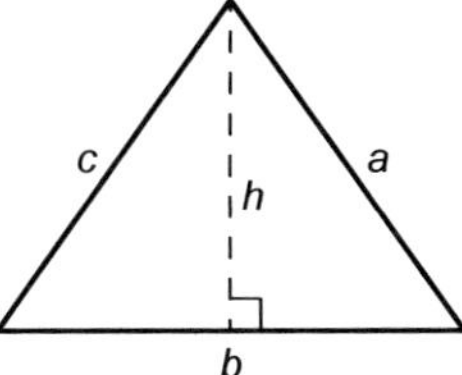

Triangle: Right

Pythagorean theorem $a^2 + b^2 = c^2$

Coordinate Geometry

Line

slope $m = \frac{\text{rise}}{\text{run}} = \frac{\text{vertical change}}{\text{horizontal change}} = \frac{y_2 - y_1}{x_2 - x_1}$

linear equation: standard form $Ax + By = C$

linear equation: slope-intercept form $y = mx + b$

linear equation: point-slope form $y - y_1 = m(x - x_1)$

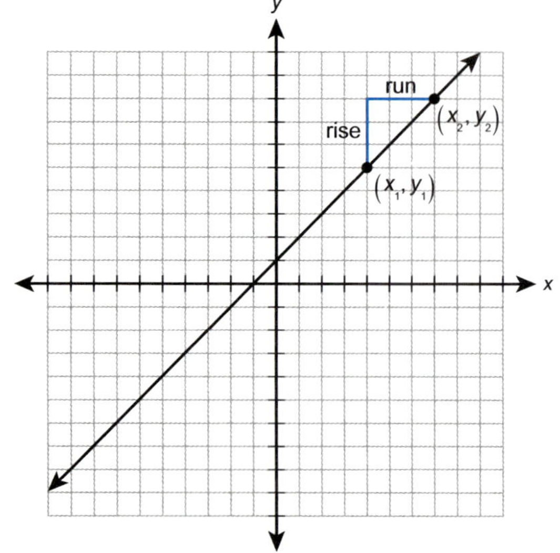

Direct Linear Variation

general formula $y = kx \quad k \neq 0$

Quadratic Variation

general formula $y = kx^2 \quad k \neq 0$

Probability

Simple Theoretical Probability

$$P(E) = \frac{\text{number of outcomes in event } E}{\text{total number of outcomes in sample space } S} = \frac{n(E)}{n(S)}$$

Probability of Mutually Exclusive Events

$$P(A \text{ or } B) = P(A) + P(B)$$

Relative Frequency of an Event (Experimental Probability)

If n is the number of trials of an experiment or number of observations in a study, then the relative frequency of an event E is

$$P(E) = \frac{\text{number of times event } E \text{ has occurred}}{n}.$$

Probability of Independent Events

For independent events A and B,

$$P(A \text{ and } B) = P(A) \bullet P(B).$$

Probability of Dependent Events

For dependent events A and B,

$$P(A \text{ and } B) = P(A) \bullet P(B \text{ after } A)$$

where $P(B \text{ after } A)$ is the probability of B knowing that event A has already occurred.

Geometric Probability

$$P(E) = \frac{\text{area of region of success}}{\text{area of entire region}}$$

Statistics

Mean

$$\overline{x} = \frac{x_1 + x_1 + \ldots + x_n}{n}$$

Absolute Deviation

The absolute deviation is the absolute value of the difference between a data value and the mean.

Mean Absolute Deviation (MAD)

The MAD is the mean of all the absolute deviations. Calculate the absolute deviation for each data value and add. Then divide the sum by the number of data value.

Means-to-MAD Ratio

$$\frac{|\overline{x}_1 + \overline{x}_2|}{\text{MAD}_{\text{larger}}}$$

Median

Arrange the values in order from least to greatest. For an

Odd number of values, use the middle value.

Even number of values, use the average of the middle two values.

Mode

The mode is the value that occurs most often in a set of data. If no one value occurs most often, then there is no mode for the set.

Conversions

Conversion for Length

English Units
1 ft = 12 in.
1 yd = 36 in.
1 yd = 3 ft
1 mi = 5280 ft

Metric Units
1 cm = 10 mm
1 m = 100 cm
1 km = 1000 m

Conversion of Cubic Units

English Units
1 ft^3 = 1728 in^3
1 yd^3 = 27 ft^3

Metric Units
1 cm^3 = 1000 mm^3
1 m^3 = 1,000,000 cm^3

General Applications

Percent of Change

$$\text{percent of change} = \frac{\text{amount of change}}{\text{original amount}} \bullet 100\%$$

Simple Interest

$$I = Prt$$

where I is the amount of interest, P is the principal, r is the annual interest rate, and t is the time in years.

Percent Error

$$\text{percent error} = \frac{|\text{measured value} - \text{actual value}|}{\text{actual value}} \bullet 100\%$$

Percent of Total Cost

$$\text{percent of total cost} = \frac{\text{individual cost}}{\text{total cost}} \bullet 100\%$$

Final Price Formula

$$\text{final price} = \text{pre-tax price} + \text{tax paid}$$

Selected Answers

CHAPTER 1 The Basics

Pages 4–6

Problem Set A

1. 22 **3.** 45 **5.** 60 **7.** 6 **9.** 2

Problem Set B

1. the sum of 12 and v **3.** the quotient of 9 and p **5.** the difference of 3 and a **7.** the product of 7 and r **9.** the quotient of k and 5 **11.** the sum of m and 0 **13.** the quotient of n and 0.8

Problem Set C

1. (a) Ryan is 6 years older than Pete. Pete is 3 years old. **(b)** Jack is 4 years older than Ryan. **3. (a)** A rectangle has a length of 4 cm. A rectangle has a width of 3 cm. **(b)** A rectangle has an area of 12 cm^2. **5. (a)** A shape has 8 sides that each measure 2 mm. **(b)** A shape has 8 angles, some obtuse and some acute.

Pages 7–11

1. (a) 6; **(b)** 1 **3. (a)** 78; **(b)** 3 **5.** 11 **7.** 5 **9.** 1 **11.** 158 **13.** 5 **15.** 34 **17.** 4 **19.** 4 **21.** $23 + 3 \cdot (5 - 1)$ **23.** $(9 + 3) \cdot 5 \div (2 + 4)$ **25.** $(17 - 5) \div (1 + 3)$ **27.** $6 + 2 \cdot 4 = 6 + 8 = 14$; The height is 14 in. **29.** $65 - (4 \cdot 6) + 10 = 65 - 24 + 10 = 41 + 10 = 51$; The final temperature is 51°F. **31.** $(2 \cdot 14) - (3 \cdot 9) = 28 - 27 = 1$; Jamal read 1 more page.

Pages 12–15

1. 67 **3.** 7 **5.** 12 **7.** 25 **9.** 24 **11.** 30 **13.** 6 **15.** 45 **17.** 3 **19.** 17 **21.** 8 **23. (a)** 3; **(b)** 3; **(c)** no reason for concern, $3 < 4$ **25.** 96 in. **27.** 561 in^3 **29.** about 2048 cm^3

Pages 16–19

For Problems 1–5, 9–11, and 15, a variable other than n can be used. **1.** $n - 15$ **3.** $n \div 7$ **5.** $25 - (6 + n)$ **7.** $6n$ **9.** $3 - 2n$ **11.** $\frac{3 + n}{n}$ **13.** $22 - x$ **15.** $5[2(n - 1)]$

For Problems 17–23, answers will vary. Answers given are possible answers. **17.** twice the difference of 3 and x **19.** 3 times the product of m and n **21.** the quotient of 2 and the sum of n and 3 **23.** the difference of the sum of a and b and the sum of twice c and d **25.** $p + (p + 1) + (p + 2) + (p + 3)$ **27.** Isaiah: $2j - 3$, Kaleb: $4(2j - 3)$ **29.** $\$0.05b + \$0.05c$ or $\$0.05(b + c)$ **31.** $0.05x$, $x + 0.05x$

Pages 20–23

1. $11 + 7 = 18$; $11 = 18 - 7$; $7 = 18 - 11$ **3.** $3 \cdot 4 = 12$; $3 = \frac{12}{4}$; $4 = \frac{12}{3}$ **5.** $35 = 7k$; $7 = \frac{35}{k}$; $k = \frac{35}{7}$ **7.** $\frac{r}{5} = 4$; $r = 5 \cdot 4$; $\frac{r}{4} = 5$ **9.** $6 + h = 13$; $6 = 13 - h$; $h = 13 - 6$ **11.** $n + 16 = 28$; $n = 28 - 16$; $16 = 28 - n$ **13.** $m = 1.8 + 0.2$; $m - 1.8 = 0.2$; $m - 0.2 = 1.8$ **15.** $g + \frac{1}{2} = 5\frac{1}{2}$; $g = 5\frac{1}{2} - \frac{1}{2}$; $\frac{1}{2} = 5\frac{1}{2} - g$ **17.** $\frac{75}{w} = 15$; $15w = 75$; $w = \frac{75}{15}$ **19.** $b \cdot 10 = 35$; $b = \frac{35}{10}$; $10 = \frac{35}{b}$ **21.** A variable other than n can be used. $n + 19 = 25$; $n = 25 - 19$; $19 = 25 - n$ **23.** $b = 27 - 14$; $b = 13$ **25.** $n = \frac{84}{4}$; $n = 21$ **27.** $r = 81 - 21$; $r = 60$ **29.** $n = \frac{39}{3}$; $n = 13$ **31.** $192 - x = 51$; $192 - 51 = x$; $141 = x$; One hundred forty-one cans were sold. **33.** Write an equation for the situation: $\frac{c}{3} = 16$. Write a related equation with c by itself on one side: $c = 16 \cdot 3$. Simplify the right side: $c = 48$. The child had 48 crayons.

Pages 24–26

1. Let m = number of monkeys, b = number of bears, and e = number of elephants. Then $m = 5b$ and $b = e - 2$. Substitute 6 for e: $b = 6 - 2 = 4$. Then substitute 4 for b: $m = 5 \cdot 4 = 20$. The zoo has 20 monkeys. **3.** Let w = number of words already written. Then she still has to write $4w$ words. Evaluate $4w$ for $w = 125$: $4 \cdot 125 = 500$. Shawna has to write another 500 words. Add this to the amount already written: $500 + 125 = 625$. The book report must have at least 625 words. **5.** Let l = length and $l - 8$ = width. Use the expression $l(l - 8)$ by substituting values for l and evaluating the expression to find the area. Lengths that give an area between 100 and 200 in^2 are 15, 16, 17, and 18 in. **7.** Let d = distance and t = time. Use the equation $d = rt$. Substitute 504 for d and 9 for t: $504 = r \cdot 9$, or $504 = 9r$. Use guess and check or write a related equation to find r: $r = \frac{504}{9}$, so $r = 56$. Mei's average rate of speed was 56 mph. **9.** First find the total distance of the loop: $3 \cdot 1820 + 2 \cdot 965 = 5460 + 1930 = 7390$. Use the expression $7390n$, where n is the number of loops Mrs. Johansson walks. Then $7390n = 7390 \cdot 2 = 14{,}780$ and $7390n = 7390 \cdot 6 = 44{,}340$. The distances are 14,780 ft and 44,340 ft. **11.** Let n, $n + 2$, and $n + 4$ represent the ages. Write an equation to represent *the sum of the youngest and oldest ages is 16*: $n + (n + 4) = 16$. Use guess and check to find that $n = 6$. The oldest cousin is $n + 4 = 6 + 4 = 10$ years old. **13.** The cost of the two adult tickets is $2 \cdot \$5 = \$10$, leaving \$40 for the children's tickets. If n = number of children's tickets, then $\$2.50n$ = cost of children's tickets. Use the equation $2.5n = 40$ to find how many children's tickets can be bought with \$40. Solve for n by writing the related equation: $n = \frac{40}{2.5} = 16$. The adults can take 16 children with them. If the cost is raised by 50¢, then the new cost is \$3 and $3n = 40$. The related equation is $n = \frac{40}{3}$, so $n \approx 13.3$. There would be enough money for 13, but not 14 children, if the price were raised. If the price were raised, they would have to take 3 fewer children. **15.** Let d = Doug's age, c = Cheryl's age, and e = Ed's age. Then $d = 2c + 1$, $e = 3d$, and $70 \le e \le 90$. Use guess and check by substituting ages for Cheryl, c, into $d = 2c + 1$ to find d, then substitute that value for d in $3d$ to find e. Cheryl is 12, 13, or 14 years old.

Pages 27–29
Solution Manual only

Pages 30–31
Solution Manual only

Pages 32–33
1. B **3.** A **5.** D **7.** D **9.** B **11.** D **13.** 72 cm³
15. The related equation with r isolated on one side of the equation is $r = \frac{54}{9}$. The value of r is $\frac{54}{9}$, or 6. **17.** Write an expression for the apple-juice sales each day: Monday $23 \cdot \$1.65$; Tuesday $19 \cdot \$1.65$; Wednesday $31 \cdot \$1.65$. Simplify each expression: Monday $23 \cdot \$1.65 = \$37.95$; Tuesday $19 \cdot \$1.65 = \$31.35$; Wednesday $31 \cdot \$1.65 = \$51.15$.

CHAPTER 2 Addition and Subtraction on a Nubmer Line

Pages 36–38

Problem Set A
1. 7 **3.** −12 **5.** 14

Problem Set B
1. 158 **3.** 441 **5.** 917 **7.** 475 **9.** 700 **11.** 23 **13.** 153

Problem Set C
1. 6.83 **3.** 31.98 **5.** 1.589 **7.** 141.089 **9.** 395.15
11. 8.345

Pages 39–44
1. −9 **3.** −1

5.
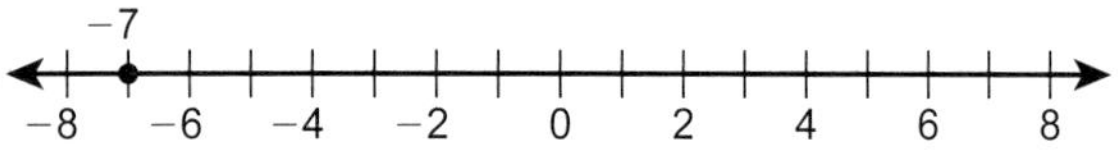

7.
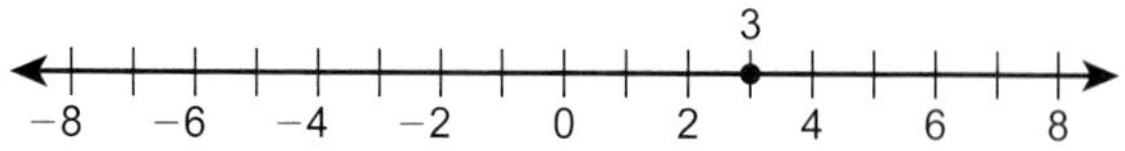

9. > **11.** < **13. (a)** 10; **(b)** −10 **15. (a)** 4; **(b)** 4
17. = **19.** < **21.** $x = 5$ and $x = -5$ **23.** $r = -5, -4, -3, -2, -1, 0, 1, 2, 3, 4, 5$ **25.** no solution **27.** $x = -2, -1, 0, 1, 2$ **29.** Haley, Buan, Trent, Jared, Alana
31. Max, Olivia, Leticia, Ramon, Emilio

Pages 45–49
1.
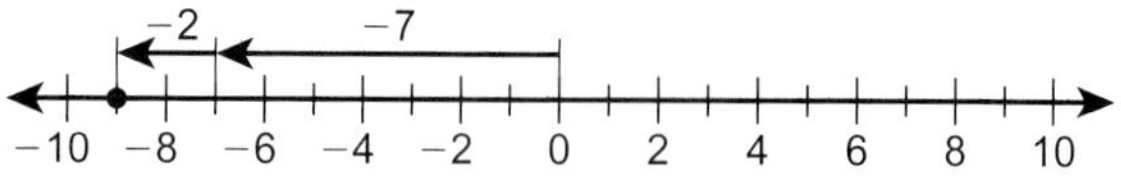

$-7 + (-2) = -9$

3.
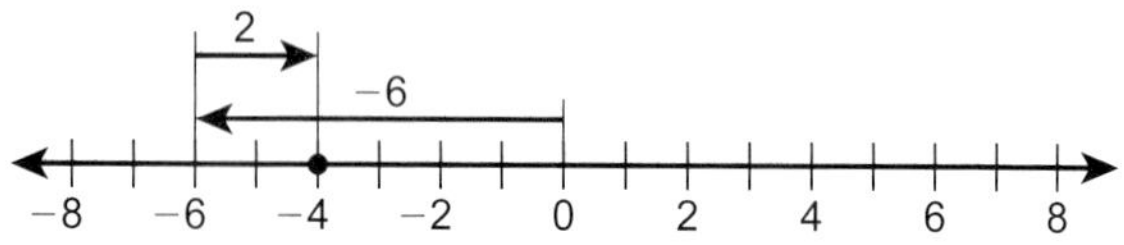

$-6 + 2 = -4$ **5.** 5 **7.** −96 **9.** −40 **11.** −4 **13.** −13
15. > **17.** = **19.** $x = 7$ **21.** $x = 0$ **23.** 39 **25.** 5
27. 20 **29. (a)** Yes; **(b)** \$72 left over; **(c)** Since 72 is a positive number, they will have money left over:
$800 + (-523) + (-125) + (-80) = 72$.

Pages 50–52
1. 1 **3.** 20 **5.** 13 **7.** 6 **9.** −10 **11.** −10 **13.** −8
15. 31 **17.** 7 **19.** 25 **21.** 8 **23.** −4 **25.** −3
27. $x = -17$ **29.** 178°F

Pages 53–55
Solution Manual only

Pages 56–60
1. −1.6 **3.** 0.2 **5.** −2.6 **7.** 0.2 **9.** −33.8 **11.** −32.6

13.
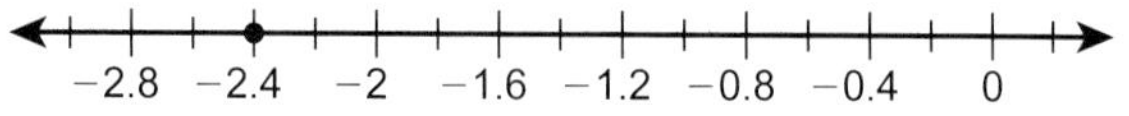

15.
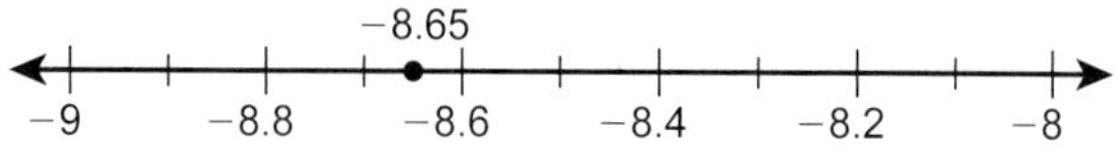

17.
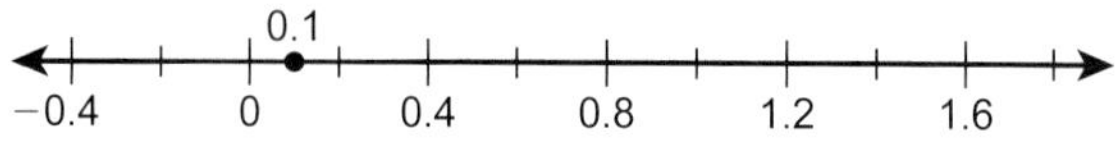

19. < **21.** > **23.** > **25.** −1.4, −0.3, 0.9, 1.3 **27.** −1.9, −0.5, 0.03, 1.7 **29.** College City, Green Valley, Snow Town, Oak Park

Pages 61–64
1. −1.6 **3.** −1.1 **5.** −1.9 **7.** −22.23 **9.** −0.52
11. 8.4 **13.** 13.123 **15.** −0.88 **17.** 34.977 **19.** −27.5
21. −7.1 **23.** −1.46 **25.** 8.455 **27.** $a = 4.8$ **29.** $z = 6.6$
31. $a = -2.5$ **33.** \$76.48

Pages 65–67
Solution Manual only

Pages 68–69

1. D **3.** D **5.** B **7.** C **9.** D **11.** D **13.** −19

15. (a)–(d) See graph.

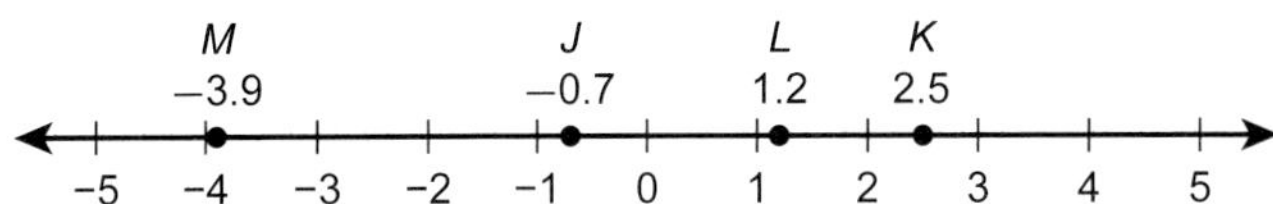

17. The submarine needs to ascend 238 m to reach sea level.

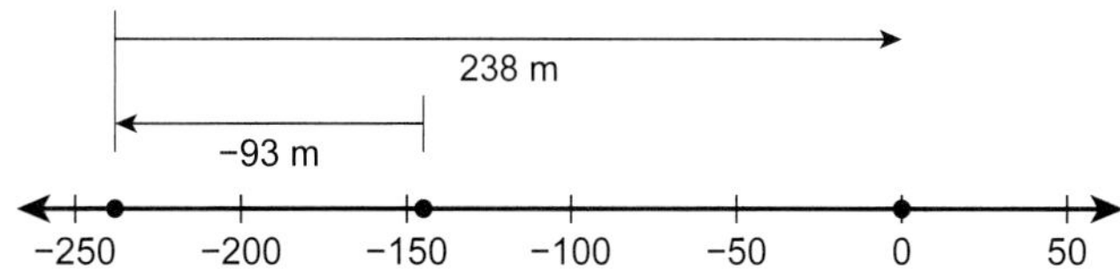

CHAPTER 3 Addition and Subtraction Properties

Pages 72–74

Problem Set A

1. 6.18 **3.** 21.27 **5.** 0.3001 **7.** 1.07 **9.** 8.33

Problem Set B

1.

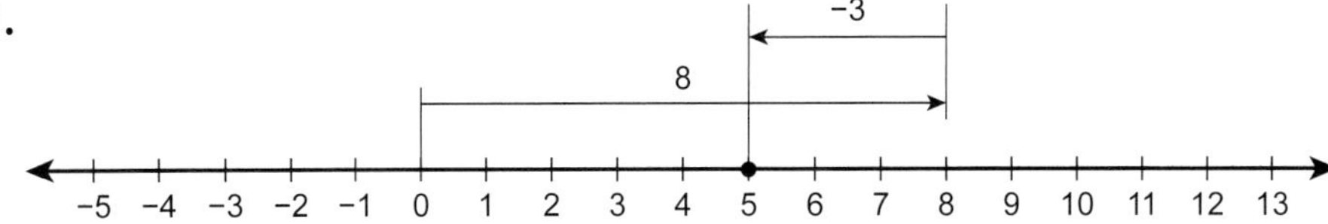

3.

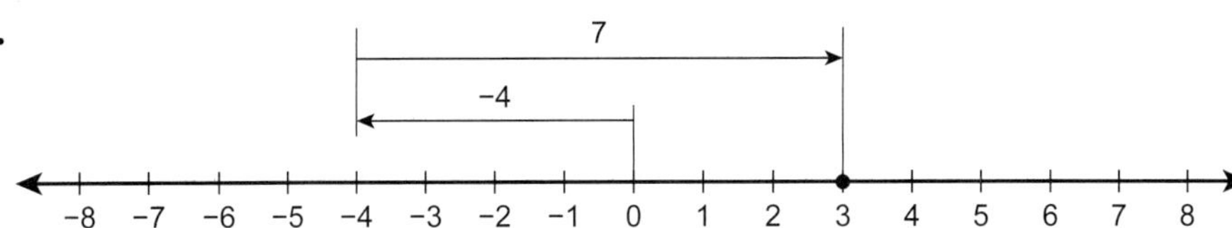

5.

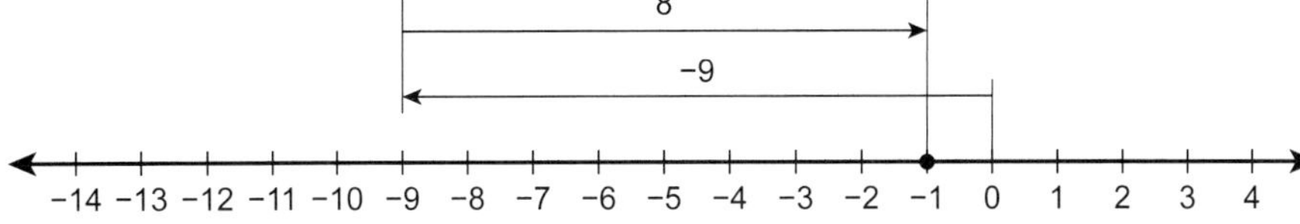

7.

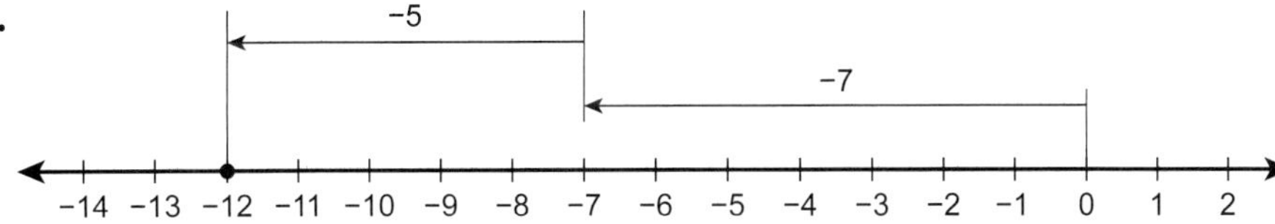

9.

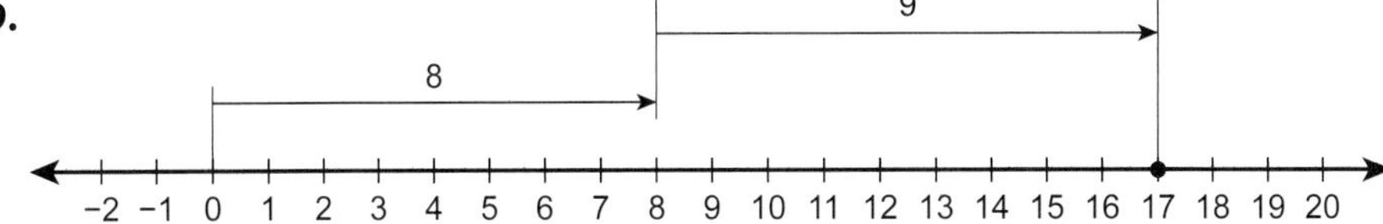

Problem Set C

1. $z = 6$ **3.** $y = 7$ **5.** $n = -2$ **7.** $x = -6$ **9.** $t = -15$
11. $p = -10$

Pages 75–78

1. 2.6 **3.** 14.4 **5.** 18.3 **7.** −1.28 **9.** −27.04 **11.** −4.42 **13.** −0.02 **15.** −194.27 **17.** 138.1 **19.** 419.77 **21.** −9.8 **23.** −6.1 **25.** 5.953 **27.** $m = 24.9$ **29.** $c = 0.9$ **31.** $d = 0$ **33.** −3.75°C

Pages 79–82

1. Opposite of a Sum **3.** Associative Property of Addition **5.** Opposite of a Sum **7.** 54 **9.** 3 **11.** −49 **13.** 87 **15.** 3 **17.** 14.32 **19.** 21.8 **21.** $m = -5$ **23.** $c = -6$ **25.** $y = 3$ **27.** $x = 12$ **29.** \$33 **31.** \$26

Pages 83–84

Solution Manual only

Pages 85–88

1. $x = -20$ **3.** $y = 17$ **5.** $k = -17$ **7.** $a = -16$ **9.** $x = -7$ **11.** $x = 19$ **13.** $z = -14$ **15.** $a = 6.8$ **17.** $k = -9$ **19.** $z = 8.0$ **21.** $m = -3.0$ **23.** $a = 9$ **25.** $z = 2$ **27.** $b = 18$ **29. (a)** $x + 14 = -26$; **(b)** $x = -40$; **(c)** The number is −40. **31. (a)** $c + 275 = 325$; **(b)** $c = 50$; **(c)** Maggie needs to buy 50 cards. **33. (a)** $8.39 - c = 7.14$; **(b)** $c = 1.25$; **(c)** The coupon was worth \$1.25.

Pages 89–93

1. −2538, −411, −156, −86, −40, −28, −12 **3.** 128 m **5.** 9261 m **7.** −44, −30, −22, −7, 23 **9.** 45°F **11.** Philadelphia **13.** The missing amount is −\$405.99. It is a withdrawal because it is a negative number. **15.** 219 ft **17.** −14 ft **19.** Sam: +9; Ella: −1; Anju: −3; Ben: −11 **21.** 20 points

Pages 94–95

Solution Manual only

Pages 96–97

1. D **3.** A **5.** B **7.** C **9.** A **11.** $|P - Q| = 6.1$ **13.** $t = -8$ **15. (a)** −127°C, −59°C, −20°C, 8°C; **(b)** 135°C; **(c)** linseed oil and formic acid; **(d)** propyl alcohol

17.

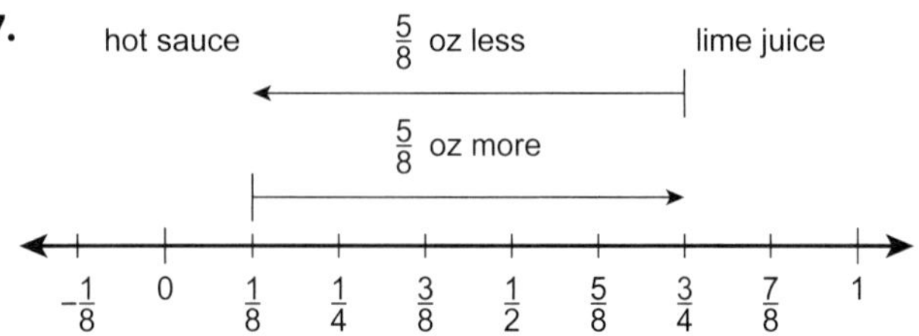

CHAPTER 4 Multiplication and Division

Pages 100–102

Problem Set A

1. 4.5 **3.** 51.6 **5.** 41.8 **7.** 9.284 **9.** 2.146

Problem Set B

1. 9 **3.** 0.09 **5.** 1.1 **7.** 40 **9.** 500

Problem Set C

1. $d = 9$ **3.** $x = -5$ **5.** $b = -16$ **7.** $z = -12$ **9.** $w = -63$ **11.** $n = 50$

Pages 103–106

1. 36 **3.** −30 **5.** 120 **7.** 72 **9.** 219 **11.** 4.2 **13.** 7.68 **15.** −9.1 **17.** 48 **19.** −15 **21.** −70 **23.** negative **25.** negative **27.** 8 **29.** −20 **31.** 8 **33.** 8.2 **35.** −3 **37.** 40

Pages 107–109

1. −7 **3.** −5 **5.** 9 **7.** −4 **9.** 0.9 **11.** 8 **13.** −1 **15.** 0.7 **17.** −30 **19.** 3 **21.** −5 **23.** −5 **25.** 12 **27.** −2 **29.** 1.25

Pages 110–114

1. Identity Property of Multiplication **3.** Reciprocal Property of Multiplication **5.** Reciprocal Property of Multiplication **7.** Zero Property of Multiplication **9.** Zero Property of Multiplication **11.** $3.5 \cdot 0 = 0$; Zero Property of Multiplication **13.** $(7 \cdot 2) \cdot 5 = 7 \cdot (2 \cdot 5) = 7 \cdot 10 = 70$; Associative Property of Multiplication **15.** $\frac{5 \cdot 0}{3 - 6} = \frac{0}{-3} = 0$; Zero Property of Multiplication and zero divided by a nonzero number equals 0 **17.** $3b \cdot 4c = 3 \cdot b \cdot 4 \cdot c = 3 \cdot 4 \cdot b \cdot c = (3 \cdot 4) \cdot (b \cdot c) = 12bc$; Commutative and Associative Properties of Multiplication **19.** $\frac{7}{8} \cdot \frac{r}{5} \cdot \frac{8}{7} = \frac{7}{8} \cdot \frac{8}{7} \cdot \frac{r}{5} = 1 \cdot \frac{r}{5} = \frac{r}{5}$; Commutative, Associative, and Reciprocal Properties of Multiplication **21.** $k = 0$ **23.** $m = 3$ **25.** $b = 9$ **27.** $z = 2.1$ **29.** $r = 2$

Pages 115–116

Solution Manual only

Pages 117–121

1. 6.25; 6.3; 6; 10 **3.** 326.00; 326.0; 326; 330 **5.** $330 + 60 + 50 = 440$ **7.** \$6 + \$14 − \$11 = \$9 **9.** $0.03 + 0.04 + 0.52 = 0.59$ **11.** \$58.60 − \$32.20 = \$26.40 **13.** C **15.** D **17.** $872 + 94 + 349 \approx 900 + 100 + 350 = 1350$; The answer is not reasonable. **19.** $235.98 \div 62.1 \approx 240 \div 60 = 4$; The answer is reasonable. **21.** 64 in^3 **23.** \$800 **25.** about 180 votes

Pages 122–125

1. $r = -2$ **3.** $b = 5$ **5.** $m = -12$ **7.** $x = \frac{15}{2}$ **9.** $g = -2.1$ **11.** $j = -14$ **13.** $b = 24$ **15.** $x = 9$ **17.** $y = -30$ **19.** $z = -8$ **21.** $b = 8$ **23.** $k = -12.8$ **25.** $w = -5$ **27.** $p = -\frac{13}{12}$ **29. (a)** $24 = 1.2x$; **(b)** $x = 20$; **(c)** Mrs. Williams had 20 students in her class last year.

Pages 126–129

1. 49 in² **3.** 5.76 cm² **5.** 48 m **7.** 5 cm² **9.** 8.06 m² **11.** 150.5 m **13.** 20 km **15.** The change is a 14% increase in price. **17.** $r = \frac{d}{t}$ **19.** $b = \frac{2A}{h}$ **21.** $a = \frac{F}{m}$ **23.** $V = IR$ **25.** 9 in. **27.** 56 mph **29.** 4 in.

Pages 130–132

Solution Manual only

Pages 133–135

Solution Manual only

Pages 136–137

1. D **3.** B **5.** C **7.** C **9.** D **11.** A **13.** −5 **15.** \$819.40, approximately \$820 **17.** 4 cm **19. (a)** $\frac{1}{8}n = 28$; **(b)** $n = 224$; 224 cups

CHAPTER 5 Fractions

Pages 140–142

Problem Set A

1. $\frac{6}{2}$ or $\frac{3}{1}$ **3.** $\frac{7}{8}$ **5.** $\frac{0}{100}$ or 0

Problem Set B

1. $P = -\frac{3}{4}, Q = \frac{5}{6}, R = \frac{7}{12}, S = -\frac{5}{12}, T = \frac{1}{12}$

3.

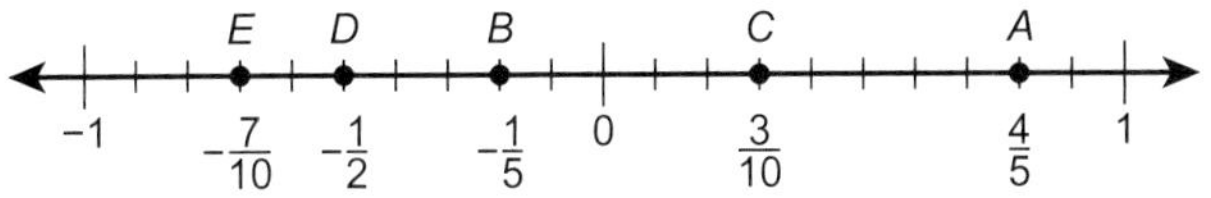

Problem Set C

1. $\frac{3}{4}$ **3.** $\frac{4}{7}$ **5.** $\frac{2}{3}$ **7.** 1

Pages 143–146

1. $\frac{2}{5}$ **3.** $\frac{1}{4}$ **5.** $\frac{13}{18}$ **7.** $\frac{9}{-10}$ **9.** $\frac{27}{32}$; already in lowest terms **11.** $\frac{12}{13}$ **13.** Yes **15.** No **17.** No **19.** No **21.** $\frac{x}{8}$ **23.** $\frac{7w}{15}$; already in simplified form **25.** $\frac{7}{8}$ in. **27.** $\frac{5}{12}$ **29.** Yes

Pages 147–150

1. $\frac{1}{16}$ **3.** $-\frac{9}{20}$ **5.** $\frac{21}{32}$ **7.** $\frac{3}{10}$ **9.** $\frac{6}{35}$ **11.** $\frac{2x}{3y}$ **13.** $\frac{1}{5}$ **15.** $\frac{3}{10}$ **17.** $\frac{3}{8}$ **19.** $\frac{3}{5}$ **21.** 1 **23.** $\frac{2}{3}$ **25.** $\frac{3}{5}$ **27.** 1 **29.** $\frac{e}{3f}$ **31. (a)** $\frac{3}{5}$; **(b)** $\frac{2}{5}$ cup **33.** $\frac{7}{32}$ mi **35.** $\frac{1}{10}$ gal **37. (a)** $\frac{15}{16}$; **(b)** $\frac{5}{32}$

Pages 151–154

1. $\frac{1}{6}$ **3.** $-\frac{3}{2}$ **5.** $\frac{9}{8}$ **7.** $\frac{y}{x}$ **9.** $\frac{2}{5}$ **11.** 9 **13.** $\frac{5}{64}$ **15.** $\frac{1}{6}$ **17.** −30 **19.** 2 **21.** $\frac{20}{27}$ **23.** $\frac{1}{4}$ **25.** $-\frac{4}{15}$ **27.** $\frac{2}{m}$ **29.** $\frac{7}{9}$ **31.** $\frac{3}{4}$ **33.** 12 **35.** $\frac{1}{8}$ **37.** $\frac{1}{16}$ ft

39.

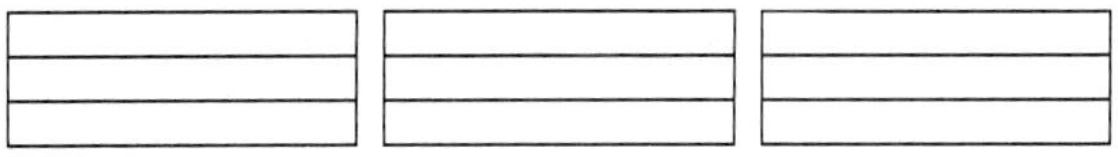

Pages 155–157

Solution Manual only

Pages 158–162

1. LCD: 6 **3.** LCD: 36 **5.** LCD: 56 **7.** LCD: 40 **9.** LCD: 42 The answers for Problems 11–17 all use the LCD. Other fractions with other denominators are also possible. **11.** $\frac{2}{4}$ and $\frac{3}{4}$ **13.** $\frac{-10}{15}$ and $\frac{9}{15}$ **15.** $\frac{20}{35}$ and $\frac{21}{35}$ **17.** $\frac{2}{16}$ and $\frac{3}{16}$ **19.** $\frac{6}{12}, \frac{4}{12}$, and $\frac{3}{12}$ **21.** $>$ **23.** $<$ **25.** $>$ **27.** $>$ **29.** Maria **31.** blue jay

Pages 163–167

1. $\frac{7}{9}$ **3.** $\frac{3}{5}$ **5.** $-\frac{1}{5}$ **7.** $\frac{3}{4}$ **9.** $\frac{5}{8}$ **11.** $\frac{1}{8}$ **13.** $\frac{41}{60}$ **15.** $-\frac{29}{150}$ **17.** $\frac{55}{63}$ **19.** $\frac{4}{9}$ **21.** $2\frac{1}{4}$ **23.** $1\frac{1}{3}$ **25.** $1\frac{1}{6}$ **27.** 5 **29.** $-3\frac{1}{5}$ **31.** $4\frac{1}{5}$ **33.** $-6\frac{3}{4}$ **35.** $3\frac{3}{4}$ **37.** D **39.** $-1\frac{7}{60}$ **41.** $-1\frac{11}{40}$ **43.** Ebenezer spent $\frac{23}{40}$ of his allowance. **45.** Roscoe drank $\frac{3}{8}$ qt more water than he drank milk and juice combined.

Pages 168–172

1. $7\frac{1}{2}$ **3.** $-4\frac{1}{3}$ **5.** $5\frac{2}{3}$ **7.** $2\frac{1}{2}$ **9.** $1\frac{13}{16}$ **11.** $3\frac{2}{15}$ **13.** $6\frac{1}{2}$ **15.** $9\frac{4}{5}$ **17.** $\frac{5}{4}$ **19.** $\frac{21}{5}$ **21.** $-\frac{11}{6}$ **23.** $-\frac{13}{5}$ **25.** $\frac{79}{8}$ **27.** $\frac{53}{9}$ **29.** $\frac{129}{13}$ **31.** $\frac{3b + a}{b}$ **33. (a)** $5\frac{1}{4} + 2\frac{5}{8} + 4\frac{1}{2} = \frac{21}{4} + \frac{21}{8} + \frac{9}{2} = \frac{42}{8} + \frac{21}{8} + \frac{36}{8} = \frac{99}{8} = 12\frac{3}{8}$; **(b)** The total amount of meat served was $12\frac{3}{8}$ lb.

35. (a) $\left(2\frac{7}{10}+3\frac{1}{2}\right)-4\frac{3}{4}=\frac{27}{10}+\frac{7}{2}-\frac{19}{4}=\frac{54}{20}+\frac{70}{20}-\frac{95}{20}$ $=\frac{29}{20}=1\frac{9}{20}$; **(b)** The group hiked $1\frac{9}{20}$ mi farther before lunch. **37. (a)** 6.75 h $=6\frac{75}{100}$ h $=6\frac{3}{4}$h; 5 h 48 min $=5\frac{48}{60}$h $=5\frac{4}{5}$h; $5\frac{1}{2}+6\frac{3}{4}+5\frac{4}{5}=\frac{11}{2}+\frac{27}{4}+\frac{29}{5}=\frac{110}{20}+\frac{135}{20}+\frac{116}{20}$ $=\frac{361}{20}=18\frac{1}{20}$; **(b)** The total time was $18\frac{1}{20}$ h.

39. (a) $3+\frac{3}{2}+\frac{3}{4}+\frac{3}{8}+\frac{3}{16}=\frac{3}{1}+\frac{3}{2}+\frac{3}{4}+\frac{3}{8}+\frac{3}{16}$ $=\frac{48}{16}+\frac{24}{16}+\frac{12}{16}+\frac{6}{16}+\frac{3}{16}=\frac{93}{16}=5\frac{13}{16}$; **(b)** The fifth term is $\frac{3}{16}$ and the sum is $5\frac{13}{16}$.

Pages 173–176

1. 12 **3.** $32\frac{1}{2}$ **5.** $7\frac{2}{9}$ **7.** $-21\frac{1}{4}$ **9.** -200 **11.** $-12\frac{15}{16}$ **13.** $1\frac{2}{5}x$ **15.** 3 **17.** 7 **19.** $3\frac{3}{10}$ **21.** 16 **23.** $3\frac{1}{8}$ **25.** $\frac{x}{10}$ **27.** $1\frac{47}{55}$ **29.** $1\frac{5}{12}$ ft **31.** 4 cups **33.** $109\frac{3}{4}$ lb

Pages 177–180

1. $x=2\frac{1}{6}$ **3.** $c=72$ **5.** $k=5\frac{2}{5}$ **7.** $m=-4\frac{13}{14}$ **9.** $a=\frac{8}{15}$ **11.** $y=\frac{2}{9}$ **13.** $d=-7\frac{8}{15}$ **15.** $q=-32$ **17.** $b=-4\frac{2}{7}$ **19.** $m=4$ **21.** $g=28$ **23.** $b=-6\frac{1}{16}$ **25. (a)** $f+2\frac{3}{4}=5\frac{1}{2}$; **(b)** $f=2\frac{3}{4}$; **(c)** Finn ran $2\frac{3}{4}$ mi. **27. (a)** $7\frac{1}{2}x=45$; **(b)** $x=6$; **(c)** There were 6 runners on the team. **29. (a)** $\frac{6\frac{1}{2}+2\frac{1}{4}+x+4\frac{3}{4}}{4}=4\frac{1}{8}$; **(b)** $x=3$; **(c)** The value of x is 3.

Pages 181–182

Solution Manual only

Pages 183–185

Solution Manual only

Pages 186–187

1. B **3.** C **5.** C **7.** C **9.** B **11.** $\frac{7}{12}$ **13.** 24 **15.** Alberto **17.** $3\frac{3}{8}$ in. **19.** $h=5\frac{1}{3}$

CHAPTER 6 Combined Operations

Pages 190–192

Problem Set A

1. 26 **3.** 24 **5.** -29 **7.** 14 **9.** 91 **11.** 5

Problem Set B

1. $x=-9$ **3.** $n=10$ **5.** $w=-1$ **7.** $p=-22$ **9.** $h=18$ **11.** $x=-5$ **13.** $z=-30$

Problem Set C

1. $x=6$ **3.** $t=7$ **5.** $h=-3$ **7.** $j=-1$ **9.** $m=3$ **11.** $w=-3$ **13.** $k=30$

Pages 193–197

1. $2(3+6)=2\cdot 3+2\cdot 6$; $2\cdot 9=6+12$; $18=18$ **3.** $-1(-3+2)=-1\cdot(-3)+(-1)\cdot 2$; $-1\cdot(-1)=3+(-2)$; $1=1$ **5.** $2(8-9)=2\cdot 8-2\cdot 9$; $2\cdot(-1)=16-18$; $-2=-2$ **7.** $5\cdot 5+5\cdot 1$ **9.** $4v+4\cdot 7$ **11.** $-9\cdot 1+(-9)\cdot y$ **13.** $3(6+9)$ **15.** $4(2-11)$ **17.** $5(8-s)$ **19.** $-2(x+y)$ **21.** 130 **23.** 594 **25.** 816 **27.** 800 **29.** 462.58 **31.** $x=3$ **33.** $n=7$ **35.** $s=-1$ **37.** 40 cm **39.** 4600 m^2 **41. (a)** $23.99; **(b)** $4.82

Pages 198–201

1. $4x$, $5x$ are like terms. $4y$, $3y$ are like terms. **3.** $3c$, $6c$ are like terms. **5.** $4ab$, $-5ab$ are like terms. 7, -5 are like terms. **7.** $9v$, $2v$ are like terms. $6uv$, $-uv$ are like terms. **9.** 3, 1, -9 are like terms. $3rs$, $8rs$ are like terms. **11.** $4w$, $4w$ are like terms. $2wxy$, $-wxy$ are like terms. **13.** $1.5s$, $2s$ are like terms. $1.5w$, $2w$ are like terms. **15.** $7a$ **17.** $2c$ **19.** $-6.2x$ **21.** 0 **23.** $\frac{1}{2}a$ **25.** $6a+5b$ **27.** $6t+5$ **29.** 6 **31.** $12z+7w$ **33.** $3r-9rs-6$ **35.** $3x+15$ **37.** $-8.5x-2.5$ **39.** $11b-5ab$ **41. (a)** $d+0.06d=1.00d+0.06d=1.06d$; $1.06d$ dollars; **(b)** $m+0.18m=1.00m+0.18m=1.18m$; $1.18m$ dollars; **(c)** $r+0.045r=1.00r+0.045r=1.045r$; $1.045r$ dollars **43. (a)** $8.85x+2.15x+35=11x+35$; $(11x+35)$ dollars; **(b)** $11x+35=11\cdot 12+35=132+35=167$; $167; **(c)** The cost of 19 shirts is $244 because $11\cdot 19+35=209+35=244$. The cost of 20 shirts is $233 because the cost per shirt is $11-0.10\cdot 11=11.00-1.10=9.90$ and $9.90\cdot 20+35=198+35=233$.

Pages 202–204

Solution Manual only

Pages 205–209

1. 9 **3.** -18 **5.** 12 **7.** -18 **9.** $20\frac{2}{3}$ **11.** 51 **13.** 2 **15.** -3 **17.** -83 **19.** -5 **21.** -26 **23.** -54 **25.** 45 **27.** $\frac{1}{2}$ **29.** $-\frac{12}{5}$ **31.** 11.68 **33.** 12.6 **35.** 0.0125 **37.** 4.45 **39.** -5 **41. (a)** 41°F; **(b)** −15°C; **(c)** −40°C

Pages 210–212

Solution Manual only

Pages 213–218

1. $x=13$; Check: $2x-12=14$; $2\cdot 13-12\stackrel{?}{=}14$; $14=14$ **3.** $x=2.5$; Check: $12.5+3x=20$; $12.5+3\cdot 2.5\stackrel{?}{=}20$; $20=20$ **5.** $x=2.5$; Check: $-1+12x=29$; $-1+12\cdot 2.5\stackrel{?}{=}29$; $29=29$ **7.** $x=4$;

Check: $-12x + 14 = -34$; $-12 \cdot 4 + 14 \stackrel{?}{=} -34$; $-34 = -34$ **9.** $x = -15$ **11.** $x = 9$ **13.** $x = 72$ **15.** $x = -8$ **17.** $x = 4$ **19.** $x = -4$ **21.** $n = -\frac{4}{3}$ **23.** $x = 11$ **25.** $a = 22.1$ **27.** $b = -3$ **29.** $x = -23$ **31.** $s = -8.2$ **33. (a)** Let n represent the number. $3n + 5 = 38$; $n = 11$; The number is 11. **(b)** Let n represent the number. $\frac{1}{3}n - 7 = 5$; $n = 36$; The number is 36. **(c)** Let n represent the number. $5n = 2n + 18$; $n = 6$; The number is 6. **35.** Let x represent the price of the sweater. $x + 0.04x = 46.28$; $x = 44.50$; The price of the sweater was \$44.50. **37.** Let x represent the amount earned by the laborer. Then $x + 0.50x$ represents the amount earned by each carpenter, and $x + 0.80x$ represents the amount earned by the supervisor. $x + (x + 0.50x) + (x + 0.50x) + (x + 0.80x) = 4205$; $x = 725$; The laborer earned \$725, each carpenter earned \$1087.50, and the supervisor earned \$1305.

Pages 219–221

Solution Manual only

Pages 222–227

1. $\{-4.8, 0, 4\}$ **3.** $\{4, 4.2, 5\}$ **5.** $\left\{-\frac{3}{5}, 0, \frac{1}{10}\right\}$

7. $x < 8$;

9. $-6 < x$;

11. $v \leq 12$;

13. $x \geq 7$;

15. $x < 16$;

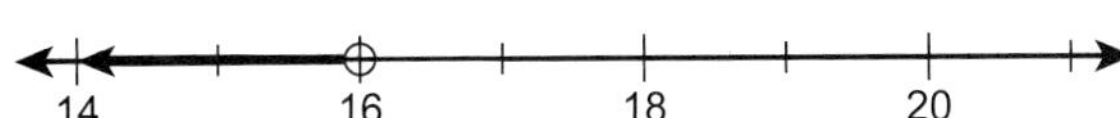

17. $d > 5$;

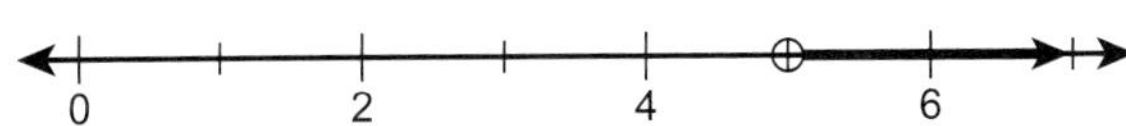

19. $-\frac{1}{4} < k$;

21. $-4 > x$;

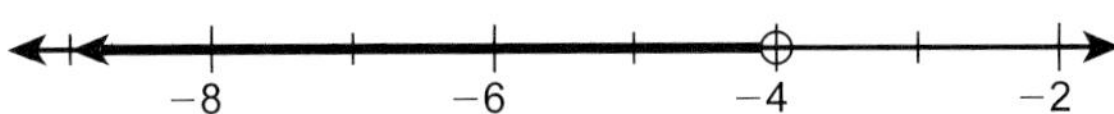

23. $-\frac{32}{7} > a$;

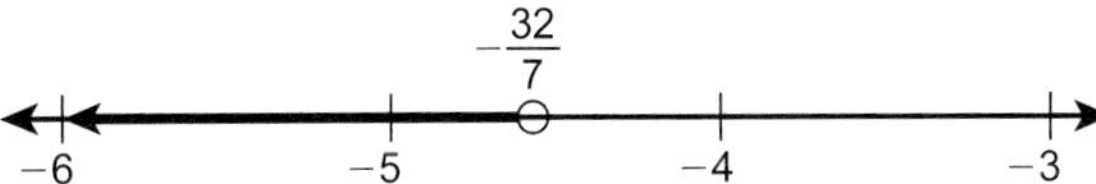

25. $-\frac{19}{2} < x$;

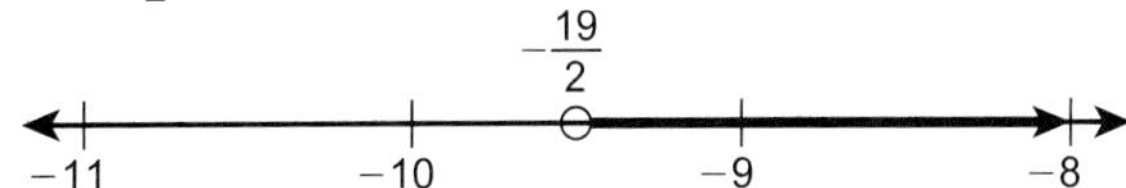

27. (a) Let $x =$ the number of pounds to be sent. cost of Ship Fast $<$ cost of Deliver Quick; $2.75 + 1.05x < 4.15 + 0.85x$; $x < 7$; It will cost less to use Ship Fast for any weight less than 7 lb. **(b)** $2.75 + 1.05x = 4.15 + 0.85x$; $x = 7$; $2.75 + 1.05 \cdot 7 = 2.75 + 7.35 = 10.10$; The two companies charge the same amount when the weight is 7 lb. That amount is \$10.10. **29. (a)** Let $x =$ the number of miles. cost of Green $<$ cost of Sedan Service; $2.15 + 1.95x < 2.90 + 1.80x$; $x < 5$; It costs less to ride a Green taxicab than a Sedan Service taxicab for any distance less than 5 mi. **(b)** $2.15 + 1.95x = 2.90 + 1.80x$; $x = 5$; $2.15 + 1.95 \cdot 5 = 2.15 + 9.75 = 11.90$; The cost is the same for a ride of 5 mi. That cost is \$11.90.

Pages 228–229

Solution Manual only

Pages 230–231

1. D **3.** D **5.** A **7.** D **9.** C **11.** 1800 **13.** B and C **15.** -2.2; First simplify the innermost parentheses in the numerator. Second simplify the parentheses in the numerator and the denominator by first multiplying and then adding. Next find the product of the two numbers in the numerator and the denominator. Lastly find the quotient. **17. (a)** $k = 5$; First use the distributive property to simplify the right side of the equation. Second move the variables to the left side of the equation and simplify. Next move the constants to the right side of the equation and simplify. Lastly divide both sides of the equation by the coefficient to isolate the variable. **(b)** $14 \neq -10$; This equation does not have a solution because, in attempting to solve it, you arrive at the false statement $14 = -10$. To arrive at this conclusion, first multiply both sides of the equation by 2 to eliminate the fraction. Second use the distributive property to simplify the right side of the equation. Next move the variables to the left side of the equation and simplify. It is at this point in the process that you arrive at the false statement. **(c)** $d=\frac{10}{3}$; First multiply both sides of the equation by 4 to eliminate the fraction, and simplify. Second move the variables to the left side of the equation and simplify. Next move the constants to the right side of the equation and simplify. Lastly divide both sides of the equation by the coefficient to isolate the variable.

CHAPTER 7 Ratio, Proportion, and Percent

Pages 234–236

Problem Set A

1. $\frac{3}{5}$ **3.** $\frac{5}{7}$ **5.** $\frac{3}{2}$ **7.** $\frac{5}{7}$ **9.** $\frac{11}{20}$ **11.** 5

Problem Set B

1. 0.4 **3.** 3.5 **5.** $0.8\overline{3}$ **7.** $\frac{1}{5}$ **9.** $\frac{27}{10}$ **11.** $\frac{54}{5}$

Problem Set C

1. $\frac{5}{14}$ **3.** $\frac{3}{16}$ **5.** $\frac{1}{4}$ **7.** $\frac{3}{2}$ **9.** $\frac{7}{3}$ **11.** $\frac{4}{35}$

Pages 237–240

1. $\frac{5}{6}$; 5 to 6; 5 : 6 **3.** $\frac{2}{3}$; 2 to 3; 2 : 3 **5.** $\frac{2}{7}$; 2 to 7; 2 : 7 **7.** $\frac{1}{3}$; 1 to 3; 1 : 3 **9.** $\frac{5}{7}$; 5 to 7; 5 : 7 **11.** $\frac{5}{1}$ or 5; 5 to 1; 5 : 1 **13.** $\frac{8}{3}$; 8 to 3; 8 : 3 **15.** $\frac{5}{3}$; 5 to 3; 5 : 3 **17.** $\frac{1}{3}$; 1 to 3; 1 : 3 **19.** $\frac{1}{6}$; 1 to 6; 1 : 6 **21.** $\frac{1}{5}$; 1 to 5; 1 : 5 **23.** $\frac{18 \div 2}{20 \div 2}=\frac{9}{10}$; 9 to 10; 9 : 10 **25.** $\frac{10 \div 10}{60 \div 10}=\frac{1}{6}$; 1 to 6; 1 : 6 **27.** $\frac{8}{7}$ **29.** $\frac{35}{16}$

Pages 241–244

1. $\frac{7 \text{ acorns}}{4 \text{ h}}$ **3.** $\frac{120 \text{ L}}{14 \text{ min}}$ **5.** $\frac{4 \text{ cars}}{22 \text{ min}}$ **7.** $\frac{\$3.96}{4 \text{ songs}}$; \$0.99/song **9.** $\frac{20 \text{ min}}{2 \text{ mi}}$; 10 min/mi **11.** $\frac{\$37.50}{5 \text{ tickets}}$; \$7.50/ticket **13.** $\frac{200 \text{ m}}{8 \text{ s}}$; 25 m/s

15. Badgers: 23.4 points/game; Senators: 21 points/game; Thunder: 24 points/game **17.** 23 points/game **19. (a)** $\frac{\$65}{10 \text{ ft}}$ or \$6.50/ft; **(b)** The unit rate that describes the cost of fencing is \$6.50/ft. **21. (a)** $\frac{30 \text{ cm}}{5 \text{ h}}$ or 6 cm/h; **(b)** The unit rate that describes the bamboo's rate of growth is 6 cm/h. **23. (a)** Burger Barn: \$0.90/hamburger; **(b)** Bargain Burger: \$0.75/hamburger; **(c)** The unit rate that describes the price per hamburger is lower at Bargain Burger. So Bargain Burger offers a better deal on its hamburgers than Burger Barn.

Pages 245–247

Solution Manual only

Pages 248–252

For Problems 1–9, answers will vary. Sample answers are given. **1.** $\frac{1}{2}$; $\frac{16}{32}$ **3.** $\frac{14}{6}$; $\frac{70}{30}$ **5.** $\frac{1}{3}$; $\frac{16}{48}$ **7.** $\frac{2}{10}$; $\frac{4}{20}$ **9.** $\frac{3}{1}$; $\frac{6}{2}$ **11.** $6 \cdot 6 = 36 \cdot 1$; Because $36 = 36$, the ratios form a proportion. **13.** $10 \cdot 11 = 5 \cdot 22$; Because $110 = 110$, the ratios form a proportion. **15.** $15 \cdot 6 = 18 \cdot 5$; Because $90 = 90$, the ratios form a proportion. **17.** $11.9 \cdot 6 = 42 \cdot 1.7$; Because $71.4 = 71.4$, the ratios form a proportion. **19.** $m = 1$ **21.** $b = 4$ **23.** $y = 6.4$ **25.** $x = 13$ **27.** $b = 22$ **29.** $n = 0.9375$ **31.** $a = 10$ **33. (a)** $\frac{93 \text{ mi}}{1.5 \text{ h}} = \frac{x \text{ miles}}{3.5 \text{ h}}$; **(b)** $x = 217$; **(c)** The car will travel 217 mi in $3\frac{1}{2}$ h. **35. (a)** $\frac{\$27.00}{3 \text{ h}} = \frac{\$x}{8 \text{ h}}$; **(b)** $x = 72$; **(c)** The employee will make \$72 in 8 h. **37. (a)** $\frac{40 \text{ pages}}{60 \text{ min}} = \frac{220 \text{ pages}}{x \text{ minutes}}$; **(b)** $x = 330$; **(c)** It will take the student 330 min to read 220 pages. **39. (a)** 3600 gal; **(b)** $73\frac{1}{3}$ h

Pages 253–257

1. 0.7 **3.** 0.6 **5.** 0.76 **7.** $\frac{3}{4}$ **9.** $1\frac{1}{2}$ **11.** $\frac{17}{50}$ **13.** 721% **15.** 3% **17.** 100.4% **19.** 0.078 **21.** 0.005 **23.** 0.1085 **25.** 16% **27.** 560% **29.** 42% **31.** $\frac{3}{5}$ **33.** $\frac{1}{20}$ **35.** $\frac{21}{25}$ **37.** 80% **39.** 0.034 **41.** 44% **43. (a)** $\frac{1}{4}$, 28%, 0.32; **(b)** 0.5%, 0.05, $\frac{1}{5}$

Pages 258–260

1. $\frac{x}{30} = \frac{76}{100}$; $x = 22.8$; So 22.8 is 76% of 30. **3.** $\frac{13}{15} = \frac{x}{100}$; $x \approx 86.7$; So 13 is about 86.7% of 15. **5.** $\frac{20}{x} = \frac{10}{100}$; $x = 200$; So 20 is 10% of 200. **7.** $\frac{17}{x} = \frac{20}{100}$; $x = 85$; So 17 is 20% of 85. **9.** $\frac{15}{30} = \frac{x}{100}$; $x = 50$; So 15 is 50% of 30. **11.** $\frac{133}{x} = \frac{35}{100}$; $x = 380$; So 133 is of 35% of 380. **13.** $\frac{99}{150} = \frac{x}{100}$; $x = 66$; So 99 is 66% of 150. **15.** $\frac{17}{85} = \frac{x}{100}$; $x = 20$; So 17 is 20% of 85. **17.** $\frac{x}{50} = \frac{34}{100}$; $x = 17$; So 17 is 34% of 50. **19.** $\frac{21}{28} = \frac{x}{100}$; $x = 75$; So 21 is 75% of 28. **21.** $\frac{7}{x}=\frac{14}{100}$; $x = 50$; So 7 is 14% of 50. **23.** $\frac{147}{210} = \frac{x}{100}$; $x = 70$; So 147 is 70% of 210. **25.** $\frac{x}{65} = \frac{150}{100}$; $x = 97.5$; So 97.5 is 150% of 65.

27. $\frac{x}{3.5} = \frac{6}{100}$; $x = 0.21$; So 0.21 is 6% of 3.5. **29.** $\frac{5.07}{65} = \frac{x}{100}$; $x = 7.8$; So 5.07 is 7.8% of 65. **31.** $\frac{x}{170} = \frac{7}{100}$; $x = 11.9$; The tax on the phone is \$11.90. **33.** $\frac{260}{x} = \frac{40}{100}$; $x = 650$; There are 650 students total. **35.** $\frac{300}{1230} = \frac{x}{100}$; $x \approx 24.4$; About 24.4% of the songs are hip-hop. **37.** $\frac{140}{420} = \frac{x}{100}$; $x \approx 33.3$; About 33.3% of the messages were from Shannon.

Pages 261–263

Solution Manual only

Pages 264–265

1. D **3.** C **5.** D **7.** C **9. (a)** $\frac{1}{5}$; **(b)** $\frac{2}{1}$; **(c)** $\frac{9}{25}$; **(d)** $\frac{5}{2}$ **11. (a)** 14.8 m/patio; **(b)** 14.8 m; The unit rate 14.8 m/patio represents that 14.8 m of fencing is needed to enclose 1 patio. **13.** 38.4 s **15.** $1\frac{13}{25}$ **17.** $\frac{51}{x} = \frac{30}{100}$; $x = 170$; A total of 170 tickets were sold.

CHAPTER 8 Proportion Applications

Pages 268–270

Problem Set A

1.

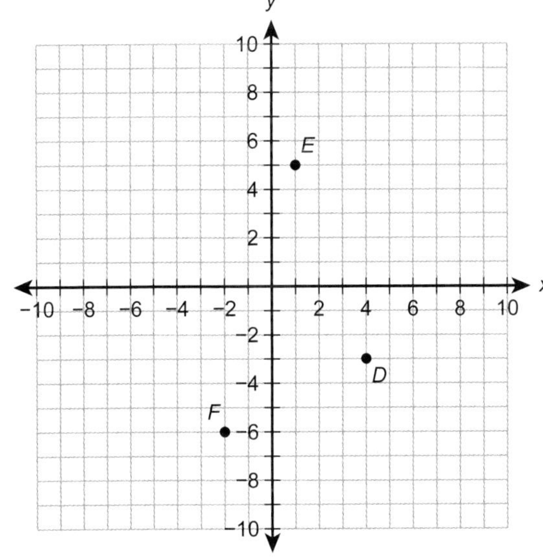

3.

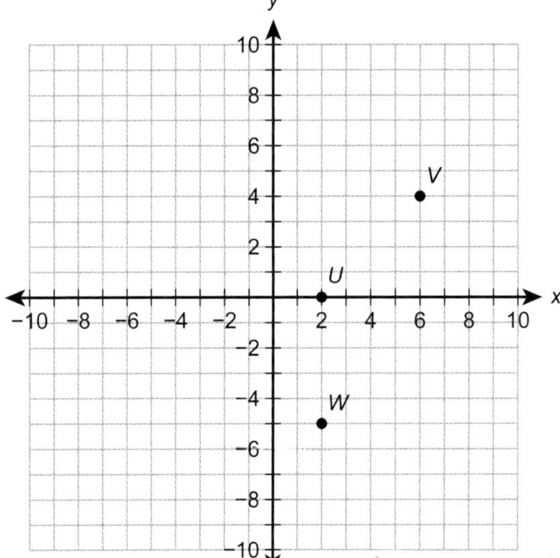

5.

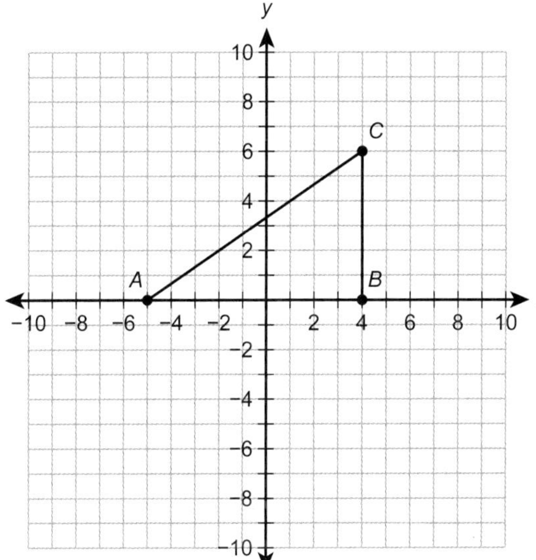

7.

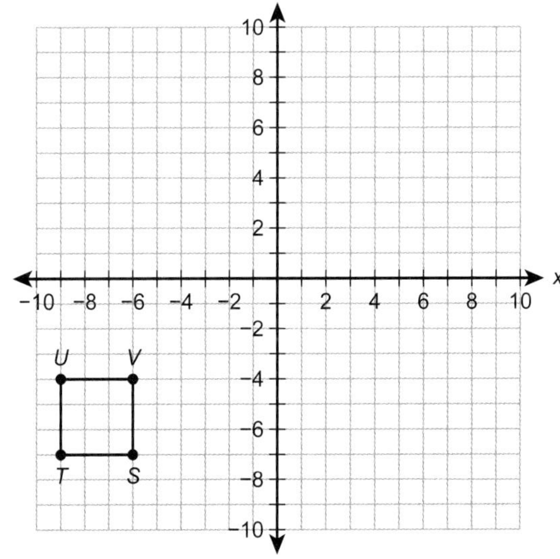

Problem Set B

1. $a = 5.5$ **3.** $f = 28$ **5.** $m = 12.5$ **7.** $p = \frac{13}{5}$ **9.** $q = 10.5$ **11.** $c = \frac{7}{9}$

Problem Set C

1. 0.9 and 90% **3.** 0.575 and 57.5% **5.** 32% and $\frac{8}{25}$ **7.** 0.625 and $\frac{5}{8}$ **9.** 4.8% and $\frac{6}{125}$ **11.** 2.45 and $\frac{49}{20}$

Pages 271–274

1. $x = 2$ **3.** $x = -1.\overline{54}$ **5.** $x = 5$ **7.** $x = 19$ **9.** $x = -1.5$ **11.** $x = -10.2$ **13. (a)** Let c represent the number of customers who preferred Cleanbiz. **(b)** $\frac{6}{10} = \frac{c}{150}$; **(c)** $c = 90$; **(d)** Of those surveyed, 90 customers preferred Cleanbiz. **15. (a)** Let c represent the new commission on the \$250,000 house. **(b)** $\frac{25{,}000}{300{,}000} = \frac{c}{250{,}000}$; **(c)** $c = 20{,}833.\overline{3}$; **(d)** The realtor would earn a \$20,833.33 commission for selling a \$250,000 house. **17. (a)** Let d represent actual distance between the class and the treasure. **(b)** $\frac{1}{3} = \frac{8.5}{d}$; **(c)** $d = 25.5$; **(d)** The treasure is 25.5 ft away from the class. **19. (a)** Let s represent shipping charges on a 50 lb package. **(b)** $\frac{15.50}{20} = \frac{s}{50}$; **(c)** $s = 38.75$; **(d)** Samir would pay \$38.75 to ship a 50 lb package. **21. (a)** Let l represent the length of the housing development. **(b)** $\frac{5}{10} = \frac{2}{l}$; **(c)** $l = 4$; **(d)** The development is 4 mi long. **23. (a)** Let g represent the number of people who answered the geography question correctly. **(b)** $\frac{4}{7} = \frac{g}{434}$; **(c)** $g = 248$; **(d)** Of those surveyed, 248 people answered the geography question correctly.

Pages 275–279

1. not similar **3.** $x = 4$ **5.** $x = 18$ **7.** scale factor: $1\frac{2}{3}$; enlargement **9.** scale factor: 1.5; enlargement **11.** 7.5 cm **13.** 44 cm

Pages 280–283

1. proportional; constant of variation of 2 **3.** proportional; constant of variation of 10 **5.** not proportional **7.** proportional; constant of variation of 4 **9.** $y = \frac{2}{3}x$; When $y = 7$, $x = \frac{21}{2}$. **11.** $h = -3d$; When $h = 4$, $d = -\frac{4}{3}$. **13.** $g = \frac{1}{4}t$; When $g = 9$, $t = 36$. **15.** $y = -\frac{1}{4}x$; When $x = 10$, $y = -\frac{5}{2}$. **17.** $y = \frac{1}{3}x$ **19.** $b = -\frac{5}{2}a$ **21.** $y = -\frac{1}{4}x$ **23.** Let m represent the number of gallons bought and c represent the total cost. $c = 2.67m$; $34.71 = 2.67m$; $m = 13$; There were 13 gal of gas purchased for \$34.71. **25.** Let m represent the number of miles and t represent time in hours. $t = 0.25m$; $t = 0.25 \cdot 5.7 = 1.425$; It will take Oni 1.425 h to run 5.7 mi. **27.** Let l represent load and s represent stretch of spring. $k = \frac{s}{l} = \frac{2.5}{7} \approx 0.3571$; $s = 0.3571l$; $5 = 0.3571l$; $l \approx 14.001$; A load of approximately 14.001 kg would stretch the spring 5 cm.

Pages 284–286

Solution Manual only

Pages 287–290

1. 0.084 **3.** 1.473 **5.** 270% **7.** 80% **9.** 70% **11.** 67.5% **13.** $\frac{24}{60} = \frac{x}{100}$; $24 \cdot 100 = 60 \cdot x$; $2400 = 60x$; $\frac{2400}{60} = \frac{60x}{60}$; $40 = x$; So 24 is 40% of 60. **15.** $\frac{x}{180} = \frac{48}{100}$; $x \cdot 100 = 180 \cdot 48$; $100x = 8640$; $\frac{100x}{100} = \frac{8640}{100}$; $x = 86.4$; So 86.4 is 48% of 180. **17.** $\frac{12}{x} = \frac{30}{100}$; $12 \cdot 100 = x \cdot 30$; $1200 = 30x$; $\frac{1200}{30} = \frac{30x}{30}$; $40 = x$; So 12 is 30% of 40. **19.** $\frac{36}{x} = \frac{40}{100}$; $36 \cdot 100 = x \cdot 40$; $3600 = 40x$; $\frac{3600}{40} = \frac{40x}{40}$; $90 = x$; So 36 is 40% of 90. **21.** $\frac{x}{325} = \frac{74}{100}$; $x \cdot 100 = 325 \cdot 74$; $100x = 24{,}050$; $\frac{100x}{100} = \frac{24{,}050}{100}$; $x = 240.5$; So 240.5 is 74% of 325. **23.** $\frac{x}{25} = \frac{30}{100}$; $x \cdot 100 = 25 \cdot 30$; $100x = 750$; $\frac{100x}{100} = \frac{750}{100}$; $x = 7.5$; So 7.5 is 30% of 25. **25. (a)** Let c represent the cash Yoshi had before he paid his bill. $\frac{28.8}{c} = \frac{36}{100}$; $c = 80$; Yoshi had \$80 before he paid his supermarket bill. **(b)** Let t represent the tip. $\frac{t}{16.50} = \frac{16}{100}$; $t = 2.64$; $16.50 + 2.64 = 19.14$; $80 - 28.80 = 51.20$; $51.20 - 19.14 = 32.06$; Yoshi had \$32.06 left after he bought dinner and tipped the server. **27.** Let q represent the number of questions Marisol answered correctly. $\frac{q}{45} = \frac{80}{100}$; $q = 36$; Marisol answered 36 questions correctly. **29. (a)** Let v represent the percent of students who voted for Carlos. $\frac{75}{250} = \frac{v}{100}$; $v = 30$; So 30% of the eligible students voted for Carlos. **(b)** Let l represent the number of students that voted for LaToya. $\frac{l}{250} = \frac{32}{100}$; $l = 80$; LaToya received 80 votes. **(c)** $75 + 80 = 155$;

Carlos and LaToya had 155 votes. $250 - 155 = 95$; There were 95 students whose votes were not yet accounted for. Let s represent the number of votes Stephanie received. $\frac{s}{95} = \frac{60}{100}$; $s = 57$; Stephanie received 57 votes.
(d) LaToya received the most votes and won the election.

Pages 291–295

1. 40% decrease **3.** about 36.8% decrease **5.** about 53.3% increase **7.** 60% decrease **9.** 406.4% increase **11.** about 16.3% increase **13.** about 42.9% increase **15.** about 69.8% increase **17.** 125% increase **19.** about 21.2% increase **21.** 5% increase **23.** November and December because $\frac{33 - 28}{33} = \frac{5}{33} \approx 15.2\%$ **25.** 1250 min **27.** about 46.2% **29.** about 6.8% **31.** about 6.7%

Pages 296–297

Solution Manual only

Pages 298–301

1. \$75 **3.** \$1600 **5.** \$3500 **7.** 2.9% **9.** 3.5 years **11.** \$202.50 **13.** 9 years **15.** about \$883.33 **17.** 4% **19.** about \$713.33 **21.** 6.5 years **23.** \$4000 **25.** \$220.80 **27.** \$11,200 **29. (a)** \$5150 after 1 year; \$5300 after 2 years; \$5450 after 3 years; **(b)** about 34 years

Pages 302–303

Solution Manual only

Pages 304–305

Solution Manual only

Pages 306–307

1. B **3.** C **5.** D **7.** B **9.** D **11.** 17.5 N **13.** approximately 9% **15.** 3.5% **17. (a)** The x-coordinate represents 12 almonds in the mixture, and the y-coordinate represents 48 peanuts in the mixture. The ratio of the number of peanuts to the number of almonds in the mixture is $\frac{y}{x}$, equal to the rate $\frac{48 \text{ peanuts}}{12 \text{ almonds}}$.
(b) The x-coordinate represents 1 almond in the mixture, and the y-coordinate represents 4 peanuts in the mixture. The ratio of the number of peanuts to the number of almonds in the mixture is $\frac{y}{x}$, equal to the unit rate 4 peanuts/almond.
(c) For both points, the ratio of $\frac{y}{x}$ is equal to 4: point (12, 48): $\frac{48}{12} = 4$, point $\frac{4}{1} = 4$. Because the ratio of y to x is constant at 4, the number of peanuts in the mixture varies directly with the number of almonds in the mixture, with a constant of variation of 4.

CHAPTER 9 Plane Figures

Pages 310–312

Problem Set A

1. $\overleftrightarrow{SD}$, $\overleftrightarrow{DS}$ **3.** $\overleftrightarrow{PC}$, $\overleftrightarrow{CP}$ **5.** line a and line b **7.** $\overleftrightarrow{AH}$, $\overleftrightarrow{HW}$, $\overleftrightarrow{AW}$

Problem Set B

1. $\angle O$, $\angle NOP$, $\angle PON$ **3.** $\angle 2$, $\angle S$

Problem Set C

1. regular **3.** none of these **5.** none of these

Pages 313–317

1. alternate interior **3.** adjacent **5.** alternate exterior **7.** alternate exterior **9.** corresponding **11. (a)** 72°; **(b)** 108°; **(c)** 72°; **(d)** 108° **13. (a)** 38°; **(b)** 142°; **(c)** 142°; **(d)** 38° **15.** Answers will vary. Sample answer: $\angle 2$ is adjacent to the angle labeled 65°, the sum of the two angle measures is 180°, and $180 - 65 = 115$, so $m\angle 2 = 115°$. $\angle 1$ forms a pair of corresponding angles with $\angle 2$, and $m\angle 2 = 115°$, so $m\angle 1 = 115°$. Another possible answer: $\angle 3$ forms a pair of corresponding angles with the angle labeled 65°, so $m\angle 3 = 65°$. $\angle 1$ is adjacent to $\angle 3$, and the sum of the two angle measures is 180°, and $180 - 65 = 115$, so $m\angle 1 = 115°$. **17. (a)** alternate exterior: transversal b; **(b)** alternate interior: transversal c; **(c)** corresponding: transversal a; **(d)** corresponding: transversal d
19. The definitions are equivalent because if two lines are not in the same plane, they cannot intersect. Any two lines can be classified in exactly one of the three ways because any two lines are either in the same plane or not in the same plane. If they are in the same plane, then they either intersect or they are parallel. If they are not in the same plane, then they are skew.

Pages 318–322

1. obtuse **3.** right **5.** obtuse **7.** $x = 17$ **9.** $x = 45$ **11.** $x = 58$ **13.** $x = 55$ **15.** $b = 39$ **17.** $d = 34$

Pages 323–326

1.

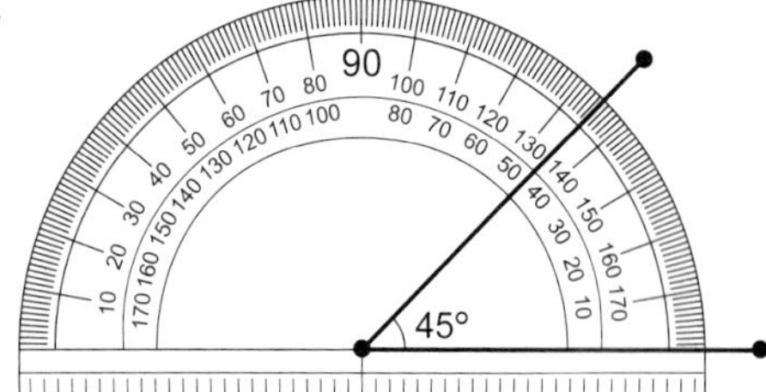

3.

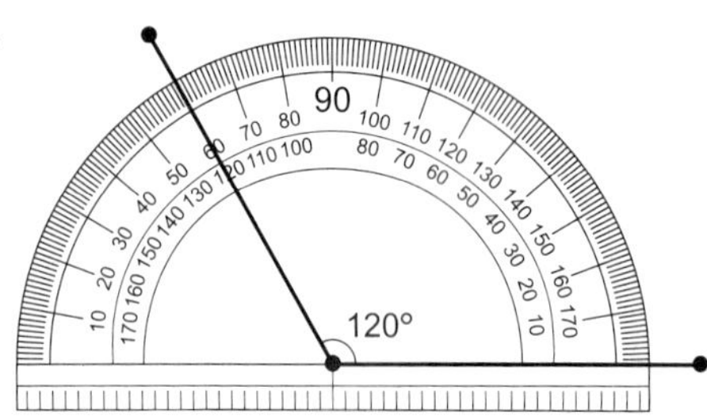

5.

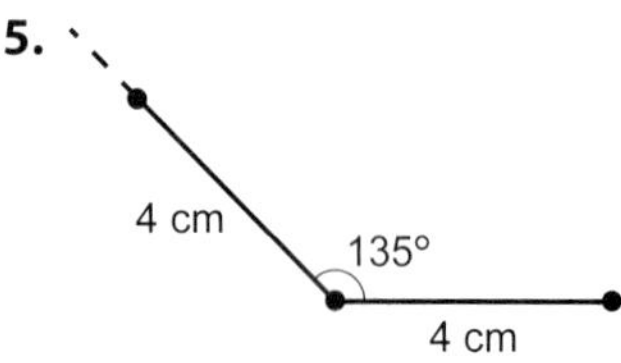

7.

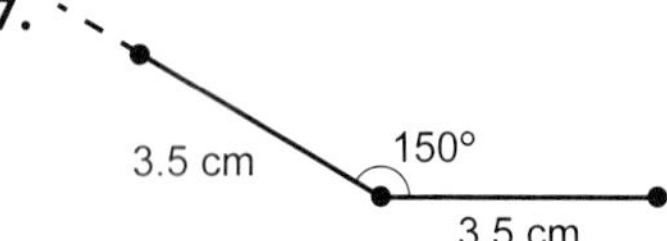

9.

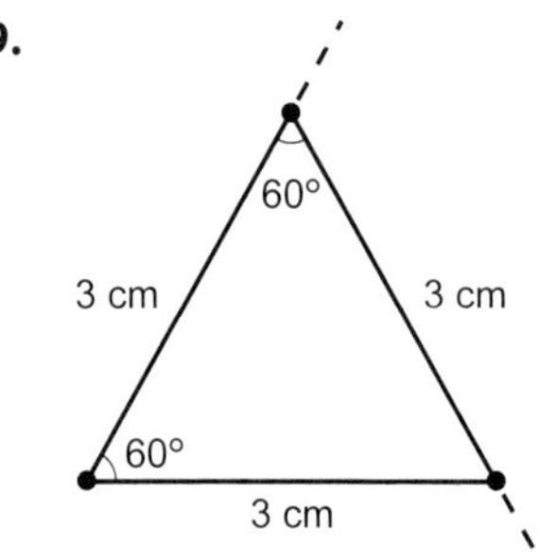

11.

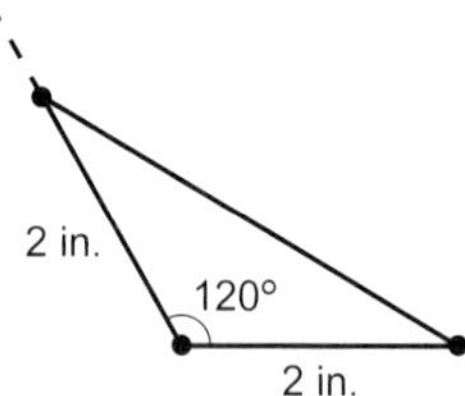

13.

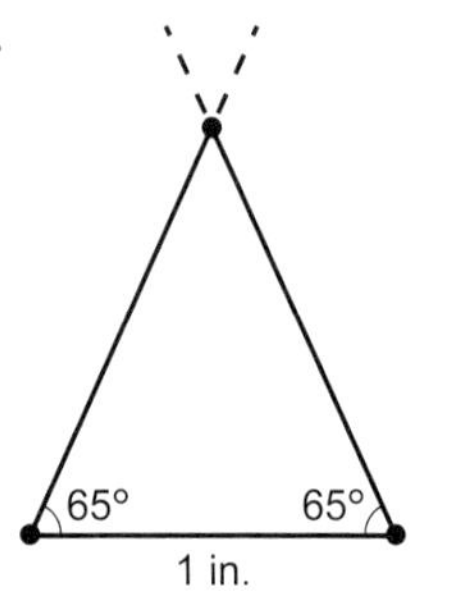

15.

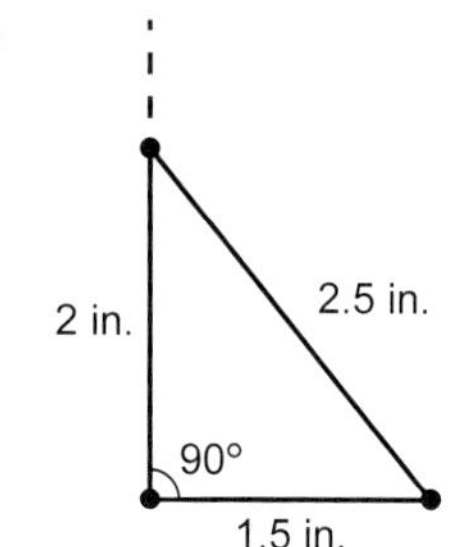

17.

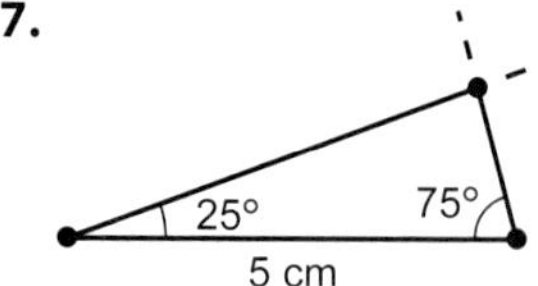

Pages 327–332

1. 144 m^2 **3.** 10.8 m^2 **5.** 414 cm^2 **7.** $1\frac{11}{16}$ m^2 **9.** 13 in^2 **11.** 6 units **13.** 9 m **15.** 24 ft **17.** 28 m **19.** 522 yd^2 **21.** 154 mm^2 **23.** 84 in^2 **25.** 32 cm^2 **27.** $75.60 **29.** If the formula for the area of a rectangle is written as $A = bh$, where b is the length and h is the width, then the formula for the area of a triangle is one-half of it, because any rectangle can be divided into two congruent triangles by connecting opposite vertices.

Pages 333–337

1. 396 km^2 **3.** 900 $unit^2$ **5.** 59.5 $unit^2$ **7.** 330 in^2 **9.** $37\frac{1}{8}$ m^2 **11.** xy mm^2 **13.** 6 units **15.** 20 m **17.** 5 cm **19.** 728 mm^2 **21.** 174 in^2 **23.** 18 $unit^2$ **25.** $78 **27.** 5.25 ft^2

Pages 338–342

1. 585 $unit^2$ **3.** 213.3 cm^2 **5.** 10.8 m^2 **7.** 85 $unit^2$ **9.** 108 $unit^2$ **11.** 5166.6 cm^2 **13.** Find the area of the shaded and unshaded regions. The unshaded region is a triangle whose base and height are the same as the base and height of the rectangle. The area of the unshaded region is $\frac{1}{2} \cdot 11 \cdot 6 = 33$. The shaded region is equivalent to a rectangle with a triangle removed.

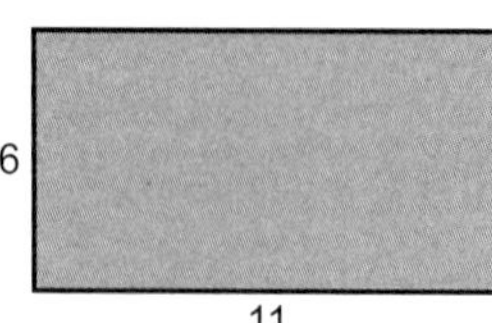

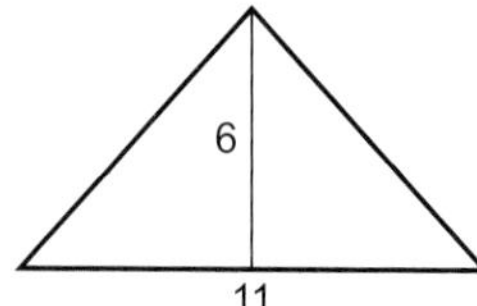

The area of the shaded region is the area of the rectangle minus the area of the triangle: $(11 \cdot 6) - 33 = 33$ $unit^2$. The area of the unshaded region equals the area of the shaded region.

Pages 343–345

Solution Manual only

Pages 346–347

1. D **3.** C **5.** B **7.** D

9.

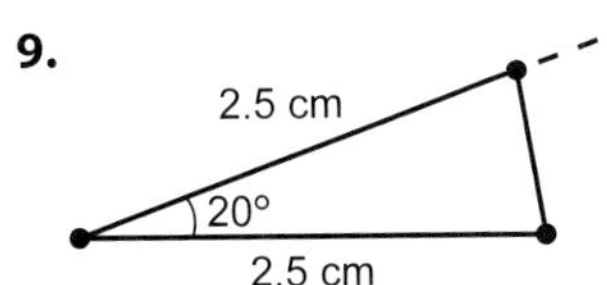

11. 96 unit^2 **13. (a)** There are two possible shapes of the sign. First the base angles could measure 40°, which means that the vertex equals $180° - (40° + 40°) = 100°$. Or the vertex angle could measure 50°, which means that the sum of the base angles is $180° - 40° = 140°$ and each base angle measures 70°. **(b)** First construct a triangle with two congruent sides with a length of 5 in. and an included angle of 100°.

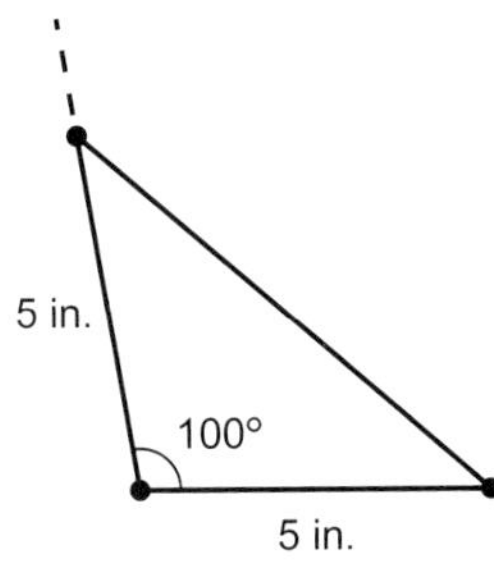

Then construct a triangle with two congruent sides with a length of 5 in. and an included angle of 40°.

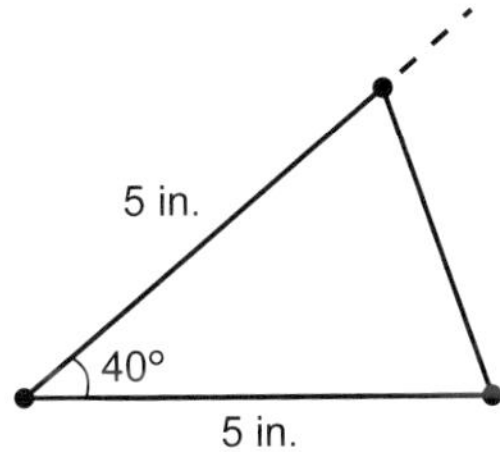

CHAPTER 10 Circles and Measurement

Pages 350–352

Problem Set A

1. approximately equal to 44 **3.** approximately equal to $\frac{11}{14}$ **5.** approximately equal to $7\frac{6}{7}$ **7.** approximately equal to 24 **9.** approximately equal to 39

Problem Set B

1. approximately equal to 47.1 **3.** approximately equal to $1\frac{4}{7}$ **5.** approximately equal to $7\frac{6}{7}$ **7.** approximately equal to 3.8 **9.** approximately equal to 9

Problem Set C

1. approximately equal to 78.5 **3.** approximately equal to $\frac{11}{56}$ **5.** approximately equal to $1\frac{25}{63}$ **7.** approximately equal to $28\frac{2}{7}$ **9.** approximately equal to $21\frac{13}{32}$

Pages 353–356

1. (a) $\overline{QK}, \overline{QT}, \overline{QR}$; **(b)** $\overline{MR}, \overline{KR}$; **(c)** $\overline{KR}$ **3. (a)** $\overline{RP}, \overline{RF}$; **(b)** $\overline{PF}$; **(c)** none **5. (a)** $\overline{FL}, \overline{FR}, \overline{FD}, \overline{FA}$; **(b)** $\overline{LR}, \overline{LA}, \overline{DR}, \overline{DA}$; **(c)** $\overline{LA}, \overline{DR}$ **7.** True **9.** False **11.** True **13.** $6\frac{1}{2}$ ft **15.** 69 cm **17.** The name of the circle is the center point of the circle. Because $\overline{KR}$ is a chord that passes through the center, it must be a diameter.

19. 15 **21. (a)** $\overline{AB}, \overline{CD}, \overline{EF}, \overline{AD}, \overline{AF}$; **(b)** Answers will vary. Sample answer: $\angle 1$ forms a pair of alternate interior angles with the angle labeled 22°, and those angles are formed by a transversal and two parallel lines, so $m\angle 1 = 22°$. $\angle BAF$ forms a pair of alternate interior angles with the angle labeled 54°, and those angles are formed by a transversal and two parallel lines, so $m\angle BAF = 54°$. And $54° - 22° = 32°$, so $m\angle 3 = 32°$. $\angle 1$, $\angle 2$, and $\angle 3$ are angles of a triangle, so the sum of their measures is 180°. And $180° - 22° - 32° = 126°$, so $m\angle 2 = 126°$.

Pages 357–362

1. 4π cm, or about 12.6 cm **3.** 18π ft, or about 56.5 ft **5.** 2π units, or about 6.28 units **7.** 8π units, or about 25.1 units **9.** 9.5 in. **11.** 66 m **13.** about 56.5 cm **15.** about 28 units **17.** about 50.1 km **19.** 8.5π m, or about 26.7 m **21.** about 5.02 cm **23.** about 11.1 mm **25.** about 7.64 km **27.** 1.5π in., or about 4.71 in. **29.** about 4.19 m

Pages 363–368

1. 36π cm^2, or about 113 cm^2 **3.** 256π ft^2, or about 804 ft^2 **5.** π unit^2, or about 3.14 unit^2 **7.** 2.25π unit^2, or about 7.07 unit^2 **9.** 9π unit^2, or about 28.3 unit^2 **11.** 4 m **13.** about 4 cm **15.** 190 in^2 **17.** 75.2 unit^2 **19.** 145 cm^2 **21.** about 55 ft^2 **23.** about 84.3 km^2 **25.** 36π m^2, or about 113 m^2 **27.** 18 in. pizza: about \$0.090/in^2; 16 in. pizza: about \$0.094/in^2; The 18 in. pizza is the better deal. **29.** circle: about 78.5 km; square: 100 km; The square has the greater area. Also, a circle with a diameter of 10 km fits inside a square with a side length of 10 km, with room left over in the corners. **31.** Draw segments at the top and bottom of the figure to form a rectangle. Then subtract the area of the two semicircles in the rectangle.

Pages 369–371

Solution Manual only

Pages 372–373

1. B **3.** D **5.** B **7.** B **9. (a)** 1.5 in.; **(b)** 8 **11.** about 40.3 units **13.** about 55.7 unit^2 **15. (a)** Let $2r$ represent the diameter of the semicircular shape.

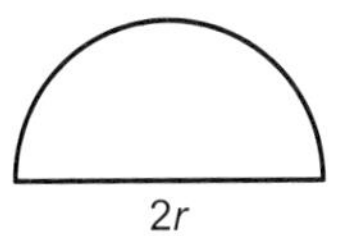

The perimeter of the shape can be written as $P = 2r + \pi r = r(2 + \pi)$. Substitute the perimeter into the formula and solve for r: $10\pi + 10 = r(2 + \pi)$; $10 \cdot 3.14 + 10 \approx r(2 + 3.14)$; $41.4 \approx 5.14r$; $8.05 \approx r$. The radius of the semicircular figure is about 8.05 units. **(b)** about 203 unit^2

CHAPTER 11 Solid Figures

Pages 376–378

Problem Set A

1. 432 in^2 **3.** 0.004685 km^2 **5.** $35.6\overline{3}$ yd^2 **7.** 42,000 mm^2

Problem Set B

1. 2 gal **3.** 0.047 m^3 **5.** 4 pt **7.** 65,400,000 cm^3

Problem Set C

1. 8 cm^3 **3.** 8 ft^3

Pages 379–381

1. 64 in^3 **3.** 1331 ft^3 **5.** 125 in^3 **7.** 216 ft^3 **9.** 29.791 m^3 **11.** 421,875 cm^3 **13.** 13,824 in^3

Pages 382–385

1. 36 in^3 **3.** 12,000 ft^3 **5.** 330 in^3 **7.** 360 in^3 **9.** 54 m^3 **11.** 112 m^3 **13.** 154 cm^3 **15.** 2992.98 cm^3

Pages 386–388

1. If the plane slicing the pyramid passed through the vertex, then the cross section would be a triangle. However, the plane slicing the pyramid does not pass through the vertex, so the cross section is in the shape of a trapezoid.

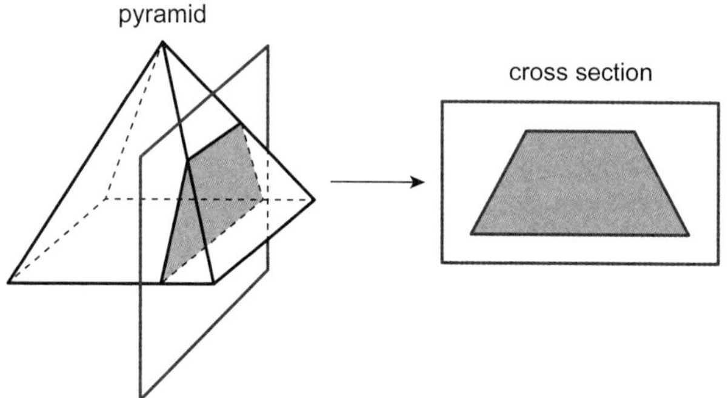

3. If the plane slicing the cone were parallel to the base, then the cross section would be a circle. However, the plane slicing the cone is tilted at an angle relative to the base, so the cross section is in the shape of an ellipse.

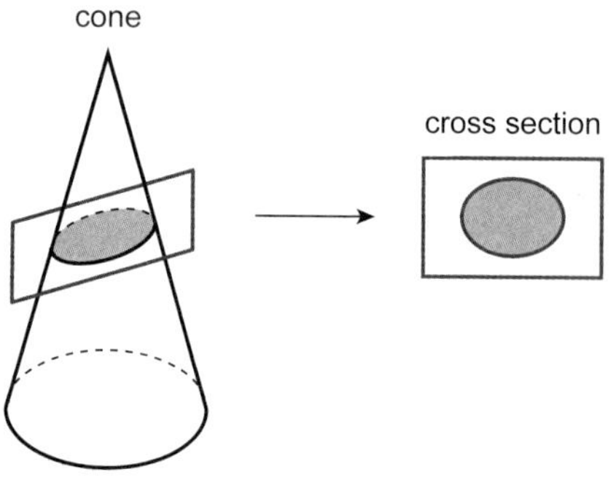

5. The plane slicing the pyramid is parallel to the base of the pyramid, so the cross section is in the shape of a rectangle that is smaller than and similar to the base of the pyramid.

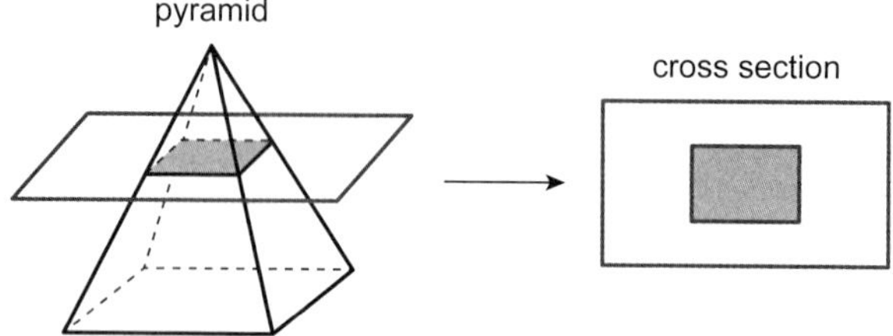

7. The plane slices through the cone vertically, creating a triangle perpendicular to the base of the cone. The triangle is isosceles, with height equal to the height of the cone.

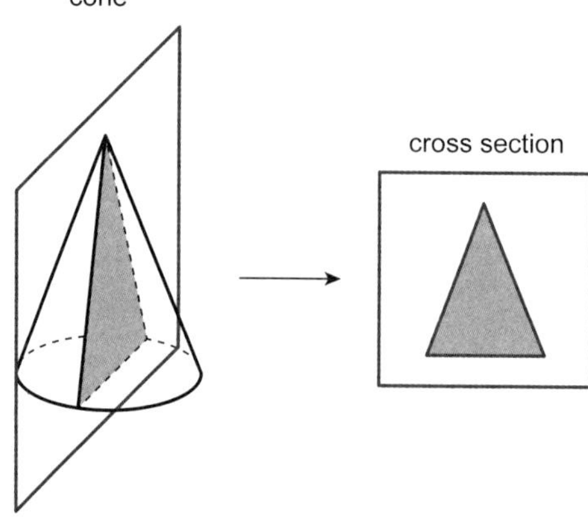

Pages 389–395

1. 24 m^2 **3.** 73.5 mm^2 **5.** 2904 in^2 **7.** 170 m^2 **9.** 96 m^2 **11.** 400 mm^2 **13.** 1694 cm^2 **15.** 152 m^2 **17.** 3552 mm^2 **19.** 304 in^2 **21.** 108 cm^2 **23.** 152 m^2 **25.** 256 ft^2 **27.** 670 cm^2

Pages 396–399

1. 52 m^2 **3.** 360 cm^2 **5.** 1288 m^2 **7.** 443.2 in^2 **9.** 468 cm^2

11. $\frac{SA}{V} = \frac{6}{1}$ **13.** $\frac{SA}{V} = \frac{3}{5}$ **15.** $\frac{SA}{V} = \frac{13}{5}$ **17.** $\frac{SA}{V} = \frac{6}{s}$

Pages 400–403

1. The surface area does not change. A square centimeter is larger than a square millimeter, so the number would decrease. The number representing the surface area would decrease. **3.** The surface area does not change. A square centimeter is smaller than a square meter, so the number would increase. The number representing the surface area would increase. **5.** 972 in^2 **7.** 7500 yd^2 **9.** 72 ft^2 **11.** 17,664 m^2 **13.** Rectangular prisms with dimensions of 3 m × 2 m × 4 m and 6 m × 2 m × 2 m have the same volume of 24 cm^3 but different surface areas. **15.** Rectangular prisms with dimensions of 2 mm × 4 mm × 4 mm and 8 mm × 4 mm × 1 mm have the same volume of 32 mm^3 but different surface areas. **17.** Rectangular prisms with dimensions of 2 ft × 4 ft × 10 ft and 4 ft × 5 ft × 4 ft have the same volume of 80 ft^3 but different surface areas. **19.** Rectangular prisms with dimensions of 2 m × 2 m × 10 m and 2 m × 4 m × 5 m have the same volume of 40 m^3 but different surface areas. **21.** Rectangular prisms with dimensions of 2 cm × 3 cm × 9 cm and 3 cm × 3 cm × 6 cm have the same volume of 54 cm^3 but different surface areas. **23.** Rectangular prisms with dimensions of 2 m × 9 m × 9 m and 3 m × 6 m × 9 m have the same volume of 162 m^3 but different surface areas. **25.** Rectangular prisms with dimensions of 3 cm × 5 cm × 15 cm and 5 cm × 5 cm × 9 cm have the same volume of 225 cm^3 but different surface areas. **27.** Rectangular prisms with dimensions of 2 cm × 4 cm × 67 cm and 67 cm × 8 cm × 1 cm have the same volume of 536 cm^3 but different surface areas. **29.** D

Pages 404–407

Solution Manual only

Pages 408–409

1. C **3.** B **5.** C **7.** A **9.** 156 cm^3 **11.** 17.6 cm^2 **13.** Rectangular prisms with dimensions of 2 m × 2 m × 10 m and 2 m × 4 m × 5 m have the same volume of 40 m^3 but different surface areas.

CHAPTER 12 Probability and Statistics

Pages 412–414

Problem Set A

1. 7 **3.** 5.4 **5.** 29 **7.** 6.79 **9.** 180.5 **11.** 3.751

Problem Set B

1. 60% **3.** 22.2% **5.** 66.7% **7.** 23.3% **9.** 5.3% **11.** 0.28% **13.** 1.06% **15.** 60.1% **17.** 9.96%

Problem Set C

1. 90% **3.** 65% **5.** 41.65% **7.** 82% **9.** 35.71%

Pages 415–419

1. mean: 93.6; median: 96; mode: 96 **3.** mean: $5\frac{1}{3}$; median: 5.5; mode: 2 **5.** mean: about 99.3; median: 100; modes: 92 and 106 **7.** mean: 45; median: 45; no mode **9.** mean: 100; median: 102; mode: 102 **11.** mean: about 0.83; median: 1; mode: 1 **13.** mean: 0; median: −0.5; no mode **15.** mean: $\frac{21}{40}$; median: $\frac{1}{2}$; mode: $\frac{1}{2}$ **17.** Because 32 is a potential outlier, the best measure of center is the median. There is no mode. **19.** Because there are no potential outliers, the best measure of center is either the mean or the median. There is no mode. **21.** Because there are so many values of 1, the best measure of center is either the median or the mode. **23.** Because there are no potential outliers, the best measure of center is either the mean or the median. The mode is 0, but there are several values above that, so the mode may not be the best measure of center. **25.** Because the mode is much smaller than the other values in the set, the best measure of center is either the mean or the median. **27.** Because there are no potential outliers, the best measure of center is either the mean or the median. There is no mode. **29.** Class A **31.** Class B **33.** 1.85 oz **35.** Because the mean and median of Class B are very different, Class B is most likely to have an outlier. The outlier would be a very low test score that caused the mean to be much less than the median. **37.** Answers will vary. Sample answer: 1, 2, 3, 4, 5

Pages 420–423

1. 2.5 **3.** about 3.4 **5.** 15.1 **7.** 3.5 **9.** about 0.4 s **11.** about 2.5°C **13.** 169.5 m; Juan overestimated.

15. A MAD of 0 represents no deviation from the mean value of 1. Therefore, all of the data values in the set are equal to the mean, or 1.

Pages 424–427

1. The sample is likely biased because many people who ski might not be home to answer the phone—they might be out skiing. **3.** There is no reason to believe the sample is biased. Every tenant has an equal chance of being selected. **5.** There is no reason to believe the sample is biased. The method of selecting voters to survey should result in a representative sample. **7.** There is no reason to believe the sample is biased. Everyone at the game has an equal chance of being selected. **9.** The sample is likely biased because people who go to school or work are not likely to be in the supermarket at that time. There is likely to be a greater percentage of stay-at-home parents and retired citizens in the sample than in the population. **11.** There is no reason to believe the sample is biased. Every item produced on the assembly line has an equal chance of being selected. **13. (a)** about 5132; **(b)** about 157,338 **15. (a)** about 267; **(b)** about 1333 **17. (a)** Potential source of bias: People who order entrées with the sauce probably already like hot and spicy foods.

Possible change: Ask every fifth customer to sample the sauce, regardless of the entrée they order. **(b)** Potential source of bias: Odd-numbered houses tend to be on one side of the street and even-numbered houses tend to be on the other. One side of a street might get more sunlight, allowing those residents to use less energy. Possible change: Choose the same number of even-numbered and odd-numbered houses. **(c)** Potential sources of bias: Due to wind, more debris might be at one end of the lake than the other. Due to the effects of sunlight and air temperature, water near the surface will be different from water near the bottom. Possible change: Collect samples from random locations in the lake and from random depths.

Pages 428–432

1. (a)

Value	Frequency
50	2
51	4
52	2

(b) estimated mean: 51; **(c)** estimated MAD: 0.5

3. (a)

Value	Frequency
76	3
77	1
79	2
80	1
82	2
83	1

(b) estimated mean: 79; **(c)** estimated MAD: 2.2

5. (a)

Value	Frequency
92	1
93	2
94	4
95	3
96	4

(b) estimated mean: 94.5; **(c)** estimated MAD: about 1.07

7. (a) Sample 3; **(b)** Sample 3 could be biased because the farmer took all the samples from an area that either received more or less water than the entire crop of corn, or that was damaged in some way. **9. (a)** Sample 2, Sample 5; **(b)** Sample 2 and Sample 5 could be biased by how Deepika randomly selected students. She could have selected a population that was biased toward either a younger or older age, or that was biased toward males or females.

11. The estimated mean number of rides that a person who attended the fair went on that day is 2.8 rides or about 3 rides. **13. (a)** Both the mean and the median are a good representation of the number of pieces of mail received by a house that day. **(b)** The mean of the sample is about 5 pieces of mail and the MAD is about 2 pieces of mail. Since the houses were selected at random, the results represent the total number of houses. Therefore, you can infer that, on average, a house received 5 pieces of mail on that day.

Pages 433–436

1. (a) Data Set 1: about 4; Data Set 2: about 9; **(b)** low
3. (a) Data Set 1: about 61; Data Set 2: about 67; **(b)** none

5. (a) **Rockville**

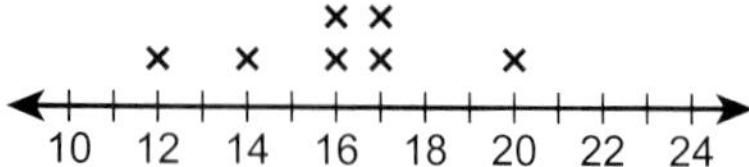

Center City

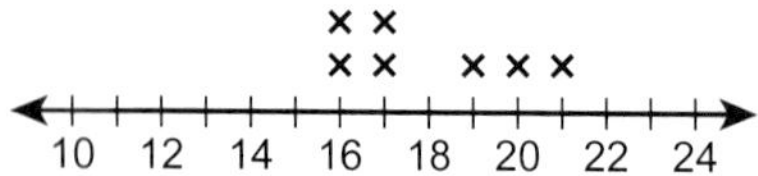

(b) Rockville mean: 16; Center City mean: 18;
(c) Rockville MAD: about 1.7; Center City Mad: about 1.7;
(d) moderate

7. (a)

Song 1

Song 2

(b) Song 1 mean: 126; Song 2 mean: 105;
(c) Song 1 MAD: 6; Song 2 MAD: 6; **(d)** no overlap

9. (a) **Beagle**

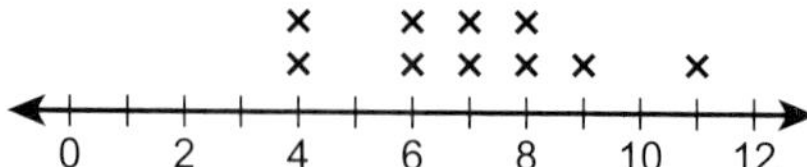

Border collie

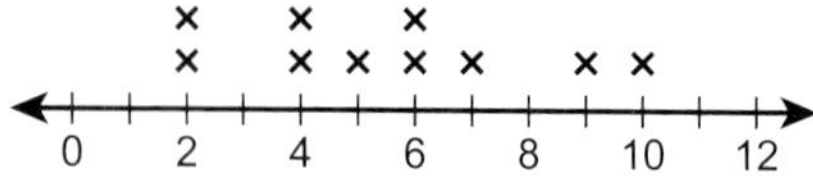

(b) beagle mean: 7; border collie mean: 5.5; **(c)** beagle MAD: 1.6; border collie MAD: 2.1; **(d)** high

11. (a) **Sandy Cay**

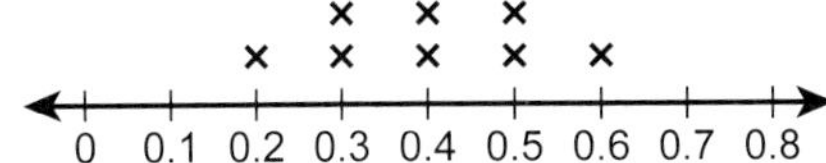

Crab Beach

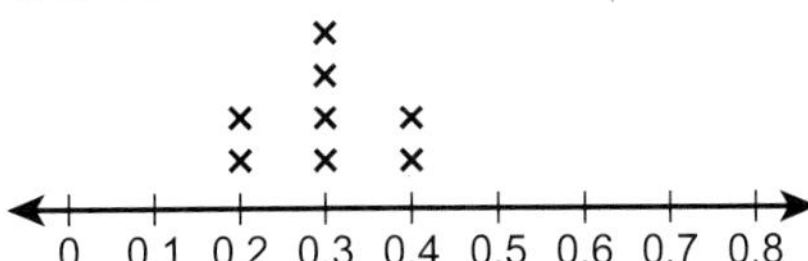

(b) Sandy Cay mean diameter is 0.4 mm, and the MAD is 0.1 mm. Crab Beach mean diameter is 0.3 mm, and the MAD is 0.05 mm. **(c)** The difference between the two means is $0.4 - 0.3 = 0.1$. This difference is equal to or slightly more than either MAD. The degree of overlap between the two distributions is high.

Pages 437–441

1. (a) Set 1 has a mean of 5, with a MAD of 3. Set 2 has a mean of 6, with a MAD of 3. **(b)** With a means-to-MAD ratio of $\frac{1}{3} \approx 0.3$, you can conclude that the distributions are similar. **3. (a)** Set 1 has a mean of 27, with a MAD of 1.2. Set 2 has a mean of 26, with a MAD of 1.8. **(b)** With a means-to-MAD ratio of $\frac{1}{1.8} \approx 0.56$, you can conclude that the distributions are similar. **5. (a)** Set 1 has a mean of 63, with a MAD of about 1.56. Set 2 has a mean of 74, with a MAD of about 0.89. **(b)** With a means-to-MAD ratio of $\frac{11}{1.56}$ ≈ 7.05, you can conclude that the distributions are different.

7. (a) **Second year**

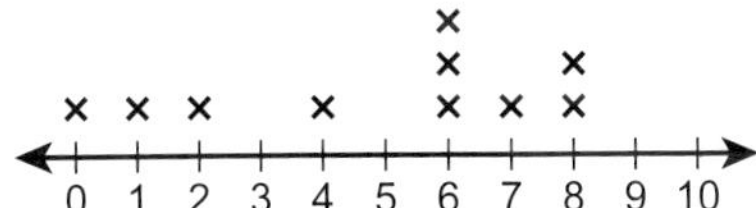

Third year

(b) The means-to-MAD ratio is $\frac{|4.8 - 4|}{2.8} = \frac{0.8}{2.8} \approx 0.29$.

(c) With a means-to-MAD ratio of about 0.29, you can conclude that the distributions are similar. Alyssa cannot conclude that second-year students were more likely than third-year students to attend a basketball game.

9. (a) **Intersection 1**

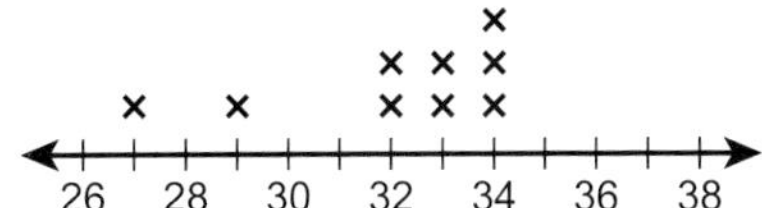

Intersection 2

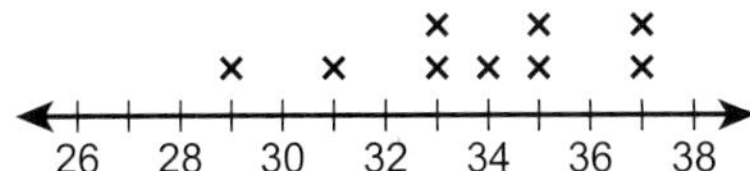

(b) The means-to-MAD ratio is $\frac{|32 - 33.8|}{1.91} \approx 0.94$.

(c) With a means-to-MAD ratio of about 0.94, you can conclude that the distributions are similar. You cannot infer that cars passed through Intersection 2 faster than through Intersection 1.

11. (a) **Demi to Renae**

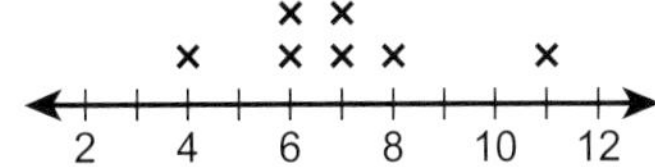

Renae to Demi

(b) The means-to-MAD ratio is $\frac{|7 - 6|}{1.4} \approx 0.7$.

(c) With a means-to-MAD ratio of about 0.7, you can conclude that the distributions are similar. In other words, on average, both girls sent about the same number of text messages each day. **13. (a)** 2010 mean: 34.2, MAD: 5.44; 2011 mean: 34, MAD: 8.4; **(b)** With a means-to-MAD ratio of $\frac{|34.2 - 34|}{8.4} \approx 0.02$, you can conclude that the distributions are similar. On average, the top five finishers in both years performed about the same.

Pages 442–445

Note: H represents heads and T represents tails. **1.** H, T **3.** HHH, HHT, HTH, HTT, THH, THT, TTH, TTT **5.** H1, H2, H3, H4, H5, H6, T1, T2, T3, T4, T5, T6 **7.** AA, AB, AC, AD, BA, BB, BC, BD, CA, CB, CC, CD, DA, DB, DC, DD

9. (a) $n(S) = 25$; **(b)** $P(\text{white}) = \frac{7}{25}$; **(c)** $P(\text{red}) = \frac{3}{5}$; **(d)** $P(\text{green}) = 0$; **(e)** $P(\text{not red}) = \frac{2}{5}$ **11. (a)** $n(S) = 12$; **(b)** $P(\text{heads and } 4) = \frac{1}{12}$; **(c)** $P(\text{tails and even number}) = \frac{1}{4}$; **(d)** $P(\text{heads and number} > 2) = \frac{1}{3}$ **13.** $P(\text{not answered}) = \frac{23}{70} \approx 33\%$ **15.** $\frac{1}{120}$

Pages 446–450

1. $\frac{16}{52} \approx 0.31 = 31\%$ **3.** $\frac{22}{52} \approx 0.42 = 42\%$ **5.** $\frac{36}{52} \approx 0.69 = 69\%$

7.

Peas per pod	7	8	9	10	11
Relative frequency	$\frac{1}{40} = 0.025 = 2.5\%$	$\frac{4}{40} = 0.1 = 10\%$	$\frac{18}{40} = 0.45 = 45\%$	$\frac{15}{40} = 0.375 = 37.5\%$	$\frac{2}{40} = 0.05 = 5\%$

9. $\frac{5}{40} = 0.125 = 12.5\%$ **11. (a)** $\frac{7}{30} \approx 0.233 = 23.3\%$; **(b)** $\frac{15}{30} = 0.5 = 50\%$; **(c)** $P(2) = \frac{1}{6} \approx 0.167 = 16.7\%$; **(d)** The relative frequency of rolling the number 2 is $\frac{4}{30} \approx 0.133 = 13.3\%$, which is different from the theoretical probability $P(2) = 16.7\%$. The relative frequency doesn't always equal the theoretical probability since theoretical probability represents what is expected to happen, and relative frequency represents what actually happens in an experiment.

13. (a)

Outcome	**Number of trials**		
	10	**25**	**100**
boy	$\frac{4}{10} = 0.4 = 40\%$	$\frac{11}{25} = 0.44 = 44\%$	$\frac{47}{100} = 0.47 = 47\%$
girl	$\frac{6}{10} = 0.6 = 60\%$	$\frac{14}{25} = 0.56 = 56\%$	$\frac{53}{100} = 0.53 = 53\%$

(b) You don't know how many boys or girls attend the school, so you cannot calculate the theoretical probability that a boy will be chosen to read the morning announcements. **(c)** According to the law of large numbers, the relative frequency of an event is close to the theoretical probability of the event for a large number of trials. As n increases from 10 to 100, the relative frequency of a girl reading the morning announcements decreases and seems to approach about 50%. Based on the pattern, about 50% of the school's population is girls.

Pages 451–456

1. Yes; A number is either even or odd; it is not both. **3.** Yes; The multiples of 2 are not multiples of 5. **5.** No; Two queens are black cards. **7.** $P(1 \text{ or } 12) = \frac{1}{6}$

9. $P(\text{multiple of 4 or multiple of 5}) = \frac{5}{12}$

11. $P(\text{baby blue or deep blue}) = \frac{1}{6}$

13. $P(\text{any blue or off white}) = \frac{11}{15}$ **15.** dependent

17. independent **19.** dependent **21.** $P(\text{heads and heads}) = \frac{1}{4}$

23. $P(\text{heads and odd number}) = \frac{1}{4}$

25. $P(\text{6 on roll and 2 on spinner}) = \frac{1}{24}$

27. $P(\text{001, 002, 003, then 004}) = \frac{1}{1{,}552{,}438{,}800}$

29. $P(\text{correct and correct and correct}) = \frac{1}{8}$

Pages 457–459

Solution Manual only

Pages 460–461

1. A **3.** B **5.** B **7.** A **9. (a)** MAD: 6.9; **(b)** The MAD is a measure of the variation in the number of new users about their mean of 52 users. On average, the values in the data set vary from the mean of 52 users by about 6.9 users.

11. $P(\text{red and even}) = \frac{5}{26}$

13. (a) Set A

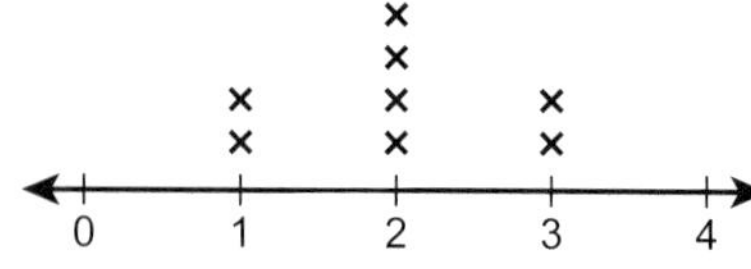

Set B

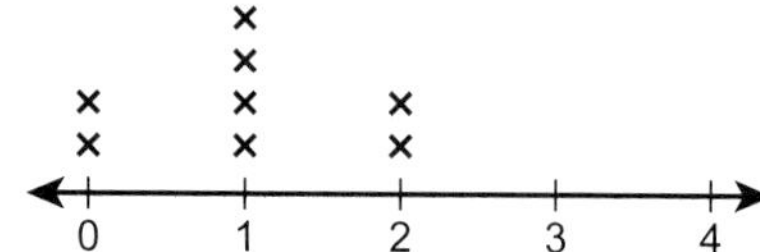

Set A: 2; Set B: 1; **(b)** moderate

Illustrations Credits

All illustrations © K12 Inc. unless otherwise noted

Front and back cover: © Tobik/Shutterstock

Chapter 1: 3 © sack/iStockphoto.com

Chapter 2: 35 © iStockphoto/Thinkstock

Chapter 3: 71 © iStockphoto/Thinkstock

Chapter 4: 99 © Martin Harvey/Alamy

Chapter 5: 139 © Marc Romanelli/Alamy

Chapter 6: 189 © DLILLC/Corbis

Chapter 7: 233 © Povl Eskild/age fotostock

Chapter 8: 267 © Mark E. Gibson/Corbis

Chapter 9: 309 © Jon McIntosh/iStockphoto.com

Chapter 10: 349 © euroluftbild.de/age fotostock

Chapter 11: 375 © Kevin Phillips/Getty Images

Chapter 12: 411 © Jonathan Larsen/Diadem Images/Alamy

Data Sources

CHAPTER 2 Addition and Subtraction on a Number Line

Information Please Database. 2007a. "Record Lowest Temperatures by State." Pearson Education publishing as Infoplease. Accessed March 6, 2014. http://www.infoplease.com/ipa/A0113527.html.

———. 2007b. "Record Highest Temperatures by State." Pearson Education publishing as Infoplease. Accessed March 6, 2014. http://www.infoplease.com/ipa/A0001416.html.

———. 2007c. "World Land Areas and Elevations." Pearson Education publishing as Infoplease. Accessed March 6, 2014. http://www.infoplease.com/ipa/A0001763.html.

CHAPTER 3 Addition and Subtraction Properties

All-Athletics.com. 2009a. "Randy Barnes." Accessed March 6, 2015. http://www.all-athletics.com/node/78431.

———. 2009b. "Helena Fibingerová." Accessed March 6, 2015. http://www.all-athletics.com/node/290933.

Guinness World Records. 2015. "Greatest Temperature Range in Day." Accessed March 6, 2015. http://www.guinnessworldrecords.com/world-records/greatest-temperature-range-in-day.

Havana Journal. 2004. "Javier Sotomayor Now Jumping to a Fast, New Beat." Accessed March 6, 2015. http://havanajournal.com/culture/entry/javier_sotomayor_now_jumping_to_a_fast_new_beat/.

Information Please Database. 2007a. "Record Lowest Temperatures by State." Pearson Education publishing as Infoplease. Accessed March 6, 2014. http://www.infoplease.com/ipa/A0113527.html.

———. 2007b. "Record Highest Temperatures by State." Pearson Education publishing as Infoplease. Accessed March 6, 2014. http://www.infoplease.com/ipa/A0001416.html.

Minshull, Phil. 2014. "Renaud Lavillenie Sets Pole Vault World Record of 6.16M in Donetsk," International Association of Athletics Federations. Accessed March 6, 2015. http://www.iaaf.org/news/news/renaud-lavillenie-pole-vault-world-record.

USA Track & Field. 2009. "Alan Webb." Accessed March 6, 2015. http://www.usatf.org/athletes/bios/TrackAndFieldArchive/2009/Webb_Alan.asp.

CHAPTER 7 Ratio, Proportion, and Percent

National Geographic. 2015. "Asian Elephant." Accessed March 9, 2015. http://animals.nationalgeographic.com/animals/mammals/asian-elephant/.

Index

Page references in **bold** indicate definitions and formulas.

F

G

H

I

L

M

N

O

P

Q

R

S

T

U

V

W

Z